Windows PowerShell™ 2.0

Best Practices

Ed Wilson
with the Windows PowerShell Teams at Microsoft

D1511502

PUBLISHED BY
Microsoft Press
A Division of Microsoft Corporation
One Microsoft Way
Redmond, Washington 98052-6399

Library of Congress Control Number: 2009938599

Printed and bound in the United States of America.

2 3 4 5 6 7 8 9 10 11 QGT 5 4 3 2 1 0

Distributed in Canada by H.B. Fenn and Company Ltd.

A CIP catalogue record for this book is available from the British Library.

Microsoft Press books are available through booksellers and distributors worldwide. For further information about international editions, contact your local Microsoft Corporation office or contact Microsoft Press International directly at fax (425) 936-7329. Visit our Web site at www.microsoft.com/mspress. Send comments to msinput@microsoft.com.

Microsoft, Microsoft Press, Access, Active Accessibility, Active Directory, ActiveX, Authenticode, Excel, Expression, Forefront, Groove, Hyper-V, IntelliSense, Internet Explorer, MSDN, OneNote, Outlook, ReadyBoost, Segoe, SharePoint, Silverlight, SQL Server, Visual Basic, Visual SourceSafe, Visual Studio, Win32, Windows, Windows Media, Windows NT, Windows PowerShell, Windows Server, and Windows Vista are either registered trademarks or trademarks of the Microsoft group of companies. Other product and company names mentioned herein may be the trademarks of their respective owners.

The example companies, organizations, products, domain names, e-mail addresses, logos, people, places, and events depicted herein are fictitious. No association with any real company, organization, product, domain name, e-mail address, logo, person, place, or event is intended or should be inferred.

Acquisitions Editor: Martin DelRe
Developmental Editor: Karen Szall
Project Editor: Melissa von Tschudi-Sutton
Editorial Production: Custom Editorial Productions, Inc.
Technical Reviewer: Randall Galloway; Technical Review services provided by Content Master, a member of CM Group, Ltd.
Cover: Tom Draper Design

Body Part No. X16-38608

This book is dedicated to Teresa Wilson, my best friend, life companion, inspiration, and wife. You made me so happy when you said yes.

Contents at a Glance

Contents

What do you think of this book? We want to hear from you!

Microsoft is interested in hearing your feedback so we can continually improve our
books and learning resources for you. To participate in a brief online survey, please visit:

microsoft.com/learning/booksurvey

PART IV   TESTING AND DEPLOYING

PART V OPTIMIZING

Chapter 16 Logging Results   577

What do you think of this book? We want to hear from you!

Microsoft is interested in hearing your feedback so we can continually improve our books and learning resources for you. To participate in a brief online survey, please visit:

microsoft.com/learning/booksurvey

Acknowledgments

It always seems that I am sideswiped when working on a book project. At the outset of a project, I think, "I know this subject pretty well. This should be easy." Then I begin the outline and am confronted with my ignorance of the subject. I have worked on this book for more than 14 months—the longest of any of my eight books. Luckily, I have been aided in the project by nearly one hundred people, each of whom has expressed enthusiastic support for a project that they all acknowledged was both vitally needed and critically important.

The outline: At least once a month, I receive an e-mail, phone call, instant message, comment on Facebook, or tweet that asks me how I go about writing a book. I cannot even call my own brother without discussing the book-writing process: he is finishing his first book (on baseball). So what does this have to do with the outline? Well, I always begin with an outline. This particular outline took me more than one month to write. I had significant help in the development of the outline from Jeffrey Snover, James Brundage, Marco Shaw, Bill Mell, Jit Banerjie, Chris Bellée, and Pete Christensen.

The sidebars: One of the cool things about a Best Practices book is the sidebars. Sidebars are short text pieces that are written by well-known industry experts as well as members of the Windows PowerShell product group. I have been extremely fortunate to have developers, test engineers, architects, field engineers, network administrators, and consultants contribute sidebars for this book. They wrote because they believed in the value of creating a book on best practices and not because it was their job or because they were otherwise compensated. These contributors are current and former employees of Microsoft. Some are Microsoft MVPs, and others will probably become Microsoft MVPs in the future. Some are moderators for the Official Scripting Guys forum, and others are moderators for other scripting forums. I even rounded up a few former Microsoft Scripting Guys. In every case, my colleagues were happy to supply a sidebar. I enjoyed reading the sidebars as much as I am sure you will enjoy them.

The following people provided assistance, suggestions, and/or contributions to sidebars for the book: Alexander Riedel, Andrew Willett, Andy Schneider, Ben Pearce, Bill Mell, Bill Stewart, Brandon Shell, Chris Bellée, Clint Huffman, Dan Harman, Daniele Muscetta, Dave Schwinn, Dean Tsaltas, Don Jones, Enrique Cedeno, Georges Maheu, Hal Rottenberg, James Brundage, James Craig Burley, James Turner, Jeffrey Hicks, Jeffrey Snover, Juan Carlos Ruiz Lopez, Keith Hill, Lee Holmes, Luís Canastreiro, Osama Sajid, Peter Costantini, Rahul Verma, Richard Norman, Richard Siddaway, Vasily Gusev, Alex K. Angelopoulos, David Zazzo,

Glenn Seagraves, Joel Bennett, Marco Shaw, Oisín Grehan, Pete Christensen, and Thomas Lee.

Special mention goes to Melissa von Tschudi-Sutton for all of her patience and guidance. During the writing of this book, I went from traveling every week (with a significant amount of international travel to Australia, Canada, Germany, Denmark, Portugal, and Mexico) to my current position as the Microsoft Scripting Guy. This change caused some disruption to my work schedule. Additionally, this project also saw a nearly two-month hiatus due to a surgery-inducing accident that I suffered in my woodworking shop. Throughout all of these changes, Melissa was a real trouper, and I could not have asked for a more understanding editor. She was awesome!

Randall Galloway, who is a Microsoft Technical Account manager and my technical editor on this book, was great. He went beyond the call of duty by even responding to style and grammar questions posed by Jan Clavey, who was my copy editor. Rose Marie Kuebbing and Megan Smith-Creed, who were project managers for this book, also contributed in significant ways to keeping the book on schedule. As the content development manager, Karen Szall did a wonderful job of helping me quickly come up to speed on all of the new features of a Best Practices book. I extend a hearty "well done" to all of you!

Windows PowerShell 2.0 Best Practices would not exist without the tireless efforts of my agent and friend, Claudette Moore, of the Moore Literary Agency. Claudette is amazing! That she can navigate all of the intricacies of a book contract and negotiate with editors and publishers while still keeping her sanity is truly an art form. Martin DelRe, my acquisitions editor from Microsoft Press, is a staunch supporter of scripting technology and makes me feel as if my book is the most important book to be published this year. His personal attention to the project is truly appreciated.

My biggest acknowledgment, however, must go to Teresa Wilson, who is my number one editor, critic, and fan. Nothing I write—whether an e-mail to John Merril (my manager at Microsoft), a Hey Scripting Guy! article, or a book for Microsoft Press—leaves our house without her careful scrutiny. She has read every word of every book that I have ever written. Incidentally, she is an accounting type of person and not a script guru or a wordsmith, even though she is sometimes referred to as "the scripting wife" in some of my Hey Scripting Guy! articles.

Even with all of this help from my friends and colleagues, I am absolutely certain that there will be a few errors in this book. All of those belong to me.

Introduction

One of the great things about being the Microsoft Scripting Guy is the interaction I have with customers—people who are using Windows PowerShell to manage enterprise networks of every size and description: pure Microsoft networks, heterogeneous networks, and even networks running software that is obsolete and no longer supported. Within all of these interactions with customers runs a common thread: "How can I more efficiently manage my network?"

Windows PowerShell is the Microsoft answer to the question of more effective and efficient network management. At TechEd 2009 in Los Angeles, the Windows PowerShell sessions were the most heavily attended of all of the sessions offered. While I was manning the Microsoft Scripting Guys booth, nearly all of the questions I received were about Windows PowerShell. My Friday afternoon talk on using Windows PowerShell to manage the Windows 7 desktop saw the highest attendance of any session offered during that time slot. Quite frankly, I was surprised that anyone attended because the convention center was a scant 15 miles from Disneyland. I felt like I was competing with Mickey Mouse for the attendees' attention after a week of sessions.

Why I Wrote This Book

"Windows administrators do not script." I have heard this truism for years. Prior to becoming the Microsoft Scripting Guy, I delivered workshops to Microsoft Premier Customers around the world on VBScript, Windows Management Instrumentation (WMI), and Windows PowerShell. Because these workshops were so popular, I had to train other instructors to assist with the demand for training. These scripting workshops were the highest-rated workshops offered through Microsoft Premier Services. There is definitely a demand and an interest in scripting. Over the years, the questions we fielded began to repeat themselves: "What is the best way to do this?" or "What is the best way to do that?" The scripting instructors formed a work group as we researched answers to these common questions. At one point, we discussed the creation of a scripting Best Practices workshop, and much of that work has been incorporated into this book.

On Form and Function

To a very large extent, the use of your script will dictate the form that it takes. Will all of the best practices in this book apply to every script that you write? No. The goal of administrative scripting is to do work, and anything that enables you to efficiently accomplish your task is probably acceptable. However, there is a point when a quickly hobbled-together script can be more trouble than it is worth, particularly if it introduces security concerns or reliability issues.

Several benefits can be derived from following best practices. The first is that a well-crafted script will be easier to understand. If it is easier to read and understand, it will be easier to modify when the time comes to add capability to the script. If a problem arises with the script, it will also be easier to troubleshoot.

For Whom Is This Book?

Windows PowerShell 2.0 Best Practices is aimed at experienced IT professionals including IT architects, engineers, administrators, and support professionals who are working in large organizations and in the enterprise. IT pros who work in smaller companies would also benefit from most of the guidelines concerning the structuring of code, many of the tips and tricks, and much of the "how to" sections regarding common everyday problems. The audience is expected to have obtained the level of Windows PowerShell understanding presented in *Microsoft Windows PowerShell Step by Step* (Microsoft Press, 2007). The audience is assumed to know and understand the basics of Windows PowerShell: fundamental looping constructs, basic decision-making code blocks, and a rudimentary understanding of the use of cmdlets, which is the type of information they would obtain in a three-day class. In this book, there are two level-setting chapters as well as references back to topics covered in more detail in *Microsoft Windows PowerShell Step by Step*. This book is a 300-level book, but the planning and managing section will be very useful to IT managers seeking guidance on establishing scripting procedures for an enterprise organization.

How Is This Book Organized?

This book is organized into five sections as listed here:

- Part I: Introduction
- Part II: Planning
- Part III: Designing
- Part IV: Testing and Deploying
- Part V: Optimizing

The first four chapters introduce many of the new features of Windows PowerShell 2.0. In Chapter 1, I cover a variety of the new cmdlets that are introduced in Windows PowerShell 2.0 as well as best practices for deploying Windows PowerShell 2.0 to different portions of the network. In Chapter 2, I discuss the new

WMI features in Windows PowerShell 2.0 and provide tips for incorporating these features into a management strategy for your network. Chapters 3 and 4 cover Active Directory.

I begin the planning section of the book in Chapter 5 by identifying scripting opportunities. Here I talk about the different types of technology available to the scripter. In Chapters 6 and 7, I present best practices for configuring the scripting environment and avoiding scripting pitfalls. Chapter 8 concludes the planning section by discussing best practices for engendering scripting collaboration within the corporate IT environment.

In the section about design, I go into a great amount of detail about functions and help. There are significant new features in Windows PowerShell 2.0 that will ratchet your enterprise scripts to a new level of functionality. Chapter 11 covers modules, which are another new Windows PowerShell 2.0 feature that provides the ability to store, share, and deploy functions and other program elements in an easy-to-reuse manner. Because there are so many methods to get data into and out of a Windows PowerShell script, I provide some guidelines to help you determine the best methodology for your particular application. You cannot always predict what the environment will be when your script is run. Therefore, in Chapter 13, I discuss best practices for handling errors.

Of course, many errors can be avoided if a script is thoroughly tested prior to deployment, so I've included a section on testing and deploying. Script testing is discussed in Chapter 14, including the types of tests to run and the type of environment to use for your script testing. In Chapter 15, I discuss best practices for running scripts. Here I talk about working with the script execution policy, code signing, and other topics that are often confusing.

In the final section of the book, I cover optimization. In Chapter 16, I present different options for implementing logging in your script. I conclude *Windows PowerShell 2.0 Best Practices* with Chapter 17, where I cover the new troubleshooting and debugging tools included in Windows PowerShell 2.0. There are many choices for you to use, and I provide quite a bit of guidance, tips, and best practices to effectively troubleshoot a Windows PowerShell script.

> **NOTE** Sidebars are provided by individuals in the industry as examples for informational purposes only and may not represent the views of their employers. No warranties, express, implied, or statutory, are made as to the information provided in sidebars.

What This Book Is Not

In *Windows PowerShell 2.0 Best Practices*, I assume that you have a basic understanding of Windows PowerShell. While I go to great lengths to explain the new features of Windows PowerShell 2.0, I do not always devote the same detail to the features of Windows PowerShell 1.0. Even though I think you can learn to use Windows PowerShell from reading this book, it is not a comprehensive text, nor is it a tutorial or even a Windows PowerShell reference book. The organization of the book, while appropriate for dealing with Windows PowerShell best practices, is not optimal for learning Windows PowerShell from scratch. I therefore recommend the following books as either prereading prior to approaching this book or, at a minimum, as supplemental reading while you are perusing this book:

- *Microsoft Windows PowerShell Step by Step* (Microsoft Press, 2007)
- *Windows PowerShell Scripting Guide* (Microsoft Press, 2008)

DIGITAL CONTENT FOR DIGITAL BOOK READERS If you bought a digital-only edition of this book, you can enjoy select content from the print edition's companion media. Visit *http://go.microsoft.com/fwlink/?LinkId=169554* to get your downloadable content. This content is always up to date and available to all readers.

System Requirements

This book is designed to be used with the following software:

- Windows XP or later
- 512 MB of RAM
- P4 processor or higher
- 100 MB of available disk space
- Internet Explorer 6.0 or later
- Windows PowerShell 2.0 or later

The following list details the minimum system requirements needed to run the companion media provided with this book:

- Windows XP, with the latest service pack installed and the latest updates from Microsoft Update Service
- CD-ROM drive
- Display monitor capable of 1024 × 768 resolution

- Microsoft Mouse or compatible pointing device
- Adobe Reader for viewing the eBook (Adobe Reader is available as a download at *http://www.adobe.com.*)

Support for This Book

Every effort has been made to ensure the accuracy of this book. As corrections or changes are collected, they will be added to a Microsoft Knowledge Base article accessible via the Microsoft Help and Support site. Microsoft Press provides support for books, including instructions for finding Knowledge Base articles, at the following Web site: *http://www.microsoft.com/learning/support/books/.*

If you have questions regarding the book that are not answered by visiting the site above or viewing a Knowledge Base article, send them to Microsoft Press via e-mail to *mspinput@microsoft.com.* Please note that Microsoft software product support is not offered through these addresses.

We Want to Hear from You

We welcome your feedback about this book. Please share your comments and ideas via the following short survey: *http://www.microsoft.com/learning/booksurvey.* Your participation will help Microsoft Press create books that better meet your needs and your standards.

> **NOTE** We hope that you will give us detailed feedback via our survey. If you have questions about our publishing program, upcoming titles, or Microsoft Press in general, we encourage you to interact with us via Twitter at *http://twitter.com/MicrosoftPress.* For support issues, use only the e-mail address shown above.

About the Companion Media

On this book's companion media, I include all of the scripts that are discussed in the book. The scripts are stored in folders that correspond to the chapters in the book. There is also a folder named Extras that contains extra scripts that I wrote while working on the chapters.

Writing extra scripts has become a tradition for me throughout all of the five scripting books that I have written. Some of these are simply modifications of the scripts in the chapters, while others are scripts that I wrote for fun that I wanted to share. You will also find some planning templates and other tools that might be useful to you as you develop your corporate scripting standards. Last but certainly not least, you will find a document that contains a summary of the best practices from this book. It is my sincere hope that this document will become a quick reference that you can use to refer to the best practices for scripting when you have a question while writing a script.

PART I

Introduction

Assessing the Scripting Environment

With the release of Windows PowerShell 2.0, a number of enterprise customers are relying on a single-script environment to provide all of their script solutions. The advantage to this approach, at first glance, seems obvious: You no longer need to support multiple-script platforms. Is this a valid approach? You will examine the pros and cons to this seeming scripting utopia in this chapter. Along the way, you will look at the requirements for performing such an upgrade and hear from people in the field about their experiences in migrating to Windows PowerShell 2.0.

Why Use Windows PowerShell 2.0?

In my mind, a better question is: Why not use Windows PowerShell 2.0? If you are talking about your personal computer, there may be little reason not to use Windows PowerShell 2.0. After all, it is a very small, free download from the Microsoft Download Center (*http://www.microsoft.com/downloads/*). But as you will see, some dependencies must be met, and it is the dependencies that may tilt the scale in one direction or the other.

Clearly, the main reason to use Windows PowerShell 2.0 is for the new features, and some features are very compelling. At the top of that list is *remoting*, which is the ability to run Windows PowerShell commands against remote computers. Remoting happens to be the feature that causes the most difficulty on upgrade due to its dependence on Windows Remote Management (WinRM) 2.0.

Perhaps second on the list of new features for Windows PowerShell 2.0 is the graphical scripting console. The *graphical scripting console* is like a script editor, and it has been a highly requested feature from the field since the earliest beta of Windows PowerShell 1.0. The requirement for this feature is Microsoft .NET Framework 3.5. However, this is a nonissue in most cases because, with any upgrade to the .NET Framework, you will want to test compatibility issues with existing applications. This testing will slow your migration to Windows PowerShell 2.0 on a global basis.

Comparison with Windows PowerShell 1.0

If you dread learning a new version of Windows PowerShell because you just got comfortable with PowerShell 1.0, you do not need to worry. You can use Windows PowerShell 2.0 in exactly the same manner as you use PowerShell 1.0, with the advantages being better performance and fewer unexpected surprises. Gradually, you may want to use some of the new features, such as remoting and access to diagnostic logs, and some of the more advanced features, such as modules and script cmdlets, to create more robust and powerful scripts. These can be added to your scripting repertoire as required by the scripting needs of your environment.

Backward Compatibility

A major design goal for Windows PowerShell 2.0 is that it be 100 percent backward-compatible. In other words, any script written for Windows PowerShell 1.0 will run on PowerShell 2.0. Because Windows PowerShell 1.0 and PowerShell 2.0 cannot be installed on the same computer at the same time, it is necessary to ensure that your scripts will still work after an upgrade.

There are three ways in which this backward compatibility is achieved.

- No Windows PowerShell 1.0 cmdlets or commands are renamed.
- No changes to Windows PowerShell 1.0 parameters are permitted.
- The version tag is introduced.

NOTE Technically, the version tag existed in Windows PowerShell 1.0, and this is why you can use it in your scripts. However, prior to the introduction of Windows PowerShell 2.0, there was no need to use the version tag.

Using the Version Tag

To maintain compatibility with Windows PowerShell 1.0, you can use the version tag. Strictly speaking, the version tag is not a requirement to enable Windows PowerShell scripts to execute. For example, you do not use the version tag in QueryEventLogForTimeErrors.ps1, a script that was written on a Windows PowerShell 2.0 computer. However, this script does not use any new features from Windows PowerShell 2.0. As a result, it is a script that can run equally well on either Windows PowerShell 1.0 or PowerShell 2.0.

QueryEventLogForTimeErrors.ps1

```
Get-EventLog -LogName system |
Where-Object { $_.timegenerated -ge [datetime]::today -AND $_.source -eq 'w32time' } |
Format-Table -Property TimeGenerated, entrytype, message -AutoSize -Wrap
```

As shown in Figure 1-1, the requested information is returned on a Windows PowerShell 1.0 computer, and the script runs without errors. Any script that is written on a Windows PowerShell 1.0 computer will run on any computer on which PowerShell 2.0 is installed. However, only scripts that do not use new Windows PowerShell features when written on PowerShell 2.0 will run on a PowerShell 1.0 computer. To ensure compatibility, it is recommended that you use the version tag.

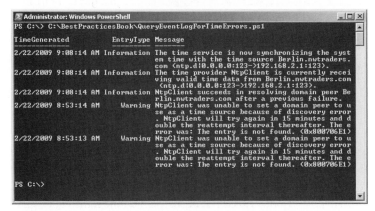

FIGURE 1-1 A script written on Windows PowerShell 2.0 will run on a PowerShell 1.0 computer if it does not use any new features.

The script in this figure is rather inefficient due to the way it operates. It gets all of the events from the entire system event log and passes them to the Where-Object cmdlet, where the filtering takes place. On my laptop, this script takes nearly 12 seconds to run. You can do better than that by using one of the new parameters that was added to the Get-EventLog cmdlet—the *source* parameter. The revised script that uses the new Windows PowerShell 2.0 features is shown here.

QueryEventLogForTimeErrorsV2.ps1

```
#requires -version 2.0
Get-EventLog -LogName system -source w32time|
Where-Object { $_.timegenerated -ge [datetime]::today } |
Format-Table -Property TimeGenerated, entrytype, message -AutoSize -Wrap
```

There are actually two benefits to the revised script. The first benefit is that the code is much simpler to understand. You now have a single WHERE clause instead of the more complicated compound WHERE clause. The second benefit pertains to how quickly the script runs. This script completes in half the time on my laptop.

As mentioned earlier, the *#requires –version 2.0* tag is not a requirement to enable the use of the new features of Windows PowerShell 2.0. If all of your computers are running Windows PowerShell 2.0 and you never share your scripts with another person, there is no real need to have the *#requires –version 2.0* tag present in your code.

The problem comes into play when a version 2.0 script is run on a computer running Windows PowerShell 1.0. As shown in Figure 1-2, the error message can be a bit misleading.

FIGURE 1-2 A script written for Windows PowerShell 2.0 that does not contain a *#requires –version 2.0* tag generates an ambiguous error message.

From a troubleshooting perspective, an error stating that the *source* parameter cannot be found can be a bit confusing. Additionally, if the script is run on a computer on which Windows PowerShell 2.0 is installed, the script runs without generating any errors. This type of error can cause a network administrator or a help desk person to waste hours trying to duplicate the error and determine the root cause of the problem. To forestall such an eventuality, you can use the *#requires –version 2.0* tag. When this tag is present, the script still generates an error when run on a Windows PowerShell 1.0 computer; however, the error is more understandable in that it specifically informs the user that the script is being run on an incorrect version of Windows PowerShell. This error message is shown in Figure 1-3. As a best practice, I recommend setting the *#requires –version 2.0* tag in any script that uses a feature from Windows PowerShell 2.0.

FIGURE 1-3 When the *#requires –version 2.0* tag is present in a script, the error message points to version incompatibility.

Deploying Windows PowerShell

Rahul Verma, Senior Systems Engineer
Microsoft Corporation

As a senior systems engineer at Microsoft, I work on a network with thousands of servers that consists of both Microsoft Windows Server 2003 and Windows Server 2008. When we began our deployment of Windows PowerShell across the network, most of the network was running .NET Framework 2.0, and we knew we needed to perform some updates. This of course necessitated some compatibility testing with our deployment. Here is how we did it.

1. We deployed Windows PowerShell on our test/staging environment to make sure it was not going to affect any production properties. During this time, we performed our .NET Framework updates as part of the package. For us, this simplified the testing scenario.

2. We selectively deployed Windows PowerShell on the production servers and made other operations teams and dev/test teams aware of this configuration. This was a pilot that happened with a small number of locations.

3. We fully deployed Windows PowerShell on specific properties. This was also an open beta period in which properties were given the opportunity to opt-in if desired.

4. We made Windows PowerShell an optional component on our bulk installation method. (We have about 200 properties, and each property seems to have different production methods, architectures, and application requirements.)

As a result of our testing, we found no compatibility issues other than a rather obscure one involving Microsoft SQL Server 2000 running on 64-bit hardware and running a job in Windows PowerShell that invokes PowerShell x86. From a deployment perspective, we used a series of custom-built tools to deploy our package to the different servers, which was required due to the sheer size of our production facilities. Additionally, there is no off-peak time for us because we are a global entity. The closest we come to an off-peak period is a slight reduction in computing load during the off hours in the United States, which is handled by redundancy that is built into the network. Fortunately, because Windows PowerShell was available as an update and because our deployment solution was already aware of the process involved in the deployment of Windows-based hotfixes and updates, there was very little custom work required for this particular deployment. The first phase of deployment was accomplished during a maintenance window, and the second phase was done during the monthly update cycle.

From a timing perspective, the entire project was rather simple. The actual installation of the package took only 5 to 10 minutes depending on the hardware configuration and exact server load. With so many servers, we obviously did not update them all at the exact same time; rather, we took a "fan-out" approach. The following time lines define our specific project phases.

- Phase 1: 1 month
- Phase 2: 1 month
- Phase 3: 1 month
- Phase 4: 3 months

A number of people in the following roles were involved in the Windows PowerShell deployment project. It is important to make sure that the operations team is brought up to speed early in the project.

- Deployment team
- Operating system imaging team
- Operations team (tier 2, tier 3)
- Dev groups
- Test groups

The main advantage we were hoping to gain from the Windows PowerShell deployment was the ability to manage servers remotely and to quickly gather information via Windows Management Instrumentation (WMI). The most difficult aspect of the project was convincing the operations team of the benefits of running Windows PowerShell in production. They offered some resistance in moving from VBScript, which they were very familiar with, to Windows PowerShell, which to them looked like C#. I helped them overcome this potential problem by providing numerous "canned" scripts to replace existing VBScripts, which really helped them to transition from VBScript to Windows PowerShell.

New Features of Windows PowerShell 2.0

The new features of Windows PowerShell 2.0 fall into three main areas: new cmdlets, modified cmdlets, and architectural changes. This section provides an overview of some of the more important changes in each of these areas; this is not a comprehensive discussion of all of the new features.

New cmdlets

The number of cmdlets in Windows PowerShell 2.0 has nearly doubled from the number that shipped with the original product. The number of cmdlets available to an IT Pro is not limited to those inside Windows PowerShell 2.0 because many of the features and roles in Windows Server 2008 R2 include new cmdlets written specifically to provide exciting automation capabilities. Many of these cmdlets are for use with remoting and the underlying WS-Management (WSMan) technology.

Some of the new cmdlets allow for easier use of WMI to manage and configure your computer systems. These cmdlets are listed as follows:

- **Invoke-WmiMethod** Calls WMI methods. Depending on the method you are trying to perform, you need to either specify the path to the object or call the method directly. The following two examples demonstrate this. The first example deletes a share named fso by specifying the path to the share. The name of the method in this example is the *delete* method. In the second example, instead of connecting to a specific process, the Invoke-WmiMethod cmdlet creates a process. The name of the method is *create*, and the argument it passes to the *create* method is the name of the process to *create*.

  ```
  Invoke-WmiMethod -path "win32_share.name='fso'" -Name delete
  Invoke-WmiMethod -Class win32_process -Name create -ArgumentList notepad.exe
  ```

- **Register-WmiEvent** Registers for an event with the WMI eventing subsystem. To use this cmdlet, write an event query using the WMI Query Language (WQL) syntax. (For more information on event-driven queries, refer to *Microsoft Windows Scripting with WMI: Self-Paced Learning Guide* [Microsoft Press, 2005]). In the following example, you create an event that will tell you when a new process starts. The notification contains the message, "A new process has started." To receive this message, you need to use the Get-PSEvent cmdlet. This process is detailed in the "Working with WMI" section in Chapter 2, "Survey of Windows PowerShell Capabilities."

  ```
  Register-WMIEvent -query "Select * From __InstanceCreationEvent within 3 Where `
  TargetInstance ISA 'Win32_Process'" -messageData "A new process has started."
  -sourceIdentifier "New Process"
  ```

- **Remove-WmiObject** Deletes WMI classes and instances. By using the Remove-WmiObject cmdlet, you have another way to delete instances of classes. As an example, to remove a share, you can use the *delete* method of the *Win32_Share* WMI class as illustrated earlier in the examination of the Invoke-WmiMethod cmdlet. However, you can also perform the query to find the class and pipeline the resulting WMI object to the Remove-WmiObject cmdlet as shown here. You may prefer this syntax for simplicity's sake.

  ```
  Get-WmiObject -Class win32_share -Filter "name = 'fso'" | Remove-WmiObject
  ```

- **Set-WmiInstance**   Creates or modifies instances of WMI classes. Use the `Set-WmiInstance` cmdlet in places where you would have used the *SpawnInstance* method from within VBScript. Here you create a new environmental variable by using the *Win32_Environment* WMI class. Because the class has no methods, you need to create a new instance of the class to create a new environmental variable, which is rather easy to do using the `Set-WmiInstance` cmdlet. The only tricky part is the way the *arguments* parameter needs to be specified: use a hash table. Each property from the *Win32_Environment* WMI class to which you need to assign a value becomes a key value within the hash table. The code is shown here.

```
Set-WmiInstance -class win32_environment -arguments `
@{Name="testvar";VariableValue="testvalue";UserName="<SYSTEM>"}
```

One area that historically has been a problem for network administrators is dealing with event logs. This problem became even more severe with the introduction of Windows Vista and the new types of event logs, as well as the difficulty of keeping up with the sheer numbers of the logs. A number of the new cmdlets are designed to address these concerns.

- **Clear-EventLog**   Deletes all entries from specified event logs on local or remote computers. The following example clears the contents of the application log on the local computer.

```
Clear-EventLog -LogName application
```

- **Get-Event**   Gets events from event logs and event-tracing log files on local and remote computers. This cmdlet runs only on Windows Vista and later versions of Windows. As a best practice, use the `Get-EventLog` cmdlet when accessing the classic event logs. Use the `Get-Event` cmdlet when working with the newer diagnostic and tracing logs.

As shown in Figure 1-4, Windows Vista and later versions have many diagnostic logs.

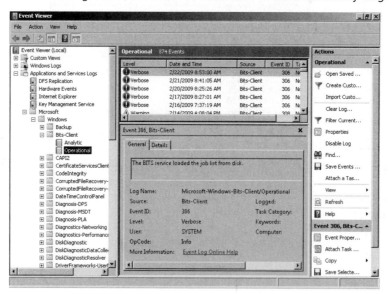

FIGURE 1-4 Windows-based diagnostic logs can be read by using the Get-Event cmdlet.

The actual names for these diagnostic logs can be rather long. The name of the log in Figure 1-4 is Microsoft-Windows-Bits-Client/operational. The easiest way to refer to the logs is by using a wildcard character as shown here.

```
Get-Event -LogName *bits*
```

- **Limit-EventLog** Sets the event log properties that limit the size of the event log and the age of its entries on a local or remote computer. To set the retention policy for a computer, use the *retention* parameter as shown here.

```
Limit-EventLog -LogName application -Retention 8
```

- **New-EventLog** Creates a new event log and a new event source on a local or remote computer. To create a new event log, you need to specify both a name and a source for the log. If you leave out the *–computername* parameter, it is assumed to be local. The following example creates a new event log named forScripting with a named source called ScriptErrors. This log will be created on a remote computer named berlin. The custom event log created by this command is shown in Figure 1-5.

```
New-EventLog -LogName forScripting -Source ScriptErrors -ComputerName berlin
```

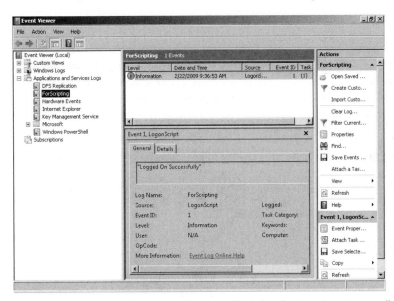

FIGURE 1-5 Custom event logs are easily created by using the New-EventLog cmdlet.

- **Remove-EventLog** Deletes an event log or unregisters an event source on a local or remote computer. To remove an event log, use the Remove-EventLog cmdlet, and specify the log name and the computer name, if applicable.

```
Remove-EventLog -LogName forscripting –computername berlin
```

- **Show-EventLog**   Displays the event logs of a local or remote computer in Event Viewer. This command is the same as typing **eventvwr** inside the Windows PowerShell console. To use the Show-EventLog cmdlet, type the name of the cmdlet, and specify the name of the computer whose event logs you want to display in the Event Viewer console as illustrated here.

```
Show-EventLog  -ComputerName berlin
```

- **Write-EventLog**   Writes an event to an event log.

```
Write-EventLog -LogName forScripting -EventId 1000 -Source ScriptErrors `
-EntryType information -Message "Script Completed" -ComputerName berlin
```

You can find a complete listing of new cmdlets and a description of their use in this book's Appendices section.

Modified cmdlets

Several cmdlets in Windows PowerShell 2.0 have new parameters. Perhaps the most immediately useful parameter is the *–computername* parameter, which allows you to work with computers in a remote fashion. The following modified cmdlets now add the *–computername* parameter.

- **Get-EventLog**   Gets the events in an event log or a list of the event logs on local or remote computers. The following command uses the *–computername* parameter with the Get-EventLog cmdlet to retrieve the most recent event from the application log on a remote computer named berlin.

```
Get-EventLog -ComputerName berlin -LogName application -Newest 1
```

- **Get-Process**   Gets the processes that are running on a local or remote computer. The following command uses the new *–computername* parameter with the Get-Process cmdlet to obtain a listing of the processes currently running on a remote computer named berlin.

```
Get-Process -ComputerName berlin
```

- **Get-Service**   Gets the services on a local or remote computer. By using the *–computername* parameter with the Get-Service cmdlet, you can obtain a listing of the status of all of the services that are defined on a remote computer named berlin.

```
Get-Service -ComputerName berlin
```

- **Set-Service**   Starts, stops, and suspends a service and changes its properties. The Set-Service cmdlet also has been updated to include the *–computername* parameter. As shown here, the new parameter is used to connect to a remote computer named berlin and to change the startup type of the service to manual. Because the Set-Service cmdlet is modifying the system state, it uses the *–confirm* switch to ensure that you are working with both the correct computer and the correct service.

```
Set-Service -ComputerName berlin -Name bits -StartupType manual –Confirm
```

Alternate Credentials and the Windows PowerShell Providers

The *–credential* parameter was present in Windows PowerShell 1.0 in the `Get-WmiObject` cmdlet only. It has since been added to several cmdlets, such as Add-Content and `Get-Content`. This parameter allows for the use of alternate credentials when making remote connections. However, when I tested this by trying to access a file on a remote computer, it came back with an error as shown in Figure 1-6.

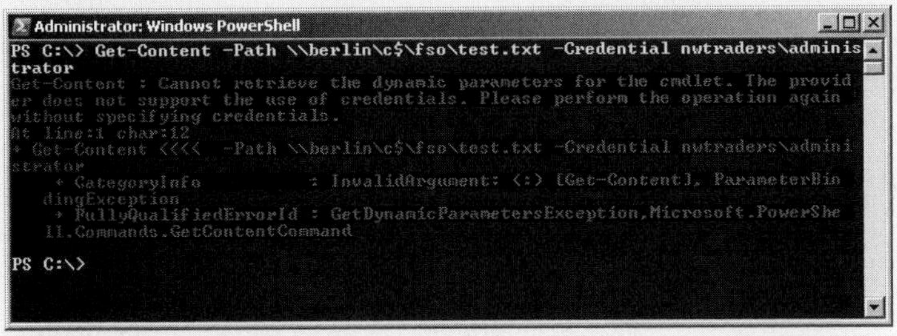

FIGURE 1-6 To use the *–credential* parameter, the provider must support it.

I investigated this error by examining the capabilities of the providers. To see what types of capabilities the providers could support, I used the *GetValues()* static method from the *System.Enum* .NET Framework class. The *GetValues()* method takes one argument—the name of the .NET Framework class from which it is to retrieve the enumeration values. The *System.Management.Automation.Provider.ProviderCapabilities* class contains the enumeration values. The following code obtains these values.

```
[enum]::getValues("System.Management.Automation.Provider.
ProviderCapabilities")
```

The result was the following list of provider capabilities.

```
None
Include
Exclude
Filter
ExpandWildcards
ShouldProcess
Credentials
Transactions
```

Now that I had a listing of the capabilities available to providers, I needed to see which default Windows PowerShell 2.0 providers support the *Credentials* capability. (This *Credentials* capability will be implemented by the cmdlets as a *–credential* parameter.) To see this, I used the `Get-PSProvider` cmdlet. As shown here, none of the default Windows PowerShell 2.0 providers support the use of capabilities.

```
Get-PSProvider
Name                   Capabilities                   Drives
----                   ------------                   ------
Alias                  ShouldProcess                  {Alias}
Environment            ShouldProcess                  {Env}
FileSystem             Filter, ShouldProcess          {C, D, dle,
apw...}
Function               ShouldProcess                  {Function}
Registry               ShouldProcess, Transactions    {HKLM, HKCU,
HKCR}
Variable               ShouldProcess                  {Variable}
Certificate            ShouldProcess                  {cert,
certCU}
WSMan                  None                           {WSMan}
```

Architectural Changes

Perhaps the most exciting additions to Windows PowerShell are in the area of architectural changes, including the ability to run a script remotely. There are five ways in which you can do remoting within Windows PowerShell 2.0, listed here.

- **The –*computername* parameter of certain cmdlets** This is the easiest remoting to do and was discussed earlier in the "Modified cmdlets" section of this chapter.

- **Remote interactive session** Establish a remote session by using the `Enter-PSSession` cmdlet.

- **Remote command execution** Execute a remote command by using the `Invoke-Command` cmdlet.

- **Persistent connection** Use the `New-PSSession` cmdlet to create a persistent connection prior to using `Invoke-Command` to execute remote commands.

- **Remote script execution** Use `Invoke-Command` to execute a locally stored script on a remote computer.

Remote Interactive Session

When you have a series of commands to enter or some work to accomplish on a remote server or workstation, a remote interactive session is the remote tool you need to use. A remote interactive session turns the Windows PowerShell session on your machine into a PowerShell session on a remote machine. All commands that you type are executed as if they were typed on the console of the remote computer.

> **NOTE** Be careful with *–path* parameter in a remote interactive session because it resolves to the remote computer, which can be very confusing at first.

You are allowed to have only one remote interactive session running from your Windows PowerShell console. It is permissible, however, to have multiple Windows PowerShell consoles open and for each to have a remote interactive session running. To begin an interactive Windows PowerShell session, use the `Enter-PSSession` cmdlet. You do not need to rely on passthrough authentication because the cmdlet supports the *–credential* parameter. This syntax is illustrated here.

```
Enter-PSSession -ComputerName Berlin -Credential nwtraders/administrator
```

Remote Command Execution

If you have only a few commands that you want to execute on the remote computer, you can use the `Invoke-Command` cmdlet. When using the `Invoke-Command` cmdlet, a remote connection is established on the remote computer, the command is executed, data is returned to the originating computer, and the connection is broken. A subsequent command to the remote computer creates a new temporary connection in the same manner as the first. There is no persistent connection, data, or shared state between the connections. The following code executes the `Get-Host` cmdlet on a remote server named berlin. The results from berlin are returned to the host computer.

```
PS C:\> Invoke-Command -ComputerName berlin -ScriptBlock { get-host }
Name             : ServerRemoteHost
Version          : 1.0.0.0
InstanceId       : 4bef95fc-7ee4-4be6-93b8-be7ea9ed3757
UI               : System.Management.Automation.Internal.Host.InternalHostUserInterf
                   ace
CurrentCulture   : en-US
CurrentUICulture : en-US
PrivateData      : PSComputerName    : berlin
```

Persistent Connection

If you want to run a series of commands on multiple computers and maintain the ability to share data between the commands, you need to first make a persistent connection prior to using the `Invoke-Command` cmdlet. To create the persistent session, you use the `New-PSSession` cmdlet and specify the name of the computer. You will need to save the returned connection object in a variable. You then use this connection when running the remote command. In the example here, the command first establishes a persistent session with a computer named berlin. The command then stores the returned session object in a variable named *$session*. On the next line in the example, the *–session* parameter is used by the `Invoke-Command` cmdlet to run two commands. The script block for the first command uses the `Get-Command` cmdlet to get a collection of commands from the remote computer. The *command* objects are stored in a variable named *$a*. On the next line of the example, the persistent connection continues to be used as the session object stored in the *$session* variable is once again supplied to the Invoke-Command cmdlet. This time, the *$a* variable is shared between the running of the two commands. The objects contained in the *$a* variable pass to the Get-Help cmdlet. This sharing of variables between commands in a single session can add great flexibility to your ability to work remotely.

```
$session = New-PSSession -ComputerName berlin
Invoke-Command -Session $session -ScriptBlock { $a = Get-Command }
Invoke-Command -Session $session -ScriptBlock { $a | get-help }
```

Remote Script Execution

In the past, if you needed to execute a script on a remote computer but the script was stored locally on your host machine, you had to physically copy the script to the remote computer and then use something to execute the remote computer, such as the *create* method from the *Win32_Process* class. In Windows PowerShell 2.0, you can use the Invoke-Command cmdlet to execute a script that is stored locally and have it run on a remote computer. When the script is run, the results of the script are returned to the local computer.

As a best practice, you can use a remote interactive session when you want to perform multiple commands on a single remote computer. If you want to run one or two commands on multiple remote computers, you can use remote command execution. If you want to execute multiple commands on multiple computers, you can use a persistent connection. If you need to run a script that does not exist on a remote computer, you can use remote script execution.

The example shown here uses the Invoke-Command cmdlet to run a script named GetBios.ps1 on a remote computer named berlin. The *–filepath* parameter is used to tell the Invoke-Command cmdlet where to find the script. This path must resolve locally.

```
PS C:\> Invoke-Command -ComputerName berlin -FilePath C:\fso\getBios.ps1
SMBIOSBIOSVersion : 080002
Manufacturer       : American Megatrends Inc.
Name               : BIOS Date: 02/22/06 20:54:49  Ver: 08.00.02
SerialNumber       : 2096-1160-0447-0846-3027-2471-99
Version            : A M I  - 2000622
PSComputerName     : berlin
```

Comparing Windows PowerShell 2.0 to VBScript

Comparing Windows PowerShell 2.0 to VBScript may seem like comparing oranges with bananas, but it is a comparison that companies need to make as they determine where to invest their future scripting efforts.

The Learning Curve

At first glance, Windows PowerShell seems to be overly complicated. The syntax is strange to most network administrators. The hyphen in the cmdlet names is annoying at first, as is the use of the braces (curly brackets, or squiggly things).

VBScript just seems to be a bit more natural, despite its admittedly wordy syntax. Perhaps the biggest reason for this perception is simply the amount of exposure it has received. Network administrators have been looking at VBScript files for more than 10 years, while even the most ardent Windows PowerShell fan has been using PowerShell for less than one-third of that time frame. What is also daunting at first is the interactive nature of Windows PowerShell. VBScript is a scripting language and does not behave in an interactive fashion. To run a command that is not native to VBScript, you must use the *exec* method from the *WshShell* object. This process is not needed within Windows PowerShell; external commands are native. In this manner, Windows PowerShell behaves more like an old-fashioned batch file. In fact, in its most basic form, a Windows PowerShell script is exactly like a batch file. It's simply a collection of commands that can be typed interactively from the prompt. Bill Mell, a senior systems administrator from Ohio in the United States, shares his experience in the following sidebar.

NOTES FROM THE FIELD

Learning Windows PowerShell

Bill Mell, MCSE, Senior Systems Administrator
Ohio Shared Information Systems

When I first saw Windows PowerShell, I was really struck by how different the command line is compared to working with the command prompt. Second, I was confronted with how difficult it is to get a script to run.

As I began to dig into Windows PowerShell, I saw that this program is definitely good. I like being able to chain different commands together by using the pipeline. At first, I used Windows PowerShell with Microsoft Exchange 2007, and I am now using it to replace as many of my existing VBScripts as I can. However, I have not found another method that I can use in Windows PowerShell to modify folder permissions that works as well for me as what I have already established in VBScript.

Most of my new development is done on Windows PowerShell because I can spend one-third of the time in development and obtain two or three times as much information from my computer systems compared to working with VBScript. The ability to create new cmdlets via scripting is pretty cool, but I have not really noticed a big demand for script cmdlets yet.

The most difficult challenge that I have confronted is trying to create a scheduled task to run a series of Windows PowerShell commands. I was initially a bit baffled,

> but after spending some time doing research on the Internet and then experimenting, it ended up being very easy.
>
> All in all, I can say I love Windows PowerShell. The biggest benefits it has given to me are ease of development and rapid access to vital system configuration information. It is quickly becoming my go-to tool of choice for system administration.

Component Object Model (COM) Support

When working with Windows PowerShell, you often have a choice between two or more ways of doing essentially the same task. Often, the method you choose does not really matter as long as the job gets done. If you are really comfortable with VBScript, you may prefer to use the *FileSystemObject* object as shown in the following CreateFolder.ps1 script.

CreateFolder.ps1
```
$fso = New-Object -ComObject scripting.filesystemobject
$fso.CreateFolder("C:\fso2")
```

When you become more comfortable with Windows PowerShell, you can perform the same action in a single line as shown here.

```
New-Item -Path C:\fso2 -ItemType directory
```

So, which is better? One way to make this determination is to see which command performs the fastest. To measure the length of time that elapses from running each command, you can use the Measure-Object cmdlet. The following command measures the amount of time spent running the CreateFolder.ps1 script.

```
Measure-Command -Expression {  $fso = New-Object -ComObject scripting.filesystemobject ;
$fso.CreateFolder("C:\fso2") }
```

Here are the results from this measurement.

```
Days              : 0
Hours             : 0
Minutes           : 0
Seconds           : 0
Milliseconds      : 1
Ticks             : 15452
TotalDays         : 1.78842592592593E-08
TotalHours        : 4.29222222222222E-07
TotalMinutes      : 2.57533333333333E-05
TotalSeconds      : 0.0015452
TotalMilliseconds : 1.5452
```

One millisecond is pretty quick! Let's see how the native Windows PowerShell commands fare. Once again, you can use the `Measure-Command` cmdlet. Here is the code to measure your command.

```
Measure-Command -Expression { New-Item -Path C:\fso2 -ItemType directory }
```

When you run this command, you obtain the following results.

```
Days              : 0
Hours             : 0
Minutes           : 0
Seconds           : 0
Milliseconds      : 3
Ticks             : 34692
TotalDays         : 4.01527777777778E-08
TotalHours        : 9.63666666666667E-07
TotalMinutes      : 5.782E-05
TotalSeconds      : 0.0034692
TotalMilliseconds : 3.4692
```

With this run, the results indicate that the Windows PowerShell method is three times slower than using *FileSystemObject*. As a best practice, when using the `Measure-Command` cmdlet, you should not make decisions about the capabilities of commands based on milliseconds. Rewrite your task in the form of a script that performs several thousand iterations of the command and time that task.

Now, write a few scripts to test your results. The first script is named CreateFolders.ps1, and it creates 10,000 subfolders under the C:\fso2 folder on your computer. This script is shown here.

```
CreateFolders.ps1
for( $i = 1 ; $i -le 10000 ; $i++)
{
    new-item -path c:\fso2 -name "Folder_$i" -itemtype director
}
```

To use the `Measure-Command` cmdlet to measure how long it takes for the script to complete, you must use the `Invoke-Expression` cmdlet. This cmdlet executes your script and allows you to see how long the command takes to complete, essentially measuring the execution time of your script. Here is the command to execute and measure the time to completion of the script.

```
Measure-Command -Expression { Invoke-Expression "C:\FSO\createFolders.ps1" }
```

When this script finally completes after approximately 40 seconds, the following results are presented.

```
Days              : 0
Hours             : 0
```

```
Minutes            : 0
Seconds            : 40
Milliseconds       : 449
Ticks              : 404494371
TotalDays          : 0.00046816478125
TotalHours         : 0.01123595475
TotalMinutes       : 0.674157285
TotalSeconds       : 40.4494371
TotalMilliseconds  : 40449.4371
```

Now, use the *FileSystemObject* object in a script and see how long it takes to create 10,000 subfolders. Here is the script, named CreateFoldersFSO.ps1.

CreateFoldersFSO.ps1
```
$fso = New-Object -ComObject scripting.filesystemobject
for( $i = 1 ; $i -le 10000 ; $i++)
{
  $fso.CreateFolder("C:\fso2\Folder_$i")
}
```

Use the same command to measure the execution time of the script. The only change you must make is to point to the new script as shown here.

```
Measure-Command -Expression { Invoke-Expression "C:\FSO\CreateFoldersFSO.ps1" }
```

The results are rather surprising. The script that uses *FileSystemObject* is nearly seven times faster. The CreateFoldersFSO.ps1 script completes in about 7 seconds as shown here.

```
Days               : 0
Hours              : 0
Minutes            : 0
Seconds            : 7
Milliseconds       : 428
Ticks              : 74287808
TotalDays          : 8.59812592592593E-05
TotalHours         : 0.00206355022222222
TotalMinutes       : 0.123813013333333
TotalSeconds       : 7.4287808
TotalMilliseconds  : 7428.7808
```

From a performance perspective, *FileSystemObject* is clearly faster than the corresponding .NET Framework classes that Windows PowerShell relies on. Which is easier to use? There is one extra step involved in using a Component Object Model (COM) object as opposed to the native Windows PowerShell command. When working directly from the command line and creating a small number of folders, I prefer to use the New-Item cmdlet because it is easier to use. However, when creating a large number of folders, I fall back on using *FileSystemObject* due to its inherent speed. As a best practice, I prefer to use the native Windows PowerShell cmdlets over corresponding COM objects because they are generally easier to use. The only exception is when a COM object has a clear speed advantage over the Windows PowerShell cmdlet.

Perhaps the biggest decision maker as to whether you can abandon VBScript is support for COM objects. Because Windows PowerShell is based on the .NET Framework, it does not have native COM support. However, this does not mean that you cannot use COM objects. For simple COM objects, the support is good. To create an instance of a COM object, use the New-Object cmdlet and specify the program ID to the –ComObject parameter. Windows PowerShell expects a string value for this parameter, and quotation marks are not required. Store the returned COM object in a variable named $wshShell. On the next line, use the *item* method to obtain the path to the user's desktop folder as shown here.

```
PS MRED C:\>$wshShell = new-object -ComObject wscript.shell
PS MRED C:\>$wshShell.SpecialFolders.Item("desktop")
C:\Users\edwilson\Desktop
```

If you are not interested in using anything else from the COM object, you do not need to go through the intermediate step of storing the object and accessing the object from a variable. You can rewrite the previous line of code to create the object and use the object at the same time. As a best practice, be very careful when using the inline method of working with COM objects. Inline code, in which you both create and use the object at the same time, can quickly become difficult to read. Stylistically, you should prefer the *block* method, in which you create the object and store it in a variable. Then, in the next line, you use the methods or properties from that object. This warning aside, here is the one-line version of the script.

```
PS MRED C:\>(new-object -ComObject wscript.shell).specialfolders.item("desktop")
C:\Users\edwilson\Desktop
```

Comparing Windows PowerShell 2.0 to the Command Shell

Many companies that have never used VBScript have invested heavily in the use of .bat files. In most cases, existing .bat files can be translated into Windows PowerShell. At times, the translation can be as simple as changing the extension from .bat to .ps1 as shown in the following example.

```
CopyAndLog.bat
md c:\fso2
copy c:\fso\* c:\fso2 > c:\fso2\auditLog.txt
c:\fso2\auditlog.txt
```

All of the commands in the CopyAndLog.bat script are legal commands within Windows PowerShell. The *md* alias creates a directory. The *copy* alias copies files from one folder to another, and typing the path to the text file causes it to open in the Notepad program. The difference is discovered when the Auditlog.txt file is opened. When the Copy command is used in the cmd prompt, it prints the path of each file as it is copied. When using the *copy* alias in

Windows PowerShell, it does not print the path of each file. To achieve the same functionality as the CopyAndLog.bat script, you need to modify the script a bit as shown here.

```
CopyAndLog.ps1
md c:\fso2
Copy C:\fso\* C:\fso2  -passthru |
foreach { $_.fullname >> c:\fso2\auditlog.txt}
c:\fso2\auditlog.txt
```

In the CopyAndLog.ps1 script, the first change you need to make from the CopyAndLog.bat script is to add the *passthru* parameter, which tells Windows PowerShell to allow the object to pass over the pipe (the | character) to enable you to continue to work with the object. Because you will have several objects coming over the pipe, you need to use the ForEach cmdlet to obtain the *FullName* property of the file objects. You then redirect and append the names and paths of all of the files that are copied to the Auditlog.txt file. The braces signify the start and end of a code block that will be executed for each file that comes over the pipe. The *$_* automatic variable is used to refer to each individual file in succession.

Deployment Requirements for Windows PowerShell 2.0

Depending on the version of Windows that is running on your network, the deployment of Windows PowerShell 2.0 can be rather easy. For example, with Windows Server 2008 R2, Windows PowerShell is already installed. On the Windows Server 2008 server, you need to update the version of the .NET Framework if you did not install the .NET Framework 3.0 feature. If you installed the Windows PowerShell 1.0 feature, you need to uninstall PowerShell 1.0. Before delving into all of the deployment details, let's look at the requirements for Windows PowerShell 2.0.

.NET Framework

There are actually two dependencies on the .NET Framework. If you want to use Windows PowerShell 2.0 in the same manner that you used PowerShell 1.0, all that you need is .NET Framework 3.0, which ships with Windows Vista and is included on the DVD with Windows Server 2008. On Microsoft Windows XP and Windows Server 2003, you more than likely need to perform an upgrade to the .NET Framework to at least version 3.0 because neither of these operating systems shipped with version 3.0 of the .NET Framework. This level of the .NET Framework allows you to work in an interactive fashion from within Windows PowerShell.

If you install .NET Framework 3.5 while you are installing .NET Framework 3.0, you also gain access to the graphical user interface (GUI) version of Windows PowerShell. This graphical console has many script editor–like features, including IntelliSense. The Windows PowerShell Integrated Scripting Environment (ISE) uses features from .NET Framework 3.5.

In general, there are very few compatibility issues between different versions of the .NET Framework. You will probably be safe installing .NET Framework 3.5 directly because, technically, .NET Framework 3.5 is considered to be an update to version 2.0 of the .NET Framework. You can directly apply the .NET Framework 3.5 package to your existing installation, which permits you to bypass installing .NET Framework 3.0 and 3.0 Service Pack 1 (SP1).

Service Dependencies

Two services need to be running to install Windows PowerShell 2.0. Because Windows PowerShell is delivered as an update to the operating system, you need both the Background Intelligent Transfer Service (BITS) and the Windows Update Service. This is generally not an issue because both services typically start by default. However, it was common in the past for both services to be disabled in an enterprise environment when software updating used alternatives to Windows Update. Windows Remote Management (WinRm) needs to be running version 2.0 and to be properly configured. On both Windows Vista and Windows Server 2008, you need to update WinRM. On Windows XP and Windows Server 2003, you need to install WinRm. On Windows Server 2008 R2, no update is required. Once installed, WinRm also needs to be configured. A cmdlet, `Enable-PSRemoting`, can be used to configure WinRM.

Deploying Windows PowerShell 2.0

Deploying Windows PowerShell 2.0 can be somewhat complicated depending on the number of different operating systems on your network. Additionally, the complications are exacerbated depending on whether you have stayed current with all of the updates to the .NET Framework. The following list details some of the considerations and paths that you can take to get Windows PowerShell 2.0 up and running on your system. The process is not quite as complicated as it looks. Basically, if you are running Windows PowerShell 1.0, you need to uninstall it. If you want to use remoting, you need WinRM 2.0. If you want to use the Windows PowerShell ISE, you need .NET Framework 3.5. The details are listed here.

> **IMPORTANT** Prior to deploying Windows PowerShell 2.0, you must decide whether you will be taking advantage of the remoting features and using the Windows PowerShell ISE. If the answer is no on both counts, you can skip the download of WinRM 2.0 and .NET Framework 3.5.

- **Windows XP** Windows XP needs to be at Service Pack 2.0 and needs an update to the .NET Framework. In addition, if Windows PowerShell 1.0 is installed, it must be uninstalled. WinRM 2.0 needs to be installed prior to the installation of Windows PowerShell 2.0.

- **Windows Server 2003** Windows Server 2003 needs to be at SP1 and needs an update to the .NET Framework. In addition, if Windows PowerShell 1.0 is installed, it must be uninstalled. WinRM 2.0 needs to be installed prior to the installation of Windows PowerShell 2.0.

- **Windows Vista** Windows Vista needs an update to the .NET Framework. If Windows PowerShell 1.0 is installed, it must be uninstalled. You need to install WinRM 2.0 prior to the installation of Windows PowerShell 2.0.

- **Windows Server 2008** Windows Server 2008 needs an update to the .NET Framework. If Windows PowerShell 1.0 is installed, it must be uninstalled. You need to install WinRM 2.0 prior to the installation of Windows PowerShell 2.0. Windows PowerShell 2.0 cannot be installed on Windows Server 2008 Core Edition.

- **Windows Server 2008 R2 and Windows 7 operating systems** Windows PowerShell 2.0 is included in both the server and client versions of Windows Server 2008 R2. No configuration changes are required. For Windows Server 2008 R2 Core Edition, Windows PowerShell 2.0 and the corresponding .NET Framework requirement can both be added as features.

 ON THE COMPANION MEDIA This information is summarized in the Windows PowerShell_Requirements spreadsheet in the Job Aids folder on the companion media.

Where to Deploy Windows PowerShell 2.0

One of the main decisions facing network administrators and consultants is where to deploy Windows PowerShell 2.0. As you saw in the previous section, Windows PowerShell can be installed on a wide variety of platforms. From a decision standpoint, the easy approach is to deploy it everywhere. However, as detailed in the previous section, the number of dependencies and the wide variety of test matrixes required to ensure a zero-impact deployment across the entire network may not justify deploying it everywhere.

How Do You Anticipate Using Windows PowerShell 2.0?

Part of the decision to deploy Windows PowerShell 2.0 will be influenced largely by how you decide to use it. Once you have installed Windows Server 2008 R2 everywhere, the decision to deploy Windows PowerShell is a nonissue because it is already included. The following list highlights ways in which Windows PowerShell can be used in the enterprise.

- Schedule jobs
- Run scripts
- Run remote commands to make configuration changes
- Query settings
- Parse setup logs
- Parse event logs

Depending on which features you need, you may deploy to the desktop, to the server farm, or only to selected machines. Some network administrators consider it a large problem to deploy Windows PowerShell 2.0 to the desktop, with the main consideration being the issue of updating the .NET Framework to the required levels. Depending on your philosophy of desktop management, Windows PowerShell can be an awesome tool to use to administer desktop computers. It can be heavily used by help desk personnel. However, if you have a 30-minute image rule (if a problem is not solved in 30 minutes, you re-image the desktop), it is possible that the help desk is not greatly involved in troubleshooting. Because of its ability to access event logs, diagnostic logs, and system settings in a quick and efficient manner, Windows PowerShell should find a place in your standard troubleshooting arsenal.

Most enterprises that I have worked with have deployed Windows PowerShell to the server farm first. It seems that network administrators are more comfortable with Windows PowerShell and, once trained on its use, they naturally want to use it to perform both simple and complex configuration tasks and auditing. Because servers are more closely managed than desktops in most enterprises, Windows PowerShell makes a nice addition to the server.

Some companies have deployed Windows PowerShell to a few machines. The biggest problem with this scenario is that it is easy to become addicted to Windows PowerShell, and it then becomes indispensible. An analogy to partial Windows PowerShell deployment comes from the early days of VBScript. When VBScript was not available everywhere, you could not depend on it. When you needed to use VBScript, you were confronted with a download-and-install scenario on a server. This meant putting VBScript into change control, requesting approval for the installation, providing justification and cost return on investment calculations, and scheduling downtime for the server. By the time you were done with all of these steps, the "simple change" of adding VBScript to a server had become a project. The presenting problem that prompted you to seek VBScript assistance was easier to do manually, even if it meant making 150 changes via the GUI. This exact scenario is occurring today with Windows PowerShell. Until Windows PowerShell is ubiquitous in your environment, you will be hesitant to rely on its power. As a best practice, you should initially deploy Windows PowerShell to servers where you can more than likely see the greatest benefit because servers are more heavily managed than desktops, and Windows PowerShell can provide assistance in configuration management. Once ensconced in the server farm, you should deploy to the desktop and begin using Windows PowerShell to assist in troubleshooting desktop issues. Training should follow deployment—that is, server administrators first and then help desk personnel.

Additional Resources

- Windows PowerShell is a free download from the Microsoft Download Center at *http://www.microsoft.com/downloads/*.
- For information on event-driven queries, refer to the Microsoft Press book, *Microsoft Windows Scripting with WMI: Self-Paced Learning Guide* (Microsoft Press, 2006).
- On the companion media, you can find the Windows PowerShell_Requirements spreadsheet in the Job Aids folder.

## CHAPTER 2

Survey of Windows PowerShell Capabilities

While this chapter presents a survey of some of the basic capabilities of Windows PowerShell 2.0, it also presents some pretty cool best practices for using them. Windows PowerShell issues in a raft of new and exciting features, many of which will completely change the way you have used Windows PowerShell in the past.

Using the Interactive Command Line

Once Windows PowerShell 2.0 is installed on a workstation or server, it is quite natural to open the PowerShell prompt and begin to work. In fact, a lot of information can be obtained quickly, efficiently, and easily. As an example, if you are concerned about the processes running on a computer, you can type the following command at the Windows PowerShell prompt.

```
PS C:\> Gps
```

Three little letters, and you receive back the following information (trimmed for clarity).

Handles	NPM(K)	PM(K)	WS(K)	VM(M)	CPU(s)	Id	ProcessName
300	5	1636	1552	23	50.35	416	csrss
101	4	872	3288	36	1.45	1260	ctfmon
377	9	13596	20480	74	32.15	912	explorer
0	0	0	16	0		0	Idle
376	9	3692	1928	40	1.87	572	lsass
211	5	29320	24560	127	0.74	492	powershell
286	7	4272	5612	55	4.23	560	services

In this example, an alias (shortcut name) is used for the Get-Process cmdlet. However, if you type the entire cmdlet name, it does not involve a tremendous amount of effort to retrieve a significant piece of information. While it is true that you can obtain similar information from the Windows Task Manager utility, you are limited in your ability to store the information and to filter and sort the data that is returned. With Windows PowerShell, there is no such limitation. In this example, you find only processes that have a CPU time of more than five seconds and that write the results to a text file named FilteredProcess.txt. When this command is run, there is no screen output. As you can see in Figure 2-1, you now have a text file that you can use at a later date for comparison purposes on your server.

```
PS C:\> Get-Process | Where-Object { $_.cpu -gt 5 } |
Out-File -FilePath C:\fso1\FilteredProcess.txt
```

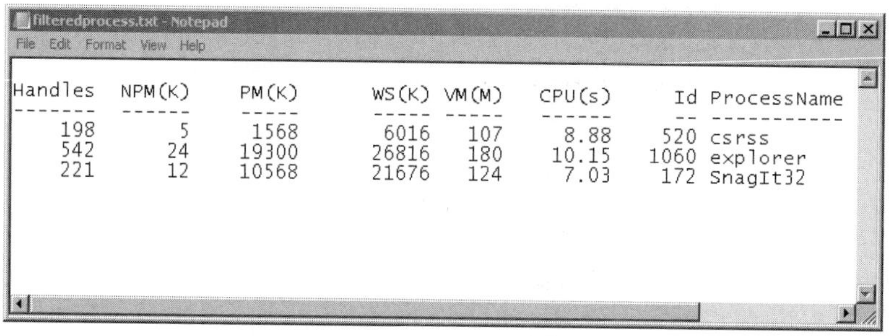

FIGURE 2-1 One of the advantages of Windows PowerShell is the ease of storing results.

In other scripting languages, formatting output can consume a significant amount of time and resources. With Windows PowerShell 2.0, there are a number of cmdlets that ease the burden of formatting output.

If you are interested in the status of services running on your computer, you can use the Get-Service cmdlet. When working interactively from the Windows PowerShell 2.0 console, you can type the following command.

```
PS C:\> gsv
```

You are rewarded with a listing of services installed on your computer. You can see the status of the service, the name of the service, and the display name of the service as shown here (truncated for readability).

```
Status   Name            DisplayName
------   ----            -----------
Running  1-vmsrvc        Virtual Machine Additions Services ...
Stopped  AeLookupSvc     Application Experience
Stopped  ALG             Application Layer Gateway Service
Stopped  Appinfo         Application Information
Stopped  AppMgmt         Application Management
Stopped  AudioEndpointBu... Windows Audio Endpoint Builder
Stopped  Audiosrv        Windows Audio
Running  BFE             Base Filtering Engine
Running  BITS            Background Intelligent Transfer Ser...
```

The display of this information is important owing to the difference between the name of the service and the display name of the service. As an example, the name of the BITS service is BITS; however, the display name is Background Intelligent Transfer Service. When using the Services snap-in, the name that is shown is the display name and not the actual name of the service. This causes confusion when trying to manage a service from the command line or from the graphical Services tool. The Services tool is shown in Figure 2-2.

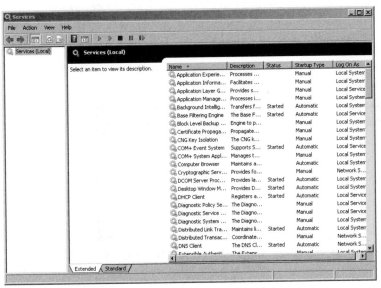

FIGURE 2-2 The Services snap-in arranges services by display name rather than by name.

Be Careful with Performance

Georges Maheu, DESS, MCSE, CISSP, Security Operations Consultant
Microsoft Canada Services

When I am working with Windows PowerShell, I spend 100 percent of my time writing scripts. However, I always have the console open so that I can look up information, test syntax, or use help. The thing to keep in mind is that Windows PowerShell can go from simple (using a cmdlet with no parameters) to complex scripts very quickly. Yet, the same can be said of VBScript; I have seen both simple VBScripts and very convoluted scripts. Be careful when writing scripts because you can easily peg the processor if you write a bad Windows Management Instrumentation (WMI) query. A poorly written script can bring a server to its knees.

The Easiest cmdlets

With more than 200 cmdlets in Windows PowerShell 2.0, it may seem overwhelming at first glance. Where do you begin? Some people begin using Windows PowerShell by using the "low-hanging fruit" methodology: What can I type and get back information? The following are some easy-to-use cmdlets. Every cmdlet returns information and requires no parameters or additional information. Keep in mind that on Windows Vista and later, the `Get-ComputerRestorePoint` cmdlet requires administrative rights, or it will fail with access denied.

- **Get-Acl**   Gets the security descriptor for a resource, such as a file or registry key. When used without any parameters, it displays access permissions for the C: drive. This command returns a *System.Security* class.

- **Get-Alias**   Gets the aliases for the current session. When used without any parameters, it produces a listing of all aliases that are defined in the current session of Windows PowerShell. This command returns a *System.Management.Automation.Aliasinfo* object.

- **Get-ChildItem**   Gets the items and child items in one or more specified locations. When used without any parameters, it produces a listing of files and folders from the root drive. This command returns a *System.Io.Fileinfo* and a *System.Io.Directoryinfo* object.

- **Get-Command**   Gets basic information about cmdlets and other elements of Windows PowerShell commands. When used without any parameters, it produces a listing of all cmdlets available during the current Windows PowerShell session. This command returns a *System.Management.Automation.Cmdletinfo* object.

- **Get-Culture**   Gets the current culture set in the operating system. When used without any parameters, it returns the current culture settings. This command returns a *System. Globalization.CultureInfo* object.

- **Get-Date**   Gets the current date and time. When used without any parameters, it produces a listing of the current date and time. This command returns a *System.DateTime* object.

- **Get-Host**   Gets a reference to the current console host object. It displays the Windows PowerShell version and regional information by default. This command returns a *System.Management.Automation.Internal.Host.Internalhost* object.

- **Get-HotFix**   Returns a *System.Management.ManagementObject* object that points to the *Win32_QuickFixEngineering* WMI class.

- **Get-ComputerRestorePoint**   Returns a *System.Management.ManagementObject* object that points to the *Win32_SystemRestore* WMI class.

- **Get-Process**   Gets the processes that are running on a local or remote computer. This command returns information from the *System.Diagnostics.Process* class.

- **Get-Random**   Gets a random number or selects objects randomly from a collection. This command returns a random number that is an instance of *System.Int32*. This number is generated by the *System.Random* class.

- **Get-Service**   Gets the services on a local or remote computer. This command returns information from the *System.ServiceProcess.ServiceController* class.

- **Get-UICulture**   Gets the current user interface culture set in the operating system. This command returns information from the *Microsoft.PowerShell.VistaCultureInfo* class on Windows Vista and Windows Server 2008. On Windows Server 2003 and Windows XP, it returns an instance of the *System.Globalization.CultureInfo* class.

The Most Important cmdlets

How do you determine which cmdlets are the most important? One approach is to find the cmdlets that will enable you to become productive in working with Windows PowerShell 2.0. Most Windows PowerShell experts agree that the three most important or foundational cmdlets are Get-Help, Get-Command, and Get-Member. When taken together, you not only can use Windows PowerShell 2.0 in a productive manner, but you have the tools to learn how to effectively use any set of cmdlets produced by any PowerShell application.

- **Get-Help**   Displays information about Windows PowerShell cmdlets and concepts. There are two kinds of help. Each cmdlet has a Help file that displays information about parameters and syntax, as well as technical information about the cmdlet. Most cmdlets also have examples that illustrate various methods of using them. The Get-Help cmdlet returns a *MamlCommandHelpInfo* object when producing cmdlet help. When returning a conceptual help article, it returns a *System.String* object.

- **Get-Command**   Gets basic information about cmdlets and other elements of Windows PowerShell commands. The Get-Command cmdlet allows you to search for cmdlets. This capability is important whether you are using native cmdlets or snapped-in additional cmdlets. The two most basic ways of locating cmdlets are by either the verb portion or the noun portion of their names. As mentioned earlier, the Get-Command cmdlet returns a *System.Management.Automation.Cmdletinfo* object.

- **Get-Member**   Gets the properties and methods of objects. The use of Get-Member provides insight into the object-oriented nature of Windows PowerShell. Everything in Windows PowerShell is an object, and Get-Member can be used to display the properties and methods that the objects provide. The judicious application of this cmdlet can open many new areas for exploration and exploitation within the scripting environment.

  As an example, suppose you have the following string.

  ```
  $string = "string"
  ```

By itself, it seems rather boring. But when you pipeline the *$string* variable to the Get-Member cmdlet, you reveal many properties and methods for the *System.String* class as shown here.

```
$string | Get-Member
```

Once you display the members of the *System.String* Microsoft .NET Framework class, you can examine the methods and properties to find the capability that you might want to implement in your script. For example, you might want to display the string in all capital letters, which is easily accomplished by using the *ToUpper()* method as shown here.

```
$string.ToUpper()
```

Once you have an idea of the basic capabilities of Windows PowerShell and are feeling comfortable with the command line, it is time to add two more cmdlets to the command line. These two cmdlets assist in handling and filtering output and are listed here.

- **Where-Object** Creates a filter that controls which objects are passed along a command pipeline. In the GetThreads.ps1 script, you use the Where-Object cmdlet to filter threads based on the process ID of the Explorer.exe process. Using this information, you can reduce the amount of information that is returned when you query the *Win32_Thread* WMI class. The GetThreads.ps1 script is shown here.

```
GetThreads.ps1
$name = "explorer"
$processHandle = (Get-Process -Name $name).id
$Threads = Get-WmiObject -Class Win32_Thread |
Where-Object { $_.ProcessHandle -eq $processHandle }
"The $name process has $($threads.count) threads"
$threads | Format-Table -Property priority, thread*, User*Time, kernel*Time
```

Once the GetThreads.ps1 script is run, it prints the count of the number of threads that make it through the filter. The resultant thread objects are stored in the *$threads* variable that gets piped to the Format-Table cmdlet. You choose a group of properties to be displayed. The resultant output is shown here.

```
The explorer process has 23 threads
Priority  ThreadState  ThreadWaitReason  UserModeTime  KernelModeTime
--------  -----------  ----------------  ------------  --------------
10        5            13                590           911
9         5            13                3424          12528
10        5            6                 120           140
```

- **Format-List** Formats the output as a list of properties in which each property appears on a new line. You can use this cmdlet when you are interested in a series of properties and values that would be too crowded for a table. An example of using the

Format-List cmdlet is the GetExplorer.ps1 script, which uses the Get-WmiObject cmdlet to retrieve information from the *Win32_Process* WMI class. This class uses the *–filter* parameter to reduce the information returned as only data from the Explorer.exe process. The resulting management object is pipelined to the Format-List cmdlet where only a few properties are selected. Format-List is designed to allow the use of wildcard characters when selecting properties to display. The GetExplorer.ps1 script is shown here.

```
GetExplorer.ps1
Get-WmiObject -Class win32_process -Filter "name = 'explorer.exe'" |
Format-List -Property name, ProcessID, page*, peak*, w*
```

When the GetExplorer.ps1 script is run, the output includes other properties from the object that are matched as shown here.

```
name                 : explorer.exe
ProcessID            : 1388
PageFaults           : 50788
PageFileUsage        : 17465344
PeakPageFileUsage    : 17764352
PeakVirtualSize      : 126586880
PeakWorkingSetSize   : 23097344
WS                   : 15151104
WindowsVersion       : 5.1.2600
WorkingSetSize       : 15151104
WriteOperationCount  : 114
WriteTransferCount   : 1923825
```

The complete *Win32_Process* management object is shown in Table 2-1.

TABLE 2-1 Members of the Win32_Process Management Object

NAME	MEMBERTYPE	DEFINITION
Handles	AliasProperty	"Handles = Handlecount"
ProcessName	AliasProperty	"ProcessName = Name"
VM	AliasProperty	"VM = VirtualSize"
WS	AliasProperty	"WS = WorkingSetSize"
AttachDebugger	Method	"System.Management.ManagementBaseObject AttachDebugger()"
GetOwner	Method	"System.Management.ManagementBaseObject GetOwner()"
GetOwnerSid	Method	"System.Management.ManagementBaseObject GetOwnerSid()"

NAME	MEMBERTYPE	DEFINITION
SetPriority	Method	"System.Management.ManagementBaseObject SetPriority(System.Int32 Priority)"
Terminate	Method	"System.Management.ManagementBaseObject Terminate(System.UInt32 Reason)"
Caption	Property	"System.String Caption {get;set;}"
CommandLine	Property	"System.String CommandLine {get;set;}"
CreationClassName	Property	"System.String CreationClassName {get;set;}"
CreationDate	Property	"System.String CreationDate {get;set;}"
CSCreationClassName	Property	"System.String CSCreationClassName {get;set;}"
CSName	Property	"System.String CSName {get;set;}"
Description	Property	"System.String Description {get;set;}"
ExecutablePath	Property	"System.String ExecutablePath {get;set;}"
ExecutionState	Property	"System.UInt16 ExecutionState {get;set;}"
Handle	Property	"System.String Handle {get;set;}"
HandleCount	Property	"System.UInt32 HandleCount {get;set;}"
InstallDate	Property	"System.String InstallDate {get;set;}"
KernelModeTime	Property	"System.UInt64 KernelModeTime {get;set;}"
MaximumWorkingSetSize	Property	"System.UInt32 MaximumWorkingSetSize {get;set;}"
MinimumWorkingSetSize	Property	"System.UInt32 MinimumWorkingSetSize {get;set;}"
Name	Property	"System.String Name {get;set;}"
OSCreationClassName	Property	"System.String OSCreationClassName {get;set;}"
OSName	Property	"System.String OSName {get;set;}"
OtherOperationCount	Property	"System.UInt64 OtherOperationCount {get;set;}"
OtherTransferCount	Property	"System.UInt64 OtherTransferCount {get;set;}"
PageFaults	Property	"System.UInt32 PageFaults {get;set;}"
PageFileUsage	Property	"System.UInt32 PageFileUsage {get;set;}"
ParentProcessId	Property	"System.UInt32 ParentProcessId {get;set;}"
PeakPageFileUsage	Property	"System.UInt32 PeakPageFileUsage {get;set;}"
PeakVirtualSize	Property	"System.UInt64 PeakVirtualSize {get;set;}"

NAME	MEMBERTYPE	DEFINITION
PeakWorkingSetSize	Property	"System.UInt32 PeakWorkingSetSize {get;set;}"
Priority	Property	"System.UInt32 Priority {get;set;}"
PrivatePageCount	Property	"System.UInt64 PrivatePageCount {get;set;}"
ProcessId	Property	"System.UInt32 ProcessId {get;set;}"
QuotaNonPagedPoolUsage	Property	"System.UInt32 QuotaNonPagedPoolUsage {get;set;}"
QuotaPagedPoolUsage	Property	"System.UInt32 QuotaPagedPoolUsage {get;set;}"
QuotaPeakNonPaged-PoolUsage	Property	"System.UInt32 QuotaPeakNonPagedPoolUsage {get;set;}"
QuotaPeakPagedPoolUsage	Property	"System.UInt32 QuotaPeakPagedPoolUsage {get;set;}"
ReadOperationCount	Property	"System.UInt64 ReadOperationCount {get;set;}"
ReadTransferCount	Property	"System.UInt64 ReadTransferCount {get;set;}"
SessionId	Property	"System.UInt32 SessionId {get;set;}"
Status	Property	"System.String Status {get;set;}"
TerminationDate	Property	"System.String TerminationDate {get;set;}"
ThreadCount	Property	"System.UInt32 ThreadCount {get;set;}"
UserModeTime	Property	"System.UInt64 UserModeTime {get;set;}"
VirtualSize	Property	"System.UInt64 VirtualSize {get;set;}"
WindowsVersion	Property	"System.String WindowsVersion {get;set;}"
WorkingSetSize	Property	"System.UInt64 WorkingSetSize {get;set;}"
WriteOperationCount	Property	"System.UInt64 WriteOperationCount {get;set;}"
WriteTransferCount	Property	"System.UInt64 WriteTransferCount {get;set;}"
__CLASS	Property	"System.String __CLASS {get;set;}"
__DERIVATION	Property	"System.String[] __DERIVATION {get;set;}"
__DYNASTY	Property	"System.String __DYNASTY {get;set;}"
__GENUS	Property	"System.Int32 __GENUS {get;set;}"
__NAMESPACE	Property	"System.String __NAMESPACE {get;set;}"
__PATH	Property	"System.String __PATH {get;set;}"
__PROPERTY_COUNT	Property	"System.Int32 __PROPERTY_COUNT {get;set;}"

NAME	MEMBERTYPE	DEFINITION
__RELPATH	Property	"System.String __RELPATH {get;set;}"
__SERVER	Property	"System.String __SERVER {get;set;}"
__SUPERCLASS	Property	"System.String __SUPERCLASS {get;set;}"
ConvertFromDateTime	ScriptMethod	"System.Object ConvertFromDateTime();"
ConvertToDateTime	ScriptMethod	"System.Object ConvertToDateTime();"
Delete	ScriptMethod	"System.Object Delete();"
GetType	ScriptMethod	"System.Object GetType();"
Put	ScriptMethod	"System.Object Put();"
Path	ScriptProperty	"System.Object Path {get=$this.ExecutablePath;}"

Grouping and Sorting Output

Prior to presenting output from a script, it is often advantageous to group or sort the data. The proper sort or group can allow you to discover previously unseen relationships in data obtained by a Windows PowerShell cmdlet or WMI query. In previous scripting languages, complicated merging algorithms involving multiple arrays or dictionaries were required to provide grouped information, and many sorts involved using a bubble-sorting routine that, while accurate, is a rather inefficient means of sorting data.

Windows PowerShell has the Group-Object and Sort-Object cmdlets, both of which accept pipelined data and are therefore easy to use. In the AnalyzeApplicationLog.ps1 script, you can use the Get-EventLog cmdlet to connect to the application log on the local computer and retrieve all of the events. You can then sort the returned collection of event log entries based on the *source* property. You can pipeline the sorted list of event log entries to the Group-Object cmdlet, which produces a listing of the number of event log entries. You then pipeline the resulting object into another Sort-Object cmdlet and specify the *descending* parameter to group the most prevalent entries first. The resulting output from the AnalyzeApplicationLog.ps1 script is shown in Figure 2-3.

```
AnalyzeApplicationLog.ps1
Get-EventLog -logname application |
Sort-Object -property source |
Group-Object -property source |
Sort-Object -Property count -Descending
```

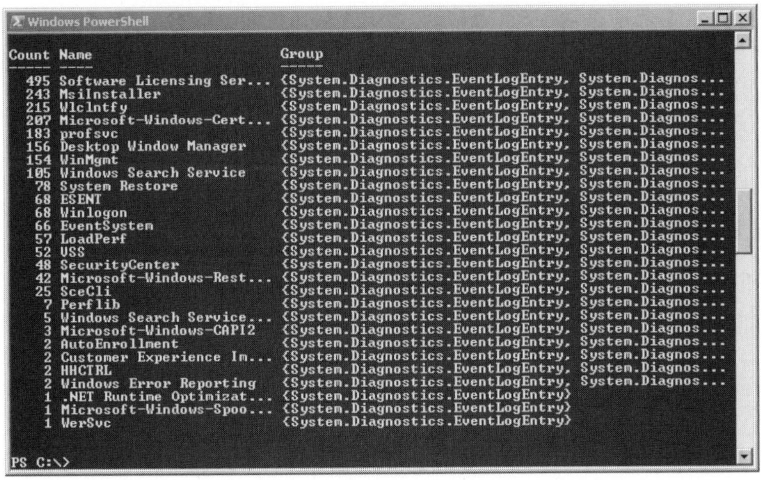

FIGURE 2-3 Grouping and sorting cmdlets lend insight to the application log.

Group-Object

This cmdlet groups objects that contain the same value for specified properties. The Group-Object cmdlet produces output that displays a numerical count of the number of times that an object meeting specific criteria occurs. The following example produces a list that tells you how many aliases exist for which cmdlets.

```
GroupAliases.ps1
Get-Alias |
Group-Object –property definition |
Sort-Object –Property count –Descending
```

Sort-Object

This cmdlet sorts objects by property values. The Sort-Object cmdlet is useful in organizing a listing of data. Once data is grouped by property, it is often beneficial to sort the data as well. The *descending* switched parameter displays the sorted list from largest numbers to smallest. In the GetGroupPolicyProcessingError.ps1 script, you can retrieve Group Policy processing failure events from the Microsoft-Windows-GroupPolicy operational log by using the Get-Event cmdlet. You can then pipeline the results to the Where-Object cmdlet to filter out only instances of the event ID 7001, which states that Group Policy processing failed for a particular user. You then pipeline the collection of event log entries to the Sort-Object cmdlet where you can perform a descending sort based on the time the error occurred.

```
GetGroupPolicyProcessingError.ps1
Get-Event -LogName *group* |
Where-Object { $_.id -eq 7001 } |
Sort-Object -Property timecreated -descending
```

Saving Output to Files

The following three cmdlets are useful in saving output to files:

- **Out-File**   Sends output to a file. If you need to create a text file, you can use the *redirection* operator. As shown here, the *redirection* operator creates a file that does not exist or overwrites a previously existing file.

  ```
  Get-Process > c:\fso\process.txt
  ```

  If you need to append to a text file, you can use the double arrow to redirect to a file and append to it. The following example illustrates this process by appending to the previously created text file. If the file did not exist, it would be created.

  ```
  Get-Process >> c:\fso\process.txt
  ```

  With the ease of creating files using the *redirection* operator, why do you need a cmdlet that does the same job? The answer is: You don't. If you are only creating or appending to a file, you can use redirection. The primary reason for using the Out-File cmdlet is to take advantage of the additional parameters that are offered, which are *width*, *encoding*, and *noclobber*.

- **Export-Clixml**   Creates an XML-based representation of an object or objects and stores it in a file.

- **Export-CSV**   Converts .NET Framework objects into a series of comma-separated, variable-length (CSV) strings and saves the strings in a CSV file.

Working with WMI

Windows Management Instrumentation (WMI) is part of Microsoft's strategic management direction and has been since its appearance more than a decade ago. Microsoft continues to invest heavily in WMI technology and the development of new classes, as well as the addition of new methods and properties to existing classes. At first glance, some network administrators may shy away from WMI in Windows PowerShell 2.0: "After all, we now have Windows PowerShell. We do not need WMI anymore." They may even point to Get-Process, Get-Service, and Get-HotFix as examples of the new and improved Windows PowerShell model. Yet, both Get-Process and Get-Service lack the functionality that is achieved by *Win32_Process* and *Win32_Service*, and, amusingly enough, Get-HotFix simply calls WMI's *Win32_QuickFixEngineering* class to retrieve its information. So, WMI is still with us.

Much of the management you will need to do involves using WMI. As a result, Windows PowerShell 2.0 has added new cmdlets to make the work involved with using WMI less onerous. WMI support in Windows PowerShell 1.0 was good, but it is much better in PowerShell 2.0. On Windows Vista, there are more than 2,000 WMI classes on the computer; compare this with approximately 200 Windows PowerShell cmdlets. In numbers alone, the coverage via WMI is ten times as great. It was not the intention of the Windows PowerShell team to write cmdlets that duplicate existing WMI classes; rather, it was their intention to write cmdlets to allow you to access WMI in an easy fashion. The WMI cmdlets that are in Windows PowerShell are detailed here.

- **Get-WmiObject**   Gets instances of WMI classes or information about available classes. This is the fundamental WMI cmdlet and the one you will likely reach for first. By using the Get-WmiObject cmdlet, you can query properties of WMI classes, set properties, and call methods on both local and remote computers. The following is an example of retrieving information about the C: drive.

  ```
  Get-WmiObject –class Win32_Volume –filter "name = 'c:'"
  ```

- **Invoke-WmiMethod**   Calls WMI methods. This is one of the new cmdlets for Windows PowerShell 2.0. At first glance, I did not think it would be all that useful. After all, you can easily use Get-WmiObject and call WMI methods by using the "dotted notation." After working with it for a while, however, the cmdlet excels at calling WMI methods.

- **Register-WmiEvent**   The Register-WmiEvent cmdlet is a tremendous bonus to network administrators who have used other scripting languages, such as VBScript, to write event-driven WMI scripts. To use the cmdlet, you must write a WMI query that is event-driven.

- **Remove-WmiObject**   Deletes WMI classes and instances. The Remove-WmiObject cmdlet may sound dangerous, and it can be. If you are not careful, you can easily delete an actual WMI class and damage your WMI repository. There are certain WMI classes that require you to actually delete an instance of the class; one class that comes to mind is *Win32_PrinterJob*.

- **Set-WmiInstance**   Creates or modifies instances of WMI classes. Some WMI classes require you to modify an existing instance of the class or create a new instance of the class, such as the *Win32_TcpIPPrinterPort* class.

One-Line Commands

If you want to set a property of the drive, such as the label, you can use the following command.

```
((Get-WmiObject -class Win32_Volume -filter "name = 'c:'").label = "new
drive label").put()
```

I do not prefer to write one-line commands, such as the previous one, because they are hard to read. Yet, there are some valid benefits.

- Easy to schedule. Copy the one-line command on the Actions tab in Task Scheduler.
- Easy to re-execute. Use the Up Arrow, add the *–computer* parameter, and press Enter.
- Easy to back up. Highlight the line, press Enter, and copy to Notepad.

I would prefer to assign a new volume label with three lines of code. The first line obtains the connection to the *Win32_Volume* class associated with the C: drive. The next line assigns the new value to the property, and the last line commits the changes.

```
$wmi = Get-WmiObject -class Win32_Volume -filter "name = 'c:'"
$Wmi.label = "new drive label"
$wmi.put()
```

The three-line version of the label command is much easier to read and to troubleshoot if a problem arises. The "one-liner" is less intuitive and fragile in its heavy reliance on nested parentheses.

If you want to call a method by using the Get-WmiObject cmdlet, you can do so as shown in the DefragAnalysis.ps1 script.

```
$wmi = Get-WmiObject -class Win32_Volume -filter "name = 'c:'"
$return = $wmi.DefragAnalysis()
$return.DefragAnalysis
```

To write the command in a single line, it would look like the following:

```
((Get-WmiObject -class Win32_Volume -filter "name = 'c:'").
DefragAnalysis).DefragAnalysis
```

Obtaining Information from Classes

Several different methods can be used to query WMI classes for information. The most basic method involves using the `Get-WmiObject` cmdlet and supplying a WMI class name for the *–class* parameter as shown here.

```
Get-WmiObject -class Win32_Bios
```

When you do this, the `Get-WmiObject` cmdlet retrieves a formatted display of information from the *Win32_Bios* WMI class as shown in Figure 2-4.

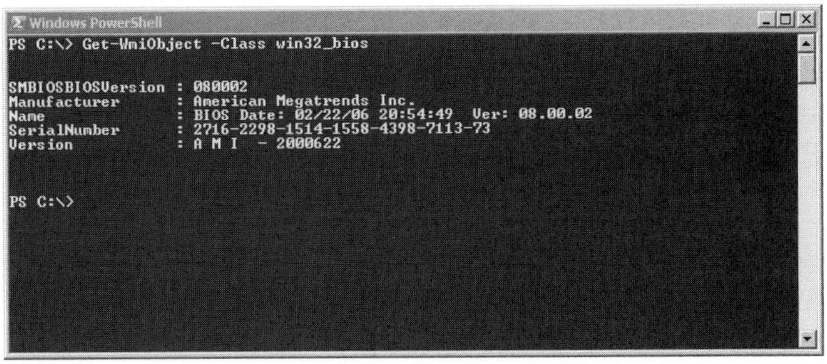

FIGURE 2-4 The *Win32_Bios* WMI class presents formatted BIOS information.

If you prefer to use the built-in alias and rely on a positional parameter, you can shorten the command as shown here.

```
Gwmi Win32_Bios
```

The advantage to this command is that it relies on less typing and can therefore make you more efficient from the command line. The disadvantage, of course, is readability and reliability. The command relies on the built-in alias, *gwmi*; this may be a reasonably valid assumption, but it is not guaranteed.

Managing Aliases

One problem in working with aliases is that they are never guaranteed to exist. Windows PowerShell 2.0 ships with two types of aliases: canonical and compatibility. Compatibility aliases are essentially mappings of various DOS and UNIX commands to their equivalent Windows PowerShell cmdlets. These aliases are not protected and can be freely deleted or modified. I know some Windows PowerShell users at Microsoft who have a command similar to this one in their PowerShell profile.

```
Get-Alias |
Where-Object { $_.options -notmatch 'readonly' } |
Remove-Item -path $_.name
```

Their logic is to remove the entire collection of compatibility aliases from Windows PowerShell and force the use of either canonical aliases or actual cmdlet names. Such a technique might prove helpful when learning Windows PowerShell because it requires you to type **Get-ChildItem** or **GCI** every time you want to obtain a directory listing instead of using the more familiar *dir* or *ls* alias. Typing **Get-ChildItem** does not involve much more typing when you take tab expansion into account; it is only five keystrokes as opposed to either three for *dir* or two for *ls*.

Aliases can be changed, deleted, or overridden by Windows PowerShell users and, as a result, should never be used in a script. For network administrators and help desk personnel who may be working on multiple systems, there are basically three different approaches. The first approach is to use no aliases. In this manner, you will always know the actual command name and be able to work on any system that has Windows PowerShell installed. The second approach to working with aliases involves establishing a corporate Windows PowerShell profile in which companywide aliases are defined. The third method creates a roaming profile by storing the profile on a shared, networked location. When the network location is available, Windows PowerShell loads the profile.

Finding WMI Classes

On a default installation of a Windows Vista computer, there are more than 3,000 WMI classes that are spread out over several different namespaces. Yet in the default WMI namespace, *root\cimv2*, there are nearly 1,000 classes. This highlights one of the hardest problems that network administrators encounter when using WMI. It is not the inability to work with WMI, nor is it the paucity of class coverage. Rather, it is the plethora of classes itself that causes the problem.

One approach to finding WMI classes is to use a tool, such as the Windows PowerShell Scriptomatic (included in the Tools folder on the companion media with this book.) The Windows PowerShell Scriptomatic makes it easy to choose a WMI namespace, select a WMI class, and then run the script to see whether the output is useful. A unique feature of the Windows PowerShell Scriptomatic is that it automatically generates WMI code to query the WMI class you selected and then executes the code to display the results of the command. If you like the results, you can save the script.

Such a method has two potential pitfalls. The first is that it can be rather tedious to manually walk through all of the WMI classes on your server. A better approach involves programmatically searching the WMI classes. To do this, you rely on the *–list* parameter from the Get-WmiObject cmdlet as shown here.

```
Get-WmiObject -List |
Where-Object { $_.name -match 'disk'}
```

You can use this technique to identify potential WMI classes that could be of benefit to you. One of the problems with the previous query is that it returns both dynamic and abstract WMI classes. You are not allowed to query abstract classes because they are unreliable. One way to reduce the number of abstracts returned is to filter out classes that begin with the letters "cim" because most abstract classes begin with these letters. There are exceptions to this, of course, but they are few in number. The revised query is shown here.

```
Get-WmiObject -List |
Where-Object { $_.name -match 'disk' -AND $_.name -notmatch '^cim' }
```

You may want the ability to query remote computers and to select different WMI namespaces other than *root\cimv2*, which is the default namespace. You can use the *-computername* and *-namespace* parameters from the Get-WmiObject cmdlet to add additional functionality to your command as shown here.

```
Get-WmiObject -List -computername 'lisbon' -namespace root\wmi |
Where-Object { $_.name -match 'disk'-AND $_.name -notmatch '^cim' }
```

Once you have set the command the way you like it, you can modify it a little further and turn it into a function. To use the function, you should pass three parameters: the related WMI classes, the computer name, and the namespace. To do this, you will cause your function to use named parameters. In the GetWmiClasses.ps1 script is a function named *GetWmiClasses*.

GetWmiClasses.ps1
```
Function GetWmiClasses(
                $Computername = 'localhost',
                $NameSpace = 'root\cimv2',
                $Class = 'disk'
                )
{
  Get-WmiObject -List -computername $computername -namespace $namespace |
  Where-Object { $_.name -match $class-AND $_.name -notmatch '^cim' }
}
```

Setting Properties

When working with WMI, a number of properties can be set. Most of these properties are read-write, but some properties are write-only. When set, they cause a change in behavior.

The value of these properties can be obtained by querying other properties. In the SetVolumeName.ps1 script, you can write a new value to the *VolumeName* property of the *Win32_LogicalDisk* WMI class. The volume name can be seen when examining the drive configuration via Windows Explorer as illustrated in Figure 2-5. To do this, first connect to a specific logical disk by using the *-filter* parameter of the Get-WmiObject cmdlet. Once you have connected to a specific instance of the WMI class, you can assign a new value for the property and use the *put* method to write the changed value back to the object. The SetVolumeName.ps1 script is shown here.

SetVolumeName.ps1

```
$wmi = Get-WmiObject -Class win32_LogicalDisk -Filter "name = 'c:' "
$wmi.VolumeName = "Local_Disk"
$wmi.Put()
```

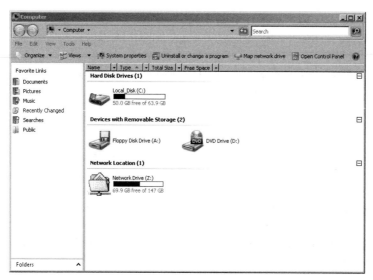

FIGURE 2-5 The volume name can be changed by editing a WMI property.

You might assume that you can modify the *VolumeName* property in a single line by using a combination of parentheses and piling parameters together. If you did, the command would look something like the following:

```
PS C:\> ((Get-WmiObject -Class win32_LogicalDisk -Filter "name = 'c:' ").volumeName =
 "c Drive").put()
Method invocation failed because [System.String] doesn't contain a method named 'put
'.
At line:1 char:93
+ ((Get-WmiObject -Class win32_LogicalDisk -Filter "name = 'c:' ").volumeName = "c D
rive").put <<<< ()
```

The reason the previous command fails is that you need a WMI object to be able to call the *put* method. The problem arises because you are working with a string. To write the command in a single line, you need to use a variable to store the connection into WMI. This command looks like the following:

```
PS C:\> $wmi = (Get-WmiObject -Class win32_logicaldisk -Filter "name = 'c:'");
$wmi.volumename = "sea Drive" ; $wmi.put()
```

The semicolon is a logical line separator in Windows PowerShell. While the command spans a single line in the Windows PowerShell console and can technically be considered to be a single line of code, the semicolon actually masks three separate lines of code. This command is three separate commands and can be written as follows:

```
PS C:\> $wmi = (Get-WmiObject -Class win32_logicaldisk -Filter "name = 'c:'");
$wmi.volumename = "sea Drive" ;
$wmi.put()
```

If I was to go through the trouble of entering three different lines of code, I believe I would turn the series of commands into a script. The SetVolumeName.ps1 script was shown earlier in this chapter.

As a best practice, if you need to modify a property on a WMI object and the command needs to be a single line, use the Set-WmiInstance cmdlet.

Calling Methods

One of the most obvious areas for exploration in WMI involves methods. Much of WMI allows you to query and to obtain a great deal of information about the operating system and hardware of the computing device. Methods allow you to make changes to the operating system or hardware. One way to call a method is to use the Get-WmiObject cmdlet to return a management object at the appropriate level and then call the method, which you can do in a single line. The example shown here returns an instance of the *Win32_OperatingSystem* WMI class and then calls the *ShutDown* method.

```
(Get-WmiObject -Class win32_operatingsystem -EnableAllPrivileges).ShutDown()
```

You can use the Invoke-WmiMethod cmdlet to call a method. To do so, you need to specify the path to a particular instance of a WMI class. The following example makes the printer named textprinter the default printer on the computer. The key property for the class is the *DeviceID* property. The path is the name of the class, the name of the key property, and the value of the key property. The *name* parameter is the name of the method, which in this case is *SetDefaultPrinter*. When the command is run, it returns some system information by default that might not be of interest to you as shown here.

```
PS C:\> Invoke-WmiMethod -Path "win32_Printer.deviceID='textprinter'" `
-name SetDefaultPrinter
__GENUS          : 2
__CLASS          : __PARAMETERS
__SUPERCLASS     :
__DYNASTY        : __PARAMETERS
__RELPATH        :
__PROPERTY_COUNT : 1
__DERIVATION     : {}
__SERVER         :
__NAMESPACE      :
```

```
__PATH          :
ReturnValue     : 0
Properties      : {ReturnValue}
SystemProperties : {__GENUS, __CLASS, __SUPERCLASS, __DYNASTY...}
Qualifiers      : {}
ClassPath       : __PARAMETERS
Site            :
Container       :
```

To control the amount of information that is returned from the `Invoke-WmiMethod` cmdlet, you can surround the command in parentheses and select the *ReturnValue* property. This command and its results are shown here.

```
PS C:\> (Invoke-WmiMethod -Path "win32_Printer.deviceID='textprinter'" `
-name SetDefaultPrinter).returnvalue
0
```

Working with Instances

When you query a class in WMI, multiple instances of the WMI class are usually returned. As an example, the *Win32_Volume* WMI class on most computers returns multiple instances of the class. On those systems, the value of the *DeviceID* property is the drive letter you want to work with. This command is shown here.

```
PS C:\> Set-WmiInstance  -Path "win32_logicalDisk.DeviceID='c:'" `
-argument @{volumeName = 'sea_drive'}
```

If you want to set the same information for several instances of the same class, you can use a WMI query to return the instances you want to work on and pipeline the results to the `Set-WmiInstance` cmdlet. In this example, the WMI class is *Win32_LogicalDisk*, which represents logical drives on a computer. The filter selects only drives that have a *DriveType* property that is equal to 3. The enumeration value of 3 represents a fixed logical disk. You then pipeline the resulting WMI objects to the `Set-WmiInstance` cmdlet where you specify that the *VolumeName* property will have a value of *Local_Disk*. You do not need to specify the path to the WMI instance because it is received over the pipeline. This technique is illustrated here along with the associated output describing each drive that is modified.

```
PS C:\> Get-WmiObject -Class win32_logicaldisk -Filter "driveType = 3" |
Set-WmiInstance -Argument @{volumeName = 'Local_Disk'}
DeviceID     : C:
DriveType    : 3
ProviderName :
FreeSpace    : 53678329856
Size         : 68716326912
VolumeName   : Local_Disk
```

Working with Events

When something occurs, it generates an event. In Windows PowerShell 1.0, it is rather difficult to work with events. In VBScript, you can write event-driven scripts, but they are a specialized subject and are complicated to execute properly. Windows PowerShell 2.0 has changed all of that.

Windows PowerShell has the `Register-WmiEvent` cmdlet that allows you to receive events by writing a WMI event-driven query. If you use an intrinsic WMI event class, you do not even have to write an event-driven query. The following example uses the *Win32_ProcessStartTrace* intrinsic event class to generate an event when a new process is created. The *SourceIdentifier* parameter is used when retrieving events and should therefore be both unique and easy to remember.

```
Register-WmiEvent -Class win32_processStartTrace -SourceIdentifier startTrace
```

Any event that is generated is collected by the Windows PowerShell event collector. To retrieve the events, use the `Get-PSEvent` cmdlet. The following example retrieves a specific event by supplying the *EventIdentifier* property to the `Where-Object` cmdlet.

```
$psEvent = Get-PSEvent | where-object { $_.eventidentifier -eq 13 }
```

Once you obtain an instance of the *System.Management.Automation.PSEventArgs* class from the `Get-PSEvent` cmdlet, examine the *NewEvent* property from the *System.Management.EventArrivedEventArgs* object as shown here.

```
$psEvent.SourceEventArgs.NewEvent
```

The *NewEvent* property returns a *System.Management.ManagementBaseObject* object that contains a new instance of the *Win32_ProcessStartTrace* class. This is where you can find out the *ProcessID*, *ProcessName*, and other important information about the process that generated the event. A sample of the output is shown here.

```
PageDirectoryBase     : 0
ParentProcessID       : 2736
ProcessID             : 2688
ProcessName           : calc.exe
SECURITY_DESCRIPTOR   :
SessionID             : 1
Sid                   : {1, 5, 0, 0...}
TIME_CREATED          : 128649718365018915
Properties            : {PageDirectoryBase, ParentProcessID, ProcessID, ProcessName...
                        }
SystemProperties      : {__GENUS, __CLASS, __SUPERCLASS, __DYNASTY...}
Qualifiers            : {abstract, Locale}
ClassPath             : Win32_ProcessStartTrace
Site                  :
Container             :
```

Working Remotely

It is seldom that an IT Pro works on a single machine. In Windows PowerShell 2.0, the flexibility of PowerShell has been extended to working with other computers. You can always run a WMI command or talk to Active Directory on a remote computer, but in Windows PowerShell 2.0, you have the ability to connect to a remote computer directly and run PowerShell commands there. Several methods allow you to work remotely with the Windows PowerShell 2.0 environment, and they are detailed in this section.

Using *–computer*

The easiest way to work remotely is to use the *–computer* parameter. This parameter has always been available via the Get-WmiObject cmdlet, but it has been added to several other cmdlets as well as shown in the following list.

- Get-Process
- Get-Service
- Get-WinEvent
- Get-EventLog
- Restart-Computer
- Stop-Computer
- Test-Connection

Get-Process

The Get-Process cmdlet has been upgraded in Windows PowerShell 2.0 with the *–computer* parameter, which allows access to the *System.Diagnostics.Process* .NET Framework class on a remote computer. There are a number of ways in which the Get-Process cmdlet can be used. In its most basic form, this cmdlet produces a listing of processes and related information as shown here (truncated for readability).

```
PS C:\> Get-Process -ComputerName berlin
```

Handles	NPM(K)	PM(K)	WS(K)	VM(M)	CPU(s)	Id	ProcessName
379	5	1436	4700	106		436	csrss
78	4	1208	4376	103		480	csrss
288	13	15028	14560	78		1696	dfsrs
150	7	2196	5892	53		1972	dfssvc
218	13	7284	8968	66		1708	dns
0	0	0	12	0		0	Idle
129	6	1892	4792	40		1728	ismserv
171	15	7320	10980	86		920	LogonUI

The listing that is returned by default by the Get-Process cmdlet is useful; I prefer to modify the readout to enable myself to find information easier. When deciding how to modify the command, I consider how I use Windows Task Manager. In general, I sort by either CPU or memory utilization. You can produce similar results by using the Get-Process and Sort-Object cmdlets as shown here (truncated for readability).

```
PS C:\> Get-Process -ComputerName berlin | Sort-Object -Property WS -Descending
```

Handles	NPM(K)	PM(K)	WS(K)	VM(M)	CPU(s)	Id	ProcessName
985	58	24672	28988	93		576	lsass
586	13	10684	17692	83		996	svchost
288	13	15048	14580	78		1696	dfsrs
468	40	7984	12824	71		1160	svchost
171	15	7320	10980	86		920	LogonUI
231	21	5148	9620	46		1324	svchost
95	3	5436	9540	42		1012	SLsvc
218	13	7284	8968	66		1708	dns
311	10	4776	8860	83		1632	spoolsv

If I am concerned about CPU utilization on the server, I sort by CPU as shown here. The problem with this approach is that the *CPU* property does not report remotely. No error is generated, and the data is simply missing.

```
PS C:\> Get-Process -ComputerName berlin | Sort-Object -Property CPU -Descending
```

Handles	NPM(K)	PM(K)	WS(K)	VM(M)	CPU(s)	Id	ProcessName
99	4	2320	4480	39		1132	svchost
244	9	3512	7028	43		1072	svchost
234	21	5176	9632	46		1324	svchost
461	39	7944	12808	71		1160	svchost
291	10	4712	7468	44		944	svchost

To solve this problem, you can use the remoting features of Windows PowerShell 2.0 and either run the command remotely or start a remote session and execute the command from within the session.

By using the *–id* parameter of the Get-Process cmdlet, you can manage processes that may have similar names. If you use the *WshShell* object to create a process by using the *exec* method, you can then use the *ProcessID* property that is returned when the process is created and feed it to the Get-Process cmdlet to obtain diagnostic information about the newly created process. To do this, store the object that is returned by the *exec* method into a variable named *$rtnPid*. Then use the variable to obtain the *ProcessID* and pass this to the *–id* parameter of the Get-Process cmdlet as illustrated here.

```
PS C:\> $rtnPid = (New-Object -ComObject wscript.shell).exec("notepad")
PS C:\> Get-Process -Id $rtnPid.ProcessID
```

Handles	NPM(K)	PM(K)	WS(K)	VM(M)	CPU(s)	Id	ProcessName
52	2	976	3496	59	0.38	3248	notepad

This technique is great if you are working directly on a local computer. The problem is that the *WshShell* object does not remote. To use a similar technique on a remote computer, you can use the [WMICLASS] type accelerator, pass it the path to the *Win32_Process* WMI class, and call the *create* method. The path is composed of three parts: the computer name, the namespace, and the class. In the example shown here, the computer is berlin, the namespace is *root\cimv2*, and the class is *Win32_Process*.

> **NOTE** Keep in mind that when the *create* method from *Win32_Process* is used, it will not be visible even though the process is running. Therefore, the program will not be useful. This technique is valid for starting processes that perform automated tasks, but it is useless if the process displays a graphical user interface.

To create an instance of the Notepad program on a remote computer named berlin, the command is shown here.

```
$wmiReturn = ([WMICLASS]"\\berlin\root\cimv2:win32_process").create("notepad")
```

When it is time to delete the process, use the *terminate* method of the *Win32_Process* WMI class. To connect specifically to the process you created earlier, you need to use the *ProcessID*. You can use the management base object that was created when the process was created to obtain the information you need. If you try to use the object directly, the command fails due to the extra information that is stored in the object.

You need to use a subexpression to control the unraveling of the object. To do this, you can use a dollar sign and a set of parentheses. Place the *$( )* around *$wmiReturn.ProcessId*. By using the subexpression, you can control the amount of information that is returned when you query the *ProcessID* property that you stored in the *$wmiReturn* variable during the previous command.

To delete the process, use the [WMI] type accelerator and give it the path to the exact instance of the class you want to delete. To do this, use the WMI path and include the key property. In the command below, the computer is berlin, the namespace is *root\cimv2*, the class is *Win32_Process*, the key property is *handle*, and the value of the *handle* property is contained in the *$wmiReturn.ProcessId* property. Once you have connected to the specific instance, call the *terminate* method.

```
([WMI]"\\berlin\root\cimv2:win32_process.handle=$($wmiReturn.ProcessId)").terminate()
```

If you want to use the `Invoke-WmiMethod` cmdlet, you still need to be able to connect to the key property of the class, the *handle* property. To find the key property for a WMI class, you can use the Windows Management Instrumentation Tester (WbemTest) program. Press the Open Class button after you connect to WMI on the computer. In the Get Class Name dialog box that appears, type the name of the WMI class (**Win32_Process** for this example). You then press the Instances button from the right side of the screen, and the Query Result dialog box shown in Figure 2-6 appears.

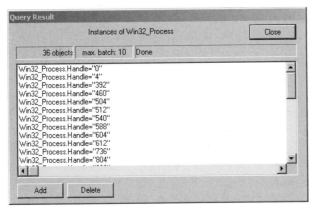

FIGURE 2-6 The Windows Management Instrumentation Tester displays key values for WMI classes.

If you have stored the handle to the process in a variable, it is not too difficult to work with it. If you have not stored the handle, you need to perform another query to obtain the handle. You can use the `Get-Process` cmdlet to obtain this information.

```
$processID = Get-Process -ComputerName berlin -Name notepad
```

Once you have the process ID, you can use it with the `Invoke-WmiMethod` cmdlet. The main advantage of the `Invoke-WmiMethod` cmdlet is that it spares you from typing the obscure *computername**namespace* type of syntax that is required by the [WMI] type accelerator. It also contains other advanced features that you will look at later in Chapter 7, "Avoiding Scripting Pitfalls."

```
Invoke-WmiMethod -ComputerName berlin -Path "win32_process.handle=$($processID.id)" '
-name terminate
```

Get-Service

If you need to check the status of a service on a remote computer, you can use the `Get-Service` cmdlet. There are essentially three ways to use this cmdlet. The easiest way is to simply use the *–computername* parameter to produce a listing of the status of all services defined on the remote computer. This process is shown here with a truncated output.

```
PS C:\> Get-Service -ComputerName berlin

Status    Name              DisplayName
------    ----              -----------
Running   1-vmsrvc          Virtual Machine Additions Services ...
Running   AeLookupSvc       Application Experience
Stopped   ALG               Application Layer Gateway Service
Stopped   Appinfo           Application Information
```

If you are interested in the status of a particular service, there are two ways to obtain the information. If you know the actual name of the service, you can use the *–name* parameter as shown here.

```
PS C:\> Get-Service -Name bits

Status    Name              DisplayName
------    ----              -----------
Stopped   BITS              Background Intelligent Transfer Ser...
```

Often, you do not know the actual name of the service because this name is not always displayed. The problem with some display names is that, while they are easy to read, they are not easy to type. A good example is the BITS service shown earlier. You can use the *–DisplayName* parameter to gain the advantage of using the friendly name; to ease the typing burden, you can use wildcards to shorten the name as shown here.

```
PS C:\> Get-Service -DisplayName background*

Status    Name              DisplayName
------    ----              -----------
Stopped   BITS              Background Intelligent Transfer Ser...
```

If you are working on a local computer, you can use the Start-Service cmdlet to start the service. However, the Start-Service cmdlet does not have the *–computername* parameter and therefore does not remote. You can use the underlying .NET Framework *System.ServiceProcess.ServiceController* class as shown here.

```
$service = New-Object ServiceProcess.ServiceController("BITS","berlin")
$service.Start()
```

If you need to stop a service on a remote server, you also need to use the *System.ServiceProcess.ServiceController* class because the Stop-Service cmdlet does not have the *–computername* parameter as shown here.

```
$service = New-Object ServiceProcess.ServiceController("BITS","berlin")
$service.Stop()
```

What if you need to start a service and the service is disabled? In this case, you cannot use the *start* method from the *System.ServiceProcess.ServiceController* class because there is no *ChangeStartMethod* method associated with this class. You are not allowed to override the *disabled* property of the service. One problem with the *System.ServiceProcess.ServiceController* .NET Framework class is that there is no property that displays the start mode of the service. When you attempt to start the disabled service as shown here, you generate an error.

```
PS C:\> $service = New-Object ServiceProcess.ServiceController("BITS","berlin")
PS C:\> $service.Start()
Exception calling "Start" with "0" argument(s): "Cannot start service BITS on
computer 'berlin'."At line:1 char:15+ $service.Start <<<< ()
```

Unfortunately, the error does not indicate the reason that the service failed to start. As a best practice, when starting services, I prefer to check the status of the service. If the service is stopped, I check the *startmode* property of the service by using the *Win32_Service* WMI class. If the service is disabled, I change the start mode of the service to manual and then start the service. An example of this technique can be seen in the GetStatusAndStartService.ps1 script.

```
GetStatusAndStartService.ps1
$computerName = "berlin"
$serviceName = "bits"
$remoteService = Get-Service -ComputerName $computerName -Name $serviceName
if($remoteService.status -ne 'running')
{
 $service = [wmi]"\\$computerName\root\cimv2:Win32_service.name=""$serviceName"""
    if($($service.startmode) -eq "disabled")
    {
    $service.changeStartMode("manual")
    $service.startService()
    }
    ELSE
    {
    $service.startService()
    }
}
```

Get-EventLog

The Get-EventLog cmdlet works with traditional event logs such as the System, Application, and Security logs. In addition to these three logs that have existed since the inception of Windows NT, a few additional event logs also fall into the traditional category. This is not due to their longstanding existence, but rather because they use the traditional event log format. To see which event logs the Get-EventLog cmdlet is capable of viewing, you can use the Get-EventLog cmdlet with the *–list* parameter. This can be done on a local machine or remotely by using the *–computername* parameter. If you use the command remotely, you might very well find additional event logs. In the following example, we use the Get-EventLog cmdlet on the local computer, which is running Windows Vista.

```
PS C:\> Get-EventLog -List
```

Max(K)	Retain	OverflowAction	Entries	Name
20,480	0	OverwriteAsNeeded	2,499	Application
512	7	OverwriteOlder	0	DFS Replication
20,480	0	OverwriteAsNeeded	0	Hardware Events
512	7	OverwriteOlder	0	Internet Explorer
20,480	0	OverwriteAsNeeded	0	Key Management Service
20,480	0	OverwriteAsNeeded	9,040	Security
20,480	0	OverwriteAsNeeded	21,813	System
15,360	0	OverwriteAsNeeded	1,584	Windows PowerShell

When the command is run on a remote computer that is running Windows Server 2008 and is configured as a domain controller and Domain Name System (DNS) server, you will notice some additional event logs displayed.

```
PS C:\> Get-EventLog -List -ComputerName berlin
```

Max(K)	Retain	OverflowAction	Entries	Name
20,480	0	OverwriteAsNeeded	1,190	Application
15,168	0	OverwriteAsNeeded	355	DFS Replication
512	0	OverwriteAsNeeded	395	Directory Service
16,384	0	OverwriteAsNeeded	233	DNS Server
20,480	0	OverwriteAsNeeded	0	Hardware Events
512	7	OverwriteOlder	0	Internet Explorer
20,480	0	OverwriteAsNeeded	0	Key Management Service
131,072	0	OverwriteAsNeeded	56,928	Security
20,480	0	OverwriteAsNeeded	7,419	System
15,360	0	OverwriteAsNeeded	200	Windows PowerShell

If you want to view the two most recent entries from the DNS server log, you need to use the –*logname* parameter and the –*computername* parameter from the Get_EventLog cmdlet. One factor to keep in mind is that the logs that have spaces in the name must be placed in quotation marks. If you do not, an error is generated as shown in Figure 2-7.

FIGURE 2-7 Use quotation marks for log names that include spaces when querying with Get-EventLog.

Get-WinEvent

The GetWinEvent cmdlet is new for Windows PowerShell 2.0 and is designed to replace the Get-EventLog cmdlet. While it is a bit more difficult to use, the Get-WinEvent cmdlet includes both the functionality of the Get-EventLog cmdlet and additional functionality as well. One of the new features of Windows Vista was the inclusion of new event logs. The Windows Event Log Service (code-named "Crimson") is a standardized service that allows you to create and publish events in standard event logs. These logs are primarily used for diagnostics and auditing. Event Tracing for Windows (ETW) logs are of a higher performance and are used primarily to monitor application performance. ETW was introduced in Microsoft Windows 2000, but improvements have been made in every version of Windows since that time. The Get-WinEvent cmdlet can read both types of logs.

To find the logs that are available to the Get-WinEvent cmdlet, you can use the *–listlog* parameter with a wildcard as shown in the ListEventLogs.ps1 script.

ListEventLogs.ps1
```
Get-WinEvent -ListLog * |
Format-Table -Property logname, RecordCount -AutoSize
```

When you run the ListEventLogs.ps1 script, between 50 and 60 event logs are returned depending on the version of the operating system and the types of applications installed on the machine as shown in Figure 2-8.

FIGURE 2-8 The number of event logs returned by Get-Event depends on the version of the operating system and the type of applications installed.

To see classic event logs with the `Get-WinEvent` cmdlet, you can use the ListClassicEventLogs.ps1 script. The script begins with the `Get-WinEvent` cmdlet and uses the *–listlog* parameter with a wildcard. It then pipelines the resulting *System.Diagnostics.Eventing.Reader.EventLogConfiguration* object to the `Where-Object` cmdlet where it filters the Boolean value *IsClassicLog*. If the log is a classic event log, the script chooses several properties and formats the output as a table. The ListClassicEventLogs.ps1 script is shown here.

ListClassicEventLogs.ps1
```
Get-WinEvent -ListLog * |
Where-Object { $_.isClassicLog } |
Format-Table -Property logname, MaximumSize*, *count –AutoSize
```

The members of the *EventLogConfiguration* class are shown in Table 2-2.

TABLE 2-2 Members of the *EventLogConfiguration* Class

NAME	MEMBERTYPE	DEFINITION
Dispose	Method	System.Void Dispose()
Equals	Method	System.Boolean Equals(Object obj)
GetHashCode	Method	System.Int32 GetHashCode()
GetType	Method	System.Type GetType()
SaveChanges	Method	System.Void SaveChanges()
ToString	Method	System.String ToString()
FileSize	NoteProperty	FileSize=null
IsLogFull	NoteProperty	IsLogFull=null
LastAccessTime	NoteProperty	LastAccessTime=null
LastWriteTime	NoteProperty	LastWriteTime=null
OldestRecordNumber	NoteProperty	OldestRecordNumber=null
RecordCount	NoteProperty	RecordCount=null
IsClassicLog	Property	System.Boolean IsClassicLog {get;}
IsEnabled	Property	System.Boolean IsEnabled {get;set;}
LogFilePath	Property	System.String LogFilePath {get;set;}
LogIsolation	Property	System.Diagnostics.Eventing.Reader. EventLogIsolation LogIsolation {get;}
LogMode	Property	System.Diagnostics.Eventing.Reader. EventLogMode LogMode {get;set;}

NAME	MEMBERTYPE	DEFINITION
LogName	Property	System.String LogName {get;}
LogType	Property	System.Diagnostics.Eventing.Reader. EventLogType LogType {get;}
MaximumSizeInBytes	Property	System.Int64 MaximumSizeInBytes {get;set;}
OwningProviderName	Property	System.String OwningProviderName {get;}
ProviderBufferSize	Property	System.Nullable'1[[System.Int32 mscorlib Version =2.0.0.0 Culture=neutral PublicKeyToken =b77a5c561934e089]] ProviderBufferSize {get;}
ProviderControlGuid	Property	System.Nullable'1[[System.Guid mscorlib Version =2.0.0.0 Culture=neutral PublicKeyToken =b77a5c561934e089]] ProviderControlGuid {get;}
ProviderKeywords	Property	System.Nullable'1[[System.Int64 mscorlib Version =2.0.0.0 Culture=neutral PublicKeyToken =b77a5c561934e089]] ProviderKeywords {get;set;}
ProviderLatency	Property	System.Nullable'1[[System.Int32 mscorlib Version =2.0.0.0 Culture=neutral PublicKeyToken= b77a5c561934e089]] ProviderLatency {get;}
ProviderLevel	Property	System.Nullable'1[[System.Int32 mscorlib Version =2.0.0.0 Culture=neutral PublicKeyToken =b77a5c561934e089]] ProviderLevel {get;set;}
ProviderMaximum-NumberOfBuffers	Property	System.Nullable'1[[System.Int32 mscorlib Version =2.0.0.0 Culture=neutral PublicKeyToken= b77a5c561934e089]] ProviderMaximumNumberOfBuffers {get;}
ProviderMinimum-NumberOfBuffers	Property	System.Nullable'1[[System.Int32 mscorlib Version =2.0.0.0 Culture=neutral PublicKeyToken= b77a5c561934e089]] ProviderMinimumNumberOfBuffers {get;}
ProviderNames	Property	System.Collections.Generic. IEnumerable'1[[System.String mscorlib Version=2.0.0.0 Culture=neutral PublicKeyToken =b77a5c561934e089]] ProviderNames {get;}
SecurityDescriptor	Property	System.String SecurityDescriptor {get;set;}

The Get-Event cmdlet does not have a *–newest* parameter like the Get-EventLog cmdlet has; however, this does not preclude using such a syntax. Due to the pipelining nature of Windows PowerShell, you can use the Get-Event cmdlet and pipeline the results to the Select-Object cmdlet, where you have access to a *–last* parameter as shown here.

```
PS C:\> Get-WinEvent -logname *bits*op* | Select-Object -Last 3
```

TimeCreated	ProviderName	Id	Message
8/7/2007 10:34:2...	Microsoft-Window...	3	The BITS service...
8/7/2007 10:21:4...	Microsoft-Window...	306	The BITS service...
8/7/2007 1:07:39 PM	Microsoft-Window...	306	The BITS service...

When querying event logs with the Get-WinEvent cmdlet, you can use partial parameters to reduce typing and to maintain the readability of the code. If a partial parameter matches several parameters, the cmdlet returns an error as shown in Figure 2-9.

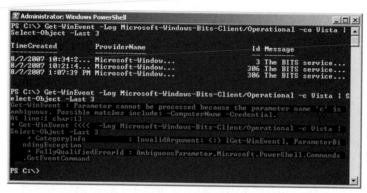

FIGURE 2-9 Partial parameters need to be unique to avoid errors.

When you use the Get-WinEvent cmdlet to retrieve entries from an event log that does not contain any entries, a record count of 0 is returned. Because no error is generated, this simplifies working from the command line. This process is shown in Figure 2-10.

FIGURE 2-10 Empty event logs list 0 records in the counter.

It is a best practice to check the record count of the event log prior to attempting access. This technique is illustrated in the DisplayEventsCheckCount.ps1 script. Because the script uses the Get-WinEvent cmdlet, which only exists in Windows PowerShell 2.0, it begins with the #requires –version 2.0 version tag. The log name can use wildcards, and considering the length of some of the event log names, I recommend the liberal use of wildcards as long as they do not interfere with the readability of the script. The $numberLogs variable is used to hold the number of log entries you want to retrieve from the script. The key to the script is using the `Get-WinEvent` cmdlet to retrieve the *RecordCount* property. The *RecordCount* property is treated like a Boolean value. The number 0 is false, and if *RecordCount* is anything but 0, then the expression is evaluated to true and you can proceed to query the event log. The DisplayEventsCheckCount.ps1 script is shown here.

DisplayEventsCheckCount.ps1
```
#requires -version 2.0
$logname = "*bits*op*"
$numberLogs = 3
if((Get-WinEvent -ListLog $logname).recordCount)
{
 "Displaying the last $numberLogs events from log $logName"
 Get-WinEvent -LogName $logname |
 Select-Object -last $numberLogs
}
```

Test-Connection

With the presence of Ping.exe and the *Win32_PingStatus* WMI class, you really do not need the `Test-Connection` cmdlet. But since you have it, go ahead and use it. One of the primary advantages of *Win32_PingStatus* is that you can target a remote computer and have it ping a different destination, which provides a tremendous amount of flexibility when troubleshooting network connectivity problems. This can be done with the `Test-Connection` cmdlet as well.

Another powerful feature of *Win32_PingStatus* is the ease with which you can create an array and have it ping a series of computers that are within the array. This can also be easily done with `Test-Connection`. Both of these techniques are shown in Figure 2-11.

FIGURE 2-11 Test-Connection works locally or remotely.

When you pipe the results from `Test-Connection` into `Get-Member`, you can see why the `Test-Connection` cmdlet reproduces the functionality of *Win32_PingStatus*—the cmdlet wraps the WMI class. The members of the *Win32_PingStatus* WMI class are shown in Table 2-3.

TABLE 2-3 Members of the *Win32_PingStatus* WMI Class

NAME	MEMBERTYPE	DEFINITION
Address	Property	System.String Address {get;set;}
BufferSize	Property	System.UInt32 BufferSize {get;set;}
NoFragmentation	Property	System.Boolean NoFragmentation {get;set;}
PrimaryAddress-ResolutionStatus	Property	System.UInt32 PrimaryAddressResolutionStatus {get;set;}
ProtocolAddress	Property	System.String ProtocolAddress {get;set;}
ProtocolAddress-Resolved	Property	System.String ProtocolAddressResolved {get;set;}
RecordRoute	Property	System.UInt32 RecordRoute {get;set;}
ReplyInconsistency	Property	System.Boolean ReplyInconsistency {get;set;}
ReplySize	Property	System.UInt32 ReplySize {get;set;}
ResolveAddressNames	Property	System.Boolean ResolveAddressNames {get;set;}
ResponseTime	Property	System.UInt32 ResponseTime {get;set;}
ResponseTimeToLive	Property	System.UInt32 ResponseTimeToLive {get;set;}
RouteRecord	Property	System.String[] RouteRecord {get;set;}
RouteRecordResolved	Property	System.String[] RouteRecordResolved {get;set;}
SourceRoute	Property	System.String SourceRoute {get;set;}
SourceRouteType	Property	System.UInt32 SourceRouteType {get;set;}
StatusCode	Property	System.UInt32 StatusCode {get;set;}
Timeout	Property	System.UInt32 Timeout {get;set;}
TimeStampRecord	Property	System.UInt32[] TimeStampRecord {get;set;}
TimeStampRecord-Address	Property	System.String[] TimeStampRecordAddress {get;set;}
TimeStampRecord-AddressResolved	Property	System.String[] TimeStampRecordAddressResolved {get;set;}
TimeStampRoute	Property	System.UInt32 TimeStampRoute {get;set;}
TimeToLive	Property	System.UInt32 TimeToLive {get;set;}
TypeofService	Property	System.UInt32 TypeOfService {get;set;}
__CLASS	Property	System.String __CLASS {get;set;}
__DERIVATION	Property	System.String[] __DERIVATION {get;set;}
__DYNASTY	Property	System.String __DYNASTY {get;set;}

NAME	MEMBERTYPE	DEFINITION
__GENUS	Property	System.Int32 __GENUS {get;set;}
__NAMESPACE	Property	System.String __NAMESPACE {get;set;}
__PATH	Property	System.String __PATH {get;set;}
__PROPERTY_COUNT	Property	System.Int32 __PROPERTY_COUNT {get;set;}
__RELPATH	Property	System.String __RELPATH {get;set;}
__SERVER	Property	System.String __SERVER {get;set;}
__SUPERCLASS	Property	System.String __SUPERCLASS {get;set;}
ConvertFromDateTime	ScriptMethod	System.Object ConvertFromDateTime();
ConvertToDateTime	ScriptMethod	System.Object ConvertToDateTime();

Restart-Computer

Once again with Windows PowerShell 2.0, we suffer from an embarrassment of riches. There are several ways to reboot a remote or local computer, but few of them are as easy to use as the Restart-Computer cmdlet. This cmdlet follows the Windows PowerShell development model exactly and contains virtually no learning curve. To reboot a remote computer named vista, type the following command.

```
Restart-Computer –computername vista
```

To restart you own computer, you use the following command:

```
Restart-Computer
```

If someone is logged on or has open programs, an error is generated when the command is executed remotely. To bypass the error, you need to use the –*force* parameter (which is consistent with normal Windows PowerShell behavior). This process is shown in Figure 2-12.

FIGURE 2-12 Use the –*force* parameter to reboot a computer that has open files or active user sessions.

Stop-Computer

The Stop-Computer cmdlet is used to shut down a computer, which can be done on a local machine or via the *–computername* parameter. If the account on which you are logged on does not have rights on the remote computer, you can use the *–credential* parameter to specify an account that does have the rights to shut down the machine. The *–credential* parameter only works for a remote shutdown. It does not allow a low-rights user to shut down the local computer because alternate credentials are not permitted for local connections. To shut down the local computer, you only need to type the command shown here.

```
Stop-Computer
```

If you want to shut down a remote computer, you can use the *–computername* parameter as shown here.

```
Stop-Computer -computername Berlin
```

To use alternate credentials when shutting down the remote computer, you can use the *–credential* parameter and supply the user name that you want to use. You cannot embed a password in the command because the *–credential* parameter requires a *credential* object and not just a user name/password combination. When you use the *–credential* parameter with the user name, a dialog box appears that prompts you to type in the password as shown in Figure 2-13.

FIGURE 2-13 The *–credential* parameter causes a dialog box to appear to permit entry of passwords.

Creating a Remote Interactive Session

If you need to run several commands on a remote computer, you can create a new Windows PowerShell session based on the other computer. When you start a remote Windows PowerShell session, the prompt includes the name of the other computer as shown in Figure 2-14.

FIGURE 2-14 When starting a remote Windows PowerShell session, the prompt includes the name of the remote computer.

Two cmdlets that are used when working with a remote interactive session are Enter-PSSession and Exit-PSSession.

> **NOTE** There is an alias for **Enter-PSSession** named *Start-PSSession*. This alias works, but one indicator that it is not an actual cmdlet is that tab expansion does not work for it.

A large number of parameters can be supplied for Enter-PSSession, but only one is required—the name of the remote computer. This syntax is illustrated here.

```
PS C:\> Enter-PSSession -ComputerName berlin
[berlin]: PS C:\Windows\System32>
```

Once you have ended your session, it is important to properly exit the remote Windows PowerShell session. To do this, use the Exit-PSSession cmdlet as shown here.

```
[berlin]: PS C:\Windows\System32> Exit-PSSession
PS C:\>
```

Running a Remote Command

If you want to execute a single command, you can use the Invoke-Command cmdlet. The easiest way to use this cmdlet is to supply two parameters: *–computername* and *–ScriptBlock*. The *–computername* parameter accepts an array of computer names, and the *–ScriptBlock* parameter accepts the code that will be run. The following example runs the Ipconfig command on the remote computer named berlin.

```
PS C:\> Invoke-Command -ComputerName berlin -ScriptBlock { ipconfig }
Windows IP Configuration
Ethernet adapter Local Area Connection:
   Connection-specific DNS Suffix  . :
   Link-local IPv6 Address . . . . . : fe80::e920:225c:1154:bf8f%10
   IPv4 Address. . . . . . . . . . . : 192.168.2.1
```

```
        Subnet Mask . . . . . . . . . . . : 255.255.255.0
        Default Gateway . . . . . . . . . : 0.0.0.0

Tunnel adapter Local Area Connection* 8:
    Media State . . . . . . . . . . : Media disconnected
    Connection-specific DNS Suffix  . :
```

Because the Invoke-Command cmdlet accepts an array for the computer name, you can supply multiple computer names when calling the cmdlet as shown here.

```
PS C:\> Invoke-Command -ComputerName berlin, hamburg -ScriptBlock { hostname }
Berlin
Hamburg
```

Additional Resources

- The TechNet Script Center at *http://www.microsoft.com/technet/scriptcenter* has many examples of Windows PowerShell scripts.

- The TechNet Script Center Windows PowerShell hub at *http://www.microsoft.com /technet/scriptcenter/hubs/msh.mspx* has a plethora of PowerShell resources.

- The MSDN Windows PowerShell library at *http://msdn.microsoft.com/en-us/library /bb905330.aspx* includes detailed documentation of the internals of PowerShell.

- On the companion media, you will find the Windows PowerShell Scriptomatic.

- On the companion media, you will find all of the scripts referred to in this chapter.

Survey of Active Directory Capabilities

Active Directory Domain Services provides security as well as storage of network objects, such as users, groups, and computers, to distributed networks built on Windows Server–based operating systems beginning with Microsoft Windows Server 2000. You may have referred to Active Directory Domain Services in the past as simply Active Directory. Active Directory is now considered to be a legacy term. Any network administrator will need to work with Active Directory Service Interfaces (ADSI). In fact, many ordinary users interact with Active Directory on a daily basis through various applications, such as Microsoft Office Outlook, or through self-provisioning of such processes as password reset. As tempting as it may be to think of Active Directory primarily in terms of user management (assigning users, groups, and permissions), such a view does not take into account the scope of its application. If user management was all there was to it, there would be no need to upgrade past Windows NT (WinNT). Indeed, it is the use of other features, such as Group Policy, that provides much of the management facilities within the Windows-based world.

 ON THE COMPANION MEDIA   You will find all of the scripts, comma-separated variable (CSV) files, and Excel spreadsheets referred to in this chapter on the companion media.

Creating Users, Groups, and Organizational Units

The process of creating objects is similar for many of the items created in Active Directory directory service. The *organizational unit* (OU) is one of the most basic objects to create because it is used to group other objects within Active Directory. As seen in the CreateOu.ps1 script, you begin by establishing a connection into Active Directory. There are three parts to the connection: the [ADSI] type accelerator, the protocol, and the path to the object. The path to the object is also known as the *distinguished name* of the object. The three parts of the connection string are seen in Table 3-1.

TABLE 3-1 Parts of an ADSI Connection

[ADSI] TYPE ACCELERATOR	PROTOCOL	PATH (DISTINGUISHED NAME)
[ADSI]	LDAP://	dc=nwtraders,dc=com
[ADSI]	LDAP, WinNT, NDS, NWCOMPAT	ou=myou,dc=nwtraders,com cn=myuser,ou=myou,dc=nwtraders,com

When working with objects in Active Directory, always use the [ADSI] type accelerator to make your connection. Which protocol is used in the connection depends on the type of directory you are working with. As seen in Table 3-2, several potential protocols can be used. The most common protocols used in the Windows-based world are Lightweight Directory Access Protocol (LDAP), which is used to connect with Active Directory, and the WinNT provider, which connects to Security Account Manager (SAM) registry-based account databases. The SAM database is typically used for local accounts on workstations and stand-alone servers.

TABLE 3-2 ADSI-Supported Providers

PROTOCOL	PURPOSE
WinNT	To communicate with Windows NT 4.0 primary domain controllers (PDCs) and backup domain controllers (BDCs) and with local account databases for Microsoft Windows 2000 and newer workstations
LDAP	To communicate with LDAP servers, including Microsoft Exchange 5.x directory and Windows 2000 Active Directory
GC	To communicate with a global catalog (GC) server
IIS	To communicate with Internet Information Services (IIS) 6.0 and earlier or with 7.0 using Metabase compatability mode
NDS	To communicate with Novell Directory Services (NDS) servers
NWCOMPAT	To communicate with Novell NetWare servers

Creating Objects

Once you make the connection to the appropriate level within Active Directory, you can use the *create* method to create an instance of the object. The *create* method takes two positional arguments. The first argument is the type of object to create, and the second argument is the name of the object. The name used to create the object includes a prefix that indicates the type of object being created. Because you are creating an *OrganizationalUnit*, the prefix is ou=. When put together, the prefix and the name form a property called the *relative distinguished name* (RDN). Table 3-3 lists some of the more common RDN prefixes.

TABLE 3-3 Common Relative Distinguished Name Attribute Types

ATTRIBUTE	DESCRIPTION
dc	Domain component
cn	Common name
ou	Organizational unit
o	Organization name
street	Street address
c	Country name
uid	User ID

The CreateOU.ps1 script illustrates the three common tasks involved in creating an object in Active Directory, which are detailed here.

- Connect to the location in the directory.
- Use the *create* method.
- Call the *SetInfo* method.

The CreateOU.ps1 script is shown here.

```
CreateOu.ps1
$adsi = [adsi]"LDAP://dc=nwtraders,dc=com"
$de = $adsi.create("OrganizationalUnit","ou=MyTestOu")
$de.SetInfo()
```

When you combine the protocol used for the connection with the path to the object to which you are connecting, you get what is called the *ADsPath*. Combining the [ADSI] type accelerator with the *ADsPath* gives you a connection string. Examples of various connection strings are shown in Table 3-4.

NOTE Connection strings are not interchangeable; rather, they generally connect in different ways and to different locations. Whereas various strings may actually connect to the same location in Active Directory, most connect to different locations in Active Directory and, in some cases, actually return different types of objects as well. You should always be aware of where you are connecting prior to performing actions that change state, such as create, modify, and delete.

TABLE 3-4 ADSI Connection Strings and Their Meanings

CONNECTION STRING	MEANING
[ADSI]""	Binds to a root of an LDAP namespace.
[ADSI]"LDAP://rootdse"	Serverless binding to the directory of the current domain.
[ADSI]"LDAP://berlin"	Binds to a specific server using a NetBIOS name.
[ADSI]"LDAP://192.168.2.1"	Binds to a specific server using an IP address.
[ADSI]"LDAP://berlin:389"	Binds to a specific server using a specified port number.
[ADSI]"LDAP: //berlin:389/ DC=nwtraders,DC=com"	Binds to a specific domain through a specific server and port number.
[ADSI]"LDAP://berlin/ DC=nwtraders,DC=com"	Binds to a specific domain through a specific server using the NetBIOS name of the server.
[ADSI]"LDAP://192.168.2.1/ DC=nwtraders,DC=com"	Binds to a specific domain using the IP address of a specific server.
[ADSI]"LDAP://CN=berlin,OU=domain controllers, DC=nwtraders,dc=com"	Binds to a specific domain controller.
[ADSI]"LDAP://CN=myuser,OU= mytestou,DC=nwtraders, DC=com"	Binds to a specific user.
[ADSI]"LDAP://berlin/ CN=myuser,OU=mytestou, DC=nwtraders,DC=com"	Binds to a specific user using a specific server.
[ADSI]"LDAP://192.168.2.1/ CN=myuser,OU=mytestou,DC= nwtraders,DC=com"	Binds to a specific user using a specific server.
[ADSI]"LDAP://192.168.2.1:389/ CN=myuser,OU=mytestou, DC=nwtraders,DC=com"	Binds to a specific user via a specific server and port number.

CONNECTION STRING	MEANING
[ADSI]"LDAP://berlin:389/ CN=myuser,OU=mytestou, DC=nwtraders,DC=com"	Binds to a specific user via a specific server and port number.
[ADSI]"LDAP://berlin.nwtraders.com/ CN=myuser, OU=mytestou,DC= nwtraders,DC=com"	Binds to a specific user through a specific server. Because the fully qualified Domain Name System (DNS) server name is used, the connection will allow Kerberos authentication to take place.

Creating a User Account

To create a user account, you must follow three steps: connect to the appropriate location within the Active Directory hierarchy, specify the class of the object (*user* in this example) and the name of the user, and call the *SetInfo* method as illustrated in the CreateUser.ps1 script.

```
CreateUser.ps1
$adsi = [adsi]"LDAP://ou=MyTestOU,dc=nwtraders,dc=com"
$de = $adsi.create("User","cn=MyUser")
$de.SetInfo()
```

Creating a Group

To create a group, you must follow three steps: connect to the specific location within Active Directory, specify the class name of the object, and call the *SetInfo* method. In this example, you connect to the organizational unit named MyTestOU in the Nwtraders.com domain. The class of the object is *Group* and the name of the group is MyGroup. This technique is seen in the CreateGroup.ps1 script.

```
CreateGroup.ps1
$adsi = [adsi]"LDAP://ou=MyTestOU,dc=nwtraders,dc=com"
$de = $adsi.create("Group","cn=MyGroup")
$de.SetInfo()
```

Creating a Computer Account

If you need to create a computer account, the process is similar to creating a group, user, or organizational unit. You connect to the specific location within Active Directory where the object will reside and then use the *create* method, specifying the type of object to create and the name of the object, and call the *SetInfo* method as shown in the CreateComputer.ps1 script.

```
CreateComputer.ps1
$adsi = [adsi]"LDAP://ou=MyTestOU,dc=nwtraders,dc=com"
$de = $adsi.create("Computer","cn=MyComputer")
$de.SetInfo()
```

Let's examine another example of creating objects in Active Directory. If you want to create a contact in Active Directory, you connect to the location within Active Directory where you will store the contact. You then call the *create* method, specifying that contact as the type of object you want to create. You supply the RDN of the object and call *SetInfo* as shown in the CreateContact.ps1 script.

CreateContact.ps1

```
$adsi = [adsi]"LDAP://ou=MyTestOU,dc=nwtraders,dc=com"
$de = $adsi.create("Contact","cn=MyContact")
$de.SetInfo()
```

INSIDE TRACK

Choosing the Correct ADSI Interface

James Turner, MCSE, Senior Premier Field Engineer
Microsoft Services

As a premier field engineer for Microsoft, I come in contact with companies that work in many different industries ranging from health care to government to education and everything in between. While I am primarily based out of New York City, my travels take me all over the United States and Canada. As a result, I see customers who have differing needs, capabilities, and abilities; however, there are some similarities. For one thing, I tend to see the following tasks commonly performed by network administrators:

- Implement login scripts (for example, modify client operating system configuration; install/uninstall software, drivers, and updates)

- Provision new user accounts

- Decommission Active Directory objects

- Maintain group memberships

- Enable and provision application-specific services (for example, provision Microsoft Exchange Server messaging services)

- Automate data protection strategies

- Monitor and troubleshoot Active Directory infrastructure services

- Search for stale or unused accounts

What's interesting is that these types of tasks can all be automated. For example, the following script gives you the option to search Active Directory for disabled user accounts or accounts with expired passwords.

```
PARAM([Switch]$PasswordExpired,[Switch]$AccountDisabled, $LastLogon,$DOM
= ([ADSI]"LDAP://rootdse").defaultNamingContext)
```

```
$ADS_UF_Dont_EXPIRE_PASS                    = 65536
$ADS_UF_ACCOUNTDISABLED                     = 2
$ADS_UF_PASS_Expired                         = 8388608


#lastLogon

If ($PasswordExpired.IsPresent -eq $true)
{
 $ADQuery = "<LDAP://$DOM>;(&(ObjectCategory=Person)(ObjectClass=User)
(UserAccountControl:1.2.840.113556.1.4.803:=$ADS_UF_PASS_Expired
));ADsPath;Subtree"
} ElseIf ($AccountDisabled.IsPresent -eq $true)
{
 $ADQuery = "<LDAP://$DOM>;(&(ObjectCategory=Person)(ObjectClass=User)
(UserAccountControl:1.2.840.113556.1.4.803:=$ADS_UF_ACCOUNTDISABLED));
ADsPath;Subtree"
} Else {
 Write-Host "---> Syntax:ADStaleUsers.ps1 [-$PasswordExpired]
[-AccountDisabled]"
 Exit
}


Write-Host "Binding to AD Path [$DOM]"

$oADOConnection                                      =
New-Object -ComObject "ADODB.Connection"
$oADOCommand                                         = New-
Object -ComObject "ADODB.Command"
$oADOConnection.Open("Provider=ADsDSOObject;")
$oADOCommand.ActiveConnection                        =
$oADOConnection
$oADOCommand.CommandText                             = $ADQuery
$oRS
= $oADOCommand.Execute()



If (-not $oRS.RecordCount -or $oRS.RecordCount -eq 0) {Write-Host "No
Objects Found!"; exit}


$oRS.MoveFirst()


While ($oRS.EOF -ne $true)
{
 $oRS.Fields.item("ADsPath").value
 $oRS.MoveNext()
}
```

When I work with Active Directory, I generally have a choice of working with either the ADSI LDAP provider or the ADSI WinNT provider. The provider I choose depends on the task and on which interface better facilitates that task (that is, fewer lines of code). I notice that WinNT is more straightforward and requires fewer lines of code. I use the WinNT interface to change passwords, create enabled users, create groups, and easily disable/enable user accounts by using the property methods that allow me to pass the friendly property name as the parameter instead of a bit mask, as with the *UserAccountControl* property. Also, WinNT can access the local SAM account database, which LDAP cannot. On the other hand, I can bind to a location in Active Directory using LDAP and retrieve/access a much greater volume of Active Directory properties than when using WinNT. With little modification, I can access all naming contexts and special Active Directory objects using LDAP (for example, RootDSE). When using LDAP, I can also use different authentication methods, such as Kerberos. WinNT has access to more object types and interfaces. I tend to prefer WinNT over LDAP if I have a choice (that is, if both providers can facilitate the same tasks).

Look at the following code.

```
PS C:\> $ADBind = [ADSI]"LDAP://cn=James Turner,cn=Users,DC=contoso,DC=c
om"
PS C:\> $ADBind.PsBase.InvokeSet("AccountDisabled", $false)
PS C:\> $ADBind.PsBase.CommitChanges()
```

To bind to my user account in my test lab using the LDAP provider, I must know the full distinguished name of my Active Directory object. This usually means that I need to use a tool such as Ldp, Adsiedit, or Active Directory Users and Computers (to view the object path and copy to my script).

```
PS C:\> $ADBind = [ADSI]"WinNT://contoso/jaturn"
PS C:\> $ADBind.psbase.invokeset("AccountDisabled",$true)
PS C:\> $ADBind.psbase.CommitChanges()
```

To bind to my user account using the WinNT provider, all I need to know is my *SamAccountName* that I use to log in every day. This is one of the many nuances of WinNT that makes it my preferred provider.

When I need to create an Active Directory script, I use the [ADSI] type accelerator from Windows PowerShell (used for binding to objects) and an ActiveX Data Object (ADO) Component Object Model (COM) object (that I use in VBScript for searching a directory). I do not use [ADSISearcher] (DirectorySearcher from .NET) to conduct a search due to my limited .NET experience. This leads me to both create from scratch when I want to bind using the accelerator and to rewrite VBScripts in Windows PowerShell to search Active Directory when using ADO because it is familiar to me.

The biggest challenge is knowing what methods are available for a given object. To this end, I use a variety of sources of information that are available to anyone seeking to use Windows PowerShell. The following are some of my favorites:

- TechNet Script Center
- Jeffrey Snovers Windows PowerShell blog
- Scripting Guys
- MSDN
- Microsoft Windows Server 2008 Software Development Kit (SDK)
- Windows PowerShell Help Guide (.chm) PowerShell Documentation Pack

I admit that there are some issues in trying to use the MSDN documentation. For instance, you need to know the keywords to use when searching for information. You really need to think your way through the problem in an orderly fashion to come up with the information. At times, you can find information related to legacy interfaces. Using MSDN can become confusing unless you understand how Windows PowerShell uses an adapter system to return these COM objects in a .NET wrapper object. For instance, when you bind to an Active Directory user object using ADSI via VB/VBScript, it returns an IADsUser interface. If you use the [ADSI] accelerator for Windows PowerShell, you need to be knowledgeable about the .NET *System.DirectoryServices.DirectoryEntry* class. Also, some errors may refer to Interface Association Descriptors (IADs).

When using ADSI in Windows PowerShell, certain methods and properties are hidden from the Get-Member cmdlet; this has been improved in PowerShell 2.0. This cmdlet still confuses newcomers and can be highly frustrating. Some actions I can perform directly with the property within Active Directory Domain Services, and other actions require me to use some type of adapter method. Through practice, research, and collaboration with peers and communities, I was able to gain an understanding of Windows PowerShell and ADSI. The techniques involved in accessing the hidden properties are not as clearly explained as they should be, and articles about accessing those properties are hard to find (again, without the right keyword, you won't find articles).

Windows PowerShell scripting is far more efficient and reliable than Active Directory Users and Computers. You can quantify how much time it takes to manage users, groups, and computers. Consider the following example.

You want to create a user. Your company has a set of mandatory attributes that must be set on all users in the directory to facilitate directory lookups and Human Resources (HR) activity. Let's say that more than 20 attributes must be set, and more than half of these attributes are common to all users within a geographical location or workgroup. Your current process is to receive a spreadsheet from HR and the IT help desk containing the information required to create user objects and populate the necessary attributes. The users were processed by HR yesterday and processed by the IT help desk this morning. You receive the e-mail containing the spreadsheet right after lunch, and you review it. Using the user interface, you open Active Directory Users and Computers and locate the appropriate Active Directory container where the user will be created. You invoke the Create User dialog box and begin the painful process of manually entering all of the necessary common and unique information for that user, which takes approximately 15 to 20 minutes at a minimum. Now, imagine performing that process for 10, 20, 30, or even 100 or more users at one time within a time-related deadline. It would take hours to complete if you were solely dedicated to the task. However, it would take days to complete this task if you have other duties to perform, not to mention the time that the company already spent while waiting for the IT help desk to process the new employee and to relay the administrative task of creating the user to you. Using this process, it would take more than 24 hours to create a user account. Why do this when you can automate the entire process?

What if you could automate the process of periodically connecting (in 1-hour intervals) to the HR SQL database to detect new employees that are approved for an Active Directory user account? On connection, you detect that a new employee requires a user account. Your script checks Active Directory for an existing account with the same name. If it does not find one, it retrieves the necessary properties from the HR database, reads the IT database for IT-specific requirements (that is, password info), and creates the user account using ADSI. Once complete, the script verifies that all domain controller update sequence numbers (USNs) in the region of the user are synchronized. It then sends an e-mail, text, or voice mail to the user using Exchange Server or Unified Messaging (UM), informing the user that his account is ready and providing the minimum required information to log in. Depending on Active Directory convergence time, the polling interval, and the time that the new employee was entered into the HR system, this process may take only 30 minutes to 4 hours to complete. Moreover, neither you nor the IT help desk was tied up in the process. This is a huge PLUS.

Additionally, automation promotes the following benefits:

- Provides consistency in process implementation, especially if you need it done right the first time
- Facilitates business-, corporate-, legal-, and security-related compliance
- Provides automation
- Lowers total cost of ownership (TCO)
- Incurs less administrative overhead

Deriving the Create Object Pattern

As you have no doubt begun to realize by now, the process of creating an object in Active Directory incorporates the same three steps: make the connection to the appropriate location within Active Directory, use the *create* method while specifying both the name and type of object to create, and then call the *SetInfo* method. If you can abstract the items that may change within the process of creating an object into variables, you are left with a block of code that can be used to create an object in Active Directory. Consequently, you never have to write this block of code again because it is completely reusable.

As a first attempt, you can choose one of the previous scripts that create an object in Active Directory and begin to abstract every potential value that can be supplied to the script. You find that the items that change—the variable items—are the path to the location within the Active Directory hierarchy, the class of the object, and the name of the object. Everything else within the various scripts that you previously reviewed is the same; the process of connecting to Active Directory, the method you used to create the objects, and the necessity of using the *SetInfo* method did not change. The resulting script is CreateObject_1.ps1 as shown here. Notice that the variable items that changed are now stored in variables. The values that did not change between the different scripts are the items that use the variables.

CreateObject_1.ps1

```
$path = "dc=nwtraders,dc=com"
$class = "OrganizationalUnit"
$name = "ou=testou"
$adsi = [adsi]"LDAP://$path"
$de = $adsi.Create($class,$name)
$de.SetInfo()
```

Modifying the Variables

If you want to create a user now, all you need to do is modify the appropriate values that are stored in variables. You do not need to modify the value stored in the *$path* variable. Simply append the ou=path portion to the name value if desired, which simplifies the number of values that need to be modified to run the script as shown in the example in the CreateUser_1.ps1 script.

CreateUser_1.ps1

```
$path = "dc=nwtraders,dc=com"
$class = "user"
$name = "cn=myuser,ou=testou"
$adsi = [adsi]"LDAP://$path"
$de = $adsi.Create($class,$name)
$de.SetInfo()
```

Constant vs. Read-Only Variables

If you create a variable (in most normal circumstances, the value of the variable never changes), you can turn that variable into either a *constant* variable or a *read-only* variable. To do this, use the New-Variable cmdlet. After specifying the value and the name of the variable, use the *–option* parameter and either of the following keywords: read-only or constant. The difference between a read-only variable and a constant variable is that a constant variable is constant; you cannot change it or delete it. A constant exists forever within the scope in which it is defined. If you do not have a compelling reason for creating a constant, I recommend as a best practice that you create a read-only variable. The revised CreateUser_1.ps1 script is now named CreateUser_2.ps1, and you have defined a constant variable for the path.

```
CreateUser_2.ps1
New-Variable -name path -value "dc=nwtraders,dc=com" -option constant
$class = "user"
$name = "cn=myuser,ou=testou"
$adsi = [adsi]"LDAP://$path"
$de = $adsi.Create($class,$name)
$de.SetInfo()
```

Creating a Utility Script

Opening and editing a script if there are only two or three variables that might need to be modified is a little foolish and certainly not a practical solution for an enterprise network administrator. You can use your basic design pattern to your advantage and easily create a few scripts that might be a bit more robust. You can modify the script so that it accepts command-line parameters, which provide you with a utility script that you can use to create various objects quickly and easily from the command line. Given the form of the CreateObject_1.ps1 script shown earlier in this chapter, your basic task is to use the *Param* statement and surround your variables with parentheses. While you are at it, it is a good idea to create a minimal form of help for the script. I consider it a best practice to always include a help function when defining command-line parameters, which greatly enhances the usability and discoverability of the script. We will call the newly created script CreateObject_Param.ps1.

Your next task is to move the code into functions. This paves the way for a modular form of script design and makes it easier to modify the code in the future. As a best practice, I recommend using a verb/noun form for the function names; this is in keeping with the overall design of Windows PowerShell and promotes discoverability. Try to use standard verbs if at all possible because this also simplifies reading the script.

One other addition to make to the CreateObject_Param.ps1 script is adding a *–debug* switched parameter. You will then be able to access *debug* statements by using the Write-Debug cmdlet. When the script is run using the *–debug* parameter, you write out some debugging information to the command line. This process is useful from two perspectives. First, it simplifies writing the script in the first place. If errors are occurring at different stages of the script development process, it is often helpful to see what values are actually getting passed to the variables. Once you finish writing the script, you typically do not need such information. In VBScript, it is common to use *wscript.echo* to print the values of the variables in the script. The process is almost a wasted effort due to the time spent typing in the code to print the values and the subsequent time spent deleting that code. In Windows PowerShell, however, you can leave the *debug* statements in the code. This introduces the second helpful aspect of using the `Write-Debug` cmdlet, which occurs at run time. If a user types in command-line parameters and receives errors, he can add the *–debug* parameter to see what is getting passed to the script; it may point him in the direction of a typo.

In the CreateObject_Param.ps1 script, you do this very thing.

```
CreateObject_Param.ps1
Param(
        $path = "dc=nwtraders,dc=com",
        $class = "OrganizationalUnit",
        $name,
        [switch]$debug,
        [switch]$help
    )
Function GetHelp()
{
  "SYNTAX: CreateObject_Param.ps1 -name `'cn=myuser,ou=testou`' -class user"
} #end GetHelp
Function CreateAdObject()
{
  Write-Debug "Connecting to $path"
  $adsi = [adsi]"LDAP://$path"
  Write-Debug "Creating $class, $name"
  $de = $adsi.Create($class,$name)
  $de.SetInfo()
} #end CreateAdObject
# *** Entry Point ***
if($debug) { $DebugPreference = "continue" }
If($help) { GetHelp ; exit }
if($name) { CreateAdObject ; exit }
if(!$name) { "Missing name of object!" ; GetHelp ; exit }
```

Using CSV Files to Create Multiple Objects

You can use the create object pattern to simplify the process of creating multiple objects in Active Directory. Windows PowerShell can work with comma-separated value (CSV) files in a native fashion by using the `Import-CSV` cmdlet. The CSV file itself is merely a text file that has one row of column headers and then a series of rows that supply values for the column headers. Such a CSV file named Objects.csv is shown in Figure 3-1.

FIGURE 3-1 A CSV file in Notepad uses the first row for columns and the remaining rows for data.

When working with CSV files in Notepad, keep in mind that items such as dc=nwtraders,dc=com show up as two columns when they are imported in Windows PowerShell. To force the item to be interpreted as a single string instead of two values for two columns, you need to surround the two pieces with quotation marks as shown here: "dc=nwtraders,dc=com". When working with CSV files, they are a bit easier to read if you have a space between the commas. However, if you intend to open and read the files in Microsoft Office Excel, then you do not want the spaces because they cause the columns not to line up properly as shown in Figure 3-2.

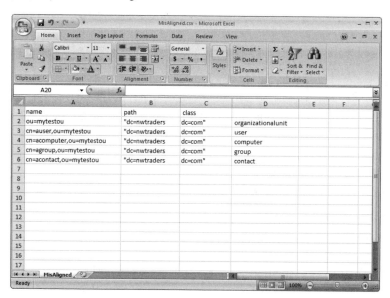

FIGURE 3-2 Misaligned Office Excel file splits the domain name into two columns and leaves object class without a column head.

Due to the finicky nature of both the quotation rules and the spacing issues, I consider it a best practice to create and maintain CSV files in Excel and to allow the application to handle the details. If you are proficient with Excel, you can use the auto-completion suggestions and auto-fill features to create a large file much quicker than is possible using Notepad. The only issue with creating CSV files in Excel is the infinite loop you may encounter when trying to save the sheet as a CSV file. It is easy to end up with an XLS-formatted sheet in addition to a CSV-formatted file if you do not read the prompts carefully. Such a warning message is shown in Figure 3-3.

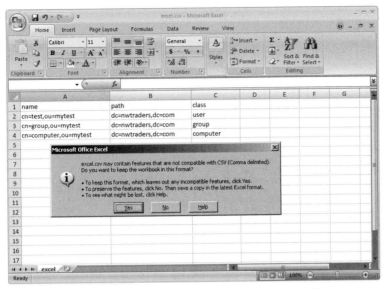

FIGURE 3-3 Excel warns of compatibility issues when saving a CSV file.

Once you click Yes from the dialog box shown in Figure 3-3, everything seems to be fine. You can continue to work, or you can choose to exit Excel. If you decide to exit Excel, a dialog box asks whether you want to save your work. This prompt appears even if you have previously saved your work. When you click Yes, you are presented with the Save As dialog box. The name of your file is populated for you. Clicking Save presents you with the Confirm Save As dialog box shown in Figure 3-4.

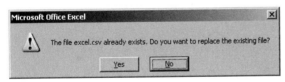

FIGURE 3-4 Saving a CSV file from Excel prompts you to replace the file.

By clicking Yes, you are once again confronted with the Excel dialog box with the message "Excel.csv May Contain Features That Are Not Compatible With CSV (Comma Delimited)," as shown in Figure 3-5.

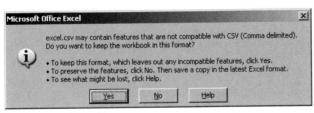

FIGURE 3-5 When trying to save a CSV file from within Excel, you will likely see this dialog box a few times.

Using Microsoft Office Excel and CSV Files

If you seem to be going around in circles, you probably are. The first few times I tried to use Excel to work with CSV files, I became frustrated by the multiple warnings and thought I must have done something wrong. So, I slowed down, paid close attention to the dialog boxes, and concluded that what I was seeing was the intended user experience.

The necessity of having Excel installed on a computer prior to being able to take advantage of its neat organizational features and superior text-processing capabilities is something you need to be concerned about. The question is: Where do you install Microsoft Office so you can take advantage of Excel? You can certainly install Microsoft Office on desktop machines and use it there, but you are not allowed to install Microsoft Office products on production servers except in extremely limited circumstances. The rationale is that Microsoft Office products are user productivity tools and not server productivity tools; therefore, they are not supported on production servers. However, there is a workaround. By using ADO in either the classic COM version or the .NET variety, you can easily access data that is stored in the spreadsheet. Keep in mind that to programmatically access Excel files, they must be saved in compatibility mode. An example Excel.xls spreadsheet is included on the companion media and is shown in Figure 3-6.

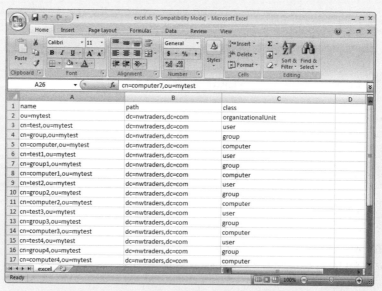

FIGURE 3-6 A native mode Excel spreadsheet provides a simple way to manage the creation of objects.

Testing a Script

The CreateObject_AdoNet.ps1 script illustrates retrieving data from Excel and creating objects in Active Directory. Due to the design of the script, it does not produce any output by default, which can be rather frustrating if you are not sure whether the script works. If you prefer to see output, you can run the script with the *–verbose* parameter. There are checks in several places in the script that will output confirmation messages to the screen. The *–verbose* parameter is shown here.

```
Param([switch]$verbose)
```

All of the logic is incorporated into separate functions, and the entry point of the script merely launches each of the different functions. This modular type of design makes the script easier to maintain.

The first function is the *TestPath* function that checks the path to the Excel spreadsheet. If the file is found and the script was run with the *–verbose* parameter, the file name is printed to the command line. If the script was not run with the *–verbose* parameter, nothing is printed if the Excel spreadsheet is found. If the file is not found, the file name is printed in red and the script exits. The *TestPath* function is shown here.

```
Function TestPath($FilePath)
{
 If(Test-Path -path $FilePath)
   {
     if($verbose) { "$filePath found" }
   } #end if
 ELSE
   {
    Write-Host -foregroundcolor red "$filePath not found."
    Exit
   } #end else
} #end TestPath
```

Configuring the Connection to the Database

You can use either ADO.NET or classic ADO COM objects to query your Excel spreadsheet; which methodology you use when reading from an Excel spreadsheet is a matter of preference. In general, when working with Windows PowerShell, I prefer to use the Microsoft .NET Framework classes if possible. When working with ADO.NET or using classic ADO, there could be performance issues. With the OLEDB .NET provider, you basically wrap the COM objects so that the performance advantage is not as large. To test this process for your systems, you can use the Measure-Command cmdlet to quickly and easily time the execution of two very similar scripts as shown below. You will need to modify the path to point to the actual location of the files on your system.

```
Measure-Command -Expression { &("C:\Bestpractices\CreateObject_AdoCOM.ps1") }
```

Using ADO.NET

The next function you create is the *SetConnectionString* function, which is used to configure all of the values that are required to make your ADO connection to the database. You specify the path to the Excel spreadsheet, the name of the spreadsheet, and the provider name. Two things to keep in mind are the following:

- The spreadsheet name must be followed by a dollar sign ($).
- The provider you are using is the Microsoft.Jet.OleDB.4.0 provider.

You need to specify the data source as the path to the spreadsheet, and you must choose to use extended properties that are equal to Excel 8.0. It does not matter what version of Microsoft Office you are running because you will use Excel 8.0 properties; these properties have not been updated for newer versions of Microsoft Office. Keep in mind that the Excel 2007 spreadsheets need to be saved in compatibility mode to work. You next define a rudimentary query: Select * from [$strSheetName]. Note that the spreadsheet name is surrounded in square brackets. This section of code is shown here.

```
Function SetConnectionString()
{
 $strFileName = $FilePath
 $strSheetName = 'Excel$'
 $strProvider = "Provider=Microsoft.Jet.OLEDB.4.0"
 $strDataSource = "Data Source = $strFileName"
 $strExtend = "Extended Properties=Excel 8.0"
 $strQuery = "Select * from [$strSheetName]"
 NewAdoConnection
} #end SetConnectionString
```

Once you configure all of the connection string parameters, you call the *NewAdoConnection* function, which creates two objects. The first object is the *System.Data.OleDb.OleDbConnection* object. When you create this object, you need to give it the provider, the data source, and the extended properties as the constructor. The second object you create is the *System.Data.OleDb.OleDbCommand* object. This class receives a query for the constructor. Now, you need to wire up the connection by specifying the *connection* object to the *connection* property of the *command* object and then open the *connection* object. Once the connection is open, you can use the *ExecuteReader* method to return a *DataReader* object; this object is an instance of the *System.Data.OleDb.OleDbDataReader* class. One item to notice is that the variables you intend to use later in other functions are specified as script-level variables, which places them into the script scope where they can be accessed anywhere within the script. The *NewAdoConnection* function is shown here.

```
Function NewAdoConnection()
{
 $Script:objConn = New-Object System.Data.OleDb.OleDbConnection(`
 "$strProvider;$strDataSource;$strExtend")
 $sqlCommand = New-Object System.Data.OleDb.OleDbCommand($strQuery)
 $sqlCommand.Connection = $objConn
```

```
$Script:objConn.open()
$Script:DataReader = $sqlCommand.ExecuteReader()
} #end NewAdoConnection
```

Once you create your instance of the *OleDbDataReader* class, you need to read the data and assign the values to variables that you can use when creating objects in Active Directory. In the *ReadData* function, you can use a *While* statement to control the execution of the data reader. By using the *Read* method of the *OleDbDataReader* class (as long as there is data in the data reader), you can retrieve the first three columns from the current row. You can use the *ToString* method to ensure that the data is a string, and you can populate the variables that will be used to create the objects in Active Directory. The three values to use are the name of the object, the path where the object will reside, and the class of object to create. Once you populate the appropriate variables, you call the *CreateObject* function to create the objects in Active Directory. The *ReadData* function is shown here.

```
Function ReadData()
{
 While($Script:DataReader.read())
  {
   $Script:Name = $Script:DataReader[0].Tostring()
   $Script:Path = $Script:DataReader[1].Tostring()
   $Script:Class = $Script:DataReader[2].Tostring()
   CreateObject
  } #end while
} #end ReadData
```

The *CreateObject* function is used to actually create the objects in Active Directory. At this point in the script, you have received all of the information you need from the constants and variables as well as the data retrieved from the Excel spreadsheet. If you are running the script in –verbose mode, you can print a message that states the class of the object, the name, and the path that will be used to create the object in Active Directory. If you are not running in –verbose mode, no confirmation message is displayed. You are now back at your abstracted three lines of code that you first saw in the CreateUser_1.ps1 script earlier in this chapter. You can connect to the appropriate location in Active Directory, use the *create* method while specifying the class and name of the object, and call the *SetInfo* method to write the information to Active Directory. The *CreateObject* function is shown here.

```
Function CreateObject()
{
 If($verbose)
  {
    "Creating $Script:Class $Script:Name,$Script:Path"
  } #end if verbose
 $adsi = [adsi]"LDAP://$Script:path"
 $de = $adsi.Create($Script:class,$Script:name)
 $de.SetInfo()
} #end CreateObject
```

Lastly, you must clean up after the script by closing the data reader and closing the connection. To do this, you use the *Close* method from both the *OleDbDataReader* class and the *OleDbConnection* class. The *CloseAdoConnection* function is shown here.

```
Function CloseAdoConnection()
{
 $Script:dataReader.close()
 $Script:objConn.close()
}
```

The last item in the script is the first item that is executed when the script is run. At the entry point to the script, you can specify the path to the Excel spreadsheet and call the *TestPath* function. By calling the *TestPath* function, you pass the path to the spreadsheet to the function as an argument. If you pass the *TestPath* function, you call the *SetConnectionString* function, then the *ReadData* function, and finally the *CloseAdoConnection* function. The entry point to the script is shown here.

```
$FilePath = "C:\BestPractices\excel.xls"
TestPath($FilePath)
SetConnectionString
ReadData
CloseAdoConnection
```

The completed CreateObject_AdoNet.ps1 script is shown here.

```
CreateObject_AdoNet.ps1
Param([switch]$verbose)
Function TestPath($FilePath)
{
 If(Test-Path -path $FilePath)
   {
    if($verbose) { "$filePath found" }
   } #end if
 ELSE
   {
    Write-Host -foregroundcolor red "$filePath not found."
    Exit
   } #end else
} #end TestPath
Function SetConnectionString()
{
 $strFileName = $FilePath
 $strSheetName = 'Excel$'
 $strProvider = "Provider=Microsoft.Jet.OLEDB.4.0"
 $strDataSource = "Data Source = $strFileName"
 $strExtend = "Extended Properties=Excel 8.0"
 $strQuery = "Select * from [$strSheetName]"
```

```
  NewAdoConnection
} #end SetConnectionString
Function NewAdoConnection()
{
 $Script:objConn = New-Object System.Data.OleDb.OleDbConnection(`
 "$strProvider;$strDataSource;$strExtend")
 $sqlCommand = New-Object System.Data.OleDb.OleDbCommand($strQuery)
 $sqlCommand.Connection = $objConn
 $Script:objConn.open()
 $Script:DataReader = $sqlCommand.ExecuteReader()
} #end NewAdoConnection
Function ReadData()
{
 While($Script:DataReader.read())
  {
   $Script:Name = $Script:DataReader[0].Tostring()
   $Script:Path = $Script:DataReader[1].Tostring()
   $Script:Class = $Script:DataReader[2].Tostring()
   CreateObject
  } #end while
} #end ReadData
Function CreateObject()
{
 If($verbose)
  {
    "Creating $Script:Class $Script:Name,$Script:Path"
  } #end if verbose
 $adsi = [adsi]"LDAP://$Script:path"
 $de = $adsi.Create($Script:class,$Script:name)
 $de.SetInfo()
} #end CreateObject
Function CloseAdoConnection()
{
 $Script:dataReader.close()
 $Script:objConn.close()
}
# *** Entry Point ***
$FilePath = "C:\BestPractices\excel.xls"
TestPath($FilePath)
SetConnectionString
ReadData
CloseAdoConnection
```

Using ADO COM Objects

You may not want to use ADO.NET to query the Excel spreadsheet. In this case, you can rewrite the CreateObject_AdoNet.ps1 script to use ADO COM objects. The advantage of the modular approach in the way the previous script was written is that you only need to modify the *NewAdoConnection* function and the *ReadData* function in the script. Everything else remains the same.

In the *NewAdoConnection* function, you first create an instance of a *connection* object by using the New-Object cmdlet. Specify that you are creating a ComObject and give it the *ADODB.Connection* program ID. Next, you create an instance of a *command* object. You can use the *ADODB.Command* program ID with the New-Object cmdlet to create the object. Once you have the two objects, you can open the *connection* object and specify the provider, data source, and extended properties. You can then specify the active connection as the connection you created and stored in the script-scope *$objConn* variable. You can use the query string as the command text and then use the *Execute* method. The revised *NewAdoConnection* function is shown here.

```
Function NewAdoConnection()
{
 $Script:objConn = New-Object -comObject "ADODB.Connection"
 $Command = New-Object -comObject "ADODB.Command"
 $Script:objConn.open("$strProvider;$strDataSource;$strExtend")
 $Command.ActiveConnection = $script:objConn
 $Command.Commandtext = $strQuery
 $Script:RecordSet = $Command.Execute()
} #end NewAdoConnection
```

Second, the *ReadData* function needs to be modified. The first step is to move the record pointer to the first position in the record set. To do this, you can use the *MoveFirst* method on the *RecordSet* object. This time, you can use a *Do Until* loop instead of the *While* statement that was used in the previous version of the script. Next, you can use the *Fields* property of the *RecordSet* object and the *Item* method to retrieve the specific column from the spreadsheet. You then query the *Value* property to see the data stored there, call the *CreateObject* function, and then move to the next record in the record set. The revised *ReadData* function is shown here.

```
Function ReadData()
{
 $Script:RecordSet.MoveFirst()
 Do
 {
  $Script:Name = $Script:RecordSet.Fields.Item("name").Value
  $Script:Path = $Script:RecordSet.Fields.Item("path").Value
  $Script:Class = $Script:RecordSet.Fields.Item("class").Value
  CreateObject
  $Script:RecordSet.MoveNext()
```

```
    }
  Until($Script:recordSet.eof)
} #end ReadData
```

With the previous two modifications made to the script, the completed
CreateObject_AdoCOM.ps1 script is seen here.

CreateObject_AdoCOM.ps1
```
Param([switch]$verbose)
Function TestPath($FilePath)
{
  If(Test-Path -path $FilePath)
    {
      if($verbose) { "$filePath found" }
    } #end if
  ELSE
    {
      Write-Host -foregroundcolor red "$filePath not found."
      Exit
    } #end else
} #end TestPath
Function SetConnectionString()
{
  $strFileName = $FilePath
  $strSheetName = 'Excel$'
  $strProvider = "Provider=Microsoft.Jet.OLEDB.4.0"
  $strDataSource = "Data Source = $strFileName"
  $strExtend = "Extended Properties=Excel 8.0"
  $strQuery = "Select * from [$strSheetName]"
  NewAdoConnection
} #end SetConnectionString
Function NewAdoConnection()
{
  $Script:objConn = New-Object -comObject "ADODB.Connection"
  $Command = New-Object -comObject "ADODB.Command"
  $Script:objConn.open("$strProvider;$strDataSource;$strExtend")
  $Command.ActiveConnection = $script:objConn
  $Command.Commandtext = $strQuery
  $Script:RecordSet = $Command.Execute()
} #end NewAdoConnection
Function ReadData()
{
  $Script:RecordSet.MoveFirst()
  Do
    {
      $Script:Name = $Script:RecordSet.Fields.Item("name").Value
      $Script:Path = $Script:RecordSet.Fields.Item("path").Value
```

```
    $Script:Class = $Script:RecordSet.Fields.Item("class").Value
    CreateObject
    $Script:RecordSet.MoveNext()
   }
  Until($Script:recordSet.eof)
} #end ReadData
Function CreateObject()
{
  If($verbose)
   {
     "Creating $Script:Class $Script:Name,$Script:Path"
   } #end if verbose
  $adsi = [adsi]"LDAP://$Script:path"
  $de = $adsi.Create($Script:class,$Script:name)
  $de.SetInfo()
} #end CreateObject
Function CloseAdoConnection()
{
  $Script:recordSet.close()
  $Script:objConn.close()
}
# *** Entry Point ***
$FilePath = "C:\BestPractices\excel.xls"
TestPath($FilePath)
SetConnectionString
ReadData
CloseAdoConnection
```

Modifying Properties

The process of modifying the properties of the objects in Active Directory generally involves three steps. You must establish a connection to the object, use the *put* method to put the data into the attribute, and use the *SetInfo* method to write the data back to Active Directory. The following list summarizes these steps.

- Connect to the object by using the [ADSI] type accelerator and the *ADsPath*.

- Use the *put* method while supplying the attribute name and attribute value.

- Use the *SetInfo* method.

In the code shown here, you make a connection to an object named *myuser* that resides in the Organizational Unit named MyTestOU in the Nwtraders.com domain. The *DistinguishedName* attribute for the object is therefore cn=myuser,ou=mytestou, dc=nwtraders,dc=com. Next, you can use the *put* method to put the value of *lastname* into the *sn* attribute and then call the *SetInfo* method to write the information back to Active Directory. This code was typed directly inside the Windows PowerShell console and illustrates the fact that you can work interactively with Active Directory if desired.

```
PS C:\> $user = [ADSI]"LDAP://cn=myuser,ou=mytestou,dc=nwtraders,dc=com"
PS C:\> $user.Put("sn","lastName")
PS C:\> $user.SetInfo()
```

Using Excel to Update Attributes

A more productive way to update the various attributes of user objects is to populate an Excel spreadsheet with the values you want to supply for the attributes. In this way, it is relatively easy to type the information into the spreadsheet, and you can then easily read the data from the spreadsheet by using ADO. Figure 3-7 presents a spreadsheet that contains the attribute names on the second row; the first row includes the tab names. The actual data begins on the third row. With the user name, ou name, and domain name in the first three columns of the spreadsheet, it is very easy to create the *DistinguishedName* attribute that is required for the *ADsPath* connection to be able to modify object attributes in Active Directory. The ModifyUsers.xls spreadsheet can easily be read and used to populate Active Directory attributes.

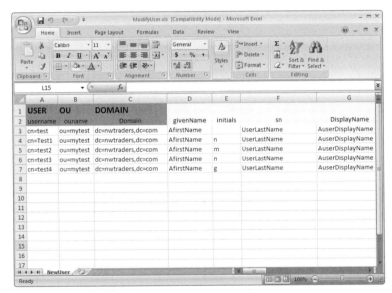

FIGURE 3-7 The ModifyUsers.xls spreadsheet contains user object attribute names.

In the ModifyProperties_AdoNet.ps1 script, you begin with the *Param* statement that defines a single command-line parameter: *–verbose*. The *–verbose* parameter is a switched parameter that has an effect on the script only when it is present. If the *–verbose* parameter is specified when the script is run, the various Write-Verbose cmdlets used throughout the script will print detailed information that enables you to track the progress of the script if desired. The *Param* statement is shown here.

```
Param([switch]$verbose)
```

Next, you must define a function named *TestPath* in the ModifyProperties_AdoNet.ps1 script. The *TestPath* function is used to verify the existence of the ModifyUsers.xls spreadsheet by using the Test-Path cmdlet. If the spreadsheet is found and the script was launched with the *–verbose* switched parameter, the *TestPath* function prints a message stating that the spreadsheet was found. If the file is not found, the *TestPath* function displays a message stating that the file was not found, regardless of the status of the *–verbose* switch. The *TestPath* function is shown here.

```
Function TestPath($FilePath)
{
 If(Test-Path -path $FilePath)
   {
    Write-Verbose "$filePath found"
  } #end if
 ELSE
  {
   Write-Host -foregroundcolor red "$filePath not found."
   Exit
  } #end else
} #end TestPath
```

The next function seen in the ModifyProperties_AdoNet.ps1 script is the *SetConnectionString* function, which is used to supply values for the six variables that are used to configure the ADO connection to the spreadsheet. The first variable defined is the *$strFileName* variable that contains the path to the Excel spreadsheet. The second variable, *$strSheetName*, is used to hold the name of the spreadsheet you will work with from the workbook referenced in the first variable.

> **IMPORTANT** When connecting to an Excel spreadsheet by using ADO—either classic ADO COM or ADO.NET—the name of the individual spreadsheet must be followed by a dollar sign.

The next variable to be defined is *$strProvider*, which is used to hold the name of the ADO provider. This string must be written as Provider=Microsoft.OleDB.4.0. Because the value never changes, this variable can be declared as a constant. Once you specify the name of the provider to use in the connection, you need to specify the data source. The data source is always equal to the full path to the Excel workbook. The basic query that you can use is: Select everything from the name of the sheet. In the *select* statement, the sheet name must be surrounded with square brackets.

Once you have assigned values to your six variables, you can call the *NewAdoConnection* function, which is used to establish the actual ADO connection to the Excel spreadsheet. The *SetConnectionString* function is shown here.

```
Function SetConnectionString()
{
 $strFileName = $FilePath
 $strSheetName = 'NewUser$'
 $strProvider = "Provider=Microsoft.Jet.OLEDB.4.0"
 $strDataSource = "Data Source = $strFileName"
 $strExtend = "Extended Properties=Excel 8.0"
 $strQuery = "Select * from [$strSheetName]"
 NewAdoConnection
} #end SetConnectionString
```

Making the Connection

The first thing you must do to make an ADO connection is to create an instance of the *System.Data.OleDb.OleDbConnection* class by using the New-Object cmdlet. The *OleDbConnection* class needs three things to make a connection: the name of the provider, the path to the data source, and the extended provider parameters. When the *OleDbConnection* class is created, you store it in the script-level *$objConn* variable.

The next object you need to create is the *System.Data.OleDb.OleDbCommand* object. The *OleDbCommand* object only needs the query string for its constructor. You give it the query that you stored in the *$strQuery* variable and store the returned *OleDbCommand* object in the *$sqlCommand* variable.

Once you create these two objects, you need to specify the *connection* property of the *command* object by using the *connection* object you stored in the *$objConn* variable. You can open the connection by using the *open* method from the *connection* object. Once the connection is open, you can use the *ExecuteReader* method from the *command* object and store the returned *DataReader* object in the script-level *$dataReader* variable. The complete *NewAdoConnection* function is shown here.

```
Function NewAdoConnection()
{
 $Script:objConn = New-Object System.Data.OleDb.OleDbConnection `
 ("$strProvider;$strDataSource;$strExtend")
 $sqlCommand = New-Object System.Data.OleDb.OleDbCommand($strQuery)
 $sqlCommand.Connection = $objConn
 $Script:objConn.open()
 $Script:DataReader = $sqlCommand.ExecuteReader()
} #end NewAdoConnection
```

Reading the Data

Once you create the ADO connection, open the connection, and create a *DataReader* object, you need to read the data. To do this, you can use the *ReadData* function. First, in the *ReadData* function, you must create a variable named *$columns* and store the number of fields from *DataReader* in it. Next, you need to create an array named *$aryProperties* by using the *CreateInstance* static method from the *System.Array* class. You should specify that the array will contain strings and that it will be the same size as the number of fields in the *DataReader*. Next, you can create a *$rowNumber* variable that is used to keep track of the row position as you work through the *DataReader*. These first three lines of code are shown here.

```
$columns = $Script:DataReader.FieldCount
 $aryProperties = [array]::CreateInstance([string],$columns)
 $rowNumber = 0
```

You can use a *While* loop to work through the *DataReader* by stating that you will continue to read as long as there is something coming back from the *Read* method of the *DataReader*. If you are running with the *–verbose* switch, you can print the row number as shown here.

```
While($Script:DataReader.read())
 {
  Write-Verbose "Row number is $rowNumber"
```

If the row number is equal to 0 and you are running the script in –verbose mode, you can print the property numbers and the name of the property. You can add all of the values from the first row into the *$aryProperties* array, which contains all of the ADSI attribute names. You can then print the entire array of property names if you are running the script in –verbose mode. This section of code is seen here.

```
if($rowNumber -eq 0)
    {
     For($i = 0 ; $i -le $columns -1 ; $i ++)
        {
         Write-Verbose "adding property $i"
         Write-verbose $script:DataReader[$i].ToString()
         $aryProperties[$i] = $script:DataReader[$i].ToString()
        } #end for
    } #end if rownumber
  Write-verbose "printing aryProperties: $aryProperties"
```

If the row number contained in the *$rowNumber* variable is greater than or equal to 1, you can call the *ModifyObject* function. You then increment the value of the *$rowNumber* variable. This section of the code is shown here.

```
if($rowNumber -ge 1)
    {
     ModifyObject
    }
  $rowNumber ++
```

The complete *ReadData* function is shown here.

```
Function ReadData()
{
 $columns = $Script:DataReader.FieldCount
 $aryProperties = [array]::CreateInstance([string],$columns)
 $rowNumber = 0
 While($Script:DataReader.read())
  {
   Write-Verbose "Row number is $rowNumber"
   if($rowNumber -eq 0)
    {
     For($i = 0 ; $i -le $columns -1 ; $i ++)
        {
          Write-Verbose "adding property $i"
          Write-verbose $script:DataReader[$i].ToString()
          $aryProperties[$i] = $script:DataReader[$i].ToString()
        } #end for
    } #end if rownumber
   Write-verbose "printing aryProperties: $aryProperties"
   if($rowNumber -ge 1)
     {
       ModifyObject
     }
   $rowNumber ++
  } #end while
} #end ReadData
```

Making the Changes

The *ModifyObject* function is used to make changes to objects in Active Directory. The first step you must take is make a connection to the actual object in Active Directory. To do this, you read data from the first three columns of the Excel spreadsheet by using the *DataReader* object that is contained in the script-level *$dataReader* variable. These three elements make up the path to the object you want to modify in Active Directory. You store this information in the script-level variable named *$path*. If you run the script with the *–verbose* switch, you can print a message that lists the path of the object you intend to modify. These two lines of code are shown here.

```
$script:path = "$($script:DataReader[0]),$($script:DataReader[1]),
$($script:DataReader[2])"
 Write-Verbose  "Modifying $script:path"
```

Next, in the *ModifyObject* function, you can use a *for* loop to walk through the columns. You use the path you stored in the *$path* variable and pass it to the [ADSI] type accelerator to make the connection to the object. You store the returned *DirectoryEntry* object in the

$adsi variable. When running the script with the *–verbose* switch, you can print the path to the object as well as the property name and value from the *DataReader* object. These three lines of code are shown here.

```
$adsi = [adsi]"LDAP://$Script:path"
 Write-Verbose "Object: $Script:path"
 write-verbose  "Putting: $($aryProperties[$j]),$($Script:DataReader[$j])"
```

You use the *IsNullOrEmpty* static method from the *System.String* class to see whether the data stored in the *DataReader* contains data. If it is empty or null, you can print a message stating that you are missing a value for the particular property you are attempting to modify. You can also use the *IsNullOrEmpty* static method from the *System.String* class to ensure that the property name itself is contained in the array of property names. If the data passes both of these tests, you can put the data into Active Directory and then call the *SetInfo* method to commit the changes to Active Directory. This section of code is shown here.

```
if( [string]::IsNullOrEmpty($($script:DataReader[$j])) )
    { "missing value: $($aryProperties[$j]) for: $script:path" }
 ELSEif( [string]::IsNullOrEmpty($($aryProperties[$j])) )
    { "missing property for $($script:DataReader[$j]) value" }
  ELSE
  {
  $adsi.Put($($aryProperties[$j]),$($Script:DataReader[$j]))
  $adsi.SetInfo()
  }
```

Closing the Connection

The last function you need to create is the one that closes the connection you established with Active Directory once you finish writing the changes. The *CloseAdoConnection* function contains two lines of code, both of which call the *Close* method. The first line closes the *DataReader* and the second closes the *connection* object. These two lines of code are shown here.

```
$Script:dataReader.close()
$Script:objConn.close()
```

The next line contains the first code that is executed in the script. You should first check for the presence of the *$verbose* variable. If you find this variable, you can set the value of the *$verbosePreference* automatic variable to *Continue*. By default, the value of *$verbosePreference* is set to *Silently Continue*, which means that anything printed using the Write-Verbose cmdlet does not display any output as shown here.

```
if($verbose) { $verbosePreference = "continue" }
```

Once you specify the path to the spreadsheet, you can call the *TestPath* function and pass it the path to the Excel spreadsheet that you intend to use. If the *TestPath* function finds the spreadsheet, you continue the script. If it cannot find the spreadsheet, the script ends. You then call the *SetConnectionString* function to assign values to all of the variables used in establishing an ADO connection. You then call the *ReadData* function and, lastly, close the connection. This section of code is shown here.

```
$FilePath = "C:\BestPractices\ModifyUser.xls"
TestPath($FilePath)
SetConnectionString
ReadData
CloseAdoConnection
```

The completed ModifyProperties_AdoNet.ps1 script is shown here.

```
ModifyProperties_AdoNet.ps1
Param([switch]$verbose)
Function TestPath($FilePath)
{
 If(Test-Path -path $FilePath)
   {
     Write-Verbose "$filePath found"
   } #end if
 ELSE
   {
     Write-Host -foregroundcolor red "$filePath not found."
     Exit
   } #end else
} #end TestPath
Function SetConnectionString()
{
 $strFileName = $FilePath
 $strSheetName = 'NewUser$'
 $strProvider = "Provider=Microsoft.Jet.OLEDB.4.0"
 $strDataSource = "Data Source = $strFileName"
 $strExtend = "Extended Properties=Excel 8.0"
 $strQuery = "Select * from [$strSheetName]"
 NewAdoConnection
} #end SetConnectionString
Function NewAdoConnection()
{
 $Script:objConn = New-Object System.Data.OleDb.OleDbConnection `
 ("$strProvider;$strDataSource;$strExtend")
 $sqlCommand = New-Object System.Data.OleDb.OleDbCommand($strQuery)
 $sqlCommand.Connection = $objConn
 $Script:objConn.open()
 $Script:DataReader = $sqlCommand.ExecuteReader()
} #end NewAdoConnection
Function ReadData()
```

```
{
 $columns = $Script:DataReader.FieldCount
 $aryProperties = [array]::CreateInstance([string],$columns)
 $rowNumber = 0
 While($Script:DataReader.read())
 {
  Write-Verbose "Row number is $rowNumber"
  if($rowNumber -eq 0)
   {
    For($i = 0 ; $i -le $columns -1 ; $i ++)
      {
       Write-Verbose "adding property $i"
       Write-verbose $script:DataReader[$i].ToString()
       $aryProperties[$i] = $script:DataReader[$i].ToString()
      } #end for
   } #end if rownumber
  Write-verbose "printing aryProperties: $aryProperties"
  if($rowNumber -ge 1)
   {
    ModifyObject
   }
  $rowNumber ++
 } #end while
} #end ReadData
Function ModifyObject()
{
 $script:path =
"$($script:DataReader[0]),$($script:DataReader[1]),$($script:DataReader[2])"
 Write-Verbose  "Modifying $script:path"
For($j = 3 ; $j -le $columns -1 ; $j++)
{
 $adsi = [adsi]"LDAP://$Script:path"
 Write-Verbose "Object: $Script:path"
 write-verbose  "Putting: $($aryProperties[$j]),$($Script:DataReader[$j])"
 if( [string]::IsNullOrEmpty($($script:DataReader[$j])) )
    { "missing value: $($aryProperties[$j]) for: $script:path" }
 ELSEif( [string]::IsNullOrEmpty($($aryProperties[$j])) )
    { "missing property for $($script:DataReader[$j]) value" }
 ELSE
 {
  $adsi.Put($($aryProperties[$j]),$($Script:DataReader[$j]))
  $adsi.SetInfo()
 }
}
} #end ModifyObject
```

```
Function CloseAdoConnection()
{
 $Script:dataReader.close()
 $Script:objConn.close()
}
# *** Entry Point ***
if($verbose) { $verbosePreference = "continue" }
$FilePath = "C:\BestPractices\ModifyUser.xls"
TestPath($FilePath)
SetConnectionString
ReadData
CloseAdoConnection
```

Additional Resources

- The TechNet Script Center at *http://www.microsoft.com/technet/scriptcenter* has many examples of working with the ADSI interface.

- *Windows PowerShell Scripting Guide* (Microsoft Press, 2008) contains several chapters related to working with objects in Active Directory.

- On the companion media, you will find all of the scripts, CSV files, and Excel spreadsheets referred to in this chapter.

- The Active Directory Service Interfaces SDK at *http://msdn.microsoft.com/en-us/library /aa772170.aspx* has complete documentation of all of the properties and methods used in working with Active Directory.

- The Windows PowerShell team blog at *http://blogs.msdn.com/powershell/* occasionally posts articles about using PowerShell with Active Directory.

## CHAPTER 4

User Management

Examining the Active Directory Schema

Before you begin to perform user management in Active Directory, you must examine the Active Directory schema. There are several hundred classes defined within the Active Directory schema; some are rather esoteric, yet others are very useful and should be explored. The BrowseActiveDirectorySchema.ps1 script, seen here, allows you to browse the schema.

BrowseActiveDirectorySchema.ps1

```
Param($action,$class, [switch]$help)
Function GetHelp()
{
  $helpText= `
@"
 DESCRIPTION:
 NAME: BrowseActiveDirectorySchema.ps1
 Browse Active Directory Schema. Lists Classes, and properties.
 PARAMETERS:
 -Action <L(ist all classes), M(andatory), O(ptional), F(ind)>
 -Class class to search: user, computer, person, contact etc
 -Help displays this help topic
 SYNTAX:
 BrowseActiveDirectorySchema.ps1 -A L
 Lists the name of each class defined in the AD schema
 BrowseActiveDirectorySchema.ps1 -A M -c user
 Lists the mandatory properties of the user class
 BrowseActiveDirectorySchema.ps1 -A O -c computer
 Lists the optional properties of the computer class
 BrowseActiveDirectorySchema.ps1 -A F -c user
 Lists all Active Directory Classes that contain the word user
 in the actual class name
```

```
 BrowseActiveDirectorySchema.ps1 -Action Find -c user
 Lists all Active Directory Classes that contain the word user
 in the actual class name
 BrowseActiveDirectorySchema.ps1 -help
 Prints the help topic for the script
"@ #end helpText
  $helpText
} #end GetHelp
Function GetADSchema($Action, $class)
{
 $schema = [DirectoryServices.ActiveDirectory.ActiveDirectorySchema]::GetCurrentSchem
a()
 Switch ($Action)
   {
   "classes" {
              $schema.FindAllClasses() |
              Select-Object -Property Name
              }
   "Mandatory"
              {
               "Mandatory Properties of $class object"
               ($schema.FindClass("$class")).MandatoryProperties |
                Format-Table -Property Name, Syntax, IsSingleValued -AutoSize
              }
   "Optional"
              {
               "Optional Properties of $class object"
               "This might take a few seconds ..."
               ($schema.FindClass("$class")).OptionalProperties |
               Format-Table -Property Name, Syntax, IsSingleValued -AutoSize
              }
   "Find"
              {
               $schema.FindAllClasses() |
               Where-Object { $_.name -match "$class" } |
               Select-Object -property name
              }
   DEFAULT {"$action is not a valid action." ; GetHelp ; Exit}
   }
} #end GetADSchema
Function GetAllClasses()
{
 GetAdSchema("classes")
} #end GetAllClasses
Function GetMandatory($class)
```

```
{
 GetAdSchema -action "Mandatory"  -class $class
} #end GetMandatory

Function GetOptional($class)
{
 GetAdSchema -action "Optional"  -class $class
} #end GetOptional
Function FindClasses($class)
{
 GetAdSchema -action "Find" -class $class
} #end FindClasses
# *** Entry Point to Script ***
if($help) { GetHelp ; Exit }
Switch ($action)
{
 "L" {GetAllClasses ; Exit}
 "M" {GetMandatory($class) ; Exit}
 "O" {GetOptional($class) ; Exit}
 "F" {FindClasses($class) ; Exit}
 DEFAULT { "$action is not a valid action." ; GetHelp ; Exit}
}
```

The script begins with the *Param* statement, which is used to create three command-line parameters that allow you to modify the script by running it instead of editing the script to see various behaviors. For example, if you want to see the mandatory properties of the *user* class in Active Directory, you can specify *–action M* and the *–class* user as shown in Figure 4-1.

FIGURE 4-1 Mandatory properties of an Active Directory class are easily displayed.

You can just as easily choose the optional properties of the *Group* class. The advantage of using command-line parameters is that it allows you to modify the behavior of a script at run time instead of at design time. This is a best practice when writing scripts that you intend to use as utilities instead of using simple, single-purpose scripts as shown in the line of code here.

```
Param($action,$class, [switch]$help)
```

The next item you see in the BrowseActiveDirectorySchema.ps1 script is the *GetHelp* function. When you write a script that exposes command-line parameters, it is a best practice to develop a function that displays help in using the script so as to prevent users from being forced to open up and read through the text of the script to figure out what the script does. An overall guiding principle of script design is that the script should be readable, but if you include a help function, you can avoid the necessity of some of that reading. The *GetHelp* function displays information in a similar fashion to the information displayed when you use the Get-Help cmdlet. The *GetHelp* function displays three sections of text: description, parameters, and syntax. It first creates a here-string that contains the text to display, and then it displays the contents of the variable that holds the here-string. The *$helpText* variable is used to hold the contents of the here-string. The advantage of using a here-string is that it allows you to type information and format your output without worrying about quoting rules. Whatever you type in the here-string is treated as text. The *GetHelp* function is called when the script is run with the *–help* switch or when someone types in an incorrect parameter. Figure 4-2 illustrates calling the script with the *–help* switch.

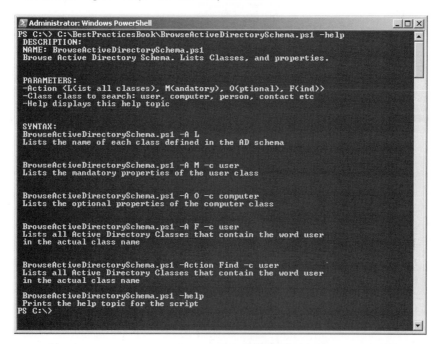

FIGURE 4-2 Detailed help information is displayed when the script is run with the *–help* switch.

The content of the *GetHelp* function is shown here.

```
Function GetHelp()
{
  $helpText= `
@"
 DESCRIPTION:
 NAME: BrowseActiveDirectorySchema.ps1
 Browse Active Directory Schema. Lists Classes, and properties.

 PARAMETERS:
 -Action <L(ist all classes), M(andatory), O(ptional), F(ind)>
 -Class class to search: user, computer, person, contact etc
 -Help displays this help topic

 SYNTAX:
 BrowseActiveDirectorySchema.ps1 -A L
 Lists the name of each class defined in the AD schema

 BrowseActiveDirectorySchema.ps1 -A M -c user
 Lists the mandatory properties of the user class

 BrowseActiveDirectorySchema.ps1 -A O -c computer
 Lists the optional properties of the computer class

 BrowseActiveDirectorySchema.ps1 -A F -c user
 Lists all Active Directory Classes that contain the word user
 in the actual class name

 BrowseActiveDirectorySchema.ps1 -Action Find -c user
 Lists all Active Directory Classes that contain the word user
 in the actual class name

 BrowseActiveDirectorySchema.ps1 -help
 Prints the help topic for the script
"@ #end helpText
  $helpText
} #end GetHelp
```

The next function to be defined is *GetADSchema*, which does most of the real work for the script. The key is using the *DirectoryServices.ActiveDirectory.ActiveDirectorySchema* Microsoft .NET Framework class. By putting the class in square brackets and following it with double colons, you can access the static methods of the class. The *DirectoryServices.ActiveDirectory. ActiveDirectorySchema* class defines two static methods: *GetSchema* and *GetCurrentSchema*. The *GetCurrentSchema* static method returns an instance of an *ActiveDirectorySchema* class that represents the schema to which you are currently connected. The members of the *ActiveDirectorySchema* class are shown in Table 4-1.

TABLE 4-1 *ActiveDirectorySchema* Members

NAME	TYPE	DEFINITION
Dispose	Method	System.Void Dispose()
Equals	Method	System.Boolean Equals(Object obj)
FindAllClasses	Method	System.DirectoryServices.ActiveDirectory. ReadOnlyActiveDirectorySchemaClassCollection FindAllClasses()
		System.DirectoryServices.ActiveDirectory. ReadOnlyActiveDirectorySchemaClassCollection FindAllClasses(SchemaClassType type)
FindAllDefunctClasses	Method	System.DirectoryServices.ActiveDirectory. ReadOnlyActiveDirectorySchemaClassCollection FindAllDefunctClasses()
FindAllDefunctProperties	Method	System.DirectoryServices.ActiveDirectory. ReadOnlyActiveDirectorySchemaPropertyCollection FindAllDefunctProperties()
FindAllProperties	Method	System.DirectoryServices.ActiveDirectory. ReadOnlyActiveDirectorySchemaPropertyCollection FindAllProperties()
		System.DirectoryServices.ActiveDirectory. ReadOnlyActiveDirectorySchemaPropertyCollection FindAllProperties(PropertyTypes type)
FindClass	Method	System.DirectoryServices.ActiveDirectory. ActiveDirectorySchemaClass FindClass (String ldapDisplayName)
FindDefunctClass	Method	System.DirectoryServices.ActiveDirectory. ActiveDirectorySchemaClass FindDefunctClass (String commonName)
FindDefunctProperty	Method	System.DirectoryServices.ActiveDirectory. ActiveDirectorySchemaProperty FindDefunctProperty(String commonName)
FindProperty	Method	System.DirectoryServices.ActiveDirectory. ActiveDirectorySchemaProperty FindProperty (String ldapDisplayName)
GetDirectoryEntry	Method	System.DirectoryServices.DirectoryEntry GetDirectoryEntry()
GetHashCode	Method	System.Int32 GetHashCode()
GetType	Method	System.Type GetType()
RefreshSchema	Method	System.Void RefreshSchema()

NAME	TYPE	DEFINITION
ToString	Method	System.String ToString()
Name	Property	System.String Name {get;}
SchemaRoleOwner	Property	System.DirectoryServices.ActiveDirectory. DirectoryServer SchemaRoleOwner {get;}

Once you create an instance of the *DirectoryServices.ActiveDirectory.ActiveDirectorySchema* .NET Framework class and store the resulting *Schema* object in the *$schema* variable, it is time to evaluate what action to perform. To do this, a *Switch* statement is used. The *Switch* statement evaluates the value that is passed to it from the *$action* variable. Based on the condition that is met, the *Switch* statement finds all of the classes in Active Directory, displays mandatory or optional properties of a specific class, or searches for a class that meets a given criterion. When using the *Switch* statement, it is a best practice to always include a default condition. The *GetADSchema* function is shown here.

```
Function GetADSchema($Action, $class)
{
$schema = [DirectoryServices.ActiveDirectory.ActiveDirectorySchema]::GetCurrentSchema()
Switch ($Action)
  {
  "classes" {
            $schema.FindAllClasses() |
            Select-Object -Property Name
            }
  "Mandatory"
            {
             "Mandatory Properties of $class object"
             ($schema.FindClass("$class")).MandatoryProperties |
              Format-Table -Property Name, Syntax, IsSingleValued -AutoSize
            }
  "Optional"
            {
             "Optional Properties of $class object"
             "This might take a few seconds ..."
             ($schema.FindClass("$class")).OptionalProperties |
             Format-Table -Property Name, Syntax, IsSingleValued -AutoSize
            }
  "Find"
            {
             $schema.FindAllClasses() |
             Where-Object { $_.name -match "$class" } |
             Select-Object -property name
            }
  DEFAULT {"$action is not a valid action." ; GetHelp ; Exit}
  }
} #end GetADSchema
```

To break up some of the code and make it easier to expand the script, a number of helper functions can be used. These functions are called based on the parameters that are passed to the script when it is run. Each of the helper functions calls the *GetADSchema* function and passes a different set of parameters depending on the value that is supplied for the *–action* parameter from the command line.

The first helper function is named *GetAllClasses*. It calls the *GetADSchema* function and passes the word *classes*. When the *Switch* statement in the *GetADSchema* function matches the word *classes*, it calls the *FindAllClasses* method from the *ActiveDirectorySchema* class. Here is the code called by the *Switch* statement.

```
"classes" {
          $schema.FindAllClasses() |
          Select-Object -Property Name'
```

The *GetAllClasses* function is shown here.

```
Function GetAllClasses()
{
 GetAdSchema("classes")
} #end GetAllClasses
```

The second helper function is *GetMandatory*, which returns mandatory properties of the object you specify in the *–class* parameter when the script is run. The *GetMandatory* function receives the value for *$class* from the command line via the *–class* parameter. When the *GetMandatory* function calls the *GetADSchema* function, it passes two parameters; therefore, I consider it a best practice to specify the full parameter name for both of the parameters, which makes the code easier to read and understand. In the *GetAllClasses* function, you do not use the *–action* parameter name when calling the *GetADSchema* function. The *classes* value was passed in a positional fashion. When the *GetADSchema* function is called, it uses the *FindClass* method from the *ActiveDirectorySchema* class to retrieve the class that is specified in the *$class* variable and then returns an instance of an *ActiveDirectorySchemaClass* class. The members of this class are shown in Table 4-2.

TABLE 4-2 Members of the *ActiveDirectorySchemaClass* Class

NAME	MEMBERTYPE	DEFINITION
Dispose	Method	System.Void Dispose()
Equals	Method	System.Boolean Equals(Object obj)
GetAllProperties	Method	System.DirectoryServices.ActiveDirectory. ReadOnlyActiveDirectorySchemaProperty Collection GetAllProperties()
GetDirectoryEntry	Method	System.DirectoryServices.DirectoryEntry GetDirectoryEntry()
GetHashCode	Method	System.Int32 GetHashCode()

NAME	MEMBERTYPE	DEFINITION
GetType	Method	System.Type GetType()
Save	Method	System.Void Save()
ToString	Method	System.String ToString()
AuxiliaryClasses	Property	System.DirectoryServices.ActiveDirectory. ActiveDirectorySchemaClassCollection AuxiliaryClasses {get;}
CommonName	Property	System.String CommonName {get;set;}
DefaultObjectSecurity-Descriptor	Property	System.DirectoryServices.ActiveDirectory Security DefaultObjectSecurityDescriptor {get;set;}
Description	Property	System.String Description {get;set;}
IsDefunct	Property	System.Boolean IsDefunct {get;set;}
MandatoryProperties	Property	System.DirectoryServices.ActiveDirectory. ActiveDirectorySchemaPropertyCollection MandatoryProperties {get;}
Name	Property	System.String Name {get;}
Oid	Property	System.String Oid {get;set;}
OptionalProperties	Property	System.DirectoryServices.ActiveDirectory. ActiveDirectorySchemaPropertyCollection OptionalProperties {get;}
PossibleInferiors	Property	System.DirectoryServices.ActiveDirectory. ReadOnlyActiveDirectorySchemaClassCollection PossibleInferiors {get;}
PossibleSuperiors	Property	System.DirectoryServices.ActiveDirectory. ActiveDirectorySchemaClassCollection PossibleSuperiors {get;}
SchemaGuid	Property	System.Guid SchemaGuid {get;set;}
SubClassOf	Property	System.DirectoryServices.ActiveDirectory. ActiveDirectorySchemaClass SubClassOf {get;set;}
Type	Property	System.DirectoryServices.ActiveDirectory. SchemaClassType Type {get;set;}

The *GetADSchema* function then queries the *MandatoryProperties* property of the object and pipelines the results to the Format-Table cmdlet, where it chooses the name, syntax, and *IsSingleValued* properties. The *–autosize* switched parameter of the Format-Table cmdlet automatically sizes the columns to avoid cutting off property values if possible. The code that runs when the "mandatory" string is matched is shown here.

```
"Mandatory"
            {
              "Mandatory Properties of $class object"
              ($schema.FindClass("$class")).MandatoryProperties |
               Format-Table -Property Name, Syntax, IsSingleValued -AutoSize
            }
```

The *GetMandatory* function is shown here.

```
Function GetMandatory($class)
{
 GetAdSchema -action "Mandatory"  -class $class
} #end GetMandatory
```

To display the optional properties of an Active Directory class, the *GetOptional* function is used. The *GetOptional* function accepts the *$class* value that was received from the command line via the *–class* parameter. Once inside the function, the *$class* value is passed to the *GetADSchema* function along with the action named Optional. When the Optional string is matched in the *Switch* statement, a message is printed on the screen within a few seconds that displays optional properties. Next, the *FindClass* method from the *ActiveDirectorySchema* class is called, and it returns an instance of an *ActiveDirectorySchemaClass* class. Querying the *OptionalProperties* property of the *ActiveDirectorySchemaClass* class returns the optional properties defined for the chosen class in Active Directory. The results are pipelined to the Format-Table cmdlet, which displays the information in the same fashion as it does for mandatory properties. This section of the code is shown here.

```
"Optional"
            {
              "Optional Properties of $class object"
              "This might take a few seconds ..."
              ($schema.FindClass("$class")).OptionalProperties |
               Format-Table -Property Name, Syntax, IsSingleValued -AutoSize
            }
```

The complete *GetOptional* function is shown here.

```
Function GetOptional($class)
{
 GetAdSchema -action "Optional"  -class $class
} #end GetOptional
```

The *FindClasses* function calls the *GetADSchema* function and passes two values. The first is the *Find* action, and the second is the class to locate. The difference here is that the *FindClasses* function is used to aid the user in identifying classes residing in the Active Directory schema that might merit further exploration. Suppose that you are interested in working with mail and want to see what classes relate to mail in Active Directory. You would consequently be interested in seeing what properties exist for that class. As shown in Figure 4-3, you first run the script with the *–action f* parameter and *–class* mail. This command returns all of the classes that have the letters mail contained somewhere within them. Once you locate the class in which you are interested, you can explore the properties of the class by choosing the *action –m* (for mandatory) and specifying the *–c* (for class) parameter followed by the exact name of the class in which you are interested.

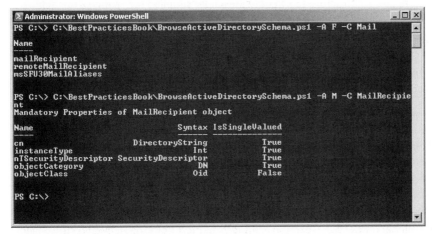

FIGURE 4-3 The BrowseActiveDirectorySchema.ps1 script often begins with a query.

When the *FindClasses* function calls *GetADSchema*, the *FindAllClasses* method is called and the resulting collection of *ActiveDirectorySchemaClass* classes is sent over the pipeline. The `Where-Object` cmdlet uses a regular expression pattern match to look for classes that match the value stored in the *$class* variable as shown here.

```
"Find"
            {
              $schema.FindAllClasses() |
              Where-Object { $_.name -match "$class" } |
              Select-Object -property name
```

The *FindClasses* function is shown here.

```
Function FindClasses($class)
{
 GetAdSchema -action "Find" -class $class
} #end FIndClasses
```

Once all of the help functions are defined, you arrive at the entry point to the script. The entry point performs only one task—it examines the command line and determines what function to call. The first item to be checked is the presence of the *–help* parameter. If the script is run with the *–h* or *–help* parameter, the script calls the *GetHelp* function to display help and then exits the script as shown here.

```
if($help) { GetHelp ; Exit }
```

If the script is not running with the *–help* parameter, the script then needs to evaluate the value supplied for the *–action* parameter. Because the *–help* parameter is searched for first, its presence on the command line trumps all other actions. The *–action* parameter is the default parameter. Whatever is typed on the command line is interpreted as a value for the *–action* parameter if no other parameter is supplied to the script, which provides the added advantage of being able to capture bogus input to the script. The *Switch* statement can be used to create the perfect structure to evaluate the values supplied for *–action*. Four actions are defined, each of which calls the appropriate function. The fifth condition that is defined is the default action. This default action displays a message that the action is not permitted, whereupon it calls the *GetHelp* function. One consideration to keep in mind about the *Switch* statement is that it might find multiple matches; for this reason, the *Exit* statement is used after each call to the functions. The *Switch* statement code is shown here.

```
Switch ($action)
{
 "L" {GetAllClasses ; Exit}
 "M" {GetMandatory($class) ; Exit}
 "O" {GetOptional($class) ; Exit}
 "F" {FindClasses($class) ; Exit}
 DEFAULT { "$action is not a valid action." ; GetHelp ; Exit}
}
```

Querying Active Directory

When working with Active Directory, it does not take long before a network administrator has the need to pose some queries. Sometimes, the need is unspoken, such as "I need to move all of the computers from one organizational unit to another organizational unit." At other times, the need is explicit: "I need to find all of the users in the Charlotte office." Anytime there is a need to work with a group of objects that may possess something in common, such as a type, location, description, or even first name, the most efficient approach to working with the group is to perform an Active Directory query.

When I speak about querying Active Directory, I am not referring to simply listing the children of an object. To obtain the children of an object, you must connect to the object by using the [ADSI] type accelerator and retrieve the *Children* property. Once you retrieve the value of the *Children* property, a collection of *System.DirectoryServices.DirectoryEntry* objects is returned. You can then work with the objects as you would with a normal *DirectoryEntry* object. The properties of the *DirectoryEntry* class are listed here.

- *accountExpires*
- *badPasswordTime*
- *badPwdCount*
- *cn*

- *codepage*
- *countryCode*
- *DistinguishedName*
- *dSCorePropagationData*
- *instanceType*
- *isCriticalSystemObject*
- *lastLogoff*
- *lastLogon*
- *localPolicyFlags*
- *logonCount*
- *name*
- *nTSecurityDescriptor*
- *objectCategory*
- *objectClass*
- *objectGUID*
- *objectSid*
- *primaryGroupID*
- *pwdLastSet*
- *sAMAccountName*
- *sAMAccountType*
- *userAccountControl*
- *uSNChanged*
- *uSNCreated*
- *whenChanged*
- *whenCreated*

Once you make the connection to a specific object in Active Directory and retrieve the collection of child objects from the organizational unit, you can access the properties listed above via the pipeline. This technique is shown here in the ListOuChildren.ps1 script.

ListOUChildren.ps1

```
([ADSI]"LDAP://ou=mytest,dc=nwtraders,dc=com").children |
Select-Object -Property cn
```

The *Children* property returns a collection of *DirectoryEntry* objects named *DirectoryEntries*. Collections often behave like arrays, but you are not allowed to index into the collection; when you attempt to do so, an error is generated as shown here.

```
PS C:\> $a = ([ADSI]"LDAP://ou=mytest,dc=nwtraders,dc=com").children
PS C:\> $a[0]
Unable to index into an object of type System.DirectoryServices.DirectoryEntries.
At line:1 char:4+ $a[ <<<< 0]
```

If you need to work with individual items via the collection, you can store the collection in a variable and iterate through the collection by using the *Foreach* statement as shown here.

```
PS C:\> $a = ([ADSI]"LDAP://ou=mytest,dc=nwtraders,dc=com").children
PS C:\> foreach($i in $a) { $i.name }
aComputer
bComputer
cComputer
```

When retrieving the value of certain properties from objects in Active Directory, you can at times receive unpredictable results. While the *Children* property returns a collection of *DirectoryEntry* objects, the *member* property of the *Group* object returns an array of strings. At first glance, the membership of a group obtained in this manner may seem to be useless, but you can use the [ADSI] type accelerator to turn the array of strings into *DirectoryEntry* objects. At this point, you can work with the *DirectoryEntry* objects in the same manner as you did in the previous example, which includes access to the properties of the *DirectoryEntry* class as shown here in the DisplayGroupMembership.ps1 script.

DisplayGroupMembership.ps1

```
$aryMembers = ([ADSI]"LDAP://cn=mygroup,ou=mytest,dc=nwtraders,dc=com").member
foreach($member in $aryMembers)
{
  [ADSI]"LDAP://$member" |
  Select-Object -Property cn
}
```

While some people may consider the previous techniques to be querying Active Directory, they really do nothing more than list the results once the value of one or more properties has been obtained. True Active Directory queries use a syntax that is more flexible than printing the value of a single attribute. In the next section, you will examine the use of query techniques to retrieve information from Active Directory.

Using ADO

The traditional method of searching Active Directory, from both the Microsoft Visual Basic Scripting Edition (VBScript) and Windows PowerShell 1.0 perspective, is to use ActiveX Data Object (ADO) technology coupled with either a Lightweight Directory Access Protocol (LDAP) dialect or a SQL dialect query submitted via the *ADSDSOObject* provider. An example of this technique, which uses the LDAP dialect query, is shown in the QueryComputersComADO.ps1 script.

First, you must assign values to the variables you will use when making an ADO connection. You can use the *$strBase* variable to hold the search base, which is the location in Active Directory where you connect and begin the query. The connection takes the form of the search protocol you are using (LDAP in this instance), followed by the path to the object you are going to connect to with your query. You can specify a domain name, organizational unit name, and the path to some other object if desired. The LDAP dialect query requires the *ADsPath* to be contained within angle brackets (< >).

You also need to define the search filter to use in the query. You can use the *$strFilter* variable to hold the search filter; in this example, the search filter is *ObjectCategory=computer*. *ObjectCategory* is the name of the Active Directory attribute, and *computer* is the value of the attribute. The search filter needs to be surrounded with parentheses. You must select the attributes you want to return in your result set. You can choose the *name* attribute and store it in the *$strAttributes* variable. You also must choose the scope of your query. In this script, you use subtree for the scope, which executes a recursive query. You connect to the root of the nwtraders.com domain and burrow down into every organizational unit looking for computers. Once you assign values to the four variables, you can put them together to form your query, which you store in the *$strQuery* variable. This section of the code is shown here.

```
$strBase = "<LDAP://dc=nwtraders,dc=com>"
$strFilter = "(ObjectCategory=computer)"
$strAttributes = "name"
$strScope = "subtree"
$strQuery = "$strBase;$strFilter;$strAttributes;$strScope"
```

Next, you must create a few objects to make an ADO connection into Active Directory. The first object to create is, in fact, the *ADODB.Connection* object. Because you are using Component Object Model (COM) objects in this script, you need to specify the *–ComObject* parameter when you use the New-Object cmdlet to create the *connection* object. You store the newly created *ADODB.Connection* object in the *$objConnection* variable. You must then create an *ADODB.Command* object, which is also a COM object, and store it in the *$objCommand* variable. Once you create the two objects, you need to open the connection into Active Directory by using the *open* method from the *connection* object stored in the *$objConnection* variable. When using the *open* method, you must specify the provider; for your Active Directory queries, you can use the *ADSDSOObject* provider.

Once the connection is open, you need to specify the active connection. You can use the *ActiveConnection* property from the *command* object stored in the *$objCommand* variable and give it the connection you just opened. You must tell the *command* object what command you want to execute; therefore, you can specify the query you stored in the *$strQuery* variable to the *CommandText* property. Once you execute the command, a record set is returned. You store the returned *RecordSet* object in the *$objRecordSet* variable as shown here.

```
$objConnection = New-Object -ComObject "ADODB.Connection"
$objCommand = New-Object -ComObject "ADODB.Command"
$objConnection.Open("Provider=ADSDSOObject;")
```

```
$objCommand.ActiveConnection = $objConnection
$objCommand.CommandText = $strQuery
$objRecordSet = $objCommand.Execute()
```

Once you have the data from your query, you must be able to walk through the *RecordSet* object. To do this, you can use the *Do ... Until* language construction. As you progress through the record set, you can use the *Item* method from the fields in the record set to choose the value of the *name* attribute. You can print this value to the screen and use the *MoveNext* method to move to the next record. Continue this process until you reach the *eof* property of the record set, where you can close the connection by using the *Close* method from the *connection* object stored in the *$objConnection* variable as shown here.

```
Do
{
    $objRecordSet.Fields.item("name").Value
    $objRecordSet.MoveNext()
}
Until ($objRecordSet.eof)

$objConnection.Close()
```

The completed QueryComputersComADO.ps1 script is shown here.

QueryComputersComADO.ps1

```
$strBase = "<LDAP://dc=nwtraders,dc=com>"
$strFilter = "(ObjectCategory=computer)"
$strAttributes = "name"
$strScope = "subtree"
$strQuery = "$strBase;$strFilter;$strAttributes;$strScope"

$objConnection = New-Object -ComObject "ADODB.Connection"
$objCommand = New-Object -ComObject "ADODB.Command"
$objConnection.Open("Provider=ADSDSOObject;")
$objCommand.ActiveConnection = $objConnection
$objCommand.CommandText = $strQuery
$objRecordSet = $objCommand.Execute()
Do
{
    $objRecordSet.Fields.item("name").Value
    $objRecordSet.MoveNext()
}
Until ($objRecordSet.eof)
$objConnection.Close()
```

Of course, you may feel more comfortable using the .NET version of ADO to query Active Directory. What is great about ADO is the way in which the syntax is structured. With only a slight change, you can modify the classic ADO script to become an ADO .NET script.

As you may have noticed in the previous script, several tasks were related to one another. Also, certain tasks must be completed prior to the execution of another task. When you see this pattern of related behavior, the related items and tasks should be investigated for inclusion into functions.

In the first function, you assign values for the variables that are used to make the connection into Active Directory. This section of the script is exactly the same as a similar section in the previous script. You assign a value for the base and filter, choose the attributes, define the scope, and create the query. You then specify the provider to use when you make the connection. The last action to perform in the function is to call the *NewADOConnection* function. This function, named *SetConnectionString*, is shown here.

```
Function SetConnectionString()
{
 $strBase = "<LDAP://dc=nwtraders,dc=com>"
 $strFilter = "(ObjectCategory=computer)"
 $strAttributes = "name"
 $strScope = "subtree"
 $strQuery = "$strBase;$strFilter;$strAttributes;$strScope"
 $strProvider = "Provider=ADSDSOObject"
 NewADOConnection
} #end SetConnectionString
```

In the next function, you create the two objects that are required to enable you to make a connection into Active Directory. The first object you create is an instance of the *OleDbConnection* class that is found in the *System.Data.OleDb* namespace. To create an instance of the *OleDbConnection* class, you can pass the provider you stored in the *$strProvider* variable as the constructor, and you can store the resulting object in a script-level variable named *$objConn*. The next object you need to create is an instance of the *OleDbCommand* class, which is also in the *System.Data.OleDb* namespace. To create the *OleDbCommand* object, you pass the query stored in the *$strQuery* variable as the constructor and then store this object in the *$sqlCommand* variable.

Now, you need to associate the connection you have in the *$objConn* variable with the connection property of the *command* object. Once this is accomplished, you can use the *open* method of the *connection* object to open the connection. Once the connection is open, you can execute your query by using the *ExecuteReader* method from the *command* object and storing the returned *OleDbDataReader* object in the script-level variable named *$dataReader*. The *OleDbDataReader* object resides in the *System.Data.OleDb* namespace. The only way to obtain an instance of this class is to use the *ExecuteReader* method; this class cannot be created otherwise. This function is named *NewADOConnection* as shown here.

```
Function NewADOConnection()
{
 $Script:objConn = New-Object System.Data.OleDb.OleDbConnection("$strProvider")
 $sqlCommand = New-Object System.Data.OleDb.OleDbCommand($strQuery)
 $sqlCommand.Connection = $objConn
 $Script:objConn.open()
 $Script:DataReader = $sqlCommand.ExecuteReader()
} #end NewADOConnection
```

Next, you can read the data by using the *ReadData* function. You use the *While* statement to loop through the *OleDbDataReader* object, which is stored in the script-level *$dataReader* variable. As long as there is something to read, you can use the *Read* method of the *OleDbDataReader* object. The *OleDbDataReader* is a forward-only stream of data; therefore, you do not need to use a *MoveNext* type of method (as you did in the COM version of ADO). Also, there is no *MovePrevious* method. You can index into a stream as you are working with it and thus pick the current item in the stream by using [0]. You can then turn the item into a string by using the *ToString* method. The *ReadData* function is shown here.

```
Function ReadData()
{
 While($Script:DataReader.read())
 {
  $Script:DataReader[0].ToString()
 } #end while
} #end ReadData
```

Last, you must close the ADO connection by using the *Close* method. Keep in mind that you need to close both the *OleDbDataReader* and the *OleDbConnection* object.

```
Function CloseADOConnection()
{
 $Script:dataReader.close()
 $Script:objConn.close()
}
```

The entry point to the script is used to control the order in which the various functions are called. Because all of your code is contained within functions, you call the *SetConnectionString* function. Once the connection is created, you call the *ReadData* function and then close the connection. This section of the script is shown here.

```
SetConnectionString
ReadData
CloseADOConnection
```

The completed QueryComputersNetADO.ps1 script is shown here.

QueryComputersNetADO.ps1

```
Function SetConnectionString()
{
 $strBase = "<LDAP://dc=nwtraders,dc=com>"
 $strFilter = "(ObjectCategory=computer)"
 $strAttributes = "name"
 $strScope = "subtree"
 $strQuery = "$strBase;$strFilter;$strAttributes;$strScope"
 $strProvider = "Provider=ADSDSOObject"
 NewADOConnection
} #end SetConnectionString
Function NewADOConnection()
{
 $Script:objConn = New-Object System.Data.OleDb.OleDbConnection("$strProvider")
 $sqlCommand = New-Object System.Data.OleDb.OleDbCommand($strQuery)
 $sqlCommand.Connection = $objConn
 $Script:objConn.open()
 $Script:DataReader = $sqlCommand.ExecuteReader()
} #end NewADOConnection
Function ReadData()
{
 While($Script:DataReader.read())
 {
   $Script:DataReader[0].Tostring()
 } #end while
} #end ReadData
Function CloseADOConnection()
{
 $Script:dataReader.close()
 $Script:objConn.close()
}
# *** Entry Point ***
SetConnectionString
ReadData
CloseADOConnection
```

Using Directory Searcher

Using the *System.DirectoryServices.DirectorySearcher* class is probably easier than employing either of the two previously discussed ADO methods for searching Active Directory.

When using the *DirectorySearcher* class, you must first define the starting point for the search. You use the *$searchRoot* variable to hold the starting location, which in this example is the "mytest" organizational unit in the nwtraders.com domain as shown here.

```
$SearchRoot = "ou=mytest,dc=nwtraders,dc=com"
```

Next, you create your filter. The filter uses the LDAP search filter syntax, in which you specify the Active Directory attribute and a value for that attribute. In this example, you are looking for a match when the value of the *ObjectCategory* attribute is equal to *computer*. This query returns all computers in the mytest organizational unit as shown in the following line of code.

```
$Filter = "ObjectCategory=computer"
```

Some of the other potential values for the *ObjectCategory* attribute are listed here.

- *User*
- *Contact*
- *PrinterQueue*
- *Group*
- *OrganizationalUnit*

You must now create an instance in the *DirectorySearcher* class. In this example, you can use the default constructor that creates a new instance of the *DirectorySearcher* class by using default values. The default values for the constructor are shown in Table 4-3.

```
$ds = New-Object -TypeName System.DirectoryServices.DirectorySearcher
```

TABLE 4-3 Default DirectorySearcher Constructor Values

PROPERTY	DEFAULT VALUE
SearchRoot	$null
Filter	"(objectClass=*)"
PropertiesToLoad	Empty StringCollection object
SearchScope	"Subtree"

You next need to define the *SearchRoot* property on the *DirectorySearcher* object because you did not supply this value when you created an instance of the object. The *SearchRoot* property must have an instance of a *DirectoryEntry* class. You can simulate this requirement by supplying an *ADsPath*. In the FindComputersDS.ps1 script, you can use a variable to hold the distinguished name for the location, which is the base of your search. You can then use expanding strings to prepend the LDAP protocol moniker to the *DistinguishedName* of your search root. You then assign the resulting *ADsPath* to the *SearchRoot* property of the *DirectorySearcher* object stored in the $ds variable as shown here.

```
$ds.SearchRoot = "LDAP://$SearchRoot"
```

It is now time to assign a value to the *Filter* property. The *Filter* property value is a string that is supplied in the LDAP search filter syntax, which is RFC2254 compliant and is in reality a Unicode string. In this section of code, the search string is stored in the *$filter* variable, and you can set the value of the *Filter* property to be equal to the string stored in the *$filter* variable.

```
$ds.Filter = $filter
```

Last, you must call the *FindAll* method, which returns an instance of a *SearchResultCollection* class. The *SearchResultCollection* class is found in the *System.DirectoryServices* namespace and contains several interesting methods, such as *Contains* and *IndexOf*, that can be used to facilitate working with the collection. This line of code is shown here.

```
$ds.FindAll()
```

The complete FindComputersDS.ps1 script is shown here.

FindComputersDS.ps1

```
$SearchRoot = "ou=mytest,dc=nwtraders,dc=com"
$Filter = "ObjectCategory=computer"
$ds = New-Object -TypeName System.DirectoryServices.DirectorySearcher
$ds.SearchRoot = "LDAP://$SearchRoot"
$ds.Filter = $filter
$ds.FindAll()
```

NOTES FROM THE FIELD

Working with Active Directory

Brandon Shell, Windows PowerShell MVP

I am not your typical Active Directory administrator, and I tend to delve very deeply into the inner workings of the technology. I typically use Windows PowerShell to analyze domain controller configurations or perform domain management tasks, such as flexible single master operation (FSMO) moves and RootDSE modifications.

I perform Active Directory searches regularly, typically because I am seeking the user count of some particular type of object. I have a very large Active Directory implementation at work (approximately 380,000 users), which often causes me to spend more time analyzing the efficiency of my LDAP filters and their effects on the network. Of the different types of searches I perform, the following is a list of the types of queries that I execute most often.

- Count Objects
- Count Objects in specific organizational units
- List computers returning DNS name
- Find "old" users

During a normal workweek and depending on my goal, I have a tendency to most often use the Active Directory Service Interface (ADSI) and classes from the *System.DirectoryServices.Protocols* .NET Framework namespace. I only use the WinNT ADSI provider for the local account management of workstations.

When writing scripts, I work strictly from scratch. I believe that once you understand Windows PowerShell and its object-oriented nature, VBScript conversions become obsolete. There is almost always a better way to do things in Windows PowerShell.

If I need to do research when writing a script, I find most of my information via Google and MSDN. Several friends of mine who work at Microsoft can help me if I need an obscure piece of information.

My biggest challenge in learning Windows PowerShell involved understanding some of the fundamental programming knowledge that is expected, including knowledge of constructors, members, classes, and static methods/fields.

I think you should make the effort to learn the wonders of working with the .NET classes contained in the *System.DirectoryServices.ActiveDirectory* namespace. Domain/forest management is a large part of the work performed by your more senior network administrators, and the classes simplify the work needed to automate many of the tasks involved in managing a more complex network.

Using [ADSISearcher]

Windows PowerShell 2.0 introduces the new [ADSISearcher] type accelerator. The advantage of the [ADSISearcher] type accelerator is that it simplifies the process of using the *System.DirectoryServices.DirectorySearcher* .NET Framework class because it allows you to bypass the step requiring you to use the New-Object cmdlet to create an instance of the class prior to use. This simplified process makes it easy to use [ADSISearcher] from the command line as shown here.

```
PS C:\> ([ADSISearcher]"ObjectCategory=computer").findall() | Select path
Path
----
LDAP://CN=BERLIN,OU=Domain Controllers,DC=nwtraders,DC=com
LDAP://CN=VISTA,CN=Computers,DC=nwtraders,DC=com
LDAP://CN=mycomputer,OU=MyTest,DC=nwtraders,DC=com
LDAP://CN=aComputer,OU=MyTest,DC=nwtraders,DC=com
LDAP://CN=bComputer,OU=MyTest,DC=nwtraders,DC=com
```

When you use the *FindAll* method from the *DirectorySearcher* class, an instance of a *System.DirectoryServices.SearchResultCollection* class is returned. The *SearchResultCollection* class is a collection, but this collection allows you to index into it. Element *0* is the first item in the collection as shown here.

```
PS C:\> ([ADSISearcher]"ObjectCategory=user").findall()[0] | Select path
Path
----
LDAP://CN=Administrator,CN=Users,DC=nwtraders,DC=com
```

If you are only interested in the first item returned from a query, such as the item returned in the previous query, then it is easier to use the *FindOne* method. This technique is shown here.

```
PS C:\> ([ADSISearcher]"ObjectCategory=user").findone() | Select path
Path
----
LDAP://CN=Administrator,CN=Users,DC=nwtraders,DC=com
```

There are essentially two occasions to use the *FindOne* method. The first occasion is when you are working from the command line, and you are not sure what type of data will be returned by your query. In this case, you probably do not want to waste several minutes watching the results from a poorly written query scroll off the screen like the opening title sequence of a futuristic intergalactic battle film from the seventies. It is far more efficient to use *FindOne* to determine whether the results contain the type of data you were expecting.

The second occasion to use the *FindOne* method is when you are certain the query will return a single-item result set. One advantage of the *FindOne* method is that the result set is returned as an instance of the *System.DirectoryServices.SearchResult* class, which happens to have a method named *GetDirectoryEntry*. What is useful about the *FindOne* method is that, when it is used, it causes the resulting object to be an instance of a *DirectoryEntry* class. Because this is a very important technique, let's take some time to explore its application.

The first step is to use a compound LDAP dialect Active Directory query and see what results are returned. You choose only the *Path* property from the *SearchResult* class. Note that an instance of the *SearchResult* class is available on the other side of the pipeline or is available via an index or a *Foreach* type of construction because the *SearchResultCollection* class does not have a *Path* property directly exposed.

To perform a compound LDAP dialect Active Directory query, you can choose two Active Directory attributes. The first Active Directory attribute is *ObjectCategory*, which is an indication of the type of object you are looking for. The second attribute is the *name* attribute, which is one of the ways to reference an object; names do not have to be unique within the Active Directory hierarchy. You first use the *FindAll* method to see whether there is more than one user in Active Directory with the name of your user. To query two attributes from within Active Directory, you can use the ampersand in front of the first attribute value pair and surround the attribute name pair with parentheses. You then put parentheses around the second attribute value pair, use an ampersand in front of the first pair, and surround the entire query with another set of parentheses, which is not nearly as complicated as it sounds. Table 4-4 provides a diagram of a compound LDAP dialect query.

TABLE 4-4 Compound LDAP Dialect Query

OPERATOR	ATTRIBUTE	OPERATOR	VALUE	ATTRIBUTE	OPERATOR	VALUE
&	objectCategory	=	User	name	=	My user

Once you define the query, you surround it entirely with parentheses and then call the *FindAll* method from the *DirectorySearcher* object. The parentheses are used to cause the code inside the parentheses to execute first, which returns the *DirectorySearcher* object and enables you to call *DirectorySearcher* methods. Next, you pipeline the *SearchResultsCollection* to the `Select-Object` cmdlet and choose the *Path* property. The result is a listing of the path of each user named "my user" in Active Directory.

```
PS C:\> ([ADSISearcher]"(&(ObjectCategory=user)(name=my user))").findall() | select path
Path
----
LDAP://CN=my user,OU=MyTest,DC=nwtraders,DC=com
```

You can see that there is only one user named "my user" in the entire Active Directory, but the query could have returned more than one user with the name "my user." You can therefore index into the *SearchResultsCollection* class and send only the first item that matches the query across the pipeline where you select the path to display. This code is only a slight modification from the previous listing.

```
PS C:\> ([ADSISearcher]"(&(ObjectCategory=user)(name=my user))").findall()[0] |
select path
Path
----
LDAP://CN=my user,OU=MyTest,DC=nwtraders,DC=com
```

Because you are able to index into a *SearchResultsCollection*, there is no reason to use the pipeline to select the *Path* property. You can shorten the previous code to include both the index number of *0* and the property name that you want to display. This process allows you to skip the use of the pipeline and to avoid using the `Select-Object` cmdlet as shown here.

```
PS C:\> ([ADSISearcher]"(&(ObjectCategory=user)(name=my user))").findall()[0].path
LDAP://CN=my user,OU=MyTest,DC=nwtraders,DC=com
```

However, there is no need to index into the collection and to display the first result by using [0] because the *FindOne* method does exactly the same thing as displaying an index value of *0*. *FindOne* returns the first item from the collection as shown here.

```
PS C:\> ([ADSISearcher]"(&(ObjectCategory=user)(name=my user))").findone().path
LDAP://CN=my user,OU=MyTest,DC=nwtraders,DC=com
```

Now that you have a path—an *ADsPath*—you can use the [ADSI] DirectoryEntry type accelerator to convert the *ADsPath* string to an instance of a *DirectoryEntry* class, which gives you a richer object to work with as shown here.

```
PS C:\> [ADSI](([ADSISearcher]"(&(ObjectCategory=user)(name=my user))").findone().path)

DistinguishedName : {CN=my user,OU=MyTest,DC=nwtraders,DC=com}
Path              : LDAP://CN=my user,OU=MyTest,DC=nwtraders,DC=com
```

Performing Account Management

When you know the *DistinguishedName* property of an object that resides in Active Directory, the process is relatively simple: you connect to the object and query or modify the properties as required. However, the life of a network administrator is seldom as simple as that scenario. It is often the case that a network administrator knows neither the exact location of an object nor the complete name of the object in question.

Locating Disabled User Accounts

To locate disabled user accounts, you must first define your filter so that you are looking for *user* objects. You can use the *$filter* variable to hold the "objectClass=user" string as shown here.

```
$filter = "objectClass=user"
```

Next, you can use the [ADSISearcher] type accelerator and the "objectClass=user" filter to create an instance of a *DirectorySearcher* object. You group the code by using parentheses and call the *FindAll* method to return a *SearchResultsCollection* object. You then send the results over the pipeline to a Foreach-Object cmdlet as shown here.

```
([ADSISearcher]$filter).findall() |
 foreach-object `
```

Next, you must obtain the value of the *userAccountControl* attribute from Active Directory. The *userAccountControl* enumeration is a 4-byte value that controls the behavior of a user account. It is not a single-string attribute but rather is a series of flags that are computed from the values listed in Table 4-5. Because of the way that the *userAccountControl* attribute is created, simply examining the numerical value is of little use unless you can decipher the individual numbers that make up the large number. When added together, these flags control the behavior of the user account on the system. This section of code is shown here.

```
$uac = ([ADSI]$_.path).psbase.invokeget("userAccountControl")
```

TABLE 4-5 User Account Control Values

ADS CONSTANT	VALUE
ADS_UF_SCRIPT	0X0001
ADS_UF_ACCOUNTDISABLE	0X0002
ADS_UF_HOMEDIR_REQUIRED	0X0008
ADS_UF_LOCKOUT	0X0010
ADS_UF_PASSWD_NOTREQD	0X0020
ADS_UF_PASSWD_CANT_CHANGE	0X0040
ADS_UF_ENCRYPTED_TEXT_PASSWORD_ALLOWED	0X0080
ADS_UF_TEMP_DUPLICATE_ACCOUNT	0X0100
ADS_UF_NORMAL_ACCOUNT	0X0200
ADS_UF_INTERDOMAIN_TRUST_ACCOUNT	0X0800
ADS_UF_WORKSTATION_TRUST_ACCOUNT	0X1000
ADS_UF_SERVER_TRUST_ACCOUNT	0X2000
ADS_UF_DONT_EXPIRE_PASSWD	0X10000
ADS_UF_MNS_LOGON_ACCOUNT	0X20000
ADS_UF_SMARTCARD_REQUIRED	0X40000
ADS_UF_TRUSTED_FOR_DELEGATION	0X80000
ADS_UF_NOT_DELEGATED	0X100000
ADS_UF_USE_DES_KEY_ONLY	0X200000
ADS_UF_DONT_REQUIRE_PREAUTH	0X400000
ADS_UF_PASSWORD_EXPIRED	0X800000
ADS_UF_TRUSTED_TO_AUTHENTICATE_FOR_DELEGATION	0X1000000

Once you determine the *userAccountControl* value, you need to examine the bit mask to determine whether the second bit is flipped (0X0002). To do this, you can use the *–band* operator to execute a bitwise *and* operation. If the second bit is flipped, it means that the account is disabled. You can use Table 4-5 to assist in the interpretation of the *userAccountControl* values obtained from the *userAccountControl* attribute. You can print a message with the distinguished name in red as shown here.

```
if($uac -band 0x2)
    {
     write-host -ForegroundColor red `
     "$($_.properties.item("DistinguishedName")) is disabled"
    }
```

Otherwise, if the *and* operation of the *userAccountControl* attribute with the 0X2 value does not match, then the account is not disabled. You can print a message with the distinguished name of the object in green as shown here.

```
ELSE
    {
     Write-Host -ForegroundColor green `
     "$($_.properties.item("DistinguishedName")) is NOT disabled"
    }
```

The complete LocateDisabledUserAccounts.ps1 script is shown here.

LocateDisabledUserAccounts.ps1

```
$filter = "objectClass=user"
([ADSISearcher]$filter).findall() |
foreach-object `
{
    $uac = ([ADSI]$_.path).psbase.invokeget("userAccountControl")
    if($uac -band 0x2)
      {
        write-host -ForegroundColor red `
        "$($_.properties.item("DistinguishedName")) is disabled"
      }
    ELSE
      {
       Write-Host -ForegroundColor green `
       "$($_.properties.item("DistinguishedName")) is NOT disabled"
      }
}
```

Moving Objects

One capability that is often needed is the ability to move objects within Active Directory. Because these types of operations are generally performed in bulk, this is a perfect opportunity to use a query. In the SearchOUMoveComputer.ps1 script, you first identify all of the computers in a particular organizational unit and then use the *MoveTo* method to move the *computer* objects to the new location. Let's look at this script in more detail.

The first step is to create your filter. You can create a variable named *$filter* and look for the *ObjectCategory* attribute that is equal to *computer*. This filter identifies only *computer* objects in Active Directory. This line of code is shown here.

```
$filter = "ObjectCategory=computer"
```

Now, you define the destination, which needs an *ADsPath* type of value. You can specify the protocol as well as the *DistinguishedName* attribute of the location you want to use for the destination of your move as shown here.

```
$destination = "LDAP://ou=mytest,dc=Nwtraders,dc=com"
```

You create the *DirectorySearcher* class by using the [ADSISearcher] type accelerator with the filter string contained in the *$filter* variable as shown here.

```
$ds = [ADSISearcher]$filter
```

You must now specify the search root, which is the location from where you begin your search. By default, the *DirectorySearcher* performs a recursive search, which is what you want to happen in this script. The *SearchRoot* property, like the destination, needs to receive an *ADsPath* value as illustrated here.

```
$ds.SearchRoot = "LDAP://ou=dumb,dc=nwtraders,dc=com"
```

Once you create the filter and specify the destination and source, you can call the *FindAll* method from the *DirectorySearcher* class. You pipeline the results from the query to the ForEach-Object cmdlet. Within the loop, you select the *path* attribute of the current item on the pipeline and use the [ADSI] type accelerator to create an instance of a *DirectoryEntry* class. You can store the instance of the *DirectoryEntry* class in the *$de* variable. Now, you can use the *MoveTo* method from the base *DirectoryEntry* object and give it the *ADsPath* representing the destination. This section of code is shown here.

```
$ds.findAll() |
ForEach-Object `
{
 $de = [ADSI]$_.path
 $de.psbase.MoveTo($destination)
}
```

The complete SearchOUMoveComputer.ps1 script is shown here.

SearchOUMoveComputer.ps1

```
$filter = "ObjectCategory=computer"
$destination = "LDAP://ou=mytest,dc=Nwtraders,dc=com"
$ds = [ADSISearcher]$filter
$ds.SearchRoot = "LDAP://ou=dumb,dc=nwtraders,dc=com"
$ds.findAll() |
ForEach-Object `
{
 $de = [ADSI]$_.path
 $de.psbase.MoveTo($destination)
}
```

Searching for Missing Values in Active Directory

Despite your best efforts as network administrators, it is inevitable that objects created in Active Directory will be missing values for attributes. Sometimes, these oversights are rather benign, such as when a user has not populated the *carLicense* attribute; at other times, the missing data has significant operational impact, such as when the *telephoneNumber* is missing. From an auditing perspective, it is nice to be able to query Active Directory and find the objects that have missing values. To do this, you must write a script that searches for *user* objects in a particular organizational unit in a specific domain and that looks at the value of the selected attribute. If the attribute value is null or empty, then you can print the distinguished name of the *user* object. The script you develop to look for missing attribute values is named SearchAdForMissingAttributeValue.ps1. The way the script is written, you can look at any object for any attribute and for any organizational unit or domain because these values are exposed via variables. Let's examine this script in detail.

In the SearchAdForMissingAttributeValue.ps1 script, you begin by including a tag specifying that version 2 of Windows PowerShell is required. The only item in the code that actually requires version 2 of Windows PowerShell is the [ADSISearcher] type accelerator. If you need to ensure that the script will also run on version 1 of Windows PowerShell, then you can replace that line of code with another, which you will examine in the next few paragraphs. As a best practice, when you write code that you know uses a feature from Windows PowerShell 2.0, make sure you include the *requires* tag as shown here.

```
#Requires -version 2.0
```

> **IMPORTANT** When using the *requires* tag to limit the execution of your script to Windows PowerShell 2.0, the tag must be the first noncommented line in your script (even though the line itself has the pound sign at the beginning).

The next two lines of the script create and define two variables. The first is the *$searchAttribute* variable that holds the ADSI attribute you want to locate. This attribute contains the value that you are inspecting to ensure that it is populated, and you can choose this attribute by finding the actual attribute name that you are interested in selecting. You can use Appendix C, "Active Directory Users and Computers to ADSI Mapping," to assist in this endeavor. As the script is written, you are going to search the *HomeDirectory* attribute to see whether it is populated; if not, then you can print the value of the distinguished name.

```
$SearchAttribute = "HomeDirectory"
$DisplayAttribute = "DistinguishedName"
```

> **NOTE** Of the hundreds of attribute values that an object in Active Directory can possess, most of them are not mandatory. One of the few attributes that is always populated is the *DistinguishedName* attribute. It is a good attribute to use when you want to locate an object because it will tell you both the name and the location of the object.

The next variable you need to populate is the *$searchRoot* variable, which contains the path to the object you will connect to for your query; in most cases, this path is an organizational unit. At times, you may want to connect to the root of a domain so that you can search the entire domain. The syntax used here is a simple value assignment.

```
$SearchRoot = "ou=testou,dc=nwtraders,dc=com"
```

You now need to create your search filter. The filter syntax was discussed earlier. See the "Using [ADSISearcher]" section earlier in this chapter. You can use the *$filter* variable to hold your filter. You are looking for objects that have the value of the *ObjectCategory* attribute set to *user*. In plain language, you are looking for users. This code is shown here.

```
$filter = "ObjectCategory=user"
```

Now you need to perform the search. To do this, you can use the *System.DirectoryServices.DirectorySearcher* class. In Windows PowerShell 2.0, you can access this .NET Framework class by using the [ADSISearcher] type accelerator. In Windows PowerShell 1.0, you need to write the code as shown here.

```
$ds = New-Object DirectoryServices.DirectorySearcher("$filter")
```

As you can see, it is not too difficult to create an instance of the *DirectorySearcher* class. Yet, when you compare the previous line of code with the one listed here, it does save a bit of typing.

```
$ds = [ADSISearcher]$filter
```

You must define the search root to be used for *DirectorySearcher*. The *SearchRoot* attribute is used to control where the search will begin. In addition to specifying the location of the search, you can also use the *SearchRoot* attribute to specify the protocol to be used. In this example, you use the LDAP protocol to search Active Directory, and you connect to the location that is stored in the *$searchRoot* variable as shown here.

```
$ds.SearchRoot = "LDAP://$SearchRoot"
```

It is now time to execute the search. You first use the *FindAll* method to return all of the items that match your search filter. Because it is possible that the query might return a large number of items, you decide to pipeline the objects rather than store them in a variable. In addition to reducing the amount of memory required for the script, it also has the advantage of being quicker by allowing items to flow into the pipeline for further processing rather than requiring the items to be returned and stored in a variable before processing. This line of code, including the pipe character, is shown here.

```
$ds.findAll() |
```

For each item that comes down the pipeline, you are going to perform some action. When you are piping information, you are using the ForEach-Object cmdlet. If you are storing information in a variable and want to iterate through the collection, then you are using the *Foreach* statement. There are advantages to using the ForEach-Object cmdlet, however, in that you have a number of parameters you can use to simplify your code and add flexibility. You must keep in mind that this cmdlet is a single command; therefore, you need to use the backtick (`) character to be able to break the command onto several lines so it will be easier to read. You begin with the ForEach-Object cmdlet and a line continuation character as shown here.

```
ForEach-Object `
```

Before you actually begin working with your data as it streams down the pipeline, you can use the –*Begin* parameter. You want to initialize a variable that will be used for counting the items you find. As a best practice, I recommend initializing these types of "throwaway" variables as close to their point of use as possible because you can use this technique to limit their scope to the localized procedure. Once the *$i* variable is initialized, you can then print a header for your output that indicates the search attribute used to produce the results. Because you are not through using the ForEach-Object cmdlet, you end the command with a backtick as shown here.

```
-Begin { $i = 0 ; "$filter missing $SearchAttribute value" } `
```

Next, you want to begin the actual processing of the data that comes down the pipeline. To do this, you can use the –*Process* parameter and trail it with a backtick as shown here.

```
-Process `
    {
```

Now, you need to find out whether the value of the search attribute is empty or null. To do this, you can use the static *IsNullOrEmpty* method from the *System.String* class, and you use the *If* statement to do the evaluation. As a best practice when evaluating an item that returns a Boolean value, such as the *IsNullOrEmpty* method, you can use the Boolean value directly instead of trying to evaluate it as true of false or as 0 or –1. You use the *$_* automatic variable to refer to the current object on the pipeline. You can use the *Properties* property to return a collection of properties, and you can use the *Item* method to retrieve the specific Active Directory attribute in which you are interested. This line of code is shown here.

```
IF([string]::isNullOrEmpty($_.properties.item($SearchAttribute)))
```

If you find an attribute with an empty value, then you want to display the attribute you selected via the *$DisplayAttribute* variable. You can then print that value on the line and increment the value of the *$i* variable as shown here.

```
    {
     $_.Properties.item($DisplayAttribute)
     $i++
    } # end if
```

When you work your way through all of the items returned by the *DirectorySearcher*, you want to display a summary that informs you of how many items are found that match your *$SearchAttribute* value. To do this, you can use the –*End* parameter from the ForEach-Object cmdlet as shown here.

```
} `
  -End { "There are $i missing the $SearchAttribute value" }
```

The completed SearchAdForMissingAttributeValue.ps1 script is shown here.

SearchAdForMissingAttributeValue.ps1

```
#Requires -version 2.0
$SearchAttribute = "HomeDirectory"
$DisplayAttribute = "DistinguishedName"
$SearchRoot = "ou=testou,dc=nwtraders,dc=com"
$filter = "ObjectCategory=user"
$ds = [ADSISearcher]$filter
$ds.SearchRoot = "LDAP://$SearchRoot"
$ds.findAll() |
ForEach-Object `
  -Begin { $i = 0 ; "$filter missing $SearchAttribute value" } `
  -Process `
  {
    IF([string]::isNullOrEmpty($_.properties.item($SearchAttribute)))
     {
      $_.Properties.item($DisplayAttribute)
      $i++
     } # end if
  } `
  -End { "There are $i missing the $SearchAttribute value" }
```

Additional Resources

- The TechNet Script Center at *http://www.microsoft.com/technet/scriptcenter* contains many examples of working with Active Directory by using both Windows PowerShell and VBScript. The VBScript examples are generally easily translated into Windows PowerShell code and should not be ignored because they illustrate good techniques.

- Take a look at *Windows PowerShell™ Scripting Guide* (Microsoft Press, 2008). Inside are two chapters devoted to working with users.

- Appendix C, "Active Directory Users and Computers to ADSI Mapping," contains screen shots from Active Directory Users and Computers and matches the display names shown in the graphical tool to the actual attribute name that is used in the Active Directory schema.

- *System.DirectoryServices.ActiveDirectory* namespace classes are detailed on Microsoft Developer Network (MSDN) at *http://msdn.microsoft.com/en-us/library/bb267453.aspx*.

- Brandon Shell's blog at *http://bsonposh.com/* has a great deal of good information about working with Active Directory.

- On the companion media, you will find all of the scripts referred to in this chapter.

## CHAPTER 5

Identifying Scripting Opportunities

Automating Routine Tasks

One of the most important tasks when developing a scripting program is to track and coordinate the development endeavors of the scripting team. This process is not done in most companies, however. As a result, much time is wasted developing multiple scripts that perform the same tasks and implement similar functionality.

This is an area in which the judicious application of collaboration tools can play a significant role. One such collaboration tool that can easily be pressed into service is the Microsoft SharePoint Portal product. The discussion forum can be used to track requests for scripts, and the library can be used as a central distribution point for released scripts.

When attempting to identify scripting opportunities, you must know which tasks are ripe for automation and which are not. In general, when making the decision to script or not to script, the most obvious requirement is repeatability. Routine tasks should nearly always be investigated for scripting. However, just because a task is repeatable does not automatically mean that it is rich for automation via scripting. Many repeatable tasks simply cannot be automated via scripting for one reason or another.

Automation Interface

One of the most obvious needs is for some type of automation interface. Automation can be implemented in many ways such as through a Component Object Model (COM) classic Application Programming Interface (API), Microsoft .NET Framework support, Windows Management Instrumentation (WMI) support, ActiveX Data Object (ADO) support in all of its various flavors, and Active Directory Services Interface (ADSI) support, not to mention Windows PowerShell cmdlets or command-line utilities, such as NetSH or NetDom. With these various avenues for automation support, identifying the proper means of performing the task can be both time consuming and overwhelming. As an example, take the simple task of reading from the registry.

If you want to identify the version of Windows PowerShell that is running on your computer, you can read the *RunTimeVersion* value from the registry. This registry key is shown in Figure 5-1.

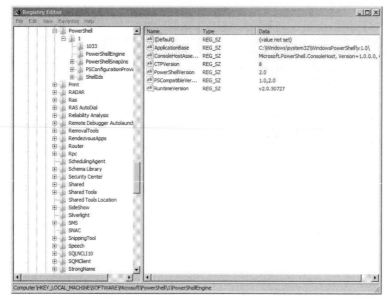

FIGURE 5-1 Identify Windows PowerShell via the registry version number.

One method to read from the registry is to use the registry provider from within Windows PowerShell and to read a registry value as you might read a property from a file or folder. To do this, you must use the HKLM PowerShell drive (HKLM: in this instance) and follow it with the path to the registry key, which is \SOFTWARE\Microsoft\PowerShell\1\PowerShellEngine. You can then select the item property in which you are interested, which is *RunTimeVersion* in this example as shown in the GetPsVersionPs.Ps1 script.

 ON THE COMPANION MEDIA All scripts in this chapter can be found on the companion media.

GetPsVersionPs.Ps1

```
$path = "HKLM:\SOFTWARE\Microsoft\PowerShell\1\PowerShellEngine"
$psv = get-itemproperty -path $path
$psv.RunTimeVersion
```

Using *RegRead* to Read the Registry

Those of you who are familiar with VBScript may wish to create the *WshShell* object and use the *RegRead* method. To do this, you can use the HKLM moniker as a shortcut to refer to the HKEY_LOCAL_MACHINE registry key.

NOTE When used with the *WshShell* object, the HKLM is case sensitive.

You store the path to the Windows PowerShell configuration information in the *$path* variable. Next, you can use the New-Object cmdlet to create an instance of the *WshShell* object. This COM object has the program ID of Wscript.Shell. You can store the returned object in the *$wshShell* variable. Once you have the *WshShell* object, you can use the *RegRead* method to read the registry key value, which you can specify by placing the path and value name in an expanding string: "$path\RunTimeVersion". This GetPsVersionRR.ps1 script is shown here.

GetPsVersionRR.ps1
```
$path = "HKLM\SOFTWARE\Microsoft\PowerShell\1\PowerShellEngine"
$WshShell = New-Object -ComObject Wscript.Shell
$WshShell.RegRead("$path\RunTimeVersion")
```

When you want to use WMI to read the registry, you need to use the *stdRegProv* WMI class, which has always been in the *root\default* WMI namespace. Beginning with Windows Vista, you also have an instance of the *stdRegProv* WMI class in the *root\cimv2* namespace (which, incidentally, really is the default namespace). This means that you can use the *stdRegProv* WMI class from either the *root\default* WMI namespace or the *root\cimv2* WMI namespace; it does not matter because it is the same WMI class. Because it does not matter which instance of the class you use, I recommend as a best practice that you use the class from the *root\default* WMI namespace (as in the GetPsVersionWmi.Ps1 script) to ensure compatibility with older versions of Windows-based operating systems.

WMI uses coded values to determine the registry tree (also known as a hive). These coded values are shown in Table 5-1.

NOTE The HKEY_DYN_DATA registry tree only exists on Microsoft Windows 95 and Windows 98.

TABLE 5-1 WMI Registry Tree Values

NAME	VALUE
HKEY_CLASSES_ROOT	2147483648
HKEY_CURRENT_USER	2147483649
HKEY_LOCAL_MACHINE	2147483650
HKEY_USERS	2147483651
HKEY_CURRENT_CONFIG	2147483653
HKEY_DYN_DATA	2147483654

You can use the value *2147483650* and assign it to the *$hklm* variable. This value points the WMI query to the HKEY_LOCAL_MACHINE registry tree. You then assign the string SOFTWARE\Microsoft\PowerShell\1\PowerShellEngine to the *$key* variable.

> **NOTE** When using WMI to read the registry, the key is not preceded with a backslash.

You assign the registry property value that you want to read to the *$value* variable. Now you can use the [WMICLASS] type accelerator to obtain an instance of the *stdRegProv* WMI class. You can choose the *root\default* WMI namespace to specify which version of the *stdRegProv* WMI class you want to use. You can also precede the namespace with the name of a computer and read the registry from a remote computer. Once you create an instance of the *stdregProv* WMI class, you can use the resulting *System.Management.Management* class to call the *GetStringValue* method. The *GetStringValue* method takes three arguments: the registry key coded value, the registry subkey string, and the property name. Two objects are returned by the method call: the *returnvalue,* which indicates the success or failure of the method call, and the *svalue,* which is the string value that is stored in the registry property. The complete GetPsVersionWmi.Ps1 script is shown here.

GetPsVersionWmi.Ps1
```
$hklm = 2147483650
$key = "SOFTWARE\Microsoft\PowerShell\1\PowerShellEngine"
$value = "RunTimeVersion"
$wmi = [WMICLASS]"root\default:stdRegProv"
($wmi.GetStringValue($hklm,$key,$value)).svalue
```

You can also use the .NET Framework classes to obtain information from the registry. To do this, you can use the *Microsoft.Win32.Registry* .NET Framework class. You can use the *GetValue* static method, which takes three parameters. The first parameter is the registry root and key name, the second parameter is the registry value you want to read, and the last parameter is the default value of the registry key value. In the GetPsVersionNet.Ps1 script, you can assign the HKEY_LOCAL_MACHINE string value to the *$hklm* variable. Next, you can assign the string representing the remainder of the registry path to the *$key* variable. The registry key property value you want to retrieve is stored in the *$value* variable. You can then use the *Microsoft.Win32.Registry* class plus two colons to signifiy that you want to use a static method and then use the *GetValue* method with the *$hklm, $key,* and *$value* variables passed to it. The GetPsVersionNet.ps1 script is shown here.

GetPsVersionNet.Ps1
```
$hklm = "HKEY_LOCAL_MACHINE"
$key = "SOFTWARE\Microsoft\PowerShell\1\PowerShellEngine"
$value = "RunTimeVersion"
[Microsoft.Win32.Registry]::GetValue("$hklm\$key",$value,$null)
```

When working with the registry, you can see that there is a Windows PowerShell provider, COM object, WMI class, and .NET Framework class. This plethora of methodologies is one of the strengths of Windows PowerShell, but it is also a significant source of confusion for those who are just learning PowerShell.

So what is the correct way to read the registry? You can never go wrong by using native Windows PowerShell providers and commands. The registry provider in Windows PowerShell is powerful and easy to use from the command line. In addition, because of the remoting features of Windows PowerShell 2.0, the need to remotely access the registry is no longer the key decision factor.

WMI gives you the ability to connect remotely to read the registry. The methodology is very similar to the way that you connect in VBScript; therefore, if you are migrating a script to Windows PowerShell from VBScript, it makes sense to stay with the WMI methodology. The *WshShell* COM object is also a good choice if you are interested in migrating legacy code to Windows PowerShell. The VBScript techniques are very similar and can therefore make a fairly straightforward translation. The .NET Framework classes offer much more flexibility than any of the other techniques explored.

INSIDE TRACK

Working with Windows PowerShell 2.0

Jeffrey Snover, Distinguished Engineer
Microsoft Corporation

Version 2 of Windows PowerShell takes advantage of the rich architecture work we did in version 1, which enables us to deliver at least as much innovation in a much shorter time period. That is why it is hard for me to pick out my favorite feature. If you make me choose just one feature, I'd have to pick remoting, but that's a bit like cheating because there are at least six separate remoting stories, which are listed here.

- You can remote to existing systems using Remote Procedure Call (RPC) and the Distributed Component Object Model (DCOM) by adding the *–computername* parameter to numerous commands.

- You can do awesome, large-scale WMI remoting by employing a new set of cmdlets that uses semi-synchronous APIs and the *–ThrottleLimit* parameter.

- You can remotely manage raw hardware and UNIX boxes by using the new *WS-Management* (WSMan) cmdlets.

- You can create remote interactive Windows PowerShell sessions on a Windows box.

- You can do fan-out command execution to a large group of machines and get results back immediately or run Windows PowerShell as a background job and collect the results at your leisure.

- You can also host Windows PowerShell as an Internet Information Services (IIS) application to support fan-in management scenarios in which service providers offer custom scripting interfaces to individual users across the Internet.

Windows PowerShell 2.0 remoting provides administrators with much more control over their environment than they ever had before. I can't wait to see what people do with it. I think that most people will perform the classic procedures with our remoting work, such as creating files and folders, making new shares, and working with the registry. Only now, they can do this on a remote machine. These types of procedures are exposed via the Windows PowerShell cmdlets and providers. I also think that a select group of people will look at our remoting capabilities and realize that we have delivered a general-purpose, distributed computing platform—and they will start doing all sorts of crazy and wonderful things with it.

Personally, when I need to work on a remote computer, I like creating PSSessions and then using the `Invoke-Command` cmdlet because it is very fast and flexible. I use this cmdlet whether I need to run a simple command or actually need a remote interactive Windows PowerShell session.

Structured Requirements

When investigating a scripting opportunity, it is important to first analyze the requirements for the script. Several of the items to be examined are listed here.

- Security requirements
- .NET Framework version requirements
- Operating system requirements
- Application requirements
- Snap-in requirements

Security Requirements

Beginning with Windows Vista, the introduction of User Account Control (UAC) has made it easier for users to run programs without having Administrator rights on their computer. While this is a boon for users and corporate security departments, it is somewhat of a headache for network administrators and others who are writing scripts that may require elevated permissions.

Windows PowerShell does not bypass security. If a script attempts to perform an action that the user is not allowed to perform, then the script fails.

In Windows PowerShell 2.0, we have improved the detection of security requirements. As shown in Figure 5-2, when a script does not contain the required rights, a failure notification is shown.

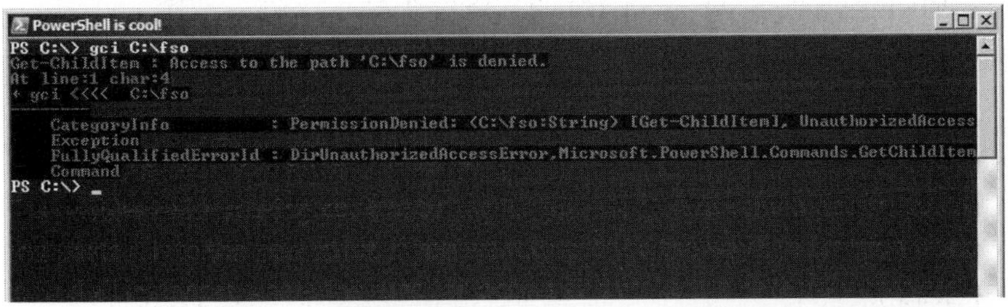

FIGURE 5-2 When a script does not have permission, it reports an access denied message.

As a best practice, a script should detect the rights it possesses when running and compare them with any requirements the script may need to run properly. To do this, you first need to obtain information about the user, which is covered in the next section.

Detecting the Current User

To provide information about currently logged-on users, you can use the *Security.Principal.WindowsIdentity* .NET Framework class. This class uses the *GetCurrent* method, which returns an instance of a *WindowsIdentity* object that represents the current user. In this example, the *WindowsIdentity* object is stored in the *$user* variable.

```
$user = [System.Security.Principal.WindowsIdentity]::GetCurrent()
```

The *WindowsIdentity* object contains the properties shown in Table 5-2.

TABLE 5-2 Properties of the *WindowsIdentity* Object

NAME	DEFINITION
AuthenticationType	System.String AuthenticationType {get;}
Groups	System.Security.Principal.IdentityReferenceCollection Groups {get;}
ImpersonationLevel	System.Security.Principal.TokenImpersonationLevel ImpersonationLevel {get;}
IsAnonymous	System.Boolean IsAnonymous {get;}
IsAuthenticated	System.Boolean IsAuthenticated {get;}
IsGuest	System.Boolean IsGuest {get;}
IsSystem	System.Boolean IsSystem {get;}
Name	System.String Name {get;}
Owner	System.Security.Principal.SecurityIdentifier Owner {get;}
Token	System.IntPtr Token {get;}
User	System.Security.Principal.SecurityIdentifier User {get;}

Once the *WindowsIdentity* object is stored in a variable, you can display the values of all of the properties shown in Table 5-2 by typing the variable at the prompt. You do not need to store the variable and can display the data directly as shown in Figure 5-3.

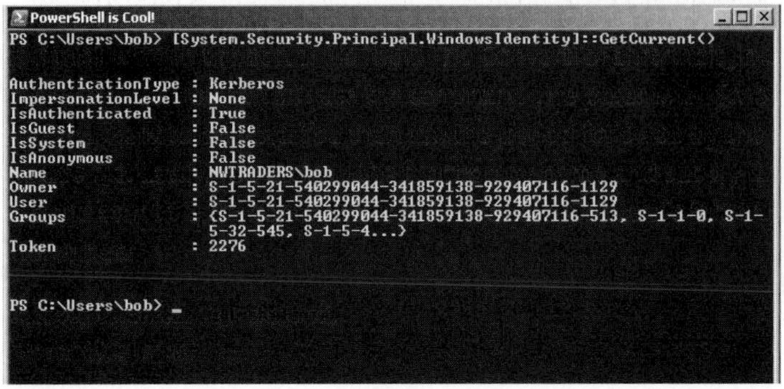

FIGURE 5-3 Windows PowerShell displays the value of the *WindowsIdentity* object.

While the display shown in Figure 5-3 is somewhat impressive and moderately useful in that it displays the user name and security identifier (SID) of the user, it does not display any information about the user rights to a particular resource or administrator rights in general. There are actually two separate requirements: does the user have access rights to a resource, and does the user have administrator rights?

To determine the rights of a user to a resource, you must examine the group information. As shown in Table 5-2, the *WindowsIdentity* class has a *Groups* property. You can easily display the contents of the *Groups* property by simply printing the value as shown here.

```
$user = [System.Security.Principal.WindowsIdentity]::GetCurrent()
```

```
$user.Groups
```

The problem with this approach is that the resulting collection of groups is not in the most readable format, as shown in Figure 5-4.

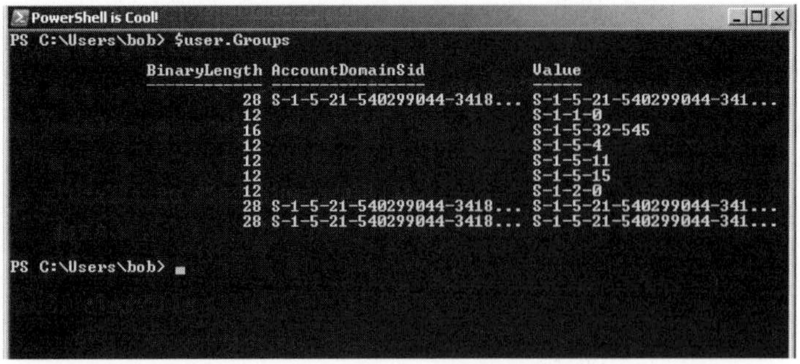

FIGURE 5-4 The *Groups* property of the *WindowsIdentity* class is subilluminating.

You need to convert the group information from a SID into something more recognizable. When you have an actual group name, it is easier to use any of the string manipulation tools provided by Windows PowerShell to determine specific group membership. You can index directly into the collection of *SecurityIdentifiers* that is returned by the *Groups* property. The following code allows you to do this.

```
$user.Groups[0]
```

Of course, there is one problem with this approach. How do you know what group[0] is? If you add the *ToString* method, you get a little bit of assistance as shown here, with the resulting display as well.

```
PS C:\Users\bob> $user.Groups[0].tostring()
```

```
S-1-5-21-540299044-341859138-929407116-513
```

At this point, you have succeeded in directly obtaining the SID of the group. In some cases, this may be enough information if you want to match group membership based on SIDs. However, most network administrators do not have this information at their fingertips, and so it is necessary to take the output to an additional level of processing.

To change a SID into a noun name, you can use the *Translate* method from the *System.Security.Principal.SecurityIdentifier* .NET Framework class. The members of this class are shown in Table 5-3.

TABLE 5-3 Members of the *SecurityIdentifier* Class

NAME	MEMBERTYPE	DEFINITION
CompareTo	Method	System.Int32 CompareTo(SecurityIdentifier sid)
Equals	Method	System.Boolean Equals(Object o) System.Boolean Equals(SecurityIdentifier sid)
GetBinaryForm	Method	System.Void GetBinaryForm(Byte[] binaryForm Int32 offset)
GetHashCode	Method	System.Int32 GetHashCode()
GetType	Method	System.Type GetType()
IsAccountSid	Method	System.Boolean IsAccountSid()
IsEqualDomainSid	Method	System.Boolean IsEqualDomainSid(SecurityIdentifier sid)
IsValidTargetType	Method	System.Boolean IsValidTargetType(Type targetType)
IsWellKnown	Method	System.Boolean IsWellKnown(WellKnownSidType type)
ToString	Method	System.String ToString()

NAME	MEMBERTYPE	DEFINITION
Translate	Method	System.Security.Principal.IdentityReference Translate(Type targetType)
AccountDomainSid	Property	System.Security.Principal.SecurityIdentifier AccountDomainSid {get;}
BinaryLength	Property	System.Int32 BinaryLength {get;}
Value	Property	System.String Value {get;}

To translate the SID from a number to a Windows group name, you must specify that you want to translate to the type of *NTAccount* by first creating an instance of an *NTAccount* type. To do this, you use a string that represents the *System.Security.Principal.NTAccount* class and then use the *–as* operator to specify the string as a [type] as shown here.

```
$nt = "System.Security.Principal.NTAccount" -as [type]
```

Once you create the *NTAccount* type, you can use it with the *Translate* method as shown here.

```
PS C:\> $user = [System.Security.Principal.WindowsIdentity]::GetCurrent()
PS C:\> $nt = "System.Security.Principal.NTAccount" -as [type]
PS C:\> $user.Groups[0].translate($nt)
Value
-----
NWTRADERS\Domain Users
```

This may seem like a bit of work to find out that the currently logged-on user is a member of the Domain Users group (you would have known that anyway). But based on the fact that a collection is returned by the *Groups* property, a looping type of cmdlet can be used to provide access to one group at a time. In this example, the ForEach-Object cmdlet is used as shown here.

```
PS C:\> $user = [System.Security.Principal.WindowsIdentity]::GetCurrent()
PS C:\> $nt = "System.Security.Principal.NTAccount" -as [type]
PS C:\> $user.Groups | ForEach-Object { $_.translate($NT) }
Value
-----
NWTRADERS\Domain Users
Everyone
BUILTIN\Users
NT AUTHORITY\INTERACTIVE
NT AUTHORITY\Authenticated Users
NT AUTHORITY\This Organization
LOCAL
NWTRADERS\moreBogus
NWTRADERS\bogus
```

Once you see that you can obtain the actual names of the groups, there are several ways to search the strings for a group match such as using the *−contains*, *−like*, or *−match* operators.

−Contains, −Like, or −Match

When searching a string, you can use at least three different operators: *−contains*, *−like*, and *−match*. The most confusing of the bunch is the *−contains* operator. This is not due to its complexity of use, but rather to an attempt at understanding when to use the operator. Perhaps a few examples will help. In the following code, an array of numbers is created and stored in the *$a* variable. Next, the *−contains* operator is used to see whether the array that is stored in the *$a* variable contains the number 1. It does, and *true* is reported. The *−contains* operator is then used to see whether the *$a* array contains the number 6. It does not, and *false* is reported as shown here.

```
PS C:\> $a = 1,2,3,4,5
PS C:\> $a -contains 1
True
PS C:\> $a -contains 6
False
```

In the next example, the number 12345 is stored in the *$b* variable. The *−contains* method is used to see whether the number stored in *$b* contains the number 4. While the number 4 is indeed present in the number 12345, *−contains* reports back *false*. The number stored in *$b* does not contain 4. Next, the *−contains* method is used to see whether *$b* contains 12345, which it does, and *true* is reported back as shown here.

```
PS C:\> $b = 12345
PS C:\> $b -contains 4
False
PS C:\> $b -contains 12345
True
```

Suppose the variable *$c* stores the following string: "This is a string." When the *−contains* method is used to look for the string "is," *false* is returned. If the *−contains* method is used to look for the string "This is a string," it returns *true* as shown here.

```
PS C:\> $c = "This is a string"
PS C:\> $c -contains "is"
False
PS C:\> $c -contains "This is a string"
True
```

For our last example of the –*contains* operator, if *$d* contains an array of strings ("This","is","a","string") when the –*contains* operator is used to look for the value of "is," then *true* is returned. When the –*contains* operator looks for "ring," it returns *false* as shown here.

```
PS C:\> $d = "This","is","a","string"
PS C:\> $d -contains "is"
True
PS C:\> $d -contains "ring"
False
```

The –*contains* operator is used to examine the elements of an array. If the array contains a particular value, the operator returns *true*. If there is not an exact match for the value, the –*contains* operator returns *false*. This process can be an easy way to locate items in an array.

The –*like* operator is used to perform a wildcard search of a string. If the *$a* variable is used to hold the string "This is a string" and the –*like* operator searches for "*ring*," the –*like* operator returns *true* as shown here.

```
PS C:\> $a = "This is a string"
PS C:\> $a -like "*ring*"
True
```

An interesting use of the –*like* operator is to search the elements of an array. If the *$b* variable is used to hold the array "This","is","a","string" and the –*like* operator searches the array for "*ring*," every match for the wildcard pattern is returned— not just a true/false answer as shown here.

```
PS C:\> $b = "This","is","a","string"
PS C:\> $b -like "*ring*"
string
```

The –*match* operator is used to perform a regular expression pattern match. When the match is found, *true* is returned. If a match is not found, *false* is returned. If the *$a* variable is assigned the value "This is a string" and the –*match* operator is used to look for the value of "is," the pattern is a match and *true* is returned as shown here.

```
PS C:\> $a = "This is a string"
PS C:\> $a -match "is"
True
```

More complex match patterns can be used. The \w character is used with regular expressions to look for any white space, such as a space before or after a letter. When the *$a* variable is used to hold the string "This is a string" and the regular expression pattern [\w a \w] is used, a match will be returned if the letter *a* is found with a space in front and a space behind the letter as shown here.

```
PS C:\> $a = "This is a string"
PS C:\> $a -match "[\w a \w]"
True
```

What about matching with an array? If the *$c* variable is used to hold the array "This","is","a","string" and the regular expression pattern match, "is," is used, two matches are found. In this example, the actual string that contains the pattern match is returned as shown here. When a match is found, an array of strings is returned as also shown here.

```
PS C:\> $c = "This","is","a","string"
PS C:\> $c -match "is"
This
is
```

The *GetMemberOf* function uses the *GetCurrent* static method from the *System.Security.Principal.WindowsIdentity* class to create a *WindowsIdentity* object. After creating an *NTAccount* type, it uses the *Groups* property to obtain a collection of security groups, whereupon it uses the ForEach-Object cmdlet to translate the group from a SID to an *NTAccount* as the groups come across the pipeline. If the group name matches the group that is used when the function is called, it displays a message stating that the user is a member of the group. The GetMemberOf.ps1 script is shown here.

GetMemberOf.ps1
```
Function GetMemberOf($group)
{
 $user = [System.Security.Principal.WindowsIdentity]::GetCurrent()
 $nt = "System.Security.Principal.NTAccount" -as [type]
 If( $user.Groups | ForEach-Object { $_.translate($NT) -match "$group"} )
  { "$($user.name) is a member of a $group group" }
}
```

An example of using the *GetMemberOf* function from the GetMemberOf.ps1 script is the UseGetMemberOf.ps1 script. This script checks to determine whether the logged-on user has rights to a folder named bogus. The security permission on the bogus folder is shown in Figure 5-5. The bogus group has full control, and no one else has permission.

The bogus group has one direct member—MyDomainAdmin. It also has two groups that are members: the moreBogus group and the Useless group. These group memberships are shown in Figure 5-6.

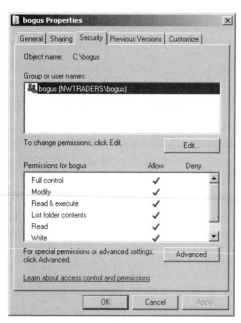

FIGURE 5-5 Only the bogus group has permission to access the bogus folder.

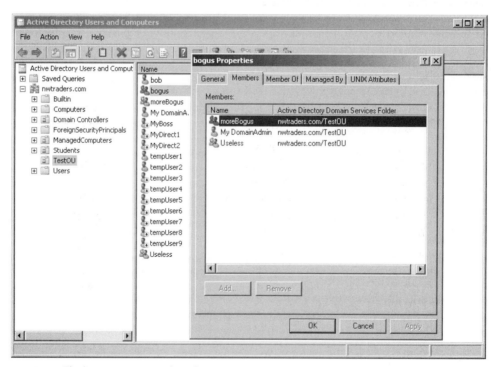

FIGURE 5-6 The bogus group contains other groups.

The logged-on user is Bob. As shown in Figure 5-6, Bob does not have direct membership in the bogus group. Bob is a member of the moreBogus group as shown in Figure 5-7.

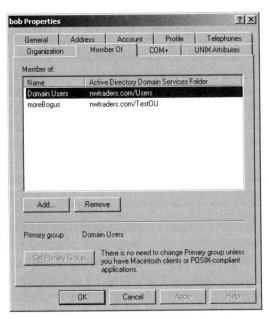

FIGURE 5-7 Bob is a member of the moreBogus group and Domain Users.

In the UseGetMemberOf.ps1 script, first an instance of the *GetCurrent* static method from the *System.Security.Principal.WindowsIdentity* class is created. You will need to store the *WindowsIdentity* object that is returned in a variable.

You next need to create an instance of an *NTAccount* type by using the *–as* operator to cast the string "System.Security.Principal.NTAccount" as a [type]. You will use this type later.

The essential portion of the script uses an *If* statement to evaluate whether the name of the user group is found within the collection of groups. The *Groups* property returns a collection of groups that is contained within the *$users* object. Each group is sent over the pipeline. Now it is time to evaluate each group from the collection by using the ForEach-Object cmdlet. Inside the code block, the *$_ automatic* variable is used to represent the current object on the pipeline. This object has the *Translate* method that accepts the *NTAccount* type created earlier and is assigned to the *$NT* variable. Now you have a translated group name and can use the *–match* operator to determine whether the group that is stored in the *$group* variable matches what is currently on the pipeline. You can treat this value as if it were a Boolean value by using the *If* statement as shown here.

```
If( $user.Groups | ForEach-Object { $_.translate($NT) -match "$group"} )
```

When a match with the group is found, you need to determine whether the file actually exists by using the Test-Path cmdlet, which receives the path stored in the *$bogusFile* variable. The Test-Path cmdlet returns a Boolean value. Here is the code to check for the existence of the file.

```
if(Test-Path -Path $bogusFile)
```

If the file exists, the script enters the code block, which adds text to the file. To write to the file, you can use the Add-Content cmdlet, which receives the path to the file and the data you want to add. At the end of the line, two special characters are used: backtick r and backtick n. The `r is a return and the `n is a new line. Together they form a carriage return and line feed that is equivalent to the VBScript vbcrlf keyword. The special characters are shown in Table 5-4.

TABLE 5-4 Special Characters

CHARACTER	DEFINITION
`0 (number zero)	Null
`a	Alert
`b	Backspace
`f	Form feed
`n	New line
`r	Carriage return
`t	Horizontal tab
`v	Vertical tab
`r`n	Carriage return line feed

Once the additional text is added to the text file, a message is displayed on the screen and the file is opened in Notepad as shown here.

```
{
 Add-Content -Path $bogusFile -Value "Added bogus content`r`n"
 "Added content to $bogusFile"
 Notepad $bogusFile
} #end if Test-Path
```

If the file does not exist, a message is printed to the screen as shown here.

```
ELSE
     {
        "Unable to find $bogusFile"
     } #end else
  } #end if user
```

If the user does not belong to a group with rights to the file, the user's name is displayed on the screen with a message regarding the lack of group membership as shown here.

```
ELSE
    {
      "$($user.name) is not a member of $group"
    }
} #end GetMemberOf
```

The completed UseGetMemberOf.ps1 script is shown here.

UseGetMemberOf.ps1
```
Function GetMemberOf($group)
{
 $user = [System.Security.Principal.WindowsIdentity]::GetCurrent()
 $nt = "System.Security.Principal.NTAccount" -as [type]
 If( $user.Groups | ForEach-Object { $_.translate($NT) -match "$group"} )
   {
     if(Test-Path -Path $bogusFile)
       {
          Add-Content -Path $bogusFile -Value "Added bogus content`r`n"
          "Added content to $bogusFile"
          Notepad $bogusFile
       } #end if Test-Path
     ELSE
       {
          "Unable to find $bogusFile"
       } #end else
   } #end if user
 ELSE
     {
       "$($user.name) is not a member of $group"
     }
} #end GetMemberOf

$bogusFile = "C:\bogus\bogus.txt"
GetMemberOf -group "bogus"
```

Changing the Way You Write Scripts

Jeffrey Snover, Distinguished Engineer
Microsoft Corporation

Version 2 has changed the way I write functions and scripts. Now, I always write functions that incorporate the version 2 cmdlet features. Before Windows PowerShell 2.0, functions were pale substitutes for cmdlets, but now they are full peers. That's right—you can now write full cmdlets in Windows PowerShell itself. That capability is a game changer. The tiny bit of extra syntax provides an incredible amount of functionality. This is the basis for what we call meta-programming, which is going to change the world. You can mark my words on that.

We can do meta-programming with the `Import-PSSession` cmdlets in which we inspect the cmdlets on a remote machine and emit local proxies for those functions on the local machine, which makes it appear as if the cmdlets are installed on the local machine. You have tab completion, help, formatting—the whole works. Yet, what happens behind the scenes is that we emit a function with cmdlet semantics that uses the remote machine to do the work. This is very powerful indeed. Once people begin to use the `Import-PSSession` cmdlet, it will be like the *2001 Space Odyssey* movie in which the large black monolith appeared, the apes figured out how to use tools, and the evolution toward mankind was initiated.

Even with all of the new command-line features in Windows PowerShell 2.0, I still write scripts. In fact, I am writing more scripts now than during my Windows PowerShell 1.0 days. Why? First and perhaps foremost—joy. It is simply a joy to write a Windows PowerShell script. It's like driving a BMW. This incredible machine goes exactly where you point it and makes you feel powerful and competent. With Windows PowerShell 2.0, you can achieve so much so easily that I tend to write a script, step back to look it, and say, "Wow! That is cool!" Let me be quick to say that I have the same experience when looking at other people's scripts. Lee Holmes, a Senior Software Development Engineer at Microsoft, just sent me a 103-line script that makes me just dizzy with excitement. I simply can't believe what he can do by using 103 lines of code. At the end of the day, it comes down to being effective at your job. Windows PowerShell makes it easy for you to be effective at your job.

Detecting the User Role

It is possible that the Windows PowerShell console that is running may not have Administrator rights. If this is the case, then even if the user is in the Administrators role for the computer, the script will fail due to insufficient rights. One way to handle this situation is to create two Windows PowerShell consoles—one that launches with ordinary user rights and one that requests elevated permissions when it launches, as shown in Figure 5-8.

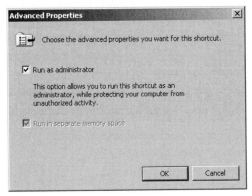

FIGURE 5-8 The Run As Administrator option causes an application to request admin rights.

You could place the *GetAdmin* function that is contained in the GetAdminFunction.ps1 script into your profile or into any script that requires administrative rights. The GetAdminFunction.ps1 script begins by declaring the *GetAdmin* function, which accepts a single value—a variable named *$isAdmin*. This variable is passed by reference, which means that you will change the value of the *$isAdmin* variable from within the function itself. You can specify that a variable is passed by reference by using the [ref] type constraint on the variable. This type constraint is required in the function declaration line of the code, as well as when you call the function from the main body of the script. The *$isAdmin* variable itself is null when it is passed to the function because it is set to null when it is declared in the main body of the script. The function declaration is shown here.

```
Function GetAdmin([ref]$isAdmin)
```

The next action in the *GetAdmin* function is to use the static *GetCurrent* method from the *Security.Principal.WindowsIdentity* .NET Framework class to retrieve an instance of the *WindowsIdentity* class that represents the current user. The returned *WindowsIdentity* object is stored in the *$currentUser* variable as shown here.

```
$currentUser = [Security.Principal.WindowsIdentity]::getCurrent()
```

Next, the *GetAdmin* function creates an instance of a *WindowsPrincipal* class that represents the current user by passing the *WindowsIdentity* object, which is stored in the *$currentUser* variable as the constructor to the *Security.Principal.WindowsPrincipal* class. Because a new object is required, the function uses the New-Object cmdlet. The resulting *WindowsPrincipal* object is stored in the *$principal* variable as shown here.

```
$principal = new-object security.Principal.windowsPrincipal($currentUser)
```

Now the static property administrator is used from the *Security.Principal.WindowsBuiltInRole* enumeration. The *administrator role value* is stored in the *$admin* variable as shown here.

```
$admin = [security.principal.WindowsBuiltInRole]::administrator
```

To be able to use the *IsInRole* method from the *WindowsPrincipal* class, you need to give it a WindowsBuiltInRole enumeration, which was created in the previous line of code and stored in the *$admin* variable. The result of the *IsInRole* method is a Boolean value: *true* or *false*, which is stored in the *Value* property of the *$isAdmin* reference type variable as shown here.

```
$isAdmin.value = $principal.IsInRole($admin)
```

The remainder of the script is used to initialize the *GetAdmin* function. First, the *$isAdmin* variable must be set to null. Then the *GetAdmin* function is called, specifying that *$isAdmin* is a reference type variable. The returned variable is then evaluated, and the appropriate string is printed to the console. Of course, you can perform other actions in any script that you intend to use this type of function. This section of the code is shown here.

```
$isAdmin = $null
GetAdmin([ref]$isAdmin)
if($isAdmin)
 { "current console has admin rights" }
ELSE
 { "current console does not have admin rights" }
```

The completed GetAdminFunction.ps1 script is shown here.

```
GetAdminFunction.ps1
Function GetAdmin([ref]$isAdmin)
{
 $currentUser = [Security.Principal.WindowsIdentity]::getCurrent()
 $principal = new-object security.Principal.windowsPrincipal($currentUser)
 $admin = [security.principal.WindowsBuiltInRole]::administrator
 $isAdmin.value = $principal.IsInRole($admin)
} #end GetAdmin function

 $isAdmin = $null
 GetAdmin([ref]$isAdmin)
 if($isAdmin)
  { "current console has admin rights" }
 ELSE
  { "current console does not have admin rights" }
```

The *Security.Principal.WindowsBuiltInRole* .NET Framework enumeration has the following possible values.

- *Administrator*

- *User*
- *Guest*
- *PowerUser*
- *AccountOperator*
- *SystemOperator*
- *PrintOperator*
- *BackupOperator*
- *Replicator*

These enumeration values are documented in reference information contained on the MSDN Web site. A link to MSDN is included in the "Additional Resources" section later in this chapter. However, you do not need to search the documentation if all you want to do is find the enumeration values. You can use Windows PowerShell to provide this information by using the static *GetNames* method from the *System.Enum* .NET Framework class. You place the *Security.Principal.WindowsBuiltInRole* enumeration class name in quotation marks to the method and press Enter to retrieve the names of all of the enumerations contained in the class as shown here.

```
PS C:\> [enum]::getnames("security.principal.WindowsBuiltInRole")
Administrator
User
Guest
PowerUser
AccountOperator
SystemOperator
PrintOperator
BackupOperator
Replicator
```

The *Enum* class also has the *GetValues* static method, which lists the values of the enumerations instead of the names of the enumerations. This would be a bit boring in this particular case because both the value and the name of the WindowsBuiltInRole enumerations are the same things. To find all of the static methods of the *Enum* class, you can use the following line of code (although the only thing I do with the *Enum* class 95 percent of the time is to use it to obtain the names of a particular .NET Framework enumeration).

```
[enum] | Get-Member -Static -MemberType method
```

Because there are no static properties defined in the *Enum* class, you can get away with omitting the *–MemberType* parameter and use the following line of code.

```
[enum] | Get-Member -Static
```

If you do not want to do that much typing, you can use the following from the console.

```
[enum] | gm -s
```

The GetAdminFunction.ps1 script can easily be modified to provide information based on the other roles available in the *Security.Principal.WindowsBuiltInRole* class. The main objective is to replace the hard-coded administrator role name with a variable as shown here.

```
$role = [security.principal.WindowsBuiltInRole]::$roleName
```

The remaining changes to the script consist of renaming variables and changing the output text slightly. The modified GetRoleFunction.ps1 script is shown here.

```
GetRoleFunction.ps1
Function GetAdmin([ref]$isInRole)
{
 $currentUser = [Security.Principal.WindowsIdentity]::getCurrent()
 $principal = new-object security.Principal.windowsPrincipal($currentUser)
 $role = [security.principal.WindowsBuiltInRole]::$roleName
 $isInRole.value = $principal.IsInRole($role)
} #end GetAdmin function

# *** Entry point to script ***

$isInRole = $null
$roleName = "User"
GetAdmin([ref]$isInRole)
if($isInRole)
  { "Current console has the $roleName role" }
ELSE
  { "Current console does not have the $roleName role" }
```

.NET Framework Version Requirements

When working with Windows PowerShell, its easy access to the .NET Framework while providing flexibility and ease of development also introduces an additional consideration—the version of the .NET Framework that is installed on the computer. There are several ways to detect the version.

To check the version of the .NET Framework system, you can use the static *GetSystemVersion* method from the *System.Runtime.InteropServices.RunTimeEnvironment* .NET Framework class as shown here.

```
[runtime.interopServices.RunTimeEnvironment]::GetSystemVersion()
```

However, when I call this method on my computer, it reports 2.0.50727, which is .NET Framework 2.0 with Service Pack 1 (SP1). The value returned occurs because of the way the Framework is installed—the service packs are considered to be extensions to the run time.

One way to determine whether a particular version of the .NET Framework has been installed is to look for the folder. For example, .NET Framework 3.5 creates a folder named v3.5. To check for the presence of the folder, you can use the Test-Path cmdlet as shown here.

```
Test-Path (Join-Path -path $env:systemroot -ChildPath microsoft.net\framework\v3.5)
```

The previous approach may be fine in most circumstances, but there is one significant problem with it. While the previous command indeed tells you whether .NET Framework 3.5 has been installed on the computer, it does not tell you whether it is still installed on the machine because the folder and accompanying install log files are left behind after uninstallation.

Another approach to finding a specific version of the .NET Framework is to check the registry. When the .NET Framework is installed, each version adds a key to the registry. You can use the code shown here to check for the presence of the .NET Framework.

```
Test-path (Resolve-Path 'HKLM:\SOFTWARE\Microsoft\NET Framework Setup\NDP\v3.5')
```

When the specific version of the .NET Framework is uninstalled, this key is removed. The presence of the .NET Framework Setup registry key for each version is therefore an indicator for the presence of the .NET Framework. The advantage to this method is that it is relatively easy to use and can be done on a local or remote computer.

The most accurate way to check for the presence of a specific version of the .NET Framework is to use the WMI *Win32_Product* class, which you can do by using the Get-WmiObject cmdlet. By using the *–filter* parameter, you can reduce the number of instances of the *Win32_Product* class that are returned. By default, *Win32_Product* returns an instance of each piece of MSI-installed software that exists on the computer; in some cases, this can result in hundreds of items returned and can also require several minutes to return any data. By using the *–filter* parameter, you do not necessarily cause the query to return more quickly, but you definitely reduce the amount of information that is returned.

```
Get-WmiObject -Class win32_product -filter "name like '%Microsoft .NET Framework 3.5%'"
```

Another way to write the previous query is to use Get-WmiObject to return the instances of the *Win32_Product* and to pipeline the results to the Where-Object cmdlet. Intuitively, it seems that using *–filter* with Get-WmiObject would be faster than pipelining. However, due to the efficiency of Windows PowerShell pipelining, there is not much difference between the performance of using the *–filter* parameter or pipelining the results. As shown here, when using the *–filter* parameter from Get-WmiObject, the command takes 19.10 seconds. When not using the *–filter* parameter but using the Where-Object cmdlet, the command takes 19.09 seconds. The second command is much easier to type and uses standard Windows PowerShell syntax.

```
PS C:\> Measure-command {Get-WmiObject -Class win32_product -filter "name like
'%Microsoft .NET Framework 3.5%'" } | select totalseconds


TotalSeconds
------------
19.1024836
PS C:\> Measure-command {Get-WmiObject -Class win32_product |
Where-Object { $_.name -match 'Microsoft .NET Framework 3.5' } } | Select TotalSeconds


TotalSeconds
------------
19.0902945
```

It is difficult to wait for nearly 20 seconds to find out which version of the .NET Framework is installed on a computer before you even begin to do anything else. One way to work around this is to use the [WMI] management object type accelerator, which allows you to retrieve information from WMI classes in much the same way that the Get-WmiObject cmdlet allows you to retrieve information. The difference is that [WMI] retrieves instance information and connects to a specific instance of a WMI class, which is great for speed. What's bad is that you need to supply [WMI] type accelerator with the specific key that identifies the instance. What's really bad is that, with the *Win32_Product* class, you have a composite key that is composed of three separate properties as listed here.

1. *IdentifyingNumber*

2. *Name*

3. *Version*

To use the [WMI] type accelerator, you use quotes around the class, the properties, and their values as shown here.

```
[WMI]"className.PropertyName=`"value`""
```

If you have a compound key for the class, the syntax looks like this.

```
[WMI]"className.PropertyName=`"value`",2ndProperty=`"value`""
```

Keep in mind that you need to escape the quotation marks, which are used to indicate the values for the properties. To do this, you can use the backtick in front of each quotation mark that is used for the property values.

```
PS C:\> [wmi]"Win32_Product.IdentifyingNumber=`"{CE2CDD62-0124-36CA-84D3-
9F4DCF5C5BD9}`",Name=`"Microsoft .NET Framework
 3.5 SP1`",Version=`"3.5.30729`""
IdentifyingNumber : {CE2CDD62-0124-36CA-84D3-9F4DCF5C5BD9}
Name              : Microsoft .NET Framework 3.5 SP1
Vendor            : Microsoft Corporation
Version           : 3.5.30729
Caption           : Microsoft .NET Framework 3.5 SP1
```

When I time this command using the Measure-Command cmdlet, it takes 180 milliseconds on my computer compared with 20 seconds, which is a dramatic improvement. However, there are problems with this approach. For one, the code needs to be updated for each version of the .NET Framework and for each service pack. For example, here is the code to check for .NET Framework 3.5 without SP1.

```
[wmi]"Win32_Product.IdentifyingNumber=`"{2FC099BD-AC9B-33EB-809C-
D332E1B27C40}`",Name=`"Microsoft .NET Framework 3.5`",Version=`"3.5.21022`""
```

You can see that every property has changed. Unfortunately, the type accelerator does not permit the use of wildcards. Wildcards can help the *name* and *version* properties, but they cannot aid in discovering the *identifyingNumber* property.

Determining .NET Framework Versions

Luís Canastreiro, Premier Field Engineer
Microsoft Portugal

When I write a script that depends on a feature from a particular version of the .NET Framework, such as version 3.5, I always like to include a test to ensure that the required version of the .NET Framework is installed. One basic test is to test the presence of the installation path: %SystemRoot%\Microsoft.NET\Framework\ v3.5. Because this folder does not exist if .NET Framework 3.5 has not been installed on the machine, this check helps me to ensure that the script will run properly.

Since the days of .NET Framework 2.0, a key has been created in the registry for each new version. I like to use this registry key because it can provide additional information such as when the version was actually installed, the path, the version number, and whether the version has been service pack installed. Figure 5-9 shows the registry key from a machine with .NET Framework version 3.5. This installation has been service pack installed.

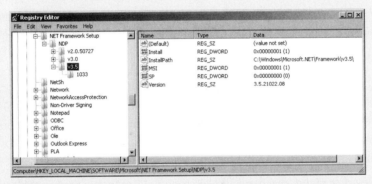

FIGURE 5-9 The registry provides an easy way to verify .NET Framework version information.

What is a bit confusing is that there is a difference between the Common Language Runtime (CLR) and the .NET Framework. It is quite possible to have a computer with the CLR 2.0 SP2 and .NET Framework 3.5 with SP1. When you install .NET Framework 3.5 SP1, you are upgrading the CLR to version 2.0 SP2. You can consider the .NET Framework as a package that includes the CLR plus a set of richly managed libraries for implementing GUIs, using Web services, accessing Windows operating system functionality, and so forth as well as the managed language compilers and tools.

Operating System Requirements

There is a wide range of operating systems on which Windows PowerShell 2.0 can be installed, ranging from Microsoft Windows XP to Windows 7, and they can all be considered for certain scripts that may rely upon the presence of a feature that only exists in particular versions of the operating system.

One way to obtain the operating system version is to use the *OSVersion* static property from the *System.Environment* .NET Framework class as shown here.

```
PS C:\> [environment]::OSVersion | Format-List *


Platform      : Win32NT
ServicePack   : Service Pack 1
Version       : 6.0.6001.65536
VersionString : Microsoft Windows NT 6.0.6001 Service Pack 1
```

As shown in the previous code, the version of the operating system is composed of a four-part number. The four parts are detailed here.

- **Major** Assemblies with the same name but different major versions are not interchangeable. For example, this part would be appropriate for a major rewrite of a product in which backward compatibility cannot be assumed.

- **Minor** If the name and major number on two assemblies are the same but the minor number is different, this indicates significant enhancement with the intention of backward compatibility. For example, this part would be appropriate on a point release of a product or a fully backward-compatible new version of a product.

- **Build** A difference in build number represents a recompilation of the same source. This part would be appropriate because of processor, platform, or compiler changes.

- **Revision** Assemblies with the same name, major, and minor version numbers but different revisions are intended to be fully interchangeable. This part would be appropriate to fix a security hole in a previously released assembly.

If you store the results of the *[environment]::OSVersion* static property into a variable, you have an instance of a *System.Version* object returned for the *version* property as shown here.

```
PS C:\> $os = [environment]::osversion
PS C:\> $os | Get-Member -MemberType property


   TypeName: System.OperatingSystem

Name          MemberType Definition
----          ---------- ----------
Platform      Property   System.PlatformID Platform {get;}
ServicePack   Property   System.String ServicePack {get;}
Version       Property   System.Version Version {get;}
VersionString Property   System.String VersionString {get;}
```

The advantage of this approach is that the *System.Version* class allows easy access to each of the different properties of the version number as shown here.

```
PS C:\> $os.Version | Get-Member -MemberType property


   TypeName: System.Version


Name            MemberType Definition
----            ---------- ----------
Build           Property   System.Int32 Build {get;}
Major           Property   System.Int32 Major {get;}
MajorRevision   Property   System.Int16 MajorRevision {get;}
Minor           Property   System.Int32 Minor {get;}
MinorRevision   Property   System.Int16 MinorRevision {get;}
Revision        Property   System.Int32 Revision {get;}
```

By using this approach, you have the ability to specify that you want the code to only run if it is on a particular version of the operating system. The GetOsVersionFunction.ps1 script illustrates this procedure. The GetOsVersionFunction.ps1 script begins with the *Get-OsVersion* function. In the function declaration, the input variable is defined as a reference type, which allows the function to return the operating system version information back to the calling portion of the script. The function declaration specifies the name of the function and any input variables as shown here.

```
Function Get-OsVersion([ref]$os)
```

The code block of the function retrieves the static *OSVersion* property from the *System.Environment* .NET Framework class and assigns it to the *Value* property of the *$os* variable as shown here.

```
$os.value = [environment]::OSVersion
```

Now, to use the *Get-OsVersion* function, you call the function by passing a reference type variable to it. The code here initializes the *$os* variable as null and then passes it to the function.

```
$os = $null
Get-OsVersion([ref]$os)
```

You can then use an *If … Else* type of statement to evaluate the major version of the operating system. To assist you in evaluating version numbers, you can refer to Table 5-5. You might find it surprising that both Windows Vista and Microsoft Windows Server 2008 have the same version numbers. If you find a match, you can then proceed to the next portion of the script; otherwise, you can exit the script as illustrated here.

```
if($os.version.major -ge 6)
  {
   "Windows Vista or greater detected"
  }
else
```

```
{
"Windows Vista or greater not detected"
exit
}
```

TABLE 5-5 Operating System Names and Versions

VERSION NUMBER	OPERATING SYSTEM NAME
5.1.2600	Windows XP
5.2.3790	Windows Server 2003
6.0.6001	Windows Vista
6.0.6001	Windows Server 2008
6.1.6801	Windows 7

The complete GetOsVersionFunction.ps1 script is shown here.

GetOsVersionFunction.ps1
```
Function Get-OsVersion([ref]$os)
{
 $os.value = [environment]::OSVersion
}


# *** entry point to script ***

$os = $null
Get-OsVersion([ref]$os)
if($os.version.major -ge 6)
 {
  "Windows Vista or greater detected"
 }
else
{
"Windows Vista or greater not detected"
exit
}
```

The *System.Environment* .NET Framework class does not have any remote features built into it. That is, you cannot give it a string and have it connect to a remote computer to retrieve information remotely. This is not an issue with Windows PowerShell 2.0. You can use the Invoke-Command cmdlet to run the command remotely as illustrated here.

```
PS C:\> $computers = "berlin","win7"
PS C:\> Invoke-Command -ComputerName $computers -ScriptBlock {[environment]::OSVersion }
```

```
PSComputerName      : berlin
RunspaceId          : d23f85ed-3f2b-465b-877a-37dd43125f40
PSShowComputerName  : True
Platform            : Win32NT
ServicePack         : Service Pack 1
Version             : 6.0.6001.65536
VersionString       : Microsoft Windows NT 6.0.6001 Service Pack 1

PSComputerName      : win7
RunspaceId          : 04b1ce80-19e9-4dde-9b8d-8725b032dfff
PSShowComputerName  : True
Platform            : Win32NT
ServicePack         :
Version             : 6.1.6801.0
VersionString       : Microsoft Windows NT 6.1.6801.0
```

INSIDE TRACK

Why Write PowerShell Scripts?

Jeffrey Snover, Distinguished Engineer
Microsoft Corporation

I think the scripting community is going to flood the world with script cmdlets because they are incredibly easy to write, share, and debug. You can post them on a blog and improve the world. Not only will people observe your functions, but they will see how you executed the function; some might even give you feedback on your script and teach you something in the process. I have certainly benefited from reading other people's scripts, and numerous people have taught me lessons in response to the scripts I've posted.

I love GUIs, but if you use a GUI all day long, you have sore arms by the end of the day. However, if you write a script, you have an artifact that you can use again and again to increase your productivity and value to your employer (and thus increase your employability and earning potential). You have an artifact that you can share with others and, in sharing, create a debt of gratitude. You have an artifact that people can review and admire and learn from using. You have an artifact that can be analyzed and critiqued and improved. When you script, you participate in a community of people who are learning with each additional script they use.

In Windows PowerShell 1.0, it is difficult to write a script because the functions do not allow you to generate the correct semantics, you cannot provide help for your functions, and it isn't easy to share scripts. With Windows PowerShell 2.0, we added extensions to functions and added modules to solve this scripting problem and make participation in the scripting community simple and easy.

I use both the command-line and the graphical versions of Windows PowerShell, but I no longer use Notepad for writing scripts. Windows PowerShell_ISE is tremendous for creating and debugging scripts.

What do I do with Windows PowerShell? I explore! What I love about Windows PowerShell is its ability to let you explore so many aspects of the system. Windows PowerShell makes it easy and safe to check such things as WMI, .NET, the registry, COM, a file—whatever. If I come across something useful, I write a script and often share it.

If you are just beginning to use Windows PowerShell, I want to tell you this: learn to learn. One of my favorite stories involves a group of novice and expert UNIX administrators who were given a written test, and the experts didn't score much higher than the novices. However, when the groups were put in front of a machine and given a hands-on examination, the experts won easily. What we learned was that, even though expert administrators may not necessarily remember more than novices, they are certainly experts at figuring out problems. Focus on learning. Learn how to use the Get-Help and Get-Member cmdlets. Learn how to use the object utilities. Then, start exploring. You'll be amazed at what you can accomplish by combining the basics, which is the point of a compositional system.

There isn't a command named DO-MYJOB. Instead, in Windows PowerShell, there is a toolkit that allows you to combine a few commands together to do your job. You need to learn how to put the pieces together and what the pieces are. Part of the process involves leveraging the community of people who are more than willing to help you with your problems if they can.

Application Requirements

Once you ensure that the script has the appropriate security rights and the correct version of the .NET Framework installed on the appropriate version of the operating system, you may still need to determine whether a particular application is running on your target machine. To check for an application, you can use either the Get-Process or Get-Service cmdlet—whichever one is appropriate.

The CheckService.ps1 script can be used to determine whether a particular service has been created on a computer and whether the service is running. To check for a service, the script uses an *If … Else* construction. Inside the *If* statement, the Get-Service cmdlet is used to obtain a list of all services that are defined on the current computer. The *–computername* parameter of the Get-Service cmdlet can be used to cause the cmdlet to retrieve information from a remote computer. Results from the Get-Service cmdlet are pipelined to the Where-Object cmdlet, which is used to filter the results. Two criteria are used inside the Where-Object cmdlet: the status of the service, which must be running, and the actual name of the service itself. This section of the code is shown here.

```
Get-Service |
Where-Object { $_.status -eq 'running' -AND $_.name -eq $serviceName }
```

If this condition is satisfied, then the script enters the code block associated with the *If* statement. In this example, the script prints the fact that the service is running. If the service does not exist or is not running, the script prints a message that the service is not running. Inside these two code blocks is where you place your code that depends on a particular state of a given service. The completed CheckService.ps1 script is shown here.

CheckService.ps1
```
$serviceName = "ZuneBusEnum"
if(
    Get-Service |
    Where-Object { $_.status -eq 'running' -AND $_.name -eq $serviceName }
  )
  {
   "$serviceName is running"
  } #end if
ELSE
  {
   "$serviceName is not running"
  } #end else
```

At other times, a particular process and not a service must be running. To verify the existence of a process, you can use the Get-Process cmdlet. The logic can be simplified because a process only exists if it is running; a compound WHERE clause is not required. The simplified logic is shown here.

```
Get-Process |
Where-Object { $_.ProcessName -eq $processName }
```

The remainder of the CheckProcess.ps1 script is similar to the CheckService.ps1 script as shown here.

CheckProcess.ps1
```
$processName = "iexplore"
if(
    Get-Process |
    Where-Object { $_.ProcessName -eq $processName }
  )
  {
   "$processName is running"
  } #end if
ELSE
  {
   "$processName is not running"
  } #end else
```

Snap-in Requirements

The extensible nature of Windows PowerShell is one of its greatest features. You can download snap-ins from the Internet that come equipped with dozens of free cmdlets. You can also purchase commercial software that solves very real mission-critical problems from major software companies. Both solutions have one thing in common: the cmdlets are delivered housed within snap-ins. There are two requirements: the snap-in must be installed and it must be loaded.

To comply with these requirements, you can use the CheckSnapin.ps1 script. The CheckSnapin.ps1 script begins with the *CheckSnapin* function, which takes the name of the snap-in you are looking for as the input parameter. The main logic of the function uses an *If* statement to determine whether the snap-in is currently running as shown here.

```
if(!(Get-PSSnapin |
    Where-Object { $_.name -eq $name }))
```

If the snap-in is loaded, then nothing happens in the script. However, if the snap-in is not running, the script checks whether it is registered. If the snap-in is not registered, it means that it is not installed. The script terminates at this point as shown here.

```
if(!(Get-PSSnapin -registered |
        Where-Object { $_.name -eq $name }))
    {
       "$name is not registered. Exiting script."
       exit
    } #end if registered
```

If the snap-in is registered but not currently running, then the script attempts to load the snap-in as shown here.

```
ELSE
    {
        add-psSnapin -name $name
    } #end else registered
 } #end if not get-pssnapin
```

However, if the snap-in is already running, the script prints this fact as shown here.

```
ELSE
  { "$name cmdlets already loaded" }
```

The complete CheckSnapin.ps1 script is shown here.

CheckSnapin.ps1

```powershell
function CheckSnapin($name)
{
 if(!(Get-PSSnapin |
     Where-Object { $_.name -eq $name }))
  {
    if(!(Get-PSSnapin -registered |
         Where-Object { $_.name -eq $name }))
     {
        "$name is not registered. Exiting script."
        exit
     } #end if registered
    ELSE
     {
        add-psSnapin -name $name
     } #end else registered
  } #end if not get-pssnapin
 ELSE
  { "$name cmdlets already loaded" }
} #end CheckSnapin

CheckSnapin("pscx")
```

Additional Resources

- The TechNet Script Center at *http://www.microsoft.com/technet/scriptcenter* contains numerous script examples.
- Take a look at *Windows PowerShell™ Scripting Guide* (Microsoft Press, 2008).
- On the companion media, you will find all of the scripts referred to in this chapter.
- A history of the .NET Framework versions can be found at *http://blogs.msdn.com/dougste/archive/2007/09/06/version-history-of-the-clr-2-0.aspx.*
- You can find help on how to determine which version of the .NET Framework is installed at *http://support.microsoft.com/kb/318785.*
- The entry point to the MSDN Web site is found at *http://msdn.microsoft.com.*

Configuring the Script Environment

Windows PowerShell 2.0 provides many ways in which the scripting environment can be customized or tailored to individual needs. This capability opens tremendous opportunities to change the way in which Windows PowerShell starts, the way it runs, and even the syntax of commonly used functions. This flexibility comes at a price, however: it's possible to customize the scripting environment to such an extent that you do not know what the commands are, how they are used, or even what you should type to find Help. In this chapter, you will examine the ways in which leading experts customize their environment and also explore options to assist both power users and corporate IT personnel in obtaining the most functionality from this rich and powerful tool.

Configuring a Profile

By default, there are no profiles when Windows PowerShell is installed. A profile can be used to configure the Windows PowerShell scripting environment, but it can also be used to make working from the PowerShell command line more convenient. The Windows PowerShell profile is a useful place to create and store four different types of items:

- Aliases
- Functions
- PSDrives
- Variables

Creating Aliases

Aliases are helpful from a usability standpoint. Consider a command, such as `Measure-Object`, that is used to count information and provide statistical information, such as the minimum and maximum values of an object. `Measure-Object` can be a bit cumbersome to type from the command line. Given the relative frequency of its use, `Measure-Object` becomes a good candidate for aliasing.

Verifying the Existence of an Alias

Prior to creating a new alias, it is a best practice to determine whether there is a suitable alias already created for the cmdlet in question. By default, Windows PowerShell ships with more than 130 predefined aliases for its 271 cmdlets. When you consider that several cmdlets have more than one alias defined, you can see that there is great opportunity for the creation of additional aliases. The ListCmdletsWithMoreThanOneAlias.ps1 script lists all of the cmdlets with more than one alias defined as shown here.

```
ListCmdletsWithMoreThanOneAlias.ps1
Get-Alias |
Group-Object -Property definition |
Sort-Object -Property count -Descending |
Where-Object { $_.count -gt 2 }
```

When the ListCmdletsWithMoreThanOneAlias.ps1 script is run, the following appears.

```
Count Name                       Group
----- ----                       -----
    6 Remove-Item                {del, erase, rd, ri...}
    3 Set-Location               {cd, chdir, sl}
    3 Get-History                {ghy, h, history}
    3 Get-ChildItem              {dir, gci, ls}
    3 Get-Content                {cat, gc, type}
    3 Move-Item                  {mi, move, mv}
    3 Copy-Item                  {copy, cp, cpi}
```

To see whether an alias for the `Measure-Object` cmdlet exists, you can use the `Get-Alias` cmdlet and the *–definition* parameter as shown here.

```
PS C:\> Get-Alias -Definition Measure-Object

CommandType     Name                                    Definition
-----------     ----                                    ----------
Alias           measure                                 Measure-Object
```

If you like the alias *measure*, you can simply begin to use that alias. However, you may decide that the readability of the alias *measure* is hampered by the fact that it only saves two key strokes. Due to the implementation of the tab expansion feature, all you need to do is type **measure-o** and press the TAB key. In general, when creating personal aliases, I prefer to sacrifice readability for ease of use. My favorite aliases are one- and two-letter aliases. I use one-letter aliases for commands I frequently use. Remember that one-letter aliases are also the most obscure and they do not always make sense unless you happen to remember why you created the alias in the first place. I use two-letter aliases for most of my other alias needs. The two-letter combination can easily correspond to the verb-noun naming convention; therefore, *mo* is a logical alias for the Measure-Object cmdlet. To ensure the availability of mo for Measure-Object, use the Get-Alias cmdlet as shown here.

```
PS C:\> Get-Alias -Name mo
```

How Many Two-Letter Aliases Are There?

The two-letter alias namespace is rather large, but how large is it really? You must take every letter in the a–z range and pair them with every other letter in the a–z range to get the answer. If you are good with math, then you already know that there are 676 possible letter combinations. However, if your math skills are a bit rusty or just for fun, you can write a Windows PowerShell script to figure out the answer. The problem with this approach is that you cannot use the *range* operator (..) to produce a range of letters. The *range* operator works with numbers; 1..10 automatically creates a range of numbers with the values 1 through 10 and can save you a great deal of typing. However, because you have ASCII numeric representations of the letters a–z, you can use the *range* operator to create a range of the letters. The ASCII value 97 is the a character, and ASCII 122 is z. Once you determine the numeric range, you can use the ForEach-Object cmdlet and convert each letter to a character by using the [char] type. You can store the resulting array of letters in the *$letters* variable. After doing two loops through the array, you can store the resulting letter combinations in the *$lettercombination* variable, which is constrained as an array by using the [array] type. The Measure-Object cmdlet is used to count the number of possible letter combinations. The ListTwoLetterCombinations.ps1 script is shown here.

```
ListTwoLetterCombinations.ps1
$letterCombinations = $null
$asciiNum = 97..122
$letters = $asciiNum | ForEach-Object { [char]$_ }
Foreach ($1letter in $letters)
{
 Foreach ($2letter in $letters)
 {
  [array]$letterCombinations += "$1letter$2letter"
```

```
    }
  }
  "There are " + ($letterCombinations | Measure-Object).count +
  " possible combinations"
  "They are listed here: "
  $letterCombinations
```

To create a new alias, you can use either the `New-Alias` or `Set-Alias` cmdlet. You can also use the `New-Item` cmdlet and target the alias drive. The problem with the latter technique is that it does not support the *–description* parameter, which allows you to specify additional information about the alias. Another problem with using `New-Item` to create an alias is that more typing is involved. So, as a best practice, I always use either the `New-Alias` or `Set-Alias` cmdlet. In choosing between the two cmdlets, which one should you use when creating a new alias? Before answering that question, I will discuss what the cmdlets are intended to be used for. The `New-Alias` cmdlet obviously creates a new alias. The `Set-Alias` cmdlet is used to modify an existing alias; if an alias does not exist, it creates the alias for you. Therefore, many people use `Set-Alias` to both create and modify an alias. The danger in using the `Set-Alias` cmdlet is that you can inadvertently modify a previously existing alias with no notification. If this is your desired behavior, however, then using the `Set-Alias` approach is fine.

A better approach is to use the `New-Alias` cmdlet when creating an alias. `New-Alias` allows you to specify the *–description* parameter and to receive notification if an alias that you are trying to create already exists. To assign a description to an alias when creating it, you can use the *–description* parameter as shown here.

```
New-Alias -Name mo -Value Measure-Object -Description "MrEd Alias"
```

In an enterprise scripting environment, many companies like to define a corporate set of aliases, which provides for a consistent environment. A network administrator working on one machine can be assured that a particular alias is available. Corporate aliases also help to ensure a predictable and consistent environment. By using the same value for the *–description* parameter of the alias, it is easy to list all corporate aliases. To do this, you can filter the list of aliases by the *–description* parameter as shown here.

```
PS C:\> Get-Alias | Where-Object { $_.description -eq 'mred alias' }
```

```
CommandType     Name                      Definition
-----------     ----                      ----------
Alias           mo                        Measure-Object
```

When using the *–eq* operator in the code block of the `Where-Object` cmdlet, the filter is case insensitive. If you need a case-sensitive operator, then you can use *–ceq*. The "c" is added to all of the operators to form a case-sensitive form of the operator—by default, the operators are case insensitive. As shown here, when using the case-sensitive operator, the filter does not return any aliases.

```
PS C:\> Get-Alias | Where-Object { $_.description -ceq 'mred alias' }
PS C:\>
```

In addition to specifying the *–description* parameter, many companies also like to use the *–option* parameter to make the alias either read-only or constant. To make the alias read-only, you supply the *read-only* keyword to the *–option* parameter as shown here.

```
New-Alias -Name mo -Value Measure-Object -Description "MrEd Alias" -Option
readonly
```

The advantage of making the alias read-only is that this offers protection against accidental modification or deletion as shown in Figure 6-1.

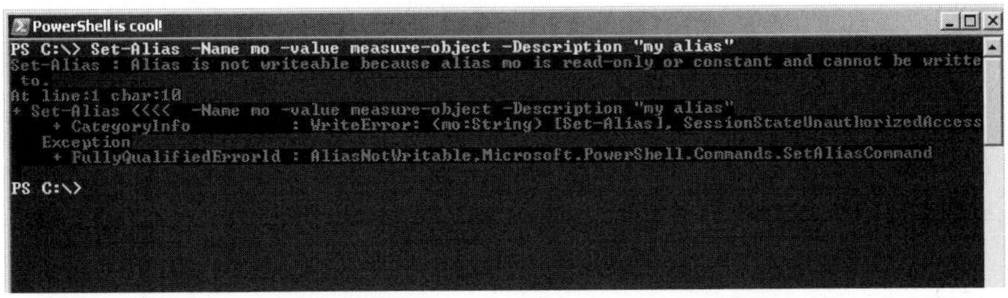

FIGURE 6-1 Attempts to modify a read-only alias generate an error message.

An additional advantage to making the alias read-only is that the alias can be modified or deleted if needed. If you want to modify the description, you can use the Set-Alias cmdlet to specify the name, value the new description, and use the *–force* parameter as shown here.

```
Set-Alias -Name mo -value measure-object -Description "my alias" -Force
```

If you need to delete a read-only cmdlet, you can use the Remove-Item cmdlet and specify the *–force* parameter as shown here.

```
Remove-Item Alias:\mo -Force
```

To create a constant alias, you can use the *constant* keyword with the *–option* parameter as shown here.

```
New-Alias -Name mo -Value Measure-Object -Description "MrEd Alias" -Option constant
```

As a best practice, you should not create constant aliases unless you are certain that you do not need to either modify it or delete it. A constant alias can neither be modified nor deleted—in effect, they really are constant. The error message is a bit misleading in that it states that the alias is either read-only or constant, and it suggests attempting to use the *–force* parameter. The reason that this is misleading is because the error message is displayed even when the command is run with the *–force* parameter. This error message is shown in Figure 6-2.

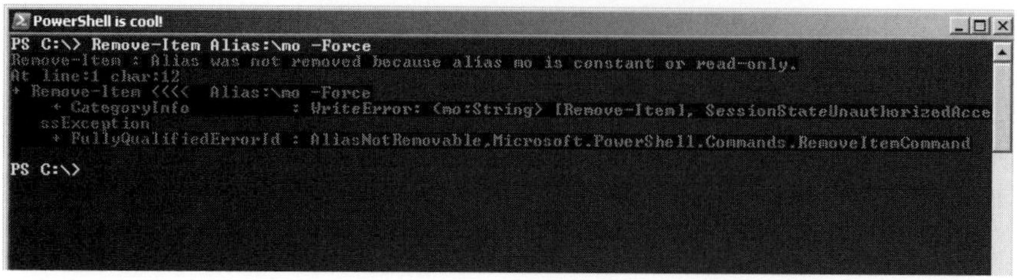

FIGURE 6-2 An error message is generated when attempting to delete a constant alias.

Creating Functions

Functions provide a nearly endless capability of customization from within Windows PowerShell. The profile is a great place to supply some of this customization. For example, when using the Get-Help cmdlet, suppose that you prefer to see the full article. However, you also know that, in most cases, the article is too long to fit on a single screen. Therefore, you like to pipeline the output to the *more* function, which provides paging control. If you are looking for information about the Get-Process cmdlet, for example, the command is shown here.

```
Get-Help Get-Process -Full | more
```

There is nothing wrong with typing the previous command; however, even when paired with tab expansion, it is more than 20 keystrokes. It will not take long before you become tired of typing such a command. Therefore, this command is a perfect candidate for a function. When naming functions, it is a best practice to use the verb-noun naming convention because this syntax is familiar to users of Windows PowerShell and because you can take advantage of tab expansion. As shown here, I named our function *Get-MoreHelp*.

Get-MoreHelp.ps1
```
Function Get-MoreHelp()
{
 Get-Help $args[0] -Full |
 more
} #end Get-MoreHelp
```

The *Get-MoreHelp* function begins by using the *Function* keyword to declare the function. After the *Function* keyword, you specify the name of the function, which in this example is Get-MoreHelp. The empty parentheses are not required after the function name; parentheses are used to define parameters, and without any parameters, the parentheses are not required. I generally include parentheses as an indicator that a parameter could be specified in the position as shown here.

```
Function Get-MoreHelp()
```

Following the *Function* keyword, the function opens the code block by using an opening curly bracket. When typing the function, I always open the code block with one curly bracket and, immediately, type the closing curly bracket on the next line. In this way, I never forget to close a code block. As a best practice, I always include a comment indicating that the bottom curly bracket closes the function. End comments are also a tremendous help when it's time to troubleshoot the script because they promote readability and make it easier to understand the delimiters of the function. In addition, if you have a long function that scrolls off of the screen, the end comment, with its repetition of the function name, makes it easier to create the alias for the function as shown here.

```
{

} #end Get-MoreHelp
```

The *Get-MoreHelp* function uses the *$args* automatic variable to hold the argument that is passed to the function when it is called. Because the Get-Help cmdlet does not accept an array for the *name* parameter, you can use [0] to index into the first element of the *$args* array. If, as is required, there is only one item passed to the function, the item is always element 0 of the array. The function passes the *–full* switched parameter to the Get-Help cmdlet. The resulting Help information is passed along the pipeline via the pipe | symbol as shown here.

```
Get-Help $args[0] -full |
```

Overriding Existing Commands

Because it is possible that the *Get-MoreHelp* function could return more than a single screen of textual information, the function pipelines the Help information to the *more* function. Because functions are first-class citizens in Windows PowerShell, they have priority over executables and even over native PowerShell cmdlets. Due to this fact, it is easy to modify the behavior of an executable or cmdlet by creating a function with the same name as an existing executable, which is illustrated by the *more* function. More.com is an executable that provides the ability to return information to the screen one page at a time—it has been available since the DOS days. The *more* function is used to modify the behavior of more.com. The content of the *more* function is shown here.

```
param([string[]]$paths)
if($paths)
{
    foreach ($file in $paths)
    {
        Get-Content $file | more.com
    }
}
else
{
    $input | more.com
}
```

By looking at the content of the *more* function, you can see that there has been a useful addition to the functionality of more.com. If you supply a path to the *more* function, it retrieves the content of the file and pipelines the result to the more.com executable as shown in Figure 6-3.

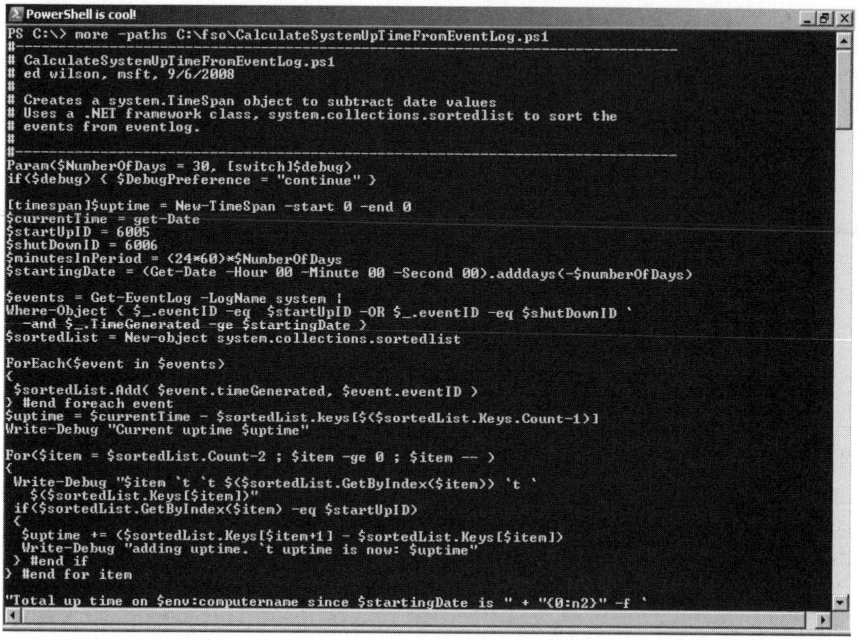

FIGURE 6-3 Passing a path to the *more* function retrieves the content and pipes the results to more.com.

Alias the Function

When I create utility functions, I generally like to create an alias to enable quick and easy access to the function. It is possible to create the function and the alias in the same script, but not within the function definition. The problem arises in that, within the function definition, the function has not yet been created; therefore, you cannot create an alias for a function that does not yet exist. However, there is nothing wrong with creating the alias and the function in the same script. Interestingly enough, you can create the alias on a line either before or after the function is declared. The position does not matter.

Get-MoreHelpWithAlias.ps1
```
Function Get-MoreHelp()
{
 Get-Help $args[0] -full |
 more
} #End Get-MoreHelp
New-Alias -name gmh -value Get-MoreHelp -Option allscope
```

Loop the Array

Because the *$args* variable returns an array, you can use *$args to* add the ability to pass two or more pieces of information and receive Help for each topic. To do this, you can use the *for* statement to loop through the elements of *$args*. The *for* statement uses three parameters: the beginning, the destination, and the method of travel. In this example, the variable *$i* is used to keep track of the position within the array. The variable *$i* is set equal to 0, and the *–le* operator, less than or equal to, is used to allow the loop to continue for the number of times represented by the number of items in *$args*. As the loop progresses, the value of *$i* is incremented by 1 during each loop by using the *$i++* construction as shown here.

```
For($i = 0 ;$i -le $args.count ; $i++)
```

One small change is required to the line of code that calls the Get-Help cmdlet. Instead of using *$args*[0], which always retrieves the first element in the array, you can change the 0 to *$i*. As the value of *$i* increases for each loop, the Get-Help cmdlet queries the next item in the array. This modified line of code is shown here.

```
Get-Help $args[$i] -full |
```

The remainder of the *Get-MoreHelp* function is the same as that found in the previous versions discussed earlier. The complete function is shown in the Get-MoreHelp2.ps1 script.

```
Get-MoreHelp2.ps1
Function Get-MoreHelp
{
 # .help Get-MoreHelp Get-Command Get-Process
 For($i = 0 ;$i -le $args.count ; $i++)
 {
  Get-Help $args[$i] -full |
  more
 } #end for
} #end Get-MoreHelp
New-Alias -name gmh -value Get-MoreHelp -Option allscope
```

To run the *Get-MoreHelp* function, you can use the *gmh* alias and supply it one or more cmdlet names to obtain Help. This process is shown in Figure 6-4 in which the function code was typed directly into the Windows PowerShell console.

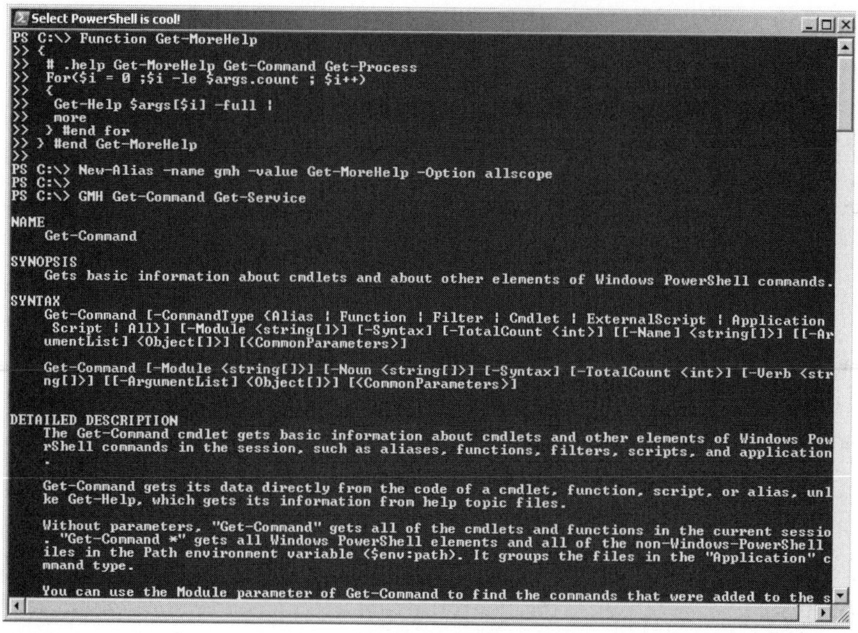

FIGURE 6-4 You can use an alias for a function to facilitate ease of use.

Passing Multiple Parameters

When using a function, it is quite common to want to accept two or more parameters for input, which adds flexibility and usefulness to the function. In Windows PowerShell, there are two choices. The first method of passing parameters is to use the *$args* automatic variable as shown in the previous section. Another way to pass parameters is to use named parameters. When named parameters are used with a script, they are preceded by the *Param* statement. To use a named parameter within a function, you do not need to use the *Param* statement. You simply supply variables in each position in which you want a parameter. The name of the variable becomes the name of the parameter. There are a few tricks to keep in mind when using both methods of passing multiple parameters. To that end, let's first examine the *$args* variable in a bit more detail.

Multiple Parameters with *$args*

One way to pass two parameters is to use the *$args* automatic variable. When passing two values to the function, you can index into the array to retrieve a specific value. In the *Get-WmiClass* function, two values are passed when calling the function. The first value is used to hold the WMI namespace to search for WMI class names, and the second value is the type of WMI class for which to search. The *Get-WmiClass* function is useful for locating WMI classes. Use of *Get-WmiClass* is shown in Figure 6-5.

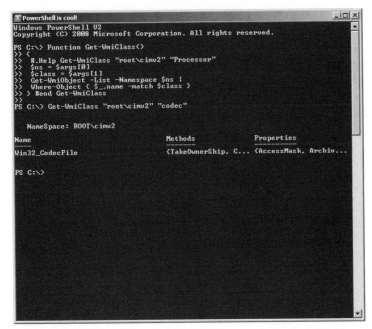

FIGURE 6-5 The *$args* variable can support positional arguments.

The *Get-WmiClass* function begins by retrieving two values from the *$args* variable. The *$args* variable is an automatic variable and is populated with whatever is fed to the function. The element from the first position is stored in the *$ns* variable, and the second element is kept in the *$class* variable as shown here.

```
$ns = $args[0]
$class = $args[1]
```

The `Get-WmiObject` cmdlet has a *–list* switched parameter that produces a listing of all WMI classes in the namespace. The namespace used is the one specified in the first position of the command that is used to call the function. The resulting listing of all WMI classes in the particular namespace is shunted to the pipeline as shown here.

```
Get-WmiObject -List -Namespace $ns |
```

To make the list of WMI classes useful, the `Where-Object` cmdlet is used to filter out the unwanted WMI class names. Inside the code block for the `Where-Object` cmdlet, the automatic *$_* variable is used to refer to the current item on the pipeline. The *–match* operator allows you to use a regular expression if desired to filter out the list of WMI class names. This line of code is shown here.

```
Where-Object { $_.name -match $class }
```

The complete Get-WmiClass.ps1 script is shown here.

Get-WmiClass.ps1

```
Function Get-WmiClass()
{
  #.Help Get-WmiClass "root\cimv2" "Processor"
  $ns = $args[0]
  $class = $args[1]
  Get-WmiObject -List -Namespace $ns |
  Where-Object { $_.name -match $class }
} #end Get-WmiClass
```

Multiple Named Parameters

When you have more than two parameters to supply to a function, it might become confusing to keep track of both the position and the meaning of the parameter. In addition, when using named parameters, you can apply type constraints to prevent basic types of errors that can occur when supplying values from the command line.

In the Get-WmiClass2.ps1 script, the *Get-WmiClass* function is rewritten to take advantage of command-line arguments. The primary change involves moving the *$ns* and *$class* variables inside the parentheses following the name of the function. In addition, because both the namespace and the class names should be strings, you can use the [string] type constraint to prevent the inadvertent entry of an illegal value, such as an integer. Because the revised function is using named parameters, the two lines that parse the *$args* variable are also removed. The Get-WmiClass2.ps1 script file is therefore shorter than the Get-WmiClass.ps1 script, and it has more capability. The first line of the *Get-WmiClass* function is shown here.

```
Function Get-WmiClass([string]$ns, [string]$class)
```

An example of the value of the type constraints is shown in Figure 6-6.

In the first example, the *Get-WmiClass* function is called with the value of 5 for the *–ns* parameter, which violates the [string] type constraint for the *–ns* parameter. The resulting error is "Invalid parameter."

In the second example shown in Figure 6-6, the *Get-WmiClass* function is called with the value of *root/cimv3* for the *–ns* parameter. Because there is no *root/cimv3* namespace in the WMI hierarchy (at least not yet), the function actually executes. The resulting error comes from WMI, which states the problem as an "invalid namespace." As a best practice, you should always apply type constraints to your function parameters. The rudimentary protection afforded by type constraints easily justifies the minimal effort required to type them in.

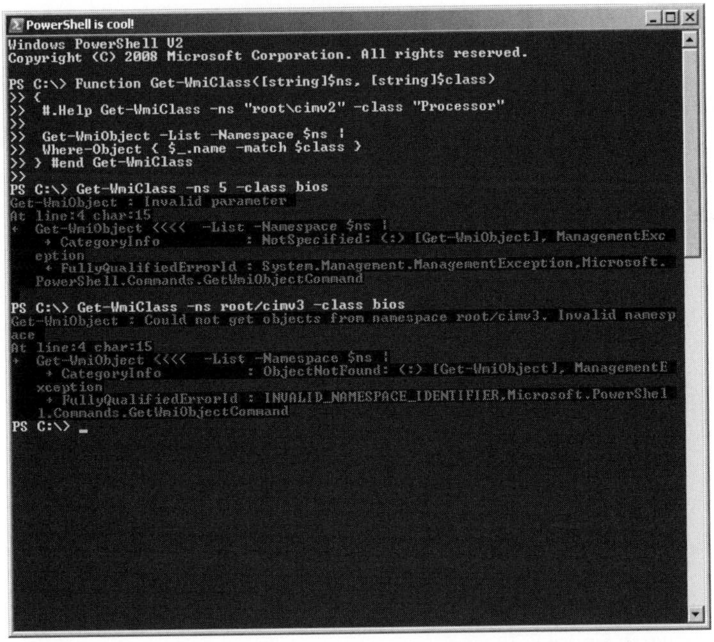

FIGURE 6-6 Type constraints placed on function parameters cause detailed error messages to display when violated.

To call the *Get-WmiClass* function, you can use the entire parameter name, a shortened unique version of the parameter name, or no parameter at all. Examples demonstrating each way to call the function are shown here. When supplying a parameter, you only need to type enough of the parameter name to ensure that it is unique. As a best practice, you should take this feature into account when naming parameters. If each parameter begins with a unique letter, users of the function can supply single-letter parameter names and still maintain a rudimentary level of readability. As an example, in the *Get-WmiClass* function, if you call the namespace *name space* and call the class name simply *name*, then you will be required to type the entire word **name** for the *–name* parameter and to type **names** for the namespace. *–Name* and *–namespace* parameters do not shorten very well as illustrated in the code shown here.

```
Get-WmiClass -ns "root\cimv2" -class "disk"
Get-WmiClass -n root\cimv2 -c disk
Get-WmiClass root\cimv2 disk
```

> **NOTE** When using named parameters with functions, you do not need to include a string inside quotation marks unless the string contains a comma, semicolon, or other special character that can be misinterpreted by the run-time engine. When working from the command line, I often take advantage of this technique to reduce typing. However, when working in a script, I like to include the quotation marks to improve readability and understandability of the code.

The complete Get-WmiClass2.ps1 script is shown here.

Get-WmiClass2.ps1
```
Function Get-WmiClass([string]$ns, [string]$class)
{
 #.Help Get-WmiClass -ns "root\cimv2" -class "Processor"

 Get-WmiObject -List -Namespace $ns |
 Where-Object { $_.name -match $class }
} #end Get-WmiClass
```

You can also create an alias for the function when you define the function. As the alias was used for the *Get-WmiClass* function, you can use the Get-Alias cmdlet to check for the existence of the chosen alias letter combination of *gwc* (selecting the first letter of each main word in the function name). You can use the following command to see whether the *gwc* alias is available.

```
Get-Alias -Name gwc
```

This is one occasion when you hope to receive an error because it means your chosen alias can be used. The error is shown in Figure 6-7.

The completed Get-WmiClassWithAlias.ps1 script is shown here.

Get-WmiClassWithAlias.ps1
```
Function Get-WmiClass([string]$ns, [string]$class)
{
 #.Help Get-WmiClass -ns "root\cimv2" -class "Processor"

 Get-WmiObject -List -Namespace $ns |
 Where-Object { $_.name -match $class }
} #end Get-WmiClass
New-Alias -Name gwc -Value Get-WmiClass -Description "Mred Alias" `
-Option readonly,allscope
```

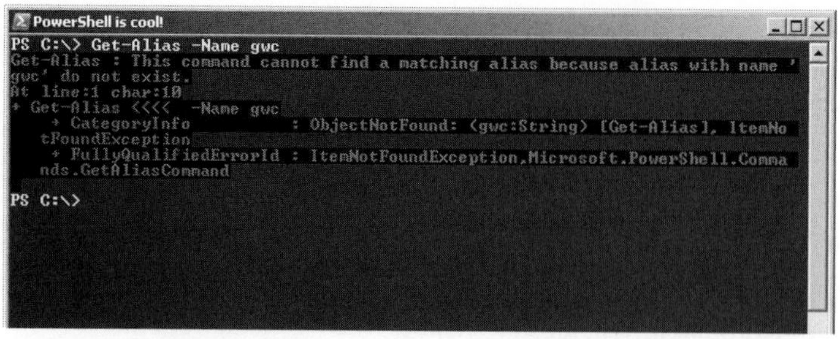

FIGURE 6-7 An error message means that the queried alias is not in use.

Creating Variables

As with creating aliases, there are several different ways to create a variable and assign a value to it. You can use the `New-Item` cmdlet on the variable drive as shown here.

```
New-Item -Name temp -Value $env:TEMP -Path variable:
```

You can also use the `Set-Item` cmdlet to create a variable. The advantage to using `Set-Item` is that it does not generate an error if the variable already exists. The following example uses `Set-Item` to create a variable. Keep in mind that the `Set-Item` cmdlet does not have a *–name* parameter.

```
Set-Item -Value $env:TEMP -Path variable:\temp
```

Neither `New-Item` nor `Set-Item` has the ability to specify the *–option* or *–description* parameter. This is an important distinction with variables because you cannot create a constant or a read-only variable without using either `Set-Variable` or `New-Variable`. If a variable already exists and you use the `Set-Variable` cmdlet, the value of the variable is overwritten if it has not been marked read-only or constant. If the variable is marked read-only, you can still modify its value by specifying the *–force* parameter. If the variable is marked as constant, the only way to modify its value is to close the Windows PowerShell console and start over with a new value.

You can also create a variable and assign a value to it at the same time. This technique is often used when the value to be stored in the variable is the result of a calculation, or concatenation. In this example, you decide to create a variable named *$wuLog* to store the path to the Windows Update Log, which is stored in a rather obscure location deep in the user's profile under a folder named AppData. While there is an environmental variable for the local application data folder, the path to the Windows Update Log continues to go on a few levels deeper prior to terminating with the WindowsUpdate.log file. As a best practice, you should use the path cmdlets when building file paths, such as `Join-Path`, to avoid concatenation errors. By using the environmental *$localappdata* variable and `Join-Path` with the *–resolve* switched parameter, you also have a formula that stores the path to the Windows Update Log file on any user's computer, which is exactly the type of variable you want to create and store in a user's Windows PowerShell profile. This command is shown here.

```
PS C:\> $wuLog = Join-Path -Path $env:LOCALAPPDATA `
-ChildPath microsoft\windows\windowsupdate.log -Resolve
PS C:\> $wuLog
C:\Users\edwils.NORTHAMERICA\AppData\Local\microsoft\windows\windowsupdate.log
```

When using a variable to hold a computed value, you are not limited to using a direct value assignment. You can use the `New-Variable` cmdlet to perform exactly the same task.

```
PS C:\> New-Variable -Name wulog -Value (Join-Path -Path $env:LOCALAPPDATA `
-ChildPath microsoft\windows\windowsupdate.log -Resolve)
```

NOTE When using the New-Variable cmdlet to create a variable that holds a computed result, you often need to use parentheses to force the value to be created prior to attempting to assign it to the *-value* parameter. You may see an error message about a missing or invalid parameter. When the New-Variable cmdlet sees a parameter outside of a set of parentheses, it attempts to locate that parameter. An example of such an error is shown in Figure 6-8.

FIGURE 6-8 An error message when creating a new variable due to missing parentheses

You can also use automatic variables when creating variables for your profile. A large number of applications place files in the user's Documents directory. While this location is convenient for applications and for users who access documents via a link off the Start menu, it is nearly impossible to locate the Documents folder via the command line. An additional problem is that the Documents folder may not be displayed from the user's Start menu. As shown in Figure 6-9, the folder may have been deselected.

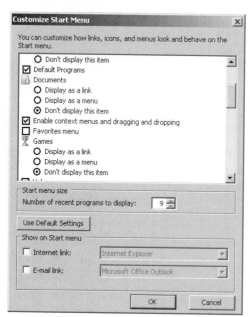

FIGURE 6-9 Users can choose not to display the Documents folder.

To facilitate ease of access to the user's Documents folder, you may decide to create a variable that can easily be used to refer to the path. This is another good opportunity to use the `Join-Path` cmdlet to aid in building the location to the Documents folder. An automatic variable already points to the user's Home directory. The Home directory on my Windows Vista laptop points to the %username% folder under the Users folder as shown here.

```
PS C:\> $home
C:\Users\edwils.NORTHAMERICA
```

Because the Documents folder resides under this Home directory as shown in Figure 6-10, you can add to this location and build the path to the Documents directory.

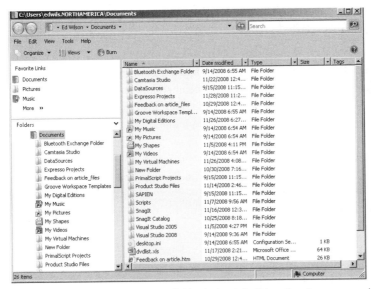

FIGURE 6-10 The user's Documents folder is the default location for many applications.

By using the `New-Variable` cmdlet, you can specify the *–value* parameter, which is contained in a set of parentheses so as to resolve the value of the `Join-Path` command prior to assigning it to the *docs* variable. The variable is read-only, which allows you to modify it if needed, but it is also protected from accidental deletion or modification. The *–description* parameter provides an easy way to keep track of all of the custom variables as shown here.

```
New-Variable -Name docs -Value (Join-Path -Path $home -ChildPath
documents) `
-Option readonly -Description "MrEd Variable"
```

> **IMPORTANT** When I was first learning Windows PowerShell, I was often frustrated when attempting to use the `New-Variable`, `Set-Variable`, and `Remove-Variable` cmdlets. This occurred because a variable is prefixed with the dollar sign when working at the command line, but the *–name* parameter does not use the dollar sign as part of the name of the variable.

Another way to obtain the path to the Documents folder is to use the *WshShell* object from VBScript. Because Windows PowerShell provides easy access to Component Object Model (COM) objects, there is no reason to avoid these objects. One way to use this *WshShell* object is to create and use the object in the same line as shown here.

```
$docs = (New-Object -ComObject Wscript.Shell).specialFolders.item("Documents")
```

From a best practice standpoint, there are at least two problems with the previous syntax. The most obvious issue is that the code is not very readable. Even though this usage is rather common and most developers employ these types of construction, common sense should prevail. It is better to split the command into two lines of code as shown here.

```
$wshShell = New-Object -ComObject Wscript.Shell
$docs = $wshShell.SpecialFolders.Item("Documents")
```

The additional advantage to the previous two-line technique is that you now have access to the entire *WshShell* object, which provides access to many useful properties and methods. As an example, in addition to resolving the path to the Documents special folder, the *WshSpecialFolders* object (returned by querying the *SpecialFolders* property of the *WshShell* object) can also be used to provide access to the following folders:

- AllUsersDesktop
- AllUsersStartMenu
- AllUsersPrograms
- AllUsersStartup
- Desktop
- Favorites
- Fonts
- Documents
- NetHood
- PrintHood
- Programs
- Recent
- SendTo
- StartMenu
- Startup
- Templates

Without creating an intermediate variable, any of the listed special folders can be resolved to the path as shown here. If the *$wshShell* object is created in the profile, the values from the *SystemFolders* property are always available for use within the scripting environment or when working from the command line.

```
$wshShell.SpecialFolders.Item("StartUp")
```

In addition to the ability to easily resolve the previously listed special folders, the *WshShell* object also provides a number of other useful properties and methods. Its members are shown in Table 6-1.

TABLE 6-1 Members of the *WshShell* Object

NAME	MEMBERTYPE	DEFINITION
AppActivate	Method	bool AppActivate (Variant, Variant)
CreateShortcut	Method	IDispatch CreateShortcut (string)
Exec	Method	IWshExec Exec (string)
ExpandEnvironmentStrings	Method	string ExpandEnvironmentStrings (string)
LogEvent	Method	bool LogEvent (Variant, string, string)
Popup	Method	int Popup (string, Variant, Variant, Variant)
RegDelete	Method	void RegDelete (string)
RegRead	Method	Variant RegRead (string)
RegWrite	Method	void RegWrite (string, Variant, Variant)
Run	Method	int Run (string, Variant, Variant)
SendKeys	Method	void SendKeys (string, Variant)
Environment	ParameterizedProperty	IWshEnvironment Environment (Variant) {get}
CurrentDirectory	Property	string CurrentDirectory () {get} {set}
SpecialFolders	Property	IWshCollection SpecialFolders () {get}

The *popup* method is useful as well as easy to use. As shown in Figure 6-11, the *popup* method produces a pop-up dialog box.

FIGURE 6-11 Pop-up message from the *WshShell* object

To create a pop-up message box, you only need to supply the first value of the method signature. This value is used for the message displayed in the middle of the pop-up box. The second value is a number that controls how long the pop-up box is displayed. The third value is used to change the title of the pop-up box. The last position of the method call controls the button configuration of the pop-up box. If you supply only the first value, you receive a pop-up box with an OK button that displays the message you supply until the user manually presses either OK or the X to close the box. The signature for the *popup* method is shown in Table 6-2.

TABLE 6-2 *WshShell Popup* Method Signature

RETURN	OBJECT.METHOD	TEXT	SECONDSTOWAIT	TITLE	TYPE
$returnValue	*$wshShell.Popup*	"message"	5	"title"	0

The title of the box refers to the Windows Script Host as shown in Figure 6-12.

FIGURE 6-12 By default, pop-up messages come from the Windows Script Host.

The code that creates the pop-up box in Figure 6-12 is shown here.

```
$wshShell.Popup("Message")
```

One useful feature of the *WshShell.popup* method is its ability to create different button configurations, which provides the ability to interact with the user in a graphical manner. To create a pop-up box that displays the Abort, Retry, and Ignore buttons, you can use the numeric value *2* in the fourth position. Common button configuration values are shown in Table 6-3. To display the pop-up message box until the user clicks one of the buttons, you can place a *0* in the second position (time argument) as shown here.

```
$wshShell.Popup("message",0,"title",2)
```

TABLE 6-3 *WshShell Popup* Button Values and Meanings

VALUE	DESCRIPTION
0	Show OK button.
1	Show OK and Cancel buttons.
2	Show Abort, Retry, and Ignore buttons.

VALUE	DESCRIPTION
3	Show Yes, No, and Cancel buttons.
4	Show Yes and No buttons.
5	Show Retry and Cancel buttons.

Of course, the entire reason for displaying different button configurations is to provide an easy way for the user to interact with the script. To interact with the user you must capture the return code, which is a value assigned to each of the different buttons. The following code produces the pop-up box shown in Figure 6-13. To evaluate the return code from the method, you must capture the return value. Return values from each of the different buttons are shown in Table 6-4. The Retry button is pressed in this example, which stores the value of 4 in the $return variable.

```
PS C:\> $return = $wshShell.Popup("message",0,"title",2)
PS C:\> $return
4
```

FIGURE 6-13 Abort, Retry, Ignore dialog box

TABLE 6-4 *WshShell Popup* Method Return Values

VALUE	DESCRIPTION
1	OK button
2	Cancel button
3	Abort button
4	Retry button
5	Ignore button
6	Yes button
7	No button

Last, you need to work with the pop-up box icons that can be displayed on any of the different box configurations. As shown in Table 6-5, the icon values seem to have little basis in reality. Additionally, it is a bit odd that the values are added to the previous button values shown in Table 6-3. To display the Stop Mark icon to an Abort, Retry, Ignore button configuration, you need to add a value of 16 for the Stop Mark icon to the value of 2 for the Abort, Retry, Ignore button display as shown in the line of code here. When the code executes, the dialog box shown in Figure 6-14 appears.

```
$return = $wshShell.Popup("message",0,"title",18)
```

TABLE 6-5 *WshShell Popup* Method Icon Values

VALUE	DESCRIPTION
16	Show Stop Mark icon.
32	Show Question Mark icon.
48	Show Exclamation Mark icon.
64	Show Information Mark icon.

FIGURE 6-14 Icon values added to the button configuration display different icon types.

Creating PSDrives

The judicious application of the creation of Windows PowerShell drives can simplify and facilitate the navigation and manipulation of data from the command line. While it is possible to use a variable to hold the path to a long folder and then change the working location to the path of the folder, this action causes you to relinquish much of the command line as shown in Figure 6-15. Although there is nothing wrong with losing a good deal of the command line, reading long commands that wrap across multiple lines can cause errors.

FIGURE 6-15 Long paths often use up too much of the command line.

One advantage of using a Windows PowerShell drive is that you can choose any location that is supported by the PowerShell provider as the root of the new drive. To create a new Windows PowerShell drive, you can use the New-PSDrive cmdlet, give the drive a name, and specify the provider and root location. The code to create a Windows PowerShell drive rooted in the C:\Data\BookDocs\PowerShellBestPractices folder is shown here.

```
New-PSDrive -Name bp -PSProvider filesystem -Root `
C:\data\BookDocs\PowerShellBestPractices -Description "MrEd Drive"
```

Once you create the Windows PowerShell drive, you can use the Set-Location cmdlet to change your working location to the newly created drive. This process allows you to reclaim your command-line real estate as shown in Figure 6-16.

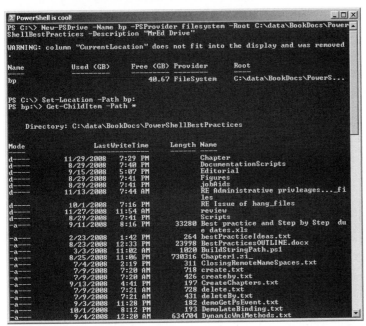

FIGURE 6-16 A Windows PowerShell drive is a good way to reclaim command-line real estate.

As a best practice, I also prefer to specify the *description* attribute when creating a Windows PowerShell drive. Setting the same –*description* parameter for all Windows PowerShell drives makes it easy to quickly identify the custom drives contained in the current PowerShell environment. Such a command might look like the following:

```
Get-PSDrive | Where-Object { $_.description -eq 'MrEd Drive' }
```

By creating Windows PowerShell drives for your most important data locations, you can easily change the working location by using the Set-Location cmdlet. If you create only a single Windows PowerShell drive that is the heart of all of your data activities, you can even use the Set-Location cmdlet to change the working location to your custom PowerShell drive as part of the profile.

Working with Profiles

Hal Rottenberg, Microsoft MVP

I put many different elements in my profile. First, I load the Windows PowerShell Community Extensions (PSCX). These cmdlets provide additional functionality and make it easier to work with Windows PowerShell. If you are not familiar with PSCX, you can find the project at *www.codeplex.com/PowerShellCX.*

Next, I create a custom prompt function and add numerous snap-ins. I create several aliases because I've been very happy with the defaults. I have a section that adds paths to *$env:path;* I never use cmd.exe anymore. Therefore, the profile is basically the core location where I maintain the %path%. The path section is also used to set some environment variables, such as *$MaximumHistoryCount.* The *$MaximumHistoryCount* variable determines the size of the command history buffer that defaults to storing 64 of your previously typed commands.

The best part of my profile is that I dot-source numerous functions I have written over the past year or so. These functions are small, reusable bits of code that make my job easier. I also create a few PSDrives. One PSDrive that I find particularly useful is called "scripts." It points to "$(split-path $profile)\scripts", which is where I store all of my function libraries and stand-alone .ps1 files. This folder is also in my path.

I also added a section to my profile that is used to load a variety of .NET assemblies. I do not use this section very often and, in fact, it is currently commented out. However, you might find it to be of interest because it loads some .NET assemblies. For example, one .NET assembly that I used had an ID3 tagging utility (for MP3 files) and one did Jabber/Extensible Messaging and Presence Protocol (XMPP) instant messaging.

The last section of my profile is used to load custom types.

I use Microsoft Live Mesh to ensure that my profile is always available. Live Mesh also serves as a backup of my entire WindowsPowerShell folder (and the aforementioned scripts, too). Other tools, such as Syncplicity (cloud), Foldershare (cloud), or Synctoy (local) can also be used for these purposes.

The coolest thing I have done in my profile is to add a ScriptProperty to the *System.Io.FileInfo* object by using Extended Type System (ETS) and .ps1 XML files in Windows PowerShell. This new ScriptProperty, named Pages, is a script that is invoked whenever the property is accessed. The script uses a little-known feature inside of the *Shell.Application* COM object to grab the number of pages in Microsoft Office Word documents. This script gives me the ability to create the following:

```
dir | ft name, length, pages
```

or even the following:

```
dir | Measure-Object -sum pages
```

Here is my profile code that loads the type (or types, if I were to add more).

```
Get-ChildItem -path $profiledir\ps1xml\*.ps1xml |
ForEach-Object {
    Update-TypeData $_
    write-host "Updating type data:`t$($_.name)"
}
```

Here are the contents of the .ps1 XML file.

```
<?xml version="1.0" encoding="utf-8" ?>
<Types>
    <Type>
        <Name>System.IO.FileInfo</Name>
        <Members>
            <ScriptProperty>
                <Name>Pages</Name>
                <GetScriptBlock>
                    $shellApp = new-object -com shell.application
                    $myFolder = $shellApp.Namespace($this.Directory.
                    FullName)
                    $fileobj = $myFolder.Items().Item($this.Name)
                    "$($myFolder.GetDetailsOf($fileobj,13))"
                </GetScriptBlock>
            </ScriptProperty>
        </Members>
    </Type>
</Types>
```

I do not use the page number capability very often. The most useful thing I have in my profile is the code to dot-source my function libraries. Note the use of the "scripts" PSDrive and "lib-" file name convention. This code makes it very easy for me to load all of the library files without touching my profile repeatedly as shown in the following code.

```
Get-ChildItem scripts:\lib-*.ps1 |
ForEach-Object {
  . $_
  write-host "Loading library file:`t$($_.name)"
}
```

I don't worry when my profile is not with me because I believe in cloud technologies. By using Live Mesh, my profile is always available. Because my primary PC is a laptop, I am not terribly concerned about profile issues.

Even though I define some aliases in my profile, I never use aliases in scripts—only at the prompt. A strong editor with cmdlet, parameter, file name, and even argument completion goes an incredible way toward making it convenient to produce very readable scripts.

I generally do some basic, simple error checking in my scripts, such as "If param is missing, throw err." However, the scripts that I publish for others usually receive a bit more treatment than that.

What I recommend to a new scripter is this: Download and install PSCX and use the default profile, which is what I did when I was new to Windows PowerShell. It's very well constructed and can serve as a great base and inspiration. Here is my personal profile.

```
# comments: $profiledir, Add-PathVariable come with PSCX


$ErrorPreference = "silentlycontinue"


# --------------------------------------------------------------------------
# Load PSCX
# --------------------------------------------------------------------------
. "$home\My Documents\WindowsPowerShell\PSCX_Profile.PS1"


# --------------------------------------------------------------------------
# Load SQL PSX
# --------------------------------------------------------------------------
# . "$home\My Documents\WindowsPowerShell\Scripts\SQLPSX\LibrarySmo.ps1"


# --------------------------------------------------------------------------
# Set prompt
# --------------------------------------------------------------------------


. $profiledir\prompt.ps1


# --------------------------------------------------------------------------
# Add third-party snapins
# --------------------------------------------------------------------------

$snapins =
  # "psmsi", # Windows Installer PowerShell Extensions
  "PshX-SAPIEN", # AD cmdlets from Sapien
  # "GetGPObjectPSSnapIn", # GPO management
```

```
    "Quest.ActiveRoles.ADManagement", # more AD stuff
  #   "Microsoft.Office.OneNote",
    "PowerGadgets",
    "VMware.VimAutomation.Core",
  #   "PoshXmpp",
  # "PSMobile",
  #"PoshHttp",
    "NetCmdlets",
    "OpenXml.PowerTools",
    "IronCowPosh"
$snapins | ForEach-Object {
  if ( Get-PSSnapin -Registered $_ -ErrorAction SilentlyContinue ) {
    Add-PSSnapin $_
  }
}


# --------------------------------------------------------------------------
# Aliases
# --------------------------------------------------------------------------
set-alias grep select-string
set-alias nsl resolve-host
Set-Alias rsps Restart-PowerShell
set-alias which get-command
Set-Alias cvi Connect-VIServer


# --------------------------------------------------------------------------
# V2 modules
# --------------------------------------------------------------------------
# dir $profiledir\modules\*.psm1 | Add-Module


# --------------------------------------------------------------------------
# Setup environment
# --------------------------------------------------------------------------
New-PSDrive -Name Scripts -PSProvider FileSystem -Root `
  $profiledir\scripts
Add-PathVariable Path $profiledir\scripts
Add-PathVariable Path $profiledir
Add-PathVariable Path "C:\Program Files\OpenSSL\bin"
Add-PathVariable Path "C:\Program Files\Reflector"
$MaximumHistoryCount = 4KB


# --------------------------------------------------------------------------
# Load function / filter definition library
# --------------------------------------------------------------------------
```

```
Get-ChildItem scripts:\lib-*.ps1 | % {
  . $_
  write-host "Loading library file:`t$($_.name)"
}
write-host


# -------------------------------------------------------------------------
# PS Drives
# -------------------------------------------------------------------------

New-PSDrive -Name Book -PSProvider FileSystem -Root 'C:\Documents and
Settings\hrottenberg\My Documents\MVP-TFM'
Write-Host


# -------------------------------------------------------------------------
# Load .NET assemblies
# -------------------------------------------------------------------------
#Get-ChildItem $profiledir\Assemblies\*.dll | % {
# [void][reflection.assembly]::LoadFrom( $_.FullName )
# write-host "Loading .NET assembly:`t$($_.name)"
#}
#Write-Host


# -------------------------------------------------------------------------
# Load custom types
# -------------------------------------------------------------------------
Get-ChildItem $profiledir\ps1xml\*.ps1xml | % {
  Update-TypeData $_
  write-host "Updating type data:`t$($_.name)"
}
Write-Host
if ($?) { Write-Host 'There were errors loading your profile.  Check the
$error object for details.' }
```

Enabling Scripting

When Windows PowerShell is first installed, the script execution policy is set to restricted.
When the execution policy is restricted, no scripts are permitted to run. Because a profile is a
.ps1 file, it is therefore a script and by default will not run. Five levels of execution policy can
be configured in Windows PowerShell by using the Set-ExecutionPolicy cmdlet, and they
are listed in Table 6-6. The restricted execution policy can be configured via Group Policy by
using the "Turn on Script Execution" Group Policy setting in Active Directory. It can be applied

to either the computer object or user object; the computer object setting takes precedence over other settings.

User preferences for the restricted execution policy can be configured by using the `Set-ExecutionPolicy` cmdlet, but the preferences do not override settings configured by Group Policy. An example of changing the current execution policy to RemoteSigned is shown here. To run the `Set-ExecutionPolicy` cmdlet, the Windows PowerShell console must be launched with admin rights. To do this, right-click on the shortcut to Windows PowerShell and select Run As Administrator. See Chapter 5, "Identifying Scripting Opportunities," for a discussion about the different ways to handle security issues. If you attempt to run the `Set-ExecutionPolicy` cmdlet, even when logged on to the computer as the administrator or as a user who is a member of the local administrators group, the error message shown in Figure 6-17 appears if you are using Windows Vista or above.

```
Set-ExecutionPolicy -ExecutionPolicy remotesigned
```

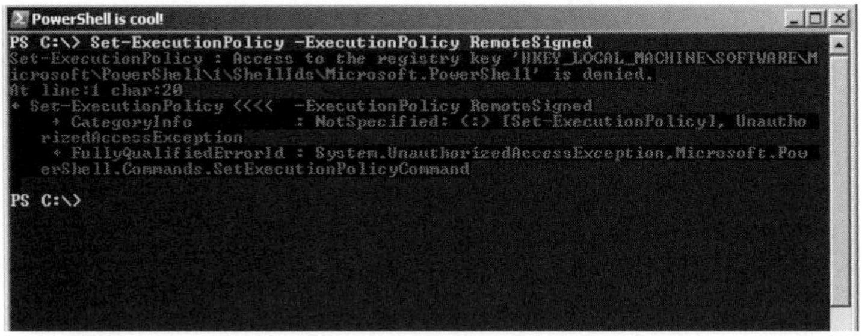

FIGURE 6-17 Attempts to change the restricted execution policy generate an error message if the Windows PowerShell console is not run as administrator.

The resultant set of restricted execution policy settings can be obtained by using the `Get-ExecutionPolicy` cmdlet.

TABLE 6-6 Execution Policy Level Settings

LEVEL	MEANING
Restricted	Does not run scripts or configuration files.
AllSigned	All scripts and configuration files must be signed by a trusted publisher.
RemoteSigned	All scripts and configuration files downloaded from the Internet must be signed by a trusted publisher.
Unrestricted	All scripts and configuration files do run. Scripts downloaded from the Internet prompt for permission prior to running.
Bypass	Nothing is blocked, and there are no warnings or prompts.

In addition to the five restricted execution policy settings, you can also configure the scope of the policy. When you set the scope of the restricted execution policy, it determines how the policy is applied by using three valid values: Process, CurrentUser, and LocalMachine. These values are detailed in Table 6-7.

TABLE 6-7 Execution Policy Scope Settings

SCOPE	MEANING
Process	The execution policy affects only the current Windows PowerShell process.
CurrentUser	The execution policy affects only the current user.
LocalMachine	The execution policy affects all users of the computer.

Creating a Profile

When Windows PowerShell is first installed, no profiles are installed on the computer. In one respect, you can consider the profile to be similar to the Autoexec.bat file from several years ago. On the one hand, the Autoexec.bat file is simply a batch file in that it only executes batch types of commands. On the other hand, because it is located in the root and has the name Autoexec.bat, it takes on an importance that is greatly out of proportion to a simple batch file because the commands that exist in the file are used to configure all types of activities, including configuring the environment and even launching Windows itself. The Windows PowerShell profile does not launch PowerShell; it is simply a PowerShell script that happens to have a special name and to exist in a special place—or, rather, it happens to have two special names and to exist in four special places! That's right. There are actually four Windows PowerShell profiles as listed in Table 6-8.

TABLE 6-8 Windows PowerShell Profiles and Locations

PROFILE	LOCATION
AllUsersAllHosts	C:\Windows\system32\WindowsPowerShell\v1.0\profile.ps1
AllUsersCurrentHost	C:\Windows\system32\WindowsPowerShell\v1.0\Microsoft.PowerShell_profile.ps1
CurrentUserAllHosts	C:\Users*UserName*\Documents\WindowsPowerShell\profile.ps1
CurrentUserCurrentHost	C:\Users*UserName*\Documents\WindowsPowerShell\Microsoft.PowerShell_profile.ps1

Choosing the Correct Profile

Two of the four profiles are used by all Windows PowerShell users on a computer. Anything placed in the All Users profiles is available to any script or any user that runs Windows PowerShell. As a result, you should be rather circumspect about what you place in the All Users profiles. However, the All Users profiles are great locations to configure aliases that you want to make available to all users, variables that you intend to use in a corporate scripting environment, or a Windows PowerShell drive or function. In fact, the items that you decide to mandate as part of the corporate Windows PowerShell environment are best placed in the All Users profiles.

The next question involves which of the two All Users profiles you should use. The AllUsersAllHosts profile applies to all of the users on the computer and to every instance of Windows PowerShell that may run on the computer including the PowerShell console, the PowerShell Integrated Scripting Environment (ISE), and any other program that may host Windows PowerShell, which can include the Exchange Management Environment, the SQL console, or any application that can host Windows PowerShell. If you are careful with the aliases you create, the variables you assign, the functions you write, and any Windows PowerShell drives you decide to make, you still need to test them to ensure compatibility. The AllUsersCurrentHost profile gives you the same ability to modify the Windows PowerShell environment for all users, but it only applies to the console host.

The two Current User profiles are used to modify the Windows PowerShell environment for the current user. The profile that is most often modified by a user to configure personal Windows PowerShell settings is the CurrentUserCurrentHost profile. This profile is referenced by the *$profile* automatic variable. On my computer, the value of the *$profile* variable is shown here.

```
PS C:\> $PROFILE
C:\Users\edwilson\Documents\WindowsPowerShell\Microsoft.PowerShell_profile.ps1
```

On a Windows Vista computer, you can see that the user's Personal folder is in the user's Documents folder. The WindowsPowerShell folder does not exist if no profile is created as shown here, where the Test-Path cmdlet is used to determine whether the parent folder that should contain the Microsoft.Powershell_profile.ps1 file exists. Because no personal profile has yet been created on this laptop, the WindowsPowerShell folder has not been created.

```
PS C:\> Test-path (Split-Path $PROFILE -Parent)
False
```

To create a CurrentUserCurrentHost profile, you can use the New-Item cmdlet as shown here. When using the New-Item cmdlet, you need to specify the *–force* parameter if the folder does not exist and to specify the itemtype as file as shown here.

```
New-Item -Path $PROFILE -ItemType file –Force
```

Once the profile is created, you can open it in Notepad or in the Windows PowerShell ISE to edit the file. If you choose to edit it in Notepad, it is as simple as typing **notepad** and giving it the *$profile* automatic variable as shown here.

```
Notepad $profile
```

After adding the functions, variables, aliases, and a Windows PowerShell drive, the CurrentUserCurrentHost profile is shown here.

CurrentUserCurrentHostProfile.ps1
```
# *** Functions go here ***


Function Set-Profile()
{
 Notepad $profile
 #MrEd function
}


Function Get-MoreHelp()
{
 #.Help Get-MoreHelp Get-Command
 Get-Help $args[0] -Full |
 more
  #MrEd function
} #end Get-MoreHelp


Function Get-WmiClass([string]$ns, [string]$class)
{
 #.Help Get-WmiClass -ns "root\cimv2" -class "Processor"
 $ns = $args[0]
 $class = $args[1]
 Get-WmiObject -List -Namespace $ns |
 Where-Object { $_.name -match $class }
  #MrEd function
} #end Get-WmiClass


# *** Aliases go here ***


New-Alias -Name mo -Value Measure-Object -Option allscope `
  -Description "MrEd Alias"
New-Alias -name gmh -value Get-MoreHelp -Option allscope `
  -Description "MrEd Alias"
New-Alias -Name gwc -Value Get-WmiClass -Option readonly,allscope `
  -Description "Mred Alias"


# *** Variables go here ***
```

```
New-Variable -Name wulog -Value (Join-Path -Path $env:LOCALAPPDATA `
  -ChildPath microsoft\windows\windowsupdate.log -Resolve) `
  -Option readonly -Description "MrEd Alias"
New-Variable -Name docs -Value (Join-Path -Path $home -ChildPath documents) `
  -Option readonly -Description "MrEd Variable"
New-Variable -name wshShell -value (New-Object -ComObject Wscript.Shell) `
  -Option readonly -Description "MrEd Alias"


# *** PSDrives go here ***


New-PSDrive -Name HKCR -PSProvider registry -Root Hkey_Classes_Root `
  -Description "MrEd PSdrive" | out-null
```

Creating Other Profiles

In addition to referencing the CurrentUserCurrentHost profile via the *$profile* variable, you can also reference all of the other profiles by using a dotted notation. To address the AllUsersAllHosts profile, you can use the *$profile* variable as shown here.

```
PS C:\> $PROFILE.AllUsersAllHosts
C:\Windows\system32\WindowsPowerShell\v1.0\profile.ps1
```

You can also easily create the AllUsersAllHosts profile by using the same technique you used for the CurrentUserCurrentHost profile.

```
New-Item -Path $PROFILE.AllUsersAllHosts -ItemType file -Force
```

One thing to keep in mind is that, on Windows Vista and above, you need to launch the Windows PowerShell console by right-clicking the icon and selecting Run As Administrator from the menu because the System32 directory is a protected area of the file system. If you do not do this, the error message shown in Figure 6-18 appears.

FIGURE 6-18 Attempts to create the All Users profile fail if Windows PowerShell is not run as an administrator.

To create the AllUsersCurrentHost profile, you again need to start the Windows PowerShell console with admin rights and then use the `New-Item` cmdlet to create the profile. This command is shown here.

```
New-Item -Path $PROFILE.AllUsersCurrentHost -ItemType file -Force
```

If you want to create the CurrentUserAllHosts profile, you can do so without using admin rights because it is stored in the user's Documents folder. A typical user, therefore, always has the rights to create the CurrentUserAllHosts and CurrentUserCurrentHost profiles. The command to create the CurrentUserAllHosts profile is shown here.

```
New-Item -Path $PROFILE.CurrentUserAllHosts -ItemType file -Force
```

When working with profiles, you should always consider the effect of the application on all of the different profiles. It is possible that items you place in a profile could be overwritten by other profiles, and the effect could very well be cumulative. Therefore, the concept of Resultant Set of Profiles (RSOP) comes into play. The four profiles are applied in the following order. The first profile is the most likely to be overwritten. The profile that is the closest to the user—the CurrentUserCurrentHost profile—is the one with the highest priority.

- All Users, All Hosts
- All Users, Current Host
- Current User, All Hosts
- Current User, Current Host

LESSONS LEARNED

Use a Standard Naming Convention to Avoid Conflict

As a best practice, when creating standard aliases and variables, you should mark them as constant to ensure that they are always available. When creating functions and Windows PowerShell drives, you should use a naming convention that is unlikely to result in naming conflicts. A company that I know uses a company name prefix for their functions as illustrated here.

```
Function CompanyAITWigitFunction() { do something interesting here }
New-Alias -Name CAWA -Value CompanyAITWigitFunction -Option constant `
-Description "CompanyA IT alias"
```

How I Use My Profile

James Brundage, Software Developer Engineer in Test
Microsoft Corporation

Profiles are an interesting trade-off. The upside of using profiles is that they can give you a consistent and personalized environment that sets up Windows PowerShell to your specifications. The downside of using profiles is that a personalized Windows PowerShell profile is always a little harder to share than a standard PowerShell profile; therefore, the way you write your profile can have a huge impact on how easy it is for others to use.

In my opinion, the ideal profile is simply a series of module imports or dot-sourcing of scripts. Both modules and script files are easy to copy from one computer to another computer, so keeping your profile in this format means that your profile remains clean and easy to understand and the scripts on which your profile depends are easy to share with the outside world. If your profiles are kept as a series of module imports or a dot-sourcing of scripts, you should be able to merely copy a module from one box to another, copy your profile, and be done.

You can also use your profile to make life more convenient. The Windows PowerShell ISE contains an object model that allows you to add tools to the environment, and PowerShell lets you customize the prompt by writing your own prompt function. If I'm adding cool things to the environment, such as a Verb menu, I always put them in my profile.

On this note, the coolest thing I ever had in my profile was the Verb menu. I built a script to create a menu hierarchy in the ISE so that I could click commands by their verb (for example, go to the Get menu, then click "Process" to run Get-Process). This type of customization is great to use in a profile because it makes life within the scripting environment easier.

I tend to shy away from using aliases in my profile because aliases make my scripts more difficult to share with the world outside of Microsoft (due to the chance that I might forget to de-alias the script before posting it to a blog). Aliases are a fine component to have in a profile if you are not scripting for public consumption, but I usually want an alias to which I can write a function with a small amount of additional effort. I believe that aliases increase the need to place your profile on every computer all of the time. Because I have a blog, I often try to minimize the dependencies of my scripts; therefore, I avoid aliases because they are a superfluous dependency.

My profile is typically short because I keep almost everything in modules. I have several more items in my *$loadedModules* variable, but the following gives you an idea of how my profile looks.

```
$loadedModules = 'DotNet',
    'WPF'
Import-Module $loadedModules –force
```

The DotNet module is very simple. It is merely a file with the .psm1 extension that dot-sources a file with a *Get-Type* function. It is placed in the ($env:UserProfile \Documents\WindowsPowerShell\Modules\DotNet).

MyDotNetmodule
```
. $psScriptRoot\Get-Type.ps1
Get-Type.ps1:
Function Get-Type() {
    [AppDomain]::CurrentDomain.GetAssemblies() | Foreach-Object {
    $_.GetTypes() }
}
```

That function is the most useful addition that I ever put into a profile. It outputs all of the types that are currently loaded so that I can search them in Windows PowerShell, such as the following:

```
Get-Type | Where-Object { $_.FullName –like "**File*" }
```

Accessing Functions in Other Scripts

After you write a large number of functions, you might like to reuse them in other scripts. Code reuse is a great idea. The easiest way to reuse code is to simply copy and paste the function from one script into another script. Suppose that you have a script containing code that performs a conversion from Celsius to Fahrenheit, and you want to use the algorithm to create another script with different capabilities. You can simply write your script and copy the code from your other script. When finished, your script might look like the ConvertToFahrenheit.ps1 script shown here.

ConvertToFahrenheit.ps1
```
Param($Celsius)
Function ConvertToFahrenheit($Celsius)
{
 "$Celsius Celsius equals $((1.8 * $Celsius) + 32) Fahrenheit"
} #end ConvertToFahrenheit
ConvertToFahrenheit($Celsius)
```

Nothing is wrong with this script. It does one thing and does it fairly well. To use the script, you supply a command-line parameter. You do not need to type the entire parameter name when calling the script as shown here.

```
PS C:\> C:\BestPracticesBook\ConvertToFahrenheit.ps1 -c 24
24 celsius equals 75.2 fahrenheit
```

Creating a Function Library

The problem with reusing code occurs when you want to use the function; you need to copy and paste it into the new script. If you want to change the way the function works, you need to find all instances where the function occurs and make the necessary changes. Otherwise, you can end up with many slightly different versions of the function, which can lead to support problems.

What is the solution? One approach is to place all of your functions into a single script, such as the ConversionFunctions.ps1 script shown here.

ConversionFunctions.ps1
```
Function ConvertToMeters($feet)
{
  "$feet feet equals $($feet*.31) meters"
} #end ConvertToMeters
Function ConvertToFeet($meters)
{
  "$meters meters equals $($meters * 3.28) feet"
} #end ConvertToFeet
Function ConvertToFahrenheit($celsius)
{
  "$celsius celsius equals $((1.8 * $celsius) + 32 ) fahrenheit"
} #end ConvertToFahrenheit
Function ConvertTocelsius($fahrenheit)
{
  "$fahrenheit fahrenheit equals $( (($fahrenheit - 32)/9)*5 ) celsius"
} #end ConvertTocelsius
Function ConvertToMiles($kilometer)
{
  "$kilometer kilometers equals $( ($kilometer *.6211) ) miles"
} #end convertToMiles
Function ConvertToKilometers($miles)
{
  "$miles miles equals $( ($miles * 1.61) ) kilometers"
} #end convertToKilometers
```

Using an Include File

If you need to use one of the conversion functions, you can include it in the script by placing a period in front of the path to the script. When you include the script containing the conversion functions, you now have access to all of the functions and can use them directly as if they were in the actual file itself. The ConvertToFahrenheit_Include.ps1 script illustrates this technique. You can still use the command-line parameter *$celsius* to supply the temperature you want to convert. You then use the period followed by the path to the script for the include file. Lastly, you can call the function by name and supply it with the value that came into the script via the command line. The revised ConvertToFahrenheit_Include.ps1 script is shown here.

ConvertToFahrenheit_Include.ps1
```
Param($Celsius)
. C:\data\scriptingGuys\ConversionFunctions.ps1
ConvertToFahrenheit($Celsius)
```

You can see that the script is much cleaner and less cluttered, and it is easier to read. Because it is easier to read, the script is easier to understand and is therefore easier to maintain. Of course, there are two downsides to this equation. The first is that the two scripts are now married. A change in one script might affect a change in the other script. More important, however, is that both scripts now must travel together because both now need to have a single working script. This outside dependency can become rather difficult to troubleshoot if you are not expecting it or have not planned for it.

One way to make the script easier to troubleshoot is to use the Test-Path cmdlet to determine whether the include file is present. If the include file is missing, you can generate a message to that effect to alert you to the missing file and simplify the troubleshooting scenario. As a best practice, I always recommend using Test-Path whenever you use the include file scenario. The revised ConvertToFahrenheit_Include2.ps1 script illustrates this technique and is shown here.

ConvertToFahrenheit_Include2.ps1
```
Param($Celsius)
$includeFile = "c:\data\scriptingGuys\ConversionFunctions.ps1"
if(!(test-path -path $includeFile))
  {
    "Unable to find $includeFile"
    Exit
  }
. $includeFile
ConvertToFahrenheit($Celsius)
```

As you can see, this process begins to become a bit ridiculous. You now have a nine-line script to allow you to use a three-line function. You must make the call if you want to use the include file. When writing a more substantial script that uses an include file, the payoff in terms of simplicity and actual code length becomes more evident. In the ConvertUseFunctions.ps1 script, a function named *ParseAction* evaluates the action and value that are supplied from the command line and then calls the appropriate function as shown here.

ConvertUseFunctions.ps1

```
Param($action,$value,[switch]$help)
Function GetHelp()
{
  if($help)
  {
    "choose conversion: M(eters), F(eet) C(elsius),Fa(renheit),Mi(les),K(ilometers) and value"
    " Convert -a M -v 10 converts 10 meters to feet."
  } #end if help
} #end getHelp
Function GetInclude()
{
 $includeFile = "c:\data\scriptingGuys\ConversionFunctions.ps1"
 if(!(test-path -path $includeFile))
   {
     "Unable to find $includeFile"
     Exit
   }
. $includeFile
} #end GetInclude
Function ParseAction()
{
 switch ($action)
 {
  "M"  { ConvertToFeet($value) }
  "F"  { ConvertToMeters($value) }
  "C"  { ConvertToFahrenheit($value) }
  "Fa" { ConvertToCelsius($value) }
  "Mi" { ConvertToKilometers($value) }
  "K"  { ConvertToMiles($value) }
  DEFAULT { "Dude illegal value." ; GetHelp ; exit }
 } #end action
} #end ParseAction
# *** Entry Point ***
If($help) { GetHelp ; exit }
if(!$action) { "Missing action" ; GetHelp ; exit }
GetInclude
ParseAction
```

Keep in mind that you need to make a change to the include file. Because you are loading the functions from within a function, the functions are scoped by default into that function's namespace. They are not available from a different function—only from child items. To avoid the inheritance issue, add a script tag to each function when it is created as shown here.

```
Function Script:ConvertToMeters($feet)
{
  "$feet feet equals $($feet*.31) meters"
} #end ConvertToMeters
```

Additional Resources

- The TechNet Script Center at *http://www.microsoft.com/technet/scriptcenter* contains numerous examples of Windows PowerShell scripts that use include files.
- Take a look at *Windows PowerShell™ Scripting Guide* (Microsoft Press, 2008).
- On the companion media, you will find all of the scripts referred to in this chapter.
- Windows PowerShell profiles are covered at *http://msdn.microsoft.com/en-us/library /bb613488(VS.85).aspx* in MSDN.
- The script execution policy is covered at *http://msdn.microsoft.com/en-us/library /bb648601(VS.85).aspx* in MSDN.

## CHAPTER 7

Avoiding Scripting Pitfalls

Knowing what you should not script is as important as knowing what you should script. There are times when creating a Windows PowerShell script is not the best approach to a problem due to the lack of support in a particular technology or to project complexity. In this chapter, you will be introduced to some of the red flags that signal danger for a potential script project.

Lack of cmdlet Support

It is no secret that cmdlet support is what makes working with Windows PowerShell so easy. If you need to check the status of the bits service, the easiest method is to use the Get-Service cmdlet as shown here.

```
Get-Service -name bits
```

To find information about the explorer process, you can use the Get-Process cmdlet as shown here.

```
Get-Process -Name explorer
```

If you need to stop a process, you can easily use the Stop-Process cmdlet as shown here.

```
Stop-Process -Name notepad
```

You can even check the status of services on a remote computer by using the *–computername* switch from the `Get-Service` cmdlet as shown here.

```
Get-Service -Name bits -ComputerName vista
```

> **IMPORTANT**   If you are working in a cross-domain scenario in which authentication is required, you will not be able to use `Get-Service` or `Get-Process` because those cmdlets do not have a *–credential* parameter. You need to use one of the remoting cmdlets, such as `Invoke-Command`, which allows you to supply an authentication context.

You can check the BIOS information on a local computer and save the information to a comma-separated value file with just a few lines of code. An example of such a script is the ExportBiosToCsv.ps1 script.

ExportBiosToCsv.ps1
```
$path = "c:\fso\bios.csv"
Get-WmiObject -Class win32_bios |
Select-Object -property name, version |
Export-CSV -path $path -noTypeInformation
```

Without cmdlet support for selecting objects and exporting them to a CSV file format, you might be tempted to use *filesystemobject* from Microsoft VBScript fame. If you take that approach, the script will be twice as long and not nearly as readable. An example of a script using *filesystemobject* is the FSOBiosToCsv.ps1 script.

FSOBiosToCsv.ps1
```
$path = "c:\fso\bios1.csv"
$bios = Get-WmiObject -Class win32_bios
$csv = "Name,Version`r`n"
$csv +=$bios.name + "," + $bios.version
$fso = new-object -comobject scripting.filesystemobject
$file = $fso.CreateTextFile($path,$true)
$file.write($csv)
$file.close()
```

Clearly, the ability to use built-in cmdlets is a major strength of Windows PowerShell. One problem with Windows Server 2008 R2 and Windows PowerShell 2.0 is the number of cmdlets that exist, which is similar to the problem experienced by Windows Exchange Server administrators. Because there are so many cmdlets, it is difficult to know where to begin. A quick perusal of the Microsoft Exchange Team's blog and some of the Exchange forums reveals that the problem is not writing scripts, but finding the one cmdlet of the hundreds of possible candidates that performs the specific task at hand. If you factor in community-developed cmdlets and third-party software company cmdlet offerings, you have a potential environment that encompasses thousands of cmdlets.

Luckily, the Windows PowerShell team has a plan to address this situation—standard naming conventions. The Get-Help, Get-Command, and Get-Member cmdlets were discussed in Chapter 1, "Assessing the Scripting Environment," but they merit mention here. If you are unaware of a specific cmdlet feature or even the existence of a cmdlet, you are forced to implement a workaround that causes additional work or that might mask hidden mistakes. Given the choice between a prebaked cmdlet and a create-your-own solution, the prebaked cmdlet should be used in almost all cases. Therefore, instead of assuming that a cmdlet or feature does not exist, you should spend time using Get-Help, Get-Command, and Get-Member before embarking on a lengthy development effort. In this chapter, you will examine some of the potential pitfalls that can develop when you do not use cmdlets.

Complicated Constructors

If you do not have support from cmdlets when developing an idea for a script, this indicates that there may be a better way to do something and should cause you to at least consider your alternatives.

In the GetRandomObject.ps1 script, a function named *GetRandomObject* is created. This function takes two input parameters: one named *$in* that holds an array of objects and the other named *$count* that controls how many items are randomly selected from the input object.

The New-Object cmdlet is used to create an instance of the *System.Random* Microsoft .NET Framework class. The new instance of the class is created by using the default constructor (no seed value supplied) and is stored in the *$rnd* variable.

A *for . . . next* loop is used to loop through the collection—once for each selection desired. The next method of the *System.Random* class is used to choose a random number that resides between the number 1 and the maximum number of items in the input object. The random number is used to locate an item in the array by using the index so that the selection of the item from the input object can take place. The GetRandomObject.ps1 script is shown here.

```
GetRandomObject.ps1
Function GetRandomObject($in,$count)
{
 $rnd = New-Object system.random
 for($i = 1 ; $i -le $count; $i ++)
 {
  $in[$rnd.Next(1,$a.length)]
 } #end for
} #end GetRandomObject


# *** entry point ***
$a = 1,2,3,4,5,6,7,8,9
$count = 3
GetRandomObject -in $a -count $count
```

While there is nothing inherently wrong with the GetRandomObject.ps1 script, you can use the Get-Random cmdlet when working with Windows PowerShell 2.0 to accomplish essentially the same objective as shown here.

```
$a = 1,2,3,4,5,6,7,8,9
Get-Random -InputObject $a -Count 3
```

Clearly, by using the native Get-Random cmdlet, you can save yourself a great deal of time and trouble. The only reason to use the GetRandomObject.ps1 script is that it works with both Windows PowerShell 1.0 and PowerShell 2.0.

One advantage of using a cmdlet is that you can trust it will be implemented correctly. At times, .NET Framework classes have rather complicated constructors that are used to govern the way the instance of a class is created. A mistake that is made when passing a value for one of these constructors does not always mean that an error is generated. It is entirely possible that the code will appear to work correctly, and it can therefore be very difficult to spot the problem.

An example of this type of error is shown in the BadGetRandomObject.ps1 script in which an integer is passed to the constructor for the *System.Random* .NET Framework class. The problem is that every time the script is run, the same random number is generated. While this particular bad implementation is rather trivial, it illustrates that the potential exists for logic errors that often require detailed knowledge of the utilized .NET Framework classes to troubleshoot.

```
BadGetRandomObject.ps1
Function GetRandomObject($in,$count,$seed)
{
 $rnd = New-Object system.random($seed)
 for($i = 1 ; $i -le $count; $i ++)
 {
   $in[$rnd.Next(1,$a.length)]
 } #end for
} #end GetRandomObject

# *** entry point ***
$a = 1,2,3,4,5,6,7,8,9
$count = 3
GetRandomObject -in $a -count $count -seed 5
```

The *System.Random* information is contained in MSDN, but it is easy to overlook some small detail because there is so much documentation and some of the classes are very complicated. When the overlooked detail does not cause a run-time error and the script appears to work properly, then you have a potentially embarrassing situation at best.

Version Compatibility Issues

While the Internet is a great source of information, it can often lead to confusion rather than clarity. When you locate a source of information, it may not be updated to include the current version of the operating system. This update situation is worsening due to a variety of complicating factors such as User Account Control (UAC), Windows Firewall, and other security factors that have so many different configuration settings that it can be unclear whether an apparent failure is due to a change in the operating system or to an actual error in the code. As an example, suppose that you decide to use the *WIN32_Volume* Windows Management Instrumentation (WMI) class to determine information about your disk drives. First, you need to realize that the WMI class does not exist on any operating system older than Microsoft Windows Server 2003; it is a bit surprising that the class does not exist on Windows XP. When you try the following command on Windows Vista, however, it generates an error.

```
Get-WmiObject -Class win32_volume -Filter "Name = 'c:\'"
```

The first suspect when dealing with Windows Vista and later versions is user rights. You open the Windows PowerShell console as an administrator and try the code again; it fails. You then wonder whether the error is caused by the differences between expanding quotes and literal quotes. After contemplation, you decide to write the filter to take advantage of literal strings. The problem is that you have to escape the quotes, which involves more work, but it is worth the effort if it works. So, you come up with the following code that, unfortunately, also fails when it is run.

```
Get-WmiObject -Class win32_volume -Filter 'Name = ''c:\'''
```

This time, you decide to actually read the error message. Here is the error that was produced by the previous command.

```
Get-WmiObject : Invalid query
At line:1 char:14
+ Get-WmiObject <<<<  -Class win32_volume -Filter "Name = 'c:\' "
    + CategoryInfo          : InvalidOperation: (:) [Get-WmiObject],
    ManagementException
    + FullyQualifiedErrorId : GetWMIManagementException,
    Microsoft.PowerShell.Commands.GetWmiObjectCommand
```

You focus on the line that says invalid operation and decide that perhaps the backslash is a special character. When this is the problem, you need to escape the backslash; therefore, you decide to use the escape character to make one more attempt. Here is the code you create.

```
Get-WmiObject -Class win32_volume -Filter "Name = 'c:`\' "
```

Even though this is a good idea, the code still does not work and once again generates an error as shown here.

```
Get-WmiObject : Invalid query
At line:1 char:14
```

```
+ Get-WmiObject <<<<   -Class win32_volume -Filter "Name = 'c:`\' "
    + CategoryInfo             : InvalidOperation: (:) [Get-WmiObject],
    ManagementException
    + FullyQualifiedErrorId : GetWMIManagementException,
    Microsoft.PowerShell.Commands.GetWmiObjectCommand
```

Next, you search to determine whether you have rights to run the query. (I know that you are running the console with Administrator rights, but some processes deny access even to the Administrator, so it is best to check.) The easiest way to check your rights is to perform the WMI query and omit the –*filter* parameter as shown here.

```
Get-WmiObject -Class win32_volume
```

This command runs without generating an error. You may assume that you cannot filter the WMI class at all and decide that the class is a bit weird. You may decide to write a different filter and see whether it will accept the syntax of a new filter, such as the following line of code.

```
Get-WmiObject -Class win32_volume -Filter "DriveLetter = 'c:'"
```

The previous command rewards you with an output similar to the one shown here.

```
PS C:\> Get-WmiObject -Class win32_volume -Filter "DriveLetter = 'c:'"


__GENUS                         : 2
__CLASS                         : Win32_Volume
__SUPERCLASS                    : CIM_StorageVolume
__DYNASTY                       : CIM_ManagedSystemElement
__RELPATH                       : Win32_Volume.DeviceID="\\\\?\\Volume{5a4a2fe5-70
                                  f0-11dd-b4ad-806e6f6e6963}\\"
__PROPERTY_COUNT                : 44
__DERIVATION                    : {CIM_StorageVolume, CIM_StorageExtent, CIM_Logic
                                  alDevice, CIM_LogicalElement...}
__SERVER                        : MRED1
__NAMESPACE                     : root\cimv2
__PATH                          : \\MRED1\root\cimv2:Win32_Volume.DeviceID="\\\\?\
                                  \Volume{5a4a2fe5-70f0-11dd-b4ad-806e6f6e6963}\\"
Access                          :
Automount                       : True
Availability                    :
BlockSize                       : 4096
BootVolume                      : True
Capacity                        : 158391595008
Caption                         : C:\
Compressed                      : False
ConfigManagerErrorCode          :
ConfigManagerUserConfig         :
```

```
CreationClassName           :
Description                 :
DeviceID                    : \\?\Volume{5a4a2fe5-70f0-11dd-b4ad-806e6f6e6963}
                              \
DirtyBitSet                 :
DriveLetter                 : C:
DriveType                   : 3
ErrorCleared                :
ErrorDescription            :
ErrorMethodology            :
FileSystem                  : NTFS
FreeSpace                   : 23077511168
IndexingEnabled             : True
InstallDate                 :
Label                       :
LastErrorCode               :
MaximumFileNameLength       : 255
Name                        : C:\
NumberOfBlocks              :
PageFilePresent             : False
PNPDeviceID                 :
PowerManagementCapabilities :
PowerManagementSupported    :
Purpose                     :
QuotasEnabled               :
QuotasIncomplete            :
QuotasRebuilding            :
SerialNumber                : 1893548344
Status                      :
StatusInfo                  :
SupportsDiskQuotas          : True
SupportsFileBasedCompression : True
SystemCreationClassName     :
SystemName                  : MRED1
SystemVolume                : False
```

NOTE When working with scripting, network administrators and consultants often use workarounds because our job is to "make things work." Sometimes, Scripting Guys end up using workarounds as well. After all, my job is to write a daily Hey Scripting Guy! column, which means that I have a deadline every day of the week. Concerning the previous *Win32_Volume* WMI class example, I always use the *DriveLetter* property when performing the WMI query. Years ago, after several hours of experimentation with this example, I determined that perhaps the *name* property was broken and therefore avoided using it when performing demonstrations when I was teaching classes. Luckily, no student ever asked me why I use *DriveLetter* instead of the *name* property in any of my queries!

If you return to the error message generated by the earlier queries, the InvalidOperation CategoryInfo field might cause you to reconsider the backslash. Your earlier attempts to escape the backslash were on the right track. The problem revolves around the strange mixture of the WMI Query Language (WQL) syntax and Windows PowerShell syntax. The *–filter* parameter is definitely Windows PowerShell syntax, but you must supply a string that conforms to WQL dialect inside this parameter. This is why you use the equal sign for an operator instead of the Windows PowerShell *–eq* operator when you are inside the quotation marks of the *–filter* parameter. To escape the backslash in the WQL syntax, you must use another backslash as found in C or C++ syntax. The following code filters out the drive based on the name of the drive.

```
Get-WmiObject -Class win32_volume -Filter "Name = 'c:\\'"
```

> **IMPORTANT**   Use of the backslash to escape another backslash is a frustrating factor when using WMI. While our documentation in MSDN is improving, we still have a way to go in this arena. Because this WMI class does not behave as you might expect, I have filed a documentation bug for the *name* property of the *Win32_Volume* class. The result will be an additional note added to the description of the property. I have since found a few more places where the backslash is used as an escape character, and I will file bugs on them as well.

As a best practice, you can write a script to return the WMI information from the *WIN32_Volume* class and hide the escape details from the user. An example of such a script is the GetVolume.ps1 script. The script accepts two command-line parameters: *–drive* and *–computer*. The drive is supplied as a drive letter followed by a colon. By default, the script returns information from the C: drive on the local computer. In the *Get-Volume* function, the *–drive* value is concatenated with the double backslash and is then submitted to the Get-WmiObject cmdlet. One interesting aspect is the use of single quotes around the *$drive* variable. Remember that, inside the *–filter* parameter, the script uses WQL syntax and not Windows PowerShell syntax. The single quote is simply a single quote, and you do not need to worry about the difference between an expanding or a literal quotation. The GetVolume.ps1 script is shown here.

GetVolume.ps1
```
Param($drive = "C:", $computer = "localhost")
Function Get-Volume($drive, $computer)
{
 $drive += "\\"
 Get-WmiObject -Class Win32_Volume -computerName $computer `
 -filter "Name = '$drive'"
}

Get-Volume -Drive $drive -Computer $computer
```

If you need to work in a cross-domain situation, you need to pass credentials to the remote computer. The Get-WmiObject cmdlet contains the *–credential* parameter that can be used in just such a situation. Because the Get-WmiObject cmdlet uses WMI in the background, the problem is that you are not allowed to pass credentials for a local connection. Local WMI scripts always run in the context of the calling user—that is, the one who is actually launching the script. This means that you cannot use the *–credential* parameter for a local script to allow a nonprivileged user to run the script with administrator rights. You can use the *–credential* parameter with remote connections. In addition, you are not allowed to have the *–credential* parameter in the Get-WmiObject cmdlet and leave it blank or null because this also generates an error. The solution is to check whether the script is running against the local computer; if it is, use the *Get-Volume* function from the previous script. If it is working remotely, the script should use a different function that supplies the *–credential* parameter as shown in the GetVolumeWithCredentials.ps1 script.

GetVolumeWithCredentials.ps1

```
Param(
        $drive = "C:",
        $computer = "localhost",
        $credential
     )
Function Get-Volume($drive, $computer)
{
 $drive += "\\"
 Get-WmiObject -Class Win32_Volume -computerName $computer `
 -filter "Name = '$drive'"
} #end Get-Volume

Function Get-VolumeCredential($drive, $computer,$credential)
{
 $drive += "\\"
 Get-WmiObject -Class Win32_Volume -computerName $computer `
 -filter "Name = '$drive'" -credential $credential
} #end Get-VolumeCredential

# *** Entry point to script
If($computer -eq "localhost" -AND $credential)
   { "Cannot use credential for local connection" ; exit }
Elseif ($computer -ne "localhost" -AND $credential)
   {
     Get-VolumeCredential -Drive $drive -Computer $computer `
     -Credential $credential
   }
Else
  { Get-Volume -Drive $drive -Computer $computer }
```

Choosing the Right Script Methodology

Luis Canastreiro, Premier Field Engineer
Microsoft Corporation, Portugal

When I am writing a script, often there are many ways of accomplishing the same task. If I am writing a VBScript, for example, I prefer to use a Component Object Model (COM) object rather than shelling out and calling an external executable because COM is native to VBScript. The same principle holds when I am writing a Windows PowerShell script. I prefer to use the .NET Framework classes if a Windows PowerShell cmdlet is not available because PowerShell is built on the .NET Framework.

Of course, my number-one preference is to use a cmdlet if it is available to me because a cmdlet will hide the complexity of dealing directly with the .NET Framework. By this I mean that there are some .NET Framework classes that at first glance appear to be simple. However, when you begin to use them, you realize that they contain complicated constructors. If you are not an expert with that particular class, you can make a mistake that will not be realized until after much testing. If a cmdlet offers the required features and if it solves my problem, then the cmdlet is my first choice.

As an example, there are several ways to read and write to the registry. You can use the *regread* and *regwrite* VBScript methods, the *stdRegProv* WMI class, the .NET Framework classes, or even various command-line utilities to gain access to the registry. My favorite method of working with the registry is to use the Windows PowerShell registry provider and the various *-item and *-itemproperty cmdlets. These cmdlets are very easy to use, and I only need to open the Windows PowerShell shell to accomplish everything I need to do with these cmdlets.

When I am writing a new script, I always like to create small generic functions, which offer a number of advantages. These functions make it easy for me to test the script while I am in the process of writing it. I only need to call the function or functions on which I am working. I can leave the other code unfinished if I need to test it later. The functions are easy to reuse or to improve as time goes by. I run the script by creating a main function whose primary purpose is to initialize the environment and manage the global flow of the script by calling the appropriate functions at the proper time.

Trapping the Operating System Version

Given the differences between the various versions of the Windows operating system, it is a best practice to check the version of the operating system prior to executing the script if you know that there could be version compatibility issues. There are several different methods to check version compatibility. In Chapter 5, "Identifying Scripting Opportunities," you used the *System.Environment* .NET Framework class to check the operating system version in the GetOsVersionFunction.ps1 script. While it is true that you can use remoting to obtain information from this class remotely, you can also achieve similar results by using the *Win32_OperatingSystem* WMI class. The advantage of this approach is that WMI automatically remotes.

The GetVersion.ps1 script accepts a single command-line parameter, *$computer,* and is set by default to the localhost computer. The entry point to the script passes the value of the *$computer* variable and a reference type *$osv* variable to the *Get-OSVersion* function. Inside the *Get-OSVersion* function, the Get-WMIObject cmdlet is first used to query the *Win32_OperatingSystem* WMI class from the computer that is targeted by the *$computer* variable. The resulting management object is stored in the *$os* variable.

The *Switch* statement is used to evaluate the *version* property of the *Win32_OperatingSystem* class. If the value of the *version* property is equal to 5.1.2600, the *Value* property of the *$osv* reference type variable is set equal to "xp". This type of logic is repeated for the value 5.1.3790, which is the build number for the Windows 2003 server.

A problem arises if the version number is 6.0.6001 because both Windows Vista and Windows Server 2008 have the same build number. This is why the script stores the entire *Win32_OperatingSystem* management object in the *$os* variable instead of retrieving only the version attribute. The *ProductType* property can be used to distinguish between a workstation and a server. The possible values for the *ProductType* property are shown in Table 7-1.

TABLE 7-1 *Win32_OperatingSystem ProductType* Values and Associated Meanings

VALUE	MEANING
1	Workstation
2	Domain controller
3	Server

Once the version of the operating system is detected, then a single word or number representing the operating system is assigned to the *Value* property of the reference variable. In the GetVersion.ps1 script, this value is displayed at the console. The complete GetVersion.ps1 script is shown here.

```
GetVersion.ps1
Param($computer = "localhost")

Function Get-OSVersion($computer,[ref]$osv)
{
 $os = Get-WmiObject -class Win32_OperatingSystem `
       -computerName $computer
 Switch ($os.Version)
  {
    "5.1.2600" { $osv.value = "xp" }
    "5.1.3790" { $osv.value = "2003" }
    "6.0.6001"
                {
                  If($os.ProductType -eq 1)
                    {
                      $osv.value = "Vista"
                    } #end if
                  Else
                    {
                      $osv.value = "2008"
                    } #end else
                } #end 6001
    DEFAULT { "Version not listed" }
  } #end switch
} #end Get-OSVersion

# *** entry point to script ***
$osv = $null
Get-OSVersion -computer $computer -osv ([ref]$osv)
$osv
```

The GetVersion.ps1 script returns a single word to indicate the version of the operating system. You can use this script from the command line to quickly check the operating system version as shown here.

```
PS C:\bp> .\GetVersion.ps1
Vista
PS C:\bp> .\GetVersion.ps1 -c berlin
2008
PS C:\bp> .\GetVersion.ps1 -c lisbon
xp
```

The GetVersion.ps1 script is written as a function to permit easy inclusion into other scripts, which allows you to perform the operating system version check and then decide whether you want to continue processing the script. An example of this approach is shown in the GetVersionGetVolume.ps1 script.

GetVersionGetVolume.ps1

```
Param($drive = "C:", $computer = "localhost")

Function Get-OSVersion($computer,[ref]$osv)
{
 $os = Get-WmiObject -class Win32_OperatingSystem `
         -computerName $computer
Switch ($os.Version)
  {
    "5.1.2600" { $osv.value = "xp" }
    "5.1.3790" { $osv.value = "2003" }
    "6.0.6001"
                   {
                       If($os.ProductType -eq 1)
                         {
                            $osv.value = "Vista"
                         } #end if
                     Else
                         {
                           $osv.value = "2008"
                         } #end else
                   } #end 6001
    DEFAULT { "Version not listed" }
  } #end switch
} #end Get-OSVersion

Function Get-Volume($drive, $computer)
{
 $drive += "\\"
 Get-WmiObject -Class Win32_Volume -computerName $computer `
 -filter "Name = '$drive'"
} #end Get-Volume

# *** entry point to script ***
$osv = $null
Get-OSVersion -computer $computer -osv ([ref]$osv)
if($osv -eq "xp") { "Script does not run on XP" ; exit }
Get-Volume -Drive $drive -Computer $computer
```

Lack of WMI Support

Windows Management Instrumentation has been in existence since the days of Microsoft Windows NT 4.0. In the years since its introduction, every new version of Windows has added WMI classes and, at times, additional methods to existing WMI classes. One advantage of WMI is its relatively consistent approach to working with software and hardware. Another advantage of WMI is that it is a well-understood technology, and numerous examples of scripts can be found on the Internet. With improved support for WMI in Windows PowerShell 2.0, there is very little that cannot be accomplished via PowerShell that can be done from inside VBScript. Before you look at some of the issues in working with WMI from Windows PowerShell, let's review some basic WMI concepts.

WMI is sometimes referred to as a *hierarchical namespace*—so named because the layers build on one another like a Lightweight Directory Access Protocol (LDAP) directory used in Active Directory or the file system structure on your hard disk drive. Although it is true that WMI is a hierarchical namespace, the term doesn't really convey its richness. The WMI model contains three sections: resources, infrastructure, and consumers. The use of these components is found in the following list:

- **WMI resources**   Resources include anything that can be accessed by using WMI: the file system, networked components, event logs, files, folders, disks, Active Directory, and so on.

- **WMI infrastructure**   The infrastructure is composed of three parts: the WMI service, WMI repository, and WMI providers. Of these parts, WMI providers are most important because they provide the means for WMI to gather needed information.

- **WMI consumers**   A consumer "consumes" the data from WMI. A consumer can be a VBScript, an enterprise management software package, or some other tool or utility that executes WMI queries.

Working with Objects and Namespaces

Let's return to the idea of a namespace introduced in the last section. You can think of a *namespace* as a way to organize or collect data related to similar items. Visualize an old-fashioned filing cabinet. Each drawer can represent a particular namespace. Inside each drawer are hanging folders that collect information related to a subset of what the drawer actually holds. For example, there is a drawer at home in my filing cabinet that is reserved for information related to my woodworking tools. Inside of this particular drawer are hanging folders for my table saw, my planer, my joiner, my dust collector, and so on. In the folder for the table saw is information about the motor, the blades, and the various accessories I purchased for the saw (such as an over-arm blade guard).

The WMI namespace is organized in a similar fashion. The namespaces are the file cabinets. The providers are drawers in the file cabinet. The folders in the drawers of the file cabinet are the WMI classes. These namespaces are shown in Figure 7-1.

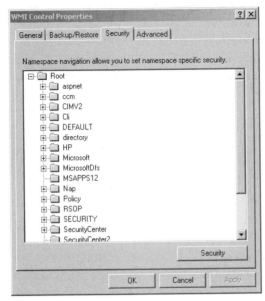

FIGURE 7-1 WMI namespaces on Windows Vista

Namespaces contain objects, and these objects contain properties that you can manipulate. Let's use a WMI command to illustrate how the WMI namespace is organized. The Get-WmiObject cmdlet is used to make the connection into the WMI. The class argument is used to specify the __Namespace class, and the namespace argument is used to specify the level in the WMI namespace hierarchy. The Get-WmiObject line of code is shown here.

```
Get-WmiObject –class __Namespace -namespace root |
Select-Object -property name
```

When the previous code is run, the following result appears on a Windows Vista computer.

```
name
----
subscription
DEFAULT
MicrosoftDfs
CIMV2
Cli
nap
SECURITY
SecurityCenter2
RSOP
WMI
```

directory

Policy

ServiceModel

SecurityCenter

Microsoft

aspnet

You can use the RecursiveWMINameSpaceListing.ps1 script to get an idea of the number and variety of WMI namespaces that exist on your computer, which is a great way to explore and learn about WMI. The entire contents of the RecursiveWMINameSpaceListing.ps1 script is shown here.

RecursiveWMINameSpaceListing.ps1
```
Function Get-WmiNameSpace($namespace, $computer)
{
 Get-WmiObject -class __NameSpace -computer $computer `
 -namespace $namespace -ErrorAction "SilentlyContinue" |
 Foreach-Object `
 -Process `
   {
     $subns = Join-Path -Path $_.__namespace -ChildPath $_.name
     $subns
     $script:i ++
     Get-WmiNameSpace -namespace $subNS -computer $computer
   }
} #end Get-WmiNameSpace


# *** Entry Point ***

$script:i = 0
$namespace = "root"
$computer = "LocalHost"
"Obtaining WMI Namespaces from $computer ..."
Get-WmiNameSpace -namespace $namespace -computer $computer
"There are $script:i namespaces on $computer"
```

The output from the RecursiveWMINameSpaceListing.ps1 script is shown here from the same Windows Vista computer that produced the earlier namespace listing. You can see that there is a rather intricate hierarchy of namespaces that exists on a modern operating system.

```
Obtaining WMI Namespaces from LocalHost ...
ROOT\subscription
ROOT\subscription\ms_409
ROOT\DEFAULT
ROOT\DEFAULT\ms_409
ROOT\MicrosoftDfs
ROOT\MicrosoftDfs\ms_409
```

```
ROOT\CIMV2
ROOT\CIMV2\Security
ROOT\CIMV2\Security\MicrosoftTpm
ROOT\CIMV2\ms_409
ROOT\CIMV2\TerminalServices
ROOT\CIMV2\TerminalServices\ms_409
ROOT\CIMV2\Applications
ROOT\CIMV2\Applications\Games
ROOT\Cli
ROOT\Cli\MS_409
ROOT\nap
ROOT\SECURITY
ROOT\SecurityCenter2
ROOT\RSOP
ROOT\RSOP\User
ROOT\RSOP\User\S_1_5_21_540299044_341859138_929407116_1133
ROOT\RSOP\User\S_1_5_21_540299044_341859138_929407116_1129
ROOT\RSOP\User\S_1_5_21_540299044_341859138_929407116_1118
ROOT\RSOP\User\S_1_5_21_918056312_2952985149_2686913973_500
ROOT\RSOP\User\S_1_5_21_135816822_1724403450_2350888535_500
ROOT\RSOP\User\ms_409
ROOT\RSOP\User\S_1_5_21_540299044_341859138_929407116_500
ROOT\RSOP\Computer
ROOT\RSOP\Computer\ms_409
ROOT\WMI
ROOT\WMI\ms_409
ROOT\directory
ROOT\directory\LDAP
ROOT\directory\LDAP\ms_409
ROOT\Policy
ROOT\Policy\ms_409
ROOT\ServiceModel
ROOT\SecurityCenter
ROOT\Microsoft
ROOT\Microsoft\HomeNet
ROOT\aspnet
There are 42 namespaces on LocalHost
```

So, what does all of this mean? It means that, on a Windows Vista machine, there are dozens of different namespaces from which you can pull information about your computer. Understanding that the different namespaces exist is the first step to begin navigating in WMI to find the information you need. Often, students and people who are new to Windows PowerShell work on a WMI script to make the script perform a certain action, which is a great way to learn scripting. However, what they often do not know is which namespace they need to connect to so that they can accomplish their task. When I tell them which namespace to work with, they sometimes reply, "It is fine for you, but how do I know that the such and such namespace even exists?" By using the RecursiveWMINameSpaceListing.ps1 script, you can easily generate a list of namespaces installed on a particular machine and, armed with that information, search MSDN to find out information about those namespaces. Or, if you like to explore, you can move on to the next topic: WMI providers.

Listing WMI Providers

Understanding the namespace assists the network administrator with judiciously applying WMI scripting to his or her network duties. However, as mentioned earlier, to access information via WMI, you must have access to a WMI provider. Once the provider is implemented, you can gain access to the information that is made available. If you want to know which classes are supported by the RouteProvider, you can click the Filter button and select RouteProvider as shown in Figure 7-2.

 ON THE COMPANION MEDIA Two Microsoft Office Excel spreadsheets with all of the providers and their associated classes from Windows XP and Windows Server 2003 are in the Job Aids folder on the companion media.

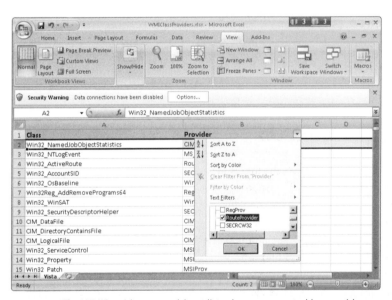

FIGURE 7-2 The WMIProviders spreadsheet lists classes supported by provider name.

Providers in WMI are all based on a template class or on a system class named __*provider*. With this information, you can look for instances of the __*provider* class and obtain a list of all providers that reside in your WMI namespace, which is exactly what the GetWMIProviders.ps1 script accomplishes.

The GetWMIProviders.ps1 script begins by assigning the string "root\cimv2" to the *$wmiNS* variable. This value is used with the `Get-WmiObject` cmdlet to specify where the WMI query takes place. It should be noted that the WMI *root\cimv2* namespace is the default WMI namespace on every Windows operating system since Microsoft Windows 2000.

The `Get-WmiObject` cmdlet is used to query WMI. The class provider is used to limit the WMI query to the *__provider* class. The namespace argument tells the `Get-WmiObject` cmdlet to look only in the *root\cimv2* WMI namespace. The array of objects returned from the *Get-WmiObject* cmdlet is pipelined into the `Sort-Object` cmdlet, where the listing of objects is alphabetized based on the *name* property. Once this process is complete, the reorganized objects are then passed to the `Format-List` cmdlet where the name of each provider is printed. The complete Get-WmiProviders.ps1 script is shown here.

Get-WmiProviders.ps1
```
Function Get-WmiProviders(

                         $namespace="root\cimv2",
                         $computer="localhost"
                         )

{
 Get-WmiObject -class __Provider -namespace $namespace `
 -computername $computer |
 Sort-Object -property Name |
 Select-Object -property Name
} #end Get-WmiProviders


Get-WmiProviders
```

Working with WMI Classes

In addition to working with namespaces, the inquisitive network administrator will also want to explore the concept of classes. In WMI parlance, there are core classes, common classes, and dynamic classes. *Core classes* represent managed objects that apply to all areas of management. These classes provide a basic vocabulary for analyzing and describing managed systems. Two examples of core classes are parameters and the *System.Security* class. *Common classes* are extensions to the core classes and represent managed objects that apply to specific management areas. However, common classes are independent of a particular implementation or technology. *CIM_UnitaryComputerSystem* is an example of a common class. Core and common classes are not used as often by network administrators because they serve as templates from which other classes are derived.

Therefore, many of the classes stored in *root\cimv2* are abstract classes and are used as templates. However, a few classes in *root\cimv2* are dynamic classes that are used to retrieve actual information. What is important to remember about *dynamic classes* is that instances of a dynamic class are generated by a provider and are therefore more likely to retrieve "live" data from the system.

To produce a simple listing of WMI classes, you can use the `Get-WMIObject` cmdlet and specify the list argument as shown here.

```
Get-WmiObject -list
```

A partial output from the previous command is shown here.

```
Win32_TSGeneralSetting                Win32_TSPermissionsSetting
Win32_TSClientSetting                 Win32_TSEnvironmentSetting
Win32_TSNetworkAdapterListSetting     Win32_TSLogonSetting
Win32_TSSessionSetting                Win32_DisplayConfiguration
Win32_COMSetting                      Win32_ClassicCOMClassSetting
Win32_DCOMApplicationSetting          Win32_MSIResource
Win32_ServiceControl                  Win32_Property
```

Working with Services

Clint Huffman, Senior Premier Field Engineer (PFE)
Microsoft Corporation

I travel a great deal, and, unfortunately, the battery life on my laptop isn't spectacular. Therefore, I've spent a fair amount of time discovering which services on my computer are consuming the I/O on my hard drive—most likely the largest consumer of battery power other than my monitor. I identified numerous services that I wouldn't need on a flight such as antivirus software, Windows Search, the Offline Files service, ReadyBoost, and so on. Because I was stopping and starting these services quite often, I decided to script the services.

WMI is a powerful object model that allows scripting languages, such as VBScript and Windows PowerShell, to perform tasks that were once only available to hardened C++ developers. Furthermore, far less code is needed to perform these tasks when scripting them makes automation relatively easy.

So, to begin this script, I need to select the correct services. WMI uses a SQL-like syntax named WMI Query Language (WQL); it is not named SQL syntax because WQL has some odd quirks that are specific to WMI. Now, I want my WQL query to return the Windows services that I identified earlier as users of frequent disk I/O such as the Offline Files service, the ReadyBoost service, my antivirus services that begin with "Microsoft ForeFront" (Microsoft Forefront Client Security Antimalware Service and Microsoft Forefront Client Security State Assessment Service), and, lastly, my personal file indexer, Windows Search.

```
$WQL = "SELECT Name, State, Caption FROM Win32_Service WHERE Caption LIKE
'Microsoft ForeFront%' OR Name = 'WSearch' OR Caption = 'Offline Files'
OR Caption = 'ReadyBoost'"
Get-WmiObject -Query $WQL
In my case, this script returns the following services as:
Offline Files
ReadyBoost
Microsoft Forefront Client Security Antimalware Service
Microsoft Forefront Client Security State Assessment Service
Windows Search
```

The *Caption* property is the text you see when you bring up Control Panel, Services, and the *name* property is the short name of the service that you might be more familiar with when using the command-line tool "Net Start" and "Net Stop." Finally, the *State* property tells me whether the service is running.

The WHERE clause allows me to limit the information that is returned. For example, if I don't use the WHERE clause, I receive all of the services as objects. This is nice if you want to know what services are on a computer, but it's not helpful when you simply want to shut down a few of them. For more information about WQL, go to "Querying with WQL" at *http://msdn.microsoft.com/en-us/library/aa392902.aspx*.

Because the *Query* parameter always returns a *collection* object, I need to enumerate the *Query* parameter to work with each item individually. This process is similar to receiving a package in the mail in a large cardboard box: before I can use what's inside, I need to open the package first. This is the point in the process in which the *Foreach* flow control statement is used. The *Foreach* statement allows me to work with one item at a time (for example, a service), which is similar to taking one item out of the cardboard box at a time. In this case, I have the Get-WmiObject cmdlet's return values go into a variable named *$CollectionOfServices* (my cardboard box). Next, I use the *Foreach* statement to work with each service, whereby the *$Service* variable becomes each service object in turn. The following code is the same as the previous code but with the addition of a *Foreach* loop.

```
$WQL = "SELECT Name, State, Caption FROM Win32_Service WHERE Caption LIKE
'Microsoft ForeFront%' OR Name = 'WSearch' OR Caption = 'Offline Files'
OR Caption = 'ReadyBoost'"
$CollectionOfServices = Get-WmiObject -Query $WQL
Foreach ($Service in $CollectionOfServices)
{
  $Service.Caption
}
```

Now that I can select specific services that I want to shut down, let's actually shut them down. I can do this by using the *StopService()* method as follows:

```
$WQL = "SELECT Name, State, Caption FROM Win32_Service WHERE Caption LIKE
'Microsoft ForeFront%' OR Name = 'WSearch' OR Caption = 'Offline Files'
OR Caption = 'ReadyBoost'"
$CollectionOfServices = Get-WmiObject -Query $WQL
Foreach ($Service in $CollectionOfServices)
{
  $Service.Caption
  $Service.StopService()
}
```

If my services don't actually stop, it is most likely because I don't have administrator rights to my customer or, if I am on Windows Vista, I need to run the script in an elevated Windows PowerShell command prompt. To make an elevated Windows PowerShell command prompt, right-click on the PowerShell icon, select Run As Administrator, and then try the script again.

Great! My unnecessary services are stopped. However, sometimes the services can be a bit tenacious and start up again the first chance they get. How do I hold them down? By setting them to disabled. How do I do that? By using the *ChangeStartMode()* method with the argument/parameter of "Disabled" as follows:

```
$WQL = "SELECT Name, State, Caption FROM Win32_Service WHERE Caption LIKE
'Microsoft ForeFront%' OR Name = 'WSearch' OR Caption = 'Offline Files'
OR Caption = 'ReadyBoost'"
$CollectionOfServices = Get-WmiObject -Query $WQL
Foreach ($Service in $CollectionOfServices)
{
  $Service.Caption
  $Service.StopService()
  $Service.ChangeStartMode("Disabled")
}
```

Now we're talking! Those pesky services are down for the count.

I've had my fun, my flight is over, and now I need to connect to my corporate network. Corporate policy does not allow me to connect unless my antivirus service is running. No problem. Two slight modifications to the script and the services are running again as follows:

```
$WQL = "SELECT Name, State, Caption FROM Win32_Service WHERE Caption LIKE
'Microsoft ForeFront%' OR Name = 'WSearch' OR Caption = 'Offline Files'
OR Caption = 'ReadyBoost'"
$CollectionOfServices = Get-WmiObject -Query $WQL
Foreach ($Service in $CollectionOfServices)
{
  $Service.Caption
  $Service.StartService()
```

```
    $Service.ChangeStartMode("Automatic")
  }
```

I replaced the *StopService()* method with *StartService()* and replaced the argument of the *ChangeStartMode()* method to "Automatic."

You might be thinking that this procedure is all well and good for your laptop battery, but what about doing massive restarts of services? Well, a great modification that you can make to the script is to run it against remote servers. For example, let's assume that you need to restart the services in a farm of 10 Web servers. You can simply modify the script slightly by adding the *–ComputerName* argument.

```
$WQL = "SELECT Name, State, Caption FROM Win32_Service WHERE Caption LIKE
'Microsoft ForeFront%' OR Name = 'WSearch' OR Caption = 'Offline Files'
OR Caption = 'ReadyBoost'"
$CollectionOfServices = Get-WmiObject -Query $WQL -ComputerName
demoserver
Foreach ($Service in $CollectionOfServices)
{
  $Service.Caption
  $Service.StartService()
  $Service.ChangeStartMode("Automatic")
}
```

These scripts have served me well, and I hope they help you too.

Changing Settings

For all of the benefits of using WMI, there are still many frustrating limitations. While WMI is good at retrieving information, it is not always very good at changing that information. The following example illustrates this point. The *Win32_Desktop* WMI class provides information about desktop settings as shown here.

```
PS C:\> Get-WmiObject Win32_Desktop
```

```
__GENUS           : 2
__CLASS           : Win32_Desktop
__SUPERCLASS      : CIM_Setting
__DYNASTY         : CIM_Setting
__RELPATH         : Win32_Desktop.Name="NT AUTHORITY\\SYSTEM"
__PROPERTY_COUNT  : 21
__DERIVATION      : {CIM_Setting}
__SERVER          : MRED1
__NAMESPACE       : root\cimv2
```

```
__PATH                   : \\MRED1\root\cimv2:Win32_Desktop.Name="NT AUTHORITY\\SY
                           STEM"
BorderWidth              : 1
Caption                  :
CoolSwitch               :
CursorBlinkRate          : 500
Description              :
DragFullWindows          : True
GridGranularity          :
IconSpacing              :
IconTitleFaceName        : Segoe UI
IconTitleSize            : 9
IconTitleWrap            : True
Name                     : NT AUTHORITY\SYSTEM
Pattern                  : (None)
ScreenSaverActive        : True
ScreenSaverExecutable : C:\Windows\system32\logon.scr
ScreenSaverSecure        : True
ScreenSaverTimeout       : 600
SettingID                :
Wallpaper                :
WallpaperStretched       : False
WallpaperTiled           :
```

As you can see from the properties and values that are returned from the `Get-WmiObject`
cmdlet, much of the information is valuable. Items such as screen saver time-out values and
secure screen saver are routine concerns to many network administrators. While it is true
that these values can, and in most cases should, be set via Group Policy, there are times
when network administrators want the ability to change these values via script. If you use
the `Get-Member` cmdlet to examine the properties of the *Win32_Desktop* WMI class, you are
greeted with the following information.

```
PS C:\> Get-WmiObject Win32_Desktop | Get-Member
    TypeName: System.Management.ManagementObject#root\cimv2\Win32_Desktop

Name                  MemberType   Definition
----                  ----------   ----------
BorderWidth           Property     System.UInt32 BorderWidth {get;set;}
Caption               Property     System.String Caption {get;set;}
CoolSwitch            Property     System.Boolean CoolSwitch {get;set;}
CursorBlinkRate       Property     System.UInt32 CursorBlinkRate {get;set;}
Description           Property     System.String Description {get;set;}
DragFullWindows       Property     System.Boolean DragFullWindows {get;set;}
GridGranularity       Property     System.UInt32 GridGranularity {get;set;}
IconSpacing           Property     System.UInt32 IconSpacing {get;set;}
IconTitleFaceName     Property     System.String IconTitleFaceName {get;set;}
IconTitleSize         Property     System.UInt32 IconTitleSize {get;set;}
```

```
IconTitleWrap            Property      System.Boolean IconTitleWrap {get;set;}
Name                     Property      System.String Name {get;set;}
Pattern                  Property      System.String Pattern {get;set;}
ScreenSaverActive        Property      System.Boolean ScreenSaverActive {get;set;}
ScreenSaverExecutable    Property      System.String ScreenSaverExecutable {get;...
ScreenSaverSecure        Property      System.Boolean ScreenSaverSecure {get;set;}
ScreenSaverTimeout       Property      System.UInt32 ScreenSaverTimeout {get;set;}
SettingID                Property      System.String SettingID {get;set;}
Wallpaper                Property      System.String Wallpaper {get;set;}
WallpaperStretched       Property      System.Boolean WallpaperStretched {get;set;}
WallpaperTiled           Property      System.Boolean WallpaperTiled {get;set;}
__CLASS                  Property      System.String __CLASS {get;set;}
__DERIVATION             Property      System.String[] __DERIVATION {get;set;}
__DYNASTY                Property      System.String __DYNASTY {get;set;}
__GENUS                  Property      System.Int32 __GENUS {get;set;}
__NAMESPACE              Property      System.String __NAMESPACE {get;set;}
__PATH                   Property      System.String __PATH {get;set;}
__PROPERTY_COUNT         Property      System.Int32 __PROPERTY_COUNT {get;set;}
__RELPATH                Property      System.String __RELPATH {get;set;}
__SERVER                 Property      System.String __SERVER {get;set;}
__SUPERCLASS             Property      System.String __SUPERCLASS {get;set;}
ConvertFromDateTime      ScriptMethod  System.Object ConvertFromDateTime();
ConvertToDateTime        ScriptMethod  System.Object ConvertToDateTime();
```

When you use the *–filter* parameter to obtain a specific instance of the *Win32_Desktop* WMI class and store it in a variable, you can then directly access the properties of the class. In this example, you need to escape the backslash that is used as a separator between NT Authority and System as shown here.

```
PS C:\> $desktop = Get-WmiObject Win32_Desktop -Filter `
>> "name = 'NT AUTHORITY\\SYSTEM'"
```

Once you have access to a specific instance of the WMI class, you can then assign a new value for the *ScreenSaverTimeout* parameter. As shown here, the value is updated immediately.

```
PS C:\> $Desktop.ScreenSaverTimeout = 300
PS C:\> $Desktop.ScreenSaverTimeout
300
```

However, if you resubmit the WMI query, you see that the *ScreenSaverTimeout* property is not updated. The get;set that is reported by the Get-Member cmdlet is related to the copy of the object that is returned by the WMI query and not to the actual instance of the object represented by the WMI class as shown here.

```
PS C:\> $desktop = Get-WmiObject Win32_Desktop -Filter `
>> "name = 'NT AUTHORITY\\SYSTEM'"
>>
PS C:\> $Desktop.ScreenSaverTimeout
600
```

Modifying Values Through the Registry

The GetSetScreenSaverTimeOut.ps1 script uses a single parameter named *debug*. This parameter is a *switched parameter*, which means that it only performs a function when it is present. The script prints detailed information when you run the script with the *debug* switch, such as letting you know which function is currently being called as shown in Figure 7-3.

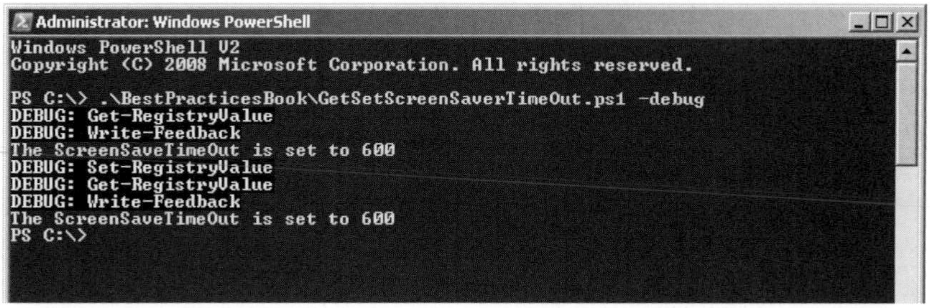

FIGURE 7-3 Detailed debug information is easily obtained when the script implements a *debug* parameter.

To create a command-line parameter, you can use the *Param* statement as shown here.

```
Param([switch]$debug)
```

Following the *Param* statement, which needs to be the first noncommented line of code in the script, the *Get-RegistryValue* function is created. In this code, the *$in* variable is passed by reference, which means that the function assigns a new value to the variable. This value is used outside of the function that assigns the value to it. To pass the variable by reference, you need to convert the *$in* variable to a reference type; you can use the [ref] type to perform this conversion. Therefore, you need to create the *$in* variable prior to calling the function because you cannot cast the variable to a reference type if it does not exist as shown here.

```
Function Get-RegistryValue([ref]$in)
```

Now you come to the first `Write-Debug` cmdlet. To write the debug information to the console prompt, the script uses the `Write-Debug` cmdlet. The `Write-Debug` cmdlet automatically formats the text with yellow and black colors (this is configurable, however), and it only writes text to the console if you tell it to do so. By default, `Write-Debug` does not print anything to the console, which means that you do not need to remove the `Write-Debug` statements prior to deploying the script. The *$DebugPreference* automatic variable is used to control the behavior of the `Write-Debug` cmdlet. By default, *$DebugPreference* is set to *SilentlyContinue* so that when it encounters a `Write-Debug` cmdlet, Windows PowerShell either skips over the cmdlet or silently continues to the next line. You can configure the *$DebugPreference* variable with one of four values defined in the *System.Management.Automation.ActionPreference* enumeration class. To see the possible enumeration values, you can either look for them on MSDN or use the *GetNames* static method from the *System.Enum* .NET Framework class as shown here.

```
PS C:\> [enum]::GetNames("System.Management.Automation.ActionPreference")
SilentlyContinue
Stop
Continue
Inquire
```

The Write-Debug cmdlet is used to print the value of the *name* property from the *System. Management.Automation.ScriptInfo* object. The *System.Management.Automation.ScriptInfo* object is obtained by querying the *MyCommand* property of the *System.Management. Automation.InvocationInfo* class. A *System.Management.Automation.InvocationInfo* object is returned when you query the *$MyInvocation* automatic variable. The properties of *System.Management.Automation.InvocationInfo* are shown in Table 7-2.

TABLE 7-2 Properties of the *System.Management.Automation.InvocationInfo* Class

PROPERTY	DEFINITION
BoundParameters	System.Collections.Generic.Dictionary`2[[System.String, mscorlib, Version=2.0.0.0, Culture=neutral, PublicKeyToken=b77a5c561934e089],[System.Object, mscorlib, Version=2.0.0.0, Culture=neutral, PublicKeyToken=b77a5c561934e089]] BoundParameters {get;}
CommandOrigin	System.Management.Automation.CommandOrigin CommandOrigin {get;}
ExpectingInput	System.Boolean ExpectingInput {get;}
InvocationName	System.String InvocationName {get;}
Line	System.String Line {get;}
MyCommand	System.Management.Automation.CommandInfo MyCommand {get;}
OffsetInLine	System.Int32 OffsetInLine {get;}
PipelineLength	System.Int32 PipelineLength {get;}
PipelinePosition	System.Int32 PipelinePosition {get;}
PositionMessage	System.String PositionMessage {get;}
ScriptLineNumber	System.Int32 ScriptLineNumber {get;}
ScriptName	System.String ScriptName {get;}
UnboundArguments	System.Collections.Generic.List`1[[System.Object, mscorlib, Version=2.0.0.0, Culture=neutral, PublicKeyToken=b77a5c561934e089]] UnboundArguments {get;}

The Write-Debug commands can be modified to include any of the properties you deem helpful to aid in troubleshooting. These properties become even more helpful when you are working with the *System.Management.Automation.ScriptInfo* object, whose properties are shown in Table 7-3.

TABLE 7-3 Properties of the *System.Management.Automation.ScriptInfo* Object

PROPERTY	DEFINITION
CommandType	System.Management.Automation.CommandTypes CommandType {get;}
Definition	System.String Definition {get;}
Module	System.Management.Automation.PSModuleInfo Module {get;}
ModuleName	System.String ModuleName {get;}
Name	System.String Name {get;}
Parameters	System.Collections.Generic.Dictionary`2[[System.String, mscorlib,Version=2.0.0.0, Culture=neutral, PublicKeyToken=b77a5c561934e089], [System.Management.Automation.ParameterMetadata, System.Management.Automation, Version=1.0.0.0, Culture=neutral, PublicKeyToken=31bf3856ad364e35]] Parameters {get;}
ParameterSets	System.Collections.ObjectModel.ReadOnlyCollection`1 [[System.Management.Automation.CommandParameterSetInfo, System.Management.Automation, Version=1.0.0.0, Culture=neutral, PublicKeyToken=31bf3856ad364e35]] ParameterSets {get;}
ScriptBlock	System.Management.Automation.ScriptBlock ScriptBlock {get;}
Visibility	System.Management.Automation.SessionStateEntryVisibility Visibility {get;set;}

The `Write-Debug` command is shown here.

```
{
Write-Debug $MyInvocation.MyCommand.name
```

To use the *$in* reference type variable, you must assign the data to the *Value* property of the variable. The `Get-ItemProperty` cmdlet creates a custom Windows PowerShell object. As you can see here, a number of properties are contained in the custom object.

```
PS C:\> $swValue = Get-ItemProperty -Path HKCU:\Scripting\Stopwatch
PS C:\> $swValue
PSPath          : Microsoft.PowerShell.Core\Registry::HKEY_CURRENT_USER\Scripting\
Stopwatch
PSParentPath    : Microsoft.PowerShell.Core\Registry::HKEY_CURRENT_USER\Scripting
PSChildName     : Stopwatch
PSDrive         : HKCU
PSProvider      : Microsoft.PowerShell.Core\Registry
PreviousCommand : 00:00:00.3153793
```

You do not have to use the intermediate variable to obtain the previous *Value* property. You can use parentheses and query the property directly. Although this may be a bit confusing, it is certainly a valid syntax as shown here.

```
PS C:\> (Get-ItemProperty -Path HKCU:\Scripting\Stopwatch).PreviousCommand
00:00:00.3153793
```

Once you have the custom object, you can query the *name* property and assign it to the *Value* property of the *$in* reference type variable as shown here.

```
$in.value = (Get-ItemProperty -path $path -name $name).$name
} #end Get-RegistryValue
```

Next, the *Set-RegistryValue* function is created. This function accepts an input variable named *$value*. As in the previous function, you first use the `Write-Debug` cmdlet to print the name of the function. Then, the `Set-ItemProperty` cmdlet is used to assign the value to the registry. This new value was passed when the function was called and is contained in the *$value* variable as shown here.

```
Function Set-RegistryValue($value)
{
 Write-Debug $MyInvocation.MyCommand.name
 Set-ItemProperty -Path $path -name $name -value $value
} #end Get-RegistryValue
```

Once the registry is updated via the *Set-RegistryValue* function, it is time to provide feedback to the user via the *Write-Feedback* function. The `Write-Debug` cmdlet is used to print debug information stating that the script is in the *Set-RegistryValue* function. This information is displayed only when the script is run with the *–debug* switch. The next line of the script is always used to display feedback. One interesting item is the *subexpression*, which is used to force the evaluation of the *Value* property to return the reference type object. This may seem a bit confusing until you understand that there are two types of string characters in Windows PowerShell. The first is a literal string, which is represented with single quotation marks. In a literal string, what you see is what you get and a variable is not expanded inside single quotation marks as shown here.

```
PS C:\> $a = "this is a string"
PS C:\> 'This is what is in $a'
This is what is in $a
```

When you use an expanding string, which is represented by double quotation marks, the value of the variable is expanded and printed as shown here.

```
PS C:\> $a = "this is a string"
PS C:\> "This is what is in $a"
This is what is in this is a string
```

While frustrating at first, the expanding string behavior can be used to your advantage to avoid concatenation of strings and variables. Once you are aware of the two strings, you can use the backtick character to suppress variable expansion when desired and proceed as follows:

```
PS C:\> $a = "this is a string"
PS C:\> "This is what is in `$a: $a"
This is what is in $a: this is a string
```

If you do not have expanding strings, you need to concatenate the output as shown here.

```
PS C:\> $a = "this is a string"
PS C:\> 'This is what is in $a: ' + $a
This is what is in $a: this is a string
```

So what does the expanding string behavior have to do with your code? When an object is expanded in an expanding string, it tells you the name of the object. If you want to see the value, you need to create a subexpression by placing the object in smooth parentheses and placing a dollar sign in front of it. This action forces evaluation of the object and returns the default property to the command line as shown here.

```
Function Write-Feedback($in)
{
 Write-Debug $MyInvocation.MyCommand.name
"The $name is set to $($in)"
} #end Write-Feedback
```

Next, the script checks to determine whether the *$debug* variable exists. If the *$debug* variable exists, it means the script was launched with the *–debug* switch. If this is the case, the script changes the value of the *$debugPreference* automatic variable from *SilentlyContinue* to *continue*. This action causes the *debug* statements created by the Write-Debug cmdlet to be emitted to the command line as shown here.

```
if($debug) { $DebugPreference = "continue" }
```

Now it is time to initialize several variables. The first variable is the path to the desktop settings, and the next variable is the name of the registry key to change. These two variables are shown here.

```
$path = 'HKCU:\Control Panel\Desktop'
$name = 'ScreenSaveTimeOut'
```

The last two variables that need to be initialized are the *$in* variable and the value assigned to the screen saver time-out as shown here.

```
$in = $null
$value = 600
```

The remainder of the script calls the functions in correct order. The first function called is the *Get-RegistryValue* function, which obtains the current value of the screen saver time-out. The *Write_Feedback* function is called to print the value of the screen saver time-out. Next, the *Set-RegistryValue* function is called, which updates the screen saver time-out. The *Get-RegistryValue* function is then called to obtain the registry value, and it is displayed with the *Write-Feedback* function as shown here.

```
Get-RegistryValue([ref]$in)
Write-Feedback($in)
Set-RegistryValue($value)
Get-RegistryValue([ref]$in)
Write-Feedback($in)
```

The completed GetSetScreenSaverTimeOut.ps1 is shown here.

GetSetScreenSaverTimeOut.ps1
```
Param([switch]$debug)
Function Get-RegistryValue([ref]$in)
{
 Write-Debug $MyInvocation.MyCommand.name
 $in.value = (Get-ItemProperty -path $path -name $name).$name
} #end Get-RegistryValue

Function Set-RegistryValue($value)
{
 Write-Debug $MyInvocation.MyCommand.name
 Set-ItemProperty -Path $path -name $name -value $value
} #end Get-RegistryValue

Function Write-Feedback($in)
{
 Write-Debug $MyInvocation.MyCommand.name
 "The $name is set to $($in)"
} #end Write-Feedback

# *** Entry Point ***
if($debug) { $DebugPreference = "continue" }
$path = 'HKCU:\Control Panel\Desktop'
$name = 'ScreenSaveTimeOut'
$in = $null
$value = 600

Get-RegistryValue([ref]$in)
Write-Feedback($in)
Set-RegistryValue($value)
Get-RegistryValue([ref]$in)
Write-Feedback($in)
```

Lack of .NET Framework Support

The ability to work with the .NET Framework from within Windows PowerShell is very exciting. Because Windows PowerShell itself is a .NET Framework application, access to the .NET Framework is very direct and natural. At times, the question is not what can be done with .NET Framework classes, but rather what cannot be done. The constructors for some of the .NET Framework classes can be both confusing and complicated. A *constructor* is used to create an instance of a class; in many cases, you must first create an instance of a class prior to using the classes. However, sometimes you do not need a constructor at all, and these methods are called static. There are both static methods and static properties.

Use of Static Methods and Properties

Static methods and properties are members that are always available. To use a static method, you place the class name in square brackets and separate the method name by two colons. An example is the *tan* method from the *System.Math* class. The *tan* method is used to find the tangent of a number. As shown here, you can use the *tan* static method from the *System.Math* class to find the tangent of a 45-degree angle.

```
PS C:\> [system.math]::tan(45)
1.61977519054386
```

When referring to *System.Math*, the word *system* is used to represent the namespace in which the "*math* class" is found. In most cases, you can drop the word *system* if you want to and the process will work exactly the same. When working at the command line, you may want to save some typing and drop the word *system*, but I consider it to be a best practice to always include the word *system* in a script. If you drop the word *system*, the command looks like the following code.

```
PS C:\> [math]::tan(45)
1.61977519054386
```

You can use the Get-Member cmdlet with the *static* switched parameter to obtain the members of the *System.Math* .NET Framework class. To do this, the command looks like the following example.

```
[math] | Get-Member –static
```

The static members of the *System.Math* class are shown in Table 7-4. These static methods are very important because you can perform most of the functionality from the class by using them. For example, there is no *tan* function built into Windows PowerShell. If you want the tangent of an angle, you must use either the static methods from *System.Math* or write your own tangent function. This occurs by design. To perform these mathematical computations, you need to use the .NET Framework. Rather than being a liability, the .NET Framework is a tremendous asset because it is a mature technology and is well documented.

TABLE 7-4 Members of the *System.Math* Class

NAME	MEMBERTYPE	DEFINITION
Abs	Method	static System.SByte Abs(SByte value) static System.Int16 Abs(Int16 value) static System.Int32 Abs(Int32 value) static System.Int64 Abs(Int64 value) static System.Single Abs(Single value) static System.Double Abs(Double value) static System.Decimal Abs(Decimal value)
Acos	Method	static System.Double Acos(Double d)
Asin	Method	static System.Double Asin(Double d)
Atan	Method	static System.Double Atan(Double d)
Atan2	Method	static System.Double Atan2(Double y Double x)
BigMul	Method	static System.Int64 BigMul(Int32 a Int32 b)
Ceiling	Method	static System.Decimal Ceiling(Decimal d) static System.Double Ceiling(Double a)
Cos	Method	static System.Double Cos(Double d)
Cosh	Method	static System.Double Cosh(Double value)
DivRem	Method	static System.Int32 DivRem(Int32 a Int32 b Int32& result) static System.Int64 DivRem(Int64 a Int64 b Int64& result)
Equals	Method	static System.Boolean Equals(Object objA Object objB)
Exp	Method	static System.Double Exp(Double d)
Floor	Method	static System.Decimal Floor(Decimal d) static System.Double Floor(Double d)
IEEERemainder	Method	static System.Double IEEERemainder(Double x Double y)
Log	Method	static System.Double Log(Double d) static System.Double Log(Double a Double newBase)
Log10	Method	static System.Double Log10(Double d)
Max	Method	static System.SByte Max(SByte val1 SByte val2) static System.Byte Max(Byte val1 Byte val2) static System.Int16 Max(Int16 val1 Int16 val2) static System.UInt16 Max(UInt16 val1 UInt16 val2) static System.Int32 Max(Int32 val1 Int32 val2) static System.UInt32 Max(UInt32 val1 UInt32 val2) static System.Int64 Max(Int64 val1 Int64 val2) static System.UInt64 Max(UInt64 val1 UInt64 val2) static System.Single Max(Single val1 Single val2) static System.Double Max(Double val1 Double val2) static System.Decimal Max(Decimal val1 Decimal val2)

NAME	MEMBERTYPE	DEFINITION
Min	Method	static System.SByte Min(SByte val1 SByte val2) static System.Byte Min(Byte val1 Byte val2) static System.Int16 Min(Int16 val1 Int16 val2) static System.UInt16 Min(UInt16 val1 UInt16 val2) static System.Int32 Min(Int32 val1 Int32 val2) static System.UInt32 Min(UInt32 val1 UInt32 val2) static System.Int64 Min(Int64 val1 Int64 val2) static System.UInt64 Min(UInt64 val1 UInt64 val2) static System.Single Min(Single val1 Single val2) static System.Double Min(Double val1 Double val2) static System.Decimal Min(Decimal val1 Decimal val2)
Pow	Method	static System.Double Pow(Double x Double y)
ReferenceEquals	Method	static System.Boolean ReferenceEquals(Object objA Object objB)
Round	Method	static System.Double Round(Double a) static System.Double Round(Double value Int32 digits) static System.Double Round(Double value MidpointRounding mode) static System.Double Round(Double value Int32 digits MidpointRounding mode) static System.Decimal Round(Decimal d) static System.Decimal Round(Decimal d Int32 decimals) static System.Decimal Round(Decimal d MidpointRounding mode) static System.Decimal Round(Decimal d Int32 decimals MidpointRounding mode)
Sign	Method	static System.Int32 Sign(SByte value) static System.Int32 Sign(Int16 value) static System.Int32 Sign(Int32 value) static System.Int32 Sign(Int64 value) static System.Int32 Sign(Single value) static System.Int32 Sign(Double value) static System.Int32 Sign(Decimal value)
Sin	Method	static System.Double Sin(Double a)
Sinh	Method	static System.Double Sinh(Double value)
Sqrt	Method	static System.Double Sqrt(Double d)
Tan	Method	static System.Double Tan(Double a)
Tanh	Method	static System.Double Tanh(Double value)
Truncate	Method	static System.Decimal Truncate(Decimal d) static System.Double Truncate(Double d)
E	Property	static System.Double E {get;}
PI	Property	static System.Double PI {get;}

Version Dependencies

One of the more interesting facets of the .NET Framework is that there always seems to be a new version available, and, of course, between versions there are service packs. While the .NET Framework is included in the operating system, updates to the .NET Framework are unfortunately not included in service packs. It therefore becomes the responsibility of the network administrators to package and deploy updates to the framework. Until the introduction of Windows PowerShell, network administrators were not keen to provide updates simply because they did not have a vested interest in the deployment of the .NET Framework. This behavior was not due to a lack of interest; in many cases, it was due to a lack of understanding of the .NET Framework. If developers did not request updates to the .NET Framework, then it did not get updated.

Lack of COM Support

Many very useful capabilities are packaged as Component Object Model (COM) components. Finding these COM objects is sometimes a matter of luck. Of course, you can always read the MSDN documentation; unfortunately, the articles do not always list the program ID that is required to create the COM object, and this is even true in articles that refer to the scripting interfaces. An example can be found in the Windows Media Player scripting object model. You can work your way through the entire Software Development Kit (SDK) documentation without discovering that the program ID is *wmplayer.ocx* and not *player*, which is used for illustrative purposes. The most natural way to work with a COM object in Windows PowerShell is to use the New-Object cmdlet, specify the *–ComObject* parameter, and give the parameter the program ID. If the program ID is not forthcoming, then you have a more difficult proposition. You can search the registry and, by doing a bit of detective work, find the program ID.

An example of a COM object whose program ID is hard to find is the object with the *makecab.makecab* program ID. The *makecab.makecab* object is used to make *cabinet files*, which are highly compressed files often used by programmers to deploy software applications. There is no reason why an enterprise network administrator cannot use .cab files to compress log files prior to transferring them across the application. The only problem is that, while the *makecab.makecab* object is present in Windows XP and Windows Server 2003, it has been removed from the operating system beginning with Windows Vista. When working with newer operating systems, a different approach is required.

To make the script easier to use, you must first create some command-line parameters by using the *Param* statement. The *Param* statement must be the first noncommented line in the script. When the script is run from within the Windows PowerShell console or from within a script editor, the command-line parameters are used to control the way in which the script executes. In this way, the script can be run without needing to edit it each time you want to create a .cab file from a different directory. You only need to supply a new value for the *–filepath* parameter as shown here.

```
CreateCab.ps1 –filepath C:\fso1
```

What is good about command-line parameters is that they use partial parameter completion, which means that you only need to supply enough of the parameter for it to be unique. Therefore, you can use command-line syntax such as the following:

```
CreateCab.ps1 –f c:\fso1 –p c:\fso2\bcab.cab –d
```

The previous syntax searches the c:\fso directory and obtains all of the files. It then creates a cabinet file named bcab.cab in the fso2 folder of the C:\ drive. The syntax also produces debugging information while it is running. Note that the *debug* parameter is a switched parameter because *debug* only affects the script when it is present. This section of the CreateCab.ps1 script is shown here.

```
Param(
        $filepath = "C:\fso",
        $path = "C:\fso\aCab.cab",
        [switch]$debug
      )
```

It is now time to create the *New-Cab* function, which will accept two input parameters. The first is the *–path* parameter, and the second is the *–files* parameter.

```
Function New-Cab($path,$files)
```

You can assign the *makecab.makecab* program ID to a variable named *$makecab*, which makes the script a bit easier to read. This is also a good place to put the first `Write-Debug` statement.

```
{
 $makecab = "makecab.makecab"
 Write-Debug "Creating Cab path is: $path"
```

You now need to create the COM object.

```
$cab = New-Object –ComObject $makecab
```

A bit of error checking is in order. To do this, you can use the *$?* automatic variable.

```
if(!$?) { $(Throw "unable to create $makecab object")}
```

If no errors occur during the attempt to create the *makecab.makecab* object, then you can use the object contained in the *$cab* variable and call the *createcab* method.

```
$cab.CreateCab($path,$false,$false,$false)
```

After you create the .cab file, you need to add files to it by using the *Foreach* statement.

```
Foreach ($file in $files)
  {
  $file = $file.fullname.tostring()
  $fileName = Split-Path -path $file -leaf
```

After you turn the full file name into a string and remove the directory information by using the Split-Path cmdlet, another Write-Debug statement is needed to let the user of the script be informed of progress as shown here.

```
Write-Debug "Adding from $file"
Write-Debug "File name is $fileName"
```

Next, you need to add a file to the cabinet file.

```
$cab.AddFile($file,$filename)
}
Write-Debug "Closing cab $path"
```

To close the cabinet file, you can use the *closecab* method.

```
$cab.CloseCab()
} #end New-Cab
```

It is now time to go to the entry point of the script. First, you must determine whether the script is being run in debug mode by looking for the presence of the *$debug* variable. If it is running in debug mode, you must set the value of the *$DebugPreference* variable to *continue*, which allows the Write-Debug statements to be printed on the screen. By default, *$DebugPreference* is set to *SilentlyContinue*, which means that no debug statements are displayed and Windows PowerShell skips past the Write-Debug command without taking any action as shown here.

```
if($debug) {$DebugPreference = "continue"}
```

Now, you need to obtain a collection of files by using the Get-ChildItem cmdlet.

```
$files = Get-ChildItem -path $filePath | Where-Object { !$_.psiscontainer }
```

After you have a collection of files, you can pass the collection to the *New-Cab* function as shown here.

```
New-Cab -path $path -files $files
```

The completed CreateCab.ps1 script is shown here. Note: The CreateCab.ps1 script will not run on Windows Vista and later versions due to lack of support for the *makecab.makecab* COM object. An alternate method of creating .cab files is explored in the "Lack of External Application Support" section later in the chapter.

```
CreateCab.ps1
Param(
        $filepath = "C:\fso",
        $path = "C:\fso\aCab.cab",
        [switch]$debug
        )
Function New-Cab($path,$files)
{
  $makecab = "makecab.makecab"
  Write-Debug "Creating Cab path is: $path"
```

```
$cab = New-Object -ComObject $makecab
if(!$?) { $(Throw "unable to create $makecab object")}
$cab.CreateCab($path,$false,$false,$false)
Foreach ($file in $files)
 {
   $file = $file.fullname.tostring()
   $fileName = Split-Path -path $file -leaf
   Write-Debug "Adding from $file"
   Write-Debug "File name is $fileName"
   $cab.AddFile($file,$filename)
 }
Write-Debug "Closing cab $path"
$cab.CloseCab()
} #end New-Cab


# *** entry point to script ***
if($debug) {$DebugPreference = "continue"}
$files = Get-ChildItem -path $filePath | Where-Object { !$_.psiscontainer }
New-Cab -path $path -files $files
```

You cannot use the *makecab.makecab* object to expand the cabinet file because it does not have an *expand* method. You also cannot use the *makecab.expandcab* object because it does not exist. Because the ability to expand a cabinet file is inherent in the Windows shell, you can use the *shell* object to expand the cabinet file. To access the shell, you can use the *Shell.Application* COM object.

You must first create command-line parameters. This section of the script is very similar to the parameter section of the previous CreateCab.ps1 script. The command-line parameters are shown here.

```
Param(
      $cab = "C:\fso\acab.cab",
      $destination = "C:\fso1",
      [switch]$debug
      )
```

After you create command-line parameters, it is time to create the *ConvertFrom-Cab* function, which will accept two command-line parameters. The first parameter contains the .cab file, and the second parameter contains the destination to expand the files as shown here.

```
Function ConvertFrom-Cab($cab,$destination)
```

You should now create an instance of the *Shell.Application* object. The *Shell.Application* object is a very powerful object with a number of useful methods. The members of the *Shell.Application* object are shown in Table 7-5.

TABLE 7-5 Members of the *Shell.Application* Object

NAME	MEMBERTYPE	DEFINITION
AddToRecent	Method	void AddToRecent (Variant, string)
BrowseForFolder	Method	Folder BrowseForFolder (int, string, int, Variant)
CanStartStopService	Method	Variant CanStartStopService (string)
CascadeWindows	Method	void CascadeWindows ()
ControlPanelItem	Method	void ControlPanelItem (string)
EjectPC	Method	void EjectPC ()
Explore	Method	void Explore (Variant)
ExplorerPolicy	Method	Variant ExplorerPolicy (string)
FileRun	Method	void FileRun ()
FindComputer	Method	void FindComputer ()
FindFiles	Method	void FindFiles ()
FindPrinter	Method	void FindPrinter (string, string, string)
GetSetting	Method	bool GetSetting (int)
GetSystemInformation	Method	Variant GetSystemInformation (string)
Help	Method	void Help ()
IsRestricted	Method	int IsRestricted (string, string)
IsServiceRunning	Method	Variant IsServiceRunning (string)
MinimizeAll	Method	void MinimizeAll ()
NameSpace	Method	Folder NameSpace (Variant)
Open	Method	void Open (Variant)
RefreshMenu	Method	void RefreshMenu ()
ServiceStart	Method	Variant ServiceStart (string, Variant)
ServiceStop	Method	Variant ServiceStop (string, Variant)
SetTime	Method	void SetTime ()
ShellExecute	Method	void ShellExecute (string, Variant, Variant, Variant, Variant)
ShowBrowserBar	Method	Variant ShowBrowserBar (string, Variant)
ShutdownWindows	Method	void ShutdownWindows ()
Suspend	Method	void Suspend ()
TileHorizontally	Method	void TileHorizontally ()
TileVertically	Method	void TileVertically ()

NAME	MEMBERTYPE	DEFINITION
ToggleDesktop	Method	void ToggleDesktop ()
TrayProperties	Method	void TrayProperties ()
UndoMinimizeALL	Method	void UndoMinimizeALL ()
Windows	Method	IDispatch Windows ()
WindowsSecurity	Method	void WindowsSecurity ()
WindowSwitcher	Method	void WindowSwitcher ()
Application	Property	IDispatch Application () {get}
Parent	Property	IDispatch Parent () {get}

Because you want to use the name of the COM object more than once, it is a good practice to assign the program ID of the COM object to a variable. You can then use the string with the New-Object cmdlet and also use it when providing feedback to the user. The line of code that assigns the *Shell.Application* program ID to a string is shown here.

```
{
 $comObject = "Shell.Application"
```

It is now time to provide some feedback to the user. You can do this by using the Write-Debug cmdlet together with a message stating that you are attempting to create the *Shell.Application* object as shown here.

```
 Write-Debug "Creating $comObject"
```

After you provide debug feedback stating you are going to create the object, you can actually create the object as shown here.

```
 $shell = New-Object -Comobject $comObject
```

Now you want to test for errors by using the *$?* automatic variable. The *$?* automatic variable tells you whether the last command completed successfully. Because *$?* is a Boolean true/false variable, you can use this fact to simplify the coding. You can use the *not* operator, *!*, in conjunction with an *If* statement. If the variable is not true, then you can use the *Throw* statement to raise an error and halt execution of the script. This section of the script is shown here.

```
 if(!$?) { $(Throw "unable to create $comObject object")}
```

If the script successfully creates the *Shell.Application* object, it is now time to provide more feedback as shown here.

```
 Write-Debug "Creating source cab object for $cab"
```

The next step in the operation is to connect to the .cab file by using the *Namespace* method from the *Shell.Application* object as shown here. This is another important step in the process, so it makes sense to use another Write-Debug statement as a progress indicator to the user.

```
$sourceCab = $shell.Namespace($cab).items()
Write-Debug "Creating destination folder object for $destination"
```

It is time to connect to the destination folder by using the *Namespace* method as shown here. You also want to use another Write-Debug statement to let the user know the folder to which you actually connected.

```
$DestinationFolder = $shell.Namespace($destination)
Write-Debug "Expanding $cab to $destination"
```

With all of that preparation out of the way, the actual command that is used to expand the cabinet file is somewhat anticlimactic. You can use the *copyhere* method from the *folder* object that is stored in the *$destinationFolder* variable. You give the reference to the .cab file that is stored in the *$sourceCab* variable as the input parameter as shown here.

```
$DestinationFolder.CopyHere($sourceCab)
}
```

The starting point to the script accomplishes two things. First, it checks for the presence of the *$debug* variable. If found, it then sets the *$debugPreference* to *continue* to force the Write-Debug cmdlet to print messages to the console window. Second, it calls the *ConvertFrom-Cab* function and passes the path to the .cab file from the *–cab* command-line parameter and the destination for the expanded files from the *–destination* parameter as shown here.

```
if($debug) { $debugPreference = "continue" }
ConvertFrom-Cab -cab $cab -destination $destination
```

The completed ExpandCab.ps1 script is shown here.

```
ExpandCab.ps1
Param(
        $cab = "C:\fso\acab.cab",
        $destination = "C:\fso1",
        [switch]$debug
        )
Function ConvertFrom-Cab($cab,$destination)
{
 $comObject = "Shell.Application"
 Write-Debug "Creating $comObject"
 $shell = New-Object -Comobject $comObject
 if(!$?) { $(Throw "unable to create $comObject object")}
 Write-Debug "Creating source cab object for $cab"
 $sourceCab = $shell.Namespace($cab).items()
 Write-Debug "Creating destination folder object for $destination"
 $DestinationFolder = $shell.Namespace($destination)
 Write-Debug "Expanding $cab to $destination"
 $DestinationFolder.CopyHere($sourceCab)
 }
```

```
# *** entry point ***
if($debug) { $debugPreference = "continue" }
ConvertFrom-Cab -cab $cab -destination $destination
```

Lack of External Application Support

Many management features still rely on the use of command-line support; a very common
example is NETSH. Another example is the MakeCab.exe utility. The *makecab.makecab* COM
object was removed from Windows Vista and later versions. To create a .cab file in Windows
Vista and beyond, you need to use the MakeCab.exe utility.

First, you need to create a few command-line parameters as shown here.

```
Param(
        $filepath = "C:\fso",
        $path = "C:\fso1\cabfiles",
        [switch]$debug
    )
```

Then you need to create the *New-DDF* function, which creates a basic .ddf file that is used
by the MakeCab.exe program to create the .cab file. The syntax for these types of files is
documented in the Microsoft Cabinet SDK on MSDN. Once you use the *Function* keyword to
create the *New-DDF* function, you can use the Join-Path cmdlet to create the file path to the
temporary .ddf file you will use. You can concatenate the drive, the folder, and the file name
together, but this might become a cumbersome and error-prone operation. As a best practice, you should always use the Join-Path cmdlet to build your file paths as shown here.

```
Function New-DDF($path,$filePath)
{
 $ddfFile = Join-Path -path $filePath -childpath temp.ddf
```

It is time to provide some feedback to the user if the script is run with the –*debug* switch
by using the Write-Debug cmdlet as shown here.

```
Write-Debug "DDF file path is $ddfFile"
```

You now need to create the first portion of the .ddf file by using an expanding here-string.
The advantage of a here-string is that it allows you not to worry about escaping special characters. For example, the comment character in a .ddf file is the semicolon, which is a reserved
character in Windows PowerShell. If you try to create the .ddf text without the advantage of
using the here-string, you then need to escape each of the semicolons to avoid compile-time
errors. By using an expanding here-string, you can take advantage of the expansion of variables. A here-string begins with an at sign and a quotation mark and ends with a quotation
mark and an at sign as shown here.

```
$ddfHeader =@"
;*** MakeCAB Directive file
;
.OPTION EXPLICIT
.Set CabinetNameTemplate=Cab.*.cab
.set DiskDirectory1=C:\fso1\Cabfiles
.Set MaxDiskSize=CDROM
.Set Cabinet=on
.Set Compress=on
"@
```

You may choose to add more feedback for the user via the `Write-Debug` cmdlet as shown here.

```
Write-Debug "Writing ddf file header to $ddfFile"
```

After providing feedback to the user, you come to the section that might cause some problems. The .ddf file must be a pure ASCII file. By default, Windows PowerShell uses Unicode. To ensure that you have an ASCII file, you must use the `Out-File` cmdlet. You can usually avoid using `Out-File` by using the file redirection arrows; however, this is not one of those occasions. Here is the syntax.

```
$ddfHeader | Out-File -filepath $ddfFile -force -encoding ASCII
```

You probably want to provide more debug information via the `Write-Debug` cmdlet before you gather your collection of files via the `Get-ChildItem` cmdlet as shown here.

```
Write-Debug "Generating collection of files from $filePath"
Get-ChildItem -path $filePath |
```

It is important to filter out folders from the collection because the MakeCab.exe utility is not able to compress folders. To filter folders, use the `Where-Object` cmdlet with a *not* operator stating that the object is not a container as shown here.

```
Where-Object { !$_.psiscontainer } |
```

After you filter out folders, you need to work with each individual file as it comes across the pipeline by using the `ForEach-Object` cmdlet. Because `ForEach-Object` is a cmdlet as opposed to a language statement, the curly brackets must be on the same line as the `ForEach-Object` cmdlet name. The problem arises in that the curly brackets often get buried within the code. As a best practice, I like to line up the curly brackets unless the command is very short, such as in the previous `Where-Object` command, but this process requires the use of the line continuation character (the backtick). I know some developers who avoid using line continuation, but I personally think that lining up curly brackets is more important because it makes the code easier to read. Here is the beginning of the `ForEach-Object` cmdlet.

```
Foreach-Object `
```

Because the .dff file used by MakeCab.exe is ASCII text, you need to convert the *FullName* property of the *System.IO.FileInfo* object returned by the Get-ChildItem cmdlet to a string. In addition, because you may have files with spaces in their name, it makes sense to ensconce the file *FullName* value in a set of quotation marks as shown here.

```
{
   '"' + $_.fullname.tostring() + '"'  |
```

You then pipeline the file names to the Out-File cmdlet, making sure to specify the ASCII encoding, and use the *–append* switch to avoid overwriting everything else in the text file as shown here.

```
   Out-File -filepath $ddfFile -encoding ASCII -append
}
```

Now you can provide another update to the debug users and call the *New-Cab* function as shown here.

```
Write-Debug "ddf file is created. Calling New-Cab function"
New-Cab($ddfFile)
} #end New-DDF
```

When you enter the *New-Cab* function, you may want to supply some information to the user as shown here.

```
Function New-Cab($ddfFile)
{
   Write-Debug "Entering the New-Cab function. The DDF File is $ddfFile"
```

If the script is run with the *–debug* switch, you can use the */V* parameter of the MakeCab.exe executable to provide detailed debugging information. If the script is not run with the *–debug* switch, you do not want to clutter the screen with too much information and can therefore rely on the default verbosity of the utility as shown here.

```
  if($debug)
     { makecab /f $ddfFile /V3 }
  Else
     { makecab /f $ddfFile }
} #end New-Cab
```

The entry point to the script checks whether the *$debug* variable is present. If it is, the *$debugPreference* automatic variable is set to *continue*, and debugging information is displayed via the Write-Debug cmdlet. Once that check is performed, the New-DDF cmdlet is called with the *path* and *filepath* values supplied to the command line as shown here.

```
if($debug) {$DebugPreference = "continue"}
New-DDF -path $path -filepath $filepath
```

The completed CreateCab2.ps1 script is shown here.

CreateCab2.ps1

```powershell
Param(
      $filepath = "C:\fso",
      $path = "C:\fso1\cabfiles",
      [switch]$debug
      )
Function New-DDF($path,$filePath)
{
 $ddfFile = Join-Path -path $filePath -childpath temp.ddf
 Write-Debug "DDF file path is $ddfFile"
 $ddfHeader =@"
;*** MakeCAB Directive file
;
.OPTION EXPLICIT
.Set CabinetNameTemplate=Cab.*.cab
.set DiskDirectory1=C:\fso1\Cabfiles
.Set MaxDiskSize=CDROM
.Set Cabinet=on
.Set Compress=on
"@
 Write-Debug "Writing ddf file header to $ddfFile"
 $ddfHeader | Out-File -filepath $ddfFile -force -encoding ASCII
 Write-Debug "Generating collection of files from $filePath"
 Get-ChildItem -path $filePath |
 Where-Object { !$_.psiscontainer } |
 Foreach-Object `
  {
    '"' + $_.fullname.tostring() + '"' |
   Out-File -filepath $ddfFile -encoding ASCII -append
  }
 Write-Debug "ddf file is created. Calling New-Cab function"
 New-Cab($ddfFile)
} #end New-DDF


Function New-Cab($ddfFile)
{
 Write-Debug "Entering the New-Cab function. The DDF File is $ddfFile"
 if($debug)
    { makecab /f $ddfFile /V3 }
 Else
    { makecab /f $ddfFile }
} #end New-Cab


# *** entry point to script ***
if($debug) {$DebugPreference = "continue"}
New-DDF -path $path -filepath $filepath
```

Additional Resources

- The TechNet Script Center at *http://www.microsoft.com/technet/scriptcenter* has numerous examples of Windows PowerShell scripts that use all of the techniques explored in this chapter.

- Take a look at *Windows PowerShell™ Scripting Guide* (Microsoft Press, 2008) for examples of using WMI and various .NET Framework classes in Windows PowerShell.

- For a good WMI reference, look at *Windows Scripting with WMI Self-Paced Learning Edition* (Microsoft Press, 2006).

- The MSDN reference library has comprehensive product documentation at *http://msdn.microsoft.com/en-us/library/default.aspx* and is the authoritative source for all Microsoft products.

- On the companion media, you will find all of the scripts referred to in this chapter.

Tracking Scripting Opportunities

It is important to track scripting opportunities to ensure that the most profitable scripts are written first. This backlog of scripting opportunities can be an effective tool for managing the scripting efforts of an enterprise. The key is to manage these scripting opportunities properly.

Evaluating the Need for the Script

Not everything in Windows PowerShell 2.0 needs to be scripted, which was also true in Windows PowerShell 1.0. When coming from a Microsoft VBScript or Perl background, some people often feel that they must write a script. However, a tremendous amount of work can be accomplished from the command line without the need for writing a script.

One of the more powerful aspects of Windows PowerShell is its ability to use language statements from the command line. The *for* statement provides the ability to control looping operations that require the creation of a script in other languages. To facilitate work from the command line, Windows PowerShell allows you to create incomplete commands on one line and continue them to the next line. When you are finished, you can press the Enter key a second time. The command shown here sends a ping command to each IP address in the range of 192.168.2.1 through 192.168.2.10.

```
PS C:\> for($i = 1 ; $i -le 10 ; $i++)
>> { Test-Connection -Destination 192.168.2.$i -Count 1 -ErrorAction
Silentlycontinue |
>> Format-Table -property Address, statusCode, ResponseTime -AutoSize }
>>
```

```
Address        statusCode ResponseTime
-------        ---------- ------------
192.168.2.1             0            1
Address        statusCode ResponseTime
-------        ---------- ------------
192.168.2.3             0            2
Address        statusCode ResponseTime
-------        ---------- ------------
192.168.2.5             0            0
Address        statusCode ResponseTime
-------        ---------- ------------
192.168.2.10            0           10
```

The previous command can become quite a bit shorter by taking advantage of a number of economies provided by the Windows PowerShell syntax such as using aliases, partial parameters, and positional arguments.

Reading a Text File

In its most basic form, a Windows PowerShell script is simply a collection of PowerShell commands stored in a file with a specific extension. If you do not want to write a script, you can store a collection of commands as a text file as shown in Figure 8-1.

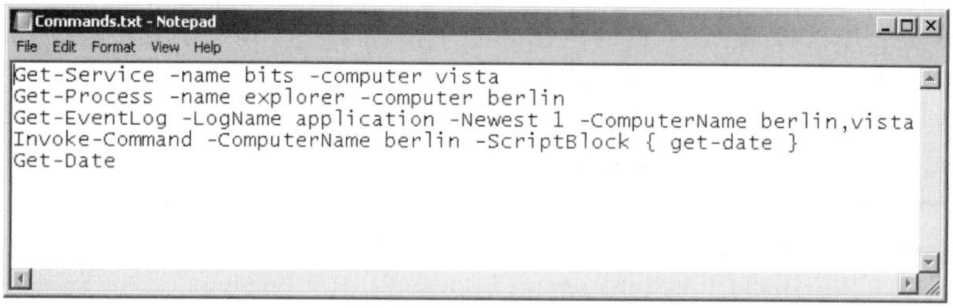

FIGURE 8-1 Text file containing a collection of Windows PowerShell commands

By using Windows PowerShell, you can easily read the commands.txt text file and execute the commands by using the Get-Content cmdlet to retrieve the commands in the text file. The default parameter for the Get-Content cmdlet is the *path* parameter; when working from the command line, it is not necessary to supply the *path* parameter. The path can be a local path or even a Universal Naming Convention (UNC) path as long as you have rights to read the text file. The best way to use this technique is to pipeline the results to the Invoke-Expression cmdlet. Each command that streams across the pipeline from the Get-Content cmdlet is executed in turn as it arrives to the Invoke-Expression cmdlet as shown here.

```
Get-Content -Path C:\fso\Commands.txt | Invoke-Expression
```

The results are shown in Figure 8-2.

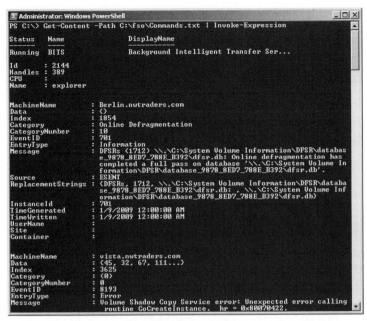

FIGURE 8-2 Windows PowerShell cmdlets can easily parse a text file and run commands.

When using the Windows PowerShell remoting features against an untrusted domain, it is easy to become confused when using cmdlets such as Get-Content. The *–path* parameter that is used refers to a path that is local to the target computer, not the launching computer. In the example that follows, the *c:\fso\commands.txt* path points to a text file named Commands.txt that must reside in the Fso folder on the C:\ drive of a computer named sydney in the Woodbridgebank.com domain. If the commands.txt file is not found in that location, the error shown here is emitted.

```
PS C:\> invoke-command -ComputerName sydney.woodbridgebank.com -Credential admin
istrator@woodbridgebank.com -ScriptBlock {get-content -Path C:\fso\Commands.txt
| Invoke-Expression}
Invoke-Command : Cannot find path 'C:\fso\Commands.txt' because it does not
exist.At line:1 char:15
+ invoke-command <<<<  -ComputerName sydney.woodbridgebank.com -Credential
administrator@woodbridgebank.com -ScriptBlock {get-content -Path
C:\fso\Commands.txt | Invoke-Expression}
    + CategoryInfo          : ObjectNotFound: (C:\fso\Commands.txt:String)
    [Get-Content], ItemNotFoundException
    + FullyQualifiedErrorId : PathNotFound,Microsoft.PowerShell.Commands.
GetContentCommand
```

You might think that you can use a UNC path and point to the Commands.txt file on the launching computer. Because the remote domain is untrusted, there is no security context that allows the remote command to access the file system of the local computer. When the command expressed in the *ScriptBlock* parameter is evaluated, it is evaluated in the context of the target computer, which in this case is the Sydney.Woodbridgebank.com computer. The local computer that is the launching point for the command is Vista.NWTraders.com. Because there is no trust relationship between these two domains, no credentials can be supplied to enable the command to run. The results of attempting to run the command are shown here.

```
PS C:\> invoke-command -ComputerName sydney.woodbridgebank.com -Credential
administrator@woodbridgebank.com -ScriptBlock {get-content -Path
'\\vista\fso\Commands.txt' | Invoke-Expression}
Invoke-Command : Cannot find path '\\vista\fso\Commands.txt' because it does
not exist.
At line:1 char:15
+ invoke-command <<<<  -ComputerName sydney.woodbridgebank.com -Credential
administrator@woodbridgebank.com -ScriptBlock {get-content -Path
'\\vista\fso\Commands.txt' | Invoke-Expression}
    + CategoryInfo          : ObjectNotFound: (\\vista\fso\Commands.txt:String)
    [Get-Content],ItemNotFoundException
    + FullyQualifiedErrorId : PathNotFound,Microsoft.PowerShell.Commands.
GetContentCommand
```

What may be confusing is that the `Get-Content` command works well when run alone. In working on a computer named vista that has a folder named Fso containing a text file named Commands.txt, the command completes successfully when it is ensconced within single quotes as shown here.

```
PS C:\> Get-Content -Path '\\vista\fso\Commands.txt'
Get-Service -Name bits -ComputerName vista
Get-Process -Name explorer -ComputerName berlin
Get-EventLog -LogName application -Newest 1 -ComputerName berlin,vista
Invoke-Command -ComputerName Berlin { Get-Date }
Get-Date
```

However, this result is expected because the logged-on user has rights to the folder and can therefore use the `Get-Content` cmdlet to read a UNC path to the Commands.txt file.

You can map a drive on the remote domain and copy the file from your local computer to the appropriate folder on the remote server. You will, of course, be required to open additional ports in the Windows Firewall, which may or may not be an acceptable solution depending on your network configuration. If you decide to use this route, you can use Windows PowerShell to perform the configuration changes as shown here.

```
PS C:\> Invoke-Command -ComputerName Sydney.WoodBridgeBank.Com -Credential
Administrator@WoodbridgeBank.com -ScriptBlock { netsh advfirewall firewall set rule
group="File and Printer Sharing" new enable=Yes }

Updated 28 rule(s).
Ok.
```

Once you enable the firewall exception, you can then map a drive by using the GUI, the Net Use command from within Windows PowerShell, or any of the other programmatic methods. After you map the drive, you can then copy the Commands.txt file to the remote server by using the Copy-Item cmdlet as shown here.

> **NOTE** When using Copy-Item to copy an item to a mapped drive, you need to keep in mind the structure of the mapped drive. It is quite common to map a drive to a share on a remote computer. The remote share is almost invariably a share of a folder and not an entire drive. Because your remote drive is a map point of a single folder, it changes the destination. The Z: drive in the following command is a share of the Fso folder on the remote server. The *–destination* parameter goes to the root of the mapped drive and not to Z:\fso.

```
Copy-Item -Path C:\fso\Commands.txt -Destination z:
```

You can now use the Commands.txt file directly in the Windows PowerShell command as shown here.

```
PS C:\> invoke-command -ComputerName Sydney.WoodbridgeBank.com -Credential
administrator@WoodBridgeBank.com -ScriptBlock { Get-Content -Path
C:\fso\Commands.txt | Invoke-Expression }
```

One solution to the dilemma of mapping drives is to use Remote Desktop, which allows you to access local resources if you want to make them available in your session. By selecting Remote Desktop, clicking the Options button, and then selecting the Local Resources tab, you can choose to allow printer connections, Clipboard access, and local drives to be available within the Remote Desktop Protocol (RDP) session. You can access Remote Desktop by going to Start, All Programs, Accessories, and selecting Remote Desktop Connection. If Remote Desktop has not been previously enabled, you are greeted with an access denied message as shown in Figure 8-3.

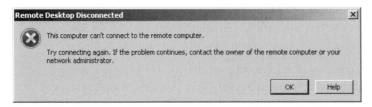

FIGURE 8-3 Access denied when attempting to connect to Remote Desktop

To enable Remote Desktop access on Microsoft Windows 2008 and Windows 2008 R2, choose Configure Remote Desktop from within Server Manager. If you are using Windows Vista or the Microsoft Windows 7 operating system, you select Remote Settings from Control Panel, then System And Maintenance, and then System. When the System Properties dialog box appears, choose the Remote tab as shown in Figure 8-4. Remote Desktop options are shown in the bottom half of the dialog box and present three different choices. By default,

Remote Desktop connections are not allowed to the local computer. The safest choice is to select Allow Connections Only From Computers Running Remote Desktop With Network Level Authentication. You are also allowed to specify which users are allowed to make the connection. By default, members of the Domain Administrators group are permitted to make connections.

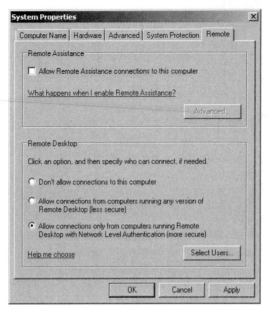

FIGURE 8-4 Remote Desktop must be enabled.

Once you enable Remote Desktop, an exception is automatically created to allow RDP traffic through the Windows Firewall. It is a good idea to double-check to ensure that the exception was permitted. The Windows Vista Firewall exception is shown in Figure 8-5.

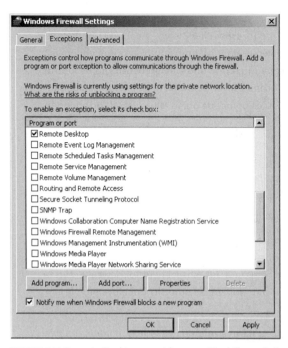

FIGURE 8-5 Remote Desktop must be permitted through the Windows Firewall.

Export Command History

Much administrative work with Windows PowerShell consists of typing a series of commands at the console. Whether you are editing the registry or stopping various processes and services, the configuration work needs to be replicated to several different servers to ensure a consistent operating environment. In the past, such duplication of effort required the creation of scripts. If the commands to be duplicated are a series of commands typed at the console, you can use the command history mechanism to replace the need for a script by using the Get-History cmdlet and exporting the commands to an .xml file as shown here.

```
Get-History | Export-Clixml -Path C:\fso\history.xml
```

The result is an .xml file that represents all of the commands typed at the console. The resulting .xml file is shown in Figure 8-6.

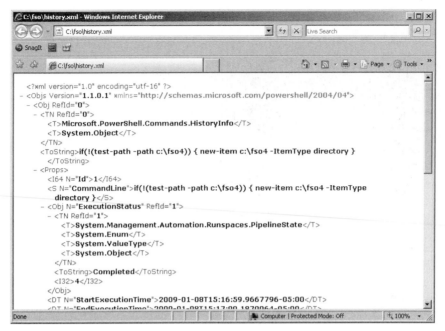

FIGURE 8-6 Command history .xml file

Once you create a command history .xml file, you can import the commands from the .xml file by using the `Import-Clixml` cmdlet. You pipeline the results of the `Import-Clixml` cmdlet to the `Add-History` cmdlet to add the commands back to the command history. The trick is to use the *–passthru* switch so that the commands go to both the `Add-History` and `ForEach-Object` cmdlets. In the `ForEach-Object` cmdlet, you can use the `Invoke-History` cmdlet to run each command in the history. The commands are shown here, as are the results of running the commands.

```
PS C:\> Import-Clixml -Path C:\fso\history.xml | Add-History -Passthru |
>> ForEach-Object { Invoke-History }
>>
 if(!(test-path -path c:\fso4)) { new-item c:\fso4 -ItemType directory }


    Directory: C:\


Mode              LastWriteTime     Length Name
----              -------------     ------ ----
d----          1/9/2009  12:33 AM          fso4
Get-Command >> C:\fso4\commands.txt
notepad C:\fso4\commands.txt
```

This technique works remotely by using the `Invoke-Command` cmdlet. Keep in mind that the *path* statement is relative to the computer that is the target, not the computer that is executing the command. If you do not keep this in mind, then an error appears, such as the one shown in Figure 8-7.

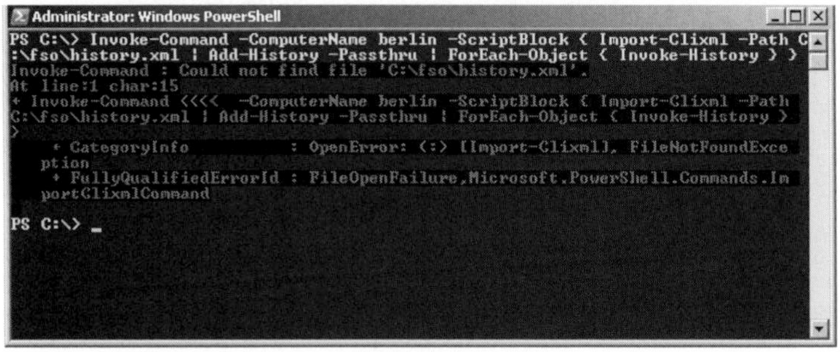

FIGURE 8-7 An error appears due to the use of local file paths.

If you copy the file to the target machine first and adjust your command line, the import and execute history technique works well. What is good about Windows PowerShell is that you can use a UNC path with the Copy-Item cmdlet. This feature actually makes the technique worthwhile because it enables you to easily move a file to a remote computer as shown here.

```
PS C:\> Copy-Item C:\fso\history.xml \\berlin\c$\fso
PS C:\> Import-Clixml -Path C:\fso\history.xml | Add-History -Passthru | ForEach
-Object { Invoke-History }
 if(!(test-path -path c:\fso4)) { new-item c:\fso4 -ItemType directory }


    Directory: C:\


Mode                LastWriteTime     Length Name
----                -------------     ------ ----
d----           1/9/2009  12:40 AM           fso4
Get-Command >> C:\fso4\commands.txt
notepad C:\fso4\commands.txt
```

Fan-out Commands

Fan-out commands are commands launched from a central computer and run against a number of remote computers. One way to perform fan-out commands is to use the Invoke-Command cmdlet as shown here.

```
PS C:\> Invoke-Command -Computer berlin,vista -Script `
>> {"$env:computername $(get-date)" }
>>
VISTA 01/09/2009 08:31:42
BERLIN 01/09/2009 08:31:47
```

You can use fan-out commands by specifying an array of computer names for the *–computername* parameter for many of the cmdlets. The problem with this approach is that the results are nearly useless. An example illustrates the issue involved. In the following command, the Get-Service cmdlet is used to obtain service configuration information from two computers. The first is a computer named vista, and the second is a server named berlin. As you can see from the partial output, the results of the command are merged, and there is no column that illustrates the computer name to which the result is associated. The results are rather interesting in that you can quickly look at the service name between two different computers and easily see divergent configurations. The fan-out command and a truncated result set is shown here.

```
PS C:\> Get-Service -ComputerName Vista, Berlin

Status    Name               DisplayName
------    ----               -----------
Running   1-vmsrvc           Virtual Machine Additions Services ...
Running   1-vmsrvc           Virtual Machine Additions Services ...
Running   AeLookupSvc        Application Experience
Stopped   AeLookupSvc        Application Experience
Stopped   ALG                Application Layer Gateway Service
Stopped   ALG                Application Layer Gateway Service
Stopped   Appinfo            Application Information
Stopped   Appinfo            Application Information
Stopped   AppMgmt            Application Management
Stopped   AppMgmt            Application Management
Stopped   AudioEndpointBu... Windows Audio Endpoint Builder
Stopped   AudioEndpointBu... Windows Audio Endpoint Builder
Stopped   Audiosrv           Windows Audio
Stopped   Audiosrv           Windows Audio
Running   BFE                Base Filtering Engine
Running   BFE                Base Filtering Engine
Running   BITS               Background Intelligent Transfer Ser...
Stopped   BITS               Background Intelligent Transfer Ser...
Stopped   Browser            Computer Browser
Running   Browser            Computer Browser
>>> Results trimmed >>>
```

You can see from the results of the Get-Service cmdlet that the AeLookupSvc service is running on the first computer and is stopped on the second computer. It is a simple matter to use the Get-Service cmdlet to connect to each of the computers and check the status of the service.

```
PS C:\> Get-Service -Name AeLookupSvc -computer vista

Status    Name               DisplayName
------    ----               -----------
Stopped   AeLookupSvc        Application Experience
```

```
PS C:\> Get-Service -Name AeLookupSvc -computer Berlin

Status    Name              DisplayName
------    ----              -----------
Running   AeLookupSvc       Application Experience
```

You might think that the first instance of the service name belongs to the computer listed first. As you can see, AeLookupSvc service is running on berlin but is stopped on vista. This is the same order shown in the original output, but the vista computer is listed first in the fan-out command. Perhaps this means that the second computer results are listed first and the first computer results are listed second—a Last In First Out (LIFO) operation. However, before assuming this to be the case, you should check another service. In the output from the original fan-out command, the BITS service was listed first as running and second as stopped. To see the status of the BITS service on berlin and on vista, you can use the following two commands.

```
PS C:\> Get-Service -Name Bits -computer berlin

Status    Name              DisplayName
------    ----              -----------
Stopped   BITS              Background Intelligent Transfer Ser...


PS C:\> Get-Service -Name Bits -computer Vista

Status    Name              DisplayName
------    ----              -----------
Running   BITS              Background Intelligent Transfer Ser...
```

You can see that the BITS service is stopped on berlin and is running on vista. The results of using Get-Service as a fan-out command by supplying an array of computer names to the –computername parameter brings back interesting results, but they are meaningless results when you need to check the exact status of a service on a remote computer. As a best practice, you should pipeline the results of the fan-out command to a Format-Table cmdlet and choose the machineName property. The value of the displayName property is the same value shown in the Services MMC in the Name column. The command and a truncated output are shown here.

```
PS C:\> Get-Service -ComputerName berlin,vista |
format-table name, status, machinename, displayName -AutoSize

Name                      Status MachineName DisplayName
----                      ------ ----------- -----------
1-vmsrvc                  Running vista       Virtual Machine Additions...
1-vmsrvc                  Running berlin      Virtual Machine Additions...
AeLookupSvc               Running berlin      Application Experience
AeLookupSvc               Stopped vista       Application Experience
ALG                       Stopped berlin      Application Layer Gateway...
```

```
ALG                          Stopped vista        Application Layer Gateway...
Appinfo                      Stopped berlin       Application Information
Appinfo                      Stopped vista        Application Information
AppMgmt                      Stopped vista        Application Management
AppMgmt                      Stopped berlin       Application Management
AudioEndpointBuilder         Stopped berlin       Windows Audio Endpoint Bu...
AudioEndpointBuilder         Stopped vista        Windows Audio Endpoint Bu...
Audiosrv                     Stopped berlin       Windows Audio
Audiosrv                     Stopped vista        Windows Audio
BFE                          Running vista        Base Filtering Engine
BFE                          Running berlin       Base Filtering Engine
BITS                         Stopped berlin       Background Intelligent Tr...
BITS                         Running vista        Background Intelligent Tr...
Browser                      Running vista        Computer Browser
Browser                      Stopped berlin       Computer Browser
```

Because the value of the *displayName* property is often quite long, it does not always fit easily within the confines of an 80-column display. If you select *displayName* early in the order of the properties to be selected by the `Format-Table` cmdlet, you should end up with several columns that are not displayed as shown here.

```
PS C:\> Get-Service -ComputerName berlin,vista | format-table name, displayname,
   status, machinename -AutoSize

WARNING: 2 columns do not fit into the display and were removed.

Name                     DisplayName
----                     -----------
1-vmsrvc                 Virtual Machine Additions Services Application
1-vmsrvc                 Virtual Machine Additions Services Application
AeLookupSvc              Application Experience
AeLookupSvc              Application Experience
```

As you can see, this code defeats the purpose of choosing the *machineName* property in the first place when the *machineName* property is left off because it does not fit on the display. To correct this potential problem, it is a best practice to always choose the property with the longest values to be displayed as the last position in the command. In this way, you allow Windows PowerShell to truncate the property value rather than filling the screen with information you can easily infer from a truncated display.

The other solution to the problem of the shrinking display output is not to use the *–autosize* parameter of the `Format-Table` cmdlet. You can use the *–Wrap* parameter instead. When the *–Wrap* parameter is used, single-line entries are allowed to wrap and form multiple lines. Depending on the information you are looking for, this output can be either helpful or annoying. Here is an example of using the *–Wrap* parameter.

```
PS C:\> Get-Service -ComputerName berlin,vista | format-table name, displayname,
 status, machinename -Wrap
```

Name	DisplayName	Status	MachineName
1-vmsrvc	Virtual Machine Add itions Services App lication	Running	vista
1-vmsrvc	Virtual Machine Add itions Services App lication	Running	berlin
AeLookupSvc	Application Experie nce	Running	berlin
AeLookupSvc	Application Experie nce	Stopped	vista

NOTE At this point in the discussion, you may think that you can solve the problem of the truncated display output by using both the –*autosize* and –*Wrap* parameters. Doing so allows the output to maximize the display real estate (the function of –*autosize*) and also to allow for multiline wrapping (the function of –*Wrap*). This procedure never works, but it does not generate an error. Windows PowerShell gives priority to the –*autosize* parameter and ignores the –*Wrap* parameter; the order in which the two parameters are typed does not matter.

Query Active Directory

To query Active Directory with Windows PowerShell 1.0, most network administrators feel that they must write a script. To an extent, this belief is a relic of the VBScript days and reflects a reliance on using ActiveX Data Object (ADO) technology to invoke a Lightweight Directory Access Protocol (LDAP) dialect query against Active Directory. While it is possible to use the *System.DirectoryServices.DirectorySearcher* class from a Windows PowerShell line, it is not extremely convenient. While there are third-party cmdlets and providers that make it possible to employ command-line queries against Active Directory, many network administrators are rightfully skeptical about installing unsupported community software on production servers. The other command-line option, using DSQuery.exe, simply does not enter most people's minds. With Windows PowerShell 2.0, however, the command-line situation has changed somewhat. By using the techniques detailed in this section, an IT Pro now has a supportable command-line solution to the problem of performing Active Directory queries.

Using [ADSISearcher]

Several options are available when querying Active Directory from the Windows PowerShell prompt. One option is to use the [ADSISearcher] type accelerator, which is a shortcut to the *System.DirectoryServices.DirectorySearcher* class. The [ADSISearcher] type accelerator merely saves you a bit of typing; you still need to give [ADSISearcher] the appropriate constructor to actually create an instance of the class. If you do not use [ADSISearcher], you need to use the New-Object cmdlet to create the object. First, you can put the New-Object command inside smooth parentheses to force the creation of the object and then call the *FindAll* method from the *DirectorySearcher* object. The resulting collection of *DirectoryEntry* objects is pipelined to the Select-Object cmdlet where the *path* property is returned as shown here.

```
PS C:\> (New-Object DirectoryServices.DirectorySearcher "ObjectClass=user").Find
All() | Select path

Path
----
LDAP://CN=Administrator,CN=Users,DC=nwtraders,DC=com
LDAP://CN=Guest,CN=Users,DC=nwtraders,DC=com
LDAP://CN=BERLIN,OU=Domain Controllers,DC=nwtraders,DC=com
LDAP://CN=krbtgt,CN=Users,DC=nwtraders,DC=com
LDAP://CN=VISTA,CN=Computers,DC=nwtraders,DC=com
LDAP://CN=VistaAdmin,OU=Students,DC=nwtraders,DC=com
List Truncated -
```

To use the [ADSISearcher] type accelerator, you still need to supply it with an appropriate constructor, which in many cases is the search filter expressed in LDAP search filter syntax. LDAP search filter syntax is defined in RFC 2254 and is represented by Unicode strings. The search filters allow you to specify search criteria in an efficient and effective manner. Some examples of using the LDAP search filter syntax are shown in Table 8-1.

TABLE 8-1 LDAP Search Filter Examples

SEARCH FILTER	DESCRIPTION
ObjectClass=Computer	All computer objects
ObjectClass=OrganizationalUnit	All organizational unit objects
ObjectClass=User	All user objects as well as all computer objects
ObjectCategory=User	All user objects
(&(ObjectCategory=User)(ObjectClass=Person))	All user objects
L=Berlin	All objects with the location of Berlin

SEARCH FILTER	DESCRIPTION
Name=*Berlin*	All objects with a name that contains Berlin
(&(L=berlin)(ObjectCategory=OrganizationalUnit))	All organizational units with the location of Berlin
(&(ObjectCategory=OrganizationalUnit)(Name=*Berlin*))	All organizational units with a name that contains Berlin
(&(ObjectCategory=OrganizationalUnit)(Name=*Berlin*)(!L=Berlin))	All organizational units with a name that contains Berlin but does not have a location of Berlin
(&(ObjectCategory=OrganizationalUnit)(Name=*Berlin*)(!L=*))	All organizational units with a name that contains Berlin but does not have any location specified
(&(ObjectCategory=OrganizationalUnit)(|(L=Berlin)(L=Charlotte)))	All organizational units with a location of either Berlin or Charlotte

As shown in the examples in Table 8-1, the search filter can be specified in two ways. The first method is a straightforward assignment filter. The attribute, the operator, and the value constitute the filter as shown here.

```
PS C:\> ([ADSISearcher]"Name=Charlotte").FindAll() | Select Path

Path
----
LDAP://OU=Charlotte,DC=nwtraders,DC=com
```

The second way to use the LDAP search filter is to combine multiple filters. The operator goes first, followed by filter A and then by filter B. You can combine multiple filters and operators as shown in the syntax examples in Table 8-1. An example of a compound filter is shown here.

```
PS C:\> ([ADSISearcher]"(|(Name=Charlotte)(Name=Atlanta))").FindAll() | Select Path

Path
----
LDAP://OU=Atlanta,DC=nwtraders,DC=com
LDAP://OU=Charlotte,DC=nwtraders,DC=com
```

The operators that you can use for either straightforward assignment filters or compound search filters are listed in Table 8-2.

TABLE 8-2 LDAP Search Filter Logic Operators

OPERATOR	DESCRIPTION
=	Equal to
~=	Approximately equal to
<=	Lexicographically less than or equal to
>=	Lexicographically greater than or equal to
&	AND
|	OR
!	NOT

Table 8-3 lists special characters. If any of these special characters must appear in a search filter as a literal character, it must be replaced by the escape sequence.

TABLE 8-3 LDAP Search Filter Special Characters

ASCII CHARACTER	ESCAPE SEQUENCE SUBSTITUTE
*	\2a
(	\28
)	\29
\	\5c
NUL	\00
/	\2f

As shown in Figure 8-8, special characters are allowed in organizational unit names in Active Directory.

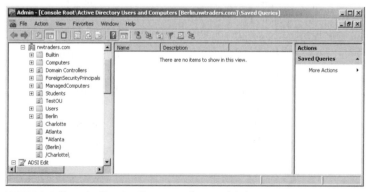

FIGURE 8-8 Organizational unit names using special characters

As shown in Figure 8-8, there is an organizational unit named *Atlanta. To retrieve this particular organizational unit, you need to use the \2a character as shown here.

```
PS C:\> ([ADSISearcher]"name=\2aAtlanta").FindAll() | Select Path
```

```
Path
----
LDAP://OU=*Atlanta,DC=nwtraders,DC=com
```

To retrieve the organizational unit named (Berlin), you need to use the \28 and \29 escape sequences as documented in Table 8-3 and as shown here.

```
PS C:\> ([ADSISearcher]"name=\28Berlin\29").FindAll() | Select Path
```

```
Path
----
LDAP://OU=(Berlin),DC=nwtraders,DC=com
```

As shown in Figure 8-8, there is also an organizational unit named /Charlotte\. The escape sequence substitute for the forward slash is \2f and for the backward slash is \5c. To retrieve the organizational unit named /Charlotte\ using the LDAP search filter and the [ADSISearcher] type accelerator, you can use a query that looks like the following:

```
PS C:\> ([ADSISearcher]"name=\2fCharlotte\5c").FindAll() | Select Path
```

```
Path
----
LDAP://OU=\/Charlotte\\,DC=nwtraders,DC=com
```

LESSONS LEARNED

Avoid Special Characters in Organizational Unit Names

I generally try to avoid using special characters in organizational unit names, user names, group names, computer names, and the like. I suspect that not all applications know how to handle special characters, and I am always afraid that a special character might not work. Also, even though you can escape the characters in searches, the process is never intuitive, and too much time can be wasted trying to figure out how to escape the special character. When you add in the fact that the problem normally occurs at 2:00 A.M. on Saturday morning (all network problems seem to occur at 2:00 A.M. on Saturday morning) when you are likely to forget to escape the special character, you have a situation that can quickly become disastrous. Just because something is permitted does not mean that it is advisable.

The LDAP search filter special characters and their associated escape sequence substitutes are documented in Table 8-3, which was shown earlier.

By using the Invoke-Command cmdlet, the [ADSISearcher] can easily be used to query the Active Directory of an untrusted forest or domain. When doing so, it is often important to provide the fully qualified domain name of the computer because it is possible that you may not have complete name resolution when using only the NetBIOS name of the server. It is also best to submit the credentials in a User Principal Name (UPN) fashion. When the command is run, the credential dialog box appears and prompts for the password, which must be typed in. The command is shown here.

```
PS C:\> Invoke-Command -ComputerName Sydney.WoodBridgeBank.Com -Credential `
administrator@WoodBridgeBank.com -ScriptBlock {([ADSISearcher]"L=Berlin").Findall()}
PSComputerName     : sydney.woodbridgebank.com
RunspaceId         : 112f974a-00aa-417c-8a13-9033a49354bd
PSShowComputerName : True
Path               : LDAP://OU=Berlin Bank,DC=woodbridgebank,DC=com
Properties         : {ou, dscorepropagationdata, whencreated, name...}
```

Using Active Directory cmdlets

Active Directory cmdlets are included with Windows Server 2008 R2. They are contained in a module and must first be loaded by using the Import-Module cmdlet. Of course, you can simply select the Active Directory Windows PowerShell icon, which starts PowerShell with the Active Directory cmdlets already loaded. It is good that the Active Directory cmdlets are contained in a module because you can use the Import-Module cmdlet to add them from a remote computer into a Windows PowerShell session that does not have the cmdlets. To do this, you need to perform the following steps:

- Establish a remote session to the server running Windows 2008 R2.
- Import the Active Directory cmdlets by using the Import-Module cmdlet.
- Perform the Active Directory query.
- Disconnect from the remote session.
- Remove the remote session.

> **NOTE** When using the Remove-PSSession cmdlet with the *–id* parameter, keep in mind that you may not always know what the session ID number actually is. The first session ID is 1, and the second session ID is 2. Windows PowerShell keeps a running tally of all of the sessions. However, you may not be aware of which session ID number you have reached. As a best practice, I always use the Get-PSSession cmdlet to obtain a listing of all of the PSSessions on the computer. I also make a habit of removing disconnected sessions that I do not expect to go back to within the near future. This process frees up the resources consumed by the session.

This technique to remove unused sessions is illustrated here.

```
PS C:\> $ps = New-PSSession -ComputerName Sydney.WoodBridgeBank.Com -Credential
administrator@WoodBridgeBank.Com
PS C:\> Enter-PSSession $ps
[sydney.woodbridgebank.com]: PS C:\> Import-Module ActiveDirectory
[sydney.woodbridgebank.com]: PS C:\> Get-ADOrganizationalUnit -Filter "L -eq 'Berlin'"


Name              : Berlin Bank
Country           : DE
PostalCode        :
City              : Berlin
ManagedBy         :
StreetAddress     :
State             : Berlin
ObjectGUID        : dde90f41-128c-4568-9822-00de5a4c96cc
ObjectClass       : organizationalUnit
DistinguishedName : OU=Berlin Bank,DC=woodbridgebank,DC=com
[sydney.woodbridgebank.com]: PS C:\> Exit-PSSession
PS C:\> Get-PSSession


    Id Name           ComputerName    State    Configuration
    -- ----           ------------    -----    -------------
     1 Session1       sydney.woodb... Broken   Microsoft.PowerShell
PS C:\> Remove-PSSession -Id 1
```

In addition to using the Active Directory filter syntax, which uses Windows PowerShell operators and supports rich type conversions, you can also use the LDAP filter syntax discussed in the previous section. To use the LDAP filter syntax, you can use the *–LDAPFilter* parameter instead of the *–filter* parameter and supply the LDAP search filter expression inside a set of single quotation marks as shown here.

```
PS C:\> Get-ADOrganizationalUnit -LDAPFilter '(L=Berlin)'


Name              : Berlin Bank
Country           : DE
PostalCode        :
City              : Berlin
ManagedBy         :
StreetAddress     :
State             : Berlin
ObjectGUID        : dde90f41-128c-4568-9822-00de5a4c96cc
ObjectClass       : organizationalUnit
DistinguishedName : OU=Berlin Bank,DC=woodbridgebank,DC=com
```

Just Use the Command Line

Many powerful commands can be executed directly from the command line by using legacy command-line utilities. There is nothing wrong with using these commands, and they are fully supported in Windows PowerShell. The fact that you can use the Get-Command cmdlet to easily search for legacy command-line utilities should be an indicator that Windows PowerShell supports using these commands. To use the Get-Command cmdlet to search for executables, you can use wildcard characters if you are not familiar with the exact name of the program as shown here.

```
PS C:\> Get-Command ds*
```

CommandType	Name	Definition
Application	ds16gt.dll	C:\Windows\system32\ds16gt.dll
Application	ds32gt.dll	C:\Windows\system32\ds32gt.dll
Application	dsa.msc	C:\Windows\system32\dsa.msc
Application	dsacls.exe	C:\Windows\system32\dsacls.exe
Application	dsadd.exe	C:\Windows\system32\dsadd.exe
Application	dsadmin.dll	C:\Windows\system32\dsadmin.dll
Application	dsauth.dll	C:\Windows\system32\dsauth.dll
Application	dsdbutil.exe	C:\Windows\system32\dsdbutil...
Application	dsdmo.dll	C:\Windows\system32\dsdmo.dll
Application	dsget.exe	C:\Windows\system32\dsget.exe
Application	dskquota.dll	C:\Windows\system32\dskquota...
Application	dskquoui.dll	C:\Windows\system32\dskquoui...
Application	dsmgmt.exe	C:\Windows\system32\dsmgmt.exe
Application	dsmod.exe	C:\Windows\system32\dsmod.exe
Application	dsmove.exe	C:\Windows\system32\dsmove.exe
Application	dsound.dll	C:\Windows\system32\dsound.dll
Application	dsprop.dll	C:\Windows\system32\dsprop.dll
Application	dsprov.dll	C:\Windows\System32\Wbem\dsp...
Application	dsprov.mof	C:\Windows\System32\Wbem\dsp...
Application	dsquery.dll	C:\Windows\system32\dsquery.dll
Application	dsquery.exe	C:\Windows\system32\dsquery.exe
Application	dsrm.exe	C:\Windows\system32\dsrm.exe
Application	dssec.dat	C:\Windows\system32\dssec.dat
Application	dssec.dll	C:\Windows\system32\dssec.dll
Application	dssenh.dll	C:\Windows\system32\dssenh.dll
Application	dssite.msc	C:\Windows\system32\dssite.msc
Application	dsuiext.dll	C:\Windows\system32\dsuiext.dll
Application	dsuiwiz.dll	C:\Windows\system32\dsuiwiz.dll
Application	dswave.dll	C:\Windows\system32\dswave.dll

The previous command returns any valid Windows PowerShell command including functions, cmdlets, and executable files. If you are specifically searching for command-line utilities, you should use the *commandtype* parameter as shown here.

```
PS C:\> Get-Command -Name ds* -CommandType application
```

CommandType	Name	Definition
Application	ds16gt.dll	C:\Windows\system32\ds16gt.dll
Application	ds32gt.dll	C:\Windows\system32\ds32gt.dll
Application	dsa.msc	C:\Windows\system32\dsa.msc
Application	dsacls.exe	C:\Windows\system32\dsacls.exe
Application	dsadd.exe	C:\Windows\system32\dsadd.exe
Application	dsadmin.dll	C:\Windows\system32\dsadmin.dll
Application	dsauth.dll	C:\Windows\system32\dsauth.dll
Application	dsdbutil.exe	C:\Windows\system32\dsdbutil...
Application	dsdmo.dll	C:\Windows\system32\dsdmo.dll
Application	dsget.exe	C:\Windows\system32\dsget.exe
Application	dskquota.dll	C:\Windows\system32\dskquota...
Application	dskquoui.dll	C:\Windows\system32\dskquoui...
Application	dsmgmt.exe	C:\Windows\system32\dsmgmt.exe
Application	dsmod.exe	C:\Windows\system32\dsmod.exe
Application	dsmove.exe	C:\Windows\system32\dsmove.exe
Application	dsound.dll	C:\Windows\system32\dsound.dll
Application	dsprop.dll	C:\Windows\system32\dsprop.dll
Application	dsprov.dll	C:\Windows\System32\Wbem\dsp...
Application	dsprov.mof	C:\Windows\System32\Wbem\dsp...
Application	dsquery.dll	C:\Windows\system32\dsquery.dll
Application	dsquery.exe	C:\Windows\system32\dsquery.exe
Application	dsrm.exe	C:\Windows\system32\dsrm.exe
Application	dssec.dat	C:\Windows\system32\dssec.dat
Application	dssec.dll	C:\Windows\system32\dssec.dll
Application	dssenh.dll	C:\Windows\system32\dssenh.dll
Application	dssite.msc	C:\Windows\system32\dssite.msc
Application	dsuiext.dll	C:\Windows\system32\dsuiext.dll
Application	dsuiwiz.dll	C:\Windows\system32\dsuiwiz.dll
Application	dswave.dll	C:\Windows\system32\dswave.dll

The ease of use and flexibility of Windows PowerShell created resurgence in the interest of command-line programs. An example is the use of DSQuery.exe, which allows the user to quickly issue a query against Active Directory. With the inclusion of the [ADSISearcher] type accelerator and various Active Directory cmdlets in Windows Server 2008 R2, you might wonder why you should use the DSQuery.exe utility. Here is the syntax to obtain a listing of the organizational units in your domain by using DSQuery.exe.

```
PS C:\> dsquery ou
"OU=Domain Controllers,DC=nwtraders,DC=com"
"OU=Students,DC=nwtraders,DC=com"
"OU=ManagedComputers,DC=nwtraders,DC=com"
"OU=TestOU,DC=nwtraders,DC=com"
```

This is the syntax to retrieve a listing of the organizational units in your domain by using the [ADSISearcher] type accelerator.

```
PS C:\> ([ADSISearcher]"objectClass=OrganizationalUnit").findall() | select-Object
-property path


Path
----
LDAP://OU=Domain Controllers,DC=nwtraders,DC=com
LDAP://OU=Students,DC=nwtraders,DC=com
LDAP://OU=ManagedComputers,DC=nwtraders,DC=com
LDAP://OU=TestOU,DC=nwtraders,DC=com
```

The syntax to obtain a listing of organizational units by using the Get-ADOrganizationalUnit cmdlet, which is included in the Active Directory module on Windows Server 2008 R2, is a bit easier to use. When working from the Active Directory Windows PowerShell prompt, you do not always need to specify parameter names. You can also use the alias name (*Select* for Select-Object) if desired. Using an alias name makes the syntax shorter but can lead to problems when it is time to modify the command. Use of the Get-ADOrganizationalUnit cmdlet is shown here.

```
PS C:\> Get-ADOrganizationalUnit -Filter "name -like '*'" | Select DistinguishedName


DistinguishedName
-----------------
OU=Domain Controllers,DC=woodbridgebank,DC=com
OU=Test1,DC=woodbridgebank,DC=com
```

If your only consideration is shortness of syntax, DSQuery.exe obviously wins. However, other considerations might come into play. DSQuery.exe returns a string, while the [ADSISearcher] type accelerator returns a *DirectoryEntry* object. The Get-ADOrganizationalUnit command returns a *Microsoft.ActiveDirectory.Management.ADOrganizationalUnit* object. Depending on what you are trying to do, one type of object may be preferable over another. Beyond the return type issue, other problems with DSQuery.exe also exist. DSQuery.exe sacrifices power for simplicity, which means that there are only a few attributes you can use as your search query. If you want to find all of the organizational units in Active Directory that contain the name Berlin in them, you can use the following syntax.

```
dsquery ou -name *berlin*
```

On the other hand, if you want to find all of the organizational units in Active Directory that have a location attribute specified as actually being in Berlin, you need to use either the Active Directory cmdlets or the [ADSISearcher] type accelerator. If you understand what DSQuery.exe can do, there is no problem at all with availing yourself of this easy-to-use tool. You can even pipeline the results from DSQuery.exe into other utilities, such as DSMove.exe. DSMove.exe moves an object to another location in Active Directory, DSMod.exe allows you to change attribute values, and DSrm.exe allows you to delete objects from Active Directory.

```
PS C:\> Get-Command ds* application
Get-Command : The command could not be retrieved because the ArgumentList
parameter can be specified only when retrieving a single cmdlet or script.
At line:1 char:12
+ Get-Command <<<< ds* application
+ CategoryInfo : InvalidArgument: (ds16gt.dLL:ApplicationInfo)
[Get-Command], PSArgumentException
+ FullyQualifiedErrorId : CommandArgsOnlyForSingleCmdlet,Microsoft.
PowerShell.Commands.GetCommandCommand
```

NOTES FROM THE FIELD

The Wonder of Modules

Keith Hill, Microsoft Windows PowerShell MVP
Microsoft Corporation

My favorite new feature in Windows PowerShell 2.0 is modules. Modules make it easier for people to package and deploy their reusable functionality, and they make it easier for end users to deploy and use that functionality.

I have not changed my process much when writing scripts in Windows PowerShell 2.0. I use modules for any script functionality that I view as "library" code, that is, script that I want to use within other scripts.

I have not really changed the number ratio between scripts and command-line interaction. I write scripts if I think I will use something over and over again; otherwise, I just write the commands out at the prompt.

Regarding remoting, I will probably use the Enter-PSSession/Exit-PSSession cmdlets because I don't have a great need for the one-to-many fan-out capabilities of Windows PowerShell remoting (I'm not an admin); however, there are times when I need to admin a build machine or a test machine. For simple operations, such as viewing running processes, I can use the *–computername* parameter to execute the command remotely. Yet, I am somewhat hampered by the fact that most of our machines run Microsoft Windows XP, and a compatible WS-Management protocol (WSMan) isn't installed on them.

There may be a simple class of cmdlets that I can use to just write the command using the advanced functions of a script cmdlet. However, I'm a C# developer, so I am fairly quick to simply develop a C#-based cmdlet instead of developing the commands as a script.

I think that modules will be tremendously useful and allow Windows PowerShell users to grow a library of easy-to-deploy functionality. The Windows PowerShell Community eXtension (PSCX) project plans to switch to a modules-based approach when PSCX 2.0 ships.

As far as using the Windows PowerShell Integrated Scripting Environment (ISE), I prefer to use the console. I use the ISE for writing, testing, and debugging scripts but not for typical interactive use.

As a software developer, I use Windows PowerShell as a tool for daily productivity needs such as searching source code, managing source code files (deleting obj dirs recursively), and managing errant processes. I also use Windows PowerShell to script our product's build process and nightly regression tests.

If I were talking to a newbie, I would say stick with it. Windows PowerShell, like other "powerful but complex" tools, has a somewhat steep learning curve. However, if you can get over the hump, your endeavors will pay big dividends on the back end. Also, tell them not to thrash—there are abundant (and passionate) Windows PowerShell gurus available to answer your questions no matter how ridiculous they may seem to you. You can visit the Network News Transfer Protocol (NNTP) newsgroup at *http://www.microsoft.com/communities/newsgroups/list/en-us /default.aspx?dg=microsoft.public.windows.powershell*, where most questions are answered within 20 minutes.

Calculating the Benefit from the Script

When considering the time consumed to write a script, test the script, and put the script into change control, a considerable amount of expense can be involved in the development process. Therefore, it is important that IT Pros spend a bit of time assessing the benefit of writing a script before launching a scripting-writing binge. As noted in this chapter, many of the traditional reasons for writing a script are no longer valid with Windows PowerShell. This does not mean that you will never need to write a script, but it does mean that a short command can usually be written that accomplishes a significant amount of work. When considering the question of whether to script or not to script, some of the benefits of a script are discussed in this section.

Repeatability

When a task needs to be repeated many times, it becomes an obvious candidate for a script (not in all situations, of course). It is quite common for an IT Pro to look at service status information, which is easily obtained by using the Get-Service cmdlet. If you want to check the status of a specific process, you need to use the *name* parameter as shown here.

```
PS C:\> Get-Process -Name powershell


Handles  NPM(K)    PM(K)     WS(K) VM(M)   CPU(s)     Id ProcessName
-------  ------    -----     ----- -----   ------     -- -----------
    661       9    42616     46024   202     3.61    880 powershell
```

If you are interested in the latest entry written to the application event log, you need to use two parameters as shown here.

```
PS C:\> Get-WinEvent -LogName application -MaxEvents 1


TimeCreated           ProviderName                          Id Message
-----------           ------------                          -- -------
1/26/2009 10:47:...   VSS                                 8193 Volume Shadow Co...
```

There is little reason to write a script for these cases because the command-line syntax is clear, easy to use, and easily discoverable if you happen to forget the exact syntax. All you need to do is use the Get-Help cmdlet.

If you need to perform a task on a routine basis and it needs to be performed against a group of computers, the task is a candidate for a script. Suppose you need to check the status of the fragmentation on a number of computers. You can probably determine a way to run the command directly from the Windows PowerShell prompt, but the next time you need to check the fragmentation on a number of computers, you will spend another 20 or 30 minutes fiddling to get the syntax just right. Instead, a script named DefragAnalysisReport.ps1 can probably be written in less than one hour. Such a script can use the *Win32_Volume* WMI class, call the *DefragAnalysis* method for each drive on the computer, and write the results to a text file.

In the DefragAnalysisReport.ps1 script, you first need to create an array of computer names and assign them to the *$arycomputer* variable. This procedure can be done either by hard-coding the literal values as shown here or by using the Get-Content cmdlet and reading the values from a text file. Next, you must assign a value for the output path of the defragmentation analysis report. This path is a folder that already exists on the computer that will be running the script; it does not need to exist on the target computer because all of the reports will be stored locally. This section of code is shown here.

```
$arycomputer = "Vista","Berlin"
$FilePath = "C:\fso"
```

You now need to walk through the array of computer names that is stored in the *$arycomputer* variable by using the *Foreach* statement as shown here.

```
Foreach($Computer in $aryComputer)
{
```

You can then use the `Get-WmiObject` cmdlet to query the *Win32_Volume* WMI class; this class exists on Windows Server 2003 and later versions. As a best practice, if you anticipate running the script on older versions of the Windows operating system, you should add some error handling to detect the operating system version and gracefully move on to the next computer. This technique is discussed in Chapter 7, "Avoiding Scripting Pitfalls." The WMI query is shown here.

```
Get-WmiObject -Class win32_volume -Filter "DriveType = 3" `
        -ComputerName $computer |
```

The results of the WMI query are pipelined to the `ForEach-Object` cmdlet. The pipelining technique normally provides performance improvements over storing the results of the query into a variable and then iterating the results through the collection because, as soon as the first object is retrieved, it is passed over the pipeline and the processing continues. The first task to perform when inside the `ForEach-Object` cmdlet is to print a message that indicates which computer is being tested by using the *–Begin* parameter as shown here.

```
ForEach-Object `
-Begin { "Testing $computer" } `
```

You can use the *Process* block to perform the actual defrag analysis, which occurs once for each drive. The *DefragAnalysis* method is called for the current object that is on the pipeline; the *$_* variable is an automatic variable that refers to that object. The *DefragAnalysis* method returns both an error report as well as an instance of the *Win32_DefragAnalysis* WMI class. Both are captured in the *$rtn* variable as shown here.

```
-Process {
    "Testing drive $($_.name) for fragmentation. Please wait ..."
    $RTN = $_.DefragAnalysis()
```

To produce the defragmentation report, you can use redirection. A single right-angle arrow (>) overwrites any previously existing reports. Because there is a strong possibility that the server might have more than one drive, it is better to use the double right-angle arrow (>>). The other option when using redirection is to use the `Out-File` cmdlet, which has the advantage of allowing you to specify what encoding to use with the file. Using the `Out-File` cmdlet is also more readable than using redirection arrows, so I generally use the `Out-File` cmdlet when writing a script. The report header section is shown here.

```
"Defrag report for $computer" >> "$FilePath\Defrag$computer.txt"
"Report for Drive $($_.Name)" >> "$FilePath\Defrag$computer.txt"
"Report date: $(Get-Date)" >> "$FilePath\Defrag$computer.txt"
"--------------------------------" >> "$FilePath\Defrag$computer.txt"
```

One of the great features of Windows PowerShell is the way in which it automatically displays the properties and values of an object. VBScript requires more than a dozen lines of code to print the value of each property. As you can see here, the *Win32_DefragAnalysis* management object that is stored in the *DefragAnalysis* property is pipelined to the Format-List cmdlet to remove the system properties of the WMI class. All system properties begin with a double underscore (__), which means that a regular expression pattern that selects properties beginning with the letters a through z that are followed by one or more characters will remove the system properties. The resulting list of properties and their values are redirected to the file in the location specified by the *$filepath* property as shown here.

```
$RTN.DefragAnalysis |
Format-List -Property [a-z]* >> "$FilePath\Defrag$computer.txt"
} `
```

Last, you can print a message indicating that testing is completed on the computer by using the *End* parameter as shown here.

```
-END { "Completed testing $computer" }
} #end foreach computer
```

The completed DefragAnalysisReport.ps1 script is shown here.

```
DefragAnalysisReport.ps1
$arycomputer = "Vista","Berlin"
$FilePath = "C:\fso"
Foreach($Computer in $aryComputer)
{
 Get-WmiObject -Class win32_volume -Filter "DriveType = 3" `
       -ComputerName $computer |
 ForEach-Object `
 -Begin { "Testing $computer" } `
 -Process {
   "Testing drive $($_.name) for fragmentation. Please wait ..."
   $RTN = $_.DefragAnalysis()
   "Defrag report for $computer" >> "$FilePath\Defrag$computer.txt"
   "Report for Drive $($_.Name)" >> "$FilePath\Defrag$computer.txt"
   "Report date: $(Get-Date)" >> "$FilePath\Defrag$computer.txt"
   "-----------------------------" >> "$FilePath\Defrag$computer.txt"
   $RTN.DefragAnalysis |
   Format-List -Property [a-z]* >> "$FilePath\Defrag$computer.txt"
 } `
 -END { "Completed testing $computer" }
} #end foreach computer
```

Documentability

A script provides assurance that certain steps have been performed in a consistent manner. This process is important when performing a series of complicated configuration tasks or even when making simple registry changes. The script documents exactly what took place during the configuration change session. If a configuration change is later discovered to have been in error, a Windows PowerShell script provides documentation for the commands that were run, and the same script can usually be easily modified to undo the changes that were made.

In the following example, a new registry key is created in the HKEY_CURRENT_USER hive that is named Scripting; another registry key named Logon is also created. Once the two registry keys are created, a property named *ScriptName* with a value of *temp* is created. The resulting registry keys are shown in Figure 8-9, and the code that creates the registry keys is shown here.

```
PS C:\> New-Item -Path HKCU:\Scripting\Logon -Force


    Hive: HKEY_CURRENT_USER\Scripting


SKC  VC Name                        Property
---  -- ----                        --------
  0   0 Logon                       {}


PS C:\> New-ItemProperty -Path HKCU:\Scripting\Logon -Name ScriptName -Value "Temp"

PSPath        : Microsoft.PowerShell.Core\Registry::HKEY_CURRENT_USER\Scripting\
                Logon
PSParentPath  : Microsoft.PowerShell.Core\Registry::HKEY_CURRENT_USER\Scripting
PSChildName   : Logon
PSDrive       : HKCU
PSProvider    : Microsoft.PowerShell.Core\Registry
ScriptName    : Temp
```

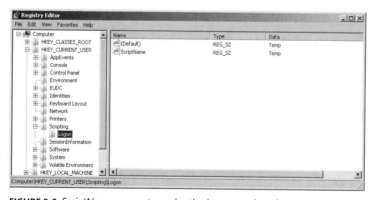

FIGURE 8-9 *ScriptName* property under the Logon registry key

If a problem arises during the creation of the registry keys and the associated property values, you must either open the Registry Editor or type an assortment of commands in the Windows PowerShell console. A script is generally easier to modify because you can see all of the code that executed at the same time. The commands that were earlier typed in the Windows PowerShell console are shown in the CreateScriptingRegistryKey.ps1 script.

CreateScriptingRegistryKey.ps1
```
New-Item -Path HKCU:\Scripting\Logon -Value "Temp" -Force
New-ItemProperty -Path HKCU:\Scripting\Logon -Name ScriptName -Value "Temp"
```

If a problem arises with the command, it is easy to create a new script based on the first script, which rolls back the changes as shown in the DeleteScriptingRegistryKey.ps1 script. The second line of the script is commented out, and the first line is changed from New-Item to Remove-Item. The *–force* parameter is changed to *Recurse*, and the *value* parameter is not required when using Remove-Item. The modified DeleteScriptingRegistryKey.ps1 script is shown here.

DeleteScriptingRegistryKey.ps1
```
Remove-Item -Path HKCU:\Scripting -Recurse
#New-ItemProperty -Path HKCU:\Scripting\Logon -Name ScriptName -Value "Temp"
```

Adaptability

Depending on the script design, the script can be used to perform other tasks. If a script is written in a modular fashion and takes advantage of functions and command-line arguments, it can be used to perform a variety of tasks. The functions themselves can be imported by dot-sourcing the script into another script. The script itself can also be converted into a module, which can then be imported into the current session by using the Import-Module cmdlet.

As an example of a modular script design, you can look at the SaveWmiInformationAsDocument.ps1 script. The essential functionality of the script is contained as functions that can easily be reused in other scripts.

Reusing Code

The ability to adapt functions from one script into another script can often justify the time and expense involved in writing the script in the first place. However, code reuse should not always be the first goal of a script writer. Writing a script in a completely modular fashion takes considerably longer than writing a script in a linear fashion. In addition, the investment of time for an undetermined possible future reuse is not always the wisest approach. Writing modular code is a good discipline and generally makes the code easier to read and modify. Both of these design goals are worthwhile endeavors, but potential code reuse alone is not enough reason to justify the extra effort.

The first function in the SaveWmiInformationAsDocument.ps1 script is named the *CreateWordDoc* function, which creates an instance of the *Word.Application* object and stores it in a script-level variable named *$word*. The function next makes the Microsoft Office Word application visible and adds a document to the document collection as shown here.

```
Function CreateWordDoc()
{
  $script:word = New-Object -ComObject word.application
  $word.visible = $true
  $Script:doc = $word.documents.add()
} #end CreateWordDoc
```

The next function is named *CreateSelection*, and it accepts a string to use in the Office Word document for a heading. To create a Word selection, the script needs an instance of the *Word.Application* object. Because the *$word* variable was created in the script-level scope, it is available inside the *CreateSelection* function. The *selection* object is created by querying the *selection* property. The heading is typed into the Word document by using the *TypeText* method. A blank paragraph is created, and the function ends as shown here.

```
Function CreateSelection($Heading)
{
  $script:selection = $word.selection
  $selection.typeText($Heading)
  $selection.TypeParagraph()
} #end CreateSelection
```

The *GetWmiData* function is used to query a WMI class, convert the output to a string, and write the information into a Word document as a selection as shown here.

```
Function GetWmiData($WmiClass)
{
 Get-WmiObject -class $wmiClass | Out-String |
 ForEach-Object {$selection.typeText($_)}
} #end GetWmiData
```

When the WMI information is retrieved, it is time to create the file path by using the *CreateFilePath* function so that the Word document can be saved. The function receives the WMI class name via the *$WmiClass* variable. It then uses the substring method from the *System.String* class to remove the first six characters from the WMI class name. The first six characters correspond to "Win32_," which is present in most of the WMI class names. To be more accurate, you need to test for other WMI class name patterns and modify the substring command according to the class name that is actually found. The function then uses the Join-Path cmdlet to build the file path that is to be used when saving the WMI documentation. This function is shown here.

```
Function CreateFilePath($wmiClass)
{
 $script:filename = $wmiClass.substring(6)
 $script:path = Join-Path -Path $folder -childpath $filename
} #end CreateFilePath
```

Next, the Word document needs to be saved. First, you must create an instance of the *Microsoft.Office.Interop.Word.WdSaveFormat* enumeration by casting the string representation of the enumeration as a type. This type is also required to be a reference type, so it is cast as a [ref]. The *saveas* method from the *Word.Document* object requires both the path and the *saveformat* to be reference types. Once the document is saved, the *Word.Application* object can be removed from memory via the *quit* method. The *SaveWordData* function is shown here.

```
Function SaveWordData($path)
{
 [ref]$SaveFormat = "microsoft.office.interop.word.WdSaveFormat" -as [type]
 $doc.saveas([ref]$path, [ref]$saveFormat::wdFormatDocument)
 $word.quit()
} #end SaveWordData
```

The entry point into the script creates some variables and calls the appropriate functions as shown here.

```
$folder = "C:\fso"
$wmiClass = "Win32_Bios"
$heading = "$wmiClass information:"
CreateWordDoc
CreateSelection($Heading)
GetWmiData($wmiClass)
CreateFilePath($wmiClass)
SaveWordData($path)
```

The completed SaveWmiInformationAsDocument.ps1 script is shown here.

SaveWmiInformationAsDocument.ps1

```
Function CreateWordDoc()
{
  $script:word = New-Object -ComObject word.application
  $word.visible = $true
  $Script:doc = $word.documents.add()
} #end CreateWordDoc


Function CreateSelection($Heading)
{
  $script:selection = $word.selection
  $selection.typeText($Heading)
  $selection.TypeParagraph()
} #end CreateSelection


Function GetWmiData($WmiClass)
{
 Get-WmiObject -class $wmiClass | Out-String |
 ForEach-Object {$selection.typeText($_)}
} #end GetWmiData


Function CreateFilePath($wmiClass)
{
 $script:filename = $wmiClass.substring(6)
 $script:path = Join-Path -Path $folder -childpath $filename
} #end CreateFilePath


Function SaveWordData($path)
{
 [ref]$SaveFormat = "microsoft.office.interop.word.WdSaveFormat" -as [type]
 $doc.saveas([ref]$path, [ref]$saveFormat::wdFormatDocument)
 $word.quit()
} #end SaveWordData


# *** Entry point ***
$folder = "C:\fso"
$wmiClass = "Win32_Bios"
$heading = "$wmiClass information:"
CreateWordDoc
CreateSelection($Heading)
GetWmiData($wmiClass)
CreateFilePath($wmiClass)
SaveWordData($path)
```

Tracking Scripting Opportunities

Chris Bellée, Premier Field Engineer
Microsoft Corporation, Australia

I often receive requests from customers to create script examples. Often their ideas are good, and I then create a script and file it away for use at a later time, by using Microsoft Notepad, which is quick and easy to use. The plain text file is compatible with all types of programs, and I do not need to worry whether I have a specific Microsoft Office application installed. When I am writing a script, I often discover a new technique or technology that causes me to write a quick sample script illustrating the new technique or technology. This is not a very formal technique, but it has the advantage of simplicity.

A database of scripts is a great idea, perhaps easily created in Microsoft Office Access. You can then categorize the scripts by topic as well as by technology and can easily create a report that will point out areas that are lacking certain types of scripts. You can then review the list and fill in the gaps in your script portfolio. You can use this database for storage as well as lookup and search. One very interesting idea is to create a script builder that is based on generic routines that are stored in a database. Of course, this does not really allow you to track scripting opportunities so much as it allows you to create new scripts based on the storage of your existing ideas. This script builder can be an extension of the Portable Script Center that is available from the Microsoft Script Center.

When I get ready to write a new script, I generally choose Microsoft .NET Framework classes if they are available instead of using an old VBScript function or even WMI classes because I am more familiar with .NET programming and because I consider this process to be a best practice. The .NET Framework is native to Windows PowerShell, and it is much easier to call Win32 Application Programming Interfaces in PowerShell 2.0. I will use these APIs when a class is not available to me from the .NET library, such as creating network shares and setting permissions on them.

Script Collaboration

While writing scripts can be fun to do and many network administrators seem to enjoy the process, it can also be time consuming. It is therefore important that the process is performed in such a way that it benefits the entire organization. You should understand that there is a difference between learning to script and writing scripts. It is true that network administrators often learn to script by writing scripts, but the two activities should be separated. Learning to script is a training function, and the time invested in learning to script should be tracked as part of the training budget. Writing scripts is an operational expense, and the time invested in writing production scripts should be tracked as an operational expense. If a network administrator takes eight hours to write a script that retrieves the amount of free disk space on a server, that network administrator does not know how to write scripts. Therefore, the eight hours should be tracked as part of the training budget and not as a production expense. It simply is not efficient for a company to have twelve different scripts that all detail the amount of free disk space on a computer. If people in different departments write the same scripts, the problem of wasted time and effort becomes compounded, which is where collaboration comes into play. Through the use of collaboration tools, scripts can be shared and requested and features can be requested. Specific personnel can be detailed to write specific scripts. The tasks of training and production can be separated, and duplication of time and effort can be avoided.

Windows SharePoint Services

Microsoft Windows SharePoint Services contains a number of features that can be used to facilitate collaboration. Numerous templates can be applied when designing a new Windows SharePoint site. I prefer to use the Document Collaboration template because it allows for the easy sharing of documents, a discussion list, links to other sites, and a shared calendar. The home page also provides a convenient place for announcements related to ongoing projects as shown in Figure 8-10.

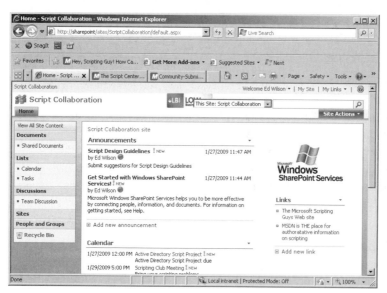

FIGURE 8-10 Script Collaboration home page using Windows SharePoint Services

You can use the Shared Documents section to form the Script library, which can be renamed Script Repository or whatever you choose to call it. You have the ability to manage permissions on a script-by-script basis. As an example, you can restrict access to certain types of troubleshooting scripts to level-two help desk personnel and permit access to the more basic scripts to ordinary users. You can check out the script when it is being modified, which allows the name of the script to still be visible but the status of the script to change to checked out. The Shared Document library is shown in Figure 8-11.

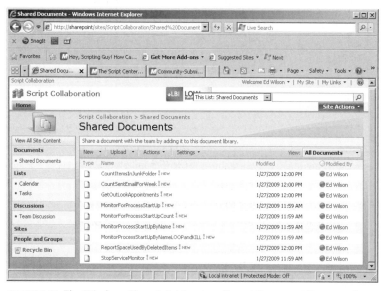

FIGURE 8-11 The Windows SharePoint Services Shared Document library makes a good script repository.

The Team Discussion site provides a good location for members of the IT team to request specific scripts. By replying to a particular script request, duplication of effort can be reduced. As shown in Figure 8-12, one person is requesting a script that will defrag hard drives on remote servers. If someone decides to write that script, they only need to reply to the posting that they will write the script. All members of the IT team should subscribe to the Script Collaboration SharePoint Services site. Subscribing to a site causes you to receive an e-mail notification when anything on the site changes such as the submission of a new script to the Shared Documents section, a reply to a request for a script, or a new event, such as scheduling a meeting of the scripting club. The Team Discussion section of the SharePoint site is shown in Figure 8-12.

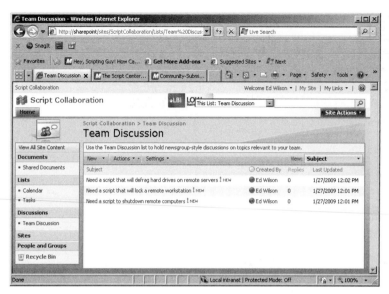

FIGURE 8-12 Team Discussion allows members to post requests for scripts and other members to sign up to write such scripts.

Microsoft Office Groove

Microsoft Office Groove is a tool that provides offline access to a shared file library. This tool allows you to group collections of scripts into different workspaces. You can then control the security on the various workspaces to permit only authorized personnel to access the script libraries. You can also publish your script standards document, which ensures that the latest version of the document is always available. Groove uses a streaming peer-to-peer method to upload and download changes to the various workspaces; as a result, it can take up to several days to ensure that the files replicate initially and populate the various workspaces. There is also a chat mechanism, presence mechanism, and discussion board that can be used for collaboration purposes. As shown in Figure 8-13, the best feature is the one that ensures offline access to documents, files, and scripts.

Live Mesh

Live Mesh is another tool that can be used to provide access to scripts and to back up your profile. This tool essentially makes a backup copy of files you publish to the Live Mesh site. You can then access the files from other computers on the network that you add to the mesh. Live Mesh provides a good way to back up your script library, your script profile, and other vital files to ensure that they are always available. Because Live Mesh is an online storage site, it requires Internet connectivity to retrieve the files. You are allowed to select the folders you want to make available. The Live Mesh Desktop is shown in Figure 8-14.

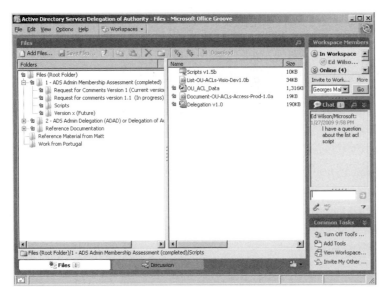

FIGURE 8-13 Groove provides offline access to scripts and documents.

FIGURE 8-14 Live Mesh Desktop provides the ability to ensure that certain folders are always available via the Internet.

Additional Resources

- The TechNet Script Center at *http://www.microsoft.com/technet/scriptcenter* contains numerous examples of the LDAP search filter syntax.

- Refer to this Knowledge Base article for information about using the NetSh Advanced Firewall commands at *http://support.microsoft.com/kb/947709*.

- LDAP search filter syntax is documented on MSDN at *http://msdn.microsoft.com/en-us /library/aa746385(VS.85).aspx*.

- Live Mesh is available at *https://www.mesh.com/Welcome/default.aspx*.

- Take a look at the *Windows PowerShell™ Scripting Guide* (Microsoft Press, 2008) for other examples of working with Active Directory.

- On the companion media, you will find all of the scripts referred to in this chapter.

Designing Functions

Clear-cut guidelines can be used to design scripts and ensure that they are easy to understand, maintain, and troubleshoot. In this chapter, you will examine the reasons for scripting guidelines and view examples of both good and bad code design.

Understanding Functions

In Windows PowerShell 2.0, functions have moved to the forefront as the primary programming element used when writing PowerShell scripts. This is not necessarily due to improvements in functions per se but rather to a combination of factors, including the maturity of Windows PowerShell script writers. In Windows PowerShell 1.0, functions were not well understood, perhaps because of a lack of clear documentation as to their use, purpose, and application.

Both subroutines and functions are found in VBScript. According to the classic definitions, a subroutine is used to encapsulate code that can perform such actions as writing to a database or creating a Microsoft Office Word document. A function is used to return a value. An example of the classic VBScript function is one that converts a temperature from Fahrenheit to Celsius. The function receives the value in Fahrenheit and returns the value in Celsius. The classic function always returns a value; if it does not, then the subroutine should be used.

To create a function, you begin with the Function keyword followed by the name of the function. As a best practice, you can use the Windows PowerShell verb-noun combination when creating functions. Pick the verb from the standard list of Windows PowerShell verbs to make your functions easier to remember. It is a best practice to avoid creating new verbs when there is an existing verb that can easily do the job. The list of recommended verbs is contained in Appendix G, "Useful COM Objects."

To obtain a better idea of the verb coverage, you can use the Get-Command cmdlet and pipe the results to the Group-Object cmdlet as shown here.

```
Get-Command -CommandType cmdlet | Group-Object -Property Verb |
Sort-Object -Property count -Descending
```

When the previous command is run, the resulting output is displayed in the following list. The command is run on Windows Vista and includes only the default cmdlets; no modules are loaded. As shown in the listing, the verb Get is used the most often by the default cmdlets, followed distantly by Set, New, and Remove.

```
Count Name                Group
----- ----                -----
   46 Get                 {Get-Acl, Get-Alias, Get-AuthenticodeSignatu...
   19 Set                 {Set-Acl, Set-Alias, Set-AuthenticodeSignatu...
   16 New                 {New-Alias, New-Event, New-EventLog, New-Ite...
   14 Remove              {Remove-Computer, Remove-Event, Remove-Event...
    8 Export              {Export-Alias, Export-Clixml, Export-Console...
    8 Write               {Write-Debug, Write-Error, Write-EventLog, W...
    7 Import              {Import-Alias, Import-Clixml, Import-Counter...
    7 Out                 {Out-Default, Out-File, Out-GridView, Out-Ho...
    6 Add                 {Add-Computer, Add-Content, Add-History, Add...
    6 Start               {Start-Job, Start-Process, Start-Service, St...
    6 Invoke              {Invoke-Command, Invoke-Expression, Invoke-H...
    6 Clear               {Clear-Content, Clear-EventLog, Clear-Histor...
    5 Test                {Test-ComputerSecureChannel, Test-Connection...
```

```
5 Stop             {Stop-Computer, Stop-Job, Stop-Process, Stop...
4 ConvertTo        {ConvertTo-Csv, ConvertTo-Html, ConvertTo-Se...
4 Register         {Register-EngineEvent, Register-ObjectEvent,...
4 Format           {Format-Custom, Format-List, Format-Table, F...
4 Disable          {Disable-ComputerRestore, Disable-PSBreakpoi...
4 Enable           {Enable-ComputerRestore, Enable-PSBreakpoint...
3 ConvertFrom      {ConvertFrom-Csv, ConvertFrom-SecureString, ...
3 Wait             {Wait-Event, Wait-Job, Wait-Process}
3 Update           {Update-FormatData, Update-List, Update-Type...
3 Select           {Select-Object, Select-String, Select-Xml}
3 Rename           {Rename-Computer, Rename-Item, Rename-ItemPr...
2 Unregister       {Unregister-Event, Unregister-PSSessionConfi...
2 Restart          {Restart-Computer, Restart-Service}
2 Move             {Move-Item, Move-ItemProperty}
2 Copy             {Copy-Item, Copy-ItemProperty}
2 Measure          {Measure-Command, Measure-Object}
1 Tee              {Tee-Object}
1 Suspend          {Suspend-Service}
1 Debug            {Debug-Process}
1 Sort             {Sort-Object}
1 Show             {Show-EventLog}
1 Checkpoint       {Checkpoint-Computer}
1 Split            {Split-Path}
1 Disconnect       {Disconnect-WSMan}
1 Use              {Use-Transaction}
1 Pop              {Pop-Location}
1 Where            {Where-Object}
1 Trace            {Trace-Command}
1 Exit             {Exit-PSSession}
1 Enter            {Enter-PSSession}
1 Undo             {Undo-Transaction}
1 Receive          {Receive-Job}
1 Read             {Read-Host}
1 Compare          {Compare-Object}
1 Convert          {Convert-Path}
1 Connect          {Connect-WSMan}
1 Join             {Join-Path}
1 Push             {Push-Location}
1 Complete         {Complete-Transaction}
1 Limit            {Limit-EventLog}
1 Resume           {Resume-Service}
1 ForEach          {ForEach-Object}
1 Send             {Send-MailMessage}
1 Reset            {Reset-ComputerMachinePassword}
1 Group            {Group-Object}
1 Restore          {Restore-Computer}
1 Resolve          {Resolve-Path}
```

In Appendix G, some verbs are marked as obsolete; thus, you should avoid using them when creating functions. Of course, nothing bad happens if you use an obsolete verb in your function name, but it is best to avoid using an obscure verb so that your functions are easy to remember.

A function is not required to accept any parameters. In fact, many functions do not require input to perform their job in the script. Let's use an example to illustrate this point. A common task for network administrators is obtaining the operating system version. Script writers often need to do this to ensure that their script uses the correct interface or exits gracefully. It is also quite common that one set of files can be copied to a desktop running one version of the operating system and a different set of files can be copied for another version of the operating system.

The first step in creating a function is to choose a name. Because the function is going to retrieve information, the best verb to use from the listing of cmdlet verbs shown earlier is Get. For the noun portion of the name, it is best to use a term that describes the information that will be obtained. In this example, a noun named OperatingSystemVersion makes sense. An example of such a function is the one shown in the Get-OperatingSystemVersion.ps1 script. The *Get-OperatingSystemVersion* function uses Windows Management Instrumentation (WMI) to obtain the version of the operating system. In this most basic form of the function, you have the Function keyword followed by the name of the function as well as a script block containing code that is delimited by curly brackets. This pattern is shown here.

```
Function Function-Name
{
 #insert code here
}
```

In the Get-OperatingSystemVersion.ps1 script, the *Get-OperatingSystemVersion* function is at the top of the script. The script uses the Function keyword to define the function followed by the name *Get-OperatingSystemVersion*. The curly brackets are opened, followed by the code. The code uses the Get-WmiObject cmdlet to retrieve an instance of the *Win32_OperatingSystem* WMI class. Because this WMI class only returns a single instance, the properties of the class are directly accessible. The version is the property in question, and parentheses force the evaluation of the code inside them. The returned management object is used to emit the version value, and the curly brackets are used to close the function. The operating system version is returned to the code that calls the function. In this example, a string that writes "This OS is version " is used. A subexpression is used to force evaluation of the function. The version of the operating system is returned to the place from where the function is called as shown here.

```
Get-OperatingSystemVersion.ps1
Function Get-OperatingSystemVersion
{
 (Get-WmiObject -Class Win32_OperatingSystem).Version
} #end Get-OperatingSystemVersion

"This OS is version $(Get-OperatingSystemVersion)"
```

In the earlier listing of cmdlet verbs, the `Read-Host` cmdlet uses the `Read` verb to obtain information from the command line. This indicates that the `Read` verb is not used to describe reading a file. There is no verb named `Display`, and the `Write` verb is used in cmdlet names such as `Write-Error` and `Write-Debug`, both of which do not really conform to the concept of displaying information. If you are writing a function that can read the content of a text file and display statistics about that file, you might call the function *Get-TextStatistics*. This is in keeping with cmdlet names such as `Get-Process` and `Get-Service`, which include the concept of emitting their retrieved content within their essential functionality. The *Get-TextStatistics* function accepts a single parameter named *–path*. What is interesting about parameters for functions is that you use a dash when you pass a value to the parameter. You use a variable when you refer to the value inside the function, such as *$path*. To call the *Get-TextStatistics* function, you have a few options. The first is to use the name of the function and put the value in parentheses as shown here.

```
Get-TextStatistics("C:\fso\mytext.txt")
```

This is a typical way to call the function. This method works when there is a single parameter but does not work when there are two or more parameters. Another way to pass a value to the function is to use the dash and the parameter name as shown here.

```
Get-TextStatistics -path "C:\fso\mytext.txt"
```

You will note from the previous example that no parentheses are required. You can also use positional arguments when passing a value by omitting the name of the parameter entirely and simply placing the value for the parameter following the call to the function as illustrated here.

```
Get-TextStatistics "C:\fso\mytext.txt"
```

TRADEOFF

Using Positional Arguments

The use of positional arguments works well when you are working from the command line and want to speed things along by reducing the typing load. This method can be a bit confusing, and I generally tend to avoid it, even when working at the command line. I avoid positional arguments because I often copy my working code from the console directly into a script; as a result, I would need to retype the command a second time to get rid of aliases and unnamed arguments. With the improvements in tab expansion in Windows Powershell 2.0, I feel that the time saved by using positional or partial arguments does not sufficiently compensate for the time involved in retyping commands when they need to be transferred to scripts. The other reason that I always use named arguments is that they help me to be aware of the exact command syntax.

One additional way to pass a value to a function is to use partial parameter names. All that is required is enough of the parameter name to disambiguate it from other parameters. This means that if you have two parameters that both begin with the letter *p*, you need to supply enough letters of the parameter name to separate it from the other parameter as illustrated here.

```
Get-TextStatistics -p "C:\fso\mytext.txt"
```

The complete text of the *Get-TextStatistics* function is shown here.

```
Get-TextStatistics.ps1Function Get-TextStatistics($path)
{
 Get-Content -path $path |
 Measure-Object -line -character -word
}
```

Between Windows PowerShell 1.0 and PowerShell 2.0, the number of verbs grew from 40 to 60. It is anticipated that the list of standard verbs should cover 80-85 percent of administrative tasks. The new verbs are listed here.

```
Checkpoint
Complete
Connect
Debug
Disable
Disconnect
Enable
Enter
Exit
Limit
Receive
Register
Reset
Restore
Send
Show
Undo
Unregister
Use
Wait
```

Once the function is named, you can create any parameters that the function may require. The parameters are contained within smooth parentheses. In the *Get-TextStatistics* function, the function accepts a single parameter named *–path*. When a function accepts a single parameter, you can pass the value to the function by placing the value for the parameter inside smooth parentheses. This command is shown here.

```
Get-TextLength("C:\fso\test.txt")
```

The "C:\fso\test.txt" path is passed to the *Get-TextStatistics* function via the *–path* parameter. Inside the function, the "C:\fso\text.txt" string is contained in the *$path* variable. The *$path* variable only lives within the confines of the *Get-TextStatistics* function and is not available outside the scope of the function; however, it is available from within child scopes of the *Get-TextStatistics* function. A child scope of *Get-TextStatistics* is one that is created from within the *Get-TextStatistics* function. In the Get-TextStatisticsCallChildFunction.ps1 script, the *Write-Path* function is called from within the *Get-TextStatistics* function, which means that the *Write-Path* function has access to variables created within the *Get-TextStatistics* function. This process involves the concept of variable scope and is an extremely important concept when working with functions. As you use functions to separate the creation of objects, you must always be aware of where the object is created and where you intend to use that object. In the Get-TextStatisticsCallChildFunction.ps1 script, the *$path* variable does not obtain its value until it is passed to the function and therefore lives within the *Get-TextStatistics* function. However, because the *Write-Path* function is called from within the *Get-TextStatistics* function, the *Write-Path* function inherits the variables from that scope. When you call a function from within another function, variables created within the parent function are available to the child function as shown in the Get-TextStatisticsCallChildFunction.ps1 script.

```
Get-TextStatisticsCallChildFunction.ps1
Function Get-TextStatistics($path)
{
 Get-Content -path $path |
 Measure-Object -line -character -word
 Write-Path
}

Function Write-Path()
{
 "Inside Write-Path the `$path variable is equal to $path"
}

Get-TextStatistics("C:\fso\test.txt")
"Outside the Get-TextStatistics function `$path is equal to $path"
```

Inside the *Get-TextStatistics* function, the *$path* variable is used to provide the path to the Get-Content cmdlet. When the *Write-Path* function is called, nothing is passed to it, yet inside the *Write-Path* function, the value of *$path* is maintained. Outside both of the functions, however, *$path* does not have any value. The output from running the script is shown here.

```
        Lines           Words        Characters Property
        -----           -----        ---------- --------
          3              41             210
Inside Write-Path the $path variable is equal to C:\fso\test.txt
Outside the Get-TextStatistics function $path is equal to
```

You then need to open and close a script block. The curly bracket is used to delimit the script block on a function. As a best practice, I always use the Function keyword when writing a function and then type in the name, input parameters, and curly brackets for the script block at the same time as shown here.

```
Function My-Function()
{
 #insert code here
}
```

In this manner, I do not forget to close the curly brackets. Trying to identify a missing curly bracket within a long script can be somewhat problematic because the error that is presented does not always correspond to the line that is missing the curly bracket. Suppose that the closing curly bracket is left off of the *Get-TextStatistics* function as shown in the Get-TextStatisticsCallChildFunction-DoesNOTWork-MissingClosingBracket.ps1 script. An error is generated as shown here.

```
Missing closing '}' in statement block.
At C:\BestPracticesBook\Get-TextStatisticsCallChildFunction-DoesNOTWork-
MissingClosingBracket.ps1:28 char:1
```

The problem is that the position indicator of the error message points to the first character on line 28. Line 28 happens to be the first blank line after the end of the script. This means that Windows PowerShell scanned the entire script looking for the closing curly bracket. Because the closing curly bracket was not found, Windows PowerShell states that the error is at the end of the script. If you place a closing curly bracket on line 28, the error in this example does go away, but the script does not work. The Get-TextStatisticsCallChildFunction-DoesNOTWork-MissingClosingBracket.ps1 script is shown here with a comment that indicates where the missing closing curly bracket should be placed. One other technique to guard against the missing curly bracket problem is to add a comment to the closing curly bracket of each function.

Get-TextStatisticsCallChildFunction-DoesNOTWork-MissingClosingBracket.ps1
```
Function Get-TextStatistics($path)
{
 Get-Content -path $path |
 Measure-Object -line -character -word
 Write-Path
# Here is where the missing bracket goes

Function Write-Path()
{
 "Inside Write-Path the `$path variable is equal to $path"
}
Get-TextStatistics("C:\fso\test.txt")
Outside the Get-TextStatistics function `$path is equal to $path"
```

Using Functions to Provide Ease of Code Reuse

When scripts are written using well-designed functions, it is easier to reuse them in other scripts and to provide access to these functions from within the Windows PowerShell console. To access these functions, you need to dot-source the containing script. An issue that arises with dot-sourcing scripts to bring in functions is that the script may often contain global variables or other items that you do not want to bring into your current environment.

An example of a good function is the ConvertToMeters.ps1 script. No variables are defined outside the function, and the function itself does not use the `Write-Host` cmdlet to break up the pipeline. The results of the conversion are returned directly to the calling code. The only problem with the ConvertToMeters.ps1 script is that when it is dot-sourced into the Windows PowerShell console, it runs and returns the data because all executable code in the script is executed. The ConvertToMeters.ps1 script is shown here.

ConvertToMeters.ps1
```
Function Script:ConvertToMeters($feet)
{
  "$feet feet equals $($feet*.31) meters"
} #end ConvertToMeters
$feet = 5
ConvertToMeters -Feet $feet
```

With well-written functions, it is trivial to collect the functions into a single script—you just copy and paste the functions from the original scripts into a new script. When you are done, you have created a Function library.

When pasting your functions into the Function library script, pay attention to the comments at the end of the function. The comments at the closing curly bracket for each function not only point to the closing curly bracket, but also provide a visual indicator for the end of each function that can be helpful when you need to troubleshoot a script. An example of such a Function library is the ConversionFunctions.ps1 script, shown here.

ConversionFunctions.ps1
```
Function Script:ConvertToMeters($feet)
{
  "$feet feet equals $($feet*.31) meters"
} #end ConvertToMeters

Function Script:ConvertToFeet($meters)
{
  "$meters meters equals $($meters * 3.28) feet"
} #end ConvertToFeet

Function Script:ConvertToFahrenheit($celsius)
{
```

```
  "$celsius celsius equals $((1.8 * $celsius) + 32 ) fahrenheit"
} #end ConvertToFahrenheit


Function Script:ConvertTocelsius($fahrenheit)
{
  "$fahrenheit fahrenheit equals $( (($fahrenheit - 32)/9)*5 ) celsius"
} #end ConvertTocelsius


Function Script:ConvertToMiles($kilometer)
{
   "$kilometer kilometers equals $( ($kilometer *.6211) ) miles"
} #end convertToMiles


Function Script:ConvertToKilometers($miles)
{
   "$miles miles equals $( ($miles * 1.61) ) kilometers"
} #end convertToKilometers
```

One way to use the functions from the ConversionFunctions.ps1 script is to use the dot-sourcing operator to run the script so that the functions from the script are part of the calling scope. To dot-source the script, you can use the dot-source operator (period or dot symbol) followed by the path to the script containing the functions you want to include in your current scope. Once done, you can call the function directly as shown here.

```
PS C:\> . C:\scripts\ConversionFunctions.ps1
PS C:\> convertToMiles 6
6 kilometers equals 3.7266 miles
```

All of the functions from the dot-sourced script are available to the current session. This can be seen by composing a listing of the function drive as shown here.

```
PS C:\> dir function: | Where { $_.name -like 'co*'} | Format-Table -Property name,
definition -AutoSize


Name                     Definition
----                     ----------
ConvertToMeters          param($feet) "$feet feet equals $($feet*.31) meters"...
ConvertToFeet            param($meters) "$meters meters equals $($meters * 3.28) feet"...
ConvertToFahrenheit param($celsius) "$celsius celsius equals $((1.8 * $celsius) + 32 )
fahrenheit"...
ConvertTocelsius      param($fahrenheit) "$fahrenheit fahrenheit equals
$( (($fahrenheit - 32)/9)*5 ) celsius...
ConvertToMiles        param($kilometer) "$kilometer kilometers equals $( ($kilometer
*.6211) ) miles"...
ConvertToKilometers param($miles) "$miles miles equals $( ($miles * 1.61) )
kilometers"...
```

Understanding Functions

Brandon Shell, Windows PowerShell MVP

In my mind, functions are, generally speaking, small, single task–based tools (like a flathead screwdriver or hammer). They do one thing, and they do that one thing reliably well. If you take this approach when writing code, you will find it easier to debug and will find yourself writing less code. Why less code? Because you'll find that you are now able to port your functions from one script to another or possibly even in your day-to-day life.

I have three basic guidelines as to when to write a function.

First guideline: I find that I am repeating the same code block over and over again. For example, I have a code block that checks several services on a computer. It may make sense to simply write a function to perform the check and then run that function against each server. This process allows me to troubleshoot the code more efficiently.

Second guideline: I find that I can use this code in other scripts. For example, if I write a nice recursive parsing block, I may want to reuse that logic in another script.

Third guideline: The code is useful outside of this script. This guideline is slightly different from the previous guideline. A good example here is a ping-server function, which is useful both in other scripts and in my day-to-day life.

When writing code, it is generally a good idea to ALWAYS consider reusing the code. This is paramount when working with functions. The sole purpose of using functions in life is for reuse, so this should be a major consideration when designing your functions. Consider how and where a function will be used., which helps to establish the parameters and defaults (if any) that it should have.

Because we design code for reuse, it is a best practice to be as verbose as possible. The basic rule of thumb is to hard-code nothing; all data should be passed by parameters. Certainly, you can have default values for the parameters, but allow the function call to specify other options without modifying the function. This comes back to the black box approach. You need to consider the effect of every change in the original function and how that change will affect the script as a whole.

In Windows PowerShell version 1.0, I always try to implement *–verbose* and *–whatif* parameters with my own switches. In version 2.0, this process is handled for you.

When designing functions, think about the looping and processing logic. This logic is generally script specific and should be implemented outside of the function. Ideally, you want to restrict logic to the party that requires the logic. For example, if you have logic to process servers in the script, keep that logic outside of the functions. There is no need to repeatedly implement that logic for each function call. On the other hand, if you have logic that is expressly the domain of the function, do not go crazy trying to rip it out just to put in the calling script.

Great functions are born from need but grow from use. As you grow in your understanding, your functions will grow with you. They are like friends who are always there when you need them, but, like friends, they need attention and care. Listed below are some features that functions should have.

Well-Defined Parameters

Your function needs to be very clear on what data it expects to generate so as to produce the data you expect. You accomplish this by establishing very specific parameters (which often includes the data type as well). If you absolutely must have a specific value to process, make sure that the value is received by the function. A great way to accomplish this is by assigning the parameter's default value to (Throw '$ThisParam is required').

Consistent and Expected Output

This feature is absolutely critical. You do not want to guess at what type of data will come from the function. You want the data to be what you expect. Design the function so that it returns one or more of a single data type (such as string, DateTime, or Boolean.) Be very cautious not to pollute the data stream with messages written using `Write-Output`.

Self-Containment

The function should NOT rely on any variables from the script. If the function needs input from outside, then make the outside value a parameter.

Portability

The single most important job of a function is to be portable. If you do not plan to reuse the code, you might as well write the code inline. A key factor to portability is to make sure that your variable names will not collide with the calling script.

Using Two Input Parameters

To create a function that uses multiple input parameters, you can use the Function keyword, specify the name of the function, use variables for each input parameter, and then define the script block within curly brackets. The pattern is shown here.

```
Function My-Function($Input1,$Input2)
{
 #Insert Code Here
}
```

An example of a function that takes multiple parameters is the *Get-FreeDiskSpace* function that is shown in the Get-FreeDiskSpace.ps1 script.

The Get-FreeDiskSpace.ps1 script begins with the Function keyword, the name of the function, and two input parameters. The input parameters are placed inside smooth parentheses as shown here.

```
Function Get-FreeDiskSpace($drive,$computer)
```

Inside the curly brackets, the *Get-FreeDiskSpace* function uses the Get-WmiObject cmdlet to query the *Win32_LogicalDisk* WMI class. The *Get-FreeDiskSpace* function connects to the computer specified in the *–computer* parameter and filters out only the drive that is specified in the *–drive* parameter. When the function is called, each parameter is specified as *–drive* and *–computer*. In the function definition, the *$drive* and *$computer* variables are used to hold the values supplied to the parameters.

Once the data from WMI is retrieved, it is stored in the *$driveData* variable. The data that is stored in the *$driveData* variable is an instance of the *Win32_LogicalDisk* class. This variable contains a complete instance of the class. The members of this class are shown in Table 9-1.

TABLE 9-1 Members of the *Win32_LogicalDisk* Class

NAME	MEMBERTYPE	DEFINITION
Chkdsk	Method	System.Management.ManagementBase-Object Chkdsk(System.Boolean FixErrors, System.Boolean VigorousIndexCheck, System.Boolean SkipFolderCycle, System.Boolean ForceDismount, System.Boolean RecoverBadSectors, System.Boolean OkToRunAtBootUp)
Reset	Method	System.Management.ManagementBaseObject Reset()
SetPowerState	Method	System.Management.ManagementBaseObject SetPowerState(System.UInt16 PowerState, System.String Time)
Access	Property	System.UInt16 Access {get;set;}
Availability	Property	System.UInt16 Availability {get;set;}
BlockSize	Property	System.UInt64 BlockSize {get;set;}
Caption	Property	System.String Caption {get;set;}

NAME	MEMBERTYPE	DEFINITION
Compressed	Property	System.Boolean Compressed {get;set;}
ConfigManagerErrorCode	Property	System.UInt32 ConfigManagerErrorCode {get;set;}
ConfigManagerUserConfig	Property	System.Boolean ConfigManagerUserConfig {get;set;}
CreationClassName	Property	System.String CreationClassName {get;set;}
Description	Property	System.String Description {get;set;}
DeviceID	Property	System.String DeviceID {get;set;}
DriveType	Property	System.UInt32 DriveType {get;set;}
ErrorCleared	Property	System.Boolean ErrorCleared {get;set;}
ErrorDescription	Property	System.String ErrorDescription {get;set;}
ErrorMethodology	Property	System.String ErrorMethodology {get;set;}
FileSystem	Property	System.String FileSystem {get;set;}
FreeSpace	Property	System.UInt64 FreeSpace {get;set;}
InstallDate	Property	System.String InstallDate {get;set;}
LastErrorCode	Property	System.UInt32 LastErrorCode {get;set;}
MaximumComponentLength	Property	System.UInt32 MaximumComponentLength {get;set;}
MediaType	Property	System.UInt32 MediaType {get;set;}
Name	Property	System.String Name {get;set;}
NumberOfBlocks	Property	System.UInt64 NumberOfBlocks {get;set;}
PNPDeviceID	Property	System.String PNPDeviceID {get;set;}
PowerManagementCapabilities	Property	System.UInt16[] PowerManagementCapabilities {get;set;}
PowerManagementSupported	Property	System.Boolean PowerManagementSupported {get;set;}
ProviderName	Property	System.String ProviderName {get;set;}
Purpose	Property	System.String Purpose {get;set;}
QuotasDisabled	Property	System.Boolean QuotasDisabled {get;set;}
QuotasIncomplete	Property	System.Boolean QuotasIncomplete {get;set;}
QuotasRebuilding	Property	System.Boolean QuotasRebuilding {get;set;}
Size	Property	System.UInt64 Size {get;set;}
Status	Property	System.String Status {get;set;}

NAME	MEMBERTYPE	DEFINITION
StatusInfo	Property	System.UInt16 StatusInfo {get;set;}
SupportsDiskQuotas	Property	System.Boolean SupportsDiskQuotas {get;set;}
SupportsFileBasedCompression	Property	System.Boolean SupportsFileBasedCompression {get;set;}
SystemCreationClassName	Property	System.String SystemCreationClassName {get;set;}
SystemName	Property	System.String SystemName {get;set;}
VolumeDirty	Property	System.Boolean VolumeDirty {get;set;}
VolumeName	Property	System.String VolumeName {get;set;}
VolumeSerialNumber	Property	System.String VolumeSerialNumber {get;set;}
__CLASS	Property	System.String __CLASS {get;set;}
__DERIVATION	Property	System.String[] __DERIVATION {get;set;}
__DYNASTY	Property	System.String __DYNASTY {get;set;}
__GENUS	Property	System.Int32 __GENUS {get;set;}
__NAMESPACE	Property	System.String __NAMESPACE {get;set;}
__PATH	Property	System.String __PATH {get;set;}
__PROPERTY_COUNT	Property	System.Int32 __PROPERTY_COUNT {get;set;}
__RELPATH	Property	System.String __RELPATH {get;set;}
__SERVER	Property	System.String __SERVER {get;set;}
__SUPERCLASS	Property	System.String __SUPERCLASS {get;set;}
PSStatus	PropertySet	PSStatus {Status, Availability, DeviceID, StatusInfo}
ConvertFromDateTime	ScriptMethod	System.Object ConvertFromDateTime();
ConvertToDateTime	ScriptMethod	System.Object ConvertToDateTime();

Obtaining Specific WMI Data

While storing the complete instance of the object in the *$driveData* variable is a bit inefficient, in reality the class is rather small, and the ease of using the Get-WmiObject cmdlet is usually worth the wasteful methodology. If performance is a primary consideration, use of the [WMI] type accelerator is a better solution. To obtain the free disk space using this method, you can use the following syntax.

```
([wmi]"Win32_logicalDisk.DeviceID='c:'").FreeSpace
```

To put the previous command into a usable function, you need to substitute the hard-coded drive letter for a variable. In addition, you also want to modify the class constructor to receive a path to a remote computer. The newly created function is contained in the Get-DiskSpace.ps1 script shown here.

```
Get-DiskSpace.ps1
Function Get-DiskSpace($drive,$computer)
{
 ([wmi]"\\$computer\root\cimv2:Win32_logicalDisk.DeviceID='$drive'").
FreeSpace
}
Get-DiskSpace -drive "C:" -computer "Office"
```

Once you make the previous changes, the code only returns the value of the *FreeSpace* property from the specific drive. If you send the output to the Get-Member cmdlet, you see that you have an integer. This technique is more efficient than storing an entire instance of the *Win32_LogicalDisk* class and then selecting a single value.

Once you store the data in the *$driveData* variable, you want to print some information to the user of the script. First, you can print the name of the computer and the drive by placing the variables inside double quotation marks. Double quotes are expanding strings, and variables placed inside double quotes emit their value and not their name as shown here.

```
"$computer free disk space on drive $drive"
```

Next, you can format the data that is returned by using the Microsoft .NET Framework format strings to specify two decimal places. You need to use a subexpression to prevent unraveling of the WMI object inside the double quotation marks of the expanding string. The subexpression uses the dollar sign and a pair of smooth parentheses to force the evaluation of the expression before returning the data to the string as shown here.

```
$("{0:n2}" -f ($driveData.FreeSpace/1MB)) MegaBytes
```

```
Get-FreeDiskSpace.ps1
Function Get-FreeDiskSpace($drive,$computer)
{
 $driveData = Get-WmiObject -class win32_LogicalDisk `
 -computername $computer -filter "Name = '$drive'"
"
 $computer free disk space on drive $drive
    $("{0:n2}" -f ($driveData.FreeSpace/1MB)) MegaBytes
"
}

Get-FreeDiskSpace -drive "C:" -computer "vista"
```

Using a Type Constraint

When accepting parameters for a function, it may be important to use a type constraint to ensure that the function receives the correct type of data. To do this, you can place the desired data type alias inside square brackets in front of the input parameter. This action constrains the data type and prevents the entry of an incorrect type of data. Allowable type shortcuts are shown in Table 9-2.

TABLE 9-2 Data Type Aliases

ALIAS	TYPE
[int]	32-bit signed integer
[long]	64-bit signed integer
[string]	Fixed-length string of Unicode characters
[char]	Unicode 16-bit character
[bool]	True/false value
[byte]	8-bit unsigned integer
[double]	Double-precision 64-bit floating point number
[decimal]	128-bit decimal value
[single]	Single-precision 32-bit floating point number
[array]	Array of values
[xml]	*Xmldocument* object
[hashtable]	*Hashtable* object (similar to a *Dictionary* object)

In the *Resolve-ZipCode* function shown in the Resolve-ZipCode.ps1 script, the *–zip* input parameter is constrained to allow only a 32-bit signed integer for input. (Obviously, the [int] type constraint eliminates most of the world's zip codes, but the Web service that the script uses only resolves U.S.-based zip codes; therefore, it is a good addition to the function.)

In the *Resolve-ZipCode* function, you can first use a string that points to the Web Services Description Language (WSDL) for the Web service. Next, the New-WebServiceProxy cmdlet is used to create a new webservice proxy for the ZipCode service. The WSDL for the ZipCode service defines a method named *GetInfoByZip*, which accepts a standard U.S.-based zip code. The results are displayed as a table. The Resolve-ZipCode.ps1 script is shown here.

```
Resolve-ZipCode.ps1
#Requires -Version 2.0
Function Resolve-ZipCode([int]$zip)
{
 $URI = "http://www.webservicex.net/uszip.asmx?WSDL"
 $zipProxy = New-WebServiceProxy -uri $URI -namespace WebServiceProxy -class ZipClass
 $zipProxy.getinfobyzip($zip).table
} #end Get-ZipCode


Resolve-ZipCode 28273
```

When using a type constraint on an input parameter, any deviation from the expected data type generates an error similar to the one shown here.

```
Resolve-ZipCode : Cannot process argument transformation on parameter 'zip'. Cannot
convert value "COW" to type "System
.Int32". Error: "Input string was not in a correct format."
At C:\Users\edwils.NORTHAMERICA\AppData\Local\Temp\tmp3351.tmp.ps1:22 char:16
+ Resolve-ZipCode <<<<  "COW"
    + CategoryInfo          : InvalidData: (:) [Resolve-ZipCode], ParameterBindin...
mationException
    + FullyQualifiedErrorId : ParameterArgumentTransformationError,Resolve-ZipCode
```

Needless to say, such an error can be distracting to users of the function. One way to handle the problem of confusing error messages is to use the Trap keyword. In the DemoTrapSystemException.ps1 script, the *My-Test* function uses [int] to constrain the *$myinput* variable to only accept a 32-bit unsigned integer for input. If such an integer is received by the function when it is called, the function returns the string "It worked." If the function receives a string for input, an error is raised similar to the previous one.

Rather than display a raw error message that most users and many IT Pros find confusing, it is a best practice to suppress the display of the error message and to perhaps inform the user that an error condition occurred, providing more meaningful and direct information that the user can then relay to the help desk. Many times, IT departments display such an error message, complete with either a local telephone number for the appropriate help desk or even a link to an internal Web page that provides detailed troubleshooting and self-help corrective steps for the user to take. You can even provide a Web page that hosts a script that the user can run that will fix the problem. This solution is similar to the "Fix it for me" Web pages introduced by Microsoft.

When an instance of a *System.SystemException* class is created (when a system exception occurs), the *Trap* statement traps the error rather than allowing the error information to display on the screen. If you query the *$error* variable, you see that the error has in fact occurred and is actually received by the error record. You also have access to the *ErrorRecord* class via the *$_* automatic variable, which means that the error record is passed along the pipeline and thus gives you the ability to build a rich error-handling solution. In this example, the string "error trapped" is displayed, and the *Continue* statement is used to continue the script execution on the next line of code. In this example, the next line of code that is executed is the "After the error" string. When the DemoTrapSystemException.ps1 script is run, the following output is shown.

```
error trapped
After the error
```

The complete DemoTrapSystemException.ps1 script is shown here.

DemoTrapSystemException.ps1
```
Function My-Test([int]$myinput)
{

 "It worked"
} #End my-test function
# *** Entry Point to Script ***

Trap [SystemException] { "error trapped" ; continue }
My-Test -myinput "string"
"After the error"
```

Using More than Two Input Parameters

When using more than two input parameters, I consider it a best practice to modify the way in which the function is structured. This modification is more of a visual change that makes the function easier to read. In the basic function pattern shown here, the function accepts three input parameters. When considering the default values and type constraints, the parameters that begin to string along are fairly long. Moving the parameters to the inside of the function body highlights the fact that they are input parameters and makes them easier to read, understand, and maintain.

```
Function Function-Name
{
  Param(
        [int]$Parameter1,
        [String]$Parameter2 = "DefaultValue",
        $Parameter3
       )
#Function code goes here
} #end Function-Name
```

An example of a function that uses three input parameters is the *Get-DirectoryListing* function. Due to the type constraints, default values, and parameter names, the function signature can be rather cumbersome to include on a single line as shown here.

```
Function Get-DirectoryListing (String]$Path,[String]$Extension = "txt",[Switch]$Today)
```

If the number of parameters is increased to four or if a default value for the *–path* parameter is desired, the signature can easily scroll to two lines. Use of the *Param* statement inside the function body also provides the ability to specify input parameters to a function.

> **NOTE**   Use of the *Param* statement inside the function body is often seen as a personal preference. Personally, I do not think it makes sense to use the *Param* statement inside the function body when there are only one or two input parameters because it requires additional work and often leaves the reader of the script wondering why it was used. Visually, the *Param* statement stands out when there are more than two parameters, and it becomes obvious why it was used in this particular manner.

Following the Function keyword and function name, the Param keyword is used to identify the parameters for the function. Each parameter must be separated by a comma, and all parameters must be surrounded with a set of smooth parentheses. If you want to assign a default value for a parameter, such as the string *.txt* value for the *Extension* parameter in the *Get-DirectoryListing* function, you can do a straight value assignment followed by a comma.

In the *Get-DirectoryListing* function, the *Today* parameter is a switched parameter. When it is supplied to the function, only files written to since midnight on the day the script is run are displayed. If the *Today* parameter is not supplied, all files matching the extension in the folder are displayed. The Get-DirectoryListingToday.ps1 script is shown here.

```
Get-DirectoryListingToday.ps1
Function Get-DirectoryListing
{
 Param(
       [String]$Path,
       [String]$Extension = "txt",
       [Switch]$Today
       )
 If($Today)
   {
    Get-ChildItem -Path $path\* -include *.$Extension |
    Where-Object { $_.LastWriteTime -ge (Get-Date).Date }
   }
 ELSE
   {
    Get-ChildItem -Path $path\* -include *.$Extension
   }
} #end Get-DirectoryListing

# *** Entry to script ***
Get-DirectoryListing -p c:\fso -t
```

IMPORTANT As a best practice, you should avoid creating functions that have a large number of input parameters because this can cause confusion. When you find yourself creating a large number of input parameters, ask yourself whether there is a better way to achieve your purpose. Using too many input parameters may be an indicator you do not have a single-purpose function. In the *Get-DirectoryListing* function, I have a switched parameter that filters the files returned by the files written to today. If I write the script for production use instead of writing it simply to demonstrate multiple-function parameters, I create another function named, for example, *Get-FilesByDate*. In this function, I have a *Today* switch and a *Date* parameter to allow a selectable date for the filter. This technique of using multiple parameters allows you to separate data-gathering from the filtering functionality. See the section titled "Using Functions to Provide Ease of Modification" later in this chapter for more discussion of this technique.

Using Functions to Encapsulate Business Logic

Script writers need to be concerned with two kinds of logic. The first is program logic, and the second is business logic. *Program logic* is the way the script works, the order in which tasks need to be done, and the requirements of code used in the script. An example of program logic is the requirement to open a connection to a database before querying the database.

Business logic is a set of rules that is a requirement of the business but not necessarily a requirement of the program or script. The script can often operate just fine regardless of the particulars of the business rule. If the script is designed properly, it should operate well no matter what is supplied for the business rules.

In the BusinessLogicDemo.ps1 script, a function named *Get-Discount* is used to calculate the discount to be granted to the total amount. Encapsulating the business rules for the discount into a function works well as long as the contract between the function and the calling code does not change. You can drop any type of convoluted discount schedule between the curly brackets of the *Get-Discount* function that the business requests including database calls to determine on-hand inventory, time of day, day of week, and total sales volume for the month, as well as the buyer's loyalty level and the square root of some random number that is used to determine the instant discount rate.

So, what is the contract with the function? The contract with the *Get-Discount* function states, "If you give me a rate number as a type of *System.Double* and a total as an integer, I will return to you a number that represents the total discount to be applied to the sale." As long as you adhere to that contract, you never need to modify the code.

The *Get-Discount* function begins with the Function keyword, the name of the function, and the definition for two input parameters. The first input parameter is the *–rate* parameter, which is constrained to be a *System.Double* class and permit you to supply decimal numbers. The second input parameter is the *–total* parameter, which is constrained to be a *System.Integer* and therefore does not allow decimal numbers. In the script block, the value of the *–total* parameter is multiplied by the value of the *–rate* parameter. The result of this calculation is returned to the pipeline.

The *Get-Discount* function is shown here.

```
Function Get-Discount([double]$rate,[int]$total)
{
  $rate * $total
} #end Get-Discount
```

The entry point to the script assigns values to both the *$total* and *$rate* variables as shown here.

```
$rate = .05
$total = 100
```

The *$discount* variable is used to hold the result of the calculation from the *Get-Discount* function. When calling the function, it is a best practice to use full parameter names. This practice makes the code easier to read and helps make the code immune to unintended problems if the function signature changes.

```
$discount = Get-Discount -rate $rate -total $total
```

IMPORTANT   The signature of a function is the order and names of the input parameters. If you typically supply values to the signature via positional parameters and the order of the input parameters changes, the code fails or, worse yet, produces inconsistent results. If you typically call functions via partial parameter names and an additional parameter is added, the script fails due to difficulty with the disambiguation process. Obviously, you should take this into account when first writing the script and the function, but the problem can arise months or years later when making modifications to the script or calling the function via another script.

The remainder of the script produces output for the screen. The results of running the script are shown here.

```
Total: 100
Discount: 5
Your Total: 95
```

The complete text of the BusinessLogicDemo.ps1 script is shown here.

BusinessLogicDemo.ps1
```
Function Get-Discount([double]$rate,[int]$total)
{
  $rate * $total
} #end Get-Discount
```

```
$rate = .05
$total = 100
$discount = Get-Discount -rate $rate -total $total
"Total: $total"
"Discount: $discount"
"Your Total: $($total-$discount)"
```

Business logic does not have to be related to business purposes. Business logic is anything arbitrary that does not affect the running of the code. In the FindLargeDocs.ps1 script, there are two functions. The first function, named *Get-Doc*, is used to find document files (files with an extension of .doc, .docx, or .dot) in a folder that is passed to the function when it is called. When used with the Get-ChildItem cmdlet, the *recurse* switch causes *Get-Doc* to look in the present folder as well as to look within child folders. This is a stand-alone function and has no dependency on other functions.

The LargeFiles piece of code is a filter. A filter is a type of special-purpose function that uses the Filter keyword rather than the Function keyword when it is created. The complete FindLargeDocs.ps1 script is shown here.

FindLargeDocs.ps1
```
Function Get-Doc($path)
{
 Get-ChildItem -Path $path -include *.doc,*.docx,*.dot -recurse
} #end Get-Doc

Filter LargeFiles($size)
{
  $_ |
  Where-Object { $_.length -ge $size }
} #end LargeFiles

Get-Doc("C:\FSO") | LargeFiles 1000
```

Using Functions to Provide Ease of Modification

It is a truism that a script is never finished. Something else can always be added to a script: a change that will improve it or additional functionality that someone requests. When a script is written as one long piece of inline code without recourse to functions, it can be rather tedious and error prone during modifications.

An example of an inline script is the InLineGetIPDemo.ps1 script. The first line of code uses the Get-WmiObject cmdlet to retrieve the instances of the *Win32_NetworkAdapterConfiguration* WMI class that IP enabled. The results of this WMI query are stored in the *$IP* variable. This line of code is shown here.

```
$IP = Get-WmiObject -class Win32_NetworkAdapterConfiguration -Filter "IPEnabled = $true"
```

Once the WMI information is obtained and stored, the remainder of the script prints information to the screen. The *IPAddress*, *IPSubNet*, and *DNSServerSearchOrder* properties are all stored in an array. This example is only interested in the first IP address and therefore prints element 0, which always exists if the network adapter has an IP address. This section of the script is shown here.

```
"IP Address: " + $IP.IPAddress[0]
"Subnet: " + $IP.IPSubNet[0]
"GateWay: " + $IP.DefaultIPGateway
"DNS Server: " + $IP.DNSServerSearchOrder[0]
"FQDN: " + $IP.DNSHostName + "." + $IP.DNSDomain
```

When the script is run, it produces output similar to the following:

```
IP Address: 192.168.2.5
Subnet: 255.255.255.0
GateWay: 192.168.2.1
DNS Server: 192.168.2.1
FQDN: vista.nwtraders.com
```

The complete InLineGetIPDemo.ps1 script is shown here.

InLineGetIPDemo.ps1
```
$IP = Get-WmiObject -class Win32_NetworkAdapterConfiguration -Filter "IPEnabled =
$true"
"IP Address: " + $IP.IPAddress[0]
"Subnet: " + $IP.IPSubNet[0]
"GateWay: " + $IP.DefaultIPGateway
"DNS Server: " + $IP.DNSServerSearchOrder[0]
"FQDN: " + $IP.DNSHostName + "." + $IP.DNSDomain
```

With just a few modifications to the script, a great deal of flexibility can be obtained. The modifications, of course, involve moving the inline code into functions. As a best practice, a function should be narrowly defined and should encapsulate a single purpose. While it is possible to move the entire previous script into a function, you do not have as much flexibility. Two purposes are expressed in the script. The first purpose is obtaining the IP information from WMI, and the second purpose is formatting and displaying the IP information. It is best to separate the gathering and displaying processes from one another because they are logically two different activities.

To convert the InLineGetIPDemo.ps1 script into a script that uses a function, you only need to add the Function keyword, give it a name, and surround the original code with a pair of curly brackets. The transformed script is now named GetIPDemoSingleFunction.ps1 and is shown here.

```
GetIPDemoSingleFunction.ps1
Function Get-IPDemo
{
 $IP = Get-WmiObject -class Win32_NetworkAdapterConfiguration -Filter "IPEnabled =
$true"
 "IP Address: " + $IP.IPAddress[0]
 "Subnet: " + $IP.IPSubNet[0]
 "GateWay: " + $IP.DefaultIPGateway
 "DNS Server: " + $IP.DNSServerSearchOrder[0]
 "FQDN: " + $IP.DNSHostName + "." + $IP.DNSDomain
} #end Get-IPDemo

# *** Entry Point To Script ***

Get-IPDemo
```

So, if you go to all of the trouble to transform the inline code into a function, what do you gain? By making this single change, you gain the following benefits.

- Easier to read

- Easier to understand

- Easier to reuse

- Easier to troubleshoot

The script is easier to read because you do not actually need to read each line of code to see what it does. You see a function that obtains the IP address, which is called from outside the function. That is all the script accomplishes.

The script is easier to understand because what you see is a function that obtains the IP address. If you want to know the details of that operation, you read that function. If you are not interested in the details, you can skip that portion of the code.

The script is easier to reuse because you can dot-source the script as shown here. When the script is dot-sourced, all of the executable code in the script is run. As a result, the following output is displayed because each of the scripts prints information.

```
IP Address: 192.168.2.5
Subnet: 255.255.255.0
GateWay: 192.168.2.1
DNS Server: 192.168.2.1
FQDN: vista.nwtraders.com

 vista free disk space on drive C:
    48,767.16 MegaBytes

This OS is version 6.0.6001
```

The DotSourceScripts.ps1 script is shown here. As you can see, this script provides you with a certain level of flexibility to choose the information required, and it also makes it easy to mix and match the required information. If each of the scripts is written in a more standard fashion and the output is standardized, the results will be more impressive. As it is, three lines of code produce an exceptional amount of useful output that can be acceptable in a variety of situations.

DotSourceScripts.ps1

```
. C:\BestPracticesBook\GetIPDemoSingleFunction.ps1
. C:\BestPracticesBook\Get-FreeDiskSpace.ps1
. C:\BestPracticesBook\Get-OperatingSystemVersion.ps1
```

The GetIPDemoSingleFunction.ps1 script is easier to troubleshoot in part because it is easier to read and understand. In addition, when a script contains multiple functions, you are able to test one function at a time, which allows you to isolate a piece of problematic code.

A better way to work with the function is to consider what the function is actually doing. There are two functions in the FunctionGetIPDemo.ps1 script. The first connects to WMI, which returns a management object. The second function formats the output. These are two completely unrelated tasks. The first task gathers data, and the second task presents information. The FunctionGetIPDemo.ps1 script is shown here.

FunctionGetIPDemo.ps1

```
Function Get-IPObject
{
 Get-WmiObject -class Win32_NetworkAdapterConfiguration -Filter "IPEnabled = $true"
} #end Get-IPObject

Function Format-IPOutput($IP)
{
 "IP Address: " + $IP.IPAddress[0]
 "Subnet: " + $IP.IPSubNet[0]
 "GateWay: " + $IP.DefaultIPGateway
 "DNS Server: " + $IP.DNSServerSearchOrder[0]
 "FQDN: " + $IP.DNSHostName + "." + $IP.DNSDomain
} #end Format-IPOutput

# *** Entry Point To Script

$ip = Get-IPObject
Format-IPOutput($ip)
```

By separating the data-gathering and presentation activities into different functions, additional flexibility is gained. You can easily modify the *Get-IPObject* function to look for network adapters that are not IP enabled. To do this, you must modify the *–filter* parameter of the Get-WmiObject cmdlet. Because you will most likely be interested only in network adapters that are IP enabled, it makes sense to set the default value of the input parameter to *true*. By default, the behavior of the revised function works exactly as it did prior to modification. The advantage is that you can now use the function and modify the objects returned by it. To do this, you supply *$false* when calling the function as illustrated in the Get-IPObjectDefaultEnabled.ps1 script.

Get-IPObjectDefaultEnabled.ps1
```
Function Get-IPObject([bool]$IPEnabled = $true)
{
 Get-WmiObject -class Win32_NetworkAdapterConfiguration -Filter "IPEnabled =
$IPEnabled"
} #end Get-IPObject

Get-IPObject -IPEnabled $False
```

By separating the gathering of information from the presentation of information, you gain flexibility not only in the type of information that is gathered but also in the way the information is displayed. When gathering network adapter configuration information from a network adapter that is not enabled for IP, the results are not as impressive as information from an adapter that is enabled for IP. Therefore, you might decide to create a different display to list only the pertinent information. Because the function that displays information is different than the one that gathers information, a change can easily be made that customizes the information that is most germane. The Begin section of the function is run once during the execution of the function. This is the perfect place to create a header for the output data. The Process section executes once for each item on the pipeline; in this example, it executes for each of the non–IP-enabled network adapters. The Write-Host cmdlet is used to easily write the data out to the Windows PowerShell console. The backtick t ("`t") character is used to produce a tab.

> **NOTE** The backtick t character (`t) is a string character and as such works with cmdlets that accept string input.

The Get-IPObjectDefaultEnabledFormatNonIPOutput.ps1 script is shown here.

Get-IPObjectDefaultEnabledFormatNonIPOutput.ps1
```
Function Get-IPObject([bool]$IPEnabled = $true)
{
 Get-WmiObject -class Win32_NetworkAdapterConfiguration -Filter "IPEnabled =
$IPEnabled"
} #end Get-IPObject

Function Format-NonIPOutput($IP)
{
  Begin { "Index #  Description" }
 Process {
  ForEach ($i in $ip)
```

```
  {
   Write-Host $i.Index `t $i.Description
  } #end ForEach
 } #end Process
} #end Format-NonIPOutPut

$ip = Get-IPObject -IPEnabled $False
Format-NonIPOutput($ip)
```

You can use the *Get-IPObject* function to retrieve the network adapter configuration. The *Format-NonIPOutput* and *Format-IPOutput* functions can then be used to format the displayed output. If you put the functions into a single script, you create the CombinationFormatGetIPDemo.ps1 script shown here.

```
CombinationFormatGetIPDemo.ps1
Function Get-IPObject([bool]$IPEnabled = $true)
{
 Get-WmiObject -class Win32_NetworkAdapterConfiguration -Filter "IPEnabled =
$IPEnabled"
} #end Get-IPObject

Function Format-IPOutput($IP)
{
 "IP Address: " + $IP.IPAddress[0]
 "Subnet: " + $IP.IPSubNet[0]
 "GateWay: " + $IP.DefaultIPGateway
 "DNS Server: " + $IP.DNSServerSearchOrder[0]
 "FQDN: " + $IP.DNSHostName + "." + $IP.DNSDomain
} #end Format-IPOutput

Function Format-NonIPOutput($IP)
{
  Begin { "Index #  Description" }
 Process {
  ForEach ($i in $ip)
  {
   Write-Host $i.Index `t $i.Description
  } #end ForEach
 } #end Process
} #end Format-NonIPOutPut

# *** Entry Point ***
$IPEnabled = $false
$ip = Get-IPObject -IPEnabled $IPEnabled
If($IPEnabled) { Format-IPOutput($ip) }
ELSE { Format-NonIPOutput($ip) }
```

Surprising Behavior of *return*

James Craig Burley, Senior Software Development Engineer in Test
Microsoft Corporation

Our team is still coming up to speed on Windows PowerShell, and we recently "discovered" the surprising behavior that "return *expr*;" does not return the specified *expr*; to the caller, but merely "appends" *expr*; to the list of other objects that are already "returned." These other objects are returned because they are un-captured expressions that are evaluated during execution of the function body.

At first, this struck me as a design flaw in the language because every other language I've used has either required *return* to return a value,[1] used a variable name as a surrogate for the return value,[2] or defaulted to returning the most recently computed expression and optionally allowed a *return* statement to return the value.[3] No other language has built up a list (or array) of computed expressions to which an explicitly returned expression is merely appended!

On second thought, I realize that this behavior is probably unavoidable in the general case, given the intersection of the functions-as-filters feature that I like with the fact that Windows PowerShell is an interpreted language as illustrated here.

```
function myfunction { 1; 2; 3; invoke-expression $a; }
```

This problem with *return* can perhaps be better appreciated by starting with the *myfunction2* function listed here.

```
function myfunction2 { 1; sleep 1; 2; sleep 1; 3; sleep 1; return 4; }
foo2
```

When the *myfunction2* function is run, you can see how the results are available dynamically: "1" is written to the console; after a second's delay, "2" is written, and so on until "4" is written and the function exits.

The only way to avoid having the first three (1, 2, 3) elements "returned" is for Windows PowerShell to recognize the *return* keyword when parsing (before running) the function and to prevent the first elements from being returned (produced) until the return statement or the end of the procedure is hit. Windows PowerShell then either replaces or returns them, respectively.

---

[1] In C: float average(float a, float b) { float c = a * b; return c / 2.0; }.

[2] In FORTRAN 77: FUNCTION AVERAGE(A,B); C = A*B; AVERAGE=C / 2.0; END.

[3] In Common Lisp: (defun average (a b) (setf c (* a b)) (/ c 2.0)).

This scenario potentially leads to problems involving unpredictable control flow and expectations. At run time, until the interpreter knows whether a *return* is going to be executed, Windows PowerShell must save (but not produce) these uncaptured results. Once it reaches a point where it is certain to either hit or not hit a *return* statement, it can then discard and stop saving the results or produce all saved results and continue producing new, uncaptured results. Such behavior is fairly surprising when encountered, but most code works as expected.

Yet, what happens when you throw in an `Invoke-Expression` cmdlet that might (or might not) attempt to expand to include execution of a *return* statement? Now the situation becomes more problematic! In the general case, Windows PowerShell cannot know what will be invoked until it executes that statement. The expression might or might not contain a *return* statement, which will not be determined until just before the `Invoke-Expression` cmdlet is executed. Therefore, the mere presence of the `Invoke-Expression` cmdlet or its equivalent amounts to an unpredictable control-flow sequence that might or might not involve executing a *return* statement.

Having Windows PowerShell silently save up instead of produce uncaptured results (but optimize those cases in which no action is necessary) might seem like a temptingly good idea to meet traditional expectations of users of computer languages. But is it really a good idea? Consider what might happen if the code that is executed on prompt delivery of uncaptured results affects the code path and/or variables leading up to the determination as to whether *return* is executed. For example:

```
function bletch { 1; sleep 1; 2; sleep 1; 3; sleep 1; invoke-expression
$a; }
$a = "5;"
bletch | %{ if ($_ -eq 3) { $a = "return 4;" }; $_; }
```

Although this example is certainly contrived, the caller of *bletch* determines, only after seeing the third object produced by *bletch*, that the expression *bletch* is to invoke at the end of the sequence is a *return 4;* statement instead of a *5;* statement.

Because *bletch* cannot reliably predict whether callers (consumers) rely on having uncaptured results or objects streamed to them as they are produced, *bletch* cannot simply withhold, or save up, those uncaptured objects so as to change the state of the system (not just the Windows PowerShell interpreter but also files, registry settings, and so on). *Bletch* must produce/stream the uncaptured results to its consumer right away, as expected.

Therefore, there is also no way for Windows PowerShell to provide a statement that means "wipe the slate clean and then return." Uncaptured results are not being saved; they're being produced (or passed back to the caller, who is the next object in the pipeline). Therefore, the preceding values are already out of the gate by the time Windows PowerShell realizes that there's a *return* statement in the mix. Saving uncaptured results until Windows PowerShell knows whether they are to be produced or flushed defeats one of the primary advantages of using PowerShell— immediacy of results. In addition, saving uncaptured results breaks other code that depends on those results being streamed to determine the next steps for their producer.

Cool architecture thus leads to sometimes astonishing results. Windows PowerShell strikes me as a mix of Lisp-like expressiveness (Lisp-like languages tend to have the return value be the last expression evaluated by the function) and shell-like immediacy (print/produce results as you receive them), resulting in an unexpected and counterintuitive behavior for the *return* expression statement.

One workaround is simply to cast every uncaptured value (that is not to be returned to the caller) to [void]. That is, the function author must simply recognize and constantly be aware of the fact that the function is really a producer of objects and not merely the evaluator of some expression that ultimately returns a single monolithic value.

What if a function already contains a great deal of code that is simply too difficult to decapture in this way? Or, what if the author of the function wants to ensure that only the final value is actually returned in case there are still some uncaptured results? The following function illustrates a workable solution (although I'm not convinced that it's exactly correct or as terse as it should be, it seems to work for basic cases).

```
function return-last { begin { $rtn = @{}; } process { $rtn = $_; } end
{ $rtn; } }
```

You can wrap your function's code in another ampersand-prefixed pair of braces and then pipe that into the *Return-Last* function as shown here.

```
PS C:\> function foo2-last { &{ 1; sleep 1; 2; sleep 1; 3; sleep 1; 4;
}|
return-last }
PS C:\> foo2-last
4
PS C:\>
```

This technique discards all but the last object produced by the function's inner statement body; on termination of that body, this technique returns (produces) the last (final) object it produced.

Or, as Louis Clausen, another Senior Software Development Engineer in Test, pointed out, a simple array-reference wrapper will suffice in lieu of using the *Return-Last* function.

```
PS C:\Users\jcburley> function foo2-last-quick { @(&{ 1; sleep 1; 2;
sleep 1; 3; sleep 1; 4; })[-1] }
PS C:\Users\jcburley> foo2-last-quick
4
PS C:\Users\jcburley>
```

Of course, the caller can wrap the function as shown here.

```
PS C:\Users\jcburley> @(foo2)[-1]
4
PS C:\Users\jcburley>
```

Understanding Filters

A *filter* is a special-purpose function that is used to operate on each object in a pipeline and is often used to reduce the number of objects that are passed along the pipeline. Typically, a filter does not use the *–Begin* or *–End* parameters that a function might need to use, so it is often thought of as a function that only has a process block. But then, many functions are written without using the *–Begin* or *–End* parameters, and some filters are written in such a way that they use the *–Begin* or *–End* parameters. The biggest difference between a function and a filter is a bit more subtle. When a function is used inside a pipeline, it actually halts the processing of the pipeline until the first element in the pipeline runs to completion. The function then accepts the input from the first element in the pipeline and begins its processing. When the processing in the function is completed, it then passes the results along to the next element in the script block. A function runs once for the pipelined data; a filter, on the other hand, runs once for each piece of data that is passed over the pipeline. The short definition here is that a filter streams data when in a pipeline and a function does not, which can make a big difference in performance. To illustrate this point, you will examine a function and a filter that accomplish the same objectives.

In the MeasureAddOneFilter.ps1 script, an array of 50,000 elements is created by using the 1..50000 syntax. (In Windows PowerShell 1.0, 50,000 was the maximum size of an array created in this manner. In Windows PowerShell 2.0, this ceiling is raised to the maximum size of an [*Int32*] 2146483647. The use of this size is dependent on memory.) This syntax is shown here.

```
PS C:\ > 1..[Int32]::MaxValue
The '..' operator failed: Exception of type 'System.OutOfMemoryException' was thrown..
At line:1 char:4
+ 1.. <<<< 2147483647
    + CategoryInfo          : InvalidOperation: (:) [], RuntimeException
    + FullyQualifiedErrorId : OperatorFailed
```

The array is then pipelined into the AddOne filter. The filter prints the "add one filter" string and then adds the number 1 to the current number on the pipeline. The length of time it takes to run the command is then displayed. On my computer, it takes about 2.6 seconds to run the MeasureAddOneFilter.ps1 script.

MeasureAddOneFilter.ps1
```
Filter AddOne
{
 "add one filter"
  $_ + 1
}


Measure-Command { 1..50000 | addOne }
```

The function version is shown next. In a similar fashion as the MeasureAddOneFilter.ps1 script, this version creates an array of 50,000 numbers and pipelines the results to the *AddOne* function. The "Add One Function" string is displayed. An automatic variable named *$input* is created when pipelining input to a function. The *$input* variable is an enumerator and not just a plain array. It has a *MoveNext* method that can be used to move to the next item in the collection. Because *$input* is not a plain array, you cannot index directly into it—*$input*[0] will fail. To retrieve a specific element, you can use the *$input.current* property. It takes 4.3 seconds to run the following script on my computer, which is almost twice as long as running the filter.

MeasureAddOneFunction.ps1
```
Function AddOne
{
  "Add One Function"
  While ($input.moveNext())
  {
    $input.current + 1
  }
}


Measure-Command { 1..50000 | addOne }
```

What makes the filter so much faster than the function in this example? The filter runs once for each item on the pipeline as shown here.

```
add one filter
2
add one filter
3
add one filter
4
add one filter
5
add one filter
6
```

The DemoAddOneFilter.ps1 script is shown here.

```
DemoAddOneFilter.ps1
Filter AddOne
{
  "add one filter"
   $_ + 1
}


1..5 | addOne
```

The *AddOne* function runs to completion once for all of the items in the pipeline. This approach effectively stops the processing in the middle of the pipeline until all of the elements of the array are created. All of the data is then passed to the function via the *$input* variable at one time. This type of approach does not take advantage of the streaming nature of the pipeline, which in many instances is more memory efficient.

```
Add One Function
2
3
4
5
6
```

The DemoAddOneFunction.ps1 script is shown here.

```
DemoAddOneFunction.ps1
Function AddOne
{
  "Add One Function"
  While ($input.moveNext())
    {
      $input.current + 1
    }
}

1..5 | addOne
```

To close this performance issue between functions and filters when used in a pipeline, you can write your function in such a manner that it behaves like a filter. To do this, you must explicitly call the process block. When you use the process block, you are also able to use the *$_* automatic variable instead of being restricted to using *$input*. When you do this, the script looks like DemoAddOneR2Function.ps1, the results of which are shown here.

```
add one function r2
2
add one function r2
```

```
3
add one function r2
4
add one function r2
5
add one function r2
6
```

The complete DemoAddOneR2Function.ps1 script is shown here.

```
DemoAddOneR2Function.ps1
Function AddOneR2
{
   Process {
   "add one function r2"
   $_ + 1
   }
} #end AddOneR2

1..5 | addOneR2
```

So, what does using an explicit process block do to performance? When run on my computer, it takes about 2.6 seconds, which is virtually the same amount of time that it takes the filter. The MeasureAddOneR2Function.ps1 script is shown here.

```
MeasureAddOneR2Function.ps1
Function AddOneR2
{
   Process {
   "add one function r2"
   $_ + 1
   }
} #end AddOneR2

Measure-Command {1..50000 | addOneR2 }
```

Another reason for using filters is that they visually stand out and therefore improve readability of the script. The typical pattern for a filter is shown here.

```
Filter FilterName
{
 #insert code here
}
```

The HasMessage filter found in the FilterHasMessage.ps1 script begins with the Filter keyword and the name of the filter, which is HasMessage. Inside the script block (the curly brackets), the $_ automatic variable is used to provide access to the pipeline. The $_ variable is sent to the `Where-Object` cmdlet, which performs the filter. In the calling script, the results of the HasMessage filter are sent to the `Measure-Object` cmdlet, which tells the user how many events in the application log have a message attached to them. The FilterHasMessage.ps1 script is shown here.

FilterHasMessage.ps1
```
Filter HasMessage
{
 $_ |
 Where-Object { $_.message }
} #end HasMessage


Get-WinEvent -LogName Application | HasMessage | Measure-Object
```

Just because the Filter has an implicit process block does not prevent you from using the Begin, Process, and End script block explicitly. In the FilterToday.ps1 script, a filter named IsToday is created. To make the filter a stand-alone entity with no external dependencies, such as the passing of a date time object to it, the filter needs to obtain the current date. However, if the call to the `Get-Date` cmdlet is done inside the Process block, the filter continues to work, but the call to `Get-Date` is made once for each object found in the Input folder. If there are 25 items in the folder, the `Get-Date` cmdlet is called 25 times. When you want a procedure to occur only once in the processing of the filter, you can place the procedure in a Begin block, which is only called once. The Process block is called once for each item in the pipeline. If you want any postprocessing to take place (such as printing a message stating how many files are found today), the postprocessing is placed in the End block of the filter. The FilterToday.ps1 script is shown here.

FilterToday.ps1
```
Filter IsToday
{
 Begin {$dte = (Get-Date).Date}
 Process { $_ |
          Where-Object { $_.LastWriteTime -ge $dte }
        }
}


Get-ChildItem -Path C:\fso | IsToday
```

Additional Resources

- The TechNet Script Center at *http://www.microsoft.com/technet/scriptcenter* contains numerous examples of using functions in Windows PowerShell.
- Take a look at the *Windows PowerShell™ Scripting Guide* (Microsoft Press, 2008).

- On the companion media, you will find all of the scripts referred to in this chapter.

- The Microsoft Fix It blog at *http://blogs.technet.com/fixit4me/default.aspx* provides numerous examples of self-help Web pages.

- Brandon Shell's Web site at *http://bsonposh.com/* has a variety of Windows PowerShell tips and tricks as well as a good discussion of some of its pitfalls.

Designing Help for Scripts

Although well-written code is easy to understand, easy to maintain, and easy to troubleshoot, it can still benefit from well-written help documentation. Well-written help documentation can list assumptions that were made when the script was written, such as the existence of a particular folder or the need to run as an administrator. It also documents dependencies, such as relying on a particular version of the Microsoft .NET Framework. Good documentation is a sign of a professional at work because it not only informs the user how to get the most from your script, but it also explains how users can modify your script or even use your functions in other scripts.

All production scripts should provide some form of help. But what is the best way to provide that help? In this chapter, you will look at proven methods for providing custom help in Windows PowerShell scripts.

When writing help documentation for a script, three tools are available to you. The first tool is the traditional comment that is placed within the script—the single-line comment that is available in Windows PowerShell 1.0. The second tool is the here-string. The third tool is the multiple-line comment that is introduced in Windows PowerShell 2.0. Once you understand how to use these tools, we will focus on the 13 rules for writing effective comments.

Adding Help Documentation to a Script with Single-Line Comments

Single-line comments are a great way to quickly add documentation to a script. They have the advantage of being simple to use and easy to understand. It is a best practice to provide illuminating information about confusing constructions or to add notes for future work items in the script, and they can be used exclusively within your scripting environment. In this section, we will look at using single-line comments to add help documentation to a script.

In the CreateFileNameFromDate.ps1 script, the header section of the script uses the comments section to explain how the script works, what it does, and the limitations of the approach. The CreateFileNameFromDate.ps1 script is shown here.

CreateFileNameFromDate.ps1

```
# --------------------------------------------------------------------------
# NAME: CreateFileNameFromDate.ps1
# AUTHOR: ed wilson, Microsoft
# DATE:12/15/2008
#
# KEYWORDS: .NET framework, io.path, get-date
# file, new-item, Standard Date and Time Format Strings
# regular expression, ref, pass by reference
#
# COMMENTS: This script creates an empty text file
# based upon the date-time stamp. Uses format string
# to specify a sortable date. Uses getInvalidFileNameChars
# method to get all the invalid characters that are not allowed
# in a file name. It assumes there is a folder named fso off the
# c:\ drive. If the folder does not exist, the script will fail.
#
# --------------------------------------------------------------------------
Function GetFileName([ref]$fileName)
{
  $invalidChars = [io.path]::GetInvalidFileNamechars()
  $date = Get-Date -format s
  $fileName.value = ($date.ToString() -replace "[$invalidChars]","-") + ".txt"
}

$fileName = $null
GetFileName([ref]$fileName)
new-item -path c:\fso -name $filename -itemtype file
```

In general, you should always provide information on how to use your functions. Each parameter, as well as underlying dependencies, must be explained. In addition to documenting the operation and dependencies of the functions, you should also include information that will be beneficial to those who must maintain the code. You should always assume that the person who maintains your code does not understand what the code actually does, therefore ensuring that the documentation explains everything. In the BackUpFiles.ps1 script, comments are added to both the header and to each function that explain the logic and limitations of the functions as shown here.

BackUpFiles.ps1

```
# ------------------------------------------------------------------------
# NAME: BackUpFiles.ps1
# AUTHOR: ed wilson, Microsoft
# DATE: 12/12/2008
#
# KEYWORDS: Filesystem, get-childitem, where-object
# date manipulation, regular expressions
#
# COMMENTS: This script backs up a folder. It will
# back up files that have been modified within the past
# 24 hours. You can change the interval, the destination,
# and the source. It creates a backup folder that is named based upon
# the time the script runs. If the destination folder does not exist, it
# will be created. The destination folder is based upon the time the
# script is run and will look like this: C:\bu\12.12.2008.1.22.51.PM.
# The interval is the age in days of the files to be copied.
#
# ------------------------------------------------------------------------
Function New-BackUpFolder($destinationFolder)
{
 #Receives the path to the destination folder and creates the path to
 #a child folder based upon the date / time. It then calls the New-Backup
 #function while passing the source path, destination path, and interval
 #in days.
 $dte = get-date
 #The following regular expression pattern removes white space, colon,
 #and forward slash from the date and replaces with a period to create the
 #backup folder name.
 $dte = $dte.tostring() -replace "[:\s/]", "."
 $backUpPath = "$destinationFolder" + $dte
 $null = New-Item -path $backUpPath -itemType directory
 New-Backup $dataFolder $backUpPath $backUpInterval
} #end New-BackUpFolder

Function New-Backup($dataFolder,$backUpPath,$backUpInterval)
{
 #Does a recursive copy of all files in the data folder and filters out
 #all files that have been written to within the number of days specified
 #by the interval. Writes copied files to the destination and will create
 #if the destination (including parent path) does not exist. Will overwrite
 #if destination already exists. This is unlikely, however, unless the
 #script is run twice during the same minute.
 "backing up $dataFolder... check $backUppath for your files"
 Get-Childitem -path $dataFolder -recurse |
 Where-Object { $_.LastWriteTime -ge (get-date).addDays(-$backUpInterval) } |
```

Adding Help Documentation to a Script with Single-Line Comments   CHAPTER 10   **333**

```
    Foreach-Object { copy-item -path $_.FullName -destination $backUpPath -force }
} #end New-BackUp

# *** entry point to script ***

$backUpInterval = 1
$dataFolder = "C:\fso"
$destinationFolder = "C:\BU\"
New-BackupFolder $destinationFolder
```

NOTES FROM THE FIELD

Crafting Inspired cmdlet Help

Dean Tsaltas, Microsoft Scripting Guy Emeritus

In many ways, writing cmdlet help is no different from writing any other type of help documentation. If you want to do a really good job, you must "become your user." This is easier said than done, of course—especially if you are the person who designed and implemented the cmdlets for which you are writing the help. Even though you just created the cmdlets, you can only guess at the mysterious ways in which some of your users will use and abuse your creations. That said, you must give it your all. Rent the original *Karate Kid* and watch it for inspiration. Wax on and wax off before hitting the keyboard. After crafting just the right sentences to convey a concept, remember to ask yourself, "What ambiguity is left in what I just wrote? What can my user possibly still question after reading my text?" Picture yourself explaining the concept to your users, anticipate their questions, and answer them.

For example, suppose that your cmdlet creates some type of file and takes a name or a full path that includes a name as a parameter. Anticipate the questions that users will have about that parameter: how long can it be, are any characters disallowed, how are quotes within quotes handled, will the resultant file include an extension or should I include the appropriate extension in the parameter value? Don't force your users to experiment to answer questions that you can easily anticipate and to which you can quickly provide answers. Help them.

Next, remember that a single example is worth a thousand support calls. You should aim high when it comes to examples. It is a best practice to brainstorm the top tasks that you think your users will be trying to accomplish. At a minimum, you need to include an example for each of those top tasks. Once you have established that baseline, you should aim to provide an example that exercises each and every cmdlet parameter set. Even if you simply mine your test cases for bland examples, try to provide your users with a starting point. As you well know, it's much easier to manipulate a working command line and get it to do what you want than it is to start from scratch.

It's important to consider how your users will interact with cmdlet help. They will see it at a command prompt one full screen at a time. Because that first screen is like the "above-the-fold" section of a newspaper, make sure you handle any really important issues right there in the detailed description. If you need certain privileges to use the cmdlet, let your users know that information up front. If there's an associated provider that might be useful to them, tell your users about it early.

Don't neglect the Related Links section of your help. It's very easy to simply list all of the cmdlets with the same noun, especially when you're in a rush. Yet, are those truly the only cmdlets that are related to the one you're writing about? For instance, is there another cmdlet that your users must use to generate an object that your cmdlet can accept as a parameter value? If so, this other cmdlet also deserves a place in the Related Links list. Again, imagine having a discussion with your users. What other help can you suggest that they access? Also include links to this additional help and not just to the help that is obviously related based on cmdlet naming conventions.

My last bit of advice about writing cmdlet help is to write it as early as you can in the development cycle and get it in the hands of some pre-alpha users to start the feedback cycle quickly. The only way to develop excellent cmdlet help (or any other type of technical documentation) is through iterative improvements in response to feedback. Include numerous simple examples in the help as soon as you can. Having someone use a cmdlet with no accompanying help is unlikely to help you understand what information is needed by your users to get the job done. However, providing someone with three examples will certainly elicit a user response as to what the fourth and fifth examples should be.

Using the Here-String for Multiple-Line Comments

One method that can be used in Windows PowerShell 1.0 to allow for multiline comments is to use a here-string. The here-string allows you to assign text without worrying about line formatting or escaping quotation marks and other special characters. It is helpful when working with multiple lines of text because it allows you to overlook the more tedious aspects of working with formatted text, such as escaping quotation marks. The advantage of using a here-string to store your comments is that it then becomes rather easy to use another script to retrieve all of the comments.

Constructing a Here-String

An example of working with here-strings is the Demo-HereString.ps1 script. The *$instructions* variable is used to hold the content of the here-string. The actual here-string itself is created by beginning the string with the at and double quotation mark (@") symbol. The here-string is terminated by reversing the order with the double quotation mark and the at symbol ("@). Everything between the two tags is interpreted as a string, including special characters. The here-string from the Demo-HereString.ps1 script is shown here.

```
$instructions = @"
This command line demo illustrates working with multiple lines
of text. The cool thing about using a here-string is that it allows
you to "work" with text without the need to "worry" about quoting
or other formating issues.
    It even allows you
      a sort of
        wysiwyg type of experience.
You format the data as you wish it to appear.
"@
```

TRADEOFF

Multiple-Line Comments in Windows PowerShell 1.0

If you want to include a comment in Windows PowerShell 1.0 that spans multiple lines, you can use multiple pound characters (#) as shown here.

```
# This is the first line of a multiple line comment
# This is the second line of the comment
```

This process works fine for short comments, but when you need to write a paragraph documenting a particular feature or construction in the script, this method becomes rather annoying because of the need to type all of the pound characters. If one of the comment characters is inadvertently omitted, an error is generated. Depending on the actual placement of the pound sign, the error can be misleading and cause you to waste development time by chasing down the errant line of code. In Windows PowerShell 2.0, you can still use the multiple pound character approach to adding comments if desired. The advantages to doing so are simplicity and backward compatibility with Windows PowerShell 1.0. Your code will also be easy to read because anyone familiar with Windows PowerShell will immediately recognize the lines of code as comments.

The here-string is displayed by calling the variable that contains the here-string. In the Demo-HereString.ps1 script, the response to a prompt posed by the Read-Host cmdlet is stored in the *$response* variable. The Read-Host command is shown here.

```
$response = Read-Host -Prompt "Do you need instructions? <y / n>"
```

The value stored in the *$response* variable is then evaluated by the *If* statement. If the value is equal to the letter "y," the contents of the here-string are displayed. If the value of the *$response* variable is equal to anything else that the script displays, the string displays "good bye" and exits. This section of the script is shown here.

```
if ($response -eq "y") { $instructions ; exit }
else { "good bye" ; exit }
```

The Demo-HereString.ps1 script is seen here.

```
Demo-HereString.ps1
$instructions = @"
This command line demo illustrates working with multiple lines
of text. The cool thing about using a here-string is that it allows
you to "work" with text without the need to "worry" about quoting
or other formating issues.
    It even allows you
        a sort of
            wysiwyg type of experience.
You format the data as you wish it to appear.
"@

$response = Read-Host -Prompt "Do you need instructions? <y / n>"
if ($response -eq "y") { $instructions ; exit }
else { "good bye" ; exit }
```

An Example: Adding Comments to a Registry Script

To better demonstrate the advantages of working with here-strings, consider the following example that employs the registry. A script named GetSetieStartPage.ps1 reads or modifies a few values from the registry to configure the Internet Explorer start pages. The GetSetieStartPage.ps1 script contains pertinent comments and provides a good example for working with documentation.

With Internet Explorer 7.0, there are actually two registry keys that govern the Internet Explorer start page. The registry key that is documented in the Tweakomatic program, available from the Microsoft Script Center, accepts a single string for the start page, which makes sense because traditionally you can have only a single start page. For Internet Explorer 7, an additional registry key was added to accept multiple strings (an array of strings), which in turn gives you the ability to have multiple start pages. You can use the Windows Management

Instrumentation (WMI) *stdRegProv* class to both read and edit the registry keys. The main advantage of this technique is that it gives you the ability to edit the registry remotely.

The registry keys that are involved with the settings are shown in Figure 10-1.

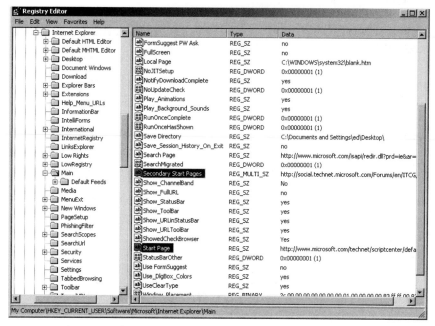

FIGURE 10-1 Internet Explorer registry keys shown in the Registry Editor

First, you must create a few command-line parameters. Two of these are switched parameters, which allow you to control the way the script operates—either by obtaining information from the registry or setting information in the registry. The last parameter is a regular parameter that controls the target computer. You are assigning a default value for the *$computer* variable of localhost, which means that the script reads the local registry by default as shown here.

```
Param([switch]$get,[switch]$set,$computer="localhost")
```

You now need to create the *Get-ieStartPage* function. The *Get-ieStartPage* function will be used to retrieve the current start page settings. To create a function, you can use the *Function* keyword and give it a name as shown here.

```
Function Get-ieStartPage()
```

After using the *Function* keyword to create the new function, you need to add some code to the script block. First, you must create the variables to be used in the script. These are the same types of variables that you use when using WMI to read from the registry in Microsoft

VBScript. You must specify the registry hive from which you plan on querying by using one of enumeration values shown Table 10-1.

TABLE 10-1 WMI Registry Tree Values

NAME	VALUE
HKEY_CLASSES_ROOT	2147483648
HKEY_CURRENT_USER	2147483649
HKEY_LOCAL_MACHINE	2147483650
HKEY_USERS	2147483651
HKEY_CURRENT_CONFIG	2147483653
HKEY_DYN_DATA	2147483654

In VBScript, you often create a constant to hold the WMI registry tree values (although a regular variable is fine if you do not change it). If you feel that you must have a constant, the following code is the syntax you need to use.

```
New-Variable -Name hkcu -Value 2147483649 -Option constant
```

The *$key* variable is used to hold the path to the registry key with which you will be working. The *$property* and *$property2* variables are used to hold the actual properties that will control the start pages. This section of the script is shown here.

```
{
$hkcu = 2147483649
$key = "Software\Microsoft\Internet Explorer\Main"
$property = "Start Page"
$property2 = "Secondary Start Pages"
```

You now need to use the [WMICLASS] type accelerator to create an instance of the *stdRegProv* WMI class. You can hold the management object that is returned by the type accelerator in the *$wmi* variable. What is a bit interesting is the path to the WMI class. It includes both the computer name, the WMI namespace followed by a colon, and the name of the WMI class. This syntax corresponds exactly to the *Path* property that is present on all WMI classes (because it is inherited from the *System* abstract class) as shown in Figure 10-2. (If you are interested in this level of detail about WMI, you can refer to *Windows Scripting with WMI: Self-Paced Learning Guide* [Microsoft Press, 2006]. All of the examples are written in VBScript, but the book applies nearly 100 percent to Windows PowerShell.)

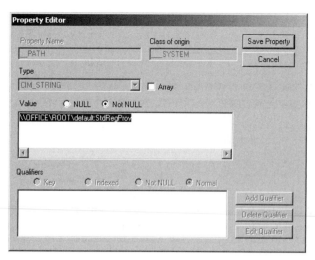

FIGURE 10-2 The WMI *Path* property seen in the WbemTest utility

Here is the line of code that creates an instance of the *stdRegProv* WMI class on the target computer.

```
$wmi = [wmiclass]"\\$computer\root\default:stdRegProv"
```

Next, you need to use the *GetStringValue* method because you want to obtain the value of a string (it really is that simple). This step can be a bit confusing when using the *stdRegProv* WMI class because of the large number of methods in this class. For each data type you want to access, you must use a different method for both writing and reading from the registry. This also means that you must know what data type is contained in the registry key property value with which you want to work. The *stdRegProv* methods are documented in Table 10-2.

TABLE 10-2 *stdRegProv* Methods

NAME	DEFINITION
CheckAccess	System.Management.ManagementBaseObject CheckAccess(System.UInt32 hDefKey, System.String sSubKeyName, System.UInt32 uRequired)
CreateKey	System.Management.ManagementBaseObject CreateKey(System.UInt32 hDefKey, System.String sSubKeyName)
DeleteKey	System.Management.ManagementBaseObject DeleteKey(System.UInt32 hDefKey, System.String sSubKeyName)
DeleteValue	System.Management.ManagementBaseObject DeleteValue(System.UInt32 hDefKey, System.String sSubKeyName, System.String sValueName)

NAME	DEFINITION
EnumKey	System.Management.ManagementBaseObject EnumKey (System.UInt32 hDefKey, System.String sSubKeyName)
EnumValues	System.Management.ManagementBaseObject EnumValues(System.UInt32 hDefKey, System.String sSubKeyName)
GetBinaryValue	System.Management.ManagementBaseObject GetBinaryValue(System.UInt32 hDefKey, System.String sSubKeyName, System.String sValueName)
GetDWORDValue	System.Management.ManagementBaseObject GetDWORDValue(System.UInt32 hDefKey, System.String sSubKeyName, System.String sValueName)
GetExpandedStringValue	System.Management.ManagementBaseObject GetExpandedStringValue(System.UInt32 hDefKey, System.String sSubKeyName, System.String sValueName)
GetMultiStringValue	System.Management.ManagementBaseObject GetMultiStringValue(System.UInt32 hDefKey, System.StringsSubKeyName, System.String sValueName)
GetStringValue	System.Management.ManagementBaseObject GetStringValue(System.UInt32 hDefKey, System.String sSubKeyName, System.String sValueName)
SetBinaryValue	System.Management.ManagementBaseObject SetBinaryValue(System.UInt32 hDefKey, System.String sSubKeyName, System.String sValueName, System.Byte[] uValue)
SetDWORDValue	System.Management.ManagementBaseObject SetDWORDValue(System.UInt32 hDefKey, System.String sSubKeyName, System.String sValueName, System.UInt32 uValue)
SetExpandedStringValue	System.Management.ManagementBaseObject SetExpandedStringValue(System.UInt32 hDefKey, System.String sSubKeyName, System.String sValueName, System.String sValue)
SetMultiStringValue	System.Management.ManagementBaseObject SetMultiStringValue(System.UInt32 hDefKey, System.StringsSubKeyName, System.String sValueName, System.String[] sValue)
SetStringValue	System.Management.ManagementBaseObject SetStringValue(System.UInt32 hDefKey, System.String sSubKeyName, System.String sValueName, System.String sValue)

The code that obtains the value of the default Internet Explorer home page is shown here.

```
($wmi.GetStringValue($hkcu,$key,$property)).sValue
```

After obtaining the value of the string that holds the default home page, you need to obtain the value of a multistring registry key that is used for the additional home pages. To do this, you can use the *GetMultiStringValue* method. What is convenient about this method is that the values of the array that are returned are automatically expanded, and you can thus avoid the for ... next gyrations required when performing this method call when using VBScript. This line of code is shown here.

```
($wmi.GetMultiStringValue($hkcu,$key, $property2)).sValue
```

Adding comments to the closing curly brackets is a best practice that enables you to quickly know where the function begins and ends.

Pairing a Comment with a Closing Curly Bracket

I once spent an entire train ride in Germany that went from Regensburg to Hamburg (nearly a five-hour trip) troubleshooting a problem with a script that occurred as the train left the central train station in Regensburg. The script was to be used for the *Windows Vista Resource Kit* (Microsoft Press, 2008), and I had a deadline to meet. The problem occurred with an edit that I made to the original script, and I forgot to close the curly bracket. The error was particularly misleading because it pointed to a line in the very long script that was unrelated to the issue at hand. It was on this train ride that I learned the value of adding a comment to closing curly brackets, which is now something that I nearly always do.

Here is the closing curly bracket and associated comment. If you always type comments in the same pattern (for example, #end with no space), they are then easy to spot if you ever decide to write a script to search for them.

```
} #end Get-ieStartPage
```

You now need to create a function to assign new values to the Internet Explorer start pages. You can call the *Set-ieStartPage* function as shown here.

```
Function Set-ieStartPage()
{
```

You must assign some values to a large number of variables. The first four variables are the same ones used in the previous function. (You could have made them script-level variables and saved four lines of code in the overall script, but then the functions would not have been stand-alone pieces of code.) The *$value* variable is used to hold the default home page, and the *$aryvalues* variable holds an array of secondary home page URLs. This section of the code is shown here.

```
$hkcu = 2147483649
$key = "Software\Microsoft\Internet Explorer\Main"
$property = "Start Page"
$property2 = "Secondary Start Pages"
$value = "http://www.microsoft.com/technet/scriptcenter/default.mspx"
$aryValues = "http://social.technet.microsoft.com/Forums/en/ITCG/threads/",
"http://www.microsoft.com/technet/scriptcenter/resources/qanda/all.mspx"
```

After assigning values to variables, you can use the [WMICLASS] type accelerator to create an instance of the *stdRegProv* WMI class. This same line of code is used in the *Get-ieStartPage* function and is shown here.

```
$wmi = [wmiclass]"\\$computer\root\default:stdRegProv"
```

You can now use the *SetStringValue* method to set the value of the string. The *SetStringValue* method takes four values. The first is the numeric value representing the registry hive to which to connect. The next is the string for the registry key. The third position holds the property to modify, and last is a string representing the new value to assign as shown here.

```
$rtn = $wmi.SetStringValue($hkcu,$key,$property,$value)
```

Next, you can use the *SetMultiStringValue* method to set the value of a multistring registry key. This method takes an array in the fourth position. The signature of the *SetMultiStringValue* method is similar to the *SetStringValue* signature. The only difference is that the fourth position needs an array of strings and not a single value as shown here.

```
$rtn2 = $wmi.SetMultiStringValue($hkcu,$key,$property2,$aryValues)
```

Now, you can print the value of the *ReturnValue* property. The *ReturnValue* property contains the error code from the method call. A zero means that the method worked (no runs, no errors), and anything else means that there was a problem as shown here.

```
"Setting $property returned $($rtn.returnvalue)"
"Setting $property2 returned $($rtn2.returnvalue)"
} #end Set-ieStartPage
```

You are now at the entry point to the script. You must first get the starting values and then set them to the new values that you want to configure. If you want to re-query the registry to ensure that the values took effect, you can simply call the *Get-ieStartPage* function again as shown here.

```
if($get) {Get-ieStartpage}
if($set){Set-ieStartPage}
```

The complete GetSetieStartPage.ps1 script is shown here.

GetSetieStartPage.ps1

```
Param([switch]$get,[switch]$set,$computer="localhost")
$Comment = @"
NAME: GetSetieStartPage.ps1
AUTHOR: ed wilson, Microsoft
DATE: 1/5/2009

KEYWORDS: stdregprov, ie, [wmiclass] type accelerator,
Hey Scripting Guy
COMMENTS: This script uses the [wmiclass] type accelerator
and the stdregprov to get the ie start pages and to set the
ie start pages. Using ie 7 or better you can have multiple
start pages.

"@ #end comment

Function Get-ieStartPage()
{
$Comment = @"
FUNCTION: Get-ieStartPage
Is used to retrieve the current settings for Internet Explorer 7 and greater.
The value of $hkcu is set to a constant value from the SDK that points
to the Hkey_Current_User. Two methods are used to read
from the registry because the start page is single valued and
the second start page's key is multi-valued.

"@ #end comment
 $hkcu = 2147483649
 $key = "Software\Microsoft\Internet Explorer\Main"
 $property = "Start Page"
 $property2 = "Secondary Start Pages"
 $wmi = [wmiclass]"\\$computer\root\default:stdRegProv"
 ($wmi.GetStringValue($hkcu,$key,$property)).sValue
 ($wmi.GetMultiStringValue($hkcu,$key, $property2)).sValue
} #end Get-ieStartPage

Function Set-ieStartPage()
{
$Comment = @"
FUNCTION: Set-ieStartPage
Allows you to configure one or more home pages for IE 7 and greater.
The $aryValues and the $Value variables hold the various home pages.
Specify the complete URL ex: "http://www.ScriptingGuys.Com." Make sure
to include the quotation marks around each URL.

"@ #end comment
```

```
$hkcu = 2147483649
$key = "Software\Microsoft\Internet Explorer\Main"
$property = "Start Page"
$property2 = "Secondary Start Pages"
$value = "http://www.microsoft.com/technet/scriptcenter/default.mspx"
$aryValues = "http://social.technet.microsoft.com/Forums/en/ITCG/threads/",
"http://www.microsoft.com/technet/scriptcenter/resources/qanda/all.mspx"
$wmi = [wmiclass]"\\$computer\root\default:stdRegProv"
$rtn = $wmi.SetStringValue($hkcu,$key,$property,$value)
$rtn2 = $wmi.SetMultiStringValue($hkcu,$key,$property2,$aryValues)
"Setting $property returned $($rtn.returnvalue)"
"Setting $property2 returned $($rtn2.returnvalue)"
} #end Set-ieStartPage

# *** entry point to script
if($get) {Get-ieStartpage}
if($set){Set-ieStartPage}
```

Retrieving Comments by Using Here-Strings

Due to the stylized nature of here-strings, you can use a script, such as
GetCommentsFromScript.ps1, to retrieve the here-strings from another script, such as
GetSetieStartPage.ps1. You are interested in obtaining three comment blocks. The first
comment block contains normal script header information: title, author, date, keywords, and
comments on the script itself. The second and third comment blocks are specifically related
to the two main functions contained in the GetSetieStartPage.ps1 script. When processed by
the GetCommentsFromScript.ps1 script, the result is automatically produced script documentation. To write comments from the source file to another document, you need to open the
original script, search for your comments, and write the appropriate text to a new file.

The GetCommentsFromScript.ps1 script begins with the *Param* statement. The *Param*
statement is used to allow you to provide information to the script at run time. The advantage
of using a command-line parameter is that you do not need to open the script and edit it to
provide the path to the script whose comments you are going to copy. You are making this
parameter a mandatory parameter by assigning a default value to the *$script* variable. The
default value you assign uses the *Throw* statement to raise an error, which means that the
script will always raise an error when run unless you supply a value for the *–script* parameter
when you run the script.

Using *Throw* to Raise an Error

Use of the *Throw* statement is seen in the DemoThrow.ps1 script. To get past the error that
is raised by the *Throw* statement in the *Set-Error* function, you first need to set the value of
the *$errorActionPreference* variable to SilentlyContinue, which causes the error to not be

displayed and allows the script to continue past the error. (This variable performs the same action as the On Error Resume Next setting from VBScript.) The *If* statement is used to evaluate the value of the *$value* variable. If there is a match, the *Throw* statement is encountered and the exception is thrown.

To evaluate the error, you can use the *Get-ErrorDetails* function. The error count is displayed first, and it will be incremented by one due to the error that was raised by the *Throw* statement. You can then take the first error (the error with the index value of 0 is always the most recent error that occurred) and send the error object to the Format-List cmdlet. You choose all of the properties. However, the invocation information is returned as an object. Therefore, you must query that object directly by accessing the invocation object via the *Invocationinfo* property of the error object. The resulting error information is shown in Figure 10-3.

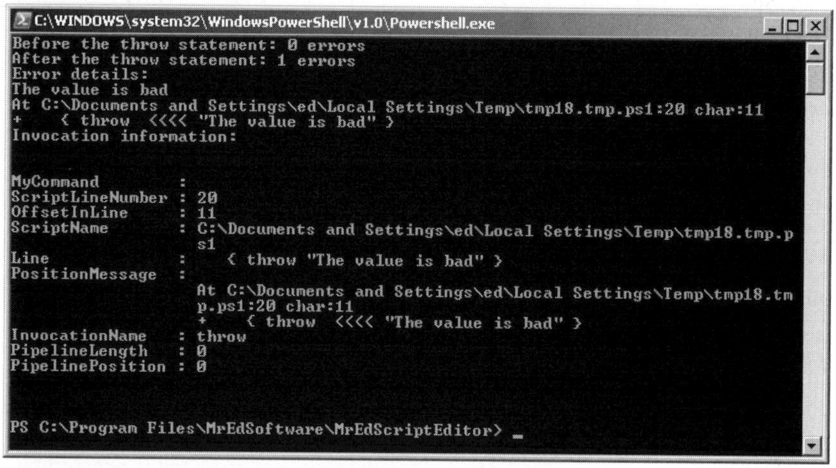

FIGURE 10-3 The *Throw* statement is used to raise an error.

The complete DemoThrow.ps1 script is shown here.

```
DemoThrow.ps1
Function Set-Error
{
 $errorActionPreference = "SilentlyContinue"
 "Before the throw statement: $($error.count) errors"
 $value = "bad"
 If ($value -eq "bad")
   { throw "The value is bad" }
} #end Set-Error

Function Get-ErrorDetails
{
 "After the throw statement: $($error.count) errors"
 "Error details:"
 $error[0] | Format-List -Property *
```

```
  "Invocation information:"
  $error[0].InvocationInfo
} #end Get-ErrorDetails

# *** Entry Point to Script
Set-Error
Get-ErrorDetails
```

The *Param* statement is shown here.

```
Param($Script= $(throw "The path to a script is required."))
```

You need to create a function that creates a file name for the new text document that will be created as a result of gleaning all of the comments from the script. To create the function, you can use the *Function* keyword and follow it with the name for the function. In your case, you can call the function *Get-FileName* in keeping with the spirit of the verb-noun naming convention in Windows PowerShell. The function will take a single input parameter that is held in the *$script* variable inside the function. The *$script* variable will hold the path to the script to be analyzed. The entry to the *Get-FileName* function is shown here.

```
Function Get-FileName($Script)
{
```

Working with Temporary Folders

Next, you can obtain the path to the temporary folder on the local computer in many different ways, including using the environmental PS drive. This example uses the static *GetTempPath* method from the *System.Io.Path* .NET Framework class. The *GetTempPath* method returns the path to the temporary folder, which is where you will store the newly created text file. You hold the temporary folder path in the *$outputPath* variable as shown here.

```
$outputPath = [io.path]::GetTempPath()
```

You decide to name your new text file after the name of the script. To do this, you need to separate the script name from the path in which the script is stored. You can use the *Split-Path* function to perform this surgery. The *–leaf* parameter instructs the cmdlet to return the script name. If you want the directory path that contains the script, you can use the *–parent* parameter. You put the Split-Path cmdlet inside a pair of parentheses because you want that operation to occur first. When the dollar sign is placed in front of the parentheses, it creates a subexpression that executes the code and then returns the name of the script. You can use .ps1 as the extension for your text file, but that can become a bit confusing because it is the extension for a script. Therefore, you can simply add a .txt extension to the returned file name and place the entire string within a pair of quotation marks.

You can use the Join-Path cmdlet to create a new path to your output file. The new path is composed of the temporary folder that is stored in the *$outputPath* variable and the file name you created using *Split-Path*. You combine these elements by using the Join-Path cmdlet. You can use string manipulation and concatenation to create the new file path, but it is much more reliable to use the Join-Path and Split-Path cmdlets to perform these types of operations. This section of the code is shown here.

```
Join-Path -path $outputPath -child "$(Split-Path $script -leaf).txt"
} #end Get-FileName
```

You need to decide how to handle duplicate files. You can prompt the user by saying that a duplicate file exists, which looks like the code shown here.

```
      $Response = Read-Host -Prompt "$outputFile already exists. Do you wish to delete
it <y / n>?"
        if($Response -eq "y")
          { Remove-Item $outputFile | Out-Null }
        ELSE { "Exiting now." ; exit }
```

You can implement some type of naming algorithm that makes a backup of the duplicate file by renaming it with an .old extension, which looks like the code shown here.

```
        if(Test-Path -path "$outputFile.old") { Remove-Item -Path "$outputFile.old" }
        Rename-Item -path $outputFile -newname  "$(Split-Path $outputFile -leaf).old"
```

You can also simply delete the previously existing file, which is what I generally choose to do. The action you want to perform goes into the *Remove-OutPutFile* function. You begin the function by using the *Function* keyword, specifying the name of the function, and using the *$outputFile* variable for input to the function as shown here.

```
Function Remove-outputFile($outputFile)
{
```

To determine whether the file exists, you can use the Test-Path cmdlet and supply the string contained in the *$outputFile* variable to the *–path* parameter. The Test-Path cmdlet only returns a *true* or *false* value. When a file is not found, it returns a *false* value, which means that you can use the *If* statement to evaluate the existence of the file. If the file is found, you can perform the action in the script block. If the file is not found, the script block is not executed. As shown here, the first command does not find the file, and *false* is returned. In the second command, the script block is not executed because the file cannot be located.

```
PS C:\> Test-Path c:\missingfile.txt
False
PS C:\> if(Test-Path c:\missingfile.txt){"found file"}
PS C:\>
```

Inside the *Remove-OutPutFile* function, you can use the *If* statement to determine whether the file referenced by *$outputFile* already exists. If it does, it is deleted by using the Remove-Item cmdlet. The information that is normally returned when a file is deleted is pipelined to the Out-Null cmdlet providing for a silent operation. This portion of the code is shown here.

```
if(Test-Path -path $outputFile) { Remove-Item $outputFile | Out-Null }

} #end Remove-outputFile
```

After you create the name for the output file and delete any previous output files that might be around, it is time to retrieve the comments from the script. To do this, you can create the *Get-Comments* function and pass it both the *$script* variable and *$outputFile* variable as shown here.

```
Function Get-Comments($Script,$outputFile)
{
```

Reading the Comments in the Output File

It is now time to read the text of the script. You can use the Get-Content cmdlet and provide it with the path to the script. When you use Get-Content to read a file, the file is read one line at a time and passed along the pipeline. If you store the result into a variable, you will have an array. You can treat the *$a* variable as any other array, including obtaining the number of elements in the array via the *Length* property and indexing directly into the array as shown here.

```
PS C:\fso> $a = Get-Content -Path C:\fso\GetSetieStartPage.ps1
PS C:\fso> $a.Length
62
PS C:\fso> $a[32]
($wmi.GetMultiStringValue($hkcu,$key, $property2)).sValue
```

The section of the script that reads the input script and sends it along the pipeline is shown here.

```
Get-Content -path $Script |
```

Next, you need to look inside each line to determine whether it belongs to the comment block. To examine each line within a pipeline, you must use the ForEach-Object cmdlet. This cmdlet is similar to a *Foreach ... next* statement in that it lets you work with an individual object from within a collection one at a time. The backtick character (`) is used to continue the command to the next line. The action you want to perform on each object as it comes across the pipeline is contained inside a script block that is delineated with a set of curly brackets (braces). This part of the *Get-Content* function is shown here.

```
Foreach-Object `
    {
```

Once you are inside the ForEach-Object cmdlet process block, it is time to examine the line of text. To do this, you can use the *If* statement. The *$_* automatic variable is used to represent the current line that is on the pipeline. You use the *−match* operator to perform a regular expression pattern match against the line of text. The *–match* operator returns a Boolean value—either *true* or *false*—in response to the pattern as shown here.

```
PS C:\fso> '$Comment = @"' -match  '^\$comment\s?=\s?@"'
True
```

The regular expression pattern you are using is composed of a number of special characters as shown in Table 10-3.

TABLE 10-3 Regular Expression Match Pattern and Meaning

CHARACTER	DESCRIPTION
^	Match at the beginning
\	Escape character so the $ sign is treated as a literal character and not the special character used in regular expressions
$comment	Literal characters
\s?	Zero or more white space characters
=	Literal character
@"	Literal characters

The section of code that examines the current line of text on the pipeline is shown here.

```
If($_ -match '^\$comment\s?=\s?@"')
```

You can create a variable named *$beginComment* that is used to mark the beginning of the comment block. If you make it past the *–match* operator, you find the beginning of the comment block. You can set the variable equal to *$true* as shown here.

```
  {
   $beginComment = $True
  } #end if match @"
```

Next, you can see whether you are at the end of the comment block by once again using the *–match* operator. You will look for the @" character sequence that is used to close a here-string. If you find this sequence, you can set the *$beginComment* variable to false as shown here.

```
  If($_ -match '"@')
    {
     $beginComment = $False
    } #end if match "@
```

After you pass the first two *If* statements—the first identifying the beginning of the here-string and the second locating the end of the here-string—you now want to grab the text that needs to be written to your comment file by setting the *$beginComment* variable to true. You also want to ensure that you do not see the @" character on the line because this designates the end of the here-string. To make this determination, you can use a compound *If* statement as shown here.

```
If($beginComment -AND $_ -notmatch '@"')
   {
```

It is now time to write the text to the output file. To do this, you can use the *$_* automatic variable, which represents the current line of text, and pipeline it to the Out-File cmdlet. The Out-File cmdlet receives the *$outputFile* variable that contains the path to the comment file. You can use the *–append* parameter to specify that you want to gather all of the comments from the script into the comment file. If you do not use the *–append* parameter, the text file will only contain the last comment because, by default, the Out-File cmdlet will overwrite the contents of any previously existing file. You can then add closing curly brackets for each of the comments that were previously opened. I consider it a best practice to add a comment after each closing curly bracket that indicates the purpose of the brace. This procedure makes the script much easier to read, troubleshoot, and maintain. This section of the code is shown here.

```
    $_ | Out-File -FilePath $outputFile -append
    } # end if beginComment
  } #end Foreach
} #end Get-Comments
```

You can now create a function named *Get-OutPutFile* that opens the output file for you to read. Because the temporary folder is not easy to find and because you have the path to the file in the *$outputFile* variable, it makes sense to use the script to open the output file. The *Get-OutPutFile* function receives a single input variable named *$outputFile*. When you call the *Get-OutPutFile* function, you pass a variable to the function that contains the path to the comment file that you want to open. That path is contained in the *$outputFile* variable. You can pass any value to the *Get-OutPutFile* function. Once inside the function, the value is then referred to by the *$outputFile* variable. You can even pass a string directly to the function without even using quotation marks around the string as shown here.

```
Function Get-outputFile($outputFile)
{
 Notepad $outputFile
} #end Get-outputFile

Get-outputFile -outputfile C:\fso\GetSetieStartPage.ps1
```

Don't Mess with the Worker Section of the Script

If I am going to gather data to pass to a function when writing a script, I generally like to encase the data in the same variable name that will be used both outside and inside the function. One reason for doing this is because it follows one of my best practices for script development: "Don't mess with the worker section of the script." In the *Get-OutPutFile* function, you are "doing work." To change the function in future scripts requires that you edit the string literal value, whereby you run the risk of breaking the code because many methods have complicated constructors. If you are also trying to pass values to the method constructors that require escaping special characters, then the risk of making a mistake becomes even worse.

By placing the string in a variable, you can easily edit the value of the variable. In fact, you are set up to provide the value of the variable via the command line or to base the value on an action performed in another function. Whenever possible, you should avoid placing string literal values directly in the script. In the code that follows, you can use a variable to hold the path to the file that is passed to the *Get-OutPutFile* function.

```
Function Get-outputFile($outputFile)
{
 Notepad $outputFile
} #end Get-outputFile


$outputFile = "C:\fso\GetSetieStartPage.ps1"
Get-outputFile -outputfile $outputFile
```

The complete *Get-OutPutFile* function is shown here.

```
Function Get-outputFile($outputFile)
{
 Notepad $outputFile
} #end Get-outputFile
```

Instead of typing in a string literal value for the path to the output file, the *$outputFile* variable receives the path that is created by the *Get-FileName* function. The *Get-FileName* function receives the path to the script that contains the comments to be extracted. The path to this script comes in via the command-line parameter. When a function has a single input parameter, you can pass it to the function by using a set of smooth parentheses. On the other hand, if the function uses two or more input parameters, you must use the *–parameter* name syntax. This line of code is shown here.

```
$outputFile = Get-FileName($script)
```

Next, you can call the *Remove-OutPutFile* function and pass it the path to the output file that is contained in the *$outputFile* variable. The *Remove-OutPutFile* function was discussed in the "Working with Temporary Folders" section earlier in this chapter. This line of code is shown here.

```
Remove-outputFile($outputFile)
```

Once you are assured of the name of your output file, you can call the *Get-Comments* function to retrieve comments from the script whose path is indicated by the *$script* variable. The comments are written to the output file referenced by the *$outputFile* variable as shown here.

```
Get-Comments -script $script -outputfile $outputFile
```

When all of the comments are written to the output file, you can finally call the *Get-OutPutFile* function and pass it the path contained in the *$outputFile* variable. If you do not want the comment file to be opened, you can easily comment the line out of your script or you can delete it and the *Get-OutPutFile* function itself from your script. If you are interested in reviewing each file prior to saving it, leave the line of code in place. This section of the script is shown here.

```
Get-outputFile($outputFile)
```

When the GetCommentsFromScript.ps1 script runs, nothing is emitted to the console. The only confirmation message that the script worked is the presence of the newly created text file displayed in Microsoft Notepad as shown in Figure 10-4.

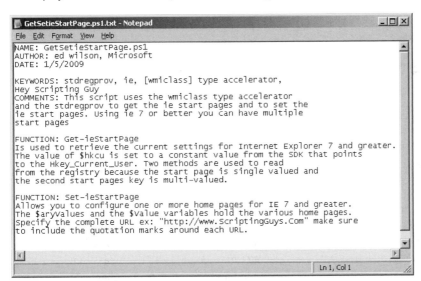

FIGURE 10-4 Comments extracted from a script by the GetCommentsFromScript.ps1 script

The complete GetCommentsFromScript.ps1 script is shown here.

```
GetCommentsFromScript.ps1
Param($Script= $(throw "The path to a script is required."))
Function Get-FileName($Script)
{
 $outputPath = [io.path]::GetTempPath()
 Join-Path -path $outputPath -child (Split-Path $script -leaf)
} #end Get-FileName


Function Remove-outputFile($outputFile)
{
  If(Test-Path -path $outputFile) { Remove-Item $outputFile | Out-Null }
} #end Remove-outputFile


Function Get-Comments($Script,$outputFile)
{
 Get-Content -path $Script |
 Foreach-Object `
  {
    If($_ -match '^\$comment\s?=\s?@"')
      {
       $beginComment = $True
      } #end if match @"
   If($_ -match '"@')
      {
       $beginComment = $False
      } #end if match "@
   If($beginComment -AND $_ -notmatch '@"')
      {
       $_ | Out-File -FilePath $outputFile -append
      } # end if beginComment
  } #end Foreach
} #end Get-Comments


Function Get-outputFile($outputFile)
{
 Notepad $outputFile
} #end Get-outputFile


# *** Entry point to script ***
$outputFile = Get-FileName($script)
Remove-outputFile($outputFile)
Get-Comments -script $script -outputfile $outputFile
Get-outputFile($outputFile)
```

Using Multiple-Line Comment Tags in Windows PowerShell 2.0

Windows PowerShell 2.0 introduces multiple-line comment tags that can be used to comment one or more lines in a script. These comment tags work in a similar fashion to here-strings or HTML tags in that, when you open a comment tag, you must also close the comment tag.

Creating Multiple-Line Comments with Comment Tags

The opening tag is the left angle bracket pound sign (<#), and the closing comment tag is the pound sign right angle bracket (#>). The pattern for the use of the multiline comment is shown here.

```
<# Opening comment tag
First line comment
Additional comment lines
#> Closing comment tag
```

The use of the multiline comment is seen in the Demo-MultilineComment.ps1 script.

```
Demo-MultilineComment.ps1
<#
Get-Command
Get-Help
#>
"The above is a multiline comment"
```

When the Demo-MultilineComment.ps1 script is run, the two cmdlets shown inside the comment tags are not run; the only command that runs is the one outside of the comment block, which prints a string in the console window. The output from the Demo-MultilineComment.ps1 script is shown here.

```
The above is a multiline comment
```

Multiline comment tags do not need to be placed on individual lines. It is perfectly permissible to include the commented text on the line that supplies the comment characters. The pattern for the alternate multiline comment tag placement is shown here.

```
<# Opening comment tag First line comment
Additional comment lines #> Closing comment tag
```

The alternate multiline comment tag placement is shown in MultilineDemo2.ps1.

```
MultilineDemo2.ps1
<# Get-Help
   Get-Command #>
"The above is a multiline comment"
```

> **NOTE** As a best practice, I prefer to place multiline comment tags on their own individual lines. This format makes the code much easier to read, and it is easier to see where the comment begins and ends.

Creating Single-Line Comments with Comment Tags

You can use the multiline comment syntax to comment a single line of code, with the advantage being that you do not mix your comment characters. You can use a single comment pattern for all of the comments in the script as shown here.

```
<# Opening comment tag First line comment #> Closing comment tag
```

An example of the single comment pattern in a script is shown in the MultilineDemo3.ps1 script.

```
MultilineDemo3.ps1
<# This is a single comment #>
"The above is a single comment"
```

When using the multiline comment pattern, it is important to keep in mind that anything placed after the end of the closing comment tag is parsed by Windows PowerShell. Only items placed within the multiline comment characters are commented out. However, multiline commenting behavior is completely different from using the pound sign (#) single-line comment character. It is also a foreign concept to users of VBScript who are used to the behavior of the single quote (') comment character in which anything after the character is commented out. A typical-use scenario that generates an error is illustrated in the following example.

```
<# --------------------------
This example causes an error
#> --------------------------
```

If you need to highlight your comments in the manner shown in the previous example, you only need to change the position of the last comment tag by moving it to the end of the line to remove the error. The modified comment is shown here.

```
<# -------------------------------
This example does not cause an error
--------------------------------- #>
```

The single pound sign (#) is still accepted for commenting, and there is nothing to prohibit its use. To perform a multiline comment using the single pound sign, you simply place a pound sign in front of each line that requires commenting. This pattern has the advantage of familiarity and consistency of behavior. The fact that it is also backward compatible with Windows PowerShell 1.0 is an added bonus.

```
# First commented line
# additional commented line
# last commented line
```

The 13 Rules for Writing Effective Comments

When adding documentation to a script, it is important that you do not introduce errors. If the comments and code do not match, there is a good chance that both are wrong. Make sure that when you modify the script, you also modify your comments. In this way, both the comments and the script refer to the same information.

Update Documentation When a Script Is Updated

It is easy to forget to update comments that refer to the parameters of a function when you add additional parameters to that function. In a similar fashion, it is easy to ignore the information contained inside the header of the script that refers to dependencies or assumptions within the script. Make sure that you treat both the script and the comments with the same level of attention and importance. In the FindDisabledUserAccounts.ps1 script, the comments in the header seem to apply to the script, but they also seem to miss the fact that the script is using the [ADSISearcher] type accelerator. In fact, the script is a modified script that was used to create a specific instance of the DirectoryServices.DirectorySearcher .NET Framework class and was recently updated. However, the comments were never updated. This oversight might make a user suspicious as to the accuracy of a perfectly useful script. The FindDisabledUserAccounts.ps1 script is shown here.

FindDisabledUserAccounts.ps1

```
# -----------------------------------------------------------------------
# FindDisabledUserAccounts.ps1
# ed wilson, 3/28/2008
#
# Creates an instance of the DirectoryServices DirectorySearcher .NET
# Framework class to search Active Directory.
# Creates a filter that is LDAP syntax that gets applied to the searcher
```

```
# object. If we only look for class of user, then we also end up with
# computer accounts as they are derived from user class. So we do a
# compound query to also retrieve person.
# We then use the findall method and retrieve all users.
# Next we use the properties property and choose item to retrieve the
# distinguished name of each user, and then we use the distinguished name
# to perform a query and retrieve the UAC attribute, and then we do a
# boolean to compare with the value of 2 which is disabled.
#
# -------------------------------------------------------------------------
#Requires -Version 2.0

$filter = "(&(objectClass=user)(objectCategory=person))"
$users = ([adsiSearcher]$Filter).findall()

 foreach($suser in $users)
  {
    "Testing $($suser.properties.item(""distinguishedname""))"
    $user = [adsi]"LDAP://$($suser.properties.item(""distinguishedname""))"

    $uac=$user.psbase.invokeget("useraccountcontrol")
      if($uac -band 0x2)
        { write-host -foregroundcolor red "`t account is disabled" }
      ELSE
        { write-host -foregroundcolor green "`t account is not disabled" }
  } #foreach
```

Add Comments During the Development Process

When you are writing a script, make sure that you add the comments at the same time you are doing the initial development. Do not wait until you have completed the script to begin writing your comments. When you make comments after writing the script, it is very easy to leave out details because you are now overly familiar with the script and those items that you looked up in documentation now seem obvious. If you add the comments at the same time that you write the script, you can then refer to these comments as you develop the script to ensure that you maintain a consistent approach. This procedure will help with the consistency of your variable names and writing style. The CheckForPdfAndCreateMarker.ps1 script illustrates this consistency problem. In reviewing the code, it seems that the script checks for PDF files, which also seems rather obvious from the name of the script. However, why is the script prompting to delete the files? What is the marker? The only discernable information is that I wrote the script back in December 2008 for a Hey Scripting Guy! article. Luckily, Hey Scripting Guy! articles explain scripts, so at least some documentation actually exists! The CheckForPdfAndCreateMarker.ps1 script is shown here.

CheckForPdfAndCreateMarker.ps1

```
# -----------------------------------------------------------------------------
# CheckForPdfAndCreateMarker.ps1
# ed wilson, msft, 12/11/2008
#
# Hey Scripting Guy! 12/29/2008
# -----------------------------------------------------------------------------
$path = "c:\fso"
$include = "*.pdf"
$name = "nopdf.txt"
if(!(Get-ChildItem -path $path -include $include -Recurse))
  {
    "No pdf was found in $path. Creating $path\$name marker file."
    New-Item -path $path -name $name -itemtype file -force |
    out-null
  } #end if not Get-Childitem
ELSE
  {
  $response = Read-Host -prompt "PDF files were found. Do you wish to delete <y>
/<n>?"
   if($response -eq "y")
    {
      "PDF files will be deleted."
      Get-ChildItem -path $path -include $include -recurse |
       Remove-Item
    } #end if response
   ELSE
    {
      "PDF files will not be deleted."
    } #end else reponse
  } #end else not Get-Childitem
```

Write for an International Audience

When you write comments for your script, you should attempt to write for an international audience. You should always assume that users who are not overly familiar with the idioms of your native language will be reading your comments. In addition, writing for an international audience makes it easier for automated software to localize the script documentation. Key points to keep in mind when writing for an international audience are to use a simple syntax and to use consistent employee standard terminology. Avoid slang, acronyms, and overly familiar language. If possible, have a colleague who is a non-native speaker review the documentation. In the SearchForWordImages.ps1 script, the comments explain what the script does and also its limitations, such as the fact that it was only tested using Microsoft Office Word 2007. The sentences are plainly written and do not use jargon or idioms. The SearchForWordImages.ps1 script is shown here.

SearchForWordImages.ps1

```
# -----------------------------------------------------------------------
# NAME: SearchForWordImages.ps1
# AUTHOR: ed wilson, Microsoft
# DATE: 11/4/2008
#
# KEYWORDS: Word.Application, automation, COM
# Get-Childitem -include, Foreach-Object
#
# COMMENTS: This script searches a folder for doc and
# docx files, opens them with Word and counts the
# number of images embedded in the file.
# It then prints out the name of each file and the
# number of associated images with the file. This script requires
# Word to be installed. It was tested with Word 2007. The folder must
# exist or the script will fail.
#
# -----------------------------------------------------------------------
#The folder must exist and be followed with a trailing \*
$folder = "c:\fso\*"
$include = "*.doc","*.docx"
$word = new-object -comobject word.application
#Makes the Word application invisible. Set to $true to see the application.
$word.visible = $false
Get-ChildItem -path $folder -include $include |
ForEach-Object `
{
 $doc = $word.documents.open($_.fullname)
 $_.name + " has " + $doc.inlineshapes.count + " images in the file"
}
#If you forget to quit Word, you will end up with multiple copies running
#at the same time.
$word.quit()
```

Consistent Header Information

You should include header information at the top of each script. This header information should be displayed in a consistent manner and indeed should be part of your company's scripting standards. Typical information to be displayed is the title of the script, author of the script, date the script was written, version information, and additional comments. Version information does not need to be more extensive than the major and minor versions. This information, as well as comments as to what was added during the revisions, is useful for maintaining a version control for production scripts. An example of adding comments is shown in the WriteBiosInfoToWord.ps1 script.

WriteBiosInfoToWord.ps1

```
# ===============================================================================
#
# NAME: WriteBiosInfoToWord.ps1
#
# AUTHOR: ed wilson , Microsoft
# DATE   : 10/30/2008
# EMAIL: Scripter@Microsoft.com
# Version: 1.0
#
# COMMENT: Uses the word.application object to create a new text document
# uses the get-wmiobject cmdlet to query wmi
# uses out-string to remove the "object nature" of the returned information
# uses foreach-object cmdlet to write the data to the word document.
#
# Hey Scripting Guy! 11/11/2008
# ===============================================================================

$class = "Win32_Bios"
$path = "C:\fso\bios"

#The wdSaveFormat object must be saved as a reference type.
[ref]$SaveFormat = "microsoft.office.interop.word.WdSaveFormat" -as [type]

$word = New-Object -ComObject word.application
$word.visible = $true
$doc = $word.documents.add()
$selection = $word.selection
$selection.typeText("This is the bios information")
$selection.TypeParagraph()

Get-WmiObject -class $class |
Out-String |
ForEach-Object { $selection.typeText($_) }
$doc.saveas([ref] $path, [ref]$saveFormat::wdFormatDocument)
$word.quit()
```

Document Prerequisites

It is imperative that your comments include information about prerequisites for running the script as well as the implementation of nonstandard programs in the script. For example, if your script requires the use of an external program that is not part of the operating system, you need to include checks within the script to ensure that the program is available when it is called by the script itself. In addition to these checks, you should document the fact that the program is a requirement for running the script. If your script makes assumptions as to the existence of certain directories, you should make a note of this fact. Of course, your script should use Test-Path to make sure that the directory exists, but you should still document this step as an important precondition for the script. An additional consideration is whether or not you create the required directory. If the script requires an input file, you should add a comment that indicates this requirement as well as add a comment to check for the existence of the file prior to actually calling that file. It is also a good idea to add a comment indicating the format of the input file because one of the most fragile aspects of a script that reads an input file is the actual formatting of that file. The ConvertToFahrenheit_include.ps1 script illustrates adding a note about the requirement of accessing the include file.

```
ConvertToFahrenheit_include.ps1
# --------------------------------------------------------------------------
# NAME: ConvertToFahrenheit_include.ps1
# AUTHOR: ed wilson, Microsoft
# DATE: 9/24/2008
# EMAIL: Scripter@Microsoft.com
# Version 2.0
#    12/1/2008 added test-path check for include file
#              modified the way the include file is called
# KEYWORDS: Converts Celsius to Fahrenheit
#
# COMMENTS: This script converts Celsius to Fahrenheit
# It uses command line parameters and an include file.
# If the ConversionFunctions.ps1 script is not available,
# the script will fail.
#
# --------------------------------------------------------------------------
Param($Celsius)
#The $includeFile variable points to the ConversionFunctions.ps1
#script. Make sure you edit the path to this script.
$includeFile = "c:\data\scriptingGuys\ConversionFunctions.ps1"
if(!(test-path -path $includeFile))
  {
    "Unable to find $includeFile"
    Exit
  }
. $includeFile
ConvertToFahrenheit($Celsius)
```

Document Deficiencies

If the script has a deficiency, it is imperative that this is documented. This deficiency may be as simple as the fact that the script is still in progress, but this fact should be highlighted in the comments section of the header to the script. It is quite common for script writers to begin writing a script, become distracted, and then begin writing a new script, all the while forgetting about the original script in progress. When the original script is later found, some-one might begin to use the script and be surprised that it does not work as advertised. For this reason, scripts that are in progress should always be marked accordingly. If you use a keyword, such as *in progress*, then you can write a script that will find all of your work-in-progress scripts. In addition to scripts in progress, you should also highlight any limitations of the script. If a script runs on a local computer but will not run on a remote computer, this fact should be added in the comment section of the header. If a script requires an extremely long time to complete the requested action, this information should be noted. If the script generates errors but completes its task successfully, this information should also be noted so that the user can have confidence in the outcome of the script. A note that indicates why the error is generated also increases the confidence of the user in the original writer. The CmdLineArgumentsTime.ps1 script works but generates errors unless it is used in a certain set of conditions and is called in a specific manner. The comments call out the special conditions, and several INPROGRESS tags indicate the future work required by the script. The CmdLineArgumentsTime.ps1 script is shown here.

CmdLineArgumentsTime.ps1

```
# ==============================================================================
#
# NAME: CmdLineArgumentsTime.ps1
# AUTHOR: Ed Wilson , microsoft
# DATE   : 2/19/2009
# EMAIL: Scripter@Microsoft.com
# Version .0
# KEYWORDS: Add-PSSnapin, powergadgets, Get-Date
#
# COMMENT: The $args[0] is unnamed argument that accepts command line input.
# C:\cmdLineArgumentsTime.ps1 23 52
# No commas are used to separate the arguments. Will generate an error if used.
# Requires powergadgets.
# INPROGRESS: Add a help function to script.
# ==============================================================================
#INPROGRESS: change unnamed arguments to a more user friendly method
[int]$inthour = $args[0]
[int]$intMinute = $args[1]
#INPROGRESS: find a better way to check for existence  of powergadgets
#This causes errors to be ignored and is used when checking for PowerGadgets
$erroractionpreference = "SilentlyContinue"
#this clears all errors and is used to see if errors are present.
$error.clear()
#This command will generate an error if PowerGadgets are not installed
Get-PSSnapin *powergadgets | Out-Null
#INPROGRESS: Prompt before loading powergadgets
If ($error.count -ne 0)
{Add-PSSnapin powergadgets}

New-TimeSpan -Start (get-date) -end (get-date -Hour $inthour -Minute $intMinute) |
Out-Gauge -Value minutes -Floating -refresh 0:0:30  -mainscale_max 60
```

Avoid Useless Information

Inside the code of the script itself, you should avoid comments that provide useless or irrelevant information. Keep in mind that you are writing a script and providing documentation for the script and that such a task calls for technical writing skills, not creative writing skills. While you might be enthralled with your code in general, the user of the script is not interested in how difficult it was to write the script. However, it is useful to explain why you used certain constructions instead of other forms of code writing. This information, along with the explanation, can be useful to people who might modify the script in the future. You should therefore add internal comments only if they will help others to understand how the script actually works. If a comment does not add value, the comment should be omitted. The DemoConsoleBeep.ps1 script contains numerous comments in the body of the script. However, several of them are obvious, and others actually duplicate information from the comments section of the header. There is nothing wrong with writing too many comments, but it can be a bit excessive when a one-line script contains 20 lines of comments, particularly when the script is very simple. The DemoConsoleBeep.ps1 script is shown here.

```
DemoConsoleBeep.ps1
# -----------------------------------------------------------------------
# NAME: DemoConsoleBeep.ps1
# AUTHOR: ed wilson, Microsoft
# DATE: 4/1/2009
#
# KEYWORDS: Beep
#
# COMMENTS: This script demonstrates using the console
# beep. The first parameter is the frequency between
# 37..32767. above 7500 is barely audible. 37 is the lowest
# note it will play.
# The second parameter is the length of time
#
# -----------------------------------------------------------------------
#this construction creates an array of numbers from 37 to 3200
#the % sign is an alias for Foreach-Object
#the $_ is an automatic variable that refers to the current item
#on the pipeline.
#the semicolon causes a new logical line
#the double colon is used to refer to a static method
#the $_ in the method is the number on the pipeline
#the second number is the length of time to play the beep
37..32000 | % { $_ ; [console]::beep($_ , 1) }
```

Document the Reason for the Code

While it is true that good code is readable and that a good developer is able to understand what a script does, some developers might not understand why a script is written in a certain manner or why a script works in a particular fashion. In the DemoConsoleBeep2.ps1 script, extraneous comments have been removed. Essential information about the range that the console beep will accept is included, but the redundant information is deleted. In addition, a version history is added because significant modification to the script was made. The DemoConsoleBeep2.ps1 script is shown here.

DemoConsoleBeep2.ps1

```
# -----------------------------------------------------------------------
# NAME: DemoConsoleBeep2.ps1
# AUTHOR: ed wilson, Microsoft
# DATE: 4/1/2009
# VERSION 2.0
# 4/4/2009 cleaned up comments. Removed use of % alias. Reformatted.
#
# KEYWORDS: Beep
#
# COMMENTS: This script demonstrates using the console
# beep. The first parameter is the frequency. Allowable range is between
# 37..32767. A number above 7500 is barely audible. 37 is the lowest
# note the console beep will play.
# The second parameter is the length of time.
#
# -----------------------------------------------------------------------

37..32000 |
Foreach-Object { $_ ; [console]::beep($_ , 1) }
```

Use of One-Line Comments

You should use one-line comments that appear prior to the code that is being commented to explain the specific purpose of variables or constants. You should also use one-line comments to document fixes or workarounds in the code as well as to point to the reference information explaining these fixes or workarounds. Of course, you should strive to write code that is clear enough to not require internal comments. Do not add comments that simply repeat what the code already states. Add comments to illuminate the code but not to elucidate the code. The GetServicesInSvchost.ps1 script uses comments to discuss the logic of mapping the *handle* property from the *Win32_Process* class to the *ProcessID* property from the *Win32_Service* WMI class to reveal which services are using which instance of the Svchost process. The GetServicesInSvchost.ps1 script is shown here.

GetServicesInSvchost.ps1

```
# ----------------------------------------------------------------------
# NAME: GetServicesInSvchost.ps1
# AUTHOR: ed wilson, Microsoft
# DATE: 8/21/2008
#
# KEYWORDS: Get-WmiObject, Format-Table,
# Foreach-Object
#
# COMMENTS: This script creates an array of WMI process
# objects and retrieves the handle of each process object.
# According to MSDN the handle is a process identifier. It
# is also the key of the Win32_Process class. The script
# then uses the handle which is the same as the processID
# property from the Win32_service class to retrieve the
# matches.
#
# HSG 8/28/2008
# ----------------------------------------------------------------------

$aryPid = @(Get-WmiObject win32_process -Filter "name='svchost.exe'") |
  Foreach-Object { $_.Handle }


"There are " + $arypid.length + " instances of svchost.exe running"

foreach ($i in $aryPID)
{
 Write-Host "Services running in ProcessID: $i" ;
 Get-WmiObject win32_service -Filter " processID = $i" |
 Format-Table name, state, startMode
}
```

Avoid End-of-Line Comments

You should avoid using end-of-line comments. The addition of such comments to your code has a severely distracting aspect to structured logic blocks and can cause your code to be more difficult to read and maintain. Some developers try to improve on this situation by aligning all of the comments at a particular point within the script. While this initially looks nice, it creates a maintenance nightmare because each time the code is modified, you run into the potential for a line to run long and push past the alignment point of the comments. When this occurs, it forces you to move everything over to the new position. Once you do this a few times, you will probably realize the futility of this approach to commenting internal code. One additional danger of using end-of-line comments when working with Windows PowerShell is that, due to the pipelining nature of language, a single command might stretch out over several lines. Each line that ends with a pipeline character continues the command to the next line. A comment character placed after a pipeline character will break the code as shown here, where the comment is located in the middle of a logical line of code. This code will not work.

```
Get-Process | #This cmdlet obtains a listing of all processes on the computer
Select-Object -property name
```

A similar situation also arises when using the named parameters of the ForEach-Object cmdlet as shown in the SearchAllComputersInDomain.ps1 script. The backtick (`) character is used for line continuation, which allows placement of the *–Begin*, *–Process*, and *–End* parameters on individual lines. This placement makes the script easier to read and understand. If an end-of-line comment is placed after any of the backtick characters, the script will fail. The SearchAllComputersInDomain.ps1 script is shown here.

SearchAllComputersInDomain.ps1
```
$Filter = "ObjectCategory=computer"
$Searcher = New-Object System.DirectoryServices.DirectorySearcher($Filter)
$Searcher.Findall() |
Foreach-Object `
   -Begin { "Results of $Filter query: " } `
   -Process { $_.properties ; "`r"} `
   -End { [string]$Searcher.FindAll().Count + " $Filter results were found" }
```

Document Nested Structures

The previous discussion about end-of-line comments should not be interpreted as dismissing comments that document the placement of closing curly brackets. In general, you should avoid creating deeply nested structures, but sometimes they cannot be avoided. The use of end-of-line comments with closing curly brackets can greatly improve the readability and maintainability of your script. As shown in the Get-MicrosoftUpdates.ps1 script, the closing curly brackets are all tagged.

Get-MicrosoftUpdates.ps1
```
# -----------------------------------------------------------------------
# NAME: Get-MicrosoftUpdates.ps1
# AUTHOR: ed wilson, Microsoft
# DATE: 2/25/2009
#
# KEYWORDS: Microsoft.Update.Session, com
#
# COMMENTS: This script lists the Microsoft Updates
# you can select a certain number, or you can choose
# all of the updates.
#
# HSG 3-9-2009
```

```
# --------------------------------------------------------------------
Function Get-MicrosoftUpdates
{
  Param(
        $NumberOfUpdates,
        [switch]$all
       )
  $Session = New-Object -ComObject Microsoft.Update.Session
  $Searcher = $Session.CreateUpdateSearcher()
  if($all)
    {
      $HistoryCount = $Searcher.GetTotalHistoryCount()
      $Searcher.QueryHistory(1,$HistoryCount)
    } #end if all
  Else
    {
      $Searcher.QueryHistory(1,$NumberOfUpdates)
    } #end else
} #end Get-MicrosoftUpdates

# *** entry point to script ***

# lists the latest update
# Get-MicrosoftUpdates -NumberofUpdates 1

# lists All updates
Get-MicrosoftUpdates -all
```

Use a Standard Set of Keywords

When adding comments that indicate bugs, defects, or work items, you should use a set of keywords that is consistent across all scripts. This would be a good item to add to your corporate scripting guidelines. In this way, a script can easily be developed that will search your code for such work items. If you maintain source control, then a comment can be added when these work items are fixed. Of course, you would also increment the version of the script with a comment relating to the fix. In the CheckEventLog.ps1 script, the script accepts two command-line parameters. One parameter is for the event log to query, and the other is for the number of events to return. If the user selects the security log and is not running the script as an administrator, an error is generated that is noted in the comment block. Because this scenario could be a problem, the outline of a function to check for admin rights has been added to the script as well as code to check for the log name. A number of TODO: tags are added to the script to mark the work items. The CheckEventLog.ps1 script is shown here.

CheckEventLog.ps1

```
# -----------------------------------------------------------------------
# NAME: CheckEventLog.ps1
# AUTHOR: ed wilson, Microsoft
# DATE: 4/4/2009
#
# KEYWORDS: Get-EventLog, Param, Function
#
# COMMENTS: This accepts two parameters the logname
# and the number of events to retrieve. If no number for
# -max is supplied it retrieves the most recent entry.
# The script fails if the security log is targeted and it is
# not run with admin rights.
# TODO: Add function to check for admin rights if
# the security log is targeted.
# -----------------------------------------------------------------------
Param($log,$max)
Function Get-log($log,$max)
{
 Get-EventLog -logname $log -newest $max
} #end Get-Log


#TODO: finish Get-AdminRights function
Function Get-AdminRights
{
#TODO: add code to check for administrative
#TODO: rights. If not running as an admin
#TODO: if possible add code to obtain those rights
} #end Get-AdminRights


If(-not $log) { "You must specify a log name" ; exit}
if(-not $max) { $max = 1 }
#TODO: turn on the if security log check
# If($log -eq "Security") { Get-AdminRights ; exit }
Get-Log -log $log -max $max
```

Document the Strange and Bizarre

The last item that should be commented in your documentation is anything that looks strange. If you use a new type of construction that you have not used previously in other scripts, you should add a comment to the effect. A good comment should also indicate the previous coding construction as an explanation. In general, it is not a best practice to use code that looks strange simply to show your dexterity or because it is an elegant solution; rather, you should strive for readable code. However, when you discover a new construction that is cleaner and easier to read, albeit a somewhat novel approach, you should always add a comment to highlight this fact. If the new construction is sufficiently useful, then it should be incorporated into your corporate scripting guidelines as a design pattern. In the GetProcessesDisplayTempFile.ps1 script, a few unexpected items crop up. The first is the *GetTempFileName* static method from the *Io.Path* .NET Framework class. Despite the method's name, *GetTempFileName* both creates a temporary file name as well as a temporary file itself. The second technique is much more unusual. When the temporary file is displayed via Notepad, the result of the operation is pipelined to the Out-Null cmdlet. This operation effectively halts the execution of the script until the Notepad application is closed. This "trick" does not conform to expected behavior, but it is a useful design pattern for those wanting to remove temporary files once they have been displayed. As a result, both features of the GetProcessDisplayTempFile.ps1 script are documented as shown here.

GetProcessesDisplayTempFile.ps1

```
# -------------------------------------------------------------------------
# NAME: GetProcessesDisplayTempFile.ps1
# AUTHOR: ed wilson, Microsoft
# DATE: 4/4/2009
# VERSION 1.0
#
# KEYWORDS: [io.path], GetTempFileName, out-null
#
# COMMENTS: This script creates a temporary file,
# obtains a collection of process information and writes
# that to the temporary file. It then displays that file via
# Notepad and then removes the temporary file when
# done.
#
# -------------------------------------------------------------------------
#This both creates the file name as well as the file itself
$tempFile = [io.path]::GetTempFileName()
Get-Process >> $tempFile
#Piping the Notepad filename to the Out-Null cmdlet halts
#the script execution
Notepad $tempFile | Out-Null
#Once the file is closed the temporary file is closed and it is
#removed
Remove-Item $tempFile
```

Teaching Your Scripts to Communicate

Peter Costantini, Microsoft Scripting Guy Emeritus

I f code was read only by computers, we could only write 1s and 0s. Even though developers would quickly go blind and insane, there's a new class of computer science majors graduating every year. Of course, the reality is that code must also be read by humans, and programming languages have been developed to mediate between humans and machines.

If one developer could write, debug, test, maintain, and field support calls for all of the code for an application, then it wouldn't be very important whether the programming language was easy for others to understand. A brilliant loner could decide to write in an obscure dialect of Lisp and name the variables and procedures in Esperanto, and that would be fine as long as the code worked.

However, that programing language may not be so fine five years later. By then, the developer's Lisp and Esperanto are a little rusty. Suddenly a call comes in that the now mission-critical application is crashing inexplicably and losing the firm billions of dollars.

"What's a few billion dollars these days? Maybe I'll get a bonus," I hear you muttering under your breath. Anyway, you're not a developer: you're a system engineer who's trying to use scripts to automate some of your routine tasks and to trouble-shoot. You thought the whole point of scripting was to let you write quick and dirty code to get a task done in a hurry.

Yes, that is a big benefit of scripting. When you first write a script to solve a problem, you're probably not concerned about producing beautiful-looking, or even comprehensible, code. You just want to make sure that it runs as expected and makes the pain stop.

However, once you decide that the script is a keeper and that you're going to run it as a scheduled task at three every Monday morning, the equation starts to change. At this point, like it or not, you really are a developer. Windows PowerShell is a programming language, albeit a dynamic one, and any code that plays an ongoing role in the functioning of your organization needs to be treated as something more than chewing gum and baling wire.

Furthermore, regardless of your personal relationship with your scripts, you probably work as part of a team, right? Other people on your team might write scripts, too. In any case, these people most likely have to run your scripts and figure out what they do. You can see where I'm going with this. But if it produces a blinding flash of insight, that's all the better for your career and your organization.

The goal is to make your scripts transparent. Your code—and the environment in which it runs—should communicate to your teammates everything they need to know to understand what your script is doing, how to use it successfully, and how to troubleshoot it if problems arise (Murphy's Law has many scripting corollaries). Clarity and readability are virtues; terseness and ambiguity are not. Consistent, descriptive variable names and white space do not make the code run any slower, but they can make the script more readable. Begin to look at transparency as an insurance policy against receiving a frantic call on your cell phone when you're lying on a beach in Puerto Vallarta sipping a margarita.

Yet, this is not just a technical and social imperative: it's an economic one as well. IT departments are pushing hard to become strategic assets rather than cost centers. The sprawling skeins of code, scripts, and all that run their operations can earn or lose figures followed by many zeros and make the difference between budget increases and layoffs. Okay, at least this year, adding good documentation to your scripts can make the budget cuts smaller.

Additional Resources

- The TechNet Script Center at *http://www.microsoft.com/technet/scriptcenter* contains numerous examples of Windows PowerShell scripts, as well as some sample documentation templates.
- Take a look at the *Windows PowerShell™ Scripting Guide* (Microsoft Press, 2008).
- The Tweakomatic can be downloaded from the TechNet Script Center at *http://www.microsoft.com/technet/scriptcenter.*
- Refer to "How Can I Delete and Manage PDF Files?" at *http://www.microsoft.com /technet/scriptcenter/resources/qanda/dec08/hey1229.mspx.*
- Refer to "How Can I Create a Microsoft Word Document from WMI Information?" at *http://www.microsoft.com/technet/scriptcenter/resources/qanda/nov08/hey1111.mspx.*
- Refer to *Windows Scripting with WMI: Self-Paced Learning Guide* (Microsoft Press, 2006).
- Script documentation guidelines are discussed in the *Microsoft Windows 2000 Scripting Guide* (Microsoft Press, 2003). This book is available online at *http://www.microsoft.com /technet/scriptcenter/guide/sas_sbp_mybu.mspx.*
- On the companion media, you will find all of the scripts referred to in this chapter.

Planning for Modules

Windows PowerShell 2.0 introduces the concept of modules. A *module* is a package that can contain Windows PowerShell cmdlets, aliases, functions, variables, and even providers. In short, a Windows PowerShell module can contain the types of items that you might put into your profile, but it can also contain items that previously required a developer to incorporate into a Windows PowerShell 1.0 snap-in.

There are several advantages to using modules instead of snap-ins. The first advantage is that anyone who can write a Windows PowerShell script can create a module. Another advantage is that you do not need to write a Microsoft Windows Installer package to install a module. In addition, administrator rights are not required to install a Windows PowerShell module. Last, the use of a module offers greater flexibility because of its ability to create a *module manifest*, which specifies exactly which functions and programming elements will be imported into the current session. These advantages should be of great interest to the IT professional.

In its most basic form, a Windows PowerShell module is a file that contains the same type of code written in a PowerShell script. Many Windows PowerShell modules begin as a PowerShell script and end as modules, with little or no modification other than changing the file extension and location of the file.

Because Windows PowerShell modules are similar to PowerShell scripts, you already know many of the essential facts surrounding the creation of modules. If you can write a function or create a variable or an alias, you can create a module. You can continue to use the scripting techniques, such as dot-sourcing and here-string help, that were examined in previous chapters.

The Benefits of Working with Modules

Andy Schneider, Systems Engineer
Author of the Get-PowerShell blog

When I first heard about Windows PowerShell modules, I was really excited to know how they would influence the PowerShell ecosystem. Modules provide the ability to easily share and distribute incredibly powerful functionality among Windows PowerShell users. In addition to making it easier to share scripts and functions, modules also provide a much better user experience for adding and removing native cmdlets written in a Microsoft .NET language. You no longer have to register a dynamic link library (DLL) or go through an installer, which makes cmdlet installations and script deployments as simple as a copy-and-paste procedure. Although there are a number of reasons why I use modules, I want to focus on just a few of them here.

- It is easy to create a module.

- You can shorten the time it takes to write and test modules by using the *–force* parameter.

- You can choose the functionality that you want to expose by using the `Export-ModuleMember` cmdlet.

I quickly realized that it is truly simple to create a module in Windows PowerShell 2.0. All you have to do is take one of your scripts, rename it from a .ps1 file to a .psm1 file (which is the file extension for a Windows PowerShell module), and move it to the modules directory. By changing only the extension, you have a bare-bones module that you can tweak and to which you can add functionality. The Windows PowerShell team has done a fantastic job of creating a smooth glidepath that enables you to easily move to the next level of scripting, whatever that level might be.

The first time I started writing, updating, and testing a module, I kept removing it and reading it with new changes and updates. I even went as far as writing a function that would remove, read and update the changes. However, I finally discovered that the `Import-Module` cmdlet has a *–force* parameter that allows you to update and overwrite your imported module without removing it first, which makes writing and testing your modules much easier.

When I wrote scripts in the past, I often created a variety of small help functions and temporary variables that my end users did not ultimately need to use directly. As an author of a script, modules allow you to expose only the functionality that you want your end users to see. If you have a module containing 15 functions but only 7 or 8 of them are useful to the end user, modules can solve this problem.

Rename your .ps1 file to a .psm1 file, and then use the Export-ModuleMember cmdlet at the end of your script. You can also think of exported functions as public functions and regard the ones that are not exposed as private functions. Exported functions also allow you as a module author to not pollute a Windows PowerShell session with a lot of useless functions and global variables.

Modules will revolutionize the way that functionality is shared within the Windows PowerShell community. Sharing a module is literally a cut-and-paste operation. I am truly looking forward to seeing how modules will be used in community-based efforts, such as PoshCode and other script/module repositories.

Locating and Loading Modules

There are two default locations for Windows PowerShell modules. The first is located in the user's home directory, and the second is located in the Windows PowerShell home directory. The modules directory in the Windows PowerShell home directory always exists. However, the modules directory in the user's home directory is not present by default but only exists in the home directory if it has been created, which does not typically happen until someone decides to create and store modules there. A nice feature of the module directory is that, when it exists, it is the first place that Windows PowerShell searches for a module. If the user's modules directory does not exist, the modules directory within the Windows PowerShell home directory is used.

NOTES FROM THE FIELD

Using the Modules Directories Effectively

Andy Schneider, Systems Engineer
Author of the Get-PowerShell blog

To be honest, modules drove me nuts when I first started playing with them in Community Technology Preview 3 (CTP3). The Get-Module cmdlet by itself doesn't show you what modules are available, so you need to use Get-Module –ListAvailable. It also took me a while to discover the modules directories, which is where you need to store module files such as .psm1s, .psd1s, and .dlls. I was digging around the variables directory and discovered the *$PSModulePath* variable. You can use the following code snippet to see the different paths.

```
((ls env:PSModulepath).value).split(";")
```

$PSModulePath is very similar to the *$path* variable. It's a series of directories separated by a semicolon, which is why I used a split at the end of the code. (For additional information about using the *split* method, see the "Creating a New Modules Folder" section later in this chapter.) I typically use the first *$PSModulePath* that is available, which in my case is C:\Users\Andys\Documents\WindowsPowerShell\Modules. However, you don't actually put your .psm1 or .psd1 files directly into the modules directory. You must create a new directory within the modules directory in which to place your .psm1 and/or .psd1 files. For example, if you write a module for Microsoft SharePoint, you will create the C:\Users\Andy\Documents\WindowsPowerShell\Modules\Sharepoint directory into which you can drop SharePoint.psm1 and/or SharePoint.psd1. Then the magic begins. Be sure to use the same name for your directory as your .psm1 and .psd1 files.

You can find out which modules are available by using Get-Module *–ListAvailable* to search for them. The *–ListAvailable* option looks in all of the modules directories for subdirectories, such as my SharePoint directory. Once the SharePoint directory is located, *–ListAvailable* looks for a .psd1 file first, then a .psm1 file, and then any .dlls. If the Get-Module cmdlet finds the module, Get-Module will list the module as available to be imported by using the Import-Module cmdlet. In this case, if I issue the Import-Module SharePoint command, I will get all of the exported functions that I wrote. After the import, I typically use the Get-Command cmdlet to determine which functions and/or cmdlets come with a module. Because there is a new Get-Command parameter named *–module*, using Get-Command –module SharePoint will list all of the exported cmdlets and functions in the SharePoint module.

Listing Available Modules

Windows PowerShell modules exist in two states: loaded and unloaded. To display a list of all loaded modules, you can use the Get-Module cmdlet without any parameters as shown here.

```
PS C:\> Get-Module
```

```
ModuleType Name            ExportedCommands
---------- ----            ----------------
Script     helloworld      {Hello-World, Hello-User}
```

If multiple modules are loaded when the Get-Module cmdlet is run, each module will be listed and its accompanying exported commands will appear on their own individual lines as shown here.

```
PS C:\> Get-Module

ModuleType Name                        ExportedCommands
---------- ----                        ----------------
Script     GetFreeDiskSpace            Get-FreeDiskSpace
Script     HelloWorld                  {Hello-World, Hello-User}
Script     TextFunctions               {New-Line, Get-TextStats}
Manifest   BitsTransfer                {Start-BitsTransfer, Remove-BitsTransfe...
Script     PSDiagnostics               {Enable-PSTrace, Enable-WSManTrace, Sta...

PS C:\>
```

If no modules are loaded, nothing is displayed to the Windows PowerShell console. No errors are displayed, and there is no confirmation that the command was actually run as shown here.

```
PS C:\> Get-Module
PS C:\>
```

To obtain a listing of all modules that are available on the system but are not loaded into the Windows PowerShell console, you can use the Get-Module cmdlet with the *–ListAvailable* parameter as shown here.

```
PS C:\> Get-Module -ListAvailable

ModuleType Name                        ExportedCommands
---------- ----                        ----------------
Manifest   GetFreeDiskSpace            Get-FreeDiskSpace
Script     HelloWorld                  {}
Script     TextFunctions               {}
Manifest   BitsTransfer                {}
Manifest   PSDiagnostics               {Enable-PSTrace, Enable-WSManTrace, Sta...
```

Name Validation and the Import-Module cmdlet

Dan Harman, Program Manager
Microsoft Corporation

With Windows PowerShell 1.0, we took the approach of exposing the function naming rules strictly as design guidelines with no enforcement mechanism or other restrictions in the PowerShell engine itself. However, we are concerned that, with the rapidly accelerating adoption of Windows PowerShell 2.0, we are going to see a proliferation of people deviating from the guidelines whether through a lack of knowledge of the guidelines, a different viewpoint about what the guidelines should be, or refusal to adhere to the guidelines for one reason or another. We spent a considerable amount of time debating what level-checking to perform and how violations should be exposed to the user. With the introduction of modules in version 2.0, we have a one-time opportunity to perform at least some level of verification on imported commands against the guidelines.

The following list is a detailed description of the name validation behavior that we added to the `Import-Module` cmdlet. `Import-Module` evaluates imported commands according to the following guidelines.

1. Hyphenated command names can have exactly one hyphen, and the hyphen symbol is typed by using a single key on the keyboard. The figure dash, en dash, em dash, horizontal bar, or other types of dashes are not to be used.

2. When a command name includes a hyphen, the characters preceding the hyphen constitute the verb and the characters following the hyphen constitute the noun.

3. Hyphenated commands can only use approved verbs.

4. Hyphenated command names cannot include characters prohibited by the cmdlet design guidelines: # , ( ) { } [ ] & - / \ $ ^ ; : " ' < > | ? @ ` * % + = ~.

5. Only hyphenated function and cmdlet names are evaluated against the naming guidelines; aliases, variables, and nonhyphenated functions or cmdlets are not evaluated.

6. Commands are evaluated against the guidelines irrespective of module type (manifest, script, or binary). However, commands from dynamic modules created with `New-Module` are not checked.

7. If `Import-Module` encounters one or more commands that violate the guidelines, the command is still imported but warnings are displayed.

8. For nonapproved verbs, the following warning is displayed.

    ```
    Some imported command names include unapproved verbs which might make
    them less discoverable. Use the Verbose parameter for more detail or
    type Get-Verb to see the list of approved verbs.
    ```

9. For restricted characters, the following warning is displayed.

    ```
    Some imported command names contain one or more of the following
    restricted characters: # , ( ) { } [ ] & - / \ $ ^ ; : " ' < > | ? @ `
    * % + = ~.
    ```

10. Only a single warning for nonapproved verbs is displayed per imported module regardless of the number of violating commands. Similarly, only a single restricted characters warning is displayed per module. Importing a module can display at most two warnings for imported commands: one for nonapproved verbs and one for restricted characters.

11. Warnings are only displayed for modules that are imported using `Import-Module` or the Windows PowerShell Application Programming Interface (API); warnings cannot be suppressed when using the API. Warnings are not displayed with nested modules imported through a manifest.

12. Using the *–verbose* switch on `Import-Module` provides additional detail on command naming violations.

13. Warnings display which commands are using restricted characters.

    ```
    The command name '<bad command>' contains one or more of the following
    restricted characters: # , ( ) { } [ ] & - / \ $ ^ ; : " ' < > | ? @ `
    * % + = ~.
    ```

14. Warnings display which commands are using nonapproved verbs.

15. For nonapproved verbs, if the verb is on the "do not use" list, the recommended approved verb is also displayed as follows.

    ```
    The command name '<bad command>' includes an unapproved verb which
    might make it less discoverable. The suggested alternative verbs are
    "<approved verb>", "<approved verb>", "<approved verb>".
    ```

16. Users can suppress warnings about command names by specifying the *DisableNameChecking* switch on `Import-Module`.

17. The *Get-Verb* function can be used to obtain the list of approved verbs.

We realize that some products might already have shipped with commands that don't adhere to the guidelines. As these products move forward in future releases, our recommendation is that the command names should be changed to adhere to the guidelines. To avoid breaking scripts that were written using the old commands, you can create aliases for the old commands that map to the new names. Because we do not perform name-checking on aliases, you won't receive a warning for these aliases as long as you've changed the underlying function/cmdlet to use approved naming conventions.

Loading Modules

Once you identify a module that you want to load, you can use the `Import-Module` cmdlet to load the module into the current Windows PowerShell session as shown here.

```
PS C:\> Import-Module -Name GetFreeDiskSpace
PS C:\>
```

If the module exists, the `Import-Module` cmdlet completes without displaying any information. If the module is already loaded, no error message is displayed as shown here. Using the up arrow retrieves the previous command, and pressing Enter executes the command. The `Import-Module` command is run three times.

```
PS C:\> Import-Module -Name GetFreeDiskSpace
PS C:\> Import-Module -Name GetFreeDiskSpace
PS C:\> Import-Module -Name GetFreeDiskSpace
PS C:\>
```

Once you import the module, you might want to use the `Get-Module` cmdlet to quickly see what functions are exposed by the module as shown here.

```
PS C:\> Get-Module -Name GetFreeDiskSpace


ModuleType Name                    ExportedCommands
---------- ----                    ----------------
Script     GetFreeDiskSpace        Get-FreeDiskSpace


PS C:\>
```

As shown in the previous example, the GetFreeDiskSpace module exports a single command, the *Get-FreeDiskSpace* function. The one problem with using the `Get-Module` cmdlet is that it only lists commands and does not include other information that can be exported by the module.

When working with modules that have long names, you are not limited to typing the entire module name. You are allowed to use wildcards. It is a best practice to type a significant portion of the module name when using wildcards to load modules so that you only match a single module from the list of modules that are available to you as shown here.

```
PS C:\> Import-Module -Name GetFree*
PS C:\>
```

> **IMPORTANT** If you use a wildcard pattern that matches more than one module name, the first matched module is loaded, and the remaining matches are discarded. This can lead to inconsistent and unpredictable results. No error message is displayed when more than one module matches a wildcard pattern.

If you want to load all of the modules that are available on your system, you can use the `Get-Module` cmdlet with the *–ListAvailable* parameter and pipeline the resulting *PSModuleInfo* objects to the `Import-Module` cmdlet as shown here.

```
PS C:\> Get-Module -ListAvailable | Import-Module
PS C:\>
```

If one of your modules uses a verb that is not on the allowed verb list, a warning message is displayed when you import the module. The functions in the module still work and the module will work, but the warning is displayed to remind you to check the authorized verb list as shown here.

```
PS C:\> Get-Module -ListAvailable | Import-Module
WARNING: Some imported command names include unapproved verbs which might make
them less discoverable. Use the Verbose parameter for more detail or type
Get-Verb to see the list of approved verbs.
PS C:\>
```

To obtain additional information about which unapproved verbs are being used, you can use the *–verbose* switch of the `Import-Module` cmdlet as shown here.

```
PS C:\> Get-Module -ListAvailable | Import-Module -Verbose
```

Results of the `Import-Module` *–verbose* command are shown in Figure 11-1.

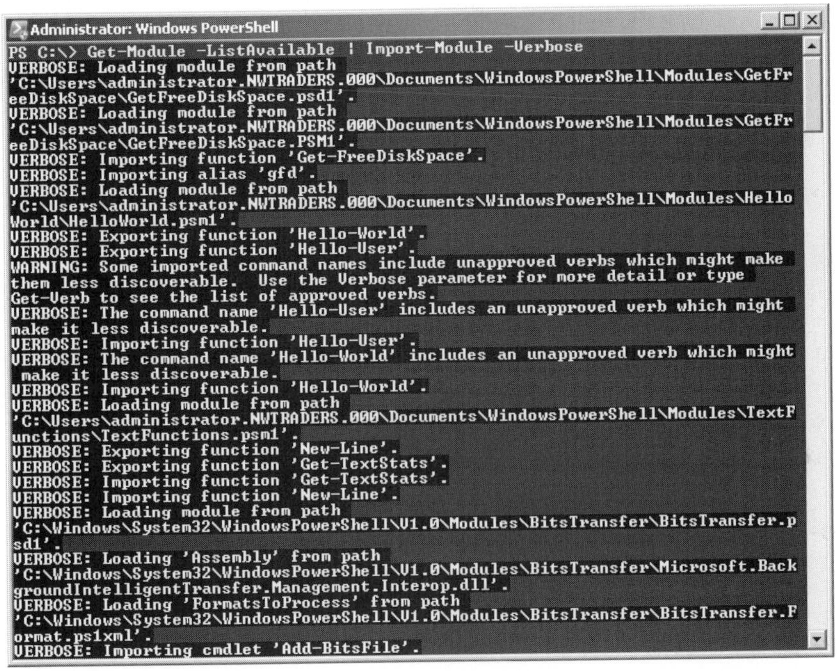

FIGURE 11-1 The *–verbose* parameter of `Import-Module` displays information about each function as well as illegal verb names.

Installing Modules

One of the features of modules is that they can be installed without elevated rights. Because each user has rights to use the Modules folder in their %UserProfile% directory, the installation of a module does not require administrator rights. An additional feature of modules is that they do not require a specialized installer. The files associated with a module can be copied by using the XCopy utility or Windows PowerShell cmdlets.

Creating a User's Modules Folder

The user's Modules folder does not exist by default. To avoid confusion, you might decide to create the modules directory in the user's profile prior to deploying modules. Or, you might simply create a module installer script that checks for the existence of the user's Modules folder, creates the folder if it does not exist, and then copies the modules.

Locating the Directory Based on the Operating System

One problem encountered when directly accessing the user's modules directory is that it can be found in a different location depending on the version of the operating system. In Microsoft Windows XP and Windows Server 2003, the user's Modules folder is located in the My Documents folder. In Windows Vista and above, the user's Modules folder is located in the Documents folder. In the Copy-Modules.ps1 script, the problem of different Modules folder locations is solved by using the *Get-OperatingSystemVersion* function, which retrieves the major version number of the operating system. The *Get-OperatingSystemVersion* function is shown here.

```
Function Get-OperatingSystemVersion
{
 (Get-WmiObject -Class Win32_OperatingSystem).Version
} #end Get-OperatingSystemVersion
```

The major version number of the operating system is used in the *Test-ModulePath* function. If the major version number is greater than 6, it means that the operating system is at least Windows Vista and therefore uses the Documents folder in the path to the modules. If the major version number of the operating system is not greater than 6, the script uses the My Documents folder for the module location. Once the version of the operating system is determined and the path to the module location is ascertained, it is time to determine whether the Modules folder exists.

INSIDE TRACK

All About Modules

James Brundage, Software Developer Engineer In Test
Microsoft Corporation

Modules make life easier in Windows PowerShell by allowing you to group code so that it's easier to pull in the code all at once and easier to isolate. Logically grouping your scripts saves you the trouble of typing. You can then run `Import-Module "WMI"` instead of dot-sourcing dozens of Windows Management Instrumentation (WMI) files. Isolating your code saves trouble so that two scripts can use a persistent variable named *$count* without interfering with each other.

A Windows PowerShell module can be one of five things.

- A module can be a single script containing functions with the extension .psm1. To access this behavior, you can simply rename a .ps1 file that contains functions with the .psm1 extension. When you import this module, the functions are pulled into your current session (similar to when you dot-source a script), but the variables and aliases are not pulled in. These single-file modules are called script modules.

```
Example .psm1 Content:
Function Get-Usb() {
    Get-WmiObject Win32_USBControllerDevice |
        Foreach-Object { [Wmi]$_.Dependent }
}
```

- A module can be a collection of scripts. To create a module in this way, you can simply take a collection of files that is normally dot-sourced and put them in a single directory. You can then create a script module (.psm1) file with a name describing the module's function (for example, WMI). In that file, you can put a number of lines of code that dot-source the .psm1 file relative to the location of the module, which will be in an environment variable named *$psScriptRoot*. This is the module type that I personally use most often because it cleanly and logically separates my scripts. These modules are called multiple-file modules.

```
Example .psm1 Content:
. $psScriptRoot\Get-USB.ps1
```

- A module can be a compiled assembly containing cmdlets, providers, hosts, or useful classes. Any Windows PowerShell 1.0 snap-in can be used as a module, but you do not need to use an install utility to install the snap-in. Thus, it becomes easier to use snap-ins because you no longer need to be an administrator to install the snap-ins and you do not need to worry whether the snap-in is running a 32-bit or 64-bit version (this is a very common mistake with third-party Windows PowerShell snap-in installers). These modules are called binary modules.

- A module can be created from a script block with the New-Module cmdlet. You can use this technique to create a function containing some persistent information without worrying about leaking the information and without defining a file for the script block to inhabit or a name for the module. These modules are called dynamic modules.

```
Example:
New-Module {
    $count =0
    function Get-Count() {
        $script:count++
        $count
    }
}
```

- A script or binary module can optionally include a module manifest (.psd1) file. Module manifests allow you to describe the properties of a script or binary module and how to load it. You can provide type or format data in a module manifest as well as declare dependencies and prerequisites. The main module to be loaded will be specified within a module manifest in the ModuleToProcess field, which should be the .psm1 or .dll of the module you're going to load. You can create a module manifest with the New-ModuleManifest cmdlet.

A module can live anywhere. However, by putting modules in one of two predefined locations, Windows PowerShell is able to import the module more easily. These locations are stored in the *$PSModulePath* environment variable (*$env:PSModulePath*), which can be changed to include additional locations. By default, *$PSModulePath* includes locations at *$psHome\Modules* and *$env:UserProfile\Documents\WindowsPowerShell\Modules*. If there's a subdirectory beneath either module path or a .psd1, .psm1, or .dll file with the same name, then Import-Module "ModuleName" imports the module. For example, if WMI. psm1 is within a directory named WMI in C:\Users\James Brundage\Documents \WindowsPowerShell\Modules, then I can simply put Import-Module "WMI" in my profile and everything included in the module will always be loaded.

By default, script modules and dynamic modules only import the functions in the file and hide any aliases or variables defined within the module. If you want to make these aliases or variables available in your Windows PowerShell session or if you want to hide a few functions, you can use the Export-ModuleMember cmdlet within the module to determine what information is exported.

```
New-Module {
    $script:count =0
    function Get-Count() {
        $script:count++
        $count
    }
    Set-Alias count Get-Count
    Export-ModuleMember -Alias count -Function Get-Count -Variable count
}
```

Checking for an Existing Folder

The best tool to use for checking the existence of folders is the Test-Path cmdlet, which returns a Boolean value. Because you are only interested in the absence of the folder, you can use the *–not* operator as shown here in the completed *Test-ModulePath* function.

```
Function Test-ModulePath
{
 $VistaPath = "$env:userProfile\documents\WindowsPowerShell\Modules"
 $XPPath =  "$env:Userprofile\my documents\WindowsPowerShell\Modules"
 if ([int](Get-OperatingSystemVersion).substring(0,1) -ge 6)
   {
     if(-not(Test-Path -path $VistaPath))
       {
          New-Item -Path $VistaPath -itemtype directory | Out-Null
       } #end if
   } #end if
 Else
   {
     if(-not(Test-Path -path $XPPath))
       {
          New-Item -path $XPPath -itemtype directory | Out-Null
       } #end if
   } #end else
} #end Test-ModulePath
```

Creating a New Modules Folder

Once the user's Modules folder is created, it is time to create a child folder to hold the new module. A module is always installed into a folder that has the same name as the module itself. The name of the module is the file name that contains the module minus the .psm1 extension. This location is shown in Figure 11-2.

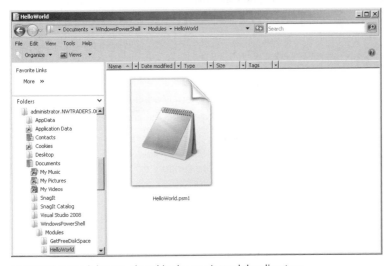

FIGURE 11-2 Modules are placed in the user's modules directory.

In the *Copy-Module* function from the Copy-Modules.ps1 script, the first action that is taken is to retrieve the value of the *$PSModulePath* environmental variable. Because there are two locations in which modules can be stored, the *$PSModulePath* environmental variable contains the path to both locations. *$PSModulePath* is stored as a string and not as an array. The value contained in *$PSModulePath* is shown here.

```
PS C:\> $env:PSModulePath
C:\Users\administrator.NWTRADERS.000\Documents\WindowsPowerShell\Modules;C:
\Windows\System32\WindowsPowerShell\V1.0\Modules\
```

If you attempt to index into the data stored in the *$PSModulePath* environmental variable, you retrieve one letter at a time as shown here.

```
PS C:\> $env:PSModulePath[0]
C
PS C:\> $env:PSModulePath[1]
:
PS C:\> $env:PSModulePath[2]
\
PS C:\> $env:PSModulePath[3]
U
```

Attempting to retrieve the path to the user's module location one letter at a time is problematic at best and error prone at worst. Because the data is a string, you can use string methods to manipulate the two paths. To break a string into an array that can be used easily, you use the *split* method from the *System.String* class. You only need to pass a single value to the *split* method—the character at which to split. Because the value stored in the *$PSModulePath* variable is a string, you can access the *split* method directly as shown here.

```
PS C:\> $env:PSModulePath.split(";")
C:\Users\administrator.NWTRADERS.000\Documents\WindowsPowerShell\Modules
C:\Windows\System32\WindowsPowerShell\V1.0\Modules\
```

As you can see from the previous output, the first string displayed is the path to the user's Modules folder, and the second path is the path to the system Modules folder. Because the *split* method turns a string into an array, you can now index into the array and retrieve the path to the user's Modules folder by using the [0] syntax. You do not need to use an intermediate variable to store the returned array of paths if you do not want to do so. You can index into the returned array directly. If you use an intermediate variable to hold the returned array and then index into the array, the code resembles the following example.

```
PS C:\> $aryPaths = $env:PSModulePath.split(";")
PS C:\> $aryPaths[0]
C:\Users\administrator.NWTRADERS.000\Documents\WindowsPowerShell\Modules
```

Because the array is immediately available once the *split* method is called, you directly retrieve the user's modules path as shown here.

```
PS C:\> $env:PSModulePath.split(";")[0]
C:\Users\administrator.NWTRADERS.000\Documents\WindowsPowerShell\Modules
```

Short Code vs. Readable Code

When writing scripts with Windows PowerShell, there is almost always another way to write the same code. In the *Copy-Module* function in the Copy-Modules.ps1 script, I needed to make a decision between storing the array that is returned by the *split* method in an intermediate variable or returning the path to the user's Modules folder directly. In this particular instance, I decided to use the shorter syntax rather than using an intermediate variable. The cost is readability. When a script is more difficult to read, it also becomes more difficult to maintain and is also harder to modify.

I consider the readability of code to be one of the most important design guidelines for scripts. What is readable for one group of Windows PowerShell script writers may not be readable for another group. Therefore, you must set forth design guidelines for your organization. As long as everyone on the team knows what is going on and understands a particular construction, there is no reason not to use the construction. However, I recommend that if you decide to use a particular construction that may be difficult to understand, you can add a comment to the script that indicates what that construction is doing. Of course, once you add additional comments to the script, the short construction is not really shorter anymore, is it?

Working with the *$ModulePath* Variable

The path that is used to store the module is found in the *$ModulePath* variable. This path includes the path to the user's Modules folder plus a child folder with the same name as the module itself. To create the new path, it is a best practice to use the Join-Path cmdlet instead of doing string concatenation and attempting to manually build the path to the new folder. The Join-Path cmdlet puts together a parent and a child path to create a new path as shown here.

```
$ModulePath = Join-Path -path $userPath `
            -childpath (Get-Item -path $name).basename
```

In Windows PowerShell 2.0, the PowerShell team added a script property named *basename* to the *System.Io.FileInfo* class that makes it easy to retrieve the name of a file without the file extension. Prior to Windows PowerShell 2.0, it was common to use the *split* method or some other string manipulation technique to remote the extension from the file name. Use of the *basename* property is shown here.

```
PS C:\> (Get-Item -Path C:\fso\HelloWorld.psm1).basename
HelloWorld
```

The last step is to create the subdirectory that will hold the module and then to copy the module files into the directory. To avoid cluttering the display with the returned information from the New-Item and Copy-Item cmdlets, the results are pipelined to the Out-Null cmdlet as shown here.

```
New-Item -path $modulePath -itemtype directory | Out-Null
Copy-item -path $name -destination $ModulePath | Out-Null
```

The entry point to the Copy-Modules.ps1 script calls the *Test-ModulePath* function to determine whether the user's Modules folder exists. The script then uses the Get-ChildItem cmdlet to retrieve a listing of all of the module files in a particular folder. The *–recurse* parameter is used to retrieve all of the module files in the path. The resulting *FileInfo* objects are pipelined to the ForEach-Object cmdlet. The *FullName* property of each *FileInfo* object is passed to the *Copy-Module* function as shown here.

```
Test-ModulePath
Get-ChildItem -Path C:\fso -Include *.psm1,*.psd1 -Recurse |
Foreach-Object { Copy-Module -name $_.fullName }
```

The complete Copy-Modules.ps1 script is shown here.

```
Copy-Modules.ps1
Function Get-OperatingSystemVersion
{
 (Get-WmiObject -Class Win32_OperatingSystem).Version
} #end Get-OperatingSystemVersion

Function Test-ModulePath
{
 $VistaPath = "$env:userProfile\documents\WindowsPowerShell\Modules"
 $XPPath =  "$env:Userprofile\my documents\WindowsPowerShell\Modules"
 if ([int](Get-OperatingSystemVersion).substring(0,1) -ge 6)
   {
     if(-not(Test-Path -path $VistaPath))
       {
         New-Item -Path $VistaPath -itemtype directory | Out-Null
       } #end if
   } #end if
 Else
   {
     if(-not(Test-Path -path $XPPath))
       {
```

```
           New-Item -path $XPPath -itemtype directory | Out-Null
        } #end if
    } #end else
} #end Test-ModulePath


Function Copy-Module([string]$name)
{
 $UserPath = $env:PSModulePath.split(";")[0]
 $ModulePath = Join-Path -path $userPath `
               -childpath (Get-Item -path $name).basename
 New-Item -path $modulePath -itemtype directory | Out-Null
 Copy-item -path $name -destination $ModulePath | Out-Null
}


# *** Entry Point to Script ***
Test-ModulePath
Get-ChildItem -Path C:\fso -Include *.psm1,*.psd1 -Recurse |
Foreach-Object { Copy-Module -name $_.fullName }
```

NOTE Scripting support does not need to be enabled in Windows PowerShell to use modules. However, you do need scripting support to run Copy-Modules.ps1 to install modules to the user's profile. To enable scripting support in Windows PowerShell, you can use the `Set-ExecutionPolicy` cmdlet. You can also use the Xcopy utility to copy modules to the user's Modules folder.

Creating a Module Drive

An easy way to work with modules is to create a few Windows PowerShell drives using the filesystem provider. Because the modules live in a location to which it is not easy to navigate from the command line and because *$PSModulePath* returns a string that contains the path to both the user's and the system's Modules folders, it makes sense to provide an easier way to work with the location of the modules. To create a Windows PowerShell drive for the user module location, you can use the `New-PSDrive` cmdlet. Specify a name (such as mymods), use the filesystem provider, and obtain the root location from the *$PSModulePath* environmental variable by using the *split* method from the .NET Framework *String* class. For the user's Modules folder, you can use the first element from the returned array as shown here.

```
PS C:\> New-PSDrive -Name mymods -PSProvider filesystem -Root `
(($env:PSModulePath).Split(";")[0])


WARNING: column "CurrentLocation" does not fit into the display and was removed.
```

```
Name              Used (GB)      Free (GB) Provider       Root
----              ---------      --------- --------       ----
mymods                              47.62 FileSystem     C:\Users\administrator....
```

The command to create a Windows PowerShell drive for the system module location is exactly the same as the one used to create a PowerShell drive for the user module location with the exception of specifying a different name, such as sysmods, and choosing the second element from the array you obtain by using the split method from the $PSModulePath variable. This command is shown here.

```
PS C:\> New-PSDrive -Name sysmods -PSProvider filesystem -Root `
(($env:PSModulePath).Split(";")[1])


WARNING: column "CurrentLocation" does not fit into the display and was removed.

Name              Used (GB)      Free (GB) Provider       Root
----              ---------      --------- --------       ----
sysmods                             47.62 FileSystem     C:\Windows\System32\Win...
```

> **NOTE** I like to create my Windows PowerShell drives for the two module locations in my personal profile. In this way, the drives are always available when I need to use them.

You can also write a script that creates Windows PowerShell drives for each of the two module locations. To do this, you first create an array of names for the Windows PowerShell drives. You can then use a *for* statement to walk through the array of Windows PowerShell drive names and call the New-PSDrive cmdlet. Because you are running the commands inside a script, the new Windows PowerShell drives by default live within the script scope. Once the script ends, the script scope goes away. This means that the Windows PowerShell drives are not available once the script ends—which defeats our purposes in creating them in the first place. To combat this scoping issue, you must create the Windows PowerShell drives within the global scope so that they will be available in the PowerShell console once the script is through running. To avoid displaying confirmation messages when creating the Windows PowerShell drives, you pipe the results to the Out-Null cmdlet.

Another function is created in the New-ModulesDrive.ps1 script. This function displays global filesystem Windows PowerShell drives. When the script is run, the *New-ModuleDrives* function is called followed by the *Get-FileSystemDrives* function. The complete New-ModulesDrive.ps1 script is shown here.

New-ModulesDrive.ps1

```
Function New-ModuleDrives
{
<#
    .SYNOPSIS
    Creates two PSDrives: myMods and sysMods
    .EXAMPLE
    New-ModuleDrives
    Creates two PSDrives: myMods and sysMods. These correspond
    to the user's Modules folder and the system Modules folder respectively.
#>
 $driveNames = "myMods","sysMods"

 For($i = 0 ; $i -le 1 ; $i++)
 {
  New-PsDrive -name $driveNames[$i] -PSProvider filesystem `
  -Root ($env:PSModulePath.split(";")[$i]) -scope Global |
  Out-Null
 } #end For
} #end New-ModuleDrives


Function Get-FileSystemDrives
{
<#
    .SYNOPSIS
    Displays global PS Drives that use the filesystem provider
    .EXAMPLE
    Get-FileSystemDrives
    Displays global PS Drives that use the filesystem provider
#>
 Get-PSDrive -PSProvider FileSystem -scope Global
} #end Get-FileSystemDrives


# *** EntryPoint to Script ***
New-ModuleDrives
Get-FileSystemDrives
```

Including Functions by Dot-Sourcing

In Windows PowerShell 1.0, you can include functions from previously written scripts by dot-sourcing the script. This technique still works in Windows PowerShell 2.0, and it offers the advantage of simplicity and familiarity. You might want to use the dot-sourcing technique to work with functions in scripts written in Windows PowerShell 1.0 because it is easier than creating a module and copying the files into the modules directory. In addition, functions that do not conform to the verb-noun naming convention and that do not use approved verbs (available by using the Get-Verbs cmdlet) will generate a warning message that is very distracting to users. For new development work, you will want to use modules because of the advantages that they offer. However, for ease of use with existing functions and scripts, the dot-source methodology is quicker and easier to use.

In this section, we examine what happens when functions are dot-sourced. Because you can dot-source functions into your modules, it is important to understand exactly what is happening when you dot-source. Due to their very nature, modules tend to be more permanent than scripts. In addition, they may not be as well understood as a script due to the way in which they are stored in special directories. Both the permanent nature and the unseen nature of the module demand that the writer of the module knows exactly what the module does and does not do.

Chapter 9, "Designing Functions," discussed the creation of functions. When functions are put into modules, you must ensure that you are following best practices in function design, naming conventions, and help.

INSIDE TRACK

cmdlet and Function Naming Guidelines

Dan Harman, Program Manager
Microsoft Corporation

In Windows PowerShell 1.0, we published a set of cmdlet design guidelines on MSDN that included direction on how to properly name cmdlets. Throughout the Windows PowerShell 2.0 development cycle, we saw an increase in cmdlet authors deviating from the standards in disconcerting ways. This led to a series of discussions on our team about an appropriate course of action for Windows PowerShell 2.0. The outcome of those discussions includes changes to the Import-Module cmdlet from which we perform name-checking on imported commands. We decided to allow unapproved verbs or characters (that is, the import succeeds), but we display a warning on the import of commands that use unapproved verbs or characters as a user-visible speed bump to more strongly encourage the right behavior. We believe we have provided improved guidance and mitigation that will help curb departures from the guidelines, reinforce the need to adhere to the prescribed naming format, and provide a clear path from version 1.0 to version 2.0 and beyond.

First, it's helpful to look at what we've done in version 2.0 as the basis for determining what guidance should be provided, both for those implementing on version 1.0 only as well as for those targeting version 2.0 or those looking to move eventually to version 2.0. In version 2.0, we're using modules as the primary mechanism to address the issues of namespaces, code isolation, and naming collisions, so this is where we've targeted some changes.

Regarding modules, we've provided a few options as described in the following guidelines.

- Name your commands using approved verbs only. While every technology has its own domain-specific language with which users of that technology are comfortable and understand, these terms have different meanings or are nonexistent when used outside that technology. This key stumbling block prevents the reuse of knowledge and skills across technology boundaries. As a broad automation and management platform that spans multiple technologies, Windows PowerShell helps break down these knowledge silos with a standard set of command verbs that are used across all technologies and domains.

- Structure your commands as verb-noun pairs. Windows PowerShell has built-in facilities, such as `Get-Command -Verb` and `Get-Command -Noun`, that make it easier to explore the system, group related commands, and find the command you're looking for to complete the task without always resorting to documentation or an in-depth knowledge of the technology.

- Prefix your nouns with a short, unique, technology-specific moniker, such as an alphanumeric moniker that doesn't include extra characters or symbols like colons or slashes. Because we don't want our built-in commands in Windows PowerShell to clash with other commands, we use the prefix PS. The Active Directory team prefixes all of their command nouns with AD, such as `Get-ADUser`, which makes it easy to use `Get-Command -Noun AD*` to find all of the AD cmdlets.

- Use a snap-in or module qualifier where name collisions exist. Since version 1.0, Windows PowerShell has the ability to reference a command using a fully qualified name. In version 1.0, this process is accomplished by specifying the snap-in that contains the command followed by a backslash followed by the command name as shown in the following example.

```
Microsoft.WSMan.Management\Connect-WSMan
Microsoft.PowerShell.Core\Get-History
```

- In version 2.0, you can also use the module name as the qualifier as shown in the following example.

```
BitsTransfer\Add-BitsFile
ServerManager\Get-WindowsFeature
```

- You can use the previously described qualifiers to ensure that scripts are always using the correct command. In version 1.0 scripts, you can use explicit naming with snap-in qualifiers. When migrating those scripts to version 2.0, no changes are required if the module name matches the snap-in name. Regarding modules in version 2.0 whose imported names collide with existing names, the last imported name overwrites or shadows the existing name. Therefore, you can alternatively add a call to `Import-Module` at the top of the script and use implicit, nonqualified names. You can still access the shadowed name using the fully qualified syntax, if necessary.

- Snap-in names are often long and unwieldy to type. However, with modules in version 2.0, you can use a module manifest to abstract long, ugly assembly names with a short, pithy module name. "BitsTransfer" is much easier to type than "Microsoft.BackgroundIntelligentTransferService.Management.Interop" as a module qualifier.

- As consumers of a module, users are given additional control with the *–Prefix* parameter in Import-Module, which allows custom prefixing on imported commands.

In the TextFunctions.ps1 script, two functions are created. The first function is named *New-Line*, and the second function is named *Get-TextStats*. The TextFunctions.ps1 script is shown here.

TextFunctions.ps1
```
Function New-Line([string]$stringIn)
{
 "-" * $stringIn.length
} #end New-Line


Function Get-TextStats([string[]]$textIn)
{
 $textIn | Measure-Object -Line -word -char
} #end Get-TextStats
```

The *New-Line* function creates a line that is the length of input text, which is helpful when you want an underline for text-separation purposes that is sized to the text. Traditional Microsoft VBScript users copy the function they need to use into a separate file and run the newly produced script. An example of using the *New-Line* text function in this manner is shown here.

CallNew-LineTextFunction.ps1
```
Function New-Line([string]$stringIn)
{
 "-" * $stringIn.length
} #end New-Line


Function Get-TextStats([string[]]$textIn)
{
 $textIn | Measure-Object -Line -word -char
} #end Get-TextStats


# *** Entry Point to script ***
"This is a string" | ForEach-Object  {$_ ; New-Line $_}
```

When the script runs, it returns the following output.

```
This is a string
----------------
```

Of course, this technique is a bit inefficient and limits your ability to use the functions. If you have to copy the entire text of a function into each new script you want to produce or edit a script each time you want to use a function in a different manner, you dramatically increase your workload. If the functions are available all of the time, you might be inclined to use the functions more often.

To make the text functions available in your current Windows PowerShell console, you need to dot-source the script containing the functions into your console. You need to use the entire path to the script unless the folder that contains the script is in your search path. The syntax to dot-source a script is very easy, so much so that it actually becomes a stumbling block for some people who are expecting a complex formula or cmdlet with obscure parameters. The command is none of that—just a period (dot) and the path to the script that contains the function, which is why it is called dot-sourcing: you have a dot and the source (path) to the functions you want to include as shown here.

```
PS C:\> . C:\fso\TextFunctions.ps1
```

Once you include the functions into your current console, all of the functions in the source script are added to the function drive as shown in Figure 11-3.

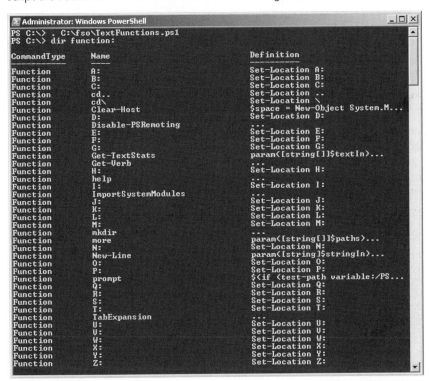

FIGURE 11-3 Functions from a dot-sourced script are available via the function drive.

Once the functions are introduced to the current console, you can incorporate them into your normal commands. This flexibility can also influence the way that you write functions. If functions are written so that they accept pipelined input and do not change the system environment (such as by adding global variables), you will be much more likely to use the functions, and they will be less likely to conflict with either functions or cmdlets that are present in the current console.

As an example of using the *New-Line* function, consider the fact that the Get-WmiObject cmdlet allows the use of an array of computer names for the *−computername* parameter. The problem is that the output is confusing because you do not know which piece of information is associated with which output as shown here.

```
PS C:\> Get-WmiObject -Class Win32_bios -ComputerName berlin, vista


SMBIOSBIOSVersion : 080002
Manufacturer      : American Megatrends Inc.
Name              : BIOS Date: 02/22/06 20:54:49  Ver: 08.00.02
SerialNumber      : 2096-1160-0447-0846-3027-2471-99
Version           : A M I  - 2000622

SMBIOSBIOSVersion : 080002
Manufacturer      : American Megatrends Inc.
Name              : BIOS Date: 02/22/06 20:54:49  Ver: 08.00.02
SerialNumber      : 2716-2298-1514-1558-4398-7113-73
Version           : A M I  - 2000622
```

You can improve the display of information returned by the Get-WmiObject cmdlet by pipelining the output to the *New-Line* function so that you can underline each computer name as it comes across the pipeline. You do not need to write a script to produce this type of display because you can type the command directly into the Windows PowerShell console. The first thing you need to do is dot-source the TextFunctions.ps1 script, which makes the functions directly available in the current Windows PowerShell console session. You then use the same *Get-WmiObject* query you used earlier to obtain BIOS information via WMI from two computers. You can pipeline the resulting management objects to the ForEach-Object cmdlet. Inside the script block section, you can use the *$_* automatic variable to reference the current object on the pipeline and retrieve the *System.Management.ManagementPath* object. From the *ManagementPath* object, you can obtain the name of the server that is supplying the information. You send this information to the *New-Line* function so that the server name is underlined, and you display the BIOS information that is contained in the *$_* variable.

> **NOTE** Revealing the *System.Management.ManagementPath* object via the *Path* property is a feature of Windows PowerShell 2.0. This example does not work in Windows PowerShell 1.0. To achieve the same results, you can use the __*Server* system property from the *System.Management.ManagementObject* class that is returned by the *Get-WmiObject* WMI query.

The command to import the *New-Line* function into the current Windows PowerShell session and use it to underline the server names is shown here.

```
PS C:\> . C:\fso\TextFunctions.ps1
PS C:\> Get-WmiObject -Class win32_Bios -ComputerName vista, berlin |
>> ForEach-Object { $_.Path.Server ; New-Line $_.Path.Server ; $_ }
```

The results of using the *New-Line* function are shown in Figure 11-4.

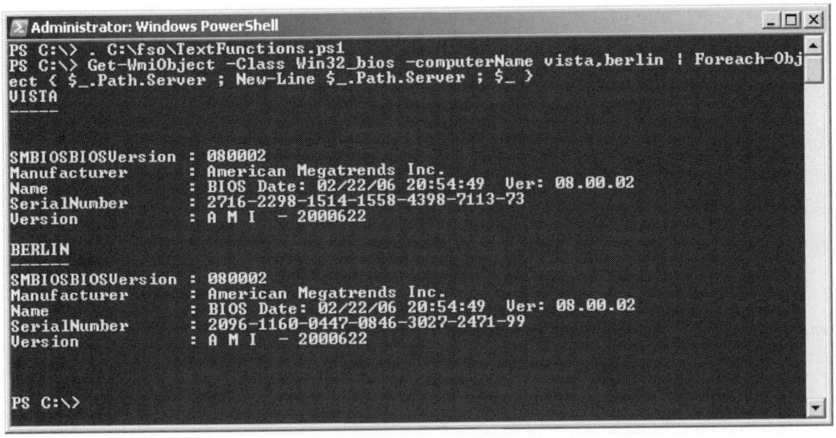

FIGURE 11-4 Functions that are written to accept pipelined input find an immediate use in your daily work routine.

Get-TextStats from the TextFunctions.ps1 script provides statistics based on an input text file or text string. Once the TextFunctions.ps1 script is dot-sourced into the current console, the statistics it returns when the function is called are word count, number of lines in the file, and number of characters. An example of using this function is shown here.

```
Get-TextStats "This is a string"
```

When the *Get-TextStats* function is used, the following output is produced.

```
      Lines              Words        Characters Property
      -----              -----        ---------- --------
        1                  4              16
```

Adding Help for Functions

Because Windows PowerShell modules contain functions that are loaded into a PowerShell environment, it is important that the parameters and use of the functions are documented. You encounter the same problem when dot-sourcing functions into the current Windows PowerShell console. Because you are not required to open the file that contains the function to use it, you might be unaware of all that the file contains. In addition to functions, the file might contain variables, aliases, Windows PowerShell drives, or any number of other possibilities. Depending on what you are actually trying to accomplish, the addition of these files may or may not be an issue. However, the need arises to have access to help information about the features provided by the Windows PowerShell script.

In Windows PowerShell 1.0, you can solve this problem by adding a *–help* parameter to the function and storing the help text within a here-string. You can use this approach in Windows PowerShell 2.0 as well, but there is a better approach to providing help for functions as shown in the next section.

Using a Here-String for Help

When documenting functions that are added to modules, you can use the classic here-string approach for help as shown in the GetWmiClassesFunction.ps1 script. This technique is covered in detail in Chapter 10, "Designing Help for Scripts." The first step is to define a switched parameter named *$help*. The second step involves creating and displaying the results of a here-string that includes help information. The GetWmiClassesFunction.ps1 script is shown here.

GetWmiClassesFunction.ps1
```
Function Get-WmiClasses(
                $class=($paramMissing=$true),
                $ns="root\cimv2",
                [switch]$help
                )
{
  If($help)
   {
    $helpstring = @"
    NAME
       Get-WmiClasses
    SYNOPSIS
       Displays a list of WMI Classes based upon a search criteria
    SYNTAX
       Get-WmiClasses [[-class] [string]] [[-ns] [string]] [-help]
    EXAMPLE
       Get-WmiClasses -class disk -ns root\cimv2"
       This command finds wmi classes that contain the word disk. The
       classes returned are from the root\cimv2 namespace.
"@
    $helpString
      break #exits the function early
   }
  If($local:paramMissing)
   {
      throw "USAGE: Get-WmiClasses -class <class type> -ns <wmi namespace>"
   } #$local:paramMissing
```

```
"`nClasses in $ns namespace ...."
Get-WmiObject -namespace $ns -list |
where-object {
                $_.name -match $class -and `
                $_.name -notlike 'cim*'
            }
    # mred function
} #end get-wmi2
```

The here-string technique works fairly well in providing function help; if you follow the cmdlet help pattern, the function looks good as shown in Figure 11-5.

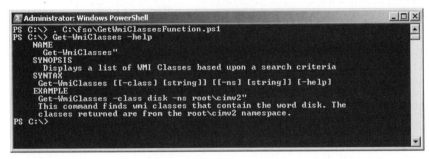

FIGURE 11-5 Manually created help can mimic the look of core cmdlet help.

The problem with manually creating help for a function is that it is tedious work. As a result, only the most important functions receive help information when using this methodology. This situation is unfortunate because it then requires the user to memorize the details of the function contract. One way to work around this scenario is to use the Get-Content cmdlet to retrieve the code that is used to create the function, which is much easier to do than searching for the script that is used to create the function and opening it in Microsoft Notepad. To use the Get-Content cmdlet to display the contents of a function, you can type **Get-Content** and supply the path to the function. All functions available to the current Windows PowerShell environment are available via the PowerShell function drive. You can therefore use the following syntax to obtain the content of a function.

```
PowerShell C:\> Get-Content Function:\Get-WmiClasses
```

The technique of using Get-Content to read the text of the function is shown in Figure 11-6.

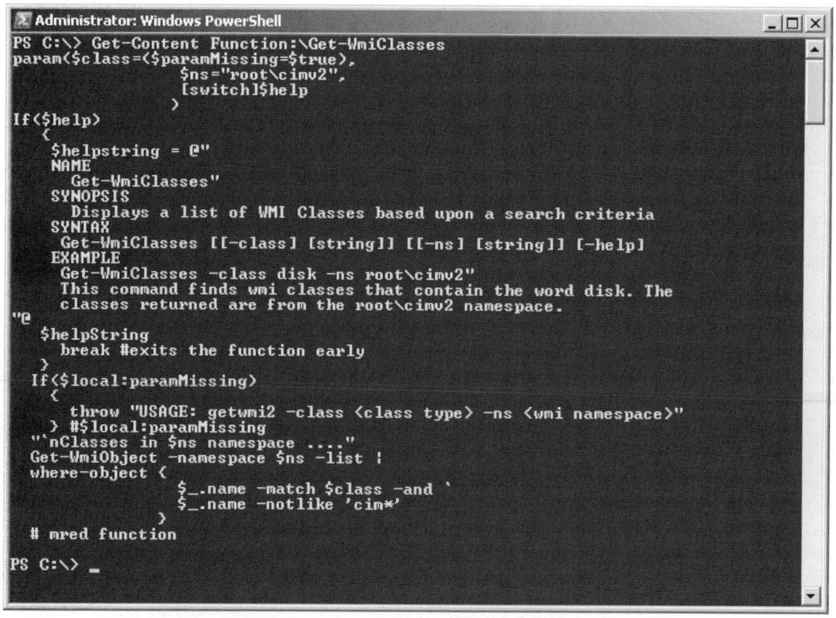

```
PS C:\> Get-Content Function:\Get-WmiClasses
param($class=($paramMissing=$true),
               $ns="root\cimv2",
               [switch]$help
               )
If($help)
   {
      $helpstring = @"
      NAME
         Get-WmiClasses"
      SYNOPSIS
         Displays a list of WMI Classes based upon a search criteria
      SYNTAX
         Get-WmiClasses [[-class] [string]] [[-ns] [string]] [-help]
      EXAMPLE
         Get-WmiClasses -class disk -ns root\cimv2"
         This command finds wmi classes that contain the word disk. The
         classes returned are from the root\cimv2 namespace.
"@
   $helpString
      break #exits the function early
   }
   If($local:paramMissing)
   {
      throw "USAGE: getwmi2 -class <class type> -ns <wmi namespace>"
   } #$local:paramMissing
"`nClasses in $ns namespace ...."
Get-WmiObject -namespace $ns -list |
where-object {
               $_.name -match $class -and `
               $_.name -notlike 'cim*'
            }
   # mred function

PS C:\> _
```

FIGURE 11-6 The Get-Content cmdlet can retrieve the contents of a function.

Using Help Function Tags to Produce Help

Much of the intensive work of producing help information for your functions is removed when you use the stylized help function tags that are available in Windows PowerShell 2.0. To use the help function tags, you place the tags inside the block comment tags when you are writing your script. Writing help information for your function by employing the help tags allows for complete integration with the Get-Help cmdlet, thus providing a seamless user experience for anyone who uses your functions. In addition, help tags promote the custom user-defined function to the same status within Windows PowerShell as native cmdlets. The experience of using a custom user-defined function is no different than using a cmdlet, and to the user, there is indeed no need to distinguish among a custom function that is dot-sourced, loaded via a module, or a native cmdlet. The help function tags and their associated meanings are shown in Table 11-1.

TABLE 11-1 Function Help Tags and Meanings

HELP TAG NAME	HELP TAG DESCRIPTION
.Synopsis	A very brief description of the function. It begins with a verb and informs the user as to what the function does. It does not include the function name or how the function works. The function synopsis tag appears in the SYNOPSIS field of all help views.

HELP TAG NAME	HELP TAG DESCRIPTION
.Description	Two or three full sentences that briefly list everything that the function can do. It begins with "The <function name> function...." If the function can receive multiple objects or take multiple inputs, use plural nouns in the description. The Description tag appears in the DESCRIPTION field of all help views.
.Parameter	Brief and thorough. Describes what the function does when the parameter is used and what legal values are set for the parameter. The Parameter tag appears in the PARAMETERS field only in the Detailed and Full help views.
.Example	Illustrates use of the function with all of its parameters. The first example is the simplest by showing only the required parameters. The last example is the most complex and should incorporate pipelining if appropriate. The Example tag only appears in the EXAMPLES field in the Example, Detailed, and Full help views.
.Inputs	Lists the .NET Framework classes of objects that the function accepts as input. There is no limit to the number of input classes you can list. The inputs tag appears only in the INPUTS field in the Full help view.
.Outputs	Lists the .NET Framework classes of objects that the function emits as output. There is no limit to the number of output classes you can list. The outputs tag appears in the OUTPUTS field only in the Full help view.
.Notes	Provides a place to list information that does not fit easily into the other sections. Notes can be special requirements required by the function, as well as author, title, version, and other information. The notes tag appear in the NOTES field only in the Full help view.
.Link	Provides links to other help topics and Internet sites of interest. Because these links appear in a command window, they are not direct links. There is no limit to the number of links you can provide. The link tag appears in the RELATED LINKS field in all help views.

You do not need to supply values for all of the help tags. As a best practice, however, you should consider supplying the .synopsis and .example tags because they contain the most critical information needed when instructing someone in how to use the function.

An example of using help tags is shown in the GetWmiClassesFunction1.ps1 script. The help information provided by using the Get-Help cmdlet is exactly the same as the information provided by the GetWmiClassesFunction.ps1 script. The difference occurs with the use of the help tags. There is no longer a need for the switched *–help* parameter due to incorporation of the code with the Get-Help cmdlet. When you no longer need to use a switched *–help* parameter, you also no longer need to test for the existence of the *$help* variable. By avoiding testing for the *$help* variable, your script can become much simpler.

The Benefits of Special Help Tags

Several bonus features are provided by using the special help tags as listed here.

- The name of the function is automatically displayed and is displayed in all help views.

- The syntax of the function is automatically derived from the parameters and is displayed in all help views.

- Detailed parameter information is automatically generated when the *–full* parameter of the Get-Help cmdlet is used.

- Common parameters information is automatically displayed when Get-Help is used with the *–detailed* and *–full* parameters.

In the GetWmiClassesFunction.ps1 script, the *Get-WmiClasses* function begins the help section with the Windows PowerShell 2.0 multiline comment block. The multiline comment block special characters begin with the left angle bracket followed by a pound sign (<#) and end with the pound sign followed by the right angle bracket (#>). Everything between the multiline comment characters is considered to be commented out. Two special help tags are included: the .SYNOPSIS tag and the .EXAMPLE tag. The other help tags listed in Table 11-1 are not used for this function.

```
<#
  .SYNOPSIS
   Displays a list of WMI Classes based upon a search criteria
  .EXAMPLE
  Get-WmiClasses -class disk -ns root\cimv2"
  This command finds wmi classes that contain the word disk. The
  classes returned are from the root\cimv2 namespace.
#>
```

Once the GetWmiClassesFunction.ps1 script is dot-sourced into the Windows PowerShell console, you can use the Get-Help cmdlet to obtain help information from the *Get-WmiClasses* function. When the Get-Help cmdlet is run with the *–full* parameter, the help display shown in Figure 11-7 appears.

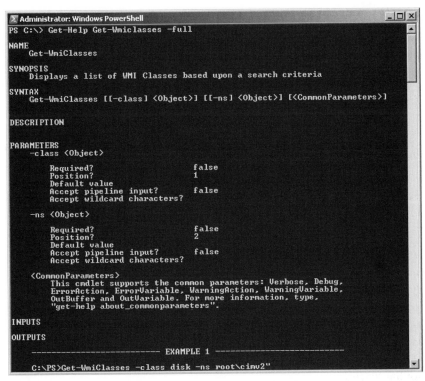

FIGURE 11-7 Full help obtained from the *Get-WmiClasses* function

The complete GetWmiClassesFunction.ps1 script is shown here.

GetWmiClassesFunction1.ps1

```
Function Get-WmiClasses(
                        $class=($paramMissing=$true),
                        $ns="root\cimv2"
                        )
{
<#
    .SYNOPSIS
      Displays a list of WMI Classes based upon a search criteria
    .EXAMPLE
      Get-WmiClasses -class disk -ns root\cimv2"
      This command finds wmi classes that contain the word disk. The
      classes returned are from the root\cimv2 namespace.
#>
  If($local:paramMissing)
    {
      throw "USAGE: getwmi2 -class <class type> -ns <wmi namespace>"
    } #$local:paramMissing
  "`nClasses in $ns namespace ...."
```

```
Get-WmiObject -namespace $ns -list |
where-object {
            $_.name -match $class -and `
            $_.name -notlike 'cim*'
        }
# mred function
} #end get-wmiclasses
```

If you intend to use the dot-source method to include functions into your working Windows PowerShell environment and modules, it makes sense to add the directory that contains your scripts to the path. You can add your function storage directory as a permanent change by using the Windows Graphical User Interface tools, or you can simply make the addition to your path each time you start Windows PowerShell by making the change via your PowerShell profile. If you decide to add your function directory by using Windows PowerShell commands, you can use the PowerShell environmental drive to access the system path variable and make the change. The code seen here first examines the path and then appends the C:\fso folder to the end of the path. Each directory that is added to the search path is separated by a semi-colon. When you append a directory to the path, you must include that semicolon as the first item that is added. You can use the += operator to append a directory to the end of the path. The last command checks the path once again to ensure that the change took place as intended.

```
PS C:\> $env:path
C:\Windows\system32;C:\Windows;C:\Windows\System32\Wbem;C:\Windows\System32
\Windows System Resource Manager\bin;C:\Windows\idmu\common;C:\Windows\system32
\WindowsPowerShell\v1.0\
PS C:\> $env:path += ";C:\fso"
PS C:\> $env:path
C:\Windows\system32;C:\Windows;C:\Windows\System32\Wbem;C:\Windows\System32
\Windows System Resource Manager\bin;C:\Windows\idmu\common;C:\Windows\system32
\WindowsPowerShell\v1.0\;C:\fso
```

A change made to the path via the Windows PowerShell environmental drive is a temporary change that only lasts for the length of the current PowerShell console session. The change takes effect immediately and therefore is a convenient method to quickly alter your current Windows PowerShell environment without making permanent changes to your system environmental settings.

> **NOTE** I personally find the ability to quickly access my scripts from the command line to be extremely useful, and I therefore add my script folder to my path environmental variable via my profile. In this manner, I always have direct access to any of my scripts via a simple dot-sourcing technique. For more information on modifying your Windows PowerShell working environment via the profile, refer to Chapter 6, "Configuring the Script Environment."

A very powerful feature of modifying the path via the Windows PowerShell environmental drive is that the changes are applied immediately and are at once available to the current PowerShell session. This means that you can add a directory to the path, dot-source a script that contains functions, and use the Get-Help cmdlet to display help information without the requirement of closing and opening Windows PowerShell. Once a directory is appended to the search path, you can dot-source scripts from that directory without the need to type the entire path to that directory. The technique of modifying the path, dot-souring a directory, and using Get-Help is illustrated here.

```
PS C:\> $env:Path += ";C:\fso"
PS C:\> . GetWmiClassesFunction1.ps1
PS C:\> Get-Help Get-WmiClasses
```

Figure 11-8 displays the results of using the technique of adding a directory to the path, dot-sourcing a script that resides in the newly appended folder, and then calling the Get-Help cmdlet to retrieve information from the newly added functions.

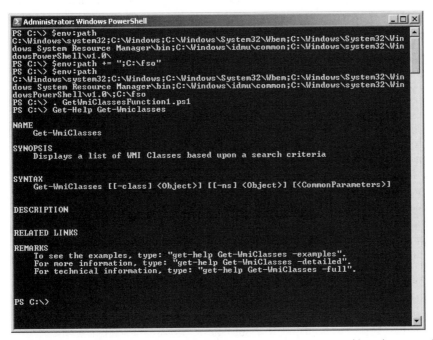

FIGURE 11-8 By appending to the path, functions can easily be dot-sourced into the current Windows PowerShell environment.

Additional Resources

- The TechNet Script Center at *http://www.microsoft.com/technet/scriptcenter* contains numerous examples of Windows PowerShell modules in the "Hey, Scripting Guy!" articles.

- Take a look at the *Windows PowerShell Scripting Guide (*Microsoft Press, 2008) for examples of working with functions.

- The Get-PowerShell blog at *http://Get-PowerShell.com* is a tremendous source of information about modules.

- Media and MicroCode at *http://blogs.msdn.com/mediaandmicrocode/* is the MSDN blog by James Brundage and features cutting-edge Windows PowerShell coverage.

- On the companion media, you will find all of the scripts referred to in this chapter.

Handling Input and Output

There are few scripts that neither receive input nor produce output. These are primarily scripts that run a series of commands in a preconfigured, batch-oriented manner. Most scripts by IT professionals, however, require either input or output, and most scripts need both. Clearly, for maximum flexibility, scripts must receive input. To maximize utility, most scripts have to produce output.

The form of input and the manner of output are part of the design process and therefore are the purview of the scriptwriter. Traditional input takes the following forms:

- Read from the command line
- Read from a text file
- Read from a database
- Read from a spreadsheet
- Read from the registry
- Read from Active Directory Domain Services

It is common for output to follow the mode of input, but it is not a requirement. The scriptwriter should not be limited by only one model of design. Consider the following scenarios:

- A script receives input from a text file and displays data to the screen.
- A script receives input from a database and writes data back to the database, but also provides confirmation of the transaction to the screen.
- A script receives input from the command line and writes data to the registry.
- A script receives input from a spreadsheet, writes to a database, records diagnostic information to a text file, and creates an event in the event log that records the exit code from the script.

■ A script receives input from the command line and writes data to a text file, but also displays the same data to the screen.

For input and output, the possibilities are varied and the potential combinations are many. Choosing the best input method and output destination is not always an exact science, and often the best solution might be dependent on external factors such as limitations of network infrastructure, ease of use, or speed of development. As a best practice, you should choose the input method that facilitates the intended use of the script. We will look at the strengths and potential use of the various input and output methods in the following section.

Choosing the Best Input Method

The selection of the best input method is the one that works for you. When it comes to best practices for input methods, it's possible to feel like the final answer is always a compromise. It might seem that using a Microsoft Office Excel spreadsheet is always the best answer because it is readily available and easy to use, but this ease of use comes with added complexity to your script. You might feel that a text file is the easiest choice because the Get-Content cmdlet makes it easy to read from a text file. Yet using and maintaining a text file comes with a maintenance cost that you might prefer to avoid. For ease of maintenance, you might be inclined to attempt to read data from Active Directory because you know the values you receive will always be up to date, but this approach adds additional complexity to the script and will not work if Active Directory is not available. In the end, your final selection will always be a compromise between usability, understandability, maintainability, and manageability. Let's begin the discussion by examining the easiest approach to receiving input—reading from the command line.

Reading from the Command Line

Reading from the command line is a traditional way to provide input to a script. It has the advantage of simplicity, which means it is easy to implement and reduces development time. If you want the ability to alter the script behavior at run time and you plan to run the script in an interactive fashion, accepting input from the command line might be the best solution for you.

Accepting input from the command line can be simple to implement. The biggest limitation of command-line input is the requirement for user intervention. You can circumvent the requirement of user interaction by assigning default values to the command-line parameters and by selecting default actions for script behavior.

Using the $args Automatic Variable

There are several ways to receive command-line input in a script. The simplest method is to use command-line arguments. When a Windows PowerShell script is run, an automatic variable, $args, is created. The $args variable will hold values supplied to the script when it is started.

Get-Bios.ps1
```
Get-WmiObject -Class Win32_Bios -computername $args
```

The Get-Bios.ps1 script starts when you call the script and supply the name of the target computer. Because $args automatically accepts a string for the input, you do not need to place the name of the target computer in quotation marks.

```
PS bp:\> .\Get-Bios.ps1 localhost
```

While the script is running, the value you supplied from the command is present on the Windows PowerShell variable drive. You can determine the value that was supplied to the script by querying the Windows PowerShell variable drive for the $args variable as shown here.

```
Get-Item -path variable:args
```

The result of running the previous query is shown here.

```
PSPath        : Microsoft.PowerShell.Core\Variable::args
PSDrive       : Variable
PSProvider    : Microsoft.PowerShell.Core\Variable
PSIsContainer : False
Name          : args
Description   :
Value         : {localhost}
Visibility    : Public
Module        :
ModuleName    :
Options       : None
Attributes    : {}
```

Even though accessing the value of $args via the Windows PowerShell variable drive provides a significant amount of information, it is easier to use the Get-Variable cmdlet.

```
Get-Variable args
```

The Dollar Sign Is Not Part of the Variable Name

When using the Get-Variable cmdlet, you do not supply a dollar sign in front of the variable name. This is extremely confusing and frustrating to beginners who assume that all variables begin with a dollar sign. While it is true that variables begin with a dollar sign, the dollar sign is not technically part of the variable name. The dollar sign is used to indicate that a particular string is to be used as a variable, but the name of the variable does not include the dollar sign. Therefore, Get-Variable will always fail when the variable is supplied with a dollar sign preceding the variable name. An error message is shown here.

```
PS bp:\> Get-Variable $args
Get-Variable : Cannot find a variable with name 'localhost'.
At C:\Users\edwils.NORTHAMERICA\AppData\Local\Temp\tmp994A.tmp.ps1:17
char:13
+ Get-Variable <<<< $args
    + CategoryInfo          : ObjectNotFound: (localhost:String)
[Get-Variable], ItemNotFoundException
    + FullyQualifiedErrorId : VariableNotFound,Microsoft.PowerShell.
Commands.GetVariableCommand
```

If you examine the error message, it states that it cannot find a variable with the name 'localhost'. This provides a clue as to what is happening under the covers. The Get-Variable cmdlet is translating the *$args* variable into the value contained within the *$args* variable and is then looking for a variable that possesses that name. This process of substituting the value of *$args* instead of looking for the *$args* variable itself can lead to unpredictable results and cause hours of frustrating troubleshooting. Suppose that you have the following code.

```
$localhost = "my computer"
Get-WmiObject -Class Win32_Bios -computername $args
Get-Variable $args
```

When the script is started as shown here, you do not receive an error. Instead, you receive the following output on your display.

```
PS bp:\> .\Get-Bios.ps1 localhost
SMBIOSBIOSVersion : 7LETB7WW (2.17 )
Manufacturer      : LENOVO
Name              : Ver 1.00PARTTBLx
SerialNumber      : L3L4518
Version           : LENOVO - 2170
Name        : localhost
Description :
Value       : my computer
```

```
Visibility  : Public
Module      :
ModuleName  :
Options     : None
Attributes  : {}
```

Of course, most of the time you are querying the variable drive only for diagnostic purposes—exactly the situation when the cloud of confusion is at its most devastating.

Supplying Multiple Values to *$args*

If you need to supply multiple values via the command line and attempt to do so by using the *$args* automatic variable, you will be greeted with the following error message that warns of a type mismatch. The error does not use the term *type mismatch*, but this is what is meant by the error. It states that you are attempting to supply an object array to a string and that the *–computername* parameter requires a string for its input.

```
Get-WmiObject : Cannot convert 'System.Object[]' to the type 'System.String' required by
parameter 'ComputerName'. Specified method is not supported.
At C:\Users\edwils.NORTHAMERICA\AppData\Local\Temp\tmp774.tmp.ps1:18 char:47
+  Get-WmiObject -Class win32_bios -computername <<<<  $args
    + CategoryInfo          : InvalidArgument: (:) [Get-WmiObject],
ParameterBindingException
    + FullyQualifiedErrorId : CannotConvertArgument,Microsoft.PowerShell.Commands.
GetWmiObjectCommand
```

The error is not caused by the array. The error is caused because the *$args* automatic variable arrives as a *System.Object* array. The Get-WmiObject cmdlet will accept an array of computer names to the *–computername* parameter. This is shown in the following script in which an array of computer names is supplied directly to the *–computername* parameter and BIOS information is retrieved via the *Win32_Bios* Windows Management Instrumentation (WMI) class.

```
PS C:\> Get-WmiObject -Class Win32_Bios -computername localhost,loopback
SMBIOSBIOSVersion : 7LETB7WW (2.17 )
Manufacturer      : LENOVO
Name              : Ver 1.00PARTTBLx
SerialNumber      : L3L4518
Version           : LENOVO - 2170

SMBIOSBIOSVersion : 7LETB7WW (2.17 )
Manufacturer      : LENOVO
Name              : Ver 1.00PARTTBLx
SerialNumber      : L3L4518
Version           : LENOVO - 2170
```

There are a few ways to solve this issue. The first is to index into the array and force the retrieval of the computer names as shown here.

Get-BiosArray1.ps1
```
Get-WmiObject -Class Win32_Bios -computername $args[0]
```

The technique of indexing directly into the *$args* automatic variable works well. Although it looks like it will only retrieve the first item in the array, *$args* in fact retrieves both items. Because Windows PowerShell automatically handles the transition between a single item and multiple items in an array, the technique of indexing into element 0 of the array works whether one or more items are supplied. The issue of the way in which the Windows PowerShell *$args* automatic variable handles an array of information is shown in the StringArgs.ps1 script.

StringArgs.ps1
```
'The value of arg0 ' + $args[0] + ' the value of arg1 ' + $args[1]
```

When the StringArgs1.ps1 script is run with the array "string1","String2" supplied from the command line, the entire array is displayed in $args[0] and nothing is displayed for $args[1].

```
PS C:\> StingArgs.ps1 "string1","String2"
The value of arg0 string1 String2 the value of arg1
PS C:\>
```

A better way to handle an array that is supplied to the *$args* automatic variable is to use the Foreach-Object cmdlet and pipeline the array to the Get-WmiObject cmdlet as shown in Get-BiosArray2.ps1.

Get-BiosArray2.ps1
```
$args | Foreach-Object {
Get-WmiObject -Class Win32_Bios -computername $_
}
```

When the Get-BiosArray2.ps1 script is started with an array of computer names from the Windows PowerShell prompt, the following output is displayed.

```
PS C:\> Get-BiosArray2.ps1 localhost,loopback
SMBIOSBIOSVersion : 7LETB7WW (2.17 )
Manufacturer      : LENOVO
Name              : Ver 1.00PARTTBLx
SerialNumber      : L3L4518
Version           : LENOVO - 2170

SMBIOSBIOSVersion : 7LETB7WW (2.17 )
Manufacturer      : LENOVO
Name              : Ver 1.00PARTTBLx
SerialNumber      : L3L4518
Version           : LENOVO - 2170
```

There are two advantages to using the Foreach-Object cmdlet. The first is readability of the code because spelling out Foreach-Object meets the principle of least shock. When people read the code and see that the script accepts an array for input via the *$args* variable, they are not surprised to see the script using the Foreach-Object cmdlet to walk through the array. Another advantage is that the script will work when a single value is supplied for the input.

Unfortunately, if the same approach is tried with the StringArgsArray.ps1 script, the value of the *$args* array is repeated twice. The StringArgsArray1.ps1 script is shown here.

StringArgsArray1.ps1
```
$args | Foreach-Object {
'The value of arg0 ' + $_ + ' the value of arg1 ' + $_
}
```

When the StringArgsArray1.ps2 script is started, the results shown here are displayed.

```
PS C:\> StingArgsArray1.ps1 "string1","String2"
The value of arg0 string1 String2 the value of arg1 string1 String2
PS C:\>
```

If you examine the output from the StringArgsArray1.ps1 script, you see that both elements of the *$args* array are displayed. If you modify the StringArgsArray1.ps1 script so that you index into the array that is contained in the $_ automatic variable (which represents the current item on the pipeline), you are able to retrieve both items from the array. The revised script is named StringArgsArray2.ps1.

StringArgsArray2.ps1
```
$args | Foreach-Object {
'The value of arg0 ' + $_[0] + ' the value of arg1 ' + $_[1]
}
```

When the script is run, the correct information is displayed.

```
PS C:\> StingArgsArray1.ps1 "string1","String2"
The value of arg0 string1 the value of arg1 String2
PS C:\>
```

A more common problem when using the *$args* automatic variable is not the need to handle multiple items from the command line but the need to handle the situation when the person running the script does not supply any values from the command line. If you run the Get-Bios.ps1 script and do not supply a value from the command line, an error is generated by the Get-WmiObject cmdlet.

```
Get-WmiObject : Cannot validate argument on parameter 'ComputerName'. The argument is
null, empty, or an element of the argument collection contains a null value. Supply a
collection that does not contain any null values and then try the command again.
At C:\Users\edwils.NORTHAMERICA\AppData\Local\Temp\tmpF8E3.tmp.ps1:16 char:46
+ Get-WmiObject -Class Win32_Bios -computername <<<< $args
```

```
    + CategoryInfo          : InvalidData: (:) [Get-WmiObject],
ParameterBindingValidationException
    + FullyQualifiedErrorId : ParameterArgumentValidationError,Microsoft.PowerShell.
Commands.GetWmiObjectCommand
```

There are two ways to handle the missing data exception, and both methods involve inspecting the *count* property from *$args*. In the first example, if the *count* property value is equal to 0, you display a message and exit the script as shown here.

Get-BiosArgsCheck1.ps1
```
If($args.count -eq 0)
  {
   Write-Host -foregroundcolor Cyan "Please supply computer name"
   Exit
  } #end if
Get-WmiObject -Class Win32_Bios -computername $args
```

You can simplify the amount of typing involved in creating a custom error message by using the *Throw* statement to raise an error, which automatically displays the output in red. This allows you to skip using the `Write-Host` cmdlet to display text in a color other than white. In the Get-BiosArgsCheck2.ps1 script, the *Throw* statement is used to raise an error. The string following the *Throw* statement is the message that is displayed on the screen. The script is further optimized by using the *not* (!) operator to determine whether the *$args* automatic variable has a count, which treats the *$args.count* as if it were a Boolean value. If the count is 0, the (*!$args.count*) expression is evaluated to *false* and the *Throw* statement is entered. The use of the *Throw* statement is shown in the Get_BiosArgsCheck2.ps1 script.

Get-BiosArgsCheck2.ps1
```
If(!$args.count)
  {
   Throw "Please supply computer name"
  } #end if
Get-WmiObject -Class Win32_Bios -computername $args
```

You should keep in mind that when you use the *Throw* statement, it generates an error. This error is populated on the *$error* object and is a *RuntimeException* class in this particular example. As a best practice, you should avoid using the *Throw* statement unless an action actually causes an error. A user omitting a parameter does not really produce an error. You have already trapped the error that would have been created as a result of not checking the *count* property of the *$args* variable.

```
PS C:\Program Files\MrEdSoftware\MrEdScriptEditor> $error
Please supply computer name
At C:\Users\edwils.NORTHAMERICA\AppData\Local\Temp\tmp72FE.tmp.ps1:17 char:9
+    Throw <<<<  "Please supply computer name"
   + CategoryInfo          : OperationStopped: (Please supply computer name:String) [],
```

```
RuntimeException
    + FullyQualifiedErrorId : Please supply computer name
```

You can use the *Trap* statement to catch a parameter binding error. If a user starts the script without supplying a computer name for the command-line argument, an error is raised. The particular error that is raised is an instance of the Microsoft .NET Framework *ParameterBindingException* class, which is located in the *System.Management.Automation* namespace. This specific error is raised when there is a problem binding the parameters that are supplied to the script. Other errors involving WMI, such as an invalid WMI class name, do not involve parameter binding and therefore do not raise the *ParameterBindingException* exception.

The advantage of using the *Trap* statement to look for a very specific error is that you can then tailor your messages to the exact problem the user encountered. Instead of glibly reply-ing that there is a problem with the script, you can provide a specific suggestion tailored to the exact error condition that is encountered. You can have multiple *Traps* in your script if you need to do so. Your script traps the error, displays a message, and exits the script gracefully. An error is still generated on the *$error* object but is not displayed to the user. An example of using the *Trap* statement to display an error message when the script is run without supplying a value for *$args* is shown in the Get-BiosArgsTrap1.ps1 script.

Get-BiosArgsTrap1.ps1
```
Trap [System.Management.Automation.ParameterBindingException]
  {
     Write-Host -foregroundcolor cyan "Supply a computer name"
     Exit
  }


Get-WmiObject -Class Win32_Bios -computername $args
```

If a *ParameterBindingException* error is encountered when the Get-BiosArgsTrap1.ps1 script is started, the script will trap the error. The output displayed from the Get-BiosArgsTrap1.ps1 script is shown here.

```
PS C:\> Get-BiosArgsTrap1.ps1
Supply a computer name
PS C:\>
```

If any other error occurs when the script runs, the error associated with that particular error condition is displayed.

You can also use *Try/Catch/Finally* to attempt an action in the *try* portion of the construc-tion. The error you will trap goes into the *catch* portion, and the action you will perform when all is completed goes into the *finally* section.

An example of using *Try/Catch/Finally* is shown in the GetBiosTryCatchFinally.ps1 script. In the *try* section of the construction, you use the `Get-WmiObject` cmdlet to retrieve BIOS information from the *Win32_Bios* WMI class. The target computer is supplied from the command line via the *$args* automatic variable, and this is the command that is attempted. If a *System.Management.Automation.ParameterBindingException* error is raised, it will be caught via the *catch* portion of the *Try/Catch/Finally* construction. When the parameter exception is raised, the code that runs is the `Write-Host` cmdlet. The string "Please enter computer name" displays on the screen in the cyan color. The code that is in the *finally* portion of *Try/Catch/Finally* always runs, and therefore the 'Cleaning up the $error object' string will be displayed to the screen in white text even if no error is raised. The error object will also be cleared, even if there are no errors to be cleared. The complete text of the GetBiosTryCatchFinally.ps1 script is shown here.

GetBiosTryCatchFinally.ps1

```
Try
    { Get-WmiObject -class Win32_Bios -computer $args }
Catch [System.Management.Automation.ParameterBindingException]
    { Write-Host -foregroundcolor cyan "Please enter computer name" }
Finally
    { 'Cleaning up the $error object' ; $error.clear() }
```

Using the *Param* Statement

Using the *$args* automatic variable is a quick and easy method to receive input to your script from the command line. As shown in the "Using the *$args* Automatic Variable" section, this simplicity is not without cost. The cost is flexibility. While the *$args* automatic variable works great for retrieving single values, it does not work as well when multiple parameters must be supplied. In addition, there is no way to make switched parameters when using the *$args* automatic variable.

The *Param* statement lets you create named arguments and switched arguments. To use the *Param* statement to create a named argument, you use the *Param* keyword, open a set of parentheses, and specify your parameter name.

```
Param($computer)
```

To specify a default value for the parameter, you use the *Param* keyword, specify the parameter name inside a set of parentheses, and use the *equality* operator to assign a value.

```
Param($computer = "localhost")
```

The *Param* statement must be the first noncommented line in the script. If you try to use the *Param* statement in another position, you will receive an error. In the example shown here, you actually receive two errors.

```
Write-Host "Param not in first position"
Param($computer = "localhost")
Get-WmiObject -Class Win32_Bios -computername $computer
```

The first is an error from WMI mentioning that the value supplied to the *–computername* parameter of the Get-WmiObject cmdlet is null. The second error states that *Param* is not recognized as a cmdlet, function, script file, or operable program. This error is shown in Figure 12-1.

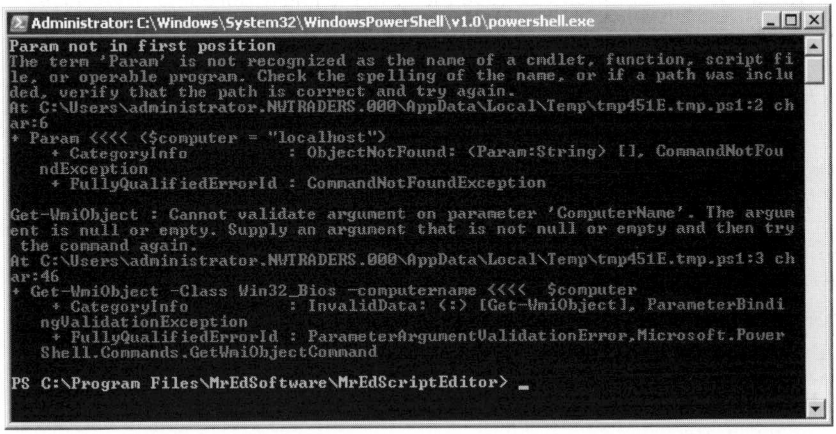

FIGURE 12-1 When the *Param* statement does not appear in the first noncommented line, an error is raised.

The Get-BiosParam.ps1 script illustrates using the *Param* keyword to create a named argument and to assign a default value for the *$computer* variable. The Get-WmiObject cmdlet uses the *Win32_Bios* WMI class to return BIOS information to the display from the computer that is specified in the *$computer* variable, which is either a computer name that was typed when the Get_BiosParam script was run or the localhost computer.

There are three different ways in which the *–computer* parameter can be supplied from the command line, as follows:

- Type the entire parameter name.
- Type a partial parameter name. You must type enough of the parameter name to uniquely identify the parameter.
- Omit the parameter name and rely on position.

These three different methods of using command-line parameters are illustrated here with the Get-BiosParam.ps1 script.

```
PS C:\> Get-BiosParam.ps1 –computer loopback

SMBIOSBIOSVersion : 7LETB7WW (2.17 )
Manufacturer      : LENOVO
Name              : Ver 1.00PARTTBLx
SerialNumber      : L3L4518
Version           : LENOVO - 2170
```

```
PS C:\> Get-BiosParam.ps1 -c loopback

SMBIOSBIOSVersion : 7LETB7WW (2.17 )
Manufacturer      : LENOVO
Name              : Ver 1.00PARTTBLx
SerialNumber      : L3L4518
Version           : LENOVO - 2170

PS C:\> Get-BiosParam.ps1 loopback

SMBIOSBIOSVersion : 7LETB7WW (2.17 )
Manufacturer      : LENOVO
Name              : Ver 1.00PARTTBLx
SerialNumber      : L3L4518
Version           : LENOVO - 2170
```

The complete Get-BiosParam.ps1 script is shown here.

Get-BiosParam.ps1
```
Param($computer = "localhost")
Get-WmiObject -Class Win32_Bios -computername $computer
```

Creating a Mandatory Parameter

You can make a parameter mandatory by using a parameter binding tag and setting the value of the *mandatory* attribute to *$true*. When the *mandatory* attribute is used to modify the command-line parameter, a prompt is displayed whenever the script is run without supplying the required value. This behavior, shown in Figure 12-2, allows the user a chance to run the script without encountering an error.

FIGURE 12-2 Windows PowerShell prompts for missing values when the *mandatory* attribute is used with a command-line parameter.

Parameter tags are a new feature of Windows PowerShell 2.0, and their use prevents interoperability with earlier versions of PowerShell. In the Get-BiosMandatoryParameter.ps1 script, the *#requires –version 2.0* tag prevents the script from attempting to start in a Windows PowerShell 1.0 environment. The *Param* statement is used to create the command-line parameters. The *[Parameter(Mandatory = $true)]* statement makes the *–computername* parameter a mandatory parameter. The *[string[]]* statement converts the *–computername* parameter into an array. When the Get-BiosMandatoryParameter.ps1 script runs without any parameters supplied, it will prompt for multiple values for the *–computername* parameter until the Enter key is pressed twice. If you want to only accept a single value for the *–computername* parameter, you should leave out the *[]* as shown here.

```
Param(
    [Parameter(Mandatory = $true)]
    [string]
    $computername)
```

When a value is supplied for the *–computername* parameter from the command line, it is converted into a string if possible because of the *[string[]]* type constraint that is placed in the parameter definition. This is, of course, the same as the *–computername* parameter from the Get-WmiObject cmdlet, which also accepts an array of strings. If you attempt to constrain the input as an integer, for example, an invalid parameter error is generated.

```
PS bp:\> .\Get-BiosMandatoryParameter.ps1 [int]12
Get-WmiObject : Invalid parameter
At C:\data\BookDocs\PowerShellBestPractices\Scripts\chapter12\Get-BiosMandatory
Parameter.ps1:20 char:14
+ Get-WmiObject <<<<  -class Win32_Bios -computername $computername
    + CategoryInfo: InvalidOperation: (:) [Get-WmiObject], ManagementException
    + FullyQualifiedErrorId : GetWMIManagementException,Microsoft.PowerShell.
Commands.GetWmiObjectCommand
```

The complete Get-BiosMandatoryParameter.ps1 script is shown here.

Get-BiosMandatoryParameter.ps1
```
#requires -version 2.0
Param(
    [Parameter(Mandatory = $true)]
    [string[]]
    $computername)


Get-WmiObject -class Win32_Bios -computername $computername
```

Using Parameter Attributes

The Get-BiosMandatoryParameter.ps1 script uses the *mandatory* parameter attribute argument to ensure that the *–computername* parameter has a value supplied for it. There are several other parameter attribute arguments that can be used to modify the default behavior of the parameter attribute of the *Param* keyword. The available parameter attribute arguments are shown in Table 12-1.

TABLE 12-1 Parameter Attribute Arguments

ARGUMENT NAME	DESCRIPTION
Mandatory	The *Mandatory* argument indicates that the parameter is required when the function is run. If this argument is not specified, the parameter is an optional parameter. **Example:** [parameter(*Mandatory=$true*)]
Position	The *Position* argument specifies the position of the parameter. If this argument is not specified, the parameter name or its alias must be explicitly specified when the parameter is set. Also, if none of the parameters of a function have positions, the Windows PowerShell run time assigns positions to each parameter based on the order in which the parameters are received. **Example:** [parameter(*Position=0*)]
ParameterSetName	The *ParameterSetName* argument specifies the parameter set to which a parameter belongs. If no parameter set is specified, the parameter belongs to all of the parameter sets defined by the function. This behavior means that each parameter set must have one unique parameter that is not a member of any other parameter set. **Example:** [parameter(*Mandatory=$true,* *ParameterSetName* = "CN")]

ARGUMENT NAME	DESCRIPTION
ValueFromPipeline	The *ValueFromPipeline* argument specifies that the parameter accepts input from a pipeline object. Specify this argument if the cmdlet accesses the complete object and not just a property of the object. **Example:** [parameter(*Mandatory=$true,* *ValueFromPipeline=$true)*]
ValueFromPipelineByPropertyName	The *ValueFromPipelineByPropertyName* argument specifies that the parameter accepts input from a property of a pipeline object. **Example:** [parameter(*Mandatory=$true,* *ValueFromPipelineByPropertyName=$true)*]
ValueFromRemainingArguments	The *ValueFromRemainingArguments* argument specifies that the parameter accepts all of the remaining arguments that are not bound to the parameters of the function. **Example:** [parameter(*Mandatory=$true,* *ValueFromRemainingArguments=$true)*]
HelpMessage	The *HelpMessage* argument specifies a message that contains a short description of the parameter. **Example:** [parameter(*Mandatory=$true, HelpMessage=* "An array of computer names.")]

Creating a Parameter Alias

The *alias* attribute of the *Param* statement can be used to make working from the command line easier. The *alias* attribute typically follows the *parameter* attribute to create an alternative to typing a long parameter name from the command line. Although partial parameter completion may be used, enough of the parameter must be typed to disambiguate it from other parameters that are defined. Consider the following *Param* statement that is used to create two parameters.

```
Param($computername, $computerIPaddress)
```

In this example, you need to type computern and computeri before the parameters are unique. In a case such as this, a parameter alias is useful. You can see how a parameter alias is used by referring to the Get-BiosMandatoryParameterWithAlias.ps1 script.

Get-BiosMandatoryParameterWithAlias.ps1
```
#requires -version 2.0
Param(
    [Parameter(Mandatory = $true)]
    [alias("CN")]
    [string[]]
    $computername)

Get-WmiObject -class Win32_Bios -computername $computername
```

Validating Parameter Input

It is more efficient to catch problems with your script by inspecting the parameters than it is to wait until the script is launched and then do parameter checking. In Windows PowerShell 2.0, there are a number of validation attributes that can be specified. Validation attributes inspect command-line parameters to ensure that they conform to certain rules. If you need to ensure that the value of a command-line parameter is within a specified range in Windows PowerShell 1.0, it is common to write a function and to call that function on entering the script as illustrated in the CheckNumberRange.ps1 script.

The *Check-Number* function in the CheckNumberRange.ps1 script ensures that the value of the *number* parameter is greater than 1 and less than or equal to 5. If *number* is within the 1 to 5 range, the *Check-Number* function returns the *true* value to the script; otherwise, it returns *false*. The *Set-Number* function multiplies the value of the *number* parameter by 2. The entry point of the script uses the *If* statement to call the *Check-Number* function. If the *Check-Number* function returns *true*, it calls the *Set-Number* function; otherwise, it displays a message stating that the value of the *$number* variable is out of bounds. The complete CheckNumberRange.ps1 script is shown here.

CheckNumberRange.ps1
```
Param($number)

Function Check-Number($number)
{
 if($number -ge 1 -And $number -le 5)
  { $true }
 Else
  { $false }
} #end check-number

Function Set-Number($number)
{
```

```
      $number * 2
} #end Set-Number

# *** Start of script ***
If(Check-Number($number))
   { Set-Number($number) }
Else
   { '$number is out of bounds' }
```

You might prefer to continue to write your own custom boundary-checking functions. This process is required if your computers are not upgraded to Windows PowerShell 2.0. A custom function might also be required if there are complicated rules that you need to enforce.

Basic boundary checking, such as that performed by the *Check-Number* function in the CheckNumberRange.ps1 script, can be accomplished in Windows PowerShell 2.0 by using one of the parameter validation attributes listed in Table 12-2, later in this chapter. The parameter validation attribute that checks the range value of a parameter is named *ValidateRange*, and its use is shown in the ValidateRange.ps1 script. In the *Param* statement, the *[ValidateRange(1,5)]* parameter attribute is used to ensure that the value supplied for the *number* parameter falls within the range of 1 to 5. If it does, the ValidateRange.ps1 script starts at the entry point to the script, which calls the *Set-Number* function. The ValidateRange.ps1 script and the CheckNumberRange.ps1 script both accomplish the same thing—they multiply an input number by 2 if that number is within the range of 1 to 5. The ValidateRange.ps1 script is shown here.

ValidateRange.ps1
```
#requires -version 2.0
Param(
       [ValidateRange(1,5)]
       $number
     )

Function Set-Number($number)
{
  $number * 2
} #end Set-Number

# *** Entry point to script ***
Set-Number($number)
```

As a best practice, you should use parameter validation attributes to inspect parameter values rather than writing your own functions to accomplish the same thing. Some of the main reasons for using parameter validation attributes are as follows:

- Reduces the complexity of your code

- Ensures that your script behaves like the core Windows PowerShell cmdlets
- Helps users of your script know how to run your script
- Promotes syntax discoverability via the Get-Help cmdlet

The most powerful parameter validation attribute is the *ValidatePattern* attribute. By using the *ValidatePattern* parameter validation attribute, you can check input to see whether it conforms to a regular expression pattern. A regular expression pattern can range from a basic pattern match that looks for a specific combination of letters within a computer name to more complex regular expression patterns. A basic pattern match is shown in the PingVistaComputers.ps1 script.

In the PingVistaComputers.ps1 script, the *ValidatePattern* parameter validation attribute is used to ensure that the string supplied for the *–computername* parameter contains the letters "vista" somewhere in the name of the computer. Valid values would include *vista*, *vistacomputer*, and even *myvistacomputer*. The requirement for a match is that the letters "vista" must appear in the string and must appear in exact order. The *Param* statement is used to allow the use of command-line parameters. The *ValidatePattern* parameter validation attribute sets the regular expression pattern that is used to validate command-line input. The *alias* attribute is used to configure an alternate name for the *–computername* parameter. The *Param* statement is shown here.

```
Param(
    [ValidatePattern("vista")]
    [alias("CN")]
    $computername
)
```

The *New-TestConnection* function uses the Test-Connection cmdlet to send a specially configured ping packet to the destination computer listed in the *–computername* parameter. The buffer size of the ping packet is reduced from the default of 32 bytes to 16 bytes, and the number of packets is reduced from the default of 4 to 2. The result is that the *New-TestConnection* function will return the status of the destination more quickly, use less network bandwidth, and complete more quickly than the standard Test-Connection cmdlet. The complete PingVistaComputers.ps1 script is shown here.

```
PingVistaComputers.ps1
#requires -version 2.0
Param(
    [ValidatePattern("vista")]
    [alias("CN")]
    $computername
)


Function New-TestConnection($computername)
{
 Test-connection -computername $computername -buffersize 16 -count 2
```

```
} #end new-testconnection

# *** Entry Point to script
New-TestConnection($computername)
```

More complicated regular expression patterns can also be used with the *ValidatePattern* parameter validation attribute. In the PingIpAddress.ps1 script, a regular expression is used to ensure that a string representing an IP address is entered. The pattern used limits input by requiring 1 to 3 numbers followed by a period, then 1 to 3 numbers followed by a period, then 1 to 3 numbers followed by a period, and then an additional 1 to 3 numbers. This pattern accepts a string such as 127.0.0.1 (a valid IP address), but it also accepts 999.999.999.999 (which is not a valid IP address). The regular expression pattern is shown here.

```
"\d{1,3}\.\d{1,3}\.\d{1,3}\.\d{1,3}"
```

In the PingIpAddress.ps1 script, the *Param* statement creates the command-line parameters. The *parameter* attribute is used to make the parameter mandatory and to specify a help message, which is available in case the script is run without typing the parameter value. The *ValidatePattern* attribute holds the regular expression pattern that is used to validate the data supplied to the script via the *–computername* parameter. An alias, *IP*, is created to allow the script to run without the need to type the *–computername* parameter name. The complete PingIpAddress.ps1 script is shown here.

PingIpAddress.ps1
```
#requires -version 2.0
Param(
    [Parameter(Mandatory=$true,
            HelpMessage="Enter a valid IP address")]
    [ValidatePattern("\d{1,3}\.\d{1,3}\.\d{1,3}\.\d{1,3}")]
    [alias("IP")]
    $computername
 )

Function New-TestConnection($computername)
{
 Test-connection -computername $computername -buffersize 16 -count 2
} #end new-testconnection

# *** Entry Point to script
New-TestConnection($computername)
```

The parameter validation attributes are shown in Table 12-2.

TABLE 12-2 Parameter Validation Attributes

ATTRIBUTE NAME	DESCRIPTION
AllowNull	The *AllowNull* attribute allows the argument of a mandatory cmdlet parameter to be set to null. **Example:** [AllowNull()]
AllowEmptyString	The *AllowEmptyString* attribute allows an empty string as the argument of a mandatory cmdlet parameter. **Example:** [AllowEmptyString()]
AllowEmptyCollection	The *AllowEmptyCollection* attribute allows an empty collection as the argument of a mandatory parameter. **Example:** [AllowEmptyCollection()]
ValidateCount	The *ValidateCount* attribute specifies the minimum and maximum number of arguments that the parameter can accept. **Example:** [ValidateCount(1,5)]
ValidateLength	The *ValidateLength* attribute specifies the minimum and maximum length of the parameter argument. **Example:** [ValidateLength(1,10)]
ValidatePattern	The *ValidatePattern* attribute specifies a regular expression that validates the pattern of the parameter argument. **Example:** [ValidatePattern("[0-9][0-9][0-9]")]
ValidateRange	The *ValidateRange* attribute specifies the minimum and maximum values of the parameter argument. **Example:** [ValidateRange(0,10)]
ValidateScript	The *ValidateScript* attribute specifies a script that is used to validate the parameter argument. The Windows PowerShell run time generates an error if the script result is false or if the script throws an exception. **Example:** [ValidateScript({$_ -lt 4})]

ATTRIBUTE NAME	DESCRIPTION
ValidateSet	The *ValidateSet* attribute specifies a set of valid values for the argument of the parameter. The Windows PowerShell run time generates an error if the parameter argument does not match a value in the set. **Example:** [ValidateSet("Steve", "Mary", "Carl")]
ValidateNotNull	The *ValidateNotNull* attribute specifies that the argument of the parameter cannot be set to null. **Example:** [ValidateNotNull()]
ValidateNotNullOrEmpty	The *ValidateNotNullOrEmpty* attribute specifies that the argument of the parameter cannot be set to null or cannot be empty. **Example:** [ValidateNotNullOrEmpty()]

Using Multiple Parameter Arguments

To use multiple parameter arguments, the *alias* attribute, and parameter validation attributes at the same time with the *Param* statement, you must keep the following rules in mind:

- Parameter arguments go inside parentheses and modify the *parameter* attribute of the *Param* statement.
- Each parameter argument is separated by a comma.
- The *parameter* attribute goes inside square brackets (just like all other parameter attributes).
- Each *parameter* attribute should be on its own line.
- *Parameter* attributes are not separated by commas.
- The command-line parameter begins with a dollar sign and is followed by a comma unless it is the last command-line parameter defined, in which case it is followed by the closing parenthesis from the *Param* statement.
- You are allowed to have an unlimited number of *parameter* attributes and parameter validation attributes.

The MultiplyNumbersCheckParameters.ps1 script illustrates the use of multiple parameter attributes. It begins with the *#requires –version 2.0* tag that is used to ensure that the script does not attempt to start on a Windows PowerShell 1.0 computer. The *Param* statement creates the command-line parameters for the script. The *parameter* attribute is used to make the *FirstNumber* parameter mandatory, assign it to the first position, and set a help message for the parameter. The *alias* attribute is used to create an alias for the *FirstNumber* parameter. The *ValidateRange* parameter validation attribute is used to ensure that the command-line *FirstNumber* parameter has a value that falls within the range of 1 to 10.

The *FirstNumber* parameter is followed by a comma, and the *parameter* attribute is used to make the *lastnumber* parameter mandatory, occupy position 1, and assign a help message for the *lastnumber* parameter. The *alias* attribute creates an alias of *ln* for the *lastnumber* parameter. The type constraint [*int16*] is used to ensure that the value of the *lastnumber* parameter is a 16-bit integer, which limits its value to 32767. The *ValidateNotNullOrEmpty* validation attribute is used to ensure that the *lastnumber* parameter is neither null nor empty. The *param* section ends by creating the *lastnumber* parameter and closing out the parentheses.

> **NOTE** An easy way to determine the capacity of certain system types is to use the static *Maxvalue* property. To obtain the maximum value of an *int32,* you can access it by using a double colon, as in [int32]::Maxvalue.

After all of the work to create the parameters, the code itself is somewhat anticlimactic: It multiplies the two command-line parameters together. The completed MultiplyNumbersCheckParameters.ps1 script is shown here.

MultiplyNumbersCheckParameters.ps1
```
#requires -version 2.0
Param(
            [Parameter(mandatory=$true,
                            Position=0,
                            HelpMessage="A number between 1 and 10")]
            [alias("fn")]
            [ValidateRange(1,10)]
            $FirstNumber,
            [Parameter(mandatory=$true,
                            Position=1,
                            HelpMessage="Not null or empty")]
            [alias("ln")]
            [int16]
            [ValidateNotNullOrEmpty()]
            $LastNumber
)

$FirstNumber*$LastNumber
```

Working with Passwords as Input

In an ideal world, you would never need to supply passwords or make passwords available to a script. Scripts would run by using impersonation and would detect whether you had rights to access data. If you had the rights, you gained access; if you did not have the rights, you would not be able to connect. To some extent, this is exactly what happens when working with a script. Issues surrounding the use of passwords come up in the following scenarios:

- Accessing information from an untrusted domain
- Accessing information from legacy databases that do not use integrated security
- Accessing information from stand-alone workstations or servers that are not joined to a domain
- Allowing a user who has no rights to run a script with alternative credentials that perform actions the user would not otherwise have permission to accomplish

There are several approaches to handling the password issue, and they are listed here as follows:

- Store the password in the script.
- Store the password in a file.
- Store the password in the registry.
- Store the password in Active Directory.
- Prompt for the password.

Store the Password in the Script

The simplest approach to handling the password problem is to store the password in the script. However, obvious concerns arise with storing the password in the script—the first of which is that the password is shown in the script in plain text, and anyone who has access to the script has access to the password.

Two things can be done to limit exposure to the password. One is to use NTFS File System (NTFS) permissions to protect the file from people who do not need to know the password. The other is to use Encrypting File System (EFS) to encrypt the script. Because Windows PowerShell is a .NET Framework application, it has the ability to use the security classes to use your EFS certificate to automatically decrypt the script and to run the encrypted script, which VBScript cannot do. Encrypted VBScripts will not run. In the QueryComputersUseCredentials.ps1 script, the *ADO* class is used to query a resource domain named nwtraders.com. The user that performs the query is named LondonAdmin, and the password is Password1. These values are stored in variables and are passed to the ADO connection object via the *password* and *user id* properties. The script then retrieves all of the computer objects from the nwtraders.com domain. The QueryComputersUseCredentials.ps1 script is shown here.

```
QueryComputersUseCredentials.ps1
$strBase = "<LDAP://dc=nwtraders,dc=msft>"
$strFilter = "(objectCategory=computer)"
$strAttributes = "name"
$strScope = "subtree"
$strQuery = "$strBase;$strFilter;$strAttributes;$strScope"
$strUser = "nwtraders\LondonAdmin"
$strPwd = "Password1"

$objConnection = New-Object -comObject "ADODB.Connection"
$objConnection.provider = "ADsDSOObject"
$objConnection.properties.item("user ID") = $strUser
$objConnection.properties.item("Password") = $strPwd
$objConnection.open("modifiedConnection")
$objCommand = New-Object -comObject "ADODB.Command"

$objCommand.ActiveConnection = $objConnection
$objCommand.CommandText = $strQuery
$objRecordSet = $objCommand.Execute()

Do
{
    $objRecordSet.Fields.item("name") |Select-Object Name,Value
    $objRecordSet.MoveNext()
}
Until ($objRecordSet.eof)

$objConnection.Close()
```

Store the Password in a Text File

Perhaps one step above storing the password in the script is to store the password in a
text file, which has the advantage of not being directly accessible from within the script. By
placing the password in a different file, you can configure different security on the password
file than the security configured on the script file itself. This might be a good solution for
those who need the ability to read the script but not the ability to run the script. Another
advantage of this approach is that it allows you to use the same script to work in different
security contexts. One example is when a script is written by network administrators from one
domain and then shared with network administrators in a different domain context. This is a
common practice when a company is composed of multiple business units, each of which has
its own separate infrastructure.

```
QueryComputersUseCredentialsFromText.ps1
$strBase = "<LDAP://dc=nwtraders,dc=msft>"
$strFilter = "(objectCategory=computer)"
$strAttributes = "name"
$strScope = "subtree"
$strQuery = "$strBase;$strFilter;$strAttributes;$strScope"
$strUser = "nwtraders\LondonAdmin"
$strPwd = Get-Content -path "C:\fso\password.txt"

$objConnection = New-Object -comObject "ADODB.Connection"
$objConnection.provider = "ADsDSOObject"
$objConnection.properties.item("user ID") = $strUser
$objConnection.properties.item("Password") = $strPwd
$objConnection.open("modifiedConnection")
$objCommand = New-Object -comObject "ADODB.Command"

$objCommand.ActiveConnection = $objConnection
$objCommand.CommandText = $strQuery
$objRecordSet = $objCommand.Execute()

Do
{
    $objRecordSet.Fields.item("name") |Select-Object Name,Value
    $objRecordSet.MoveNext()
}
Until ($objRecordSet.eof)

$objConnection.Close()
```

Store the Password in the Registry

With the ease of registry access inherent in Windows PowerShell, storing a password in the registry might make sense in some cases. Because you can set security on a registry key, you might want to store a password in the registry. The registry key can be created in a separate process. When the script is run, it accesses the registry for the password that is required for remote access.

```
QueryComputersUseCredentialsFromRegistry.ps1
$strBase = "<LDAP://dc=nwtraders,dc=msft>"
$strFilter = "(objectCategory=computer)"
$strAttributes = "name"
$strScope = "subtree"
$strQuery = "$strBase;$strFilter;$strAttributes;$strScope"
$strUser = "nwtraders\administrator"
$strPwd = (Get-ItemProperty HKCU:\Software\ForScripting\CompatPassword).password
```

```
$objConnection = New-Object -comObject "ADODB.Connection"
$objConnection.provider = "ADsDSOObject"
$objConnection.properties.item("user ID") = $strUser
$objConnection.properties.item("Password") = $strPwd
$objConnection.open("modifiedConnection")
$objCommand = New-Object -comObject "ADODB.Command"

$objCommand.ActiveConnection = $objConnection
$objCommand.CommandText = $strQuery
$objRecordSet = $objCommand.Execute()

Do
{
    $objRecordSet.Fields.item("name") |Select-Object Name,Value
    $objRecordSet.MoveNext()
}
Until ($objRecordSet.eof)

$objConnection.Close()
```

Store the Password in Active Directory Domain Services

It is relatively easy to extend the schema to create an attribute within which you can store a password that is used for certain scripts. This option provides a central location that is accessible from anywhere within the domain.

> **NOTE** If you are uncomfortable with adding an attribute to the Active Directory schema, you can use one of the configurable attributes instead of creating your own attributes. In any case, you should ensure that you use a valid object identifier (OID) number and test your changes in a test environment before deploying the changes to your live production network.

QueryComputersUseCredentialsFromADDS.ps1
```
$strBase = "<LDAP://dc=nwtraders,dc=msft>"
$strFilter = "(objectCategory=computer)"
$strAttributes = "name"
$strScope = "subtree"
$strQuery = "$strBase;$strFilter;$strAttributes;$strScope"
$strUser = "nwtraders\testUser"
$strPwd = ([adsi]"LDAP://cn=testUser,ou=myusers,dc=nwtraders,dc=com").compatPassword

$objConnection = New-Object -comObject "ADODB.Connection"
$objConnection.provider = "ADsDSOObject"
```

```
$objConnection.properties.item("user ID") = $strUser
$objConnection.properties.item("Password") = $strPwd
$objConnection.open("modifiedConnection")
$objCommand = New-Object -comObject "ADODB.Command"

$objCommand.ActiveConnection = $objConnection
$objCommand.CommandText = $strQuery
$objRecordSet = $objCommand.Execute()

Do
{
    $objRecordSet.Fields.item("name") |Select-Object Name,Value
    $objRecordSet.MoveNext()
}
Until ($objRecordSet.eof)

$objConnection.Close()
```

Prompt for the Password

The best approach is to have the script prompt you when it needs a password. There are a number of advantages to this method. The biggest advantage is that it removes your concern about storage of the password because it is not stored in the script, a file, the registry, or another location. The next advantage of having the script prompt for the password is that it reduces maintenance requirements. If a password changes on a regular basis and is stored in a text file, the file contents must be updated each time the password changes. Using a prompt makes troubleshooting the script easier. When a script must access a password from a remote location, connectivity issues and remote permissions must be considered if a script fails to execute properly. Of course, if the script contains robust error checking, the script is easier to troubleshoot; however, this introduces an additional level of complexity that can potentially increase the maintenance cost of the script. The easiest way to prompt for a password is to use the Read-Host cmdlet.

QueryComputersPromptForPassword.ps1
```
$strBase = "<LDAP://dc=nwtraders,dc=com>"
$strFilter = "(objectCategory=computer)"
$strAttributes = "name"
$strScope = "subtree"
$strQuery = "$strBase;$strFilter;$strAttributes;$strScope"
$strUser = "nwtraders\administrator"
$strPwd = Read-Host -prompt "Enter password to Connect to AD"

$objConnection = New-Object -comObject "ADODB.Connection"
$objConnection.provider = "ADsDSOObject"
```

```
$objConnection.properties.item("user ID") = $strUser
$objConnection.properties.item("Password") = $strPwd
$objConnection.open("modifiedConnection")
$objCommand = New-Object -comObject "ADODB.Command"

$objCommand.ActiveConnection = $objConnection
$objCommand.CommandText = $strQuery
$objRecordSet = $objCommand.Execute()

Do
{
    $objRecordSet.Fields.item("name") |Select-Object Name,Value
    $objRecordSet.MoveNext()
}
Until ($objRecordSet.eof)

$objConnection.Close()
```

If the cmdlet supports a *PSCredential* object, you can use the *AsSecureString* parameter from the Read-Host cmdlet. A secure string is used for text that should be kept confidential. The text is encrypted for privacy when it is used and is deleted from computer memory when it is no longer needed. The password is never revealed as plain text. The *System.Security.SecureString* .NET Framework class is invisible to the Component Object Model (COM) and therefore cannot be used with classic COM interfaces.

```
ReadHostSecureStringQueryWmi.ps1
$user = "Nwtraders\administrator"
$password = Read-Host -prompt "Enter your password" -asSecureString
$credential = new-object system.management.automation.PSCredential $user,$password
Get-WmiObject -class Win32_Bios -computername berlin -credential $credential
```

When working with a secure string, it is also possible to store the hash of the password in a text file. The advantage of this technique is that it allows you to use the password with the *PSCredential* object, but it gives you the flexibility of not having to manually enter the password each time the script is run. In addition, it allows you to give the script to another user who does not know the password for the account.

To do this, you use the Read-Host cmdlet and specify the *AsSecureString* parameter. In this example, the encrypted password is stored in a *$pwd* variable.

```
PS C:\> $pwd = Read-Host -Prompt "Enter your password" -AsSecureString
Enter your password: *********
```

If you use the *ToString* method from the *SecureString* object, the only thing that is relayed back to the Windows PowerShell console is an instance of a *System.Security.SecureString* class as shown here. If you attempt to store the output from the *ToString* method in a text file, the only words that the text file will contain are "System.Security.SecureString."

```
PS C:\> $PWD.ToString()
System.Security.SecureString
```

To be able to store the secure string in a text file, you need to use the ConvertFrom-SecureString cmdlet. As illustrated here, ConvertFrom-SecureString reveals the hash of the password.

```
PS C:\> $PWD | ConvertFrom-SecureString
01000000d08c9ddf0115d1118c7a00c04fc297eb01000000151046ea8f869541a129ff10c91b850
e000000000200000000000003660000a800000010000000aa2caba61452ffd5f973901a5dbd0e8100
00000004800000a000000100000003172c749434dfac3262616d15dea4d1018000000916d60d59
0d381bff1225663c6b4dcab536fca5920077cb414000000e92d30f80b9fbf337c1a8e5d99f50f11
8fae2d3b
```

You can write this password hash to a text file by using a pair of redirection arrows.

```
PS C:\> $PWD | ConvertFrom-SecureString >> C:\fso\passwordHash.txt
```

The passwordHash.txt file now contains the exact information that was previously displayed on the screen. This is no longer a *System.Security.SecureString* class, but is instead a string that represents the hash of a *SecureString* class. To convert the hash back to a secure string, you need to use the ConvertTo-SecureString cmdlet.

```
PS C:\> ConvertTo-SecureString (Get-Content C:\fso\passwordHash.txt)
System.Security.SecureString
```

> **NOTE** Keep in mind that you want to convert the contents of the passwordHash.txt file to a secure string and not the path to the passwordHash.txt file. The first time I attempted this operation, I used the following command: ConvertTo-SecureString C:\fso\passwordHash.txt, which does not work. I then realized that I was trying to encrypt the path to the file and not the contents of the file.

A more efficient way to create the password hash text file is to use pipelining and thus avoid the intermediate variable as shown here. When the command is run, it prompts for the password.

```
PS C:\> Read-Host -Prompt "Enter your password" -AsSecureString |
>> ConvertFrom-SecureString >> C:\fso\passwordHash.txt
```

To use this password hash text file in a script, you can use a script like the one shown here.

```
UsePasswordHashFile.ps1
$user = "Nwtraders\administrator"
$password = ConvertTo-SecureString -String (Get-content C:\fso\passwordHash.txt)
$credential = new-object system.management.automation.PSCredential $user,$password
Get-WmiObject -class Win32_Bios -computername berlin -credential $credential
```

Importing and Exporting Credentials

Lee Holmes, Senior Software Developer Engineer and Author of *Windows PowerShell Cookbook*
Microsoft Corporation

One question that comes up fairly often when dealing with Windows PowerShell scripts is how to properly handle user names and passwords. The solution is to use the `Get-Credential` cmdlet to create a *PSCredential* object. A *PSCredential* object ensures that your password stays protected in memory, unlike cmdlets that accept a straight user name/password combination.

If a parameter accepts a *PSCredential* object, Windows PowerShell supports several types of input, such as the ones that are listed here:

- **Empty** If you supply no input to a mandatory –*credential* parameter, Windows PowerShell prompts you for the user name and password.

- **String** If you supply a string to the –*credential* parameter, Windows PowerShell treats it as a user name and prompts you for the password.

- **Credential** If you supply a credential object to the –*credential* parameter, Windows PowerShell accepts it as is.

This is great for interactive use, but what if you want to write an automated script for a cmdlet that accepts a –*credential* parameter? The solution lies in passing a preconstructed *PSCredential* object. This solution is covered by recipe 16.9 in the *Windows PowerShell Cookbook*, which is excerpted here.

The first step for storing a password on disk is usually a manual one. Given a credential that you have stored in the *$credential* variable, you can safely export its password to password.txt using the following command.

```
PS >$credential.Password | ConvertFrom-SecureString |
Set-Content c:\temp\password.txt
```

In the script that you want to run automatically, add the following commands.

```
$password = Get-Content c:\temp\password.txt | ConvertTo-SecureString
$credential = New-Object System.Management.Automation.PSCredential `
    "CachedUser",$password
```

These commands create a new credential object (for the CachedUser user) and store that object in the $credential variable. When reading the solution, you might at first be wary of storing a password on disk. While it is natural (and prudent) to be cautious of littering your hard drive with sensitive information, the ConvertFrom-SecureString cmdlet encrypts this data using the Windows standard Data Protection API. This ensures that only your user account can properly decrypt its contents.

While keeping a password secure is an important security feature, you may sometimes want to store a password (or other sensitive information) on disk so that other accounts have access to it anyway. This is often the case with scripts run by service accounts or scripts that are designed to be transferred between computers. The ConvertFrom-SecureString and ConvertTo-SecureString cmdlets support this scenario by allowing you to specify an encryption key. Keep in mind that when used with a hard-coded encryption key, this technique no longer acts as a security measure. If a user can access the content of your automated script, she has access to the encryption key. If the user has access to the encryption key, she has access to the data you were trying to protect.

Although the solution stores the password in a specific named file, it is more common to store the file in a more generic location—such as the directory that contains the script or the directory that contains your profile.

```
$passwordFile = Join-Path (Split-Path $profile) password.txt
$password = Get-Content $passwordFile | ConvertTo-SecureString
```

Working with Connection Strings as Input

When working with different types of data sources, such as a Microsoft Office Access database or a password-protected Microsoft Office Word document or Office Excel spreadsheet, you are often required to supply a means to pass the credentials to the resource because these types of data sources are unable to use impersonation. The methods for passing the password have already been explored and can easily be adapted to these types of data sources. Because access to these data sources are COM based, you are not able to use the .NET Framework *System.Security.SecureString* class to pass credentials. This also means that you are not able to use the Get-Credential cmdlet due to its reliance on the *SecureString* class to encrypt the password.

As a best practice when working with connection strings to data sources, you should use variables to hold each portion of the connection string. This makes it easier to update the various components of the connection string, as well as adding additional flexibility to change the input methodology without a major rewrite of the script. An example is shown here.

OpenPasswordProtectedExcel.ps1

```
$filename = "C:\fso\TestNumbersProtected.xls"
$updatelinks = 3
$readonly = $false
$format = 5
$password = "password"
$excel = New-Object -comobject Excel.Application
$excel.visible = $true
$excel.workbooks.open($fileName,$updatelinks,$readonly,$format,$password) |
Out-Null
```

Once the *password* parameter is available via a parameter, it is trivial to revise the script
to accept the input via the command line. In the OpenPasswordProtectedWord.ps1 script,
both the file name and the password are moved to command-line parameters. The logic used
to open the password-protected Office Word document is moved into a function, and both
command-line values are marked as mandatory. The use of the *Parameter* tag is a feature that
requires Windows PowerShell 2.0, and the *#requires –version 2.0* tag is used.

OpenPasswordProtectedWord.ps1

```
#requires -version 2.0
Param(
  [Parameter(Mandatory=$true)]
  [string]$fileName,
  [Parameter(Mandatory=$true)]
  [string]$password
)
Function Open-PasswordProtectedDocument($filename,$password)
{
 $Conversion= $false
 $readOnly = $false
 $addRecentFiles = $false
 $doc = New-Object -Comobject Word.Application
 $doc.visible = $true
 $doc.documents.open($filename,$Conversion,$readOnly,$addRecentFiles,$password) |
 out-null
} #end function Open-PasswordProtectedDocument

# *** Entry Point to Script ***

Open-PasswordProtectedDocument -filename $filename -password $password
```

Prompting for Input

From the preceding discussion, you might surmise that if you can use the Read-Host cmdlet to prompt for a password, you can also use the Read-Host cmdlet prior to performing a specific action—and you would be correct. Two primary cases require input from the user. The first case requires the user to supply information to allow the script to complete. This technique is often used when the script is able to perform multiple actions. The input received from the user determines the way the script will run.

The second case that requires input from the user is more basic. It is a prompt for approval to continue. You might want to use this technique prior to deleting a file or performing an action that might tie up the resources of the computer for a significant period of time. Both of these scenarios are discussed here.

Scripts often require information from the user to customize the information that is returned to the user. In the ReadHostQueryDrive.ps1 script, the Read-Host cmdlet is used to prompt the user to enter the drive letter that will be used to request volume information from WMI. The *Switch* statement is used to evaluate the value that is typed in response to the prompt. The ReadHostQueryDrive.ps1 script is shown here.

ReadHostQueryDrive.ps1
```
$response = Read-Host "Type drive letter to query <c: / d:>"

Switch -regex($response) {
  "C" { Get-WmiObject -class Win32_Volume -filter "driveletter = 'c:'" }
  "D" { Get-WmiObject -class Win32_Volume -filter "driveletter = 'd:'" }
} #end switch
```

A more elegant approach to requesting information from the user is to use the *$host.ui.PromptForChoice* class to handle the prompting. The *PromptForChoice* class uses the choices created by the *System.Management.Auomation.Host.ChoiceDescription* class. When creating the choice descriptions, each choice is preceded by the ampersand and stored in an array. Because it is an array, each value has a numeric value that begins counting with 0 as shown in the PromptForChoice.ps1 script.

```
PromptForChoice.ps1
$caption = "No Disk"
$message = "There is no disk in the drive. Please insert a disk into drive D:"
$choices = [System.Management.Automation.Host.ChoiceDescription[]] `
@("&Cancel", "&Try Again", "&Ignore")
[int]$defaultChoice = 2
$choiceRTN = $host.ui.PromptForChoice($caption,$message, $choices,$defaultChoice)

switch($choiceRTN)
{
  0    { "cancelling ..." }
  1    { "Try Again ..." }
  2    { "ignoring ..." }
}
```

Choosing the Best Output Method

There are at least as many output methods available to the scriptwriter in Windows PowerShell 2.0 as there are input methods. If all of the output methods were added up, the list would probably be much greater than the number of input methods. In this section, you will look at outputting to the screen, to a file, and to e-mail.

Output to the Screen

When a cmdlet is used, it automatically outputs to the screen. This is one of the features that makes Windows PowerShell easy to work with from the PowerShell prompt. When you use the Get-Process cmdlet, it automatically displays output to the screen.

In many cases, you do not have to do anything more complicated than run the cmdlet. When you do, you are automatically rewarded with a nicely formatted output that is displayed to the screen as shown in Figure 12-3.

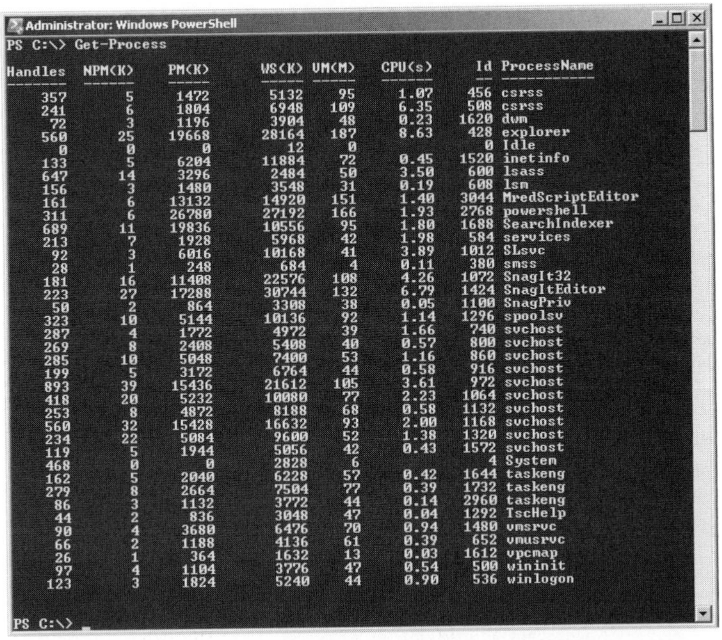

FIGURE 12-3 Output from the `Get-Process` cmdlet is automatically displayed to the Windows PowerShell console.

The reason the output is nicely formatted is that the Windows PowerShell team created several format.ps1xml files that are used to control the way in which different objects are formatted when they are displayed. These XML files are located in the Windows PowerShell install directory. Luckily, there is an automatic variable, *$pshome*, that can be used to refer to the Windows PowerShell install directory. To obtain a listing of all of the format.ps1xml files that are installed on your computer, you use the `Get-ChildItem` cmdlet and specify a path that will retrieve any file with the name format in it. Pipeline the resulting *FileInfo* objects to the `Select-Object` cmdlet, and choose the *name* property.

```
PS C:\> Get-ChildItem -Path $pshome/*format* | Select-Object -Property name
```

```
Name
----
certificate.format.ps1xml
dotnettypes.format.ps1xml
filesystem.format.ps1xml
help.format.ps1xml
powershellcore.format.ps1xml
powershelltrace.format.ps1xml
registry.format.ps1xml
```

These format.ps1xml files are used by the Windows PowerShell Extended Type System to determine how to display objects. This system is required because most objects do not know how to display themselves. Because the format files are XML files, it is possible to edit them to change the default display behavior. This process should not be undertaken lightly because the files are rather complicated. If you want to edit the files, make sure you have a good backup copy of the files before you start making changes. Direct manipulation of the format.ps1xml files can result in unexpected behavior. It is also possible to write your own format.ps1xml file, but such a project can be very complicated.

The dotnettypes.format.ps1xml file is used to control the output that is displayed by a number of the cmdlets (e.g., Get-Process, Get-Service, Get-EventLog) that return .NET Framework objects. A portion of the dotnettypes.format.ps1xml file is shown in Figure 12-4. This is the section of the file that controls the output from the Get-Process cmdlet. Under the *<TableHeaders>* section, each column heading is specified by the <TableColumnHeader> tag. Under the <TableColumnHeader>, there are additional nodes.

FIGURE 12-4 The dotnettypes.format.ps1xml file controls the display of cmdlet data.

To display information to the console, you do not need to worry about formatting XML files. You can rely on the defaults and allow Windows PowerShell to make the decision for you. To display a string, you place the string in quotation marks to display it to the console.

```
PS C:\> "this string is displayed to the console"
this string is displayed to the console
PS C:\>
```

The important thing to keep in mind is that when the string is emitted to the console, it retains its type—that is, it is still a string.

```
PS C:\> "this string is displayed to the console" | Get-Member
   TypeName: System.String
```

Name	MemberType	Definition
Clone	Method	System.Object Clone()
CompareTo	Method	int CompareTo(System.Object value), i...
Contains	Method	bool Contains(string value)
CopyTo	Method	System.Void CopyTo(int sourceIndex, c...
EndsWith	Method	bool EndsWith(string value), bool End...
Equals	Method	bool Equals(System.Object obj), bool ...
GetEnumerator	Method	System.CharEnumerator GetEnumerator()
GetHashCode	Method	int GetHashCode()
GetType	Method	type GetType()
GetTypeCode	Method	System.TypeCode GetTypeCode()
IndexOf	Method	int IndexOf(char value), int IndexOf(...
IndexOfAny	Method	int IndexOfAny(char[] anyOf), int Ind...
Insert	Method	string Insert(int startIndex, string ...
IsNormalized	Method	bool IsNormalized(), bool IsNormalize...
LastIndexOf	Method	int LastIndexOf(char value), int Last...
LastIndexOfAny	Method	int LastIndexOfAny(char[] anyOf), int...
Normalize	Method	string Normalize(), string Normalize(...
PadLeft	Method	string PadLeft(int totalWidth), strin...
PadRight	Method	string PadRight(int totalWidth), stri...
Remove	Method	string Remove(int startIndex, int cou...
Replace	Method	string Replace(char oldChar, char new...
Split	Method	string[] Split(Params char[] separato...
StartsWith	Method	bool StartsWith(string value), bool S...
Substring	Method	string Substring(int startIndex), str...
ToCharArray	Method	char[] ToCharArray(), char[] ToCharAr...
ToLower	Method	string ToLower(), string ToLower(Syst...
ToLowerInvariant	Method	string ToLowerInvariant()
ToString	Method	string ToString(), string ToString(Sy...
ToUpper	Method	string ToUpper(), string ToUpper(Syst...
ToUpperInvariant	Method	string ToUpperInvariant()
Trim	Method	string Trim(Params char[] trimChars),...
TrimEnd	Method	string TrimEnd(Params char[] trimChars)
TrimStart	Method	string TrimStart(Params char[] trimCh...
Chars	ParameterizedProperty	char Chars(int index) {get;}
Length	Property	System.Int32 Length {get;}

If you use one of the out-* cmdlets, such as Out-Host or Out-Default, you destroy the object-oriented nature of the string. That is, the output is no longer an instance of a *System.String* .NET Framework class.

```
PS C:\> "this string is displayed to the console" | Out-Host | Get-Member
this string is displayed to the console
Get-Member : No object has been specified to the get-member cmdlet.
At line:1 char:66
+ "this string is displayed to the console" | Out-Host | Get-Member <<<<
    + CategoryInfo          : CloseError: (:) [Get-Member], InvalidOperationException
    + FullyQualifiedErrorId : NoObjectInGetMember,Microsoft.PowerShell.Commands.
    GetMemberCommand


PS C:\>
```

As a best practice, you should avoid using the Out-Host or Out-Default cmdlet unless there is a reason to use it because you lose your object once you send the output to the Out-* cmdlet. The only reason for using Out-Host is to use the *–paging* parameter.

```
PS C:\> Get-WmiObject -Class Win32_process | Out-Host –Paging
```

```
__GENUS                    : 2
__CLASS                    : Win32_Process
__SUPERCLASS               : CIM_Process
__DYNASTY                  : CIM_ManagedSystemElement
__RELPATH                  : Win32_Process.Handle="0"
__PROPERTY_COUNT           : 45
__DERIVATION               : {CIM_Process, CIM_LogicalElement, CIM_ManagedSystemElement}
__SERVER                   : VISTA
__NAMESPACE                : root\cimv2
__PATH                     : \\VISTA\root\cimv2:Win32_Process.Handle="0"
Caption                    : System Idle Process
CommandLine                :
CreationClassName          : Win32_Process
CreationDate               :
CSCreationClassName        : Win32_ComputerSystem
CSName                     : VISTA
Description                : System Idle Process
ExecutablePath             :
ExecutionState             :
Handle                     : 0
HandleCount                : 0
InstallDate                :
KernelModeTime             : 151488730096
MaximumWorkingSetSize      :
MinimumWorkingSetSize      :
Name                       : System Idle Process
OSCreationClassName        : Win32_OperatingSystem
OSName                     : Microsoftr Windows VistaT Business |C:\Windows|\Device
                             \Harddisk0\Partition1
```

```
OtherOperationCount        : 0
OtherTransferCount         : 0
PageFaults                 : 0
PageFileUsage              : 0
ParentProcessId            : 0
PeakPageFileUsage          : 0
PeakVirtualSize            : 0
PeakWorkingSetSize         : 0
Priority                   : 0
PrivatePageCount           : 0
<SPACE> next page; <CR> next line; Q quit
```

If you are not using the *–paging* parameter, there is no advantage to using the Out-Host cmdlet. From a display perspective, the following commands are identical.

```
Get-Process
Get-Process | Out-Host
Get-Process | Out-Default
```

In fact, Out-Default and Out-Host do the same thing on most systems because, by default, the Out-Host cmdlet is the default outputter. The only reason to use the Out-Default cmdlet is if you anticipate changing the default outputter and do not want to rewrite the script. By using Out-Default, the output from the script will always go to the default outputter, which may or may not be the host.

Output to File

If you want to display information to the screen, you run the command. By default, the command will emit the information to the console as shown here.

```
PS C:\> Get-WmiObject -Class Win32_Bios


SMBIOSBIOSVersion : A01
Manufacturer      : Dell Computer Corporation
Name              : Default System BIOS
SerialNumber      : 9HQ1S21
Version           : DELL   - 6


PS C:\>
```

If you want to store the information in a text file, you can use the redirection arrow.

```
PS C:\> Get-WmiObject -Class Win32_Bios >c:\fso\bios.txt
PS C:\>
```

The problem is that there is no confirmation message stating that the command completed successfully, nor is there any idea of what is contained in the text file. Although you can use the Out-File cmdlet, as shown here, there is no feedback from the command.

```
PS C:\> Get-WmiObject -Class Win32_Bios | Out-File -FilePath C:\fso\bios.txt
PS C:\>
```

You can use the Get-Content cmdlet to inspect the contents of the file to ensure that it has the information you require. The thing to keep in mind is that you are not piping the information from the Out-File cmdlet to the Get-Content cmdlet. The semicolon is used to indicate that you are beginning a new command. The semicolon is the equivalent of typing the command on a new line in a script.

```
PS C:\> Get-WmiObject -Class Win32_Bios | Out-File -FilePath C:\fso\bios.txt ;
Get-Content -Path C:\fso\bios.txt


SMBIOSBIOSVersion : A01
Manufacturer      : Dell Computer Corporation
Name              : Default System BIOS
SerialNumber      : 9HQ1S21
Version           : DELL   - 6
```

Because you have already seen that using the redirection arrow is the same as using the Out-File cmdlet, for your purposes here, you can revise the command to use the redirection arrows. You can also shorten the command a bit by using the alias *cat* instead of the lengthier Get-Content cmdlet name.

```
PS C:\> Get-WmiObject -Class Win32_Bios > C:\fso\bios.txt ; cat C:\fso\bios.txt


SMBIOSBIOSVersion : A01
Manufacturer      : Dell Computer Corporation
Name              : Default System BIOS
SerialNumber      : 9HQ1S21
Version           : DELL   - 6
```

By using an alias for the Get-WmiObject cmdlet and omitting the *–class* parameter name, you can shorten the command quite a bit.

```
PS C:\> gwmi Win32_Bios > C:\fso\bios.txt ; cat C:\fso\bios.txt


SMBIOSBIOSVersion : A01
Manufacturer      : Dell Computer Corporation
Name              : Default System BIOS
SerialNumber      : 9HQ1S21
Version           : DELL   - 6
```

Splitting the Output to Both the Screen and the File

Now you have a shorter command that you can use to feed the content from the command to a text file for storage and then display the information on the console. While this is a workable solution, it is easier to use a cmdlet if it can essentially do the same thing. As it turns out, there is a cmdlet that will split the output from a cmdlet and direct it to both the screen and to a file, and this cmdlet is named Tee-Object. Most of the time, you will split the output from your command line to a file and to the console. To do this, you can use the –*filepath* parameter and specify the full path to the file. As shown here, the Tee-Object cmdlet supports a number of additional switches and parameters.

```
Tee-Object [-FilePath] <String> [-InputObject <PSObject>] [-Verbose] [-Debug]
[-ErrorAction <ActionPreference>] [-ErrorVariable <String>] [-OutVariable <String>]
[-OutBuffer <Int32>]
```

To return to the example, you can replace the redirection arrow (or the Out-File cmdlet) and the Get-Content cmdlet (*cat* alias) with the Tee-Object cmdlet. The revised code is shown here.

```
Get-WmiObject -Class Win32_Bios | Tee-Object -FilePath c:\fso\bios.txt
```

When you run the command, you receive the output shown in Figure 12-5.

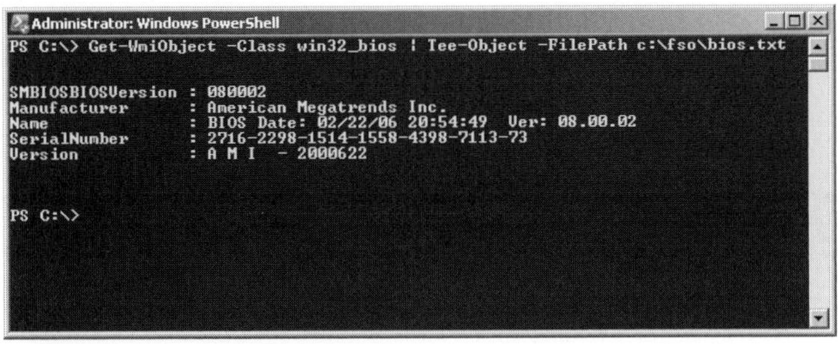

FIGURE 12-5 The Tee-Object cmdlet splits output between the text file and the Windows PowerShell console.

One thing to keep in mind when using the Tee-Object cmdlet is that it always overwrites the previous text file if the file already exists. On the other hand, if the file does not exist, the Tee-Object cmdlet creates the file, but it does not create the folder. If you attempt to use the Tee-Object cmdlet to write to a folder that does not exist, an error will be received that warns of a missing path.

```
PS C:\> Get-WmiObject -class Win32_Bios | Tee-Object -FilePath C:\fso5\bios.txt
out-file : Could not find a part of the path 'C:\fso5\bios.txt'.
PS C:\>
```

You can also use the Tee-Object cmdlet to hold the output of a command in a variable. This offers a convenient way to save the information for use later in the script. The following code shows you how to save the results of a command in a variable and then display them later without using the Tee-object cmdlet.

```
PS C:\> $bios = Get-WmiObject -class Win32_Bios
PS C:\> $bios


SMBIOSBIOSVersion : A01
Manufacturer      : Dell Computer Corporation
Name              : Default System BIOS
SerialNumber      : 9HQ1S21
Version           : DELL   - 6


PS C:\>
```

The syntax for the Tee-Object cmdlet when it is used to store the results of a pipeline in a variable is shown here.

```
Tee-Object [-InputObject <PSObject>] -Variable <String> [-Verbose] [-Debug]
[-ErrorAction <ActionPreference>] [-ErrorVariable <String>] [-OutVariable <String>]
[-OutBuffer <Int32>]
```

To store the results of your Get-WmiObject –Class Win32_Bios command in a variable named *$bios*, you can use the following command.

```
PS C:\> Get-WmiObject -class Win32_Bios | Tee-Object -Variable bios


SMBIOSBIOSVersion : A01
Manufacturer      : Dell Computer Corporation
Name              : Default System BIOS
SerialNumber      : 9HQ1S21
Version           : DELL   - 6
```

One thing to keep in mind when using the *variable* parameter with the Tee-Object cmdlet is that you do not need to use a dollar sign in front of the variable name. This makes the behavior of the cmdlet the same as the behavior when using the New-Variable cmdlet.

To see the contents of the *$bios* variable, you type **$bios** on the command line in the Windows PowerShell console.

```
PS C:\> $bios


SMBIOSBIOSVersion : A01
Manufacturer      : Dell Computer Corporation
Name              : Default System BIOS
SerialNumber      : 9HQ1S21
Version           : DELL   - 6


PS C:\>
```

One of the best features of the `Tee-Object` cmdlet is that it also passes the object through the pipeline. This means that you are not stuck with the default display of information that is returned by the previous command, such as the `Get-WmiObject` cmdlet. You can store the object in the *$bios* variable and then choose to display only the *name* property.

```
PS C:\> Get-WmiObject -class Win32_Bios | Tee-Object -Variable bios |
select name

name
----
Default System BIOS
```

To retrieve the object from the variable, you once again type the variable **$bios** on the command line or use it elsewhere in your script.

```
PS C:\> $bios

SMBIOSBIOSVersion : A01
Manufacturer      : Dell Computer Corporation
Name              : Default System BIOS
SerialNumber      : 9HQ1S21
Version           : DELL   - 6
```

You are not limited to using the `Tee-Object` cmdlet with Windows PowerShell cmdlets. You can use `Tee-Object` with ordinary command-line utilities as shown here, where the results of the ping command are displayed to the console and stored in the *$ping* variable.

```
PS C:\> ping berlin | Tee-Object -Variable ping
Pinging Berlin.nwtraders.com [192.168.2.1] with 32 bytes of data:
Reply from 192.168.2.1: bytes=32 time=11ms TTL=128
Reply from 192.168.2.1: bytes=32 time=1ms TTL=128
Reply from 192.168.2.1: bytes=32 time=1ms TTL=128
Reply from 192.168.2.1: bytes=32 time=1ms TTL=128
Ping statistics for 192.168.2.1:
    Packets: Sent = 4, Received = 4, Lost = 0 (0% loss),
Approximate round trip times in milli-seconds:
    Minimum = 1ms, Maximum = 11ms, Average = 3ms
PS C:\>
```

The advantage of this technique is that you can now use the `Select-String` cmdlet to search the contents of the variable and quickly find the information you need. If you are most interested in only the number of packets that were sent and received, you can pipe the data that is stored in the *$ping* variable to the `Select-String` cmdlet.

```
PS C:\> $ping | Select-String packet
    Packets: Sent = 4, Received = 4, Lost = 0 (0% loss),
PS C:\>
```

Working with Output

Dave Schwinn, Senior Consultant
Full Service Networking

In Windows PowerShell 2.0, there are many options when dealing with output from a script or even when working from the Windows PowerShell command shell. For example, I can easily output to a text file, a database, the screen, to HTML, XML, or a comma-separated variable (CSV) file. The choice, of course, depends on what I intend to do with the data after I obtain it.

One of the things I really enjoy doing is exporting XML from a command. I will run a command, export it to XML in a file, and then display the contents of that XML on the screen. Although this can be a hassle, the XML formatting makes it easy for me to see relationships between different data elements.

On an average day, it seems that I usually format data to the screen as a table. This view is extremely useful for allowing me to quickly work my way through a long list of related items. You can consider the table view in terms of the Get-Process or the Get-Service cmdlets, which produce a table list by default. As an example, consider the WMI *Win32_LogicalDisk* class. I can quickly use the following command to provide exactly the information I need.

```
PS C:\> Get-WmiObject Win32_LogicalDisk |
Format-Table name, size, freespace -AutoSize

name          size        freespace
----          ----        ---------
C:     158391595008 15872155648
E:
S:       1647308800  1554030592
```

If I send information to a printer, I like to use the ConvertTo-Html cmdlet because it allows me to specify details that make for a professional-looking report. However, I will often output to another cmdlet and continue using the command line.

I can also use Microsoft Visual Studio to host Windows PowerShell commands. I often write commands in a Visual Studio project that call Windows PowerShell to retrieve the data for me and then return it to my application. It is easier for me to use Windows PowerShell to retrieve the WMI objects and for me to consume the data returned by PowerShell in my application than it is for me to call the WMI classes directly from the .NET Framework. I then output the data as a dataset and parse the columns of data for my application.

I use the Export_CSV cmdlet quite frequently because I can easily open the file in Excel, which allows me to do advanced data manipulation as well as create charts and reports for various presentations. Because I work for a Microsoft solutions provider, our company has a large number of customers who use a licensing model from Microsoft whereby they basically lease the software from Microsoft. Therefore, these customers always have the right to upgrade to the latest software whenever they want to do so, and they can easily budget for their software expenses. The problem is that they must let Microsoft know how many seats of the software they are using each month. I use Windows PowerShell to query a customer's Microsoft Exchange Server by using the `Get-Mailbox` cmdlet, which gives me a listing of all of the mailboxes used on the server. I then export the list to a CSV file and pipeline it to the `Send-MailMessage` cmdlet. The report goes directly to the purchasing representative so that he can open it in Excel and determine how many seats the client must pay for that month. This type of easy automation simply was not available before Windows PowerShell, and it is the ease of formatting output that makes it all possible.

Output to E-Mail

It is a common request to be able to send information from a script to an e-mail recipient. In the past, this generally meant writing a complicated function and hoping that all of the details were put together correctly to enable this functionality to work properly. It was easier to do before spammers caused security concerns about sending e-mail from scripts. E-mail viruses have added additional layers of authentication and made the process much more confusing.

In Windows PowerShell 2.0, the `Send-MailMessage` cmdlet can be used to simplify the task of sending e-mail from a script. In some cases, this cmdlet works without any additional configuration on your network. At other times, you need to grant the user account that is being used to run the script permission to send e-mail from the script.

Output from Functions

When a function is called, it returns data to the calling code. This behavior is often not understood well by people who come to Windows PowerShell from other scripting languages. When you run the AddOne.ps1 script, the number 6 is displayed to the console. What is confusing is that data is returned from the line of code that calls the function and not from within the function itself, which is different behavior than might be expected. Most of the time, when two numbers are added together, the data is returned from the line that performs the work.

```
PS C:\> $int = 5
PS C:\> $int + 1
6
PS C:\>
```

It is therefore reasonable to expect that the number 6 is coming from inside the *AddOne* function and not from outside the function. The AddOne.ps1 script including the *AddOne* function is shown here.

```
AddOne.ps1
Function AddOne($int)
{
  $int + 1
}


AddOne(5)
```

To illustrate where the data comes from, you can modify the script to store the result of calling the function to a variable. You can then use the Get-Member cmdlet to display the information that is returned as shown in AddOne1.Ps1.

```
AddOne1.ps1
Function AddOne($int)
{
  $int + 1
}


$number = AddOne(5)
$number | get-member
'Display the value of $number: ' + $number
```

When the AddOne1.ps1 script is run, you can see that the information is returned to the code that calls the function. In the first line after the function call, the object stored in the *$number* variable is shown to be a *System.Int32* object. Following the Get-Member command, the value stored in the *$number* variable is shown to be equal to 6. The value 5 is not displayed from within the *AddOne* function.

```
   TypeName: System.Int32

Name        MemberType Definition
----        ---------- ----------
CompareTo   Method     System.Int32 CompareTo(Object value), System.Int32 Co...
Equals      Method     System.Boolean Equals(Object obj), System.Boolean Equ...
GetHashCode Method     System.Int32 GetHashCode()
GetType     Method     System.Type GetType()
GetTypeCode Method     System.TypeCode GetTypeCode()
ToString    Method     System.String ToString(), System.String ToString(Stri...
Display the value of $number: 6
```

When you use a cmdlet such as Write-Host from inside the function, you then circumvent the return process that is inherent in the design of the function. The use of Write-Host from within a function is illustrated in AddOne2.ps1.

```
AddOne2.ps1
Function AddOne($int)
{
 Write-Host $int + 1
}


$number = AddOne(5)
$number | get-member
'Display the value of $number: ' + $number
```

When the script is run, you will notice that nothing is returned from inside the function. The *$number* variable no longer contains an object.

```
5 + 1
Get-Member : No object has been specified to get-member.
At C:\Documents and Settings\ed\Local Settings\Temp\tmp6.tmp.ps1:9 char:21
+ $number | get-member <<<<
Display the value of $number:
```

Avoid Populating the Global Variable

In addition to using cmdlets, such as Write-Host, from within a function to circumvent the output from a function, it is also possible to store the results of a function to a variable. The problem with storing results from the function to a variable within the function is that when a variable is created within a function, it is not available outside of the function as shown here.

```
AddOne3.ps1
Function AddOne($int)
{
 $number =  $int + 1
}


$number = AddOne(5)
$number | get-member
'Display the value of $number: ' + $number
```

When the AddOne3.ps1 script is run, there is no object in the *$number* variable because the variable is not available outside of the *AddOne* function.

```
Get-Member : No object has been specified to get-member.
At C:\Documents and Settings\ed\Local Settings\Temp\tmp9.tmp.ps1:9 char:21
+ $number | get-member <<<<
Display the value of $number:
```

One technique that is sometimes used to provide the value of the variable from within the function to the calling script is to add a scope to the variable.

```
AddOne4.ps1
Function AddOne($int)
{
 $global:number =  $int + 1
}


AddOne(5)
$global:number | get-member
'Display the value of $global:number: ' + $global:number
```

A potential problem exists when adding a variable to the global scope—the variable continues to exist after the script has exited. As long as the Windows PowerShell console is open and until you explicitly remove the global variable, it continues to be available. This means that the variable will be available in other scripts and will always be available within the console. This might not be a problem, but it can cause scripts that use the same variable names to operate in an erratic fashion. One way to determine whether the variable persists is to check the variable drive.

```
   TypeName: System.Int32

Name           MemberType Definition
----           ---------- ----------
CompareTo      Method     System.Int32 CompareTo(Object value), System.Int32 Co...
Equals         Method     System.Boolean Equals(Object obj), System.Boolean Equ...
GetHashCode    Method     System.Int32 GetHashCode()
GetType        Method     System.Type GetType()
GetTypeCode    Method     System.TypeCode GetTypeCode()
ToString       Method     System.String ToString(), System.String ToString(Stri...
Display the value of $global:number: 6


PS C:\data\PowerShellBestPractices\Scripts\Chapter12> Get-Item Variable:\number

Name                            Value
----                            -----
number                          6
```

It is possible to remove the global variable in the last line of the script by using the Remove-Variable cmdlet, but a better approach is to use the Script-level scope instead of the Global-level scope. The Script-level variable is available inside and outside the function while the script is running. Once the script has completed, the variable is removed. The use of the Script-level scope is shown in the AddOne5.ps1 script.

```
AddOne5.ps1
Function AddOne($int)
{
 $script:number =  $int + 1
}


AddOne(5)
$script:number | get-member
'Display the value of $script:number: ' + $script:number
```

When the AddOne5.ps1 script runs, the value of the *$number* variable is available outside of the function. When the script has completed its run, an error is returned when the Get-Item cmdlet is used to attempt to retrieve the value of the variable.

```
   TypeName: System.Int32

Name        MemberType Definition
----        ---------- ----------
CompareTo   Method     System.Int32 CompareTo(Object value), System.Int32 Co...
Equals      Method     System.Boolean Equals(Object obj), System.Boolean Equ...
GetHashCode Method     System.Int32 GetHashCode()
GetType     Method     System.Type GetType()
GetTypeCode Method     System.TypeCode GetTypeCode()
ToString    Method     System.String ToString(), System.String ToString(Stri...
Display the value of $script:number: 6

PS C:\data\PowerShellBestPractices\Scripts\Chapter12> Get-Item variable:number
Get-Item : Cannot find path 'number' because it does not exist.
At line:1 char:9
+ Get-Item  <<<< variable:number
```

Using a Namespace in the Global Variable

One way to protect your Windows PowerShell console from inadvertent pollution from global variables that are created within scripts is to add a namespace tag to the variable. This process still allows you to use a global variable if required, but it also reduces variable naming conflicts. To create a global variable in a separate namespace, you can use a dollar sign, a pair of curly brackets, and the global scope tag. The separate namespace follows the colon. Finally, the variable itself is separated by a period from the namespace.

```
${Global:AddOne6.number} =  $int + 1
```

To reference the value that is stored in a global variable within a separate namespace, you can use the dollar sign, curly brackets, and the dotted notation for the namespace/variable name. You do not need to add the global tag.

```
${AddOne6.number}
```

An example of using a global variable in a separate namespace is shown in the AddOne6.ps1 script.

```
AddOne6.ps1
Function AddOne($int)
{
 ${Global:AddOne6.number} = $int + 1
}


AddOne(5)
${AddOne6.number} | get-member
'Display the value of ${AddOne6.number}: ' + ${AddOne6.number}
```

When the AddOne6.ps1 script runs, the variable can be accessed after the script runs by including the namespace and the variable name in a dotted notation.

```
   TypeName: System.Int32


Name           MemberType Definition
----           ---------- ----------
CompareTo      Method     System.Int32 CompareTo(Object value), System.Int32 Co...
Equals         Method     System.Boolean Equals(Object obj), System.Boolean Equ...
GetHashCode    Method     System.Int32 GetHashCode()
GetType        Method     System.Type GetType()
GetTypeCode    Method     System.TypeCode GetTypeCode()
ToString       Method     System.String ToString(), System.String ToString(Stri...
Display the value of ${AddOne6.number}: 6


PS C:\data\PowerShellBestPractices\Scripts\Chapter12> Get-Item Variable:\AddOne6.number


Name                           Value
----                           -----
AddOne6.number                 6
```

Windows PowerShell Requires a New Way of Thinking

Richard Norman, Senior Premier Field Engineer
Microsoft Corporation

As a premier field engineer for Microsoft, I spend a lot of time talking to customers about working with Windows PowerShell. I tell them that the number one rule when working with Windows PowerShell is: You must change some of your thinking. This is especially true for people who are migrating to Windows PowerShell from VBScript.

With Windows PowerShell, you obtain all new possibilities along with the old capabilities. The underlying premise of Windows PowerShell is the fact that you are working with objects. These objects have properties and methods that can be exploited in ways that VBScript cannot. Previously, you only dealt with results as text. To accomplish anything more, you needed to use other tools to parse and manipulate the results. With Windows PowerShell, you receive more than just a "text" representation because you are working with objects that you can manipulate in new ways. You can continue to use text parsing if that is what you are accustomed to do, but this reduces your possibilities. The next step in your thinking is to start taking advantage of the properties of the objects. As an example, you can obtain a list of files that were modified within the last week by using the object properties as shown here.

```
dir | where-object {$_.lastwritetime -ge (get-date).adddays(-7)}})
```

You should also stop thinking that the pipeline is operating on a list (called an array) of objects on the command line. You are sending these objects in a series through to the next command, and the next, and the next, and so on. This list of objects is key to understanding how Windows PowerShell works. Using the objects in your scripts reveals much of the power behind all of the cmdlets. Due to the way in which Windows PowerShell operates on objects, it can process items lazily. This means that while one command is processing, Windows PowerShell can begin processing results before the first command is finished. This procedure typically happens so fast that you aren't aware of it, but it is a process that can come in handy for larger files and lists.

Finally, remember that you can use the Windows PowerShell interpreted string to your advantage. When you use quote marks or double quotes ("..."), Windows PowerShell can interpret any variable within the quotes (variables begin with a dollar sign). This process allows you to go beyond the old ideas of using string concatenation and to instead use your variables directly within any string and script output.

The assumption that Windows PowerShell is just like other scripting languages will get you in trouble. While you can write a Windows PowerShell script code in a similar fashion to VBScript, there are differences in how you should write the script. For example, if you want to filter based on the date or some other factor, VBScript is limited and requires quite a few lines of script. In Windows PowerShell, the filtering can be accomplished in one line.

```
dir | where-object {$_.lastwritetime –ge (get-date).adddays(-14)}
```

Another example involves something as simple as converting a time stamp in Domain Name System (DNS) into a usable date and time. Using VBScript can lead to several calculations and functions. Because of the concept of Windows PowerShell objects, you can break the conversion of the date down to a single line of code.

```
get-date "1/1/1601 12:00 am GMT").addhours($timestamp)
```

Because Windows PowerShell is strongly object based, you end up simplifying some things at the expense of complicating a few others. Some functions from VBScript have direct equivalents, while others become slightly more complex in the Windows PowerShell world, such as the CMD.exe "DIR /a:d" command. This command returns a list of folders in the current directory. In Windows PowerShell, a similar command looks like the following: "DIR | Where-Object {$_.PSISContainer}". The command is a little longer, but the power you receive in other areas more than compensates for some of these shortcomings in verboseness.

Also, procedures that you commonly perform, such as using the CLS command in CMD.exe, are now an entirely new function named *Clear-Host* Windows PowerShell. I will leave this function to the reader to investigate. However, the implementation of this function is clearly more complex than the older CLS command.

I often hear that Windows PowerShell is bringing the power that developers have with the .NET Framework to the command line for administrators. Sometimes, that power can take some getting used to. For example, it is very easy to do DNS look-ups using the .NET Framework ([system.net.dns]::Resolve($address)). What is special about this scenario is that the result is not simply text to parse but an object that can be manipulated.

You can use simple strings to show you a vast amount of methods that are available to parse and manipulate the strings, such as "a string" | Get-Member. The technique of using the underlying .NET Framework classes and methods also works with many other objects such as dates, IP addresses, and Uniform Resource Identifiers (URIs). You can now use and manipulate all of these items through Windows PowerShell that were previously only available in the .NET Framework. Even user interface and Web-based .NET libraries are available to you.

When working with XML, I can now take the string and transform it into an XML document instead of doing other parsing. As an example, the following code creates an XML document from a string that can be written to a file or that can be parsed or searched using an XPath or XQuery statement.

```
$dom=[xml]"<doc><item1>value1</item1><item1>value2</item1><item1>value3
<item2>subvalue1</item2></item1></doc>"
$dom.doc
$dom | get-member
```

I can take a regular expression and, in two lines of Windows PowerShell script, determine whether a string matches that expression. By using one more line, I can list all of the matches. The ability of Windows PowerShell to use and create regular expressions is very powerful.

```
$regex=[regex]"^((6\.((1\.((98\.(10|[0-9]))|((9[0-7]|[1-8]?
[0-9])\..*)))|(0\..*)))|([0-5]\..*))$"
$regex.ismatch("6.0.84.18")
```

Additional Resources

- The Technet Script Center at *http://www.microsoft.com/technet/scriptcenter* contains numerous examples of handling input from Windows PowerShell scripts.
- Take a look at *Windows PowerShell™ Scripting Guide* (Microsoft Press, 2008).
- On the companion media, you will find all of the scripts referred to in this chapter.

Handling Errors

When it comes to handling errors in your script, you need to understand how the script will be used. The way that a script will be used is sometimes called the *use case scenario*, and it describes how the user will interact with the script.

If the use case scenario is simple, the user might not need to do anything more than type the name of the script inside the Windows PowerShell console. A script such as Get-Bios.ps1 can get by without much need for any error handling because there are no inputs to the script. The script is called, it runs, and it displays information that should always be readily available because the *Win32_Bios* Windows Management Instrumentation (WMI) class is present in all versions of Windows since Microsoft Windows 2000.

Get-Bios.ps1
```
Get-WmiObject -class Win32_Bios
```

However, if the use case scenario is complicated, the requirements for handling potential errors increase. Most scripts used in enterprise environments allow the user of the script to enter parameters from the command line. Very few scripts actually require the user to open the script in a script editor and manually change variable assignments. Instead, the user types in values from the command line, which opens up all types of potential sources for error. The most common error occurs when the user of the script does not supply a value for something basic, such as the target computer name. What happens when the user types in the name of a computer that is turned off or that does not exist in the network? Suppose you have a script that does performance monitoring on a remote computer, and you allow the user of the script to select the monitor interval.

What happens if the user chooses to read the performance counters every .1 second? This can have an adverse impact on the performance of the computer that is being tested. What about a script that attempts to read from a WMI class that does not exist on the remote computer? How does the script handle that error condition? There are some tried and true methods for dealing with each of these potential error conditions, and in this chapter we will examine each of these scenarios.

Handling Missing Parameters

When you examine the Get-Bios.ps1 script, you can see that it does not receive any input from the command line. Although this is a good way to avoid user errors in your script, it is not always practical. When your script accepts command-line input, you are opening the door for all types of potential problems. Depending on the way in which you accept command-line input, you might need to test the input data to ensure that it corresponds to the type of input that the script is expecting. Because the Get-Bios.ps1 script does not accept command-line input, you therefore avoid most potential sources of errors.

Creating a Default Value for the Parameter

There are two ways to assign default values for a command-line parameter. You can assign the default value in the *Param* declaration statement, or you can assign the value in the script itself. Given a choice between the two, I generally feel it is a best practice to assign the default value in the *Param* statement because it makes the script easier to read.

Detecting the Missing Value and Assigning It in the Script

In the Get-BiosInformation.ps1 script, the *–computername* command-line parameter is created to allow the script to target both local and remote computers. If the script is run without a value for the *–computername* parameter, the Get-WmiObject cmdlet fails because it requires a value for the *–computername* parameter. To solve the problem of the missing parameter, the Get-BiosInformation.ps1 script checks for the presence of the *$computerName* variable. If this variable is missing, then it was not created via the command-line parameter, and the script therefore assigns a value to the *$computerName* variable. Here is the line of code that populates the value of the *$computerName* variable.

```
If(-not($computerName)) { $computerName = $env:computerName }
```

The completed Get-BiosInformation.ps1 script is shown here.

```
Get-BiosInformation.ps1
Param(
  [string]$computerName
) #end param


Function Get-BiosInformation($computerName)
{
 Get-WmiObject -class Win32_Bios -computername $computername
} #end function Get-BiosName


# *** Entry Point To Script ***
If(-not($computerName)) { $computerName = $env:computerName }
Get-BiosInformation -computername $computername
```

Assigning the Value in the *Parameter* Statement

To assign a default value in the *Param* statement, use the equality operator following the parameter name and assign the value to the parameter.

```
Param(
  [string]$computerName = $env:computername
) #end param
```

The advantage of assigning the default value for the parameter in the *Param* statement is that the script is easier to read. Because the parameter declaration and the default parameter are in the same place, you can immediately see which parameters have default values and which do not. The second advantage that arises from assigning a default value in the *Param* statement is that the script is easier to write. Notice that no *If* statement is used to check for the existence of the *$computerName* variable. The complete Get-BiosInformationDefaultParam.ps1 script is shown here.

```
Get-BiosInformationDefaultParam.ps1
Param(
  [string]$computerName = $env:computername
) #end param


Function Get-BiosInformation($computerName)
{
 Get-WmiObject -class Win32_Bios -computername $computername
} #end function Get-BiosName


# *** Entry Point To Script ***


Get-BiosInformation -computername $computername
```

Making the Parameter Mandatory

The best way to handle an error is to ensure that the error does not occur in the first place. In Windows PowerShell 2.0, you can mark a parameter as mandatory. The advantage of marking a parameter as mandatory is that it requires the user of the script to supply a value for the parameter. If you do not want the user of the script to be able to run the script without making a particular selection, you want to make the parameter mandatory. To make a parameter mandatory, use the *mandatory* parameter attribute.

```
Param(
    [Parameter(Mandatory=$true)]
    [string]$drive,
    [string]$computerName = $env:computerName
) #end param
```

The complete MandatoryParameter.ps1 script is shown here.

```
MandatoryParameter.ps1
#Requires -version 2.0
Param(
    [Parameter(Mandatory=$true)]
    [string]$drive,
    [string]$computerName = $env:computerName
) #end param


Function Get-DiskInformation($computerName,$drive)
{
 Get-WmiObject -class Win32_volume -computername $computername `
-filter "DriveLetter = '$drive'"
} #end function Get-BiosName


# *** Entry Point To Script ***

 Get-DiskInformation -computername $computerName -drive $drive
```

When a script with a mandatory parameter is run without supplying a value for the parameter, an error is not generated. Instead, Windows PowerShell prompts for the required parameter value.

```
PS C:\bp> .\MandatoryParameter.ps1

cmdlet MandatoryParameter.ps1 at command pipeline position 1
Supply values for the following parameters:
drive:
```

Limiting Choices

Depending on the design of the script, there are several things that you can do to decrease the amount of error checking required. If you have a limited number of choices that you want to display to the user, you can use the *PromptForChoice* method. If you want to limit the selection to computers that are currently running, you can ping the computer prior to attempting to connect. If you want to limit the choice to a subset of computers or properties, you can parse a text file and use the *–contains* operator. In this section, you will examine each of these techniques for limiting the permissible input values from the command line.

Using *PromptForChoice* to Limit Selections

If you use the *PromptForChoice* method of soliciting input from the user, the user has a limited number of options from which to choose. You completely eliminate the problem of bad input. The user prompt from the *PromptForChoice* method is shown in Figure 13-1.

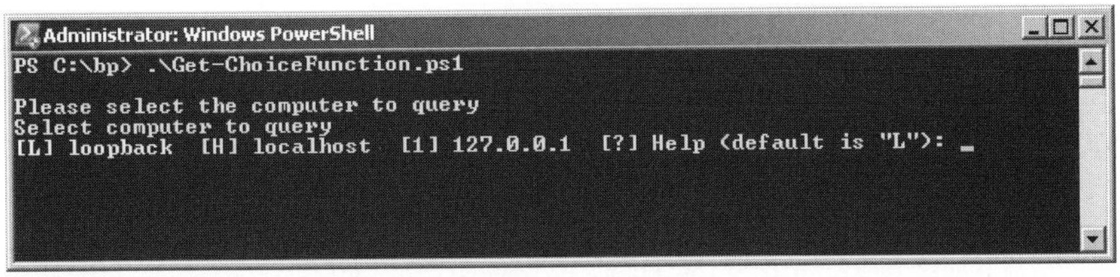

FIGURE 13-1 The *PromptForChoice* method presents a selectable menu to the user.

The use of the *PromptForChoice* method is illustrated in the Get-ChoiceFunction.ps1 script. In the *Get-Choice* function, the *$caption* variable and the *$message* variable hold the caption and the message that is used by *PromptForChoice*. The choices that are offered are instances of the Microsoft .NET Framework *ChoiceDescription* class. When you create the *ChoiceDescription* class, you also supply an array with the choices that will appear.

```
$choices = [System.Management.Automation.Host.ChoiceDescription[]] `
 @("&loopback", "local&host", "&127.0.0.1")
```

Next, you need to select a number that will be used to represent the default choice. When you begin counting, keep in mind that the *ChoiceDescription* class is an array, and the first option is numbered 0. Next, you call the *PromptForChoice* method and display the options.

```
[int]$defaultChoice = 0
$choiceRTN = $host.ui.PromptForChoice($caption,$message, $choices,$defaultChoice)
```

Because the *PromptForChoice* method returns an integer, you can use the *If* statement to evaluate the value of the *$choiceRTN* variable. The syntax of the *Switch* statement is more compact and is actually a better choice for this application. The *Switch* statement from the *Get-Choice* function is shown here.

```
switch($choiceRTN)
 {
  0     { "loopback"  }
  1     { "localhost"  }
  2     { "127.0.0.1"  }
 }
```

When you call the *Get-Choice* function, it returns the computer that was identified by the *PromptForChoice* method. You place the method call in a set of parentheses to force it to be evaluated before the rest of the command.

```
Get-WmiObject -class win32_bios -computername (Get-Choice)
```

This solution to the problem of bad input works well when your help desk personnel are working with a limited number of computers. The other caveat to this approach is that you do not want to change the choices on a regular basis. You want a stable list of computers to avoid creating a maintenance nightmare for yourself. The complete Get-ChoiceFunction.ps1 script is shown here.

```
Get-ChoiceFunction.ps1
Function Get-Choice
{
 $caption = "Please select the computer to query"
 $message = "Select computer to query"
 $choices = [System.Management.Automation.Host.ChoiceDescription[]] `
 @("&loopback", "local&host", "&127.0.0.1")
 [int]$defaultChoice = 0
 $choiceRTN = $host.ui.PromptForChoice($caption,$message, $choices,$defaultChoice)

 switch($choiceRTN)
 {
  0     { "loopback"  }
  1     { "localhost"  }
  2     { "127.0.0.1"  }
 }
} #end Get-Choice function

Get-WmiObject -class win32_bios -computername (Get-Choice)
```

Using Ping to Identify Accessible Computers

If you have more than a few computers that need to be accessible or if you do not have a stable list of computers that you will be working with, then one solution to the problem of trying to connect to nonexistent computers is to ping the computer prior to attempting to make the WMI connection.

You can use the *Win32_PingStatus* WMI class to send a ping to a computer. The best way to use the *Win32_PingStatus* WMI class is to create a function that pings the target computer. Because you are interested in a quick reply, the *Test-ComputerPath* function sends one ping only. The *Test-ComputerPath* function accepts a single input, which is the name or IP address of the target computer. To help control the information that is passed to the function, the *$computer* parameter uses a *string* type constraint to ensure that the input to the function is a string. The *Test-ComputerPath* function is shown here.

```
Function Test-ComputerPath([string]$computer)
{
 Get-WmiObject -class win32_pingstatus -filter "address = '$computer'"
} #end Test-ComputerPath
```

The entire *Win32_PingStatus* object is returned to the calling code and is shown here.

```
__GENUS                       : 2
__CLASS                       : Win32_PingStatus
__SUPERCLASS                  :
__DYNASTY                     : Win32_PingStatus
__RELPATH                     : Win32_PingStatus.Address="localhost",BufferSiz
                                e=32,NoFragmentation=FALSE,RecordRoute=0,Resol
                                veAddressNames=FALSE,SourceRoute="",SourceRout
                                eType=0,Timeout=1000,TimestampRoute=0,TimeToLi
                                ve=128,TypeofService=128
__PROPERTY_COUNT              : 24
__DERIVATION                  : {}
__SERVER                      : OFFICE
__NAMESPACE                   : root\cimv2
__PATH                        : \\OFFICE\root\cimv2:Win32_PingStatus.Address="
                                localhost",BufferSize=32,NoFragmentation=FALSE
                                ,RecordRoute=0,ResolveAddressNames=FALSE,Sourc
                                eRoute="",SourceRouteType=0,Timeout=1000,Times
                                tampRoute=0,TimeToLive=128,TypeofService=128
Address                       : localhost
BufferSize                    : 32
NoFragmentation               : False
PrimaryAddressResolutionStatus : 0
ProtocolAddress               : 127.0.0.1
ProtocolAddressResolved       :
RecordRoute                   : 0
ReplyInconsistency            : False
ReplySize                     : 32
ResolveAddressNames           : False
ResponseTime                  : 0
ResponseTimeToLive            : 128
RouteRecord                   :
RouteRecordResolved           :
```

```
SourceRoute                          :
SourceRouteType                      : 0
StatusCode                           : 0
Timeout                              : 1000
TimeStampRecord                      :
TimeStampRecordAddress               :
TimeStampRecordAddressResolved       :
TimeStampRoute                       : 0
TimeToLive                           : 128
TypeofService                        : 128
```

In the Test-ComputerPath.ps1 script, the *statusCode* property from the *Win32_PingStatus* object is evaluated. If the value is 0, the ping was successful. If the *statusCode* property is null or is equal to some other number, the ping was not successful. Because the *Win32_PingStatus* object is returned to the calling script, you can retrieve the *statusCode* property directly and use the equality operator to see whether it is equal to 0.

```
if( (Test-ComputerPath -computer $computer).statusCode -eq 0 )
```

If the *statusCode* property is equal to 0, the Test-ComputerPath.ps1 script uses the Get-WmiObject cmdlet to retrieve the BIOS information from the *Win32_Bios* WMI class.

```
Get-WmiObject -class Win32_Bios -computer $computer
```

If the target computer is unable to be reached, the Test-ComputerPath.ps1 script displays a message to the Windows PowerShell console stating the target computer is unreachable.

```
Else
 {
  "Unable to reach $computer computer"
 }
```

The complete Test-ComputerPath.ps1 script is shown here.

```
Test-ComputerPath.ps1
Param([string]$computer = "localhost")

Function Test-ComputerPath([string]$computer)
{
 Get-WmiObject -class win32_pingstatus -filter "address = '$computer'"
} #end Test-ComputerPath


# *** Entry Point to Script ***

if( (Test-ComputerPath -computer $computer).statusCode -eq 0 )
 {
  Get-WmiObject -class Win32_Bios -computer $computer
 }
Else
```

```
{
   "Unable to reach $computer computer"
}
```

Using the *–contains* Operator to Examine the Contents of an Array

To verify input that is received from the command line, you can use the *–contains* operator to examine the contents of an array of possible values. This technique is illustrated here with an array of three values that is created and stored in the *$noun* variable. The *–contains* operator is then used to see whether the array contains "hairy-nosed wombat." Because the *$noun* variable does not have an array element that is equal to the string "hairy-nosed wombat," the *–contains* operator returns false.

```
PS C:\> $noun = "cat","dog","rabbit"
PS C:\> $noun -contains "hairy-nosed wombat"
False
PS C:\>
```

If an array contains a match, the *–contains* operator returns true.

```
PS C:\> $noun = "cat","dog","rabbit"
PS C:\> $noun -contains "rabbit"
True
PS C:\>
```

The *–contains* operator returns true only when there is an exact match. Partial matches return false.

```
PS C:\> $noun = "cat","dog","rabbit"
PS C:\> $noun -contains "bit"
False
PS C:\>
```

The *–contains* operator is case insensitive. Therefore, it returns true when matched regardless of case.

```
PS C:\> $noun = "cat","dog","rabbit"
PS C:\> $noun -contains "Rabbit"
True
PS C:\>
```

If you need to perform a case-sensitive match, you can use the case-sensitive version of the *–contains* operator, *–ccontains*. It returns true only if the case of the string matches the value contained in the array.

```
PS C:\> $noun = "cat","dog","rabbit"
PS C:\> $noun -ccontains "Rabbit"
False
PS C:\> $noun -ccontains "rabbit"
True
PS C:\>
```

In the Get-AllowedComputer.ps1 script, a single command-line parameter is created that is used to hold the name of the target computer for the WMI query. The *–computer* parameter is a string, and it receives the default value from the environmental drive. This is a good technique because it ensures that the script has the name of the local computer, which can then be used in producing a report of the results. If you set the value of the *–computer* parameter to *LocalHost*, you never know which computer the results belong to.

```
Param([string]$computer = $env:computername)
```

The *Get-AllowedComputer* function is used to create an array of permitted computer names and to check the value of the *$computer* variable to see whether it is present. If the value of the *$computer* variable is present in the array, the *Get-AllowedComputer* function returns true. If the value is missing from the array, the *Get-AllowedComputer* function returns false. The array of computer names is created by using the Get-Content cmdlet to read a text file that contains a listing of computer names. The text file, servers.txt, is a plain ASCII text file that has a list of computer names on individual lines as shown in Figure 13-2.

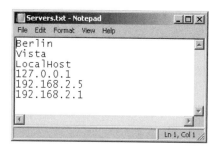

FIGURE 13-2 A text file with computer names and addresses is an easy way to work with allowed computers.

A text file of computer names is easier to maintain than a hard-coded array that is embedded into the script. In addition, the text file can be placed on a central share and used by many different scripts. The *Get-AllowedComputer* function is shown here.

```
Function Get-AllowedComputer([string]$computer)
{
 $servers = Get-Content -path c:\fso\servers.txt
 $servers -contains $computer
} #end Get-AllowedComputer function
```

Because the *Get-AllowedComputer* function returns a Boolean value (true/false), it can be used directly in an *If* statement to determine whether the value that is supplied for the *$computer* variable is on the permitted list. If the *Get-AllowedComputer* function returns true, the Get-WmiObject cmdlet is used to query for BIOS information from the target computer.

```
if(Get-AllowedComputer -computer $computer)
 {
   Get-WmiObject -class Win32_Bios -Computer $computer
 }
```

On the other hand, if the value of the *$computer* variable is not found in the *$servers* array, a string stating that the computer is not an allowed computer is displayed.

```
Else
 {
  "$computer is not an allowed computer"
 }
```

The complete Get-AllowedComputer.ps1 script is shown here.

Get-AllowedComputer.ps1
```
Param([string]$computer = $env:computername)

Function Get-AllowedComputer([string]$computer)
{
 $servers = Get-Content -path c:\fso\servers.txt
 $servers -contains $computer
} #end Get-AllowedComputer function

# *** Entry point to Script ***

if(Get-AllowedComputer -computer $computer)
 {
   Get-WmiObject -class Win32_Bios -computer $computer
 }
Else
 {
   "$computer is not an allowed computer"
 }
```

Using the *−contains* Operator to Test for Properties

You are not limited to only testing for specified computer names in the *Get-AllowedComputer* function. To test for other properties, all you need to do is add additional information to the text file as shown in Figure 13-3.

FIGURE 13-3 A text file with server names and properties adds flexibility to the script.

Only a few modifications are required to turn the Get-AllowedComputer.ps1 script into the Get-AllowedComputerAndProperty.ps1 script. The first modification is to add an additional command-line parameter to allow the user to choose which property to display.

```
Param([string]$computer = $env:computername,[string]$property="name")
```

Next, the signature to the *Get-AllowedComputer* function is changed to permit passing of the property name. Instead of directly returning the results of the *–contains* operator, the returned values are stored in variables. The *Get-AllowedComputer* function first checks to see whether the *$servers* array contains the computer name. It then checks to see whether the *$servers* array contains the property name. Each of the resulting values is stored in variables. The two variables are then added together, and the result is returned to the calling code. When two Boolean values are added together, only the true and true case is equal to true.

```
PS C:\> $true -and $false
False
PS C:\> $true -and $true
True
PS C:\> $false -and $false
False
PS C:\>
```

The revised *Get-AllowedComputer* function is shown here.

```
Function Get-AllowedComputer([string]$computer, [string]$property)
{
 $servers = Get-Content -path c:\fso\serversAndProperties.txt
 $s = $servers -contains $computer
 $p = $servers -contains $property
 Return $s -and $p
} #end Get-AllowedComputer function
```

The *If* statement is used to determine whether both the computer value and the property value are contained in the allowed list of servers and properties. If the *Get-AllowedComputer* function returns true, the Get-WmiObject cmdlet is used to display the chosen property value from the selected computer.

```
if(Get-AllowedComputer -computer $computer -property $property)
 {
   Get-WmiObject -class Win32_Bios -Computer $computer |
   Select-Object -property $property
 }
```

If the computer value and the property value are not on the permitted list, the Get-AllowedComputerAndProperty.ps1 script displays a message stating that there is a nonpermitted value.

```
Else
 {
  "Either $computer is not an allowed computer, `r`nor $property is not an allowed
property"
 }
```

The complete Get-AllowedComputerAndProperty.ps1 script is shown here.

Get-AllowedComputerAndProperty.ps1
```
Param([string]$computer = $env:computername,[string]$property="name")

Function Get-AllowedComputer([string]$computer, [string]$property)
{
 $servers = Get-Content -path c:\fso\serversAndProperties.txt
 $s = $servers -contains $computer
 $p = $servers -contains $property
 Return $s -and $p
} #end Get-AllowedComputer function


# *** Entry point to Script ***

if(Get-AllowedComputer -computer $computer -property $property)
 {
   Get-WmiObject -class Win32_Bios -computer $computer |
   Select-Object -property $property
 }
Else
 {
   "Either $computer is not an allowed computer, `r`nor $property is not an allowed
property"
 }
```

Handling Missing Rights

Another source of potential errors is a script that requires elevated permissions to work correctly. Beginning with Windows Vista, the operating system makes it much easier to run and to allow the user to work without requiring constant access to administrative rights. As a result, more users and network administrators are no longer running their computers with a user account that is a member of the local Administrators group. The User Account Control (UAC) feature makes it easy to provide elevated rights for interactive programs, but Windows PowerShell and other scripting languages are not UAC aware and therefore do not prompt when elevated rights are required to perform a specific activity. Thus, it is incumbent on the scriptwriter to take rights into account when writing scripts. The Get-Bios.ps1 script, however, does not use a WMI class that requires elevated rights. As the script is currently written, anyone who is a member of the local Users group—and that includes everyone who is logged on interactively—has permission to run the Get-Bios.ps1 script. Therefore, testing for rights and permissions prior to making an attempt to obtain information from the *Win32_Bios* WMI class is not required.

Attempting and Failing

One way to handle missing rights is to attempt the action and then fail. This action generates an error. Windows PowerShell has two types of errors: terminating and non-terminating. Terminating errors, as the name implies, will stop a script dead in its tracks. Non-terminating errors will output to the screen and the script will continue. Terminating errors are generally more serious than non-terminating errors. Normally, you receive a terminating error when you try to use .NET or a Component Object Model (COM) from within Windows PowerShell, you try to use a command that doesn't exist, or you do not provide all of the required parameters to a command. A good script handles the errors it expects and reports unexpected errors to the user. Because any good scripting language must provide decent error handling, Windows PowerShell has several ways to approach the problem. The old way is the *Trap* statement, which can sometimes be problematic. The new way (for Windows PowerShell) is to use *Try/Catch/Finally*.

INSIDE TRACK

Trapping Errors

James Brundage, Software Development Engineer
Microsoft Corporation

n Windows PowerShell 1.0, there is one and only one way to handle terminating errors: through the *Trap* statement. The *Trap* statement comes at the end of your script and lets you swallow all of the errors in the script (or all of the errors of a specific type). Most Windows PowerShell 1.0 scripts that handle errors end up looking something like the following code.

```
Do-Something
....    Do-SomethingElse
trap {
 "Something Bad Happened"
}
```

Unfortunately, the *Trap* statement is a little strange. First and foremost, it is a concept that is unfamiliar to most scripters or developers. Second, *Trap* statements don't actually allow you to easily trap errors within a few lines of code. Therefore, if you write a *Trap* because you expect errors in your script and you call some other script that also hits errors, the *Trap* statement can end up swallowing both sets of errors and leave you mystified as to why your script doesn't work.

People who are familiar with C# or JavaScript will probably be familiar with *Try/Catch/Finally*. In Windows PowerShell 2.0, we introduce *Try/Catch/Finally* to address some of the pain points surrounding error handling in PowerShell 1.0.

A try block identifies a section of code that can handle errors. A try block will attempt to execute the script within it; if any terminating errors are encountered, then the nearest catch block catches the errors. Try and catch must be paired together (you can have one and only one catch for each try, and Windows PowerShell does not allow a try without a catch), but you can also add a finally block for good measure. A finally block will run whether you have errors or not, so it's a great place to put any cleanup code.

The following is a complete example.

```
try {
    throw "Houston, We Have a Problem"
}
catch {
    Write-Error $_
    try {
        Test-System
    }
    catch [Management.Automation.CommandNotFoundException] {
        "Where's the $($_.TargetObject) command?"
    }

}
finally {
    "byebye"
}
```

In this example, the first error (*Houston, We Have a Problem*) is swallowed by the catch block and is written out with the `Write-Error` cmdlet. This turns my terminating error into a non-terminating error so that my script can continue. Inside of that catch block is another try/catch block that runs a diagnostic command (`Test-System`). If `Test-System` writes out any errors, I want to see them. However, I only want to ask the user where the command is located if and only if it's not found, so I create a catch block that catches only *CommandNotFoundExceptions* (the type of exception I see when the command is missing). The finally block is run whether there is an error or not, so I always see a polite *byebye* whenever I run the script.

Quietly reinterpreting errors is one of the handiest things you can do with try/catch blocks. I personally like to be able to see all of the errors that I hit while running a script, but I also do not like users of my scripts to see red errors (it's bad for their ulcers). Therefore, I often place something like the following in my script.

```
try {
}
catch {
    Write-Debug ($_|Out-String)
}
```

This try/catch block puts my error in the Debug stream (which is hidden by default but which I can turn on with *$DebugPreference* = *"Continue"*). The result is that my scripts almost never show an error to my user, but I obtain a view that shows me all of the errors in my script.

Checking for Rights and Exiting Gracefully

The best way to handle insufficient rights is to check for the rights and then exit gracefully. What are some of the things that can go wrong with a simple script, such as the Get-Bios.ps1 script that was examined earlier in the chapter? Well, the Get-Bios.ps1 script can fail if the Windows PowerShell script execution policy is set to Restricted. When the script execution policy is set to Restricted, Windows PowerShell scripts will not run. The problem with a restricted execution policy is that, because Windows PowerShell scripts do not run, you cannot write code to detect the restricted script execution policy. Because the script execution policy is stored in the registry, you can write a VBScript script that will query and set the policy prior to launching the Windows PowerShell script, but that is not the best way to manage the problem. The best way to manage the script execution policy is to use Group Policy to set the policy to the appropriate level for your network. On a stand-alone computer, you can set the execution policy by opening Windows PowerShell as an administrator and using the Set-ExecutionPolicy cmdlet. In most cases, the RemoteSigned setting is appropriate. You then see the command shown here.

```
PS C:\> Set-ExecutionPolicy remotesigned
PS C:\>
```

The script execution policy is generally dealt with once and then no more problems are associated with it. In addition, the error message that is associated with the script execution policy is relatively clear in that it tells you that script execution is disabled on the system. It also refers you to a help article that explains the various settings.

```
File C:\Documents and Settings\ed\Local Settings\Temp\tmp2A7.tmp.ps1 cannot be
loaded because the execution of scripts is disabled on this system. Please see
"get-help about_signing" for more details.
At line:1 char:66
+ C:\Documents` and` Settings\ed\Local` Settings\Temp\tmp2A7.tmp.ps1 <<<<
```

Handling Missing WMI Providers

About the only thing that can actually go wrong with the Get-Bios.ps1 script is if the WMI provider that supplies the *Win32_Bios* WMI class information is corrupted or missing. To check for the existence of the appropriate WMI provider, you need to know the name of the provider for the WMI class. To check for the name, you can use the Windows Management Instrumentation Tester (WbemTest) that is included as part of the WMI installation. If WMI is installed on a computer, it has Wbemtest.exe. Because WbemTest resides in the system folders, you can launch it directly from within the Windows PowerShell console by typing the name of the executable.

```
PS C:\> wbemtest
PS C:\>
```

Once WbemTest appears, the first thing you need to do is connect to the appropriate WMI namespace by pressing the Connect button. In most cases, the appropriate namespace is the *root\cimv2* namespace. On Windows Vista and later versions, *root\cimv2* is the default WMI namespace for WbemTest. On earlier versions of Windows, the default WbemTest namespace is *root\default*. Change or accept the namespace as appropriate, and press the Connect button. The display changes to a series of buttons, many of which appear to have cryptic names and functionality. To obtain information about the provider for a WMI class, you need to open the class. Press the Open Class button, and type the name of the WMI class in the Get Class Name dialog box. You are looking for the provider name for the *Win32_Bios* WMI class, so that is the name that is entered in the text box of the Get Class Name dialog box. When you press OK, the Object Editor For *Win32_Bios* WMI class now appears, as shown in Figure 13-4. The first section of the Object Editor For *Win32_Bios* lists the qualifiers. Provider is one of the qualifiers. WbemTest tells you that the provider for *Win32_Bios* is CIMWin32.

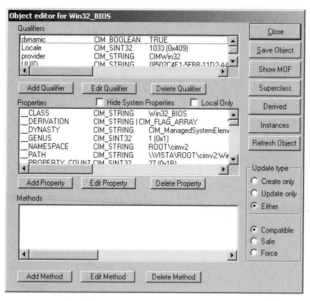

FIGURE 13-4 The Windows Management Instrumentation Tester displays WMI class provider information.

Armed with the name of the WMI provider, you can use the Get-WmiObject cmdlet to determine whether the provider is installed on the computer. To do this, you can query for instances of the *__provider* WMI class. All WMI classes that begin with a double underscore are system classes. The *__provider* WMI class is the class from which all WMI providers are derived. By limiting the query to providers with the name of CIMWin32, you can determine whether the provider is installed on the system.

```
PS C:\> Get-WmiObject -Class __provider -filter "name = 'cimwin32'"
__GENUS                  : 2
__CLASS                  : __Win32Provider
__SUPERCLASS             : __Provider
__DYNASTY                : __SystemClass
__RELPATH                : __Win32Provider.Name="CIMWin32"
__PROPERTY_COUNT         : 24
__DERIVATION             : {__Provider, __SystemClass}
__SERVER                 : OFFICE
__NAMESPACE              : ROOT\cimv2
__PATH                   : \\OFFICE\ROOT\cimv2:__Win32Provider.Name="CIMWi
                           n32"
ClientLoadableCLSID      :
CLSID                    : {d63a5850-8f16-11cf-9f47-00aa00bf345c}
Concurrency              :
DefaultMachineName       :
Enabled                  :
HostingModel             : NetworkServiceHost
ImpersonationLevel       : 1
```

```
InitializationReentrancy       : 0
InitializationTimeoutInterval :
InitializeAsAdminFirst          :
Name                            : CIMWin32
OperationTimeoutInterval        :
PerLocaleInitialization         : False
PerUserInitialization           : False
Pure                            : True
SecurityDescriptor              :
SupportsExplicitShutdown        :
SupportsExtendedStatus          :
SupportsQuotas                  :
SupportsSendStatus              :
SupportsShutdown                :
SupportsThrottling              :
UnloadTimeout                   :
Version                         :


PS C:\>
```

For the purposes of determining whether the provider exists, you do not need all of the information to be returned to the script. It is easier to treat the query as if it returned a Boolean value by using the *If* statement. If the provider exists, then you can perform the query.

```
If(Get-WmiObject -Class __provider -filter "name = 'cimwin32'")
 {
  Get-WmiObject -class Win32_bios
 }
```

If the CIMWin32 WMI provider does not exist, then you display a message stating that the provider is missing.

```
Else
 {
  "Unable to query Win32_Bios because the provider is missing"
 }
```

The completed CheckProviderThenQuery.ps1 script is shown here.

CheckProviderThenQuery.ps1
```
If(Get-WmiObject -Class __provider -filter "name = 'cimwin32'")
 {
  Get-WmiObject -class Win32_bios
 }
Else
 {
  "Unable to query Win32_Bios because the provider is missing"
 }
```

A better approach to find out whether a WMI class is available is to check for the existence of the provider. In the case of the *Win32_Product* WMI class, the class is supplied by the MSIProv WMI provider. In this section, we create the *Get-WmiProvider* function that can be used to detect the presence of any WMI provider that is installed on the system.

The *Get-WmiProvider* function contains two parameters. The first parameter is the name of the provider, and the second parameter is a switched parameter named *–verbose*. When the *Get-WmiProvider* function is called with the *–verbose* switched parameter, detailed status information is displayed to the console. The *–verbose* information provides the user of the script with information that can be useful from a troubleshooting perspective.

```
Function Get-WmiProvider([string]$providerName, [switch]$verbose)
```

After the function is declared, the first thing to do is to store the current value of the *$verbosePreference* variable because it can be set to one of four potential values. The possible enumeration values are *SilentlyContinue*, *Stop*, *Continue*, and *Inquire*. By default, the value of the *$verbosePreference* automatic variable is set to *SilentlyContinue*.

When the function completes running, you want to set it back to its original value if it is changed during the script. Therefore, the original value of the *$verbosePreference* variable is stored in the *$oldVerbosePreference* variable.

It is time to determine whether the function is called with the *–verbose* switch. If the function is called with the *–verbose* switch, a variable named *$verbose* will be present on the variable drive. If the *$verbose* variable exists, the value of the *$verbosePreference* automatic variable is set to *Continue*.

```
{
 $oldVerbosePreference = $verbosePreference
 if($verbose) { $verbosePreference = "continue" }
```

Next, you need to look for the WMI provider. To do this, the Get-WmiObject cmdlet is used to query for all instances of the *__provider* WMI system class. In most cases, they are not of much interest to IT pros, yet familiarity with them can often provide powerful tools to the scripter who takes the time to examine them. All WMI providers are derived from the *__provider* WMI class. This is similar to the way in which all WMI namespaces are derived from the *__Namespace* WMI class. The properties of the *__provider* class are shown in Table 13-1.

TABLE 13-1 Properties of the *__provider* WMI Class

PROPERTY NAME	PROPERTY TYPE
ClientLoadableCLSID	System.String
CLSID	System.String
Concurrency	System.Int32
DefaultMachineName	System.String
Enabled	System.Boolean

PROPERTY NAME	PROPERTY TYPE
HostingModel	System.String
ImpersonationLevel	System.Int32
InitializationReentrancy	System.Int32
InitializationTimeoutInterval	System.String
InitializeAsAdminFirst	System.Boolean
Name	System.String
OperationTimeoutInterval	System.String
PerLocaleInitialization	System.Boolean
PerUserInitialization	System.Boolean
Pure	System.Boolean
SecurityDescriptor	System.String
SupportsExplicitShutdown	System.Boolean
SupportsExtendedStatus	System.Boolean
SupportsQuotas	System.Boolean
SupportsSendStatus	System.Boolean
SupportsShutdown	System.Boolean
SupportsThrottling	System.Boolean
UnloadTimeout	System.String
Version	System.UInt32
__CLASS	System.String
__DERIVATION	System.String[]
__DYNASTY	System.String
__GENUS	System.Int32
__NAMESPACE	System.String
__PATH	System.String
__PROPERTY_COUNT	System.Int32
__RELPATH	System.String
__SERVER	System.String
__SUPERCLASS	System.String

The *–filter* parameter of the `Get-WmiObject` cmdlet is used to return the provider that is specified in the *$providerName* variable. If you do not know the name of the appropriate

WMI provider, you need to search for it by using WbemTest. You can start this program by typing the name of the executable inside your Windows PowerShell console.

Once the WbemTest appears, the first thing you need to do is connect to the appropriate WMI namespace by pressing the Connect button. In most cases, the appropriate namespace is the *root\cimv2* namespace. Change or accept the namespace as appropriate, and press the Connect button. Press the Open Class button, and type the name of the WMI class in the Enter Target Class Name text box of the Get Class Name dialog box. You are looking for the provider name for the *Win32_Product* WMI class, and that is the name that is entered in the text box. When you press OK, the Object Editor For *Win32_Product* WMI class now appears, as shown in Figure 13-5. The first section of the Object Editor For *Win32_Product* lists the qualifiers. Provider is one of the qualifiers. WbemTest tells you that the provider for *Win32_Product* is MSIProv.

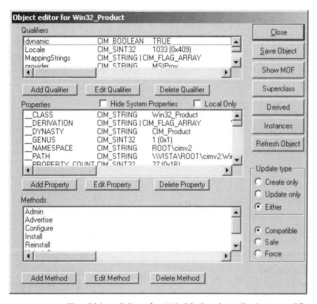

FIGURE 13-5 The Object Editor for *Win32_Product* displays qualifiers and methods.

You assign the name of the WMI provider to the *$providerName* variable.

```
$providerName = "MSIProv"
```

The resulting object is stored in the *$provider* variable.

```
$provider = Get-WmiObject -Class __provider -filter "name = '$providerName'"
```

If the provider is not found, there is no value in the *$provider* variable. Therefore, you can determine whether the *$provider* variable is null. If the *$provider* variable is not equal to null, the *CLSID* property of the provider is retrieved. The class ID of the WMI provider is stored in the *CLSID* property.

```
If($provider -ne $null)
    {
     $clsID = $provider.CLSID
```

If the function is run with the *–verbose* parameter, the *$verbosePreference* variable is set to *Continue*. When the value of *$verbosePreference* is equal to *Continue*, the `Write-Verbose` cmdlet displays information to the console. On the other hand, if the value of the *$verbosePreference* variable is equal to *SilentlyContinue*, the `Write-Verbose` cmdlet does not emit anything. This process makes it easy to implement tracing features in a function without creating extensive test conditions. When the function is called with the *–verbose* parameter, the class ID of the provider is displayed.

```
Write-Verbose "$providerName WMI provider found. CLSID is $($CLSID)"
}
```

If the WMI provider is not found, the function returns false to the calling code.

```
Else
    {
     Return $false
    }
```

Next, the function checks the registry to ensure that the WMI provider is properly registered with the Distributed Component Object Model (DCOM). Once again, the `Write-Verbose` cmdlet is used to provide feedback on the status of the provider check.

```
Write-Verbose "Checking for proper registry registration ..."
```

To search the registry for the WMI provider registration, the Windows PowerShell registry provider is used. By default, there is no Windows PowerShell drive for the HKEY_Classes_Root registry hive. However, you cannot take it for granted that someone has not created such a drive in their Windows PowerShell profile. To avoid a potential error that might arise when creating a Windows PowerShell drive for the HKEY_Classes_Root hive, the `Test-Path` cmdlet is used to check whether an HKCR: drive exists. If the HKCR: drive does exist, it will be used, and the `Write-Verbose` cmdlet is used to print a status message stating that the HKCR: drive is found and that the search is commencing for the class ID of the WMI provider.

```
If(Test-Path -path HKCR:)
    {
     Write-Verbose "HKCR: drive found. Testing for $clsID"
```

To detect whether the WMI provider is registered with DCOM, check whether the class ID of the WMI provider is present in the CLSID section of HKEY_Classes_Root. The best way to check for the presence of the registry key is to use the `Test-Path` cmdlet.

```
Test-path -path (Join-Path -path HKCR:\CLSID -childpath $clsID)
}
```

On the other hand, if there is no HKCR: drive on the computer, you can create one. You can search for the existence of a drive that is rooted in HKEY_Classes_Root and, if you find it, use the Windows PowerShell drive in your query. To discover whether there are any Windows PowerShell drives rooted in HKEY_Classes_Root, use the Get-PSDrive cmdlet.

```
Get-PSDrive | Where-Object { $_.root -match "classes" } |
Select-Object name
```

Yet, to be honest, Get-PSDrive is more trouble than it is worth. There is nothing wrong with having multiple Windows PowerShell drives mapped to the same resource. Therefore, if there is no HKCR: drive, the Write-Verbose cmdlet is used to print a message stating that the drive does not exist and will be created.

```
Else
  {
    Write-Verbose "HKCR: drive not found. Creating same."
```

To create a new Windows PowerShell drive, use the New-PSDrive cmdlet to specify the name and root location of the PowerShell drive. Because this drive is going to be a registry drive, you can use the registry provider. When a Windows PowerShell drive is created, it displays feedback to the Windows PowerShell console.

```
PS C:\AutoDoc> New-PSDrive -Name HKCR -PSProvider registry -Root HKEYClasses_Root
```

```
Name       Provider      Root                          CurrentLocation
----       --------      ----                          ---------------

HKCR       Registry      Hkey_Classes_Root
```

The feedback from creating the registry drive can be distracting. To remove the feedback, you can pipeline the results to the Out-Null cmdlet.

```
New-PSDrive -Name HKCR -PSProvider registry -Root HKEY_Classes_Root | Out-Null
```

Once the Windows PowerShell registry drive is created, it is time to look for the existence of the WMI provider class ID. But first, you can use the Write-Verbose cmdlet to provide feedback about this step of the operation.

```
Write-Verbose "Testing for $clsID"
```

The Test-Path cmdlet is used to check for the existence of the WMI provider class ID. To build the path to the registry key, the Join-Path cmdlet is used. The parent path is the HKCR: registry drive CLSID hive, and the childpath is the WMI provider class ID that is stored in the $clsID variable.

```
Test-path -path (Join-Path -path HKCR:\CLSID -childpath $clsID)
```

Once the Test-Path cmdlet is used to check for the existence of the WMI provider class ID, the Write-Verbose cmdlet is used to display a message stating that the test is complete.

```
Write-Verbose "Test complete."
```

It is a best practice to not make permanent modifications to the Windows PowerShell environment in a script. Therefore, you want to remove the Windows PowerShell drive if it was created in the script. The `Write-Verbose` cmdlet is employed to provide a status update, and the `Remove-PSDrive` cmdlet is used to remove the HKCR: registry drive. To avoid cluttering the Windows PowerShell console, the result of removing the HKCR: registry drive is pipelined to the `Out-Null` cmdlet.

```
        Write-Verbose "Removing HKCR: drive."
        Remove-PSDrive -Name HKCR | Out-Null
    }
```

The last thing to do is set the *$verbosePreference* variable back to the value that was stored in the *$oldVerbosePreference* variable. This line of code is executed even if no change to *$verbosePreference* is made.

```
    $verbosePreference = $oldVerbosePreference
} #end Get-WmiProvider function
```

The entry point to the script assigns a value to the *$providerName* variable.

```
$providerName = "MSIProv"
```

The *Get-WmiProvider* function is called, and it passes both the WMI provider name that is stored in the *$providerName* variable and the *–verbose* switched parameter. The *If* statement is used because the *Get-WmiProvider* function returns a Boolean value: true or false.

```
 if(Get-WmiProvider -providerName $providerName  -verbose )
```

If the return from the *Get-WmiProvider* function is true, the WMI class supported by the WMI provider is queried by using the `Get-WMiObject` cmdlet.

```
  {
    Get-WmiObject -class win32_product
  }
```

If the WMI provider is not found, a message stating that the WMI provider is not found is displayed to the console.

```
else
  {
    "$providerName provider not found"
  }
```

The complete Get-WmiProviderFunction.ps1 script is shown here.

Get-WmiProviderFunction.ps1

```powershell
Function Get-WmiProvider([string]$providerName, [switch]$verbose)
{
 $oldVerbosePreference = $verbosePreference
 if($verbose) { $verbosePreference = "continue" }
 $provider = Get-WmiObject -Class __provider -filter "name = '$providerName'"
 If($provider -ne $null)
   {
    $clsID = $provider.clsID
    Write-Verbose "$providerName WMI provider found. CLSID is $($CLSID)"
   }
 Else
   {
     Return $false
   }
   Write-Verbose "Checking for proper registry registration ..."
   If(Test-Path -path HKCR:)
     {
        Write-Verbose "HKCR: drive found. Testing for $clsID"
        Test-path -path (Join-Path -path HKCR:\CLSID -childpath $CLSID)
     }
   Else
     {
       Write-Verbose "HKCR: drive not found. Creating same."
       New-PSDrive -Name HKCR -PSProvider registry -Root HKEY_Classes_Root | Out-Null
       Write-Verbose "Testing for $clsID"
       Test-path -path (Join-Path -path HKCR:\CLSID -childpath $CLSID)
       Write-Verbose "Test complete."
       Write-Verbose "Removing HKCR: drive."
       Remove-PSDrive -Name HKCR | Out-Null
     }
 $verbosePreference = $oldVerbosePreference
} #end Get-WmiProvider function

# *** Entry Point to Script ***
$providerName = "msiprov"
 if(Get-WmiProvider -providerName $providerName  -verbose )
  {
    Get-WmiObject -class win32_product
  }
else
  {
    "$providerName provider not found"
  }
```

Incorrect Data Types

There are two approaches to ensure that your users enter only allowed values for the script parameters. The first approach is to offer only a limited number of values. The second approach allows the user to enter any value for the parameter. It is then determined whether that value is valid before it is passed along to the remainder of the script. In the Get-ValidWmiClassFunction.ps1 script, a function named *Get-ValidWmiClass* is used to determine whether the value that is supplied to the script is a legitimate WMI class name. In particular, the *Get-ValidWmiClass* function is used to determine whether the string that is passed via the *−class* parameter can be cast to a valid instance of the *System.Management.ManagementClass* .NET Framework class. The purpose of using the [WMICLASS] type accelerator is to convert a string into an instance of the *System.Management.ManagementClass* class. As shown here, when you assign a string value to a variable, the variable becomes an instance of the *System.String* class. The *GetType* method is used to display information about the type of object that is contained in a variable.

```
PS C:\> $class = "win32_bio"
PS C:\> $class.GetType()


IsPublic IsSerial Name                                  BaseType
-------- -------- ----                                  --------
True     True     String                                System.Object
```

To convert the string to a WMI class, you can use the [WMICLASS] type accelerator. The string value must contain the name of a legitimate WMI class. If the WMI class you are trying to create on the computer does not exist, an error is generated.

```
PS C:\> $class = "win32_bio"
PS C:\> [wmiclass]$class
Cannot convert value "win32_bio" to type "System.Management.ManagementClass".
Error: "Not found "
At line:1 char:16
+ [wmiclass]$class <<<<
```

The Get-ValidWmiClassFunction.ps1 script begins by creating two command-line parameters. The first is the *−computer* parameter that is used to allow the script to run on a local or remote computer. The second parameter is the *−class* parameter that is used to provide the name of the WMI class that will be queried by the script. The third parameter is used to allow the script to inspect other WMI namespaces. All three parameters are strings.

```
Param (
    [string]$computer = $env:computername,
    [string]$class,
    [string]$namespace = "root\cimv2"
) #end param
```

The *Get-ValidWmiClass* function is used to determine whether the value supplied for the *−class* parameter is a valid WMI class on the particular computer. This is important because certain versions of the operating system contain unique WMI classes. For example, Windows XP contains a WMI class named *NetDiagnostics* that does not exist on any other version of Windows. Windows XP does not contain the *Win32_Volume* WMI class, but Windows Server 2003 and later versions do have this class. Therefore, checking for the existence of a WMI class on a remote computer is a good practice to ensure that the script will run in an expeditious manner.

First, the *Get-ValidWmiClass* function retrieves the current value for the *$errorActionPreference* variable. There are four possible values for this variable. The possible enumeration values are *SilentlyContinue*, *Stop*, *Continue*, and *Inquire*. The error-handling behavior of Windows PowerShell is governed by these enumeration values. If the value of *$errorActionPreference* is set to *SilentlyContinue*, any error that occurs will be skipped and the script will attempt to execute the next line of code in the script. The behavior is similar to using the VBScript setting *On Error Resume Next*. Normally, you do not want to use this setting because it can make troubleshooting scripts very difficult. It can also make the behavior of a script unpredictable and even lead to devastating consequences.

Consider the case in which you write a script that first creates a new directory on a remote server. Next, the script copies all of the files from a directory on your local computer to the remote server. Last, it deletes the directory and all of the files from the local computer. Now, you enable *$errorActionPreference = SilentlyContinue* and you run the script. The first command fails because the remote server is not available. The second command fails because it cannot copy the files, but the third command completes successfully—and you have just deleted all of the files you wanted to back up instead of actually backing up the files. Hopefully, you have a recent backup of your critical data. If you set *$errorActionPreference* to *SilentlyContinue*, you must handle errors that arise during the course of running the script.

In the *Get-ValidWmiClass* function, the old *$errorActionPreference* setting is retrieved and stored in the *$oldErrorActionPreference* variable. Next, the *$errorActionPreference* variable is set to *SilentlyContinue* because it is entirely possible that errors will be generated while in the process of checking for a valid WMI class name. Then the error stack is cleared of errors. The following three lines of code illustrate this process.

```
$oldErrorActionPreference = $errorActionPreference
$errorActionPreference = "SilentlyContinue"
$Error.Clear()
```

The value stored in the *$class* variable is used with the [WMICLASS] type accelerator to attempt to create a *System.Management.ManagementClass* object from the string. Because you need to run this script on a remote computer as well as on a local computer, the value in the *$computer* variable is used to provide a complete path to the potential management object. When concatenating the variables to make the path to the WMI class, a trailing colon causes problems with the *$namespace* variable. To work around this problem, a subexpression is used to force evaluation of the variable before attempting to concatenate the remainder of the string. The subexpression consists of a leading dollar sign and a pair of parentheses.

```
[WMICLASS]"\\$computer\$($namespace):$class" | out-null
```

To determine whether the conversion from string to *ManagementClass* is successful, the error record is checked. Because the error record was cleared earlier, any error that appears indicates that the command failed. If an error exists, the *Get-ValidWmiClass* function returns false to the calling code. If no error exists, the *Get-ValidWmiClass* function returns true.

```
If($error.count) { Return $false } Else { Return $true }
```

The last thing to do in the *Get-ValidWmiClass* function is to clean up the error environment. First, the error record is cleared, and then the value of the *$errorActionPreference* variable is set back to the original value.

```
$Error.Clear()
$errorActionPreference = $oldErrorActionPreference
```

The next function in the Get-ValidWmiClassFunction.ps1 script is the *Get-WmiInformation* function. This function accepts the values from the *$computer*, *$class*, and *$namespace* variables and passes them to the Get-WmiObject cmdlet. The resulting *ManagementObject* is pipelined to the Format-List cmdlet, and all properties that begin with the letters a through z are displayed.

```
Function Get-WmiInformation ([string]$computer, [string]$class, [string]$namespace)
{
  Get-WmiObject -class $class -computername $computer -namespace $namespace|
  Format-List -property [a-z]*
} # end Get-WmiInformation function
```

The entry point to the script calls the *Get-ValidWmiClass* function; if it returns true, the script next calls the *Get-WmiInformation* function. On the other hand, if the *Get-ValidWmiClass* function returns false, a message is displayed that details the class name, namespace, and computer name. This information can be used for troubleshooting any difficulty in obtaining the WMI information.

```
If(Get-ValidWmiClass -computer $computer -class $class -namespace $namespace)
  {
    Get-WmiInformation -computer $computer -class $class -namespace $namespace
  }
Else
  {
    "$class is not a valid wmi class in the $namespace namespace on $computer"
  }
```

The complete Get-ValidWmiClassFunction.ps1 script is shown here.

Get-ValidWmiClassFunction.ps1
```
Param (
    [string]$computer = $env:computername,
    [string]$class,
    [string]$namespace = "root\cimv2"
) #end param

Function Get-ValidWmiClass([string]$computer, [string]$class, [string]$namespace)
{
 $oldErrorActionPreference = $errorActionPreference
 $errorActionPreference = "SilentlyContinue"
 $Error.Clear()
 [wmiclass]"\\$computer\$($namespace):$class" | out-null
 If($error.count) { Return $false } Else { Return $true }
 $Error.Clear()
 $errorActionPreference =  $oldErrorActionPreference
} # end Get-ValidWmiClass function

Function Get-WmiInformation ([string]$computer, [string]$class, [string]$namespace)
{
  Get-WmiObject -class $class -computername $computer -namespace $namespace|
  Format-List -property [a-z]*
} # end Get-WmiInformation function

# *** Entry point to script ***

If(Get-ValidWmiClass -computer $computer -class $class -namespace $namespace)
  {
    Get-WmiInformation -computer $computer -class $class -namespace $namespace
  }
Else
  {
    "$class is not a valid wmi class in the $namespace namespace on $computer"
  }
```

Learning to Use the Windows PowerShell Error-Handling Mechanisms

Bill Stewart, Network Administrator
Moderator for Official Scripting Guys Forum

I have written many Windows Script Host (WSH) scripts using VBScript over the years, and error handling is one of the weakest features of VBScript. For example, if a line of VBScript code throws an error, it always terminates the script unless you use the *On Error Resume Next* statement to disable the default error handler. However, the *On Error Resume Next* statement can have unforeseen consequences because it causes the VBScript interpreter to skip all subsequent lines containing errors. I cannot count the number of times I have seen questions about VBScript problems in online forums because the script's author put the *On Error Resume Next* statement at the top of the script without understanding how the VBScript error handler works.

In contrast, the Windows PowerShell error-handling mechanisms are much more flexible and powerful than those of VBScript. Because Windows PowerShell distinguishes between terminating and non-terminating errors, handling errors in PowerShell code can be more complex than in VBScript. However, once I understood the difference between terminating and non-terminating errors, it was easier to write error-handling code in Windows PowerShell scripts.

First, I usually handle non-terminating errors by setting the *$errorActionPreference* variable (or the *–ErrorAction* parameter of a cmdlet) to *SilentlyContinue* and then test the *$?* variable.

```
get-item "C:\FileDoesNotExist.txt" -erroraction SilentlyContinue
if (-not $?) {
  write-host ("Exception: " + $Error[0].Exception.GetType().FullName)
  write-host $Error[0].Exception.Message
}
```

Second, I handle terminating errors using the Windows PowerShell *Try* and *Catch* statements.

```
try {
  $searcher = [WMISearcher] "select * from Win32_NonExistentClass"
  $searcher.Get()
}
catch [System.Management.Automation.RuntimeException] {
  write-host ("Exception: " + $_.Exception.GetType().FullName)
  write-host $_.Exception.Message
}
```

Windows PowerShell 1.0 only provided the *Trap* statement to catch terminating errors, but the *Try* and *Catch* statements are clearer and easier to use.

One thing that initially confused me is that catch blocks only handle terminating errors. That is, you cannot use a catch block to handle non-terminating errors unless the *$errorActionPreference* variable (or the *–ErrorAction* parameter of a cmdlet) is set to *Stop*.

```
try {
  get-item "C:\FileDoesNotExist.txt" -ErrorAction Stop
}
catch {
  write-host ("Exception: " + $_.Exception.GetType().FullName)
  write-host $_.Exception.Message
}
```

If you omit the *–ErrorAction* parameter from this example, the Get-Item cmdlet throws a non-terminating error and the catch block is ignored.

However, there is one caveat to handling non-terminating errors using *Try/Catch*. If you set *$errorActionPreference* to *Stop* and handle the error in a catch block, the exception object's message contains the following introductory text: "Command execution stopped because the preference variable "errorActionPreference" or common parameter is set to Stop." If you don't mind this introductory text in the exception message (for example, if you're not writing the exception message any-where), this method works fine. Yet because I usually output the exception message, I prefer to set *$errorActionPreference* to *SilentlyContinue* and test the *$?* variable instead.

Out of Bounds Errors

When receiving input from a user, an allowed value is limited to a specified range of values. If the allowable range is small, it might be best to present the user with a prompt that allows selection from a few choices, as shown in the "Limiting Choices" section earlier in this chapter. However, when the allowable range of values is large, limiting the choices through a menu-type system is not practical. This is where bounds checking comes into play.

Using a Boundary Checking Function

One technique used to perform boundary checking is to use a function that determines whether the supplied value is permissible. One way to create a boundary checking function is to have the script create a hash table of permissible values. You can then use the *–contains* method to determine whether the value supplied from the command line is permissible. If the value is present in the hash table, the *–contains* method returns true. If the value is not present, it returns false. The *Check-AllowedValue* function is used to gather a hash table of volumes that reside on the target computer. This hash table is then used to verify that the volume requested from the *–drive* command-line parameter is actually present on the computer. The *Check-AllowedValue* function returns a Boolean true/false value to the calling code in the main body of the script. The complete *Check-AllowedValue* function is shown here.

```
Function Check-AllowedValue($drive, $computerName)
{
 Get-WmiObject -class Win32_Volume -computername $computerName|
 ForEach-Object { $drives += @{ $_.DriveLetter = $_.DriveLetter } }
 $drives.contains($drive)
} #end function Check-AllowedValue
```

Because the *Check-AllowedValue* function returns a Boolean value, an *If* statement is used to determine whether the value supplied to the *–drive* parameter is permissible. If the drive letter is found in the *$drives* hash table that is created in the *Check-AllowedValue* function, the *Get-DiskInformation* function is called. If the *–drive* parameter value is not found in the hash table, a warning message is displayed to the Windows PowerShell console, and the script exits. The complete GetDrivesCheckAllowedValue.ps1 script is shown here.

GetDrivesCheckAllowedValue.ps1
```
Param(
    [Parameter(Mandatory=$true)]
    [string]$drive,
    [string]$computerName = $env:computerName
) #end param

Function Check-AllowedValue($drive, $computerName)
{
 Get-WmiObject -class Win32_Volume -computername $computerName|
 ForEach-Object { $drives += @{ $_.DriveLetter = $_.DriveLetter } }
 $drives.contains($drive)
} #end function Check-AllowedValue

Function Get-DiskInformation($computerName,$drive)
{
 Get-WmiObject -class Win32_volume -computername $computername -filter "DriveLetter =
'$drive'"
} #end function Get-BiosName
```

```
# *** Entry Point To Script ***

if(Check-AllowedValue -drive $drive -computername $computerName)
  {
    Get-DiskInformation -computername $computerName -drive $drive
  }
else
  {
   Write-Host -foregroundcolor yellow "$drive is not an allowed value:"
  }
```

Placing Limits on the Parameter

In Windows PowerShell 2.0, you can place limits directly on the parameter in the *Param* section of the script. This technique works well when you are working with a limited set of allowable values. The *ValidateRange* parameter attribute creates a numeric range of allowable values, but it is also able to create a range of letters as well. Using this technique, you can greatly simplify the GetDrivesCheckAllowedValue.ps1 script by creating an allowable range of drive letters. The *Param* statement is shown here.

```
Param(
    [Parameter(Mandatory=$true)]
    [ValidateRange("c","f")]
    [string]$drive,
    [string]$computerName = $env:computerName
) #end param
```

Because you are able to control the permissible drive letters from the command line, you increase the simplicity and readability of the script by not having the requirement to create a separate function to validate the allowed values. One additional change is required in the GetDrivesValidRange.ps1 script, and that is to concatenate a colon at the end of the drive letter. In the GetDrivesCheckAllowedValue.ps1 script, you were able to include the drive letter and the colon from the command line; however, this technique does not work with the *ValidateRange* attribute. The trick to concatenating the colon to the drive letter is that it needs to be escaped.

```
-filter "DriveLetter = '$drive`:'"
```

The complete GetDrivesValidRange.ps1 script is shown here.

GetDrivesValidRange.ps1
```
Param(
    [Parameter(Mandatory=$true)]
    [ValidateRange("c","f")]
    [string]$drive,
    [string]$computerName = $env:computerName
) #end param

Function Get-DiskInformation($computerName,$drive)
{
 Get-WmiObject -class Win32_volume -computername $computername `
 -filter "DriveLetter = '$drive`:'"
} #end function Get-BiosName

# *** Entry Point To Script ***

Get-DiskInformation -computername $computerName -drive $drive
```

Additional Resources

- The TechNet Script Center at *http://www.microsoft.com/technet/scriptcenter* contains numerous examples of Windows PowerShell scripts that perform error handling.

- Take a look at *Windows PowerShell™ Scripting Guide* (Microsoft Press, 2008).

- On the companion media, you will find all of the scripts referred to in this chapter.

#### PART IV

Testing and Deploying

Testing Scripts

I f you take the time to write a script, you should take a few additional minutes to test the script. How do you know what to test in the script? For many IT professionals, testing a script is nothing more than running the script and looking for errors. If the script runs without errors, the script is considered to be a good script. As you will learn in this chapter, there is more to testing a script than determining whether it runs without errors. When testing your scripts, it is a best practice to check the basic syntax of the script. You should also measure the performance of the script to ensure that the script will meet the demands of your specific environment. If a script accepts command-line parameters, you should also test the script to see how it handles various types of input.

Using Basic Syntax Checking Techniques

Basic syntax checking can be done by running the script and looking for errors. If you have several scripts to check, it makes sense to write a script that will perform basic syntax checking for you. Test-ScriptHarness.ps1 searches a folder for all .ps1 scripts, executes each script while checking for errors, and records the length of time it takes for each script to run. The Test-ScriptHarness.ps1 script writes the results to a text file and then displays the report.

First, the Test-ScriptHarness.ps1 script determines whether the script is running inside a virtual machine. A script that is going to execute a large number of Windows Power-Shell scripts can potentially cause a significant amount of damage to your workstation depending on the actions that the scripts are performing. For example, if one of the scripts kicks off an automated installation of Windows Vista, you can potentially wipe out all of your data and end up with a fresh installation of Windows Vista. If you run the script inside a virtual machine on Microsoft Virtual PC with undo disks enabled, you are then minimizing the potential disruption that the scripts can cause.

Because the *Win32_ComputerSystem* Windows Management Instrumentation (WMI) class returns a single instance, you can directly access the properties of the class. This means that you do not need to work through a collection of instances of the class to retrieve the model property value. On Virtual PC, the model is reported as "virtual machine." If the model is not reported as "virtual machine," the script displays a prompt asking whether you want to run the script. This prompt is created by using the Read-Host cmdlet. If you type **n** in reply to the prompt, the script will exit. Any other response to the Read-Host prompt permits the script to run.

```
if((Get-WmiObject Win32_ComputerSystem).model -ne "virtual machine")
  {
    $response = Read-Host -prompt "This script is best run in a VM.
    Do you wish to continue? <y / n>"
    if ($response -eq "n") { exit }
  }
```

The path to search for Windows PowerShell scripts is stored in the *$path* variable. Depending on how you plan to run the ScriptHarness.ps1 script, you might want to change the variable to a command-line parameter.

```
$path = "C:\bp"
```

The *GetTempFileName* static method from the *System.Io.Path* Microsoft .NET Framework class is used to create a temporary file name in the Users temporary directory. The path to this temporary file name is stored in the *$report* directory. An example of a temporary file name is shown here.

```
C:\Users\administrator.NWTRADERS.000\AppData\Local\Temp\tmpC484.tmp
```

Because the file name is randomly generated each time the *GetTempFileName* method is called, it is stored in the *$report* variable for use later in the script.

```
$report = [io.path]::GetTempFileName()
```

The Get-ChildItem cmdlet shown here is used to produce a listing of all .ps1 files in the folder referenced by the *$path* variable. The *–recurse* parameter is required to permit the Get-ChildItem cmdlet to retrieve all .ps1 files in the folder. The results from the Get-ChildItem cmdlet are pipelined to the ForEach-Object cmdlet.

```
Get-ChildItem -Path $path -Include *.ps1 -Recurse |
```

The ForEach-Object cmdlet uses the *–Begin* parameter to perform an action once for all items that enter the pipeline. In this example, the starting time of the script processing is stored in the *$stime* variable (the *$stime* variable is used instead of *$startTime* because *$startTime* will be used later). The value of the *$errorActionPreference* automatic variable is set to *SilentlyContinue*, indicating that errors are not to be displayed and the script should continue processing when an error is encountered. A status message is written to the *$report* file that indicates the beginning of script testing and the time it commenced.

```
ForEach-Object -Begin `
  {
    $stime = Get-Date
    $ErrorActionPreference = "SilentlyContinue"
    "Testing ps1 scripts in $path $stime" |
      Out-File -append -FilePath $report
```

The *−Process* parameter occurs once for each object that comes through the pipeline. The first thing that is done inside the Process block is to clear all errors from the error stack to ensure that any errors that do occur are specific to the particular script that is being tested. A new time is written to the *$startTime* variable, and this time stamp will be used to calculate how long it takes the specific script to run. An entry is written to the report that indicates the name of the script and the starting time from the *$startTime* variable. The name of the script is obtained from the *$_* automatic variable, which refers to the current object on the pipeline. All of the output from this section is then pipelined to the Out-File cmdlet with the *−append* parameter to tell the script to add to the *$report* file instead of overwriting the file.

```
  } -Process `
  {
    $error.Clear()
    $startTime = Get-Date
    "  Begin Testing $_ at $startTime" |
      Out-File -append -FilePath $report
```

It is now time to run the script that is on the pipeline. To execute the script, you use the Invoke-Expression cmdlet with the *−command* parameter and provide it with the *$_* automatic variable.

```
    Invoke-Expression -Command $_
```

Once the script completes running, you should retrieve the time that the script completed. The end time of the script is then pipelined to the Out-File cmdlet with the *−append* parameter.

```
    $endTime = Get-Date
    "  End testing $_ at $endTime." |
      Out-File -append -FilePath $report
```

To continue with the report, the number of errors on the error stack is obtained and written to the *$report* file. Because the *$error* automatic variable contains an object, a subexpression is used (a dollar sign and a set of parentheses surround the *$error* variable) to force the evaluation of the *count* property from the *$error* object. This value is then sent down the pipeline to the Out-File cmdlet.

```
    "  Script generated $($error.Count) errors" |
      Out-File -append -FilePath $report
```

The DateTime object that is stored in the *$startTime* variable is subtracted from the DateTime object that is stored in the *$endTime* variable. Once again, a subexpression is used to force the evaluation of this operation. If you do not use a subexpression inside the expanding string double quotation marks, you need to use concatenation to combine the string and the DateTime objects. The time that is created by subtracting the starting time from the ending time is pipelined to the Out-File cmdlet for inclusion in the report. Once this is done, the process block of the ForEach-Object cmdlet is completed.

```
"    Elasped time: $($endTime - $startTime)" |
  Out-File -append -FilePath $report
} -end `
```

After the last script has run, the ending time is stored in the *$etime* variable. The value of the *$errorActionPreference* variable is set back to the default value of *Continue,* and the ending time is written to the report.

```
{
$etime = Get-Date
$ErrorActionPreference = "Continue"
"Completed testing all scripts in $path $etime" |
  Out-File -append -FilePath $report
```

Last, you must record the total running time for all script testing. To do this, the start time recorded in the *$stime* variable is subtracted from the time stored in the *$etime* variable. A subexpression is used to force the evaluation of the total elapsed time. The total time pipelined to the Out-File cmdlet and the entire report is displayed in Notepad.

```
"Testing took $($etime - $stime)" |
  Out-File -append -FilePath $report
}
Notepad $report
```

The complete Test-ScriptHarness.ps1 script is shown here.

Test-ScriptHarness.ps1

```
if((Get-WmiObject win32_computersystem).model -ne "virtual machine")
  {
    $response = Read-Host -prompt "This script is best run in a VM.
    Do you wish to continue? <y / n>"
    if ($response -eq "n") { exit }
  }
$path = "C:\bp"
$report = [io.path]::GetTempFileName()
Get-ChildItem -Path $path -Include *.ps1 -Recurse |
ForEach-Object -Begin `
  {
   $stime = Get-Date
   $ErrorActionPreference = "SilentlyContinue"
   "Testing ps1 scripts in $path $stime" |
     Out-File -append -FilePath $report
  } -Process `
  {
   $error.Clear()
   $startTime = Get-Date
   "  Begin Testing $_ at $startTime" |
     Out-File -append -FilePath $report
   Invoke-Expression -Command $_
   $endTime = Get-Date
   "  End testing $_ at $endTime." |
     Out-File -append -FilePath $report
   "    Script generated $($error.Count) errors" |
     Out-File -append -FilePath $report
   "    Elasped time: $($endTime - $startTime)" |
     Out-File -append -FilePath $report
  } -end `
  {
   $etime = Get-Date
   $ErrorActionPreference = "Continue"
   "Completed testing all scripts in $path $etime" |
     Out-File -append -FilePath $report
   "Testing took $($etime - $stime)" |
     Out-File -append -FilePath $report
  }

  Notepad $report
```

Figure 14-1 shows the report that is produced.

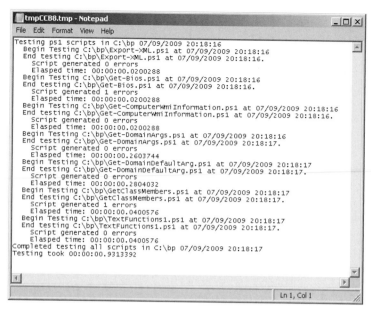

FIGURE 14-1 Log produced by the Test-ScriptHarness.ps1 script

Looking for Errors

A systematic script-testing methodology is probably not going to directly save time, and it more than likely will add time during the prerelease phase of your script. However, because you will experience fewer unexplained errors as a result of poorly written scripts, you will likely save time over the lifetime of the script.

One of the simplest ways to test a script is to run the script. Before you run the script, however, you should examine it for obvious errors and clues to its functionality. Pay attention to each section of the script. Individual sections are listed here, with details as to the type of items you should examine. You should make these checks prior to running the script.

In the Param section, focus on these things:

- The command-line parameters begin with the *param* keyword.
- Each command-line parameter is separated by a comma.
- The last parameter is not followed by a comma.
- The parentheses should open and close.
- Make sure the *Param* statement is the first noncommented line in the script.
- Look for mandatory parameters and default values of parameters.

A correctly formed *Param* statement is shown here.

```
Param(
    [string]$computer=$env:computerName,
    [switch]$disk,
    [switch]$processor,
    [switch]$memory,
    [switch]$network,
    [switch]$video,
    [switch]$all
) #end param
```

In the Function section, there are many different items on which to focus:

- The function begins by using the *function* keyword followed by the name of the function.

- The function name should follow the Verb-Noun pattern, which follows the same naming format of Windows PowerShell cmdlets.

- Input parameters to the function are placed inside a set of parentheses.

- Each *function* parameter is separated by a comma. The last parameter is not followed by a comma.

- Each opening curly bracket must have a corresponding closing curly bracket.

- How are the functions called from within the script? If a function is not used in the script, it should not be stored in the script.

- Pay particular attention to the function parameters. What types of parameters do they require?

A correctly formed function section is shown here.

```
Function Get-Disk($computer)
{
 Get-WmiObject -class Win32_LogicalDisk -computername $computer
} #end Get-Disk
```

You are now at the entry point to the script. The entry point of the script is the first code that is executed when the script runs (following the *Param* statement). This code is extremely important because it governs what the script will actually do.

- What does the entry point code actually do?

- What variables are initialized? Are the variables released at the end of the script?

- What constants are declared? In what scope are the constants created?

- What objects are created? What methods and properties are exposed by the new objects?

- What are the default actions? What happens when the script is run without using any command-line parameters?

- Does the script expose any help?

- Does the help provide any examples of using the script?

- What type of output does the script produce? Does it output to the screen, a text file, a database, e-mail, or some other location?

- Is the output location from the script accessible to the workstation that runs the script?

INSIDE TRACK

Testing with Windows PowerShell

James Brundage and Ibrahim Abdul Rahim, Software Development Engineers
Microsoft Corporation

The key point to remember about testing software in Windows PowerShell is that it is the same general task as automating the operating system with PowerShell. To test software, you must get the operating system into a good working state (for example, you might launch programs or change registry keys). You can then automate an action instead of doing it by hand and verify the result by looking at what the action does to the operating system.

Because automated software testing and systems automation use so many of the same tools, the first thing to keep in mind as a tester is to leverage the examples you find from scripters or C# developers. Windows PowerShell can easily work with all of the objects from C# (using the New-Object cmdlet) and VBScript (using the New-Object –*ComObject* parameter).

Another point to keep in mind when considering testing with Windows PowerShell is the need for a framework. Usually, software tests are automated within a testing framework. The testing framework runs a chunk of code with some parameters and writes the results to one or more logs. When you write a Windows PowerShell function, you also have a chunk of code with parameters and, within that code, a function that you can write to several logs (Output, Error, Verbose, Debug, Warning, and Progress Logs or the Event Log). Because Windows PowerShell already contains everything you need for a good framework, including an Integrated Scripting Environment, I tend to use PowerShell as my framework rather than another testing framework.

The final point to keep in mind when testing in Windows PowerShell is the importance of interactivity. The key to testing in Windows PowerShell is to interact with Application Programming Interfaces (APIs), Web pages, and user interfaces (UIs) by trying them in short scripts and then turning those short scripts into common libraries and automated tests. I recommend using the command pane of the Windows PowerShell Integrated Scripting Environment to adjust your interaction and then copy working commands into the scripting pane to create tests.

Running the Script

Once you examine the script in sufficient detail, it is time to run the script. Before running the script for the first time, consider the possible impact of running the script if it happened to blue screen your computer. (The best place to test new scripts is in a virtual machine with undo disks enabled.)

- Do you have any unsaved work?
- Close all unnecessary programs.
- Is the script that you are working on saved?
- Is the script that you are working on backed up to an external drive? (If the script completely wipes out your computer, you will have a record of what the script actually did to your computer.)
- Do you have a previously working version of the script? (If the changes to the script are radical, you might have trouble backing out the changes in case of a disaster.)
- Do you have a recent backup of your workstation?

When you run the Get-ComputerWmiInformation.ps1 script, you will notice that there is no output and no feedback from the script: no errors, no output, no feedback, and no help. You will need to determine how the script runs by examining the command-line parameters and the entry point to the script. Nearly all of the command-line parameters are switched parameters and have names such as *–disk*, *–processor*, *–memory*, and one named *–all*. From this bit of information, you might surmise that the script retrieves information about computer hardware. From the name of the script, Get-ComputerWmiInformation.ps1, you might determine that the script uses WMI to obtain information.

The entry point to the script calls the *Get-CommandLineOptions* function. An examination of the *Get-CommandLineOptions* function reveals that it tests for each of the command-line parameters and calls the appropriate function. Because there is no default behavior, the script ends without notice when it is run without any command-line parameters. The *Get-CommandLineOptions* function is shown here.

```
Function Get-CommandLineOptions
{

if($all)
  {
    Get-Disk($computer)
    Get-Processor($computer)
    Get-Memory($computer)
    Get-Network($computer)
    Get-Video($computer)
     exit
  } #end all
```

```
if($disk)
  {
    Get-Disk($computer)
  } #end disk

if($processor)
  {
    Get-Processor($computer)
  } #end processor

if($memory)
  {
    Get-Memory($computer)
  } #end memory

if($network)
  {
    Get-Network($computer)
  } #end network

if($video)
  {
    Get-Video($computer)
  } #end video
} #end function Get-CommandLineOptions
```

Multiple Test Paths

To properly test the Get-ComputerWmiInformation.ps1 script, each of the command-line parameters should be tested individually and together. In addition, the script should be run remotely and locally against a variety of operating systems. You might also consider testing it on both Windows PowerShell 1.0 and Windows PowerShell 2.0. If you find that a script only runs on Windows PowerShell 2.0, it is a best practice to include the *#requires –version 2.0* tag in your script. This is the only command that is permitted to go above the *Param* statement. However, because it begins with the pound (#) sign, it confirms to the "first noncommented line" rule that was stated earlier.

Documenting What You Did

Make sure you document how the script was tested. The version of the operating system, service pack level, and installed hotfixes all impact the way a script will run. Document all software that is installed on the computer, including management clients (such as Microsoft

System Center Operations Manager Management Packs). If you run the script from within a script editor or directly from the command line of the Windows PowerShell console, it should be noted. If you are running on a 64-bit version of the operating system, you should test the script in both 32-bit and 64-bit Windows PowerShell. The script should be run elevated with Administrator rights and with normal user rights.

The Get-ComputerWmiInformation.ps1 script is shown here.

Get-ComputerWmiInformation.ps1
```
Param(
    [string]$computer=$env:computerName,
    [switch]$disk,
    [switch]$processor,
    [switch]$memory,
    [switch]$network,
    [switch]$video,
    [switch]$all
) #end param

Function Get-Disk($computer)
{
 Get-WmiObject -class Win32_LogicalDisk -computername $computer
} #end Get-Disk

Function Get-Processor($computer)
{
 Get-WmiObject -class Win32_Processor -computername $computer
} #end Get-Processor

Function Get-Memory($computer)
{
 Get-WmiObject -class Win32_PhysicalMemory -computername $computer
} #end Get-Processor

Function Get-Network($computer)
{
 Get-WmiObject -class Win32_NetworkAdapter -computername $computer
} #end Get-Processor

Function Get-Video($computer)
{
 Get-WmiObject -class Win32_VideoController -computername $computer
} #end Get-Processor

Function Get-CommandLineOptions
{
```

```
if($all)
  {
    Get-Disk($computer)
    Get-Processor($computer)
    Get-Memory($computer)
    Get-Network($computer)
    Get-Video($computer)
     exit
  } #end all

if($disk)
  {
    Get-Disk($computer)
  } #end disk

if($processor)
  {
    Get-Processor($computer)
  } #end processor

if($memory)
  {
    Get-Memory($computer)
  } #end memory

if($network)
  {
    Get-Network($computer)
  } #end network

if($video)
  {
    Get-Video($computer)
  } #end video
} #end function Get-CommandLineOptions

# *** Entry Point to Script ***

Get-CommandLineOptions
```

Are You Safe?

Jeffrey Hicks, Microsoft PowerShell MVP
Author of Managing Active Directory with Windows PowerShell: TFM

Without a doubt, the Windows PowerShell community is growing by leaps and bounds, as is the collection of readily available scripts. However, not all scripts are written to perhaps the same level of quality that you might desire. How can you tell what the script is going to do? Is it safe to run? Or perhaps you have developed your own script that someone else will be using. Can you trust that it will be executed correctly? For example, you might have the following concerns:

- How does the script handle missing parameters?
- How does the script handle different operating systems?
- How does the script handle a wide range of values for the inputs?
- How does the script handle the different combinations of parameters?

Frankly, some of these issues can be handled during script development. In Windows PowerShell 2.0, you can use the `Set-StrictMode` cmdlet to help alleviate errors produced during development.

```
Set-StrictMode -version 2.0
```

Windows PowerShell will complain if you attempt to use an undefined variable, which is terrific for catching typos. You should also include as much error handling and trapping as you can. I always recommend providing default values for *–script* or function parameters as well as casting the parameter to the necessary type. In this way, if the user passes the wrong type of object as a parameter, Windows PowerShell will grumble. You can also use a *Throw* statement if the parameter is required but omitted. In a Windows PowerShell 1.0 script, you can use parameter syntax, such as the syntax shown here.

```
Param (
[string]$name="default",
[int]$size=$(Throw "You must enter a file size in bytes")
)
```

The previous syntax still works in Windows PowerShell 2.0, but you can also use parameter attributes to make parameter checking easier.

```
Param (
[Parameter(Position=0, Mandatory=$False, ValueFromPipeline=$False,
 HelpMessage="What is the name of the computer to backup?")]
[string]$computername=$env:computername,
)
```

And of course, you need to test *everything* in a nonproduction environment. Your script should follow the same code development process that an internally developed application will follow. I always try to think of the most ridiculous way in which someone might run the script and then test it.

But suppose the downloaded script doesn't follow your development suggestions? What can you do? Well, you still need to test the script and observe its behavior in a variety of scenarios. I don't have an automated test process yet, but I do have a script that will analyze another script and create what I refer to as a script profile. The Get-ScriptProfile.ps1 script requires Windows PowerShell 2.0. To see help for the Get-ScriptProfile.ps1 script, you can use the Get-Help cmdlet.

```
Get-Help .\get-scriptprofile.ps1 –full
```

The complete Get-ScriptProfile.ps1 script is on the companion media.

To be honest, I am still adding to the script, but most of the core functionality is complete. My script takes a Windows PowerShell script—version 1 scripts work best right now—and analyzes it. The script writes a profile report that tells you what parameters are used and their type, the lines of code that use the parameters, the names of any internally defined functions, whether the script is digitally signed, the lines of code that include a Windows PowerShell command, and, optionally, the script code itself. The profile offers me a summary of the script's critical components so that I can tell at a glance what the script will most likely attempt to accomplish. Run this command at a Windows PowerShell prompt for more information on how to run this script.

Conducting Performance Testing of Scripts

A common mistake that some people make is to use Windows PowerShell as if it were another scripting language. When you use certain constructions, such as the ones that read the contents of a file and store the results in a variable, and then iterate through the contents of the file by using a *Foreach* statement, the performance will generally be substandard. This type of store and forward construction is shown here.

```
$a = Get-Content –Path c:\fso\myfile.txt
Foreach ($i in $a)
{
 Write-Host $i
}
```

The previous construction can easily be written in Microsoft Visual Basic, VBScript, or a dozen other languages because the design pattern is exactly the same. For optimal performance and ease of development, however, it is best to take advantage of the native features of Windows PowerShell. For example, the previous code can be written as shown here.

```
Get-Content -Path c:\fso\myfile.txt
```

One of the more powerful features of Windows PowerShell is the pipeline, and when you do not take advantage of the pipeline, you are setting yourself up for disappointing results. The Windows PowerShell pipeline does not need to read the entire contents of the file before processing it. Additionally, when working with large files, you reduce the amount of memory that is required because you do not need to store the contents of the file in a variable. Due to the asynchronous nature of the pipeline and the reduced memory footprint of the operation, it is a Windows PowerShell best practice to engage the pipeline whenever it makes sense in your code.

Because you know that the Windows PowerShell pipeline is more efficient, it seems logical to always use it in your script. However, this is simply not the case. For certain types of operations, such as those that process small files and do not require large amounts of memory, the store and forward approach previously shown can actually be more efficient. The key to determining the best approach to writing a script is to test two different versions of the script and see which one is the fastest. In this section, we will look at different versions of a script to determine which one is the fastest.

Using the Store and Forward Approach

The Get-ModifiedFiles.ps1 script is used to count the number of files that were modified in a folder within a specified period of time. The *param* keyword is used to create two command-line parameters. The first parameter is the *–path* parameter that specifies the folder to search. The second parameter is the *-days* parameter that is used to create the starting date for counting modified files.

```
Param(
    $path = "C:\data",
    $days = 30
) #end param
```

The starting date needs to be a DateTime object. The Get-Date cmdlet creates an instance of a DateTime object, which exposes the *AddDays* method. By using a negative number for the number of days to be added to the current DateTime object, a point in time from the past is created. By default, the script creates a DateModified object 30 days in the past.

```
$dteModified= (Get-Date).AddDays(-$days)
```

The Get-ChildItem cmdlet is used to obtain a collection of all files and folders in the path that are specified by the *$path* variable. The *–recurse* switched parameter is used to tell the

Get-ChildItem cmdlet to burrow down into all of the subfolders. This collection of files and folders is stored in the *$files* variable.

```
$files = Get-ChildItem -path $path -recurse
```

To walk through the collection of files and folders, the *Foreach* statement is used. The variable *$file* is used as the enumerator that keeps track of the current position in the collection. The collection of files and folders is stored in the *$files* variable. Inside the *foreach* loop, the *If* statement is used to evaluate the DateTime object that is retrieved from the *LastWriteTime* property of the file object. If the value stored in the *LastWriteTime* property is greater than or equal to the DateTime value stored in the *$dteModified* variable, the value of the *$changedFiles* variable is incremented by one.

```
Foreach($file in $files)
{
   if($file.LastWriteTime -ge $dteModified)
     { $changedFiles ++ }
}
```

The last step initiated by the Get-ModifiedFiles.ps1 script is to display a message to the user stating how many modified files are found. The following command is used to display the confirmation message to the user.

```
"The $path has $changedFiles modified files since $dteModified"
```

The complete Get-ModifiedFiles.ps1 script is shown here.

Get-ModifiedFiles.ps1
```
Param(
    $path = "D:",
    $days = 30
) #end param
$dteModified= (Get-Date).AddDays(-$days)
$files = Get-ChildItem -path $path -recurse

Foreach($file in $files)
{
   if($file.LastWriteTime -ge $dteModified)
     { $changedFiles ++ }
}

"The $path has $changedFiles modified files since $dteModified"
```

When the Get-ModifiedFiles.ps1 script is run, it takes a bit of time to return on my computer. This is understandable because the D: drive on my computer consumes approximately 60 GB of disk space and contains nearly 30,000 files and 4,000 folders. It therefore does not seem to be a horrible performance considering what the script is actually doing.

Using the Windows PowerShell Pipeline

The Get-ModifiedFiles.ps1 script can be changed to take advantage of the Windows PowerShell pipeline. The *Param* statement and the creation of the DateTime object contained in the *$dteModified* variable are exactly the same. The first change comes when the results of the Get-ChildItem cmdlet are pipelined to the next command instead of being stored in the *$files* variable. This results in two performance improvements. The first improvement is that subsequent sections of the script are able to begin work almost immediately. When the results of the Get-ChildItem cmdlet are stored in a variable, this means that all 30,000 files and 4,000 folders in the previous example must be enumerated before any additional processing can begin. In addition, because the variable is stored in memory, it is conceivable that the computer might run out of memory before it finishes enumerating all of the files and folders from an extremely large drive. The change to the pipeline is shown here.

```
Get-ChildItem -path $path -recurse |
```

Instead of using the *Foreach* statement, the Get-ModifiedFilesUsePipeline.ps1 script uses the ForEach-Object cmdlet. The ForEach-Object cmdlet is designed to accept pipelined input and is more flexible than the *Foreach* language statement. The default parameter for the ForEach-Object cmdlet is the *−Process* parameter. As each object comes through the pipeline, the *$_* automatic variable is used to reference it. Here the *$_* automatic variable is acting in a similar fashion to the *$file* variable from the Get-ModifiedFiles.ps1 script. The *If* statement is exactly the same in the Get-ModifiedFilesUsePipeline.ps1 script, with the exception of the change to using *$_* instead of *$file*. The ForEach-Object section of the Get-ModifiedFilesUsePipeline.ps1 script is shown here.

```
ForEach-Object {
  if($_.LastWriteTime -ge $dteModified)
    { $changedFiles ++ }
}
```

The user message is the same as that shown in the Get-ModifiedFiles.ps1 script. The completed Get-ModifiedFilesUsePipeline.ps1 script is shown here.

```
Get-ModifiedFilesUsePipeline.ps1
Param(
    $path = "D:",
    $days = 30
) #end param

$dteModified= (Get-Date).AddDays(-$days)
Get-ChildItem -path $path -recurse |
ForEach-Object {
  if($_.LastWriteTime -ge $dteModified)
    { $changedFiles ++ }
}

"The $path has $changedFiles modified files since $dteModified"
```

Comparing the Speed of Two Scripts

When the Get-ModifiedFilesUsePipeline.ps1 script is run, it seems a little faster, but it might be hard to tell. Was the modification to the script worth the trouble? To determine whether a change to a script makes an improvement in the performance of the script, you can use the Measure-Command cmdlet. You will want to first measure the performance of the original script and then measure the performance of the revised script. To measure the performance of the original script, you supply the path to the Get-ModifiedFiles.ps1 script to the *Expression* parameter of the Measure-Command cmdlet.

```
PS C:\fso> Measure-Command -Expression { C:\fso\Get-ModifiedFiles.ps1 }
```

The Measure-Command cmdlet returns a *System.TimeSpan* .NET Framework class, which is used to measure the difference between two *System.DateTime* classes. It has a number of properties that report days, hours, minutes, seconds, and milliseconds, and these properties report the TimeSpan in units of these divisions. In Figure 14-2, you see that the Get-ModifiedFiles.ps1 script ran for 26 seconds and 141 milliseconds. The *System.TimeSpan* object also reports the TimeSpan in total units. The same TimeSpan is reported as five different units. For example, the Get-ModifiedFiles.ps1 script run time of 26 seconds and 141 milliseconds translates into 26.1411386 total seconds or 0.435685643333333 total minutes. When expressed in milliseconds, this value is 26141.1386.

FIGURE 14-2 The Measure-Command cmdlet returns a *TimeSpan* object.

The double display of time breakdown into days, hours, minutes, seconds, and milliseconds can be confusing to people who are not used to working with the *System.TimeSpan* .NET Framework class. In general, you can probably examine only the *TotalSeconds* property when testing your scripts.

It is now time to see whether the use of the pipeline makes any difference in the performance of the script. To measure the performance of the Get-ModifiedFilesUsePipeline.ps1 script, the path to the Get-ModifiedFilesUsePipeline.ps1 script is passed to the *Expression* parameter of the Measure-Command cmdlet, which results in the command line shown here.

```
PS C:\fso> Measure-Command -Expression { C:\fso\Get-ModifiedFilesUsePipeline.ps1 }
```

Once the command has run, the *TimeSpan* object shown in Figure 14-3 is displayed.

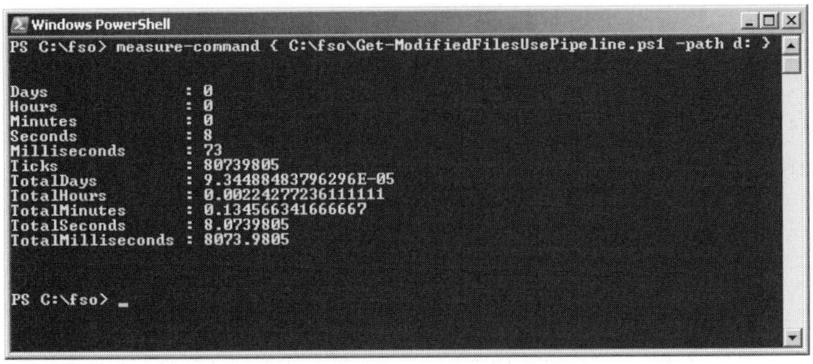

FIGURE 14-3 *TimeSpan* object displaying improvement in script speed when using the pipeline

As shown in Figure 14-3, the Get-ModifiedFilesUsePipeline.ps1 script completed in 8.0739805 total seconds. When compared to the original 26.1411386 total seconds, we see a nearly 70 percent improvement in the speed of the script; expressed another way, the Get-ModifiedFilesUsePipeline.ps1 script is nearly 3.5 times faster than the original Get-ModifiedFiles.ps1 script. This is a significant performance improvement no matter how you express it.

Reducing Code Complexity

Further changes can be made to the Get-ModifiedFilesUsePipeline.ps1 script. This is a more radical modification to the script because it requires removing the ForEach-Object cmdlet and the *If* statement. The following section of code is ripped out.

```
ForEach-Object {
   if($_.LastWriteTime -ge $dteModified)
     { $changedFiles ++ }
}
```

By removing the ForEach-Object cmdlet and the *If* statement, you can get rid of the *$changedFiles* ++ statement and take advantage of the fact that Windows PowerShell automatically returns objects from the cmdlets. The use of the single Where-Object cmdlet should be faster than the more convoluted ForEach-Object cmdlet when combined with the *If* statement. However, you will determine whether the modification is effective when you test the script with the Measure-Object cmdlet. By using a single Where-Object cmdlet, you arrive at this filter.

```
where-object { $_.LastWriteTime -ge $dteModified }
```

The result of the pipeline operation is stored in the *$changedFiles* variable, which has a *count* property associated with it. Directly reading the *count* property should be faster than incrementing the *$changedFiles* variable as was done in the Get-ModifiedFilesUsePipeline.ps1 script. The entire Get-ModifiedFilesUsePipeline2.ps1 script is shown here.

```
Get-ModifiedFilesUsePipeline2.ps1
Param(
    $path = "D:\",
    $days = 30
) #end param


$changedFiles = $null
$dteModified= (Get-Date).AddDays(-$days)
$changedFiles = Get-ChildItem -path $path -recurse |
where-object { $_.LastWriteTime -ge $dteModified }


"The $path has $($changedFiles.count) modified files since $dteModified"
```

When the Get-ModifiedFilesUsePipeline2.ps1 script is run, the script completes in 8.4052029 seconds, which is a 9.6 percent decrease in the speed of the script. In this particular example, the modification to the script was not an improvement in performance. The *TimeSpan* object that is created by running the Get-ModifiedFilesUsePipeline2.ps1 script is shown in Figure 14-4.

FIGURE 14-4 *TimeSpan* object indicating that changes were not an improvement to the script

Evaluating the Performance of Different Versions of a Script

It is relatively simple to use the Measure-Command cmdlet to check the performance of a script and monitor for moderate changes. For more extensive changes to a script, you will want to create different versions of the script. To simplify the testing scenario, it makes sense to create a script that will test the performance of two different scripts. To take into account the difference in performance between run times of the scripts that can be attributed to computer loading, resource contention, and the like, you might want the ability to run the tests multiple times and create a report on the average run time of the scripts.

The Test-TwoScripts.ps1 script allows you to run the performance test of the script multiple times. It also produces a report that details the time that was taken for each run and produces a summary evaluation of the two scripts.

Command-Line Parameters

First, the Test-TwoScripts.ps1 script creates the command-line parameters.

- The first parameter, *baseLineScript*, is the path to the script that will be the baseline for comparison. Typically, this is the script you used before you modified it.

- The second parameter is *modifiedScript*, and it is used to reference the script whose changes you want to evaluate. Note that these two scripts do not need to be related to one another.

- The third parameter is the *numberOfTests* parameter. This number controls how many times the scripts will be run. By running the scripts several times and averaging the results, a more accurate picture of the performance of the scripts can be gained.

  When testing, a script might run faster or slower on any given run. This might be due to file caching or to other performance enhancements offered by the operating system, but it might also be due to resource contention or other anomalies.

- The last parameter is the *–log* switched parameter. When the *–log* parameter is present, it causes the script to write the performance information to a temporary text file that is displayed at the end of the completion of the script.

The *Param* section of the script is shown here.

```
Param(
    [string]$baseLineScript,
    [string]$modifiedScript,
    [int]$numberOfTests = 20,
    [switch]$log
) #end param
```

Functions

The *Test-Scripts* function is used to call the `Measure-Command` cmdlet for each of the two scripts to be tested. The *Param* section of the function receives two inputs: the *baseLineScript* parameter and the *modifiedScript* parameter. These parameters are cut and pasted from the *Param* section to the script because it is easier than typing everything a second time. Cutting and pasting the parameters also ensures that you avoid typing errors as shown here.

```
Function Test-Scripts
{
    Param(
    [string]$baseLineScript,
    [string]$modifiedScript
) #end param
```

After the parameters for the *Test-Scripts* function are created, it is time to call the `Measure-Command` cmdlet, which is called twice. During the first call, the baseline script is passed to the *Expression* parameter of the `Measure-Command` cmdlet. The string that is passed to the *$baseLineScript* parameter includes the full path to the script as well as all parameters that the script requires to successfully execute. The second `Measure-Command` cmdlet is called to evaluate the performance of the modified script. The path to the modified script as well as the parameters required to set up the command are passed to the *Expression* parameter of the `Measure-Command` cmdlet.

```
Measure-Command -Expression { $baseLineScript }
Measure-Command -Expression { $modifiedScript }
} #end Test-Scripts function
```

The *Get-Change* function is used to calculate the percentage increase or decrease in total running time between the baseline script and the modified script. The *baseline* parameter contains the total number of seconds that the baseline script requires to execute. The *modified* parameter contains the total number of seconds that the modified script requires to execute. If the *Test-Scripts* function is called several times (due to the script performing multiple tests), the *$baseLine* variable and the *$modified* variable will contain the cumulative number of seconds of running time from the entire series of tests. To calculate the percentage increase or decrease in total running time, the total number of seconds contained in the *$modified* variable is subtracted from the total number of seconds contained in the *$baseLine* variable, and this number is then divided by the total number of seconds contained in the *$baseLine* variable. The result of this computation is then multiplied by 100. The *Get-Change* function is shown here.

```
Function Get-Change($baseLine, $modified)
{
  (($baseLine - $modified)/$baseLine)*100
} #end Get-Change function
```

After the *Get-Change* function is created, the *Get-TempFile* function is created. The *Get-TempFile* function calls the static *GetTempFileName* method from the *IO.Path* .NET Framework class. The *Get-TempFile* function is shown here.

```
Function Get-TempFile
{
 [io.path]::GetTempFileName()
} #end Get-TempFile function
```

After all of the functions are created, you arrive at the entry point to the script. You must first determine whether the Test-TwoScripts.ps1 script was run with the *–log* switched parameter. If it was launched with the *–log* switched parameter, the *$log* variable will exist. If the *$log* variable exists, the *Get-TempFile* function is called and the resulting temporary file name is stored in the *$logFile* variable.

```
if($log) { $logFile = Get-TempFile }
```

A *for* loop is used to count the number of tests to perform on the scripts. The number of tests is stored in the *$numberOfTests* variable. A status message is displayed to the Windows PowerShell console that indicates the test loop number. This section of the code is shown here.

```
For($i = 0 ; $i -le $numberOfTests ; $i++)
{
 "Test $i of $numberOfTests" ; start-sleep -m 50 ; cls
```

After the loop progress message is displayed, the *Test-Scripts* function is called. The *Test-Scripts* function returns two *System.TimeSpan* objects, which are stored in the *$results* variable.

```
$results= Test-Scripts -baseLineScript $baseLineScript -modifiedScript $modifedScript
```

Because the *$results* variable contains an array of two *TimeSpan* objects, you can index directly into the array and retrieve the value of the *$TotalSeconds* variable. Use [0] to retrieve the first *TimeSpan* object and [1] to retrieve the second *TimeSpan* object. The total seconds from the current test run is added to the total seconds that are stored in the *$baseLine* and *$modified* variables.

```
$baseLine += $results[0].TotalSeconds
$modified += $results[1].TotalSeconds
```

If the script is run with the *–log* switched parameter, the name of the script, the test number, and the results are written to the log file. The code that performs this action is shown here.

```
 If($log)
  {
     "$baseLineScript run $i of $numberOfTests $(get-date)" >> $logFile
     $results[0] >> $logFile
     "$modifiedScript run $i of $numberOfTests $(get-date)" >> $logFile
     $results[1] >> $logFile
  } #if $log
} #for $i
```

The complete Test-TwoScripts.ps1 script is shown here.

Test-TwoScripts.ps1
```
Param(
  [string]$baseLineScript,
  [string]$modifiedScript,
  [int]$numberOfTests = 20,
  [switch]$log
) #end param

Function Test-Scripts
{
```

```
   Param(
   [string]$baseLineScript,
   [string]$modifiedScript,
   [int]$numberOfTests,
   [switch]$log
) #end param
 Measure-Command -Expression { $baseLineScript }
 Measure-Command -Expression { $modifiedScript }
} #end Test-Scripts function


Function Get-Change($baseLine, $modified)
{
  (($baseLine - $modified)/$baseLine)*100
} #end Get-Change function


Function Get-TempFile
{
 [io.path]::GetTempFileName()
} #end Get-TempFile function


# *** Entry Point To Script
if($log) { $logFile = Get-TempFile }
For($i = 0 ; $i -le $numberOfTests ; $i++)
{
  "Test $i of $numberOfTests" ; start-sleep -m 50 ; cls
  $results= Test-Scripts -baseLineScript $baseLineScript -modifiedScript $modifedScript
  $baseLine += $results[0].TotalSeconds
  $modified += $results[1].TotalSeconds
  If($log)
   {
      "$baseLineScript run $i of $numberOfTests $(get-date)" >> $logFile
      $results[0] >> $logFile
      "$modifiedScript run $i of $numberOfTests $(get-date)" >> $logFile
      $results[1] >> $logFile
   } #if $log
} #for $i


"Average change over $numberOfTests tests"
"BaseLine: $baseLineScript average Total Seconds: $($baseLine/$numberOfTests)"
"Modified: $modifiedScript average Total Seconds: $($modified/$numberOfTests)"
"Percent Change: " + "{0:N2}" -f (Get-Change -baseLine $baseLine -modified $modified)
if($log)
{
  "Average change over $numberOfTests tests" >> $logFile
```

```
 "BaseLine: $baseLineScript average Total Seconds: $($baseLine/$numberOfTests)" >>
$logFile
 "Modified: $modifiedScript average Total Seconds: $($modified/$numberOfTests)" >>
$logFile
 "Percent Change: " + "{0:N2}" -f (Get-Change -baseLine $baseLine -modified $modified)
>> $logFile
} #if $log
if($log) { Notepad $logFile }
```

INSIDE TRACK

Testing APIs, Web Services, SOAP, and REST with Windows PowerShell

James Brundage and Ibrahim Abdul Rahim, Software Development Engineers
Microsoft Corporation

It's probably easier to test APIs in Windows PowerShell than in any other language because you can use the APIs interactively. When testing APIs, the task normally involves checking both the results from an API as well as the things that the API should have done within the system. You can easily create objects, run their methods, and get their results in Windows PowerShell. To create an existing .NET class, use the New-Object cmdlet. To load a type from disk, you can use [Reflection.Assembly]::LoadFrom(*$FullPath*) to load an assembly. To run a static method or get a static property, use [*Type*]::*PropertyOrMethod*.

In Windows PowerShell 2.0, it is easier than ever to test Web services. Web service testing is similar to API testing in that you are usually simply running some method and checking the results. However, Web tests might pay more attention to timing. To add timing to your tests, use the Measure-Command cmdlet to execute the core of the test and use the *Throw* statement or the Write-Error cmdlet to fail the test if the command takes too long to complete.

Windows PowerShell 2.0 makes testing Simple Object Access Protocol (SOAP) a snap because you can use SOAP's autodiscovery to create a type to use the Web service in PowerShell with the New-WebServiceProxy cmdlet. Because SOAP Web services use many different types, I recommend using New-WebServiceProxy in a command that is similar to the one shown here.

```
$webService =New-WebServiceProxy Url -Namespace WebServiceName
```

Once you create a proxy of the Web service, test it interactively just like any other API by trying different actions and validating the results and side effects.

Because Representational State Transfer (REST) Web Services are not discoverable, they also are not as easy to test as SOAP Web services. However, because REST Web services are straightforward to query, you can generally simply query the Web service and check the XML that it returns. Most REST Web services use a long GET query (like the one you can see in your address bar when you search via a search engine) to provide the parameters to the Web service.

To test REST in Windows PowerShell, you should first write a function to wrap the REST Web service. For example, this means that if the service takes a topic string, a count of articles to retrieve, and an offset, then you should write a function with a signature that matches the Web service (that is, function Get-RestService([string]$Topic, [int]$count = 20, [int]$offset =0) {}).

The function used to wrap REST is simple. Typically, all you need to do is use New-Object to create a *webclient*, use the *DownloadString* method to get the results, and then turn the results into an XML object by casting.

```
($client = New-Object NET.Webclient; $client.DownloadString($url) -as [xml])
```

When done, you will be able to use the Select-Xml cmdlet to query the data returned from the Web service to determine whether you should have received this data.

Displaying the Results and Creating the Log File

After writing to the log file, it is time to display information to the Windows PowerShell console. The number of tests and the average time for each test run is displayed to the console for both the baseline and the modified scripts. The portion of the script that performs this action is shown here.

```
"Average change over $numberOfTests tests"
"BaseLine: $baseLineScript average Total Seconds: $($baseLine/$numberOfTests)"
"Modified: $modifiedScript average Total Seconds: $($modified/$numberOfTests)"
```

The percentage of change between the two scripts is calculated by using the *Get-Change* function. A .NET format specifier is used to display the percentage of change to two decimal places. The {0:N2} format specifier indicates two decimal places.

```
"Percent Change: " + "{0:N2}" -f (Get-Change -baseLine $baseLine
-modified $modified)
```

The same information that was just displayed to the console is written to the log file if the script is launched with the *–log* switched parameter.

```
if($log)
{
 "Average change over $numberOfTests tests" >> $logFile
 "BaseLine: $baseLineScript average Total Seconds:
$($baseLine/$numberOfTests)" >> $logFile
 "Modified: $modifiedScript average Total Seconds:
$($modified/$numberOfTests)" >> $logFile
 "Percent Change: " + "{0:N2}" -f (Get-Change -baseLine $baseLine
-modified $modified) >> $logFile
} #if $log
```

After the log file is updated, it is displayed by using Notepad. The code that displays the log file in Notepad is shown here.

```
if($log) { Notepad $logFile }
```

The log that is produced by running the Test-TwoScripts.ps1 script is shown in Figure 14-5.

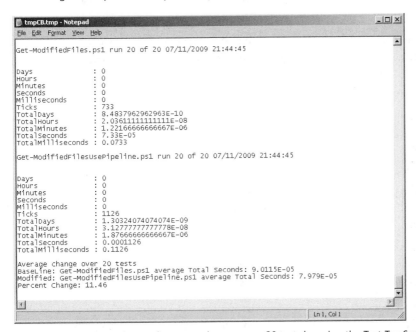

FIGURE 14-5 Log reporting performance changes over 20 tests by using the Test-TwoScripts.ps1 script

Testing Graphical Applications with Windows PowerShell

James Brundage and Ibrahim Abdul Rahim, Software Development Engineers
Microsoft Corporation

The easiest way to test Web sites in Windows PowerShell is to try scripting Windows Internet Explorer. The incredible amount of data that you can view about a Web site can help you determine whether the content is correct. To automate the Web, the main object with which you should interact is the Component Object Model (COM) *Shell.Application* object ($Shell = New-Object –ComObject Shell.Application). You can use the *ShellExecute* method of *Shell.Application* to create brand new windows, and you can use the *Shell.Windows()* method to get (and change) all of the running windows. The Internet Explorer Developer Tools (press F12 when viewing any site) will be very helpful in determining where the content that you need to automate can be found on the Web page.

Web page testing has two additional areas of special concern, one of which I can be of some help in explaining. Web pages often take one period of time to load the page and another period of time to render individual controls, which can result in the need for multiple waiting periods. In the following example, for instance, I wait once to load *Bing.com* and wait again to make sure that the search dialog box is ready for input. The other area of special concern that the Web can throw at you involves dealing with Adobe Flash or Microsoft Silverlight pages. At this point, it is significantly easier to treat the Web page as any other UI that you want to test.

Here is a quick Web test written in Windows PowerShell to search for a term on Bing.com.

```
$shell.ShellExecute("http://www.bing.com")
$timeout = New-TimeSpan -Seconds 15
$startTime = Get-Date
do {
    $window = $shell.Windows() | ? { $_.LocationUrl -eq "http://www.bing.
com/" }
} while (-not $window -and
    ($startTime + $timeout) -gt (Get-Date))
if (-not $window) {
    throw "Timed out waiting for Window to load"
}
$timeout = New-TimeSpan -Seconds 5
$startTime = Get-Date
do {
    $searchQuery = $window.Document.getElementById("sb_form_q")
```

```
} while (-not $searchQuery -and
    ($startTime + $timeout) -gt (Get-Date))
if (-not $searchQuery) {
    throw "Timed out waiting for search query box to be available"
}
$searchQuery.InnerText = "foobar"
$window.Document.getElementById("sb_form_go").Click()
```

Windows PowerShell has easy access to console applications and APIs. When dealing with GUI applications, however, Windows PowerShell needs to go through several layers before it can access information on the GUI (such as Text Box text or whether a check box is checked) and execute GUI commands, such as send keys and click buttons.

As in testing Web pages, the trick is locating the item with which you want to interact and then interacting with it. Because UI technologies can use different underlying implementations, the tricks that work for some UI types will not work for others. The APIs that you can use to access the pages include Microsoft Active Accessibility (MSAA), User Interface Automation (UIA), and C Windows APIs. C Windows APIs require Interop (Add-Type and P/Invoke), while MSAA and UIA have .NET and COM APIs. The Windows Automation Snap-in for Windows PowerShell (*http://www.codeplex.com/WASP*) can help you get started with UI testing and is based on C Windows API windows.

The trick to automating the majority of tests in UIs is to consider most interactions in terms of the keyboard when possible. By using the keyboard, you can use the SendKeys API (it's on `New-Object -ComObject WScript.Shell`) to send the sequence of actions as keys that you can type. You can then validate the UI changes by pulling out screen positions and text in the Web Application Services Platform (WASP).

If you choose not to actually automate testing, another common approach to testing Web sites is to keep a store of manual test cases. In this scenario, Windows PowerShell still possesses all that is required to be your testing framework. Windows PowerShell contains two common cmdlets that make this process easy: `Read-Host` and `Write-Host`. `Read-Host` returns what the user provided, and `Write-Host` writes out prompts for the user. By writing out the steps of a test case using `Write-Host` and checking for a fixed result from `Read-Host`, you can effectively write manual test cases for someone else to run in Windows PowerShell.

Using Standard Parameters

Windows PowerShell defines two standard parameters that are useful when testing scripts: *debug* and *–whatif*. When the *debug* parameter is implemented in a script, detailed debugging information is displayed to the Windows PowerShell console via the `Write-Debug` cmdlet. When you implement the *–whatif* parameter in a script, the parameters that are supplied to a function are displayed to the console. Both of these features provide you with useful information when testing the functionality of a script.

Using the *debug* Parameter

In Windows PowerShell 2.0, the *debug* parameter is automatically available to you because it is a standard parameter. To use the *debug* parameter, you only need to check whether it has been supplied from the command line. If the *debug* parameter is set, you need to assign the value of the automatic variable *$DebugPreference* to *Continue*.

```
if($debug) { $debugPreference = "continue" }
```

When *$DebugPreference* is set to *Continue*, it means that using the `Write-Debug` cmdlet will cause the string to be displayed on the Windows PowerShell console. If *$DebugPreference* is set to *SilentlyContinue*, which is the default value, the `Write-Debug` cmdlet is ignored. This variety provides a flexible way of displaying detailed information on the progress of the script without the need to create a debug build and a release build. As a best practice, you should use a `Write-Debug` statement before each method that you call, during value assignment, and before you call a function.

In the Add-UserToGroups.ps1 script, the `Write-Debug` cmdlet is used to provide debugging information before calling the *Add-UserToGroups* function. The information displayed indicates the action that the script is preparing to take, the function that is going to be called, and the parameters that are passed to the function.

```
Write-Debug "Adding user to group ..."
Write-Debug "Calling Add-UserToGroups function."
Write-Debug "passing: user $user group $group ou $ou domain $domain"
```

Inside the *Add-UserToGroups* function, the `Write-Debug` cmdlet is used prior to connecting to the group in Active Directory, writing to the group, and calling the *SetInfo* method.

```
write-debug "Connecting to group: LDAP://$g,$ou,$domain"
$de = [adsi]"LDAP://$g,$ou,$domain"
write-debug "Putting user: $user,$ou,$domain"
$de.putex($ads_Property_Append,"member", @("$user,$ou,$domain"))
write-Debug "Calling setinfo"
$de.SetInfo()
```

The complete Add-UserToGroups.ps1 script is shown here.

Add-UserToGroups.ps1

```
<#
   .Synopsis
   Adds a user to multiple groups
   .Description
   This script adds a user to one or more groups. User and group
    must be in same OU
   .Example
   Add-UserToGroups.ps1 -user cn=myuser -group cn=mygroup `
   -ou ou=myou -domain 'dc=nwtraders,dc=com'
   Adds the user myuser to the group mygroup in the myou ou in the
   nwtraders.com domain.
   .Example
   Add-UserToGroups.ps1 -user cn=myuser -group cn=mygroup1,cn=mygroup2 `
   -ou ou=myou -domain 'dc=nwtraders,dc=com'
   Adds the user myuser to both the mygroup1 and the mygroup2 groups in the
   myou ou in the nwtraders.com domain.
   .Example
   Add-UserToGroups.ps1 -user cn=myuser -group cn=mygroup `
   -ou ou=myou -domain      'dc=nwtraders,dc=com' -whatif
   Displays WhatIf: Add user cn=myuser,ou=myou,dc=nwtraders,dc=com to `
   cn=mygroup,ou=myou,dc=nwtraders,dc=com
   .Inputs
    [String]
   .OutPuts
    [string]
   .Notes
   NAME:  Add-UserToGroups.ps1
   AUTHOR: Ed Wilson
   LASTEDIT: 7/25/2009
   KEYWORDS: ADSI accelerator, best practices, debug
   .Link
     Http://www.ScriptingGuys.com
#Requires -Version 2.0
#>
[CmdletBinding()]
Param(
   [Parameter(Mandatory=$true)]
   [string[]]$group,
   [Parameter(Mandatory=$true)]
   [string]$user,
   [Parameter(Mandatory=$true)]
   [string]$ou,
   [Parameter(Mandatory=$true)]
   [string]$domain,
   [switch]$whatif
```

```
) #end param

# *** Functions ***
Function Add-UserToGroups
{
 Param(
   [string[]]$group,
   [string]$user,
   [string]$ou,
   [string]$domain
 ) #end param
 $ads_Property_Append = 3
 ForEach($g in $group)
 {
   write-debug "Connecting to group: LDAP://$g,$ou,$domain"
   $de = [adsi]"LDAP://$g,$ou,$domain"
   write-debug "Putting user: $user,$ou,$domain"
   $de.putex($ads_Property_Append,"member", @("$user,$ou,$domain"))
   write-Debug "Calling setinfo"
   $de.SetInfo()
 } #end foreach
} # end function Add-UserToGroups


Function Get-Whatif
{
  Param(
   [string[]]$group,
   [string]$user,
   [string]$ou,
   [string]$domain
 ) #end param
 ForEach($g in $group)
  {
    "WHATIF: Add user $user,$ou,$domain to $g,$ou,$domain"
  } #end foreach
} #end function Get-Whatif


# *** Entry Point to script ***
if($debug) { $debugPreference = "continue" }
if($whatif) { Get-Whatif -user $user -group $group -ou $ou -domain $domain ; exit }

 Write-Debug "Adding user to group ..."
 Write-Debug "Calling Add-UserToGroups function."
 Write-Debug "passing: user $user group $group ou $ou domain $domain"


Add-UserToGroups -user $user -group $group -ou $ou -domain $domain
```

When testing the Add-UserToGroups.ps1 script, you run the script with the *debug* parameter. In addition to displaying the debug information, you are prompted to confirm the action, which enables you to skip problematic sections of the code as shown in Figure 14-6.

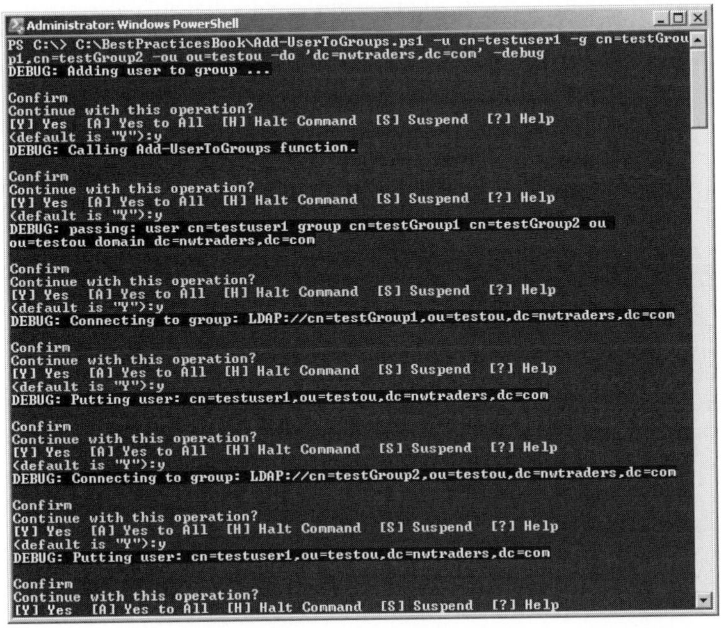

FIGURE 14-6 Debug information displayed when the script is run with the *debug* switched parameter

Using the *–whatif* Parameter

The *–whatif* parameter is not automatically created. If you want to implement the *–whatif* parameter in your script, you need to create a switched parameter named *–whatif* as well as a function that you can use to display the parameters that are passed to the function. As a best practice, you should implement the *–whatif* parameter whenever the script executes any process that changes system state. Examples of changing system state are deleting files or folders, creating folders or files, and writing values to the registry. If you display information, such as listing the properties of your mouse, this information does not change system state and therefore you should not use the *–whatif* parameter.

The first step in implementing the *–whatif* parameter is to create the switched parameter named *whatif*.

```
Param(
    [Parameter(Mandatory=$true)]
    [string]$group,
    [Parameter(Mandatory=$true)]
    [string]$ou,
    [Parameter(Mandatory=$true)]
```

```
    [string]$domain,
    [switch]$whatif
) #end param
```

You also need to create a function that accepts all of the parameters that are passed to the function. You can use any name for the *whatif* function, but it is best to use standard verbs. Because you will be displaying *whatif* information that you put together, you can used the verb *Get*. The *whatif* function is therefore called *Get-WhatIf*.

```
Function Get-Whatif
{
  Param(
    [string]$group,
    [string]$ou,
    [string]$domain
  ) #end param
  "WHATIF: Remove all members from $group,$ou,$domain"
} #end function Get-Whatif
```

When you compare the parameters for the *Get-WhatIf* function to the *Remove-AllGroupMembers* function, you will notice that they are the same. This occurs because the purpose of the *whatif* function is to display the parameters that can be passed to the *Remove-AllGroupMembers* function if it is called. The *Remove-AllGroupMembers* function is shown here.

```
Function Remove-AllGroupMembers
{
  Param(
    [string]$group,
    [string]$ou,
    [string]$domain
  ) #end param
  $ads_Property_Clear = 1
  $de = [adsi]"LDAP://$group,$ou,$domain"
  $de.putex($ads_Property_Clear,"member",$null)
  $de.SetInfo()
} # end function Remove-AllGroupMembers
```

The complete Remove-AllGroupMembers.ps1 script is shown here.

Remove-AllGroupMembers.ps1

```
<#
    .Synopsis
    Removes all members of a group
    .Description
    This script removes all members of a group
    .Example
    Remove-AllGroupMembers.ps1 -group cn=mygroup -ou ou=myou `
```

```
     -domain 'dc=nwtraders,dc=com
     Removes all members of the mygroup group in the myou organizational unit
     of the nwtraders.com domain
    .Example
     Remove-AllGroupMembers.ps1 -group cn=mygroup -ou ou=myou `
     -domain 'dc=nwtraders,dc=com' -whatif
     Displays: WHATIF: Remove all members from cn=mygroup,ou=myou,
     dc=nwtraders,dc=com
    .Inputs
     [string]
    .OutPuts
     [string]
    .Notes
     NAME:  Remove-AllGroupMembers.ps1
     AUTHOR: Ed Wilson
     LASTEDIT: 5/20/2009
     KEYWORDS: adsi, groups, powershell best practice
    .Link
       Http://www.ScriptingGuys.com
#Requires -Version 2.0
#>
[CmdletBinding()]
Param(
    [Parameter(Mandatory=$true)]
    [string]$group,
    [Parameter(Mandatory=$true)]
    [string]$ou,
    [Parameter(Mandatory=$true)]
    [string]$domain,
    [switch]$whatif
) #end param


# *** Functions ***
Function Remove-AllGroupMembers
{
 Param(
    [string]$group,
    [string]$ou,
    [string]$domain
 ) #end param
 $ads_Property_Clear = 1
 $de = [adsi]"LDAP://$group,$ou,$domain"
 $de.putex($ads_Property_Clear,"member",$null)
 $de.SetInfo()
} # end function Remove-AllGroupMembers
```

```
Function Get-Whatif
{
  Param(
    [string]$group,
    [string]$ou,
    [string]$domain
  ) #end param
  "WHATIF: Remove all members from $group,$ou,$domain"
} #end function Get-Whatif


# *** Entry Point to script ***

if($whatif) { Get-Whatif -group $group -ou $ou -domain $domain ; exit }
"Removing all members from $group,$ou,$domain"
Remove-AllGroupMembers -group $group -ou $ou -domain $domain
```

When the script is run with the –*whatif* parameter, the output shown in Figure 14-7 is displayed.

```
Administrator: Windows PowerShell                                      _|□|x|
PS C:\> C:\BestPracticesBook\Remove-AllGroupMembers.ps1 -group cn=testgroup1 -ou▲
ou=testou -domain 'dc=nwtraders,dc=com' -whatif
WHATIF: Remove all members from cn=testgroup1,ou=testou,dc=nwtraders,dc=com
PS C:\>
```

FIGURE 14-7 The –*whatif* parameter displays a script action but does not execute.

Testing Scripts

Enrique Cedeno, MCSE
Senior Network Administrator

As a senior network administrator for a large service provider, I spend a great deal of time writing scripts that are used in our server build processes. The first thing I do when testing a script is to break the script down into functions and test each function individually.

For example, if a script will be connecting to a database, I have set up a test database that has known data inside it. Each function is treated as if it were an individual script. In this way, it is easy to isolate the problem and pinpoint any issues that might arise.

A cohort on our team once wrote a script that connected to a database, but a problem emerged in one of the SQL statements. Although there was no error handling in the script, the script appeared to run okay. However, when I ran the script against the test database, I immediately noticed that the script was returning bogus data. The script was a masterpiece of spaghetti code, and it took the team three days to debug the script. This points to the value of having a database that contains known data. When you run a query and know the type of data that the query should return, you will know immediately whether your script is working properly.

In our production scripts, we trap the output of the script and write it to a log file. We use the `Write-Debug` cmdlet to provide our detailed logging for troubleshooting purposes. When we need to troubleshoot a script, we use a switch that changes the value of the *$DebugPreference* variable to turn on the `Write-Debug` cmdlet.

If we are confronted with a logic error in a script, we run the script in a known test environment and watch the data that is returned very carefully to make sure the information makes sense. Because we know the test environment, we can tell whether the script is accurate or bogus. If multiple functions are involved and we are doing unit testing, we use the `Write-Debug` cmdlet to display a message that states when the function is being entered and when it is being exited.

One of our golden rules when writing scripts is to write a ton of comments. We do this because we might not touch the script for more than six months after writing it. The comments should explain anything that is unusual, or they can even explain the logic behind the purpose of a piece of code. You should not explain the things that anyone who works with Windows PowerShell will already know how to do. Never include a comment that explains what a cmdlet does. However, always include a comment in a script that explains a particular bug that you discovered and the workaround that you put in place.

For logging errors from the script, we place code in the script that writes all errors to a log file. We use this script during development because you cannot always rely on being able to read error messages from the screen. An added bonus of writing errors to a log file is that this process makes it easy to do automated testing. When we shift the script into production, we turn off the detailed error logging but keep the code in place so we can enable the detailed error logging via a switch.

Using Start-Transcript to Produce a Log

An easy way to document the results of a script is to call the *Start-Transcript* function. Although this action will produce limited information, it is an easy way to test your scripts and provide documentation. To use this technique, use the `Start-Transcript` cmdlet to create the transcript log file. By default, the `Start-Transcript` cmdlet overwrites any log files that have the same name as the one specified by the *–path* parameter. To prevent the overwriting behavior, you can use the *Noclobber* parameter when calling the `Start-Transcript` cmdlet. In the TranscriptBios.ps1 script, the line that calls the `Start-Transcript` cmdlet is shown here.

```
Start-Transcript -path $path
```

Because the transcript log file will not contain the script name, the *$myInvocation.InvocationName* variable is used to obtain the script name. The `Start-Transcript` cmdlet copies everything that appears on the Windows PowerShell console to the log file. An easy way to get the script name in the log file is to display it to the Windows PowerShell console. Because the time when the script starts might be important, the `Get-Date` cmdlet is used to display a time stamp that will be written to the transcript log. A subexpression is used with both the *$myInvocation.InvocationName* variable and the `Get-Date` cmdlet to force the evaluation of the command and return the value to the string.

```
"Starting $($myInvocation.InvocationName) at $(Get-Date)"
```

Next, the *Get-Bios* function is called, which is a standard WMI command using the `Get-WmiObject` cmdlet. However, the *$myInvocation.InvocationName* variable is used to display the name of the function. The technique of obtaining the called function name provides useful information about the results of the script.

```
Function Get-Bios($computer)
{
 "Calling function $($myInvocation.InvocationName)"
 Get-WmiObject -class win32_bios -computer $computer
}#end function Get-Bios
```

Last, you must stop the transcript by using the `Stop-Transcript` cmdlet. No additional parameters are needed to stop the transcript.

```
Stop-Transcript
```

The complete TranscriptBios.ps1 script is shown here.

TranscriptBios.ps1
```
Param(
 [Parameter(Mandatory=$true)]
 [string]$path,
 [string]$computer = $env:computername
)#end param
```

```
# *** Functions ***

Function Get-Bios($computer)
{
 "Calling function $($myInvocation.InvocationName)"
 Get-WmiObject -class win32_bios -computer $computer
}#end function Get-Bios

# *** Entry point to script ***

Start-Transcript -path $path
"Starting $($myInvocation.InvocationName) at $(Get-Date)"

Get-Bios -computer $computer
Stop-Transcript
```

When the TranscriptBios.ps1 script is run, it creates a log in the path that is supplied when the script is run. The transcript log is shown in Figure 14-8.

FIGURE 14-8 Transcript log file documenting results of running the TranscriptBios.ps1 script

Advanced Script Testing

Although running a script and looking for errors will spot syntax problems, missing curly brackets, and even rights and permissions issues, it does not ensure that the script will perform the task it is intended to complete when the script is moved to production. To ensure that the script will work as expected in the production environment, you must test the script in a similar lab environment. The best lab environment is a complete duplication of the production network—down to the same physical infrastructure, including server models with the same BIOS revisions. Some companies maintain a duplicate infrastructure for disaster recovery purposes. If this is the case, the duplicate infrastructure can often be used for application testing.

If you do not have the luxury of working at a company that maintains a duplicate network infrastructure, you can often duplicate the existing hierarchy in virtual machines. By using Windows Server 2008 R2 Hyper-V, it is possible to create a network with several hundred virtual machines. You can then use Remote Desktop and the Hyper-V Manager console to connect to the Hyper-V server and work with multiple machines at the same time, which greatly simplifies and speeds up testing as shown in Figure 14-9.

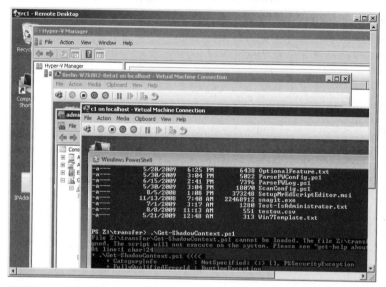

FIGURE 14-9 Using Remote Desktop to work with multiple machines on a Hyper-V system speeds up advanced script testing.

In most cases, it is not a requirement to duplicate the entire network—certainly not all of the client machines. Depending on what the script actually accomplishes, it is often sufficient to recreate the domain controller and a few servers.

Testing Scripts Against Known Data

Enrique Cedeno, MCSE
Senior Network Administrator

Our team once wrote a script to determine whether a person was a member of a particular group. If the person was a member of this group, they had to change their password every 30 days. When we were writing the script, it was returning bogus names of people. When we investigated the situation, we realized that we needed to address the way in which we were changing the date and instead subtract the date first. If we had not already known who was supposed to be in this particular group, we would not have caught the date manipulation error, which could have created a big problem and made us look ridiculous.

It is possible to write a script to create the users, groups, and organizational units that make up a typical Active Directory implementation, but it is not a requirement to do so. Every enterprise network creates backups of their domain controllers on a regular basis. It is possible to restore the domain into the test machine. As long as the test machines are isolated from the production environment, there will be no problem with the restoration. Of course, depending on how the backup tapes are made and how the files are restored, you might run into issues with hardware incompatibility; however, these issues can generally be resolved. The advantage of using the restore-from-tape method is that passwords, security identifiers (SIDs), relative identifiers (RIDs)—everything—will be exactly the same as the production environment. The disadvantages are the hardware requirements and the amount of time it takes to perform the backup and restore.

A faster solution is to use built-in tools to export only the portion of the Active Directory in which you are interested in working. Two tools can export portions of the Active Directory: the first is CSVDE, and the second is LDIFDE. (For additional information, refer to the Knowledge Base article at *http://support.microsoft.com/kb/237677*). Of the two, I prefer to use CSVDE because it exports a comma-separated value file that is easy to clean up by using Microsoft Office Excel.

The cleanup process becomes an issue when using either of the two export tools because the data is not exported in the format that will be required for a later import. Therefore, cleanup operations become a necessity, and the tool that makes it the easiest to do the cleanup is the tool that will be the most useful.

Using the CSVDE utility, you can specify the organizational unit that you want to export.

```
PS C:\fso> csvde -f testou.csv -d "ou=testou,dc=nwtraders,dc=com"
Connecting to "(null)"
Logging in as current user using SSPI
Exporting directory to file testou.csv
Searching for entries...
Writing out entries
...
Export Completed. Post-processing in progress...
3 entries exported

The command has completed successfully
```

Once the data is exported, it must be cleaned up prior to being imported into another server because a number of the properties that are exported are read-only properties that are controlled by the system. These are properties such as the *whencreated* and *whenmodified* attributes, as shown in Figure 14-10.

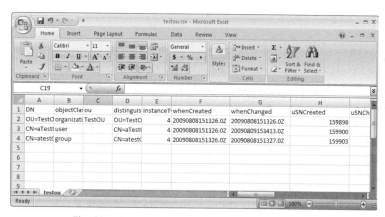

FIGURE 14-10 The CSVDE utility exports a comma-separated value file that is easily edited by using the Office Excel application.

When the CSV file is cleaned up, you can import it into your test environment. To perform the import, you use the *i* parameter (export is the default behavior of CSVDE, and there is no export parameter).

```
PS C:\fso> csvde -f testou.csv -i
Connecting to "(null)"
Logging in as current user using SSPI
Importing directory from file "testou.csv"
Loading entries....
3 entries modified successfully.

The command has completed successfully
```

Handling Passwords Inside a Virtual Machine

Neither CSVDE nor LDIFDE has the ability to export passwords from Active Directory. If your script tests passwords or authentication mechanisms, you need to use the backup and restore technique discussed earlier. If your test scenario involves noting what happens to specific users and groups, then the CSVDE technique will work for that particular application. Because the users are exported with no passwords, you have two choices. The first choice is to import all of the users in a disabled state and then use another script to enable the users and set them with the same password. However, this process seems to be a lot of work for very little value. A better approach is to change the password policy inside the virtual machine to allow empty passwords, which then allows the CSVDE scripts to work fine.

Additional Resources

- The TechNet Script Center at *http://www.microsoft.com/technet/scriptcenter* contains many examples of Windows PowerShell scripts.
- Take a look at *Windows PowerShell™ Scripting Guide* (Microsoft Press, 2008) for additional information on script testing.
- For more information on CSVDE and LDIFDE, see the following Knowledge Base article at *http://support.microsoft.com/kb/237677.*
- On the companion media, you will find all of the scripts referred to in this chapter.

Running Scripts

When it comes to running scripts in Windows PowerShell, all scripts are not equal. You are likely to have many different types of scripts within your environment. Some scripts—written quickly for a one-time use—are little more than a collection of commands that might be typed at the Windows PowerShell console. Other scripts more closely resemble applications and should be treated as such. These are the scripts that are used to perform mission-critical configuration tasks and automated deployment and that are used by the help desk to aid in troubleshooting various support issues.

However, before you can run a Windows PowerShell script, you must choose the appropriate script execution policy. Once you choose the script execution policy, you need to decide how to deploy it to the computers on your network. Because script signing can become an issue with several of the execution policies, in this chapter we will examine the techniques involved with signing scripts. We will then move on to specialized types of scripts and different techniques for maintaining version control.

Selecting the Appropriate Script Execution Policy

Choosing the right level of script support for your environment is an essential first step when it comes to deploying and using Windows PowerShell scripts. The first decision to be made involves whether to allow the use of Windows PowerShell scripts on a particular desktop or server. By default, when Windows PowerShell is installed, scripting is turned off. This action provides an additional level of protection not only from malware, but also from careless users and untrained network administrators who are unfamiliar with Windows PowerShell. To allow for the running of scripts, you must make a decision to enable script support. Once you enable support for Windows PowerShell scripting, you gain several advantages, including:

- The ability to run Windows PowerShell scripts as logon scripts (Windows Server 2008 R2 domain controller required)
- The ability to remotely administer desktops and servers through both fan-out and fan-in scenarios
- The ability to quickly apply consistent configuration changes to desktops and servers
- The ability to save a series of commands for reuse at a later point in time
- The ability to fine-tune a series of commands and optimize the performance of those commands
- The ability to use a Windows PowerShell profile
- The ability to use modules

The Purpose of Script Execution Policies

Windows PowerShell script execution policies are not a security feature—they are a convenience feature. Script execution policies are designed to raise awareness surrounding the process of running Windows PowerShell scripts. Even if you sign all of your scripts, you cannot guarantee that the script will not wreak havoc on your network. All that you can guarantee is that the script has not been tampered with since you signed it. Anyone can obtain a code-signing certificate—even people who write malware. Therefore, a certificate is not a security panacea. You still need to ensure that both the IT staff and the users are trained to pay attention to their computing environment. Even if you have the script execution policy set to restrict the execution of Windows PowerShell scripts, it is still possible to bypass the execution policy by using the *bypass* switch.

Understanding the Different Script Execution Policies

Several levels of scripting support are defined in Windows PowerShell. Each of these levels can potentially alter the ability to run scripts on a local or remote computer. In addition, some of the levels might alter the way in which scripts are written and tested. The five different execution policies and their associated policy settings are shown in Table 15-1.

TABLE 15-1 Script Execution Policy Settings

POLICY SETTING	CHANGES
Restricted	■ Default script execution policy setting ■ Runs commands interactively from the Windows PowerShell console ■ Pipeline commands permitted ■ Creating functions in the Windows PowerShell console permitted ■ Use of script blocks in commands allowed ■ All files with the extension of (.ps1) are blocked from executing, including all six of the various Windows PowerShell profiles ■ Modules are blocked (.psm1file extension) ■ Windows PowerShell configuration files are blocked (.ps1xml)
AllSigned	■ Scripts, profiles, modules, and configuration files run when signed by a trusted publisher ■ Requires all scripts to be signed, including scripts written on local computer ■ Prompts before running scripts signed by publishers that are not trusted ■ Prompts before running scripts from trusted publishers the first time the script is run
RemoteSigned	■ Local scripts, profiles, modules, and configuration files run when not signed ■ Scripts received from the Internet zone must be signed by a trusted publisher prior to running ■ Prompts before running scripts downloaded from the Internet zone from trusted publishers
Unrestricted	■ All unsigned scripts, profiles, modules, and configuration files run when not signed ■ Prompts before running scripts received from the Internet zone
Bypass	■ Nothing is blocked and no warning prompts

Understanding the Internet Zone

Windows PowerShell script execution policies rely on the Internet zone settings from Windows Internet Explorer. Certain applications, such as Microsoft Office Outlook, also use and honor the Internet Explorer Internet zone settings. On a Windows Server 2008 R2 Core Edition server (which does not include Internet Explorer), Windows PowerShell script execution policies do not have any effect because the mechanism to set and to read the Internet zone settings does not exist. The same is true for the European version of the Windows 7 client, which does not include Internet Explorer. The Internet Explorer security zones are shown in Figure 15-1.

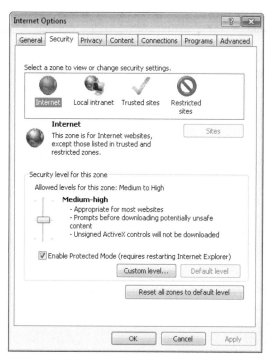

FIGURE 15-1 Windows PowerShell uses the Internet Explorer security zone settings to determine whether a script came from a local or remote location.

Internet Explorer adds a tag to the alternate file stream of the script file. When a script is received via Office Outlook (assuming that the antivirus software does not remove the file), a tag is also added to the alternate data stream of the script file. Any application can choose to honor the Internet Explorer definition of Internet zone settings and either add the tag or read the tag that is placed on the file. To view the alternate data stream of the file, you can use the Streams.exe Windows SysInternals utility, which has the ability to both read and delete the Internet zone tag. To search for files with alternate data streams, you can use the –s switch and specify the path to a folder. All files in the specified folder that contain alternate data streams will be returned.

```
PS C:\data\streams> .\streams.exe -s c:\fso

Streams v1.5 - Enumerate alternate NTFS data streams
Copyright (C) 1999-2003 Mark Russinovich
Sysinternals - www.sysinternals.com

c:\fso\InternetScript.ps1:
    :Zone.Identifier:$DATA        26
```

The Zone.Identifier tag is used to indicate that the file was downloaded from the Internet. Attempts to run the InternetScript.ps1 script will be blocked. However, by using the *-d* switch from the Streams.exe utility, the Internet zone tag is removed. When using the Streams.exe utility to remove the alternate data stream from the file, you must supply the path to the script by name.

```
PS C:\data\streams> .\streams.exe -d C:\fso\InternetScript.ps1

Streams v1.5 - Enumerate alternate NTFS data streams
Copyright (C) 1999-2003 Mark Russinovich
Sysinternals - www.sysinternals.com

C:\fso\InternetScript.ps1:
    :Zone.Identifier:$DATA        26
PS C:\data\streams> .\streams.exe -s c:\fso

Streams v1.5 - Enumerate alternate NTFS data streams
Copyright (C) 1999-2003 Mark Russinovich
Sysinternals - www.sysinternals.com
```

Once the alternate data stream is removed from the file, the file is considered to have originated from the local computer and will no longer be blocked. This technique can be used to remove the Internet location from compiled help files (CHM) files, as well as from scripts and other files that are routinely blocked when they are downloaded from the Internet zone.

If a script is copied from a Web page and saved into a .ps1 file (by using the Windows PowerShell Integrated Scripting Environment [ISE] or Notepad), the file is considered to be in the local Trusted zone because the file was created locally. The only time that a script is tagged as remote is if it is actually downloaded from the Internet—not when the content is cut and pasted from the Internet. This can affect files other than Windows PowerShell files. When Windows PowerShell scripts (that are compressed by certain file compression utilities) are downloaded from the Internet zone as a compressed file, the script is tagged as remote when it is expanded. This is a function of the compression software honoring the Internet Explorer zone settings and therefore does not occur with all compressed files. If the Windows PowerShell script files are packaged by using an executable software installer, the scripts will not pick up the remote location setting because the scripts are considered local once they are installed.

When changing the Windows PowerShell script execution policy to RemoteSigned, scripts that are determined to have come from the Internet zone must be signed prior to executing. Internet Explorer is very aggressive in determining the boundaries for the Internet zone. By default, Universal Naming Convention (UNC) shares are determined to be in the Internet zone, which means that scripts downloaded from an internal share will not execute unless they are signed. Because many companies store their script repositories on an internal file share, a major problem is created. The solution is to add the script share to the Trusted Sites zone in Internet Explorer. To do this, you can directly add the site by using Internet Explorer, adding the location to the registry, or using Group Policy to make the change. In a corporate enterprise, using Group Policy is obviously the best approach.

Deploying the Script Execution Policy

When deploying the script execution policy, you have several choices. While it is possible to edit the registry to modify the script execution policy, this is generally not the best approach due to the potential for making mistakes and corrupting the registry. Additionally, in most cases, it is simply too much unnecessary work. If you want to modify the script execution policy on a local computer, it is a best practice to use the Set-ExecutionPolicy cmdlet to make the change because it is easy to use and you can be assured that it will make the change correctly.

If you have more than a few computers, it is a best practice to use Group Policy to modify the Windows PowerShell script execution policy. Using Group Policy has the advantage of being easily reversible as well as centrally controlled. If you do not use Group Policy, you can use a logon script to make the changes.

Modifying the Registry

It is possible to modify the registry to enable or disable the script execution policy. You might want to take this approach if you are working in an environment that does not have Group Policy deployed. If the Windows PowerShell script execution policy is not modified to enable the use of PowerShell scripts, you might think you are limited to using VBScript or a batch .BAT file to deploy the registry modification. Because Windows PowerShell includes the *bypass* switch, you will be able to run a Windows PowerShell script in bypass mode and make the requisite changes to the registry. The registry key, HKEY_LocalMachine\Software \Microsoft\PowerShell\1\ShellIDs\Microsoft.PowerShell\ExecutionPolicy, is shown in Figure 15-2.

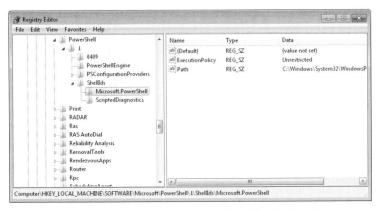

FIGURE 15-2 Windows PowerShell script execution policy in the registry

If you are creating a Microsoft Installer (MSI) package to deploy a standardized profile to your computers, you might also want to modify the registry via the MSI package. Such a scenario is more likely to be the exception rather than the rule, and you should generally avoid directly editing the registry.

Using the Set-ExecutionPolicy cmdlet

The Set-ExecutionPolicy cmdlet can be used to set the Windows PowerShell script execution policy. This cmdlet must be executed from an elevated Windows PowerShell prompt because it modifies the registry. Modifying the registry or using the Set-ExecutionPolicy cmdlet both perform the same task: they change the value of the registry key. When Windows is first installed, the registry keys that control the Windows PowerShell script execution policy do not exist. The default value of the script execution policy is Restricted, but this value is not shown in the registry unless it has been changed. To properly modify the registry entails checking for the existence of the registry key, creating it if it does not exist, or modifying the value if it does exist. The checking and modifying process is a bit tedious and in most cases presents unnecessary work. It is far better to use the Set-ExecutionPolicy cmdlet and avoid the manual registry work.

Using the Set-ExecutionPolicy cmdlet on a Local Computer

To modify the Windows PowerShell script execution policy on a local computer, you must run the PowerShell console as an administrator if your operating system is Windows Vista or a later version (see Figure 15-3).

FIGURE 15-3 To run the Set-ExecutionPolicy cmdlet,
Windows PowerShell must be launched with admin rights.

If the user does not have admin rights, the command will generate an error.

```
PS C:\Users\edwils> Set-ExecutionPolicy -ExecutionPolicy remotesigned


Execution Policy Change
The execution policy helps protect you from scripts that you do not trust. Changing the
execution policy might expose you to the security risks described in the about_
Execution_
Policies help topic. Do you want to change the execution policy?
[Y] Yes  [N] No  [S] Suspend  [?] Help (default is "Y"): y
Set-ExecutionPolicy : Access to the registry key 'HKEY_LOCAL_MACHINE\SOFTWARE\Microsoft
\PowerShell\1\ShellIds\Microsoft.PowerShell'
is denied. At line:1 char:20
+ Set-ExecutionPolicy <<<<  -ExecutionPolicy remotesigned
    + CategoryInfo          : NotSpecified: (:) [Set-ExecutionPolicy],
  UnauthorizedAccessException
    + FullyQualifiedErrorId : System.UnauthorizedAccessException,Microsoft.PowerShell.
Commands.SetExecutionPolicyCommand
```

When the command completes successfully, nothing is displayed.

```
PS C:\> Set-ExecutionPolicy -ExecutionPolicy unrestricted
PS C:\>
```

The changes take effect immediately. You can therefore test the script execution policy by attempting to run a script or by using the `Get-ExecutionPolicy` cmdlet. The Test-Script.ps1 script combines both approaches.

Test-Script.ps1
```
"This test script displays the script execution policy."
Get-ScriptExecutionPolicy
```

Using the Set-ExecutionPolicy cmdlet via a Logon Script

If your network does not use Group Policy and you do not relish the idea of hacking the registry, you can still set the Windows PowerShell script execution policy. The easiest way to do this is to add a command to your logon script. Because the logon script is being run anyway, you already have the necessary infrastructure in place to configure the script execution policy. To set the script execution policy to RemoteSigned from within a logon script, use the following command.

```
powershell -command &{Set-ExecutionPolicy remotesigned}
```

If the logon script is a batch file, the previous command works directly. On the other hand, if the logon script is a VBScript file, you need to do a bit more work. You can use the *run* method from the *WshShell* object to use the Set-ExecutionPolicy cmdlet to set the Windows PowerShell script execution policy on all of the workstations. The SetScriptExecutionPolicy.vbs script sets the script execution policy to RemoteSigned, but it can easily be modified to set any other policy that is required. Keep in mind that this script must run with admin rights because the Set-ExecutionPolicy cmdlet modifies the registry.

SetScriptExecutionPolicy.vbs
```
Set WshShell = CreateObject("WScript.Shell")
WshShell.Run("powershell -Noninteractive -command &{Set-ExecutionPolicy
remotesigned}")
```

NOTES FROM THE FIELD

Working with Windows PowerShell Security

Richard Siddaway, Microsoft PowerShell MVP
UK PowerShell User Group Chairman

"Windows PowerShell doesn't work. I can't run scripts."

I can't remember the number of times I have seen this sentiment on the forums. It's a question that comes up so often that I always cover it when speaking publicly. The answer is "Yes, it does work" and "You need to change the execution policy."

Scripting has had bad press in certain quarters since the "I Love You" virus of 2000. This virus enticed the user to open an attachment, which sent a copy of the virus using VBScript to all members of the user's address list as well as doing other damage. Strictly speaking, this is a social engineering issue rather than a scripting issue, but Windows PowerShell is designed to counter these threats.

When Windows PowerShell is first installed, it can be used interactively, but it won't run scripts because the execution policy is set to the default of Restricted. We can view the execution policy with the Get-ExecutionPolicy cmdlet. Accounts with administrator privileges can modify the policy with the following code.

```
Set-ExecutionPolicy -ExecutionPolicy RemoteSigned
```

This is a good compromise because it allows local scripts to run, but it blocks scripts from the Internet or UNC mapped drives unless they are signed with a code-signing certificate that the system can accept. Other options include AllSigned (all scripts must be signed) and Unrestricted (any script can run, but a warning is generated if scripts are running from the Internet). AllSigned should be used if you have a code-signing infrastructure. Unrestricted is not recommended. Windows PowerShell 2.0 introduces Bypass, which does not block any scripts and does not issue warnings. You can use Bypass when Windows PowerShell is built into an application or when there is another security model in place for the programs.

Another cause for complaint is that Windows PowerShell scripts cannot be run by double-clicking. If this operation is attempted, the scripts are opened in the default editor. Again, this process occurs by design to help prevent rogue scripts from damaging your systems.

The final "speed bump" to running scripts is that the current folder is not on the path. If you type a script name, Windows PowerShell will not search in the current folder. You need to force access to the local folder using the following command.

```
./myscript.ps1
```

So, do these settings make Windows PowerShell totally secure? Of course not. It is always possible for the Windows PowerShell settings to be changed by human intervention. On the forums, numerous people have asked how to make Windows PowerShell run by double-clicking a script. Just because you *can* do it doesn't mean you should! My advice is to set the script execution policy to the setting that best fits your organization—AllSigned ideally, but RemoteSigned is the next best choice. Don't change the other settings.

There are a lot of "people" out there who want to compromise your system. Don't help them. Leave the settings as they are. A great deal of thought went into the Windows PowerShell configuration, and these settings exist for a reason, as we have seen. Enjoy Windows PowerShell, but keep it secure.

Using Group Policy to Deploy the Script Execution Policy

The best way to define the Windows PowerShell script execution policy is to use Group Policy. In Windows Server 2008 R2, a Group Policy object (GPO) for Windows PowerShell contains a setting named Turn On Script Execution. This GPO can be applied to the computer or to the user. As shown in Figure 15-4, there is only one option—the execution policy. Three values can be selected in the Turn On Script Execution GPO, and these three values correspond to the Set-ExecutionPolicy settings of Signed, RemoteSigned, and Unrestricted. You are not allowed to set the Bypass policy from within Group Policy.

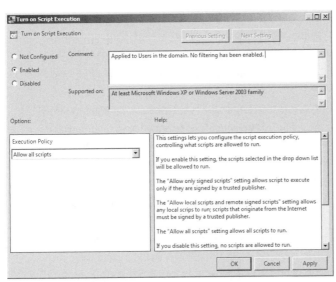

FIGURE 15-4 Group Policy settings to control Windows PowerShell script execution allow you to choose the execution policy.

When a Group Policy setting is in effect, you are not allowed to override the setting. This is true even if you want to configure a stricter policy or if you launch the Windows PowerShell console with admin rights. If you attempt to modify the execution policy and the script execution policy GPO is currently in effect, an error is displayed to the Windows PowerShell console. This error is somewhat misleading because it begins by stating that the command completed successfully (see Figure 15-5).

FIGURE 15-5 Attempts to change the script execution policy when it is managed via a GPO generate an error.

Working with Script Execution

Daniele Muscetta, Premier Field Engineer
Microsoft Corporation, Italy

Scripting is a powerful tool that allows you to do amazing things, such as integrate and automate, in new ways. Yet, with great power comes great responsibilities.

We have seen abuse of scripting power before—VBScript viruses. Someone sends an e-mail message, the user clicks on it, and it is already too late. Microsoft did not want to make the same mistakes. That's why, for example, .ps1 files are not executed by default, unlike .vbs files.

Also by default, Windows PowerShell scripts are not executed even if you intentionally call them from within the shell. This behavior is determined by a feature called the execution policy. The execution policy should not be considered to be a security feature that will prevent all evils. In fact, the administrator or a user can decide to disable it. The script execution policy is more like a convenience, such as the seatbelts in your car—it is better to keep them fastened at all times, but you always have the option to take them off.

The Windows PowerShell installer configures the execution policy to Restricted as a safe default because most users will never run a PowerShell script in their life. Restricted means that absolutely no script is allowed to run. It is therefore a safe default but not a very useful default if you actually want to run scripts on your machines (and you do, or you would not be reading this).

Therefore, you can use the other commonly used options:

- RemoteSigned means that all scripts and configuration files that are downloaded from the Internet must be signed by a trusted publisher.

- Unrestricted means that the shell is allowed to load all configuration files and run all scripts. If you run an unsigned script that was downloaded from the Internet, you are prompted for permission before it runs.

Scripters and system administrators are usually very careful when running scripts that they did not personally write, and they either deeply trust the author or have reviewed the script itself. Therefore, they usually relax the execution policy for their machine to either RemoteSigned or Unrestricted. This action might be okay on their development or testing machines, where the script can be checked to determine that it is not harmful. But what do you do about using scripts in a production environment, that is, on your servers and clients?

If you administered Windows XP, Windows PowerShell might not have been on the system if you did not install it, so the possibilities for management were limited. With Windows Vista and Windows Server 2008, Windows PowerShell 1.0 is available in the operating system. With Windows 7 and Windows Server 2008 R2, you even get Windows PowerShell 2.0 by default. Windows PowerShell allows for a great deal of flexibility in using the shell for your automations and administrative tasks, but it also means that you need to consider a safe way to prevent users from running untrusted scripts.

The AllSigned execution policy is the setting that most people consider to be the safe option. AllSigned requires that all scripts and configuration files are signed by a trusted publisher, including scripts that you write on the local computer. If you are a system administrator, you might want to set the execution policy to AllSigned for your nontechnical users so that they are allowed to run a subset of safe scripts. Non-technical users who are administered by you will then be allowed to execute only the scripts that you have signed for them (just like keeping them buckled in their seatbelt). Yet, you will be able to operate with a more relaxed execution policy while writing and testing your own scripts before actually releasing them to production.

At the end of the day, an administrator can use any of the execution policy options to configure her own computer by using the Set-ExecutionPolicy cmdlet, which ultimately stores the execution policy setting in a registry value under HKEY_LOCAL_MACHINE\SOFTWARE\Microsoft\PowerShell\1\ShellIds \Microsoft.PowerShell\Executionpolicy. Now that the execution policy has a registry setting, the setting can also be applied to client workstations centrally by using some handy Group Policy templates (ADM files) that set the registry value for you en masse. These ADM files have already been written for you by the Windows team and are available on the Microsoft Download Center.

You have even more execution policy options with Windows PowerShell 2.0 compared to the options just described for PowerShell 1.0. First, Windows PowerShell 2.0 introduces the concept of scopes, in which you can set an execution policy that is effective only in a particular scope. The valid scopes are Process, CurrentUser, and LocalMachine.

LocalMachine is the default when setting an execution policy. However, an adminis-trator can change her execution policy just for the purpose of testing a script with-out changing the entire policy on the machine for all users. She can simply change the policy for her scope—for the current Process (the current session in the current Windows PowerShell process). This setting can be volatile and will stop its effect when the session in which the policy is set is finally closed. Alternatively, she can set a policy that only affects her own user profile by using CurrentUser and having the policy setting stored under her HKEY_CURRENT_USER registry hive. You can even execute different policies for different users on the same computer by using scopes.

Second, Windows PowerShell 2.0 has a few brand-new execution policy settings:

- **Undefined** is used when an execution policy is not defined at all in one or more scopes. If that is the case, the execution policy that you apply depends on the policies set in other scopes (e.g., if no execution policy is defined for CurrentUser but a policy is defined for LocalMachine, then the execution policy for LocalMachine takes precedence). Of course, if there are no policies set for any scope, then the execution policy always defaults to Restricted.

- **Bypass** is an even more relaxed policy than Unrestricted in that nothing is blocked, and no warnings or prompts are presented to the user when trying to run a script. This execution policy is designed for configurations in which a Windows PowerShell script is built into a larger application or for configurations in which Windows PowerShell is the foundation for a program that has its own security model.

With all of these available options, an administrator can truly choose what is safest/best for his clients/users while still being allowed the flexibility to test and debug his own scripts with ease.

Understanding Code Signing

Working with signed scripts in Windows PowerShell is relatively easy and pain free because there are two cmdlets that allow you to sign scripts and verify the script signature. The two cmdlets are Get-AuthenticodeSignature and Set-AuthenticodeSignature. To use the Set-AuthenticodeSignature cmdlet, you must have a code-signing certificate. You can use the Certificate Manager utility, shown in Figure 15-6, to ensure that you have the proper code-signing certificate.

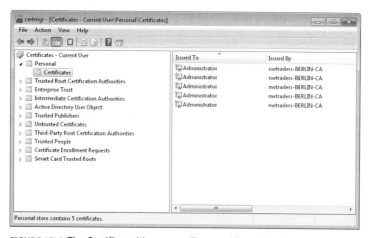

FIGURE 15-6 The Certificate Manager utility provides a view into the user's certificate stores.

To request a code-signing certificate from the enterprise certification authority (CA), you can use the Certificate Manager utility to submit the request. The Certificate Enrollment Wizard from the Certificate Manager utility is shown in Figure 15-7.

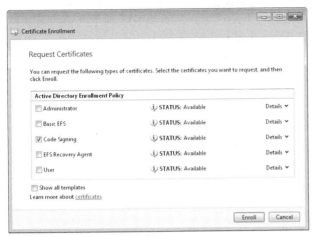

FIGURE 15-7 The Certificate Manager utility can be used to request certificates if automatic enrollment is not enabled for the domain.

Logon Scripts

In Windows PowerShell 1.0, you cannot use a PowerShell script as a logon script because the PowerShell script is not executable. If you double-click the Windows PowerShell script, it opens in Notepad. There is no file association between the .ps1 extension and the PowerShell.exe executable. In Windows Server 2008 R2, you can use a Windows PowerShell script as a logon script, a logoff script, a startup script, or a shutdown script. All of these script options can be configured using Group Policy from within an Active Directory domain as shown in Figure 15-8, but they can also be configured by using the local Group Policy editor.

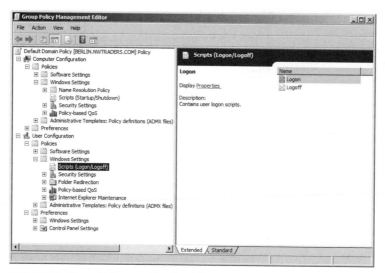

FIGURE 15-8 Group Policy provides the ability to manage startup, shutdown, logon, and logoff scripts.

What to Include in Logon Scripts

Because many of the configuration items that were traditionally performed in logon scripts have migrated to Group Policy preferences, many network administrators run their networks without logon scripts. If you can use Group Policy and avoid the hassle of creating and maintaining logon scripts, you remove one source of potential errors. Most networks are sufficiently complex and have enough legacy applications that they are not able to avoid the use of logon scripts. In the past, it was common to use logon scripts for the following purposes:

- Map user drives
- Set default printers

With the ability to use Windows PowerShell for logon scripts, many new and exciting opportunities present themselves within this area of scripting. Simple auditing can be done as well as logging to facilitate the ability to track potential errors. An example is shown in Logon.ps1 in which a new registry key is created to record the user name and time the user logs on to the computer. The newly created registry key is shown in Figure 15-9.

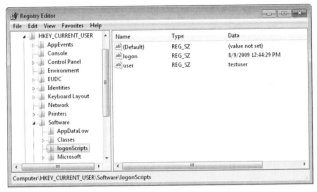

FIGURE 15-9 Windows PowerShell logon scripts can write auditing information to the registry.

Another useful item accomplished by the Logon.ps1 script is creating a new event log named Logonscripts. The script then writes the full path to the logon script and the time it was executed, which is vital information when troubleshooting logon scripts. One of the key problems is trying to identify which logon script is executing. The Logonscripts event log is shown in Figure 15-10. The full UNC logon script path is stored as a hyperlink. By clicking on the hyperlink in the event log details pane, the actual logon script is opened, providing you with the ability to make changes to the logon script if modifications are required. The ability to view the text of the logon script from within the event log makes it easy to troubleshoot logon scripts.

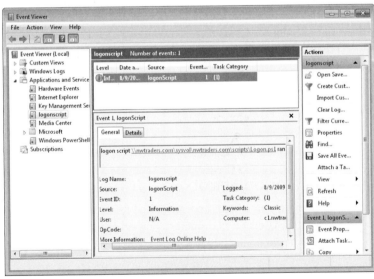

FIGURE 15-10 Windows PowerShell logon scripts can write logging information to a custom event log.

The complete Logon.ps1 logon script is shown here.

Logon.ps1
```
$ErrorActionPreference = "SilentlyContinue"
if(-not(Test-path -path HKCU:\Software\logonScripts))
 {
  new-Item -path HKCU:\Software\logonScripts
  new-Itemproperty -path HKCU:\Software\logonScripts -name logon `
   -Value $(get-date).tostring() -Force
  new-Itemproperty -path HKCU:\Software\logonScripts -name user `
   -Value $env:USERNAME -Force
 }
else
 {
  set-Itemproperty -path HKCU:\Software\logonScripts -name logon `
   -Value $(get-date).tostring() -Force
  set-Itemproperty -path HKCU:\Software\logonScripts -name user `
   -Value $env:USERNAME -Force
 }

try
{
 New-EventLog -source logonscript -logname logonscript
}
Catch{ [System.Exception] }
Finally
{
 Write-EventLog -LogName logonscript -Source logonScript `
  -EntryType information `
  -EventId 1 `
  -Message "logon script $($myinvocation.invocationName) ran at $(get-date)"
}
$ErrorActionPreference = "Continue"
```

Methods of Calling the Logon Scripts

Logon scripts are commonly called during the logon process. In the past, logon scripts were assigned to the user via Active Directory Users And Computers; however, logon scripts assigned via Active Directory Users And Computers do not understand how to run Windows PowerShell scripts.

You should assign scripts from within Group Policy. You can assign logon, logoff, startup, and shutdown scripts. The great thing about using either a logoff or a shutdown script is that it can be used to unmap drives and printers, which can significantly improve the performance of a computer when it starts up and is unable to find the default printer or some remote share.

Script Folder

Windows PowerShell scripts can be stored in any folder. They can be stored locally or on a remote file share. If they are stored on a remote file share, the file share should be added to the Trusted Internet zone to enable you to run the scripts without interruption to the scripting environment. If you do not add your remote file share to the Trusted Internet zone, you will be prompted to do so the first time you open the script. If you choose to trust the script, you will then be permitted to work with the script. You can also choose to set the script execution policy to Bypass, which suppresses Internet zone warning messages.

Deployed Locally

One way to avoid the issue of network trusted zones is to store the scripts in a local folder on local workstations. This is also an important consideration if you want to use logon and logoff scripts that might not be available if the scripts are stored remotely. One additional consideration for storing the scripts locally is to improve performance by avoiding the network copy operation that occurs when you attempt to launch the script across the network. The problem with maintaining a local store of scripts is ensuring that the collection of scripts is kept up to date. You can keep the scripts up to date by maintaining version identification for the script collection. You can store the version of the script collection in the registry and check the collection version during the logon process. If the version has been superseded, new scripts can then be copied to the local workstation.

MSI Package Deployed Locally

If scripts are copied from a network share and the share is not added to the Trusted Internet zone, the scripts will not be able to run unless the Windows PowerShell script execution policy is set to Bypass or Unrestricted. If the scripts are installed on the local computer, the scripts will be placed into the local Internet zone. An easy way to deploy the scripts is to create an MSI package that creates the script folder and copies the scripts to the folder. You can then use Group Policy to deploy the MSI package.

Stand-Alone Scripts

Stand-alone scripts do not have any external dependencies. They will always run because they do not rely on modules that might or might not be loaded or deployed. They do not use include files because the included file might not always be available. Stand-alone scripts tend to be longer than other types of scripts because they must include all functions, constants, variables, and aliases that the script requires to run without errors.

In an enterprise environment where you have total control over the desktop, you have the ability to ensure that requisite modules, constants, variables, and aliases will be present for the script. You can check for the presence of the module and, if it is missing, you have the option of copying it from a network share and installing or writing an error to a log file. Additionally, you can send an e-mail to the help desk and report the missing dependencies.

Diagnostics

Diagnostic scripts are written for the purpose of troubleshooting a particular error condition. Often, diagnostic scripts make use of the Windows Management Instrumentation (WMI) performance counter classes and the appropriate Windows PowerShell cmdlets. These types of scripts are typically run only on demand and can be run either remotely or locally as the situation dictates.

Reporting and Auditing

Reporting scripts gather information from the target computer. These scripts are often launched in a fan-out type of configuration, and they write to a centralized database. These scripts can be called from within logon scripts or from logoff scripts as the need arises, but they can also be launched directly from the Windows PowerShell console and use the fan-out–type technology.

Help Desk Scripts

Help desk scripts are a special class of stand-alone scripts because they often need to be able to perform multiple tasks from a single script. At a minimum, help desk scripts must be able to target different computers when they are run. While many scripts write to databases, text files, comma-separated variable (CSV) files, or Web pages, most help desk scripts display information to the Windows PowerShell console because the information that is generated must be used during the resolution of the help desk call. As such, the data is not persisted to other formats.

Avoid Editing

A well-designed help desk script should expose all essential functionality through command-line parameters. It is a best practice to avoid editing help desk scripts due to the potential for introducing errors or changing the designed functionality of the script. Help desk scripts should be seen as utilities that provide custom diagnostic information and remediation to localized problems. One way to ensure that the scripts remain unaltered is to sign help desk scripts. When a script is signed, any alteration to the script invalidates the signature of the script. The script will need to be re-signed once it is modified.

To provide the functionality to troubleshoot remote computers, help desk scripts should expose a *–computer* parameter as well as other parameters that improve the functionality of the script.

Provide a Good Level of Help Interaction

Because the help desk script might expose multiple command-line parameters, it is imperative that the help desk script provides help that explains each parameter, the allowed range of values, and a sample of the required syntax. The DisplayProcessor.ps1 script uses help tags to display the synopsis, description, examples, and other information about the script and its use. The DisplayProcessor.ps1 script is fully integrated with the Get-Help cmdlet and supports the standard parameters shown here.

```
Get-Help DisplayProcessor.ps1
Get-Help DisplayProcessor.ps1 –full
Get-Help DisplayProcessor.ps1 –detailed
Get-Help DisplayProcessor.ps1 –examples
```

The complete DisplayProcessor.ps1 script is shown here.

DisplayProcessor.ps1

```
<#
    .Synopsis
    Displays Processor information for the computer processor.
    .Description
    This script displays processor information for the local or
    remote computer. This includes Processor utilization, processor
    speed, L2 cache size, number of cores, and architecture.
    .Example
    DisplayProcessor.ps1
    Displays processor information for the local computer.
    .Example
    DisplayProcessor.ps1 -computer berlin
    Displays Processor information for a remote computer named berlin.
    .Inputs
    [string]
    .OutPuts
    [string]
    .Notes
    NAME:  Windows PowerShell Best Practices
    AUTHOR: Ed Wilson
    LASTEDIT: 5/20/2009
    VERSION: 1.0.0
    KEYWORDS:
    .Link
      Http://www.ScriptingGuys.com
#Requires -Version 2.0
#>
param(
  [Parameter(position=0)]
  [string]
```

```
    [alias("CN")]
    $computer=$env:computername
) #end param


# Begin Functions
function New-Underline
{
<#
.Synopsis
 Creates an underline the length of the input string
.Example
 New-Underline -strIN "Hello world"
.Example
 New-Underline -strIn "Morgen welt" -char "-" -sColor "blue" -uColor "yellow"
.Example
 "this is a string" | New-Underline
.Notes
 NAME:
 AUTHOR: Ed Wilson
 LASTEDIT: 5/20/2009
 VERSION: 1.0.0
 KEYWORDS:
.Link
 Http://www.ScriptingGuys.com
#>
[CmdletBinding()]
param(
      [Parameter(Mandatory = $true,Position = 0,valueFromPipeline=$true)]
      [string]
      $strIN,
      [string]
      $char = "=",
      [string]
      $sColor = "Green",
      [string]
      $uColor = "darkGreen",
      [switch]
      $pipe
) #end param
$strLine= $char * $strIn.length
if(-not $pipe)
 {
  Write-Host -ForegroundColor $sColor $strIN
  Write-Host -ForegroundColor $uColor $strLine
 }
```

```
    Else
    {
    $strIn
    $strLine
    }
} #end New-Underline function

Function funQueryProcessor ($computer)
{
 get-wmiobject -class win32_processor -computername $computer |
 foreach-object `
  {
   New-Underline("Processor details for $computer")
   $_.psobject.properties |
   foreach-object `
    {
     If($_.value)
      {
       if ($_.name -match "__"){}
       ELSE
        {
         $Processor +=@{ $($_.name) = $($_.value) }
        } #end else
      } #end if
    } #end foreach property
    $Processor   ; $Processor.clear()
   } #end foreach Processor
  exit
} #end funQueryProcessor
# Entry Point

funQueryProcessor -computer $computer
```

Why Version Control?

Version control involves tracking changes made to production scripts. There are several reasons for maintaining version control of production scripts, including the following:

- Avoids introducing errors into existing production scripts
- Enables accurate troubleshooting of production scripts
- Tracks changes in production scripts
- Maintains a master listing of production scripts
- Maintains compatibility with other scripts

Control Your Source

Don Jones, Microsoft PowerShell MVP
ConcentratedTech.com

Unfortunately, some people don't take their scripts seriously. For me, a script is the result of long work at the command line and becomes something that I want to save forever. I don't want the script ruined because a coworker mangled the code or because I lost the only copy of the script that I had. Software developers discovered a solution years ago and named it *source control*. If you take your scripts seriously, you should avail yourself of source control; if you don't take your scripts seriously enough to protect them in this fashion, then why are you scripting at all?

Source control repositories keep *every* past version of your script so that you can revert to a previous version at any time. Most source control repositories require that you check out scripts if you want to change them, although some simply keep every version you save, thereby eliminating messy "check-in" and "check-out" steps. Ideally, you have already found yourself a quality script editor—and a *quality* script editor includes source control connectivity, which means that it will interact with popular source control systems.

If your company already has a source control repository, that's great. It's probably based on Microsoft Visual SourceSafe, Microsoft Team Server, or CSV/Subversion, which are open-source solutions. Use your company's source control repository—simply set yourself up with a "Windows PowerShell" project and check all of your scripts into it. If your company does not have a source control solution, consider something a little simpler to set up and use than those big-iron, developer-oriented solutions. SAPIEN Technologies offers ChangeVue, for example, and a Web search for "easy source control" will turn up several source control solutions, including some with fun names such as FileHamster, Git, and History Explorer. There are also online source control hosting services, such as BeanstalkApp.com and Unfuddle.com as well as hundreds of others, that require only a Subversion client (and that functionality might be included in higher-end script development environments).

If your data is important enough to save in a .ps1 file, then that .ps1 file is important enough to save in a source control repository. Scripting in Windows PowerShell *without* version control is like driving without a seatbelt. You can do it—and plenty of people don't regret it—but when you *do* regret it, you regret it a *lot*.

Avoid Introducing Errors

It is unlikely that a person can make a change to a script without introducing an error. The process of writing scripts is often reduced to making changes to the code and looking for errors. Whether making minor or major changes to an existing script, the potential for breaking a working production script is great. If the change is substantial and the error is major, it is possible that the script will never work again. By maintaining version control, you work on a copy of the existing script. When the script modifications are completed and tested, the new version of the script becomes the production model of the script. If subsequent use of the script reveals an unexpected problem, you can revert to the previous version of the script. At no time is the production version of the script altered. All changes are tracked, and the changes are made on copies of the script.

Enable Accurate Troubleshooting

If you track your scripts by file name only, it quickly becomes impossible to tell one version of a script from another version. If a problem is discovered with a particular script and there is no version control, you must carefully read and compare one version of the script with another version. You cannot be certain which version is the most recent or which script to actually deploy. By maintaining file versions, you can quickly discern that you want to deploy one particular version of the script instead of another version.

If a user of the script files reports a problem with the script and you are maintaining version control, you only need to ask the user which version of the script is being used to detect whether the user has an out-of-date copy of the script or whether the user discovered a new bug in the production version of the code.

Track Changes

Unfortunately, not all changes that are made to production scripts improve the reliability, performance, security, and ease of use of the script. It is a sad fact of the scripting life that some changes introduce errors, diminish performance, and complicate previously easy to use scripts. If a particular modification to a script is serious, the changes must be backed out and removed from the production code.

If version control is being maintained, the solution to backing out suboptimal script changes is to revert to the most recent working version of the script. If version control is not being maintained, the solution is to edit the production script and attempt to remove all of the changed lines in the script. If the modifications were not properly commented, then your only choice is to try to find a previous version of the script in the backup software or the previous version's utility.

Maintain a Master Listing

If you maintain proper version control of your production scripts, you will be able to produce a report that details which scripts are released to production and which scripts are still in progress. If you find a script that is not on the released-to-production list, you will know that the script is not yet authorized for release.

Maintain Compatibility with Other Scripts

As your script library grows, it is likely that you will begin to develop dependencies on other scripts. This can occur because functions contained in the script are used by other scripts or because the script produces output that is used by another script. In either case, if a script is used either directly or indirectly by other scripts, then changes must be tracked carefully and testing must be thorough to ensure that breaking changes are not introduced into multiple scripts.

Internal Version Number in the Comments

One simple way to maintain version control is to add a version number of the script into the comments. In this way, you can examine the comments of the script to reveal the version of the script. This technique relies on the person who modifies the internal version number of the script when changes are made.

Two challenges are present with this approach to version control. Maintaining an internal version number is a manual approach to versioning and relies on the editor of the script to make a version number change for each modification to the script. There is a real temptation to not tamper with modifying the version number when making minor changes to the script, such as updating comments.

The second challenge with manual version control is that the previous version of the script needs to be renamed so that the current version of the script can be stored. This challenge can be overcome by keeping each version of the script in its own folder. The most recent version of the script is the one in the most recent folder. The Get-ScriptVersion.ps1 script retrieves the version of the script and the last date that the script was edited. It relies on both the version and the last-edit information being stored in the header of the script as shown here.

```
.Notes
NAME:  Windows PowerShell Best Practices
AUTHOR: Ed Wilson
LASTEDIT: 5/20/2009
VERSION: 1.0.0
KEYWORDS:
.Link
Http://www.ScriptingGuys.com
```

The complete Get-ScriptVersion.ps1 script is shown here.

Get-ScriptVersion.ps1

```
function get-ScriptVersion ([string]$path)
{
 $scripts = Get-ChildItem -Path $path -recurse
 ForEach($script in $scripts)
 {
  $info = New-Object psobject
  $scriptText = Get-Content $script.fullname
  $info |
  Add-Member -Name "name" -Value $script.name -MemberType noteproperty
  $lastedit = $scriptText |
  Select-String -Pattern "\s\d{1,1}/\d{1,2}/\d{1,4}"

  if($lastedit.count -gt 1)
   {
     $info |
     Add-Member -Name "LastEdit" -Value $lastedit[0].matches[0].value `
     -membertype noteproperty
   }
  if($lastedit.matches.count -gt 0)
   {
    $info |
    Add-Member -Name "LastEdit" -Value $lastedit.matches[0].value `
    -membertype noteproperty
   }
  $version = $scriptText |
  Select-String -Pattern "\s\d\.\d\.\d"

  if($version.count -gt 1)
   {
    $info |
    Add-Member -Name version -Value $version[0].matches[0].value `
    -membertype noteproperty
   }
  if($version.matches.count -gt 0)
   {
    $info |
    Add-Member -Name version -Value $version.matches[0].value `
    -membertype noteproperty
   }
  $info
  $version = $lastedit = $scriptText = $null
 } #end foreach
```

```
} #end function get-ScriptVersion

# *** Entry Point ***

Get-ScriptVersion -path C:\W7_ResKitScripts\Chapter1|
Format-Table -Property * -AutoSize
```

When the Get-ScriptVersion.ps1 script runs, it produces a listing similar to the one shown in Figure 15-11.

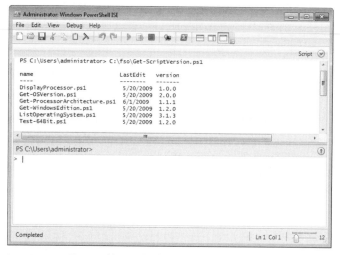

FIGURE 15-11 By searching script files for the last-edit date and the version, a master list of scripts can be produced.

Incrementing Version Numbers

When adding version identification numbers to scripts, it is not typically necessary to go beyond three decimal places. The first number usually represents the major version of the script. A 1.0.0 version number denotes the first release of the script, with no minor versions and no revisions. A major version change is one that involves a number of substantial changes to the script. Typically, these changes create new functionality that requires a major re-write of the script. A minor version change, such as version 1.1.0, involves less drastic changes and improvements to the script, such as a change that involves performance tuning of the script or that improves the flow of the script. If you are correcting misspelled words, fixing bugs, or improving error handling to the script, you might change the version to 1.1.1.

Deleting the Wrong Version of the Script

Keep in mind that every change you make to the script should involve a version change. I constantly come across multiple versions of the same script with no easy way to differentiate between the two copies. You should keep the working copy of the script, and rename the previous versions of the script in a manner that is readily identifiable. Inside the script, you should maintain a version table and list what has changed between version numbers. In this manner, you can avoid accidentally deleting the wrong edition of the script.

Tracking Changes

When making version changes to your script, you should include a comment indicating the changes that were made to the script. This comment can be included in the Notes section of the header portion of the script. As shown in the Get-WindowsVersion.ps1 script, each version of the script is listed, the date that it was current, and the change that was made that caused the version to be modified. The version table of the script is shown here.

```
.Notes
    NAME: Get-WindowsEdition.ps1
    AUTHOR: Ed Wilson
    LASTEDIT: 5/20/2009
    VERSION: 1.2.0 Added Help tags
             1.1.1 4/2/1009 Added link to http://www.ScriptingGuys.com
             1.1.0 4/1/2009 Modified to use regex pattern
    KEYWORDS: Windows PowerShell Best Practices
```

The complete Get-WindowsEdition.ps1 script is shown here.

Get-WindowsEdition.ps

```
<#
    .Synopsis
    Gets the version of Windows that is installed on the local computer
    .Description
    Gets the version of Windows that is installed on the local computer. This
    is information such as Windows 7 Enterprise.
    .Example
    Get-WindowsEdition.ps1
    Displays version of windows on local computer.
    .Inputs
    none
    .OutPuts
    [string]
```

```
   .Notes
    NAME:  Get-WindowsEdition.ps1
    AUTHOR: Ed Wilson
    LASTEDIT: 5/20/2009
    VERSION: 1.2.0 Added Help tags
            1.1.1 4/2/1009 Added link to http://www.ScriptingGuys.com
            1.1.0 4/1/2009 Modified to use regex pattern
    KEYWORDS: Windows PowerShell Best Practices
   .Link
     Http://www.ScriptingGuys.com
#Requires -Version 2.0
#>


$strPattern = "version"
$text = net config workstation

switch -regex ($text)
{
  $strPattern { Write-Host $switch.current }
}
```

Version Control Software

The easiest way to perform Windows PowerShell version control is to use a version control software package. Previous versions of Microsoft Visual Studio contained a source control software package named Visual SourceSafe (VSS). However, for many scripters, VSS was too complicated for a scripting environment. At any rate, VSS is no longer supplied with Visual Studio and is no longer an option.

Third-party version control software packages are available, but most target commercial software developers and are not a good fit for enterprise scripters. The Microsoft SharePoint Server can be used to maintain a master repository for scripts, and it does have checkout and versioning features that will work; however, it needs to be modified to allow Windows PowerShell and VBScripts to be natively stored on the SharePoint site. A better solution is one that integrates directly with the script editor and provides automatic versioning.

Using Version Control Software

Alexander Riedel, Vice President
SAPIEN Technologies

Ever since Microsoft introduced the Script Encoder for the Windows Script Host and SAPIEN Technologies added the ability to package scripts into executable files within PrimalScript, one question has become quite commonplace on our support forums: *"Can you please help me retrieve my script?"*

While some of the causes for this usually panic-stricken request are the lack of backup combined with a failed hard drive, an exploding laptop battery, or a teenager who causes a virus infection on his dad's work computer, much more common are the following comments:

"A previous employee at my company wrote the script, and I don't know where the original is located."

"The script used to work, but now it doesn't. The only thing that still works is the script in the .exe file."

"Somebody changed it, I and don't know what they did to it."

Quite obviously, a simple backup won't help with these types of problems. You need to find out what actually changed. For a software developer, none of these scenarios are usually troublesome. Over the past several decades, the software development industry has created tools and adopted best practices that prevent these types of problems from becoming disasters. However, because script developers often don't view themselves as "developers," they sometimes do not observe code development best practices.

From experience, we also know that even the best intentions toward backing up scripts don't always help to protect scripts from accidental modification or deletion. Consider the following, for example: when did **your** last script backup occur? That is why SAPIEN added a file history function to PrimalScript and created a simple, yet powerful version control system named ChangeVue. The file history feature creates versions of your file automatically and stores them in a .zip file that resides in the folder where the original file is located. This feature saves a daily version and stores up to five versions. Therefore, if you find yourself in a predicament, you can go back a few days to a previous version and see what you actually did.

ChangeVue 2009 is a full-featured version control system that plugs right into PrimalScript, Visual Studio, and other major integrated development environments (IDEs) and editors. An easy-to-use and streamlined repository explorer, along with command-line tools and Windows PowerShell cmdlets, allow you to create a safe haven not only for your scripts, source code, and configuration files but also for any binary file that you need to preserve.

ChangeVue is self-contained and does not require any additional database software or a dedicated administrative staff. Even for a single developer, scripting or otherwise, ChangeVue is simple to set up and use. If you use PrimalScript in combination with ChangeVue, you can set the check-out and check-in parameters automatically and then forget about the version control system until you need it. If you keep your repository on a network or external drive, you can accomplish the tasks of receiving backup and version control together.

Notice that the operative word here is "automatically." Set up your environment to automatically back up and track changes to your vital files, and you won't need to call anyone again with panic in your voice.

Additional Resources

- The Technet Script Center at *http://www.microsoft.com/technet/scriptcenter* contains numerous examples of logon scripts and help desk scripts.

- Take a look at *Windows PowerShell™ Scripting Guide* (Microsoft Press, 2008) for additional examples of logon scripts and working with code signing.

- On the companion media, you will find all of the scripts referred to in this chapter.

- PrimalScript and ChangeVue can be found at *http://www.primaltools.com*.

- Administrative templates for Windows PowerShell can be found at *http://www.microsoft.com/downloads*.

- Additional information on code signing can be found on MSDN at *http://msdn.microsoft.com/en-us/library/ms537361.aspx*.

Optimizing

Logging Results

Once your scripts are written, deployed, and executed on a system, you need to know whether the scripts ran successfully. The best way to make this determination is to log the results of the scripts. There are many options for logging script results, and we'll look at them in this chapter.

Logging results from scripts is a basic technique. Quite often, you will want to store the results of a script. While there are many options for data storage that range in complexity from writing to a database to creating Web pages, three techniques are used so often that they should be part and parcel of the IT professional's scripting toolkit. These techniques are so critical that Windows PowerShell 2.0 has designed cmdlets to simplify the task of logging from the script. The three main logging tools at your disposal are the text file, the event log, and the registry. In this chapter, we will cover best practices that govern choosing one technique over another.

Logging to a Text File

Despite the advances in XML documents, HTML documents, Microsoft Office documents, and other storage mechanisms, the plain text file remains an often-used format for logging purposes. The text file is simple to use, compact, portable, and causes no compatibility issues. The easiest way to write logging information to a text file is to use the redirection operators, of which there are two—the single and the double. The single redirection operator writes to a text file. If the file does not exist, it will be created and the data written to it. If the file already exists, the file will be overwritten.

```
PS C:\> Get-Process > C:\data\FSO\process.txt
```

The double redirection operator will create a file if it does not exist. If the file does exist, it will append to the file.

```
PS C:\> Get-Process >> C:\data\FSO\process.txt
```

Designing a Logging Approach

One of the design decisions that you will make when implementing logging to a text file is whether you will append to the log file or whether you will overwrite the file. There are several decision points that govern the use of overwriting or appending to the log file, as covered in Table 16-1.

TABLE 16-1 Logging to Text File Decision Guide

MODE	NEED	EXAMPLE
Append	Maintain history	Log multiple changes made by script
Append	Maintain audit	A logon script that documents when a user logged on
Append	Maintain tracing	A script that writes error information to a file for each operation it performs
Overwrite	Capture return code	A script that writes the success or error returns code from the script to a file
Overwrite	Display information that is too wide to fit in the Windows PowerShell console	A script that displays the members of an object
Overwrite	Display information that the user might need to scroll or search	A script that displays a detailed log file in which a user might want to use Notepad or some other tool to search for keywords or to scroll through the file contents

Overwriting the Log

You might decide to overwrite the log file on each occasion if your logging goal is to know whether a particular operation succeeded or failed. This one-time logging approach is useful from a troubleshooting perspective in which historical data is not important and the maintenance of a change log is not desired.

A typical use for a one-time log is the logon script. Once the user successfully logs on to the system, there is little need for the log file. However, if the user has problems with his system and is unable to print to his network printer or to access files from his network share, the log becomes an important troubleshooting device.

An example of a logon script with built-in logging is the LogonScriptWithLogging.ps1 script. First, the LogonScriptWIthLogging.ps1 script uses the $errorActionPreference variable to configure Windows PowerShell to not display any errors to the console while the script is running. Hiding errors from the user during the logon process is generally a best practice because it avoids confusing the user and reduces help desk calls. Next, the script clears the error object; as a result, the only errors that will be present on the error object are errors generated from the logon script. Several variables are initialized to null to avoid possible pollution from the scripting environment.

```
$errorActionPreference = "SilentlyContinue"
$error.Clear()
$startTime = $endTime = $Message = $logResults = $null
```

The Test-Path cmdlet is used to ensure that the logging directory is present on the computer. If the logging directory is not present, it is created by using the New-Item cmdlet. The Join-Path cmdlet is used to build the complete path to the log file.

```
$logDir = "c:\fso"
if(-not(Test-Path -path $logdir))
  { New-Item -Path $logdir -ItemType directory | Out-Null }
$logonLog = Join-Path -Path $logDir -ChildPath "logonlog.txt"
```

An important item in any log file is a time stamp that informs you of the time that the operation ran. In general, it is a best practice to log the start time of the script as well as the end time to give you an indication as to how long it takes the script to run. If a script that normally completes in 3 seconds suddenly takes 35 seconds, it can indicate a problem. The LogonScriptWithLogging.ps1 script uses the *WshNetwork* object to map network drives and set the default printer. After each operation in the script completes, the operation and any resulting errors are written to the *$message* variable.

```
$startTime = (Get-Date).tostring()
$WshNetwork = New-Object -ComObject wscript.network
$WshNetwork.MapNetworkDrive("f:","\\berlin\studentShare")
$message += "`r`nMapping drive f to \\berlin\student share `r`n$($error[0])"
$WshNetwork.SetDefaultPrinter("berlinPrinter")
$message += "`r`nSetting default printer to berlinPrinter `r`n$($error[0])"
```

Once all actions defined in the script are performed, the script end time is obtained from the Get-Date cmdlet and the output message is formatted. Because all of the errors, operations, and time stamps are collected into variables, a single output message can easily be created. The collecting of messages during script operation is a best practice because a single I/O (input/output) operation can be undertaken to create the log file, which is much more efficient than writing to the log file multiple times during the script's progress. A here-string is used to create the log results message, and the single redirection operator writes to the log file.

```
$endTime = (Get-Date).tostring()
$logResults = @"
**Starting script: $($MyInvocation.InvocationName) $startTime.
  $message
**Ending logon script $endTime.
**Total script time was $((New-TimeSpan -Start $startTime `
  -End $endTime).totalSeconds) seconds.
"@
$logResults > $logonLog
```

The complete LogonScriptWithLogging.ps1 script is shown here.

LogonScriptWithLogging.ps1

```
$errorActionPreference = "SilentlyContinue"
$error.Clear()
$startTime = $endTime = $Message = $logResults = $null

$logDir = "c:\fso"
if(-not(Test-Path -path $logdir))
  { New-Item -Path $logdir -ItemType directory | Out-Null }
$logonLog = Join-Path -Path $logDir -ChildPath "logonlog.txt"

$startTime = (Get-Date).tostring()
$WshNetwork = New-Object -ComObject wscript.network
$WshNetwork.MapNetworkDrive("f:","\\berlin\studentShare")
$message += "`r`nMapping drive f to \\berlin\student share `r`n$($error[0])"
$WshNetwork.SetDefaultPrinter("berlinPrinter")
$message += "`r`nSetting default printer to berlinPrinter `r`n$($error[0])"

$endTime = (Get-Date).tostring()
$logResults = @"
**Starting script: $($MyInvocation.InvocationName) $startTime.
 $message
**Ending logon script $endTime.
**Total script time was $((New-TimeSpan -Start $startTime `
  -End $endTime).totalSeconds) seconds.
"@
$logResults > $logonLog
```

When the LogonScriptWithLogging.ps1 script is run, the log shown in Figure 16-1 is created in the C:\fso directory.

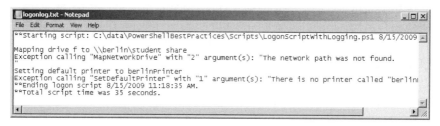

FIGURE 16-1 Script log showing logon time and status of operation

Appending to the Log

If your logging scenario needs to maintain historical data from either a security perspective or from a long-term troubleshooting stance, you will append to your log. You might also decide to append to the log if the script completes a number of discrete operations and you want to maintain a log of each operation's results. Appending might be an important technique if it is possible for the operation to fail midway through the script.

Using Logging for Troubleshooting

When I was writing the 200 scripts for the *Windows 7 Resource Kit*, I needed to produce documentation that described each script and its parameters and that illustrated samples of command syntax. Because I had written help for each script, I wrote a documentation script that gathered a list of all of the *Windows 7 Resource Kit* scripts from their folders and called the Get-Help cmdlet on each of the scripts. I then used the double redirection arrows to append to the Windows7_Script_Documentation.txt file. As I looked over the documentation file, I noticed that the last documented script was not from the last chapter in the book. I became curious as to why the scripts were being documented out of order. I also noticed that the documentation for several scripts was missing. I looked at the last script on the list and found no problems with that script. When I examined the next script in the folder, however, I noticed that it was not in the documentation text file. When I used the Get-Help cmdlet on the script, an error was produced. Once I solved the error and re-ran the create documentation script, the problem was solved. By appending the results of multiple operations to a single text file, I created not only documentation but also a good troubleshooting tool.

When working with a more complex script, you might want to instrument the script to provide detailed logging information. The LogChartProcessWorkingSet.ps1 script is an example of instrumenting a script. The script uses the *Param* keyword to create a switched command-line parameter named *trace*. When the script is run with the *trace* switch, statements are written to a Tracelog.txt file in the C:\fso directory. The *$errorActionPreference* variable is set to *SilentlyContinue*, and any errors are cleared from the error object. The *$startTime* and *$endTime* variables are set to null. The initialization section of the script is shown here.

```
Param([switch]$trace)
$trace=$true
$errorActionPreference = "SilentlyContinue"
$error.Clear()
$startTime = $endTime = $null
```

The presence of the log directory is checked; if it is not present, it is created. The path to the Tracelog.txt file is created, and the start time of the script is recorded as a string in the *$startTime* variable.

```
$logDir = "c:\fso"
if(-not(Test-Path -path $logdir))
  { New-Item -Path $logdir -ItemType directory | Out-Null }
$traceLog = Join-Path -Path $logDir -ChildPath "Tracelog.txt"
$startTime = (Get-Date).tostring()
```

The script looks for the presence of the *$trace* variable. If the *$trace* variable is found, logging information is written to the Tracelog.txt file. If the *$trace* variable is not found, no logging is done.

```
If($trace)
  {"**Starting script: $($MyInvocation.InvocationName) $startTime" >> $traceLog}
```

Once the script completes the creation of the chart, the number of errors that are generated is written to the log file. The *Foreach* statement is used to walk through the collection of errors, and each error is written to the log file.

```
"*** LISTING $($error.count) Errors ***" >> $traceLog
 Foreach ($e in $error) { $e >> $tracelog }
```

The completed LogChartProcessWorkingSet.ps1 script is shown here.

```
LogChartProcessWorkingSet.ps1
Param([switch]$trace)
$errorActionPreference = "SilentlyContinue"
$error.Clear()
$startTime = $endTime = $null

$logDir = "c:\fso"
if(-not(Test-Path -path $logdir))
  { New-Item -Path $logdir -ItemType directory | Out-Null }
$traceLog = Join-Path -Path $logDir -ChildPath "Tracelog.txt"
$startTime = (Get-Date).tostring()

If($trace)
  {"**Starting script: $($MyInvocation.InvocationName) $startTime" >> $traceLog}
If($trace)
  {"Creating msgraph.application object" >> $traceLog}
$chart = New-Object -ComObject msgraph.application
$chart.visible = $true
If($trace)
  {"Adding chart column labels" >> $traceLog}
$chart.datasheet.cells.item(1,1) = "Process Name"
$chart.datasheet.cells.item(1,2) = "Working Set"
If($trace)
  {"Adding Data to chart" >> $traceLog}
$r = 2
If($trace)
```

```
{"Obtaining process information" >> $traceLog}


Get-Process |
ForEach-Object {
  $chart.datasheet.cells.item($r,1) = $_.name
  $chart.datasheet.cells.item($r,2) = $_.workingSet
  $r++
} # end foreach process


$endTime = (Get-Date).tostring()
If($trace)
  {"**ending script $endTime. " >> $traceLog}
If($trace)
  {"**Total script time was $((New-TimeSpan -Start $startTime `
  -End $endTime).totalSeconds) seconds`r`n" >> $traceLog}
"*** LISTING $($error.count) Errors ***" >> $traceLog
  Foreach ($e in $error) { $e >> $tracelog }
```

When the script is run, the log shown in Figure 16-2 is produced.

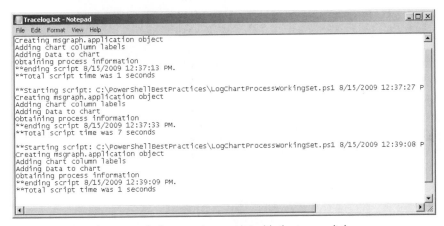

FIGURE 16-2 Trace log created when running a script with the *trace* switch

Using the Out-File cmdlet

In addition to using the redirection operators, you can also use the Out-File cmdlet to
create a text file. Both methods create text files, and both methods work in a similar fashion
because, inside Windows PowerShell, the redirection operators actually map to Out-File. The
difference between the two is that the Out-File cmdlet is configurable and the redirection
operators are not. The default values for the redirection operators are listed here.

- The redirection operators use Unicode.

- The redirection operators use the Windows PowerShell console dimensions when writing to files.

Both the redirection operators and the Out-File cmdlet send output through the Windows PowerShell formatter prior to writing to a file. In some cases, the Windows PowerShell formatter can add or change the output in such a way as to cause corruption in certain binary data types.

To change the output encoding of a file, you can use the *Encoding* parameter when creating the file.

```
PS C:\> (Get-Acl -Path C:\fso\access.txt).AccessToString |
Out-File -FilePath C:\fso\outFile.Txt -Encoding ASCII
```

If your output is truncated in the Windows PowerShell console, such as the output shown in Figure 16-3, you can save the output in a text file and use the *Width* parameter to capture all of the information.

FIGURE 16-3 Truncated output in the Windows PowerShell console is indicated by three dots.

If you use a semicolon to separate commands when working at the Windows PowerShell console or in a Windows PowerShell script, you can call Notepad at the same time that you create the file. You can then use the Notepad utility to display all of the information and scroll as required to see the information that is truncated.

By pipelining the results of the process information to the Get-Member cmdlet, the members of the objects are displayed. The content is too wide for the Windows PowerShell console and is truncated. By specifying a width of 200 for the Out-File cmdlet, the member definition will fit on the lines of the file.

```
PS C:\> Get-Process |
Get-Member |
Out-File -FilePath C:\fso\processMembers.txt -Width 200 ;
notepad C:\fso\processMembers.txt
```

The resulting text file is shown in Figure 16-4.

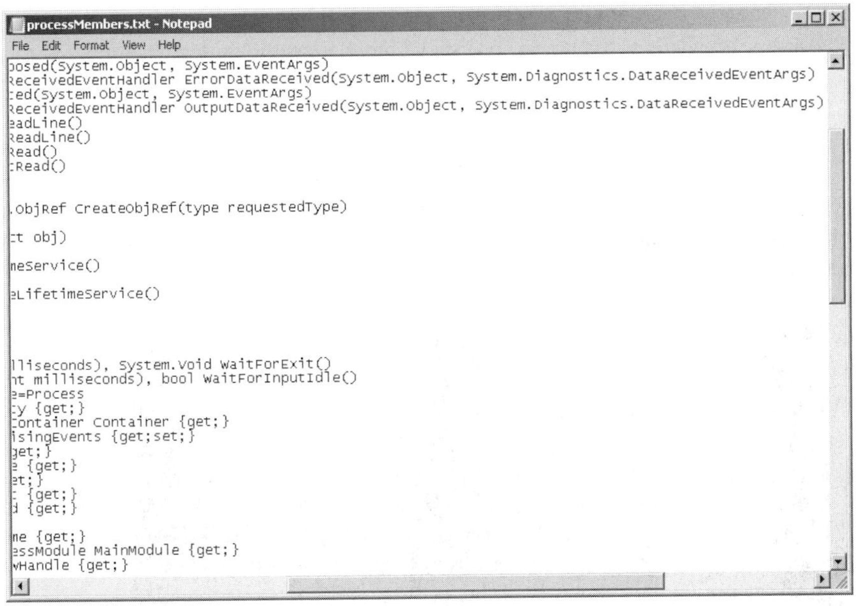

FIGURE 16-4 Notepad allows viewing of wide text files.

INSIDE TRACK

Building Maintainable Scripts

Ben Pearce, Premier Field Engineer
Microsoft Corporation, United Kingdom

When I'm writing scripts, there are typically two types that I create. The first type is scripts that are quick, dirty, and automate a task that will probably only be run a few times. The second type is scripts that will be deployed in a production environment, will be run by many people, and might have a very long life. When developing these "production-ready" scripts, much more thought should be given to script performance, script maintainability, and how to troubleshoot the script in the future. It is essential that code is well commented and that you have put a provision in place for script logging. In subsequent years when you troubleshoot a problem with a script, life is a lot easier if you can simply put the script in "logging" mode and receive detailed logs of what actions the script is taking.

So what should you log? Depending on what the script does, there can be many things to log. However, the key information should be user name, script start time, script finish time, key tasks completed, and errors that occurred. So where should you write your log and in what format? Well, that's the great thing about Windows PowerShell—it is really easy to write to a text file, comma-separated variable (CSV) file, HTML file, or even a database, depending on your need. A simple text file will often suffice, a CSV file is better, and a centralized database is the perfect solution, allowing administrators to analyze the logs in bulk.

Let me give you an example: A large enterprise customer with whom I worked had very slow logon times. After some logon analysis, it turned out they had more than twenty VBScript login scripts running at startup from many sources: User GPO, Computer GPO, AD User Account, and the Run key in the registry. We had no idea which scripts were running and when, and what's more, the script comments were written in a different language. Wouldn't it have been great if all of those scripts had been put in debug mode to write their key information to logs? It would have saved us hours of poring through old scripts. After some careful planning, we modified the logon scripts to include logging that wrote various pieces of information to a centralized SQL database, which helped us to identify key problems with the scripts and actually baseline the entire login process.

Windows PowerShell makes logging even easier than it was before! Useful cmdlets for generating logs include Add-Content, Out-File, Export-CSV, and ConvertTo-HTML, and useful variables for checking the success of operations are *$error* and *$?*.

Text Location

One of the decisions that must be made when working with text files is the location to store the output. This decision is easy if you have a directory in which to store the output, and this is the approach taken in the LogChartProcessWorkingSet.ps1 script. The C:\fso folder is created and used to hold log files. If the user does not have rights to create a folder or to write to the log folder, the logging operation will fail. Another issue encountered when creating a designated log file folder is that the user might not always be available. Because the target folder might not always be available, you must always check for the existence of the folder and create it if it does not exist. An additional problem with using a specific folder is that, in some instances, the system drive is not always C:\. To be safe, you should always check for the system drive and use that location in the script.

All of the potential problems of creating a special log folder can be avoided if you use a folder that always exists on the user's computer. If you use a folder to which the user always has rights to write to, it is even better. Many folders are automatically created on a user's system that can be used to store log files that are created from within a script. The path to special folders is automatically resolved by the system and therefore will always be accurate regardless of the current user name or the drive letter of the system drive. The path to special folders is cumbersome to manually derive; therefore, it is a best practice to use the Microsoft .NET Framework environment class to resolve the path.

In the Get-CountryByIP.ps1 script, the `Tee-Object` cmdlet is used to display output to the Windows PowerShell console and to also write information to a text file. The Get-CountryByIP.ps1 script uses a Web service and the `Get-WebServiceProxy` cmdlet to resolve an IP address to the country of origin. Besides being fun to play with, the script can be used to automatically detect and configure localization settings.

The Get-CountryByIP.ps1 script begins by using help tags to provide command-line help. In the help section, the synopsis, Description, Example, inputs, outputs, and notes tags are used to provide detailed help for the script. The help section of the script is shown here.

```
<#
    .Synopsis
    Gets country location by IP address
    .Description
    This script gets country location based upon an IP address. It uses
    a Web service, and therefore must be connected to Internet.
    .Example
    Get-CountryByIP.ps1 -ip 10.1.1.1, 192.168.1.1 -log iplog.txt
    Writes country information to %mydocuments%\iplog.txt and to screen
    .Inputs
    [string]
    .OutPuts
    [PSObject]
    .Notes
    NAME: Get-CountryByIP.ps1
    AUTHOR: Ed Wilson
    VERSION: 1.0.0
    LASTEDIT: 8/20/2009
    KEYWORDS: New-WebServiceProxy, IP, New-Object, PSObject
    .Link
      Http://www.ScriptingGuys.com
#requires -version 2.0
#>
```

The script uses cmdlet binding and creates some command-line parameters. The *ip* parameter is configured as an array of strings and is used to specify the IP address that will be resolved to a country. The *–log* parameter supplies the name of the script. The *folder* parameter designates the special folder to use. The parameter section of the script is shown here.

```
[CmdletBinding()]
Param(
    [Parameter(Mandatory = $true,Position = 0,ValueFromPipeline = $true)]
    [string[]]$ip,
    [string]$log = "ipLogFile.txt",
    [string]$folder = "Personal"
)#end param
```

The main portion of the code is contained in the *Get-CountryByIP* function. The function begins by specifying the Uniform Resource Identifier (URI) that is used to point to the Web Service Definition Language (WSDL) for the Web service. The New-WebServiceProxy cmdlet is used to create the proxy to the Web service. Once the Web service proxy is created, the object is stored in the variable *$proxy*. The *GetGeoIP* method is called from the object, and the returned data is stored in the *$rtn* variable.

```
Function Get-CountryByIP($IP)
{
 $URI = "http://www.webservicex.net/geoipservice.asmx?wsdl"
 $proxy = New-WebServiceProxy -uri $URI -namespace WebServiceProxy -class IP
 $RTN = $proxy.GetGeoIP($IP)
```

To make it easier to work with the returned data, a new *PSObject* is created by using the New-Object cmdlet. The newly returned object is stored in the *$ipReturn* variable. Once the *PSObject* is created, the Add-Member cmdlet is used to add the IP address, country name, and country code to the *PSObject* that is stored in the *$ipReturn* variable. When the object is created, it is returned to the calling code.

```
 $ipReturn = New-Object PSObject
 $ipReturn | Add-Member -MemberType noteproperty -Name ip -Value $rtn.ip
 $ipReturn | Add-Member -MemberType noteproperty -Name countryName -Value $rtn.
CountryName
 $ipReturn | Add-Member -MemberType noteproperty -Name countryCode -Value $rtn.
CountryCode
 $ipReturn
} #end Get-CountryByIP
```

The output folder that will be used to store the newly created text file is determined by using the *GetFolderPath* static method from the *Environment* .NET Framework class. The *GetFolderPath* static method must receive an *Environment.SpecialFolder* enumeration value. The *Get-Folder* function is used to return the path to the specified special folder.

```
Function Get-Folder($folderName)
{
 [Environment]::GetFolderPath([environment+SpecialFolder]::$folderName)
} #end function Get-Folder
```

The entry point to the script passes the IP address that is stored in the *$IP* variable and pipelines it to the Foreach-Object cmdlet, where the *Get-CountryByIP* function passes the current item on the pipeline to the function via the *ip* parameter. The returned custom *PSObject* is then pipelined to the Tee-Object cmdlet, and the resulting object is displayed to the Windows PowerShell console and stored in the *$results* variable. The *$results* variable is then pipelined to the Out-File cmdlet, and the file path is created by using the Join-Path cmdlet that receives the string returned from the *Get-Folder* function. The path to the special folder and the file name are put together to create the path for the output file.

```
$ip |
Foreach-Object { Get-CountryByIP -ip $_ } |
Tee-Object -Variable results

$results |
Out-File -FilePath `
  (Join-Path -Path (Get-Folder -folderName $folder) -childPath $log)
```

The complete Get-CountryByIP.ps1 script is shown here.

Get-CountryByIP.ps1
```
<#
    .Synopsis
    Gets country location by IP address
    .Description
    This script gets country location based up an IP address. It uses
    a Web service, and therefore must be connected to Internet.
    .Example
    Get-CountryByIP.ps1 -ip 10.1.1.1, 192.168.1.1 -log iplog.txt
    Writes country information to %mydocuments%\iplog.txt and to screen
    .Inputs
    [string]
    .OutPuts
    [PSObject]
    .Notes
    NAME: Get-CountryByIP.ps1
    AUTHOR: Ed Wilson
    VERSION: 1.0.0
    LASTEDIT: 8/20/2009
    KEYWORDS: New-WebServiceProxy, IP, New-Object, PSObject
    .Link
      Http://www.ScriptingGuys.com
#requires -version 2.0
#>
[CmdletBinding()]
Param(
    [Parameter(Mandatory = $true,Position = 0,ValueFromPipeline = $true)]
    [string[]]$ip,
    [string]$log = "ipLogFile.txt",
    [string]$folder = "Personal"
)#end param

# *** Function below ***
Function Get-CountryByIP($IP)
{
 $URI = "http://www.webservicex.net/geoipservice.asmx?wsdl"
 $Proxy = New-WebServiceProxy -uri $URI -namespace WebServiceProxy -class IP
```

```
$RTN = $proxy.GetGeoIP($IP)

 $ipReturn = New-Object PSObject
 $ipReturn | Add-Member -MemberType noteproperty -Name ip -Value $rtn.ip
 $ipReturn | Add-Member -MemberType noteproperty -Name countryName -Value $rtn.
CountryName
 $ipReturn | Add-Member -MemberType noteproperty -Name countryCode -Value $rtn.
CountryCode
 $ipReturn
} #end Get-CountryByIP


Function Get-Folder($folderName)
{
 [Environment]::GetFolderPath([environment+SpecialFolder]::$folderName)
} #end function Get-Folder


# *** Entry Point to Script ***

$ip |
ForEach-Object { Get-CountryByIP -ip $_ } |
Tee-Object -Variable results


$results |
Out-File -FilePath `
   (Join-Path -Path (Get-Folder -folderName $folder) -childPath $log)
```

Networked Log Files

At times, it might be more convenient to store the logs in a central shared folder instead of storing them on a local computer. This approach can solve many of the problems identified earlier in this chapter that are associated with creating and maintaining a folder on each computer. There are two methods of handling networked log files. The first method is to write directly to the file, and the second is to write to a temporary file on the local host machine and copy the file to the network location. As a best practice, any file that is very large or that might potentially involve large amounts of data should be created locally first and then copied to the network location. In this section, you will examine both approaches.

Writing Directly to the File

The simplest approach to working with networked log files is to write directly to the file. The Out-File cmdlet is able to use a Universal Naming Convention (UNC) path or a mapped network drive path. The UNC path is the most convenient approach because it does not require the creation and maintenance of mapped network drives.

```
Get-Process | Out-File -FilePath \\berlin\netshare\processes.txt
```

For small amounts of data on a well-connected network, the writing directly approach works fine. For larger amounts of data or when working on a network that might have unreliable or limited connectivity, a different approach is required.

Writing to the Local File and Copying to the Network

Because the creation and the writing to files on a network share is not an optimized operation, you can experience performance problems when writing directly to a networked file share. Writing to local files is an optimized scenario, and copying files to a network share is also a performance operation. Because of the different caveats involved in working with local files and folders, it is a best practice to write to a temporary file in the temporary directory and then copy the temporary file to the networked share. This is not a difficult process, and it will greatly improve the performance of networked logging.

The easiest way to write to a temporary file is to use the *getTempFileName* method from the *Io.Path* .NET Framework class. The *getTempFileName* method creates a temporary file name in the user's temporary directory in a location that looks similar to the one shown here.

```
C:\Users\edwilson\AppData\Local\Temp\tmpE7C6.tmp
```

The New-TempFile.ps1 script illustrates using a local temporary file for output and displaying the results of the operation in Notepad. The New-TempFile.ps1 script creates a function named *New-TempFile* that uses *CmdletBinding* and creates a single input parameter that accepts an array of *PSObjects* in the *$inputObject* variable. The script then calls the *getTempFileName* static method from the *Io.Path* .NET Framework class. The temporary file name is stored in the *$tmpFile* variable. The data contained in the *$inputObject* variable is pipelined to the Out-File cmdlet and then to the temporary file specified in the *$tmpFile* variable. The file path to the temporary file is then returned to the calling code.

```
Function New-TempFile
{
 [CmdletBinding()]
 Param(
  [Parameter(Position=0,ValueFromPipeline=$true)]
  [PSObject[]]$inputObject
 )#end param
  $tmpFile = [Io.Path]::getTempFileName()
  $inputObject | Out-File -filepath $tmpFile
  $tmpFile
} #end function New-TempFile
```

The entry point to the script illustrates how you might interact with this function. It calls the *New-TempFile* function and passes the results of the Get-Service cmdlet to the function via the *inputObject* parameter. The returned file path is stored in the *$rtn* variable. Once the temporary file is created, inside the *New-TempFile* function, the file is moved to a file share on a remote server and renamed by using the Move-Item cmdlet.

```
$destination = "\\berlin\fileshare\services.txt"
$rtn = New-TempFile  -inputObject (Get-Service)
Move-Item -path $rtn -destination $destination
```

The complete New-TempFile.ps1 script is shown here.

New-TempFile.ps1

```
Function New-TempFile
{
 [CmdletBinding()]
 Param(
  [Parameter(Position=0,ValueFromPipeline=$true)]
  [PSObject[]]$inputObject
 )#end param
  $tmpFile = [Io.Path]::getTempFileName()
  $inputObject | Out-File -filepath $tmpFile
  $tmpFile
} #end function New-TempFile

# *** Entry Point to Script ***
 $destination = "\\berlin\fileshare\services.txt"
 $rtn = New-TempFile  -inputObject (Get-Service)
 Move-Item -path $rtn -destination $destination
```

NOTES FROM THE FIELD

Logging in Windows PowerShell

Andrew Willett, Systems Architect
Unitrans Logistics, Steinhoff Group

You have written a Windows PowerShell script, tested it on your PC, and deployed it to run on your network—except that something is wrong. But what?

Logging—or as our developer friends call it, instrumentation—is both an invaluable tool for testing and debugging your scripts as well as a key part of their life cycle. Logging can tell you when a script succeeds or fails to run as expected, what causes an exception to occur, or can tell you more detailed information, such as how long it takes a script to execute and why.

Implementing a basic form of logging is simple and is similar to what you might do at the command line. Similar to using > to send the console output to a text file, you can use the Tee-Object cmdlet to store the output in a variable as well as in a text file.

```
Get-Service | Tee-Object -filepath c:\services.txt
```

Using the `Tee-Object` cmdlet might be easy for individual commands, but it does not work very well for entire scripts. The next logical step is to use `Tee-Object` where necessary and append the output to the file. Unfortunately, while `Tee-Object` is only able to overwrite a file, Windows PowerShell encapsulates this functionality and a whole lot more in the `Start-Transcript` cmdlet. Using the transcript functionality requires two lines of code—one at the start and one at the end—that turn logging on and off, respectively.

```
Start-Transcript -path c:\scriptoutput.txt
    (...)
Stop-Transcript
```

A few useful parameters for `Start-Transcript` are *–append*, which appends the log to the existing file, and *Noclobber*, which prevents the default behavior of overwriting an existing file (unix admins might recognize this behavior). The call to the `Stop-Transcript` cmdlet is implicit, so if you forget to use the command or your code exits through a different path or exception, the script will still close correctly.

Both of these logging cmdlets can be very useful when diagnosing the root cause of a problem with your script in the field or for debugging your script while you are developing and testing it. However, digging through a verbose log of your script is not very helpful when you want to know at a glance whether the script succeeded or whether a failure was simply due to a time-out.

While developing your script, you will be aware of a subset of reasons as to why it might fail, such as connectivity or a lack of system resources or permissions, as well as how to determine whether it succeeded in its desired function. In addition, your script might look up or determine certain parameters at run time rather than being hard-coded, such as the available network bandwidth, whether the user is running with administrator privileges, or whether the computer is on battery power. Diagnosing a problem after the event can be difficult if you can only *assume* what parameters the script was running at the time. Calling out some of this key information, perhaps appended by the full verbose log, will save you a great deal of time—something I know that many people desire when digging through Windowsupdate.log!

Viewing instrumentation as an entire collection of technology means thinking about the storage and delivery of this information—a text file sitting on the hard disk collecting dust is not very helpful! When you know which pieces are salient pieces of output information, you should decide what to do with this information based on the effects that a failure might cause, whether action needs to be taken and by whom, and how time-critical the issue might be. If the log output is to be used for archive purposes, then you should consider where to store the data—such as in the file system, the event log, or on the network—based on the write permissions of the user and your need for a retention period.

The following are some tricks of the trade that you might find useful, along with some examples with which to get started.

- E-mailing logging information back to the administrator can proactively tell you when a problem has occurred and why—you can even e-mail logging information to your help desk software and have the software set up an incident.

```
$to = "helpdesk@contoso.com"
$from = "scripts@contoso.com"
$subject = "Permissions Error in Script"
$body = "The script could not run as user " + (Get-Content env:username) +
" was not a member of the required security group."
$server = "smtp.contoso.com"
$smtp = New-Object Net.Mail.SmtpClient($server)
$smtp.Send($from, $to, $subject, $body)
```

- Outputting the text file to a network file share is a useful way to collate diagnostic information in a central store, especially when you want to view a list of computers and determine when the script was last executed. When a file name is composed of the computer name and date/time in seconds, you can be assured that the file name will always be unique and that a file name–based sort in Windows Explorer, albeit crude, will sort the files chronologically.

```
$path = "\\fileserver\logs\script1\" + (Get-Content env:computername) +
" " + (Get-Date -f "yyyy-MM-dd HHmmss") + ".txt"
Start-Transcript -path $path
```

- Calling out specific errors in the event log is a great way to bubble instrumentation data to the surface, for this is often the first place that technicians will look when diagnosing a problem. The event log can also be monitored by tools commonplace in larger IT shops, such as Microsoft System Center Operations Manager or the Event Collector service.

You can set the log level to Information, Warning, or Error depending on the severity (or lack of severity) attached to the data, and you can even assign granular error codes based on the root cause of the issue. The only caveat is that administrator privileges are required to set up your own event log source. If you need to use an event log in these scenarios, you must either ensure that the event log is created in advance or commandeer one of the pre-existing Windows sources for your needs.

```
$source = "MyScript"
$log = "Application"
$message = "The script could not run as user " + (Get-Content
env:username) +
" was not a member of the required security group."
```

```
$type = "Error"
$id = 1

if (![System.Diagnostics.EventLog]::SourceExists($source)) { [System.
Diagnostics.EventLog]::CreateEventSource($source, $log) }

$eventLog = New-Object System.Diagnostics.EventLog
$eventLog.Log = $log
$eventLog.Source = $source
$eventLog.WriteEntry($message, $type, $id)
```

Logging to the Event Log

Windows event logs provide a convenient place to store short status and diagnostic information. You can use the .NET Framework classes directly to create event sources, event logs, and event log entries, or you can use cmdlets. The New-EventLog cmdlet can be used to create a new event log and event log source. To write to an event log, you must supply both a log name and a log source.

To create a new event log and event source requires administrative rights. The error shown here will be generated if administrative rights are not present.

```
PS C:\> New-EventLog -LogName scripting -Source processAudit
New-EventLog : Access is denied. Please try with an elevated user permission.
At line:1 char:13
+ New-EventLog <<<<  -LogName scripting -Source processAudit
    + CategoryInfo          : InvalidOperation: (:) [New-EventLog], Exception
    + FullyQualifiedErrorId : AccessIsDenied,Microsoft.PowerShell.Commands.
NewEventLogCommand
```

To start either the Windows PowerShell console or the Windows PowerShell Integrated Scripting Environment (ISE), you right-click the icon and choose Run As Administrator from the action menu. In a script, you want to use a function, such as *Test-IsAdministrator*, to determine rights prior to attempting to create a new event log. The TestAdminCreateEventLog.ps1 script contains the *Test-IsAdministrator* function. This function begins by creating a minimal amount of help: the synopsis, description, and an example of using the function.

```
function Test-IsAdministrator
{
    <#
    .Synopsis
        Tests if the user is an administrator
    .Description
        Returns true if a user is an administrator,
        false if the user is not an administrator
```

```
.Example
    Test-IsAdministrator
#>
```

The function uses the *GetCurrent* static method from the *Security.Principal.WindowsIdentity* .NET Framework class. This method returns a *WindowsIdentity* object that represents the current user. The *WindowsIdentity* object is passed to the *System.Principal.WindowsPrincipal* .NET Framework class where it is used to generate an instance of a *WindowsPrincipal* class. The *IsInRole* method receives a *WindowsBuiltinRole* enumeration value that is used to determine whether the user is in the Administrator role.

```
$currentUser = [Security.Principal.WindowsIdentity]::GetCurrent()
(New-Object Security.Principal.WindowsPrincipal $currentUser).IsInRole `
    ([Security.Principal.WindowsBuiltinRole]::Administrator)
} #end function Test-IsAdministrator
```

The *Test-IsAdministrator* function returns a Boolean value. If the function is true, the user is in the Administrator role; if it is false, the user is not elevated and the script will exit. If the user is in the Administrator role, the script creates a new event log and source.

```
If(-not (Test-IsAdministrator)) { "Admin rights are required for this script" ; exit }
New-EventLog -LogName scripting -Source processAudit
```

The complete TestAdminCreateEventLog.ps1 script is shown here.

TestAdminCreateEventLog.ps1
```
function Test-IsAdministrator
{
    <#
    .Synopsis
        Tests if the user is an administrator
    .Description
        Returns true if a user is an administrator,
        false if the user is not an administrator
    .Example
        Test-IsAdministrator
    #>
    param()
    $currentUser = [Security.Principal.WindowsIdentity]::GetCurrent()
    (New-Object Security.Principal.WindowsPrincipal $currentUser).IsInRole `
        ([Security.Principal.WindowsBuiltinRole]::Administrator)
} #end function Test-IsAdministrator


# *** Entry Point to Script ***
If(-not (Test-IsAdministrator)) { "Admin rights are required for this script" ; exit }
New-EventLog -LogName scripting -Source processAudit
```

Using the Application Log

The easiest log to use is the Application log because it is always present on the system and because administrative rights are not required. A source must exist in the event log. If you choose a source that exists but an event ID that does not exist, no error will be generated, but the event details will contain a message about a missing source description.

```
PS C:\> Write-EventLog -LogName application -Source certenroll -EntryType information `
-EventId 0 -Message "test"
PS C:\> Get-EventLog -LogName application -Newest 1 | Format-List *
```

```
EventID            : 0
MachineName        : EDWILSON.microsoft.com
Data               : {}
Index              : 6130
Category           : (1)
CategoryNumber     : 1
EntryType          : Information
Message            : The description for Event ID '0' in Source 'certenroll' cannot be
found. The local computer may not have the necessary registry information or message
DLL files to display the message or you may not have permission to access them. The
following information is part of the event:'test'
Source             : certenroll
ReplacementStrings : {test}
InstanceId         : 0
TimeGenerated      : 8/17/2009 12:03:52 PM
TimeWritten        : 8/17/2009 12:03:52 PM
UserName           :
Site               :
Container          :
```

Creating a Custom Event Log

The best way to use event log logging is to create your own custom event log with its own custom sources. Because the Application log is heavily used by numerous sources, retrieving events involves sorting through thousands of entries. With a custom event log, you are in complete control of how many events are written, the number of sources that are defined, and the level of logging that is done. This means that it is generally easier to retrieve event log entries from a custom event log than from System or Application logs. To create a new event log, use the New-EventLog cmdlet to specify the log name and the source for the events.

```
PS C:\> New-EventLog -LogName ForScripting -Source scripting
```

To write to the event log, use the Write-EventLog cmdlet. You need to specify the log name, the source, the type of entry, and the event ID and message, which can all be accomplished on a single line.

```
PS C:\> Write-EventLog -LogName ForScripting -Source scripting -EntryType information `
-EventId 0 -Message test
```

To retrieve event log entries, you can use the Get-EventLog cmdlet and specify the event log name.

```
PS C:\> Get-EventLog -LogName ForScripting
```

```
Index Time          EntryType    Source            InstanceID Message
----- ----          ---------    ------            ---------- -------
    1 Aug 17 12:42  Information  scripting                  0 test
```

Logging to the Registry

The registry is an ideal location to store small pieces of information, such as exit codes and time stamps. Due to the nature of the registry, you do not want to store large amounts of data here. In addition, you will need to remove the object-oriented nature of the objects when you write to the registry by pipelining the object to the Out-String cmdlet or by calling one of the *ToString* methods.

The best place to write to the registry is in the Hkey_Current_User hive because the current user has rights to write to the Current_User registry hive, and you therefore avoid rights and permissions issues. This process is illustrated in the CreateRegistryKey.ps1 script, which is used to create a registry key named ForScripting in the Hkey_Current_User hive. A property named *forscripting* is created with the value of *test* assigned to it.

The CreateRegistryKey.ps1 script contains a function named *Add-RegistryValue* that accepts two parameters—the *$key* and the *$value* variables. The function can be further expanded to include the registry root as well. The value of the *$scriptRoot* variable is used to determine where the registry key value will be created. If the path to the *$scriptRoot* registry key does not exist, it will be created, and the registry property value will be added as well. The Test-Path cmdlet is used to ensure that the path to the *$scriptRoot* registry key exists. The New-Item cmdlet is used to create the registry key, and the New-ItemProperty cmdlet is used to create the new registry property and assign its value. The Out-Null cmdlet is used to keep the results of creating the registry key and value from cluttering the Windows PowerShell console.

```
Function Add-RegistryValue($key,$value)
{
 $scriptRoot = "HKCU:\software\ForScripting"
 if(-not (Test-Path -path $scriptRoot))
   {
    New-Item -Path HKCU:\Software\ForScripting | Out-Null
    New-ItemProperty -Path $scriptRoot -Name $key -Value $value `
    -PropertyType String | Out-Null
   }
```

If the registry key does exist, the `Set-ItemProperty` cmdlet is used to either create the registry property value or change its value. Once again, the results of the cmdlet are pipelined to the `Out-Null` cmdlet.

```
Else
  {
   Set-ItemProperty -Path $scriptRoot -Name $key -Value $value | `
   Out-Null
  }
```

The entry point to the script calls the *Add-RegistryValue* function and passes the registry key name and the value to modify.

```
Add-RegistryValue -key forscripting -value test
```

The complete CreateRegistryKey.ps1 script is shown here.

CreateRegistryKey.ps1
```
Function Add-RegistryValue($key,$value)
{
 $scriptRoot = "HKCU:\software\ForScripting"
 if(-not (Test-Path -path $scriptRoot))
   {
    New-Item -Path HKCU:\Software\ForScripting | Out-Null
    New-ItemProperty -Path $scriptRoot -Name $key -Value $value `
    -PropertyType String | Out-Null
   }
  Else
  {
   Set-ItemProperty -Path $scriptRoot -Name $key -Value $value | `
   Out-Null
  }

} #end function Add-RegistryValue

# *** Entry Point to Script ***
Add-RegistryValue -key forscripting -value test
```

When the CreateRegistryKey.ps1 script is run, nothing is displayed on the screen. The ForScripting registry key is created with the *forscripting* registry property, which is set to a value of *test* as shown in Figure 16-5.

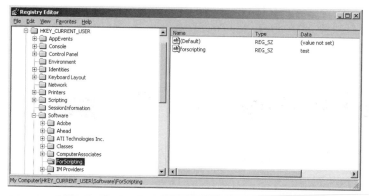

FIGURE 16-5 The Current_User registry hive is a great place to store small amounts of data.

Additional Resources

- The Technet Script Center at *http://www.microsoft.com/technet/scriptcenter* contains numerous examples of writing to files, the event log, and the registry.

- Take a look at Chapter 3 in *Windows PowerShell™ Scripting Guide* (Microsoft Press, 2008) for more information about how to log script results.

- On the companion media, you will find all of the scripts referred to in this chapter.

Troubleshooting Scripts

A well-designed, well-written script rarely needs troubleshooting. This is not to say that all scripts are perfect or that all scripts run without errors the first time they are executed—or even the second time. Yet, a good script should be organized in a manner that makes it easy to read and easy to understand. By default, the two best practices of readability and understandability reduce the amount of troubleshooting necessary to fix errors in a script because they make errors easier to spot. When problems do crop up, however, you will want to know how to debug your script. In this chapter, we will look at the commands to produce a trace of your script, to step through the commands of the script, and to debug the script and will examine the best practices involved in choosing tracing, stepping, or debugging commands for identifying errors in scripts. Debugging cmdlets represent a new feature in Windows PowerShell 2.0, and they might completely replace the way you debugged scripts in the past.

Using the Set-PSDebug cmdlet

The Set-PSDebug cmdlet was available in Windows PowerShell 1.0 and has not changed in Windows PowerShell 2.0. To do basic debugging in a quick and easy fashion, you cannot beat the combination of features that are available with the Set-PSDebug cmdlet. Three things can be accomplished with this cmdlet. You can trace script execution in an automated fashion, step through the script in an interactive fashion, and enable StrictMode. Each of these features will be examined in this section. The Set-PSDebug cmdlet is not designed to do heavy debugging; it is a lightweight tool that is useful when you want to produce a quick trace or rapidly step through the script.

Tracing the Script

One of the simplest ways to debug a script is to turn on level tracing. By doing this, each executed command is displayed to the Windows PowerShell console. By watching the commands as they are displayed to the console, you can determine whether a line of code in your script executes or whether it is being skipped. To enable script tracing, you use the Set-PSDebug cmdlet and specify one of three levels for the *trace* parameter (listed in Table 17-1).

TABLE 17-1 Set-PSDebug Trace Levels

TRACE LEVEL	MEANING
0	Turns script tracing off.
1	Traces each line of the script as it is executed. Lines in the script that are not executed are not traced. Does not display variable assignments, function calls, or external scripts.
2	Traces each line of the script as it is executed. Displays variable assignments, function calls, and external scripts. Lines in the script that are not executed are not traced.

To illustrate the process of tracing a script as well as the differences between the trace levels, look at the CreateRegistryKey.ps1 script. This script contains a single function named *Add-RegistryValue*. In the *Add-RegistryValue* function, the Test-Path cmdlet is used to determine whether the registry key exists. If the registry key exists, a property value is set. If the registry key does not exist, the registry key is created and a property value is set. The *Add-RegistryValue* function is called when the script executes. The complete CreateRegistryKey.ps1 script is shown here.

```
CreateRegistryKey.ps1
Function Add-RegistryValue($key,$value)
{
 $scriptRoot = "HKCU:\software\ForScripting"
 if(-not (Test-Path -path $scriptRoot))
   {
    New-Item -Path HKCU:\Software\ForScripting | Out-Null
    New-ItemProperty -Path $scriptRoot -Name $key -Value $value `
    -PropertyType String | Out-Null
   }
 Else
   {
    Set-ItemProperty -Path $scriptRoot -Name $key -Value $value | `
    Out-Null
   }

} #end function Add-RegistryValue

# *** Entry Point to Script ***
Add-RegistryValue -key forscripting -value test
```

Working with Trace Level 1

When the trace level is set to 1, each line in the script that executes is displayed to the Windows PowerShell console. To set the trace level to 1, you use the Set-PSDebug cmdlet, use the *trace* parameter, and assign the value of 1 to it. When you press Enter, you are immediately presented with three lines of output. These three lines of output are commands that are executed by the Windows PowerShell console host and are used to provide suggestions when the user inputs incorrect commands. These commands are displayed to the Windows PowerShell console because every command supplied to the Windows PowerShell console is traced. Each trace is preceded with the word DEBUG: and a line number that is followed by a plus sign. Input to the command is preceded by a series of four left arrows (<<<<). These three trace lines can be safely ignored.

```
PS C:\> Set-PSDebug -trace 1
DEBUG:    2+          $foundSuggestion = <<<<  $false
DEBUG:    4+          if <<<< ($lastError -and
DEBUG:    15+         $foundSuggestion <<<<
PS C:\>
```

Once the trace level is set, it applies to everything that is typed in the Windows PowerShell console. If you run an interactive command, run a cmdlet, or execute a script, it will be traced. When the CreateRegistryKey.ps1 script is run and no registry key is present, the first command debug line displays the path to the script that is being executed. Because Windows PowerShell parses from the top down, the next line that is executed is the line that creates the *Add-RegistryValue* function. This command is on line 7 of the script because the actual script that executed contains six lines that are commented out. When you add the status bar to Notepad (View/Status Bar), the status bar at the lower-right corner of Notepad displays the line number, as shown in Figure 17-1.

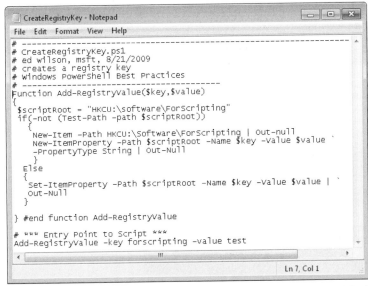

FIGURE 17-1 The Notepad status bar at the lower-right corner of Notepad displays line numbers.

After the function is created, the next line of the script that executes is line 25. Line 25 of the CreateRegistryKey.ps1 script follows the comment that points to the entry point to the script (this last line is shown in Figure 17-1) and calls the *Add-RegistryValue* function by passing two values for the *$key* and *$value* parameters.

```
PS C:\> y:\CreateRegistryKey.ps1
DEBUG:     1+  <<<< y:\CreateRegistryKey.ps1
DEBUG:     7+ Function Add-RegistryValue <<<< ($key,$value)
DEBUG:    25+  <<<< Add-RegistryValue -key forscripting -value test
```

Once inside the *Add-RegistryValue* function, the HKCU:\Software\ForScripting string is assigned to the *$scriptRoot* variable.

```
DEBUG:     9+  $scriptRoot = <<<<  "HKCU:\Software\ForScripting"
```

The *If* statement is now evaluated. If the Test-Path cmdlet is unable to find the *$scriptRoot* location in the registry, the *If* statement is entered and the commands inside the associated script block are executed. In this example, the *$scriptRoot* is located and the commands inside the script block are not executed.

```
DEBUG:    10+  if <<<< (-not (Test-Path -path $scriptRoot))
```

The Set-ItemProperty cmdlet is called on line 18 of the CreateRegistryKey.ps1 script.

```
DEBUG:    18+     <<<< Set-ItemProperty -Path $scriptRoot -Name $key -Value
$value | `
```

Once the Set-ItemProperty cmdlet is executed, the script ends. The Windows PowerShell console parser now enters with the same three lines of feedback that were seen when tracing was first enabled.

```
DEBUG:     2+         $foundSuggestion = <<<<  $false
DEBUG:     4+         if <<<< ($lastError -and
DEBUG:    15+         $foundSuggestion <<<<
PS C:\>
```

By setting the debug trace level to 1, a basic outline of the execution plan of the script is produced. This technique is good for quickly determining the outcome of branching statements (such as the *If* statement) to note whether a script block is being entered as shown in Figure 17-2.

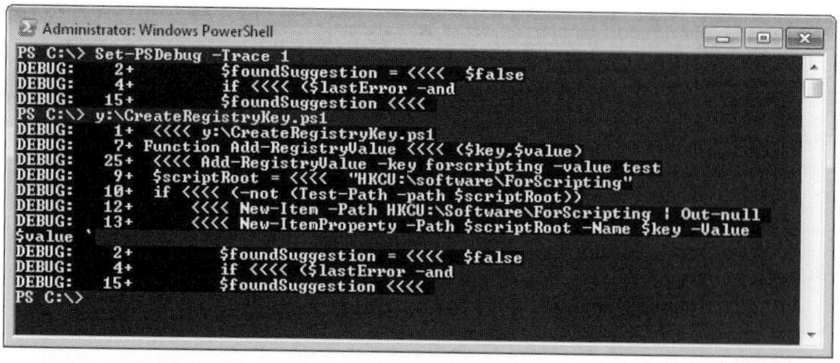

FIGURE 17-2 Script level 1 tracing displays each executing line of the script.

Working with Trace Level 2

When the trace level is set to 2, each line in the script that executes is displayed to the Windows PowerShell console. In addition, each variable assignment, function call, and outside script call is displayed. These additional tracing details are all prefixed with an exclamation mark to make them easier to spot. When the Set-PSDebug *trace* parameter is set to 2, an extra line is displayed indicating a variable assignment.

```
PS C:\> Set-PSDebug -Trace 2
DEBUG:    1+  <<<< Set-PSDebug -Trace 2
DEBUG:    2+         $foundSuggestion = <<<<  $false
DEBUG:    ! SET $foundSuggestion = 'False'.
DEBUG:    4+         if <<<< ($lastError -and
DEBUG:   15+         $foundSuggestion <<<<
```

When the CreateRegistryKey.ps1 script is run, the function trace points first to the script, stating that it is calling a function named CreateRegistryKey.ps1. Calls to functions are prefixed with *! CALL*, making them easy to spot. Windows PowerShell treats scripts as functions. The next function that is called is the *Add-RegistryValue* function. The trace also states where the function is defined by indicating the path to the file.

```
PS C:\> y:\CreateRegistryKey.ps1
DEBUG:    1+  <<<< y:\CreateRegistryKey.ps1
DEBUG:    ! CALL function 'CreateRegistryKey.ps1'  (defined in file
'y:\CreateRegistryKey.ps1')
DEBUG:    7+ Function Add-RegistryValue <<<< ($key,$value)
DEBUG:   25+  <<<< Add-RegistryValue -key forscripting -value test
DEBUG:    ! CALL function 'Add-RegistryValue'  (defined in file
'y:\CreateRegistryKey.ps1')
```

The *! SET* keyword is used to preface variable assignments. The first variable that is assigned is the *$scriptRoot* variable.

```
DEBUG:    9+  $scriptRoot = <<<<  "HKCU:\software\ForScripting"
DEBUG:    ! SET $scriptRoot = 'HKCU:\software\ForScripting'.
DEBUG:   10+  if <<<< (-not (Test-Path -path $scriptRoot))
DEBUG:   18+   <<<< Set-ItemProperty -Path $scriptRoot -Name $key -Value
$value | `
DEBUG:    2+         $foundSuggestion = <<<<  $false
DEBUG:    ! SET $foundSuggestion = 'False'.
DEBUG:    4+         if <<<< ($lastError -and
DEBUG:   15+         $foundSuggestion <<<<
PS C:\>
```

When the CreateRegistryKey.ps1 script is run with trace level 2, the detailed tracing shown in Figure 17-3 is displayed.

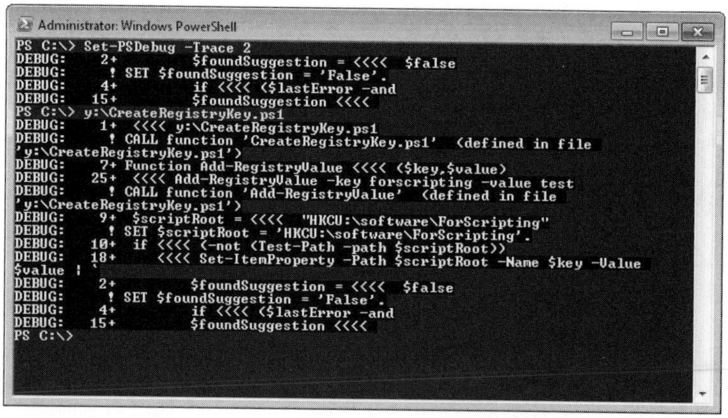

FIGURE 17-3 Script level 2 tracing adds variable assignments, function calls, and external script calls.

Stepping Through the Script

Watching the script trace the execution of the lines of code in the script can often provide useful insight that can lead to a solution for a misbehaving script. If a script is more complicated and comprises several functions, a simple trace might not be a workable solution. For those occasions when your script is more complex and comprises multiple functions, you will want the ability to step through the script. When you step through a script, you are prompted before each line of the script is run. An example of a script that you might want to step through is the BadScript.ps1 script, shown here.

BadScript.ps1

```
# -----------------------------------------------------------------------
# NAME: BadScript.ps1
# AUTHOR: ed wilson, Microsoft
# DATE: 8/22/2009
#
# KEYWORDS: template
#
# COMMENTS: This script has a couple of errors in it
# 1. TimesOne function multiplies by 2
# 2. Script pipelines input but function does not take pipe
# 3. Script divides by 0
#
#
# -----------------------------------------------------------------------

Function AddOne([int]$num)
{
 $num+1
} #end function AddOne
```

```
Function AddTwo([int]$num)
{
 $num+2
} #end function AddTwo

Function SubOne([int]$num)
{
 $num-1
} #end function SubOne

Function TimesOne([int]$num)
{
  $num*2
} #end function TimesOne

Function TimesTwo([int]$num)
{
 $num*2
} #end function TimesTwo

Function DivideNum([int]$num)
{
 12/$num
} #end function DivideNum

# *** Entry Point to Script ***

$num = 0
SubOne($num) | DivideNum($num)
AddOne($num) | AddTwo($num)
```

The BadScript.ps1 script contains a number of functions that are used to add, subtract, multiply, and divide numbers. There are some problems with the way in which the script runs because it contains several errors. It is possible for you to set the trace level to 2 and examine the trace of the script, but with the large number of functions and the types of errors that are contained in the script, it might be difficult to spot the problems. By default, the trace level is set to level 1 when stepping is enabled, and in nearly all cases, it is the best solution for the trace level.

You might prefer to be able to step through the script as each line executes. There are two benefits to using the *step* parameter from the Set-PSDebug cmdlet. The first benefit is that you are able to watch what happens when each line of the script executes, which allows you to very carefully walk through the script. With the trace feature of Set-PSDebug, it is possible to miss important clues to help solve troubleshooting problems because everything is displayed on the Windows PowerShell console. With the prompt feature, you are asked to choose a response before each line in the script executes. The default choice is *Y* for "yes, continue the operation," but you have other choices. When you respond *Y*, the debug line is displayed to the Windows PowerShell console. This is the same debug statement that you saw in the trace output, and it is governed by your debug trace level settings. Step prompting is shown here.

```
PS C:\> Set-PSDebug -Step


Continue with this operation?
   2+          $foundSuggestion = <<<< $false
[Y] Yes  [A] Yes to All  [N] No  [L] No to All  [S] Suspend  [?] Help
(default is "Y"):y
DEBUG:    2+          $foundSuggestion = <<<< $false


Continue with this operation?
   4+          if <<<< ($lastError -and
[Y] Yes  [A] Yes to All  [N] No  [L] No to All  [S] Suspend  [?] Help
(default is "Y"):y
DEBUG:    4+          if <<<< ($lastError -and


Continue with this operation?
   15+          $foundSuggestion <<<<
[Y] Yes  [A] Yes to All  [N] No  [L] No to All  [S] Suspend  [?] Help
(default is "Y"):y
DEBUG:    15+          $foundSuggestion <<<<
PS C:\> Y:\BadScript.ps1


Continue with this operation?
   1+ <<<< Y:\BadScript.ps1
[Y] Yes  [A] Yes to All  [N] No  [L] No to All  [S] Suspend  [?] Help
(default is "Y"):y
DEBUG:    1+ <<<< Y:\BadScript.ps1


Continue with this operation?
   16+ Function AddOne <<<< ([int]$num)
[Y] Yes  [A] Yes to All  [N] No  [L] No to All  [S] Suspend  [?] Help
(default is "Y"):y
DEBUG:    16+ Function AddOne <<<< ([int]$num)
```

The second benefit to using the *step* parameter with the Set-PSDebug cmdlet is the ability to suspend script execution, run additional Windows PowerShell commands, and then return to the script execution. The ability to return the value of a variable from within the Windows PowerShell console can offer important clues to the problems inherent in the script. When you choose *S* (for "suspend") at the prompt, you are dropped into a nested Windows PowerShell prompt. From there, you retrieve the variable value in the same way as when working at a regular Windows PowerShell console—by typing the name of the variable; tab expansion even works. When you are finished retrieving the value of the variable, you type **exit** to return to the stepping trace.

```
Continue with this operation?
   48+ $num = <<<<  0
[Y] Yes  [A] Yes to All  [N] No  [L] No to All  [S] Suspend  [?] Help
(default is "Y"):y
DEBUG:    48+ $num = <<<<  0

Continue with this operation?
   49+  <<<< SubOne($num) | DivideNum($num)
[Y] Yes  [A] Yes to All  [N] No  [L] No to All  [S] Suspend  [?] Help
(default is "Y"):s
PS C:\>>> $num
0
PS C:\>>> exit
```

If you want to see what happens if you run continuously from the point you just inspected, you can choose *A* (for "yes to all"), and the script will run to completion without further prompting. If the script runs to completion, then you have found the problem. It is also possible that you might notice an error, such as the one shown here, when the script attempts to divide by zero.

```
Continue with this operation?
   1+  <<<< Y:\BadScript.ps1
[Y] Yes  [A] Yes to All  [N] No  [L] No to All  [S] Suspend  [?] Help
(default is "Y"):y
DEBUG:    1+  <<<< Y:\BadScript.ps1

Continue with this operation?
   16+ Function AddOne <<<< ([int]$num)
[Y] Yes  [A] Yes to All  [N] No  [L] No to All  [S] Suspend  [?] Help
(default is "Y"):A
DEBUG:    16+ Function AddOne <<<< ([int]$num)
Attempted to divide by zero.
At Y:\BadScript.ps1:43 char:5
+  12/ <<<< $num
    + CategoryInfo          : NotSpecified: (:) [], RuntimeException
    + FullyQualifiedErrorId : RuntimeException


2
PS C:\>
```

Once you find a specific error, you might want to change the value of a variable from within the suspended Windows PowerShell console to see whether it corrects the remaining logic. To do this, run the script again and choose *S* (for "suspend") at the line that caused the error. This is the point where some careful reading of the error messages comes into play.

When you chose *A* ("yes to all") in the previous example, the script ran until it came to line 43. The line number indicator follows a colon after the script name. The plus (+) sign indicates the command, which is 12/ $num. The four left arrows indicate that it is the value of the *$num* variable that is causing the problem.

```
Attempted to divide by zero.
At Y:\BadScript.ps1:43 char:5
+    12/ <<<< $num
```

You will need to step through the code until you come to the prompt for line 43. This prompt is shown as 43+ 12/ <<<< $num, which means that you are at line 43 and the operation (+) is to divide 12 by the value of the number contained in the *$num* variable. At this point, you want to press *S* (for "suspend") to drop into a nested Windows PowerShell prompt. Inside the prompt, you can query the value contained in the *$num* variable and change it to a number, such as 2. You exit the nested Windows PowerShell prompt and are returned to the stepping trace. At this point, you should continue to step through the code to see whether any other problems arise. If they do not, you know that you have located the source of the problem.

```
Continue with this operation?
   28+    $num- <<<< 1
[Y] Yes  [A] Yes to All  [N] No  [L] No to All  [S] Suspend  [?] Help
(default is "Y"):y
DEBUG:     28+    $num- <<<< 1


Continue with this operation?
   43+   12/ <<<< $num
[Y] Yes  [A] Yes to All  [N] No  [L] No to All  [S] Suspend  [?] Help
(default is "Y"):s
PS C:\>>> $num
0
PS C:\>>> $num = 2
PS C:\>>> exit


Continue with this operation?
   43+   12/ <<<< $num
[Y] Yes  [A] Yes to All  [N] No  [L] No to All  [S] Suspend  [?] Help
(default is "Y"):y
DEBUG:     43+   12/ <<<< $num
6


Continue with this operation?
   50+ <<<< AddOne($num) | AddTwo($num)
[Y] Yes  [A] Yes to All  [N] No  [L] No to All  [S] Suspend  [?] Help
(default is "Y"):
```

Of course, locating the source of the problem is not the same as solving the problem, but the previous example points to a problem with the value of *$num*. Your next step is to look at how *$num* is being assigned its values.

A few annoyances emerge when working with the Set-PSDebug tracing features. The first problem is to step through the three lines of output created by the commands that executed by the Windows PowerShell console host that provide suggestions when the user inputs incorrect commands. The prompts and output will use half of the Windows PowerShell console window. If you use Clear-Host to attempt to clear the host window, you will spend several minutes attempting to step through all of the commands used by Clear-Host. This is also true if you attempt to set the debug trace level to 2. By default, the trace level is set to 1 by the Set-PSDebug *step* parameter. The second problem with the Set-PSDebug *step* parameter occurs when you attempt to bypass a command in the script. You are not allowed to step over a command. Instead, the stepping session ends with an error displayed to the Windows PowerShell console as shown in Figure 17-4.

FIGURE 17-4 Set-PSDebug *–step* does not allow you to step over functions or commands.

To turn off stepping, you use the *off* parameter. You will be prompted to step through this command as well.

```
PS C:\> Set-PSDebug -Off
Continue with this operation?
   1+ Set-PSDebug -Off
[Y] Yes  [A] Yes to All  [N] No  [L] No to All  [S] Suspend  [?] Help
(default is "Y"):y
DEBUG:    1+ Set-PSDebug -Off
PS C:\>
```

Enabling StrictMode

Variables that are used incorrectly, that are nonexistent, or that are incorrectly initialized can cause problems in a script. A simple typing error is a common mistake, and simple typing errors can also cause problems when contained in a large, complex script. StrictMode can aid in detecting these common problems. When enabled, StrictMode forces you to assign values to your variables. Noninitialized variables and misspelled variables will automatically be detected, which can save hours of frustrating troubleshooting when working with a large, complex script.

Using Set-PSDebug –*Strict*

An example of a simple typing error in a script is shown in the SimpleTypingError.ps1 script.

```
SimpleTypingError.ps1
$a = 2
$b = 5
$d = $a + $b
'The value of $c is: ' + $c
```

When the SimpleTypingError.ps1 script is run, it produces the following output.

```
PS C:\> y:\SimpleTypingError.ps1
The value of $c is:
PS C:\>
```

As you can see, the value of the *$c* variable is not displayed. If you use the *strict* parameter from the Set-PSDebug cmdlet, an error is generated. The error tells you that the value of *$c* has not been set.

```
PS C:\> Set-PSDebug -Strict
PS C:\> y:\SimpleTypingError.ps1
The variable $c cannot be retrieved because it has not been set yet.
At y:\SimpleTypingError.ps1:4 char:27
+ 'The value of $c is: ' + $c <<<<
PS C:\>
```

When you return to the SimpleTypingError.ps1 script and examine it, you will see that the sum of *$a* and *$b* is assigned to *$d* and not assigned to *$c*. The way to correct the problem is to assign the sum of *$a* and *$b* to *$c* and not to *$d* (which was probably the original intention). It is possible to include the Set-PSDebug –*Strict* command in your scripts to provide a quick check for uninitialized variables while you are actually writing the script and therefore avoid the error completely.

If you routinely use an expanding string to display the value of your variables, you need to be aware that an uninitialized variable is not reported as an error. The SimpleTypingErrorNotReported.ps1 script uses an expanding string to display the value of the *$c* variable. The first instance of the *$c* variable is escaped by using the backtick character, which causes the variable name to be displayed and does not expand its value. The second occurrence of the *$c* variable is expanded as shown in the following line of code.

```
"The value of `$c is: $c"
```

When the SimpleTypingErrorNotReported.ps1 script is run, the following is displayed.

```
PS C:\> Set-PSDebug -Strict
PS C:\> y:\SimpleTypingErrorNotReported.ps1
The value of $c is:
PS C:\>
```

The complete SimpleTypingErrorNotReported.ps1 script is shown here.

SimpleTypingErrorNotReported.ps1
```
$a = 2
$b = 5
$d = $a + $b
"The value of `$c is: $c"
```

To disable StrictMode, use the `Set-PSDebug` *–off* command.

Using the Set-StrictMode cmdlet

The `Set-StrictMode` cmdlet can also be used to enable StrictMode. It has the advantage of being scope aware. Where the `Set-PSDebug` cmdlet applies globally, if the `Set-StrictMode` cmdlet is used inside a function, StrictMode is enabled for that function only. There are two modes of operation that can be defined when using the `Set-StrictMode` cmdlet. The first mode is version 1, which behaves in the same way as the `Set-PSDebug` *–strict* command (except that scope awareness is enforced).

```
PS C:\> Set-StrictMode -Version 1
PS C:\> y:\SimpleTypingError.ps1
The variable '$c' cannot be retrieved because it has not been set.
At y:\SimpleTypingError.ps1:4 char:28
+ 'The value of $c is: ' + $c <<<<
    + CategoryInfo          : InvalidOperation: (c:Token) [], RuntimeException
    + FullyQualifiedErrorId : VariableIsUndefined
PS C:\>
```

The `Set-StrictMode` cmdlet is not able to detect the uninitialized variable contained in the expanding string that is shown in the SimpleTypingErrorNotDetected.ps1 script.

When version 2 mode is enacted, the technique of calling a function, such as a method, is enforced. The AddTwoError.ps1 script passes two values to the *Add-Two* function using method notation. Because method notation is allowed when calling functions, no error is typically generated. However, the method notation of passing parameters for functions works only when there is a single value to pass to the function. To pass multiple parameters, the function notation must be used as shown here.

```
Add-Two 1 2
```

Another way to correctly call the *Add-Two* function is to use the parameter names when passing the values.

```
Add-Two -a 1 -b 2
```

Either of the two syntaxes will produce the correct result. The method notation of calling the function displays incorrect information but does not generate an error. When an incorrect value is returned from a function and no error is generated, it can take a significant amount of time to debug. The method notation of calling the *Add-Two* function is used in the AddTwoError.ps1 script.

```
Add-Two(1,2)
```

When the script is run and the `Set-StrictMode` *–Version 2* command is not enabled, no error is generated. The output seems confusing because the results of adding the two variables *$a* and *$b* are not displayed.

```
PS C:\> y:\AddTwoError.ps1
1
2
PS C:\>
```

Once the `Set-StrictMode` *–Version 2* command is entered and the AddTwoError.ps1 script is run, an error is generated. The error that is generated states that the function was called as if it were a method. The error points to the exact line where the error occurred and shows the function call that caused the error. The function call is preceded by a + sign, followed by the name of the function, and then followed by four arrows that indicate what was passed to the function. The error message is shown here.

```
PS C:\> Set-StrictMode -Version 2
PS C:\> y:\AddTwoError.ps1
The function or command was called as if it were a method. Parameters should be
 separated by spaces. For information about parameters, see the about_Parameters
Help topic.
At Y:\AddTwoError.ps1:7 char:8
+ Add-Two <<<< (1,2)
    + CategoryInfo          : InvalidOperation: (:) [], RuntimeException
    + FullyQualifiedErrorId : StrictModeFunctionCallWithParens
PS C:\>
```

The complete AddTwoError.ps1 script is shown here.

AddTwoError.ps1
```
Function Add-Two ($a,$b)
{
 $a + $b
}


Add-Two(1,2)
```

Debugging Scripts

The new debugging features of Windows PowerShell 2.0 make the use of the `Set-PSDebug` cmdlet seem rudimentary or even cumbersome. When you become more familiar with the debugging features of Windows PowerShell 2.0, you might decide to never look at the `Set-PSDebug` cmdlet again. Several new cmdlets were created to enable debugging from both the Windows PowerShell console and from the Windows PowerShell Integrated Scripting Environment (ISE). The *Windows PowerShell ISE* is an integrated scripting environment that includes a Windows PowerShell console and a Windows PowerShell script editor in a single tool. Some people refer to the Windows PowerShell ISE as "graphical Windows PowerShell."

The new debugging cmdlets are listed in Table 17-2.

TABLE 17-2 Windows PowerShell Debugging cmdlets

CMDLET NAME	CMDLET FUNCTION
`Set-PSBreakpoint`	Sets breakpoints on lines, variables, and commands
`Get-PSBreakpoint`	Gets breakpoints in the current session
`Disable-PSBreakpoint`	Turns off breakpoints in the current session
`Enable-PSBreakpoint`	Re-enables breakpoints in the current session
`Remove-PSBreakpoint`	Deletes breakpoints from the current session
`Get-PSCallStack`	Displays the current call stack

NOTES FROM THE FIELD

Debugging in Windows PowerShell

Andy Schneider, Systems Engineer
Author of Get-PowerShell Blog

I have always found the origin of words to be fascinating. Apparently, the terms "bug" and "debugging" in regard to computers are attributed to Admiral Grace Hopper in the 1940s.

> *While she was working on a Mark II Computer at Harvard University, her associates discovered a moth stuck in a relay and thereby impeding operation, whereupon she remarked that they were "debugging" the system. –Wikipedia*

When I first started scripting and writing a little code, the concept of debugging something seemed to be a very daunting task. However, I have found that by using a few simple steps and thinking through the code, I can debug most of my scripts fairly quickly.

Ninety-nine percent of the time, debugging scripts requires the ability to watch a variable at some point in a script or a function. Have you ever written a function and thought, "If only I knew what *x* was before *y* started messing with it?" A former boss of mine used to tell me when I was troubleshooting network issues to "be the bit." You have to know exactly where you came from and exactly what your next hop is. Debugging code is similar, but you have to "be the variable."

Windows PowerShell 2.0 offers some great tools for watching variables: the breakpoints. Breakpoints allow you to pause running code in the middle of execution and poke around to see what's happening. The Windows PowerShell ISE makes using breakpoints even easier. You can set a breakpoint on any line in the ISE by using the Debug menu and choosing Toggle Breakpoint or by using the F9 shortcut key.

One thing to be aware of that wasn't immediately intuitive to me is that, when you set a breakpoint in the ISE, it highlights the line on which you set the breakpoint. However, the script will run up to the beginning of that line, but the line itself will not be executed. Remember that you must add the breakpoint after the last line you want to execute. From that point, you can use the Step Into function in the ISE and walk through the rest of your code.

Another feature that I have used is setting a breakpoint based on a variable. Rather than specifying a breakpoint on line 45 column 1, you can create a breakpoint that is triggered any time that a particular variable is accessed. You can do this by using the Set-PSBreakpoint cmdlet and the *variable* parameter. Be sure that when you specify the variable, such as *$var*, that you use only the name of the variable (*var*) and not the dollar sign (*$var*).

One last bit of information that I didn't notice right away was how to navigate within the nested prompt once I hit a breakpoint. If you type **?** or **h**, you will see some usage information that explains how to navigate within this "mini shell." It is interesting that the "nested>" prompt displays this usage information when you press **?**. Under typical circumstances, **?** is an alias for the Where-Object cmdlet, as shown when you type **?** at a normal prompt. Within the nested prompt, there are shortcuts to all of the items in the ISE Debug menu.

The bottom line is that you should not be intimidated by debugging code. With a methodical approach and the tools offered by Windows PowerShell 2.0, the line of code that is causing you grief will bubble up to the top fairly quickly.

Setting Breakpoints

The new debugging features in Windows PowerShell use breakpoints. A breakpoint is very familiar to developers who have used products such as Microsoft Visual Studio in the past. Yet for IT professionals who come from a VBScript background, the concept of a breakpoint is somewhat foreign. A *breakpoint* is a spot in the script where you want the execution of the script to pause. Because the script pauses, it is similar to the stepping functionality shown earlier in this chapter. However, because you control where the breakpoint will occur instead of halting on each line of the script, the stepping experience of breakpoints is much faster. In addition, because there are numerous methods to use to set the breakpoint (instead of merely stepping through the script line by line), the breakpoint can be tailored to reveal precisely the information for which you are looking.

Setting a Breakpoint on a Line Number

To set a breakpoint, you use the Set-PSBreakpoint cmdlet. The easiest way to set a break-point is to set it on line 1 of the script. To set a breakpoint on the first line of the script, you use the *line* parameter and *–script* parameter. When you set a breakpoint, an instance of the *System.Management.Automation.LineBreak* Microsoft .NET Framework class is returned and lists the *ID*, *Script*, and *Line* properties that were assigned when the breakpoint was created.

```
PS C:\> Set-PSBreakpoint -line 1 -script Y:\BadScript.ps1
  ID Script            Line Command        Variable        Action
  -- ------            ---- -------         --------        ------
   0 BadScript.ps1        1
```

This breakpoint causes the script to break immediately. You can then step through the function in the same way as when using the Set-PSDebug cmdlet with the *step* parameter. When you run the script, it hits the breakpoint that is set on the first line of the script, and Windows PowerShell enters the script debugger. Windows PowerShell enters the debugger every time that the BadScript.ps1 script is run from the Y: drive. When Windows PowerShell enters the debugger, the Windows PowerShell prompt changes to [DBG]: PS C:\>>> to visually alert you that you are inside the Windows PowerShell debugger. To step to the next line in the script, you type **s**. To quit the debugging session, you type **q**. The debugging commands are not case sensitive.

```
PS C:\> Y:\BadScript.ps1
Hit Line breakpoint on 'Y:\BadScript.ps1:1'

BadScript.ps1:1    #
-----------------------------------------------------------------------
[DBG]: PS C:\>>> s
BadScript.ps1:16   Function AddOne([int]$num)
[DBG]: PS C:\>>> s
BadScript.ps1:21   Function AddTwo([int]$num)
[DBG]: PS C:\>>> s
BadScript.ps1:26   Function SubOne([int]$num)
[DBG]: PS C:\>>> s
BadScript.ps1:31   Function TimesOne([int]$num)
[DBG]: PS C:\>>> s
BadScript.ps1:36   Function TimesTwo([int]$num)
```

```
[DBG]: PS C:\>>> s
BadScript.ps1:41   Function DivideNum([int]$num)
[DBG]: PS C:\>>> s
BadScript.ps1:48   $num = 0
[DBG]: PS C:\>>> s
BadScript.ps1:49   SubOne($num) | DivideNum($num)
[DBG]: PS C:\>>> s
BadScript.ps1:28      $num-1
[DBG]: PS C:\>>> s
BadScript.ps1:43    12/$num
[DBG]: PS C:\>>> s
                              if ($_.FullyQualifiedErrorId -ne
"NativeCommandErrorMessage" -and $ErrorView -ne "CategoryView")
{[DBG]: PS C:\>>> q
PS C:\>
```

LESSONS LEARNED

When you specify a breakpoint on a script, keep in mind that breakpoints are dependent on the location of the specific script. When you create a breakpoint for a script, you specify the location to the script for which you want to set a breakpoint. I often have several copies of a script that I keep in different locations (for version control). I sometimes become confused when in a long debugging session and open up the wrong version of the script to debug it. This doesn't work. If the script is identical in all respects except for the path to the script, the script will not break. If you want to use a single breakpoint that applies to a specific script that is stored in multiple locations, you can set the breakpoint for the condition inside the Windows PowerShell console, and you do not use the *–script* parameter.

Setting a Breakpoint on a Variable

Setting a breakpoint on line 1 of the script is useful for easily entering a debug session, but setting a breakpoint on a variable can often make a problem with a script easy to detect. Of course, this is especially true when you have already determined that the problem pertains to a variable that is either being assigned a value or is being ignored. Three modes can be configured when the breakpoint is specified for a variable, and the modes are specified by using the *mode* parameter. The three modes of operation are listed in Table 17-3.

TABLE 17-3 Variable Breakpoint Access Modes

ACCESS MODE	MEANING
Write	Stops execution immediately before a new value is written to the variable.
Read	Stops execution when the variable is read, that is, when its value is accessed to be either assigned, displayed, or used. In read mode, execution does not stop when the value of the variable changes.
Readwrite	Stops execution when the variable is read or written.

To determine when the BadScript.ps1 script writes to the *$num* variable, you can use the write mode. When you specify the value for the *variable* parameter, do not include the dollar sign in front of the variable name. To set a breakpoint on a variable, you only need to supply the path to the script, the name of the variable, and the access mode. When a variable breakpoint is set, the *System.Management.Automation.LineBreak* .NET Framework class object that is returned does not include the access mode value. This is true even if you use the Get-PSBreakpoint cmdlet to directly access the breakpoint. If you pipeline the *System.Management.Automation.LineBreak* .NET Framework class object to the Format-List cmdlet, you will be able to see that the access mode property is available. In this example, we set a breakpoint when the *$num* variable is written to in the Y:\BadScript.ps1 script.

```
PS C:\> Set-PSBreakpoint -Variable num -Mode write -Script Y:\BadScript.ps1
  ID Script            Line Command      Variable        Action
  -- ------            ---- -------      --------        ------
   3 BadScript.ps1                       num

PS C:\> Get-PSBreakpoint
  ID Script            Line Command      Variable        Action
  -- ------            ---- -------      --------        ------
   3 BadScript.ps1                       num

PS C:\> Get-PSBreakpoint  | Format-List * -Force
AccessMode : Write
Variable   : num
Action     :
Enabled    : True
HitCount   : 0
Id         : 3
Script     : Y:\BadScript.ps1
```

When you run the script after setting the breakpoint (if the other breakpoints have been removed or deactivated, which will be discussed later), the script will enter the Windows PowerShell debugger when the breakpoint is hit, that is, when the value of the *$num* variable is written to. If you step through the script by using the *s* command, you will be able to follow the sequence of operations. Only one breakpoint is hit when the script is run, which is on line 48 when the value is set to 0.

```
PS C:\> Y:\BadScript.ps1
Hit Variable breakpoint on 'Y:\BadScript.ps1:$num' (Write access)

BadScript.ps1:48   $num = 0
[DBG]: PS C:\>>> $num
[DBG]: PS C:\>>> Write-Host $num

[DBG]: PS C:\>>> s
BadScript.ps1:49  SubOne($num) | DivideNum($num)
[DBG]: PS C:\>>> $num
0
```

To set a breakpoint on a read operation for the variable, specify the *variable* parameter and the name of the variable, specify the *–script* parameter with the path to the script, and set *read* as the value for the *mode* parameter.

```
PS C:\> Set-PSBreakpoint -Variable num -Script Y:\BadScript.ps1 -Mode read
```

ID Script	Line Command	Variable	Action
4 BadScript.ps1		num	

When you run the script, a breakpoint is displayed each time you hit a read operation on the variable. Each breakpoint is displayed in the Windows PowerShell console as Hit Variable breakpoint followed by the path to the script and the access mode of the variable. In the BadScript.ps1 script, the value of the *$num* variable is read several times. The truncated output is shown here.

```
PS C:\> Y:\BadScript.ps1
Hit Variable breakpoint on 'Y:\BadScript.ps1:$num' (Read access)

BadScript.ps1:49   SubOne($num) | DivideNum($num)
[DBG]: PS C:\>>> s
Hit Variable breakpoint on 'Y:\BadScript.ps1:$num' (Read access)

BadScript.ps1:49   SubOne($num) | DivideNum($num)
[DBG]: PS C:\>>> s
BadScript.ps1:28   $num-1
[DBG]: PS C:\>>> s
Hit Variable breakpoint on 'Y:\BadScript.ps1:$num' (Read access)

BadScript.ps1:28   $num-1
[DBG]: PS C:\>>> s
```

If you set readwrite as the access mode for the *mode* parameter for the variable *$num* for the BadScript.ps1 script, you receive the feedback shown here.

```
PS C:\> Set-PSBreakpoint -Variable num -Mode readwrite -Script Y:\BadScript.ps1
```

ID Script	Line Command	Variable	Action
-- ------	---- -------	--------	------
6 BadScript.ps1		num	

When you run the script (assuming that you have disabled the other breakpoints), you will hit a breakpoint each time that the *$num* variable is read to or written to. If you get tired of typing **s** and pressing Enter while you are in the debugging session, you can press Enter to repeat your previous *s* command as you continue to step through the breakpoints. When the script has stepped through the code and hit the error in the BadScript.ps1 script, **q** is typed to exit the debugger.

```
PS C:\> Y:\BadScript.ps1
Hit Variable breakpoint on 'Y:\BadScript.ps1:$num' (ReadWrite access)

BadScript.ps1:48   $num = 0
[DBG]: PS C:\>>> s
BadScript.ps1:49   SubOne($num) | DivideNum($num)
[DBG]: PS C:\>>>
Hit Variable breakpoint on 'Y:\BadScript.ps1:$num' (ReadWrite access)

BadScript.ps1:49   SubOne($num) | DivideNum($num)
[DBG]: PS C:\>>>
Hit Variable breakpoint on 'Y:\BadScript.ps1:$num' (ReadWrite access)

BadScript.ps1:49   SubOne($num) | DivideNum($num)
[DBG]: PS C:\>>>
BadScript.ps1:28   $num-1
[DBG]: PS C:\>>>
Hit Variable breakpoint on 'Y:\BadScript.ps1:$num' (ReadWrite access)

BadScript.ps1:28   $num-1
[DBG]: PS C:\>>>
BadScript.ps1:43   12/$num
[DBG]: PS C:\>>>
Hit Variable breakpoint on 'Y:\BadScript.ps1:$num' (ReadWrite access)

BadScript.ps1:43   12/$num
[DBG]: PS C:\>>>
                                if ($_.FullyQualifiedErrorId -ne
"NativeCommandErrorMessage" -and $ErrorView -ne "CategoryView") {
[DBG]: PS C:\>>> q
PS C:\>
```

When using the readwrite access mode of the *mode* parameter for breaking on variables, the breakpoint does not tell you whether the operation is a read operation or a write operation. You must look at the code that is being executed to determine whether the value of the variable is being written or read.

By specifying a value for the *–action* parameter, you can include regular Windows PowerShell code that executes when the breakpoint is hit. For example, if you are trying to follow the value of a variable within the script and you want to display the value of the variable each time the breakpoint is hit, you might want to specify an *–action* parameter that uses the Write-Host cmdlet to display the value of the variable. By using the Write-Host cmdlet, you can also include a string that indicates the value of the variable being displayed. This process is crucial for detecting variables that never initialize because it is easier to notice the displayed value than it is to spot a blank line. The technique of using the Write-Host cmdlet in an *–action* parameter is shown here.

```
PS C:\> Set-PSBreakpoint -Variable num -Action { write-host "num = $num" ;
Break } -Mode readwrite -script Y:\BadScript.ps1


  ID Script            Line Command       Variable       Action
  -- ------            ---- -------       --------       ------
   5 BadScript.ps1                        num            write-host "...
```

When you run Y:\BadScript.ps1 with the breakpoint set, you receive the following output inside the Windows PowerShell debugger.

```
PS C:\> Y:\BadScript.ps1
num =
Hit Variable breakpoint on 'Y:\BadScript.ps1:$num' (ReadWrite access)

BadScript.ps1:48   $num = 0
[DBG]: PS C:\>>> s
BadScript.ps1:49   SubOne($num) | DivideNum($num)
[DBG]: PS C:\>>> s
Set-PSBreakpoint -Variable num -Action { write-host "num = $num" ; break }
-Mode readwrite -script Y:\BadScript.ps1
[DBG]: PS C:\>>> s
num = 0
Set-PSBreakpoint -Variable num -Action { write-host "num = $num" ; break }
-Mode readwrite -script Y:\BadScript.ps1
[DBG]: PS C:\>>> c
Hit Variable breakpoint on 'Y:\BadScript.ps1:$num' (ReadWrite access)

BadScript.ps1:49   SubOne($num) | DivideNum($num)
[DBG]: PS C:\>>>
```

Setting a Breakpoint on a Command

To set the breakpoint on a command, you use the *–command* parameter. You can break on a call to a Windows PowerShell cmdlet, function, or external script. You can use aliases when setting breakpoints. When you create a breakpoint for a cmdlet on an alias, the debugger will hit on the use of the alias only and not the actual command name. In addition, you do not have to specify a script for the debugger to break. If you do not type a path to a script, the debugger will be active for any scripts within the Windows PowerShell console session. Every occurrence of the *Foreach* command will cause the debugger to break. Because *Foreach* is a language statement as well as an alias for the Foreach-Object cmdlet, you might wonder whether the Windows PowerShell debugger will break on both the language statement and the use of the alias for the cmdlet—the answer is no. You can set breakpoints on language statements, but the debugger will not break on a language statement. As shown here, the debugger breaks on the use of the *Foreach* alias, but not on the use of the Foreach-Object cmdlet.

```
PS C:\> Set-PSBreakpoint -Command foreach

 ID Script          Line Command      Variable      Action
 -- ------          ---- -------      --------      ------
 10                      foreach

PS C:\> 1..3 | Foreach-Object { $_}
1
2
3
PS C:\> 1..3 | foreach { $_ }
Hit Command breakpoint on 'foreach'

1..3 | foreach { $_ }
[DBG]: PS C:\>>> c
1
Hit Command breakpoint on 'foreach'

1..3 | foreach { $_ }
[DBG]: PS C:\>>> c
2
Hit Command breakpoint on 'foreach'

1..3 | foreach { $_ }
[DBG]: PS C:\>>> c
3
```

When creating a breakpoint for the *DivideNum* function used by the Y:\BadScript.ps1 script, you can omit the path to the script because it is the only script that uses the *DivideNum* function. Although doing this makes the command easier to type, it might become confusing when looking through a collection of breakpoints. If you are debugging multiple scripts in a single Windows PowerShell console session, it might become confusing if you do not specify the script to which the breakpoint applies—unless, of course, you are specifically debugging the function as it is used in multiple scripts. Creating a command breakpoint for the *DivideNum* function is shown here.

```
PS C:\> Set-PSBreakpoint -Command DivideNum


ID Script           Line Command        Variable      Action
-- ------           ---- -------        --------      ------
 7                        DivideNum
```

When you run the script, it hits a breakpoint when the *DivideNum* function is called. When BadScript.ps1 hits the *DivideNum* function, the value of *$num* is 0. As you step through the *DivideNum* function, you assign the value of 2 to the *$num* variable; the result of 6 is displayed, and then the 12/$num operation is carried out. Next, the *AddOne* function is called, and the value of *$num* is once again 0. When the *AddTwo* function is called, the value of *$num* is also 0.

```
PS C:\> Y:\BadScript.ps1
Hit Command breakpoint on 'DivideNum'

BadScript.ps1:49  SubOne($num) | DivideNum($num)
[DBG]: PS C:\>>> s
BadScript.ps1:43    12/$num
[DBG]: PS C:\>>> $num
0
[DBG]: PS C:\>>> $num =2
[DBG]: PS C:\>>> s
6
BadScript.ps1:50  AddOne($num) | AddTwo($num)
[DBG]: PS C:\>>> s
BadScript.ps1:18    $num+1
[DBG]: PS C:\>>> $num
0
[DBG]: PS C:\>>> s
```

```
BadScript.ps1:23    $num+2
[DBG]: PS C:\>>> $num
0
[DBG]: PS C:\>>> s
2
PS C:\>
```

The Best Debugging

Juan Carlos Ruiz Lopez, Senior Premier Field Engineer
Microsoft Corporation Spain

Fortunately (or unfortunately depending on your perspective), my experience with the Windows PowerShell debugger is a bit limited. Because the Windows PowerShell scripting language is really powerful, most of the loops required by other scripting languages are not needed. In many cases, each cmdlet silently performs the needed looping. These automatic looping features result in less complicated scripts that often translate into less debugging.

In previous scripting languages, a condition such as an out-of-range loop often necessitated extensive debugging to track down. With Windows PowerShell, you are not immediately faced with these looping problems when running scripts. The best debugging occurs when you don't need debugging. Of course, there are still some classical situations when debugging is a necessity, such as when you call SomeFunction(Param1,param2) with the wrong syntax. For most of these situations, adding a `Write-Debug` statement and showing the received variables or parameters will generally suffice. Even better, you can create your own *MyDebug* function so that you can control the colors and formatting that are displayed when you print the information.

I still recommend that you spend some time playing with breakpoints because they really are easy to use and should be learned. You might not need to use them often, but the minimal effort put forth to learn debugging skills is worth it. Even if you never use the Windows PowerShell debugger, you will gain more insight into how Windows PowerShell works.

My favorite Windows PowerShell debugging command is the *k* command, which calls the `Get-PSCallStack` cmdlet. I like to use the *k* command because it is very nice to see who is calling the commands, which is especially important when you have a constantly changing script library and the function you just called seems to be in the wrong module.

Responding to Breakpoints

When the script reaches a breakpoint, control of the Windows PowerShell console is turned over to you. Inside the debugger, you can type any legal Windows PowerShell command and even run cmdlets, such as `Get-Process` or `Get-Service`. In addition, several new debugging commands can be typed into the Windows PowerShell console when a breakpoint is reached. The available debug commands are listed in Table 17-4.

TABLE 17-4 Windows PowerShell Debugger Commands

KEYBOARD SHORTCUT	COMMAND NAME	COMMAND MEANING
s	Step-into	Executes the next statement and then stops.
v	Step-over	Executes the next statement, but skips functions and invocations. The skipped statements are executed but not stepped through.
o	Step-out	Steps out of the current function and up one level if nested. If the command occurs in the main body, it continues to the end of the script or the next breakpoint. The skipped statements are executed but not stepped through.
c	Continue	Continues to run until the script is complete or until the next breakpoint is reached. The skipped statements are executed but not stepped through.
l	List	Displays the part of the script that is executing. By default, it displays the current line, five previous lines, and 10 subsequent lines. To continue listing the script, press Enter.
l <m>	List	Displays 16 lines of the script beginning with the line number specified by <m>.
l <m> <n>	List	Displays <n> lines of the script beginning with the line number specified by <m>.
q	Stop	Stops executing the script and exits the debugger.
k	Get-PSCallStack	Displays the current call stack.
<Enter>	Repeat	Repeats the last command if it was Step-into (*s*), Step-over (*v*), or List (*l*). Otherwise, represents a submit action.
h or *?*	Help	Displays the debugger command Help.

Using the *DivideNum* function as a breakpoint, when the BadScript.ps1 script is run, the script breaks on line 49 when the *DivideNum* function is called. The *s* debugging command is used to step into the next statement and to stop prior to actually executing the command. The *l* debugging command is used to list the five previous lines of code from the BadScript.ps1 script and the 10 lines of code that follow the current line in the script.

```
PS C:\> Y:\BadScript.ps1
Hit Command breakpoint on 'Y:\BadScript.ps1:dividenum'

BadScript.ps1:49  SubOne($num) | DivideNum($num)
[DBG]: PS C:\>>> s
BadScript.ps1:43    12/$num
[DBG]: PS C:\>>> l

    38:    $num*2
    39:  } #end function TimesTwo
    40:
    41:  Function DivideNum([int]$num)
    42:  {
    43:*   12/$num
    44:  } #end function DivideNum
    45:
    46:  # *** Entry Point to Script ***
    47:
    48:  $num = 0
    49:  SubOne($num) | DivideNum($num)
    50:  AddOne($num) | AddTwo($num)
    51:
```

After reviewing the code, the *o* debugging command is used to step out of the *DivideNum* function. The remaining code in the *DivideNum* function is still executed, and therefore the divide by zero error is displayed. There are no more prompts until the next line of executing code is met. The *v* debugging statement is used to step over the remaining functions in the script, which are still executed. The results are displayed at the Windows PowerShell console.

```
[DBG]: PS C:\>>> o
Attempted to divide by zero.
At Y:\BadScript.ps1:43 char:5
+   12/ <<<< $num
    + CategoryInfo          : NotSpecified: (:) [], RuntimeException
    + FullyQualifiedErrorId : RuntimeException

BadScript.ps1:50  AddOne($num) | AddTwo($num)
[DBG]: PS C:\>>> v
2
PS C:\>
```

Listing Breakpoints

Once you set several breakpoints, you might want to know where they are created. One thing to keep in mind is that breakpoints are stored in the Windows PowerShell environment and not in the individual script. Using the debugging features does not involve editing the script or modifying your source code, and the debugging features enable you to debug any script without worrying about corrupting the code. However, because you might have set several breakpoints in the Windows PowerShell environment during a typical debugging session, you might want to know what breakpoints have already been defined. To find out this information, you can use the Get-PSBreakpoint cmdlet.

```
PS C:\> Get-PSBreakpoint
   ID Script            Line Command      Variable      Action
   -- ------            ---- -------      --------      ------
   11 BadScript.ps1          dividenum
   13 BadScript.ps1          if
    3 BadScript.ps1                       num
    5 BadScript.ps1                       num
    6 BadScript.ps1                       num
    7                        DivideNum
    8                        foreach
    9                        gps
   10                        foreach
PS C:\>
```

If you are interested in which breakpoints are currently enabled, you need to use the Where-Object cmdlet and pipeline the results of the Get-PSBreakpoint cmdlet.

```
PS C:\> Get-PSBreakpoint | where { $_.enabled }

   ID Script            Line Command      Variable      Action
   -- ------            ---- -------      --------      ------
   11 BadScript.ps1          dividenum

PS C:\>
```

You can also pipeline the results of Get-PSBreakpoint to a Format-Table cmdlet.

```
PS C:\> Get-PSBreakpoint |
Format-Table -Property id, script, command, variable, enabled -AutoSize

Id Script          Command   variable Enabled
-- ------          -------   -------- -------
11 Y:\BadScript.ps1 dividenum          True
13 Y:\BadScript.ps1 if                False
 3 Y:\BadScript.ps1           num      False
 5 Y:\BadScript.ps1           num      False
 6 Y:\BadScript.ps1           num      False
 7                 DivideNum           False
 8                 foreach             False
 9                 gps                 False
10                 foreach             False
```

Because the creation of the custom formatted breakpoint table requires a bit of typing and because the display is extremely helpful, you might consider placing the code into a function that can be included in your profile or in a custom debugging module. Such a function is shown here stored in the Get-EnabledBreakpointsFunction.ps1 script.

```
Get-EnabledBreakpointsFunction.ps1
Function Get-EnabledBreakpoints
{
  Get-PSBreakpoint |
  Format-Table -Property id, script, command, variable, enabled -AutoSize
}

# *** Entry Point to Script ***

Get-EnabledBreakpoints
```

Enabling and Disabling Breakpoints

While you are debugging a script, you might need to disable a particular breakpoint to see how the script runs. To do this, you can use the Disable-PSBreakpoint cmdlet.

```
Disable-PSBreakpoint -id 0
```

On the other hand, you might also need to enable a breakpoint. To do this, you can use the Enable-PSBreakpoint cmdlet.

```
Enable-PSBreakpoint -id 1
```

As a best practice while in a debugging session, you can selectively enable and disable breakpoints to see how the script is running in an attempt to troubleshoot the script. To keep track of the status of breakpoints, you can use the Get-PSBreakpoint cmdlet as illustrated in the previous section.

Debugging Scripts

Vasily Gusev, Systems Administrator, MCSE: Security/Messaging,
MCITP: Enterprise/Server Administrator, Microsoft MVP: Windows PowerShell
Microsoft Corporation

In Windows PowerShell 2.0, new useful debugging features are added. First, take a look at the `Set-PSBreakpoint` cmdlet, which you can use to assign breakpoints to selected lines of scripts and execute cmdlets, functions, or variables.

When I do Windows PowerShell debugging, for example, instead of modifying the body of my script commands to include a number of Write-Debug commands that will output a value of *$var* to the console, I simply assign a breakpoint to the event of its value change. This is a much simpler process and does not require additional cleanup of the script afterward to remove all of the additional commands.

```
Set-PSBreakpoint -Variable var -Mode write
```

After I set the breakpoint inside the Windows PowerShell console and before each change in the value of the *$var* variable, PowerShell stops the execution of commands and enters into debug mode. I can distinguish when I am in debug mode because the prompt changes to include [DBG] at the beginning of each line. In this mode, I can execute all of the usual Windows PowerShell commands as well as view and change variable values.

Yet, the main advantage of debug mode is that special debugging commands are available, such as Step-into, Step-over, and Step-out, that allow me to move through the executing code without ever leaving debug mode. The Continue command exits from debug mode and executes all of the remaining code. The Quit command exits the debugger and halts the execution of the script.

Also in the arsenal of Windows PowerShell debugging commands is one that I find very useful while doing command-line debugging—the List command. The List command displays the current position of the debugger and, by default, also displays the five lines of code before the active line and 10 lines of code after it.

The Enter key feature simplifies working from the command line when debugging because it repeats the last command entered into the debugger. I can execute a Step-into command, and the Step-into command will execute again each time I press Enter.

I can obtain a list of all debugger commands and their descriptions by typing the letter **h** or using the question mark **?** symbol. This list is useful when I need to quickly refresh myself on the available commands.

The same breakpoints can be set to the event of calling specific commands and functions by using the *–command* switch when creating the breakpoint via the Set-PSBreakpoint cmdlet. You might have guessed that parameters such as *line* and *column* are used for setting breakpoints in the body of a script. Of course, they will work only if you also specify a script to debug by using the *–script* parameter.

Instead of pausing a script and entering the debugger, I can associate almost any action with a breakpoint. For example, if I need to debug a long-running script and cannot sit near the console at all times waiting for errors to occur, I can order the debugger to dump all variables into an XML file and continue running the script.

```
Set-PSBreakpoint -Variable var -Mode write -Action {Get-Variable |
Export-Clixml C:\dump.clixml}
```

Later, I can load this XML to perform variable analysis as shown here.

```
$Variables = Import-Clixml c:\dump.clixml
```

I can also specify a conditional expression when creating a breakpoint that will take an action if a certain condition is true. For example, the command shown here will set up a breakpoint that only works if the value of the *$DebugIsOn* variable is set to *$true*.

```
Set-PSBreakpoint -Variable var -Mode write -Action `
{if ($DebugIsOn){break}}
```

It is possible to manage breakpoints after they are created by using other cmdlets that contain the PSBreakpoint noun. The names of these cmdlets are very intuitive. For example, the following command removes all breakpoints from the current session.

```
Get-PSBreakpoint | Remove-PSBreakpoint
```

You can also disable and enable breakpoints without removing the breakpoints by using the Disable-PSBreakpoint and Enable-PSBreakpoint cmdlets, respectively.

Deleting Breakpoints

When you are finished debugging the script, you will want to remove all of the breakpoints that were created during the Windows PowerShell session. There are two ways to do this. The first is to close the Windows PowerShell console. Although this is a good way to clean up the environment, you might not want to do this because you might have remote Windows PowerShell sessions defined or variables that are populated with the results of certain queries. To delete all of the breakpoints, you can use the Remove-PSBreakpoint cmdlet. Unfortunately, there is no *all* switch for the `Remove-PSBreakpoint` cmdlet. When deleting a breakpoint, the `Remove-PSBreakpoint` cmdlet requires the breakpoint ID number. To remove a single breakpoint, specify the ID number for the *–id* parameter.

```
Remove-PSBreakpoint –id 3
```

If you want to remove all of the breakpoints, pipeline the results from `Get-PSBreakpoint` to `Remove-PSBreakpoint`.

```
Get-PSBreakpoint | Remove-PSBreakpoint
```

If you want to remove only the breakpoints from a specific script, you can pipeline the results through the `Where-Object` cmdlet.

```
(Get-PSBreakpoint | Where-Object (ScriptName – eq "C:\Scripts\Test.ps1")) |
Removebreakpoint
```

INSIDE TRACK

Debugging Scripts with the Windows PowerShell ISE

Osama Sajid, Program Manager: Windows Manageability
Microsoft Corporation

The Windows PowerShell ISE is a complete script editor and debugger. If you have a script file (ps1) loaded in an ISE, you can set a breakpoint on a line using F9. When the script is run, the execution will stop at that line, and the ISE will allow you to perform one of the following common debugging tasks.

- Execute the line – Step Over (F10)
- Go inside a function – Step Into (F11)
- Execute the rest of the function and come out (Shift-F11)

Pressing F5 continues the execution of the script until the next breakpoint or until the end. These debug commands are also available through the Debug menu.

When the debugger is stopped at a breakpoint, you can view the value assigned to a variable by hovering the cursor on the variable. There is also a debugger prompt (>>>) in the command pane that allows you to execute commands. For example, you can get/set the value of a variable or execute a cmdlet.

Setting a breakpoint on a line is the simplest and most common way of debugging; however, complex situations can arise when you want to stop executing a script if the value of a variable changes or a particular command is executed. Although there is no direct way to halt the execution from the Windows PowerShell ISE user interface, there is a cmdlet that allows you to perform this action.

```
Set-PSBreakpoint  -variable val -Mode ReadWrite
```

This command sets a breakpoint on the variable named *val* and uses the *mode* parameter with a value of *ReadWrite* to stop execution when the value of the variable is read and just before the value changes.

```
Set-PSBreakpoint -command Get-Process
```

This command sets a breakpoint on the execution of the `Get-Process` cmdlet. Whenever Windows PowerShell executes the cmdlet, it will give control to the debugger.

Another interesting thing about the Windows PowerShell debugger is its capability to execute a script block when a breakpoint is hit.

```
 Set-PSBreakpoint -Variable val -Mode Read -Action `
{Write-Host "Alert: Value of X = $x"; if($val-eq 5){break}}
```

Use of the Windows PowerShell ISE makes debugging very easy. However, all Windows PowerShell debugging can be done from the command line without ISE menus and shortcuts. For example, you can obtain a list of all breakpoints by running `Get-PSBreakpoint` or by disabling a breakpoint using `Disable-PSBreakpoint`. Once the script execution stops on a breakpoint, you can use the following debugger commands in Windows PowerShell.

- *s*, Step-into
- *v*, Step-over
- *o*, Step-out
- *c*, Continue
- *q*, Stop

For more information about debugger commands, you can read "about_debuggers" in Windows PowerShell help.

Additional Resources

- The TechNet Script Center at *http://www.microsoft.com/technet/scriptcenter* contains numerous examples of debugging Windows PowerShell scripts.
- Take a look at Appendix E in *Windows PowerShell™ Scripting Guide* (Microsoft Press, 2008) for more information about troubleshooting scripts.
- On the companion media, you will find all of the scripts referred to in this chapter.

Windows PowerShell 2.0 cmdlets

WINDOWS POWERSHELL 2.0 SHIPS with some very interesting cmdlets. However, with more than 250 cmdlets on a default installation of Windows 7 (with modules loaded), the number of cmdlets can be a bit overwhelming. The following table contains a listing of the cmdlets and a description of their use.

TABLE A-1 Windows Powershell 2.0 cmdlets

NAME	SYNOPSIS
Add-BitsFile	Adds one or more files to an existing Background Intelligent Transfer Service (BITS) transfer job.
Add-Computer	Adds the local computer to a domain or workgroup.
Add-Content	Adds content to the specified items, such as adding words to a file.
Add-History	Appends entries to the session history.
Add-Member	Adds a user-defined custom member to an instance of a Windows PowerShell object.
Add-PSSnapin	Adds one or more Windows PowerShell snap-ins to the current session.
Add-Type	Adds a Microsoft .NET Framework type (a class) to a Windows PowerShell session (PSSession).
Checkpoint-Computer	Creates a system restore point on the local computer.
Clear-Content	Deletes the contents of an item, such as deleting the text from a file, but does not delete the item.
Clear-EventLog	Deletes all entries from specified event logs on the local or remote computers.
Clear-History	Deletes entries from the command history.

NAME	SYNOPSIS
Clear-Item	Deletes the contents of an item but does not delete the item.
Clear-ItemProperty	Deletes the value of a property but does not delete the property.
Clear-Variable	Deletes the value of a variable.
Compare-Object	Compares two sets of objects.
Complete-BitsTransfer	Completes a BITS transfer job.
Complete-Transaction	Commits the active transaction.
Connect-WSMan	Connects to the Windows Remote Management (WinRM) service on a remote computer.
ConvertFrom-CSV	Converts object properties in comma-separated value (CSV) format into CSV versions of the original objects.
ConvertFrom-SecureString	Converts a secure string into an encrypted standard string.
ConvertFrom-StringData	Converts a string containing one or more key/value pairs to a hash table.
Convert-Path	Converts a path from a Windows PowerShell path to a PowerShell provider path.
ConvertTo-CSV	Converts .NET Framework objects into a series of CSV variable-length strings.
ConvertTo-Html	Converts .NET Framework objects into HTML that can be displayed in a Web browser.
ConvertTo-SecureString	Converts encrypted standard strings to secure strings. It can also convert plain text to secure strings. It is used with ConvertFrom-SecureString and Read-Host.
ConvertTo-XML	Creates an XML-based representation of an object.
Copy-Item	Copies an item from one location to another within a namespace.
Copy-ItemProperty	Copies a property and value from a specified location to another location.
Debug-Process	Debugs one or more processes running on the local computer.
Disable-ComputerRestore	Disables the System Restore feature on the specified file system drive.
Disable-PSBreakpoint	Disables breakpoints in the current console.

NAME	SYNOPSIS
Disable-PSSessionConfiguration	Denies access to the session configurations on the local computer.
Disable-WSManCredSSP	Disables Credential Security Service Provider (CredSSP) authentication on a client computer.
Disconnect-WSMan	Disconnects the client from the WinRM service on a remote computer.
Enable-ComputerRestore	Enables the System Restore feature on the specified file system drive.
Enable-PSBreakpoint	Enables breakpoints in the current console.
Enable-PSRemoting	Configures the computer to receive remote commands.
Enable-PSSessionConfiguration	Enables session configurations on the local computer.
Enable-WSManCredSSP	Enables CredSSP authentication on a client computer.
Enter-PSSession	Starts an interactive session with a remote computer.
Exit-PSSession	Ends an interactive session with a remote computer.
Export-Alias	Exports information about currently defined aliases to a file.
Export-Clixml	Creates an XML-based representation of an object or objects and stores it in a file.
Export-Console	Exports the names of snap-ins in the current session to a console file.
Export-Counter	Takes *PerformanceCounterSampleSet* objects and exports them as counter log files.
Export-CSV	Converts .NET Framework objects into a series of CSV variable-length strings and saves the strings in a CSV file.
Export-FormatData	Saves formatting data from the current session in a formatting file.
Export-ModuleMember	Specifies the module members that are exported.
Export-PSSession	Imports commands from another session and saves them in a Windows PowerShell module.
ForEach-Object	Performs an operation against each of a set of input objects.
Format-Custom	Uses a customized view to format the output.
Format-List	Formats the output as a list of properties in which each property appears on a new line.
Format-Table	Formats the output as a table.

NAME	SYNOPSIS
Format-Wide	Formats objects as a wide table that displays only one property of each object.
Get-Acl	Gets the security descriptor for a resource, such as a file or registry key.
Get-Alias	Gets the aliases for the current session.
Get-AppLockerFileInformation	Gets the AppLocker file information from a list of files or an event log.
Get-AppLockerPolicy	Gets the local, effective, or domain AppLocker policy.
Get-AuthenticodeSignature	Gets information about the Authenticode signature in a file.
Get-BitsTransfer	Retrieves the associated *BitsJob* object for an existing BITS transfer job.
Get-ChildItem	Gets the items and child items in one or more specified locations.
Get-Command	Gets basic information about cmdlets and other elements of Windows PowerShell commands.
Get-ComputerRestorePoint	Gets the restore points on the local computer.
Get-Content	Gets the content of the item at the specified location.
Get-Counter	Gets performance counter data from local and remote computers.
Get-Credential	Gets a credential object based on a user name and password.
Get-Culture	Gets the current culture set in the operating system.
Get-Date	Gets the current date and time.
Get-Event	Gets the events in the event queue.
Get-EventLog	Gets the events in an event log, or a list of the event logs, on the local or remote computers.
Get-EventSubscriber	Gets the event subscribers in the current session.
Get-ExecutionPolicy	Gets the execution policies for the current session.
Get-FormatData	Gets the formatting data in the current session.
Get-Help	Displays information about Windows PowerShell commands and concepts.
Get-History	Gets a list of the commands entered during the current session.

NAME	SYNOPSIS
Get-Host	Gets an object that represents the current host program. Also displays Windows PowerShell version and regional information by default.
Get-HotFix	Gets the hotfixes that are applied to the local and remote computers.
Get-Item	Gets the item at the specified location.
Get-ItemProperty	Gets the properties of a specified item.
Get-Job	Gets Windows PowerShell background jobs that are running in the current session.
Get-Location	Gets information about the current working location.
Get-Member	Gets the properties and methods of objects.
Get-Module	Gets the modules that are imported or that can be imported into the current session.
Get-PfxCertificate	Gets information about .pfx certificate files on the computer.
Get-Process	Gets the processes that are running on the local computer or a remote computer.
Get-PSBreakpoint	Gets the breakpoints that are set in the current session.
Get-PSCallStack	Displays the current call stack.
Get-PSDrive	Gets the Windows PowerShell drives in the current session.
Get-PSProvider	Gets information about the specified Windows PowerShell provider.
Get-PSSession	Gets the Windows PSSessions in the current session.
Get-PSSessionConfiguration	Gets the registered session configurations on the computer.
Get-PSSnapin	Gets the Windows PowerShell snap-ins on the computer.
Get-Random	Gets a random number or selects objects randomly from a collection.
Get-Service	Gets the services on a local or remote computer.
Get-TraceSource	Gets the Windows PowerShell components that are instrumented for tracing.
Get-Transaction	Gets the current (active) transaction.
Get-TroubleshootingPack	Gets information about a troubleshooting pack and can generate an answer file.

NAME	SYNOPSIS
Get-UICulture	Gets the current user interface (UI) culture settings in the operating system.
Get-Unique	Returns the unique items from a sorted list.
Get-Variable	Gets the variables in the current console.
Get-WinEvent	Gets events from event logs and event tracing log files on local and remote computers.
Get-WmiObject	Gets instances of Windows Management Instrumentation (WMI) classes or information about the available classes.
Get-WSManCredSSP	Gets the CredSSP-related configuration for the client.
Get-WSManInstance	Displays management information for a resource instance specified by a Uniform Resource Identifier (URI).
Group-Object	Groups objects that contain the same value for specified properties.
Import-Alias	Imports an alias list from a file.
Import-Clixml	Imports a CLIXML file and creates corresponding objects within Windows PowerShell.
Import-Counter	Imports performance counter log files (.blg, .csv, .tsv) and creates the objects that represent each counter sample in the log.
Import-CSV	Converts object properties in a CSV file into CSV versions of the original objects.
Import-LocalizedData	Imports language-specific data into scripts and functions based on the UI culture that is selected for the operating system.
Import-Module	Adds modules to the current session.
Import-PSSession	Imports commands from another session into the current session.
Invoke-Command	Runs commands on local and remote computers.
Invoke-Expression	Runs commands or expressions on the local computer.
Invoke-History	Runs commands from the session history.
Invoke-Item	Performs the default action on the specified item.
Invoke-TroubleshootingPack	Executes a troubleshooting pack in interactive or unattended mode to fix a problem and then generates a results report.
Invoke-WmiMethod	Calls WMI methods.

NAME	SYNOPSIS
Invoke-WSManAction	Invokes an action on the object that is specified by the Resource URI and by the selectors.
Join-Path	Combines a path and a child path into a single path. The provider supplies the path delimiters.
Limit-EventLog	Sets the event log properties that limit the size of the event log and the age of its entries.
Measure-Command	Measures the time it takes to run script blocks and cmdlets.
Measure-Object	Calculates the numeric properties of objects and the characters, words, and lines in string objects, such as files of text.
Move-Item	Moves an item from one location to another.
Move-ItemProperty	Moves a property from one location to another.
New-Alias	Creates a new alias.
New-AppLockerPolicy	Creates a new AppLocker policy from a list of file information and other rule creation options.
New-Event	Creates a new event.
New-EventLog	Creates a new event log and a new event source on a local or remote computer.
New-Item	Creates a new item.
New-ItemProperty	Creates a new property for an item and sets its value. For example, you can use New-ItemProperty to create and change registry values and data, which are properties of a registry key.
New-Module	Creates a new dynamic module that exists only in memory.
New-ModuleManifest	Creates a new module manifest.
New-Object	Creates an instance of a Microsoft .NET Framework or Component Object Model (COM) object.
New-PSDrive	Creates a Windows PowerShell drive in the current session.
New-PSSession	Creates a persistent connection to a local or remote computer.
New-PSSessionOption	Creates an object that contains advanced options for a PSSession.
New-Service	Creates a new Windows service.

NAME	SYNOPSIS
New-TimeSpan	Creates a *TimeSpan* object.
New-Variable	Creates a new variable.
New-WebServiceProxy	Creates a Web service proxy object that lets you use and manage the Web service in Windows PowerShell.
New-WSManInstance	Creates a new instance of a management resource.
New-WSManSessionOption	Creates a WS-Management session option hash table to use as input parameters to the following WS-Management cmdlets: Get-WSManInstance Set-WSManInstance Invoke-WSManAction Connect-WSMan
Out-Default	Sends the output to the default formatter and to the default output cmdlet.
Out-File	Sends output to a file.
Out-GridView	Sends output to an interactive table in a separate window.
Out-Host	Sends output to the command line.
Out-Null	Deletes output instead of sending it to the console.
Out-Printer	Sends output to a printer.
Out-String	Sends objects to the host as a series of strings.
Pop-Location	Changes the current location to the location most recently pushed onto the stack. You can pop the location from the default stack or from a stack that you create by using the Push-Location cmdlet.
Push-Location	Adds the current location to the top of a list of locations (a stack).
Read-Host	Reads a line of input from the console.
Receive-Job	Gets the results of the Windows PowerShell background jobs in the current session.
Register-EngineEvent	Subscribes to events that are generated by the Windows PowerShell engine and by the New-Event cmdlet.
Register-ObjectEvent	Subscribes to the events that are generated by a Microsoft .NET Framework object.
Register-PSSessionConfiguration	Creates and registers a new session configuration.
Register-WmiEvent	Subscribes to a WMI event.

NAME	SYNOPSIS
Remove-BitsTransfer	Cancels a BITS transfer job.
Remove-Computer	Removes the local computer from a workgroup or domain.
Remove-Event	Deletes events from the event queue.
Remove-EventLog	Deletes an event log or unregisters an event source.
Remove-Item	Deletes the specified items.
Remove-ItemProperty	Deletes the property and its value from an item.
Remove-Job	Deletes a Windows PowerShell background job.
Remove-Module	Removes modules from the current session.
Remove-PSBreakpoint	Deletes breakpoints from the current console.
Remove-PSDrive	Removes a Windows PowerShell drive from its location.
Remove-PSSession	Closes one or more Windows PSSessions.
Remove-PSSnapin	Removes Windows PowerShell snap-ins from the current session.
Remove-Variable	Deletes a variable and its value.
Remove-WmiObject	Deletes an instance of an existing WMI class.
Remove-WSManInstance	Deletes a management resource instance.
Rename-Item	Renames an item in a Windows PowerShell provider namespace.
Rename-ItemProperty	Renames a property of an item.
Reset-ComputerMachinePassword	Resets the machine account password for the computer.
Resolve-Path	Resolves the wildcard characters in a path and displays the path contents.
Restart-Computer	Restarts (reboots) the operating system on local and remote computers.
Restart-Service	Stops and then starts one or more services.
Restore-Computer	Starts a system restore on the local computer.
Resume-BitsTransfer	Resumes a BITS transfer job.
Resume-Service	Resumes one or more suspended (paused) services.
Select-Object	Selects specified properties of an object or set of objects. It can also select unique objects from an array of objects, or it can select a specified number of objects from the beginning or end of an array of objects.
Select-String	Finds text in strings and files.

NAME	SYNOPSIS
Select-XML	Finds text in an XML string or document.
Send-MailMessage	Sends an e-mail message.
Set-Acl	Changes the security descriptor of a specified resource, such as a file or registry key.
Set-Alias	Creates or changes an alias (alternate name) for a cmdlet or other command element in the current Windows PSSession.
Set-AppLockerPolicy	Sets the AppLocker policy for the specified Group Policy object (GPO).
Set-AuthenticodeSignature	Adds an Authenticode signature to a Windows PowerShell script or other file.
Set-BitsTransfer	Modifies the properties of an existing BITS transfer job.
Set-Content	Writes or replaces the content in an item with new content.
Set-Date	Changes the system time on the computer to a time that you specify.
Set-ExecutionPolicy	Changes the user preference for the Windows PowerShell execution policy.
Set-Item	Changes the value of an item to the value specified in the command.
Set-ItemProperty	Creates or changes the value of a property of an item.
Set-Location	Sets the current working location to a specified location.
Set-PSBreakpoint	Sets a breakpoint on a line, command, or variable.
Set-PSDebug	Turns script debugging features on and off, sets the trace level, and toggles StrictMode.
Set-PSSessionConfiguration	Changes the properties of a registered session configuration.
Set-Service	Starts, stops, and suspends a service and changes its properties.
Set-StrictMode	Establishes and enforces coding rules in expressions, scripts, and script blocks.
Set-TraceSource	Configures, starts, and stops a trace of Windows PowerShell components.
Set-Variable	Sets the value of a variable. Creates the variable if one with the requested name does not exist.
Set-WmiInstance	Creates or updates an instance of an existing WMI class.

NAME	SYNOPSIS
Set-WSManInstance	Modifies the management information that is related to a resource.
Set-WSManQuickConfig	Configures the local computer for remote management.
Show-EventLog	Displays the event logs of the local or a remote computer in Event Viewer.
Sort-Object	Sorts objects by property values.
Split-Path	Returns the specified part of a path.
Start-BitsTransfer	Creates a new BITS transfer job.
Start-Job	Starts a Windows PowerShell background job.
Start-Process	Starts one or more processes on the local computer.
Start-Service	Starts one or more stopped services.
Start-Sleep	Suspends the activity in a script or session for the specified period of time.
Start-Transaction	Starts a transaction.
Start-Transcript	Creates a record of all or part of a Windows PSSession in a text file.
Stop-Computer	Stops (shuts down) local and remote computers.
Stop-Job	Stops a Windows PowerShell background job.
Stop-Process	Stops one or more running processes.
Stop-Service	Stops one or more running services.
Stop-Transcript	Stops a transcript.
Suspend-BitsTransfer	Suspends a BITS transfer job.
Suspend-Service	Suspends (pauses) one or more running services.
Tee-Object	Saves command output in a file or variable and displays it in the console.
Test-AppLockerPolicy	Tests whether the input files are allowed to run for a given user based on the specified AppLocker policy.
Test-ComputerSecureChannel	Tests and repairs the secure channel between the local computer and its domain.
Test-Connection	Sends Internet Control Message Protocol (ICMP) echo request packets (pings) to one or more computers.
Test-ModuleManifest	Verifies that a module manifest file accurately describes the contents of a module.
Test-Path	Determines whether all elements of a path exist.

NAME	SYNOPSIS
Test-WSMan	Tests whether the WinRM service is running on a local or remote computer.
Trace-Command	Configures and starts a trace of the specified expression or command.
Undo-Transaction	Rolls back the active transaction.
Unregister-Event	Cancels an event subscription.
Unregister-PSSessionConfiguration	Deletes registered session configurations from the computer.
Update-FormatData	Updates the formatting data in the current session.
Update-List	Adds items to and removes items from a property value that contains a collection of objects.
Update-TypeData	Updates the current extended type configuration by reloading the *.types.ps1xml files into memory.
Use-Transaction	Adds the script block to the active transaction.
Wait-Event	Waits until a particular event is raised before continuing to run.
Wait-Job	Suppresses the command prompt until one or all of the Windows PowerShell background jobs running in the session are complete.
Wait-Process	Waits for the processes to be stopped before accepting more input.
Where-Object	Creates a filter that controls which objects will be passed along a command pipeline.
Write-Debug	Writes a debug message to the console.
Write-Error	Writes an object to the error stream.
Write-EventLog	Writes an event to an event log.
Write-Host	Writes customized output to a host.
Write-Output	Sends the specified objects to the next command in the pipeline. If the command is the last command in the pipeline, the objects are displayed in the console.
Write-Progress	Displays a progress bar within a Windows PowerShell command window.
Write-Verbose	Writes text to the verbose message stream.
Write-Warning	Writes a warning message.

Common Windows PowerShell Verbs

TABLE B-1 PROVIDES A list of common Windows PowerShell verbs and their associated grouping. Use these verbs when creating functions that will be placed into modules to avoid nonstandard verb warning messages.

TABLE B-1 Windows PowerShell Verbs

VERB	GROUP
Add	Common
Clear	Common
Close	Common
Copy	Common
Enter	Common
Exit	Common
Find	Common
Format	Common
Get	Common
Hide	Common
Join	Common
Lock	Common
Move	Common
New	Common
Open	Common
Pop	Common
Push	Common
Redo	Common

VERB	GROUP
Remove	Common
Rename	Common
Reset	Common
Search	Common
Select	Common
Set	Common
Show	Common
Skip	Common
Split	Common
Step	Common
Switch	Common
Undo	Common
Unlock	Common
Watch	Common
Backup	Data
Checkpoint	Data
Compare	Data
Compress	Data
Convert	Data
ConvertFrom	Data
ConvertTo	Data
Dismount	Data
Edit	Data
Expand	Data
Export	Data
Group	Data
Import	Data
Initialize	Data
Limit	Data
Merge	Data
Mount	Data

VERB	GROUP
Out	Data
Publish	Data
Restore	Data
Save	Data
Sync	Data
Unpublish	Data
Update	Data
Approve	Lifecycle
Assert	Lifecycle
Complete	Lifecycle
Confirm	Lifecycle
Deny	Lifecycle
Disable	Lifecycle
Enable	Lifecycle
Install	Lifecycle
Invoke	Lifecycle
Register	Lifecycle
Request	Lifecycle
Restart	Lifecycle
Resume	Lifecycle
Start	Lifecycle
Stop	Lifecycle
Submit	Lifecycle
Suspend	Lifecycle
Uninstall	Lifecycle
Unregister	Lifecycle
Wait	Lifecycle
Debug	Diagnostic
Measure	Diagnostic
Ping	Diagnostic
Repair	Diagnostic

VERB	GROUP
Resolve	Diagnostic
Test	Diagnostic
Trace	Diagnostic
Connect	Communications
Disconnect	Communications
Read	Communications
Receive	Communications
Send	Communications
Write	Communications
Block	Security
Grant	Security
Protect	Security
Revoke	Security
Unblock	Security
Unprotect	Security
Use	Other

Useful COM Objects

MANY COMPONENT OBJECT MODEL (COM) objects are included in a typical installation of any version of the Windows operating system. Many of these objects serve special purposes and are therefore of little value to a scripter. However, many are extremely useful, and others provide the only scripting means to perform a particular task. Table C-1 lists some of the more useful COM objects.

TABLE C-1 COM Objects and How They Are Used

COM OBJECT	OBJECT USE
Access.Application	The *Application* object refers to the active Microsoft Office Access application.
ADODB.Command	Defines a specific command that you intend to execute against a data source.
ADODB.Connection	Represents an open connection to a data source.
ADODB.Recordset	Represents the entire set of records from a base table or the results of an executed command. At any time, the *Recordset* object refers to only a single record within the set as the current record.
ADSystemInfo	The *ADSystemInfo* object returns an instance of the IADsADSystemInfo interface. The IADsADSystemInfo interface retrieves data about the local computer, such as the domain, site, and distinguished name of the local computer.
Excel.Application	The Microsoft Office Excel *Application* object is the top-level object in the Office Excel object model. The *Application* object is used to determine or specify application-level properties or execute application-level methods. The *Application* object is also the entry point into the rest of the Excel object model.
GPMgmt.gpm	Allows you to define the criteria to use for search operations when using Group Policy Management Console (GPMC) interfaces.
HnetCfg.FwMgr	Returns the INetFwMgr interface that provides access to the firewall settings for a computer.

COM OBJECT	OBJECT USE
HNetCfg.FwPolicy2	Returns the INetFwPolicy interface that provides access to a firewall policy.
InternetExplorer.Application	Obtains the automation object for Windows Internet Explorer.
Microsoft.FeedsManager	Exposes methods that provide access to the Common Feed List, which is a hierarchy of Really Simple Syndication (RSS) feeds to which the user is subscribed.
Microsoft.Update.AutoUpdate	Returns the IAutomaticUpdates interface that contains the functionality of Automatic Updates.
Microsoft.Update.Installer	Returns the IUpdateInstaller interface that installs or uninstalls updates from or onto a computer.
Microsoft.Update.Searcher	Returns the IUpdateSearcher interface that searches for updates on a server.
Microsoft.Update.Session	Returns the IUpdateSession interface that represents a session in which the caller can perform operations that involve updates.
Microsoft.Update.UpdateColl	Returns the IUpdateCollection interface that represents an ordered list of updates.
MSGraph.Application	Represents the entire Microsoft Graph application. The *Application* object represents the top level of the object hierarchy and contains all of the objects, properties, and methods for the application.
MSGraph.Chart	Represents the specified Graph chart.
MSScriptControl.ScriptControl	Provides the ability to run other script code, such as VBScript, from within a Windows PowerShell script.
MSXML.DOMdocument	Returns an instance of a Document Object Model (DOM) document for MSXML 2.0.
MSXML2.DOMdocument	Returns an instance of a DOM document for MSXML 3.0.
Outlook.Application	Represents the entire Microsoft Office Outlook application.
SAPI.SpVoice	Returns the ISpTTSEngineSite interface that is used to write audio data and events.
Schedule.Service	Creates a *taskservice* object that provides access to the Task Scheduler service for managing registered tasks.
Scripting.FileSystemObject	Creates the *FileSystemObject* that provides access to files and folders.
Shell.Application	Provides access to scriptable shell objects.

COM OBJECT	OBJECT USE
WbemScripting.SWbemLocator	Returns the Windows Management Instrumentation (WMI) *SWbemLocator* object that contains the *ConnectServer* method for connecting to namespaces on remote computers.
Word.Application	Represents the Microsoft Office Word application. The *Application* object includes properties and methods that return top-level objects.
WScript.Network	Returns the *WshNetwork* object that provides access to the shared resources on the network to which your computer is connected.
WScript.Shell	Returns the *WshShell* object that provides access to the native Windows shell.
WSMan.Automation	Returns the automation object for Windows Remote Management. Windows Remote Management can be used to retrieve data exposed by WMI.

APPENDIX D

Useful WMI Classes

WITH MORE THAN 2,000 Windows Management Instrumentation (WMI) classes installed on a modern Windows operating system, the problem is not what you can use in a script but rather what you should script. Some WMI classes return a lot of information, but for all practical purposes, the information is basically useless. It makes sense to hone in on the WMI classes that produce the most valuable information. The lists in this appendix are not exhaustive lists of classes but rather are lists of the WMI classes that I have used repeatedly over the last few years.

TABLE D-1 Cooling Device Classes

CLASS	PROPERTIES	METHODS
Win32_Fan	22	3
■ Represents the properties of a fan device in the computer system.		
Win32_HeatPipe	20	2
■ Represents the properties of a heat pipe cooling device.		
Win32_Refrigeration	20	2
■ Represents the properties of a refrigeration device.		
Win32_TemperatureProbe	35	2
■ Represents the properties of a temperature sensor (electronic thermometer).		

TABLE D-2 Input Device Classes

CLASS	PROPERTIES	METHODS
Win32_Keyboard	23	2
■ Represents a keyboard installed on a Windows system.		
Win32_PointingDevice	33	2
■ Represents an input device used to point to and select regions on the display of a Windows computer system.		

TABLE D-3 Mass Storage Classes

CLASS	PROPERTIES	METHODS
Win32_AutochkSetting	4	0
■ Represents the settings for the autocheck operation of a disk.		
Win32_CDROMDrive	48	2
■ Represents a CD-ROM drive on a Windows computer system.		
Win32_DiskDrive	49	2
■ Represents a physical disk drive as seen by a computer running the Windows operating system.		
Win32_FloppyDrive	30	2
■ Manages the capabilities of a floppy disk drive.		
Win32_PhysicalMedia	23	0
■ Represents any type of documentation or storage medium.		
Win32_TapeDrive	40	2
■ Represents a tape drive on a Windows computer.		

TABLE D-4 Motherboard, Controller, and Port Classes

CLASS	PROPERTIES	METHODS
Win32_1394Controller	23	2
■ Represents the capabilities and management of a 1394 controller.		
Win32_1394ControllerDevice	7	0
■ Relates the high-speed serial bus (IEEE 1394 Firewire) controller and the *CIM_LogicalDevice* instance connected to it.		
Win32_AllocatedResource	2	0
■ Relates a logical device to a system resource.		
Win32_AssociatedProcessorMemory	3	0
■ Relates a processor and its cache memory.		
Win32_BaseBoard	29	1
■ Represents a baseboard (also known as a motherboard or system board).		

CLASS	PROPERTIES	METHODS
Win32_BIOS	27	0
■ Represents the attributes of the computer system's BIOS that are installed on the computer.		
Win32_Bus	21	2
■ Represents a physical bus as seen by a Windows operating system.		
Win32_CacheMemory	53	2
■ Represents cache memory (internal and external) on a computer system.		
Win32_ControllerHasHub	7	0
■ Represents the hubs downstream from the universal serial bus (USB) controller.		
Win32_DeviceBus	2	0
■ Relates a system bus and a logical device using the bus.		
Win32_DeviceMemoryAddress	11	0
■ Represents a device memory address on a Windows system.		
Win32_DeviceSettings	2	0
■ Relates a logical device and a setting that can be applied to it.		
Win32_DMAChannel	19	0
■ Represents a direct memory access (DMA) channel on a Windows computer system.		
Win32_FloppyController	23	2
■ Represents the capabilities and management capacity of a floppy disk drive controller.		
Win32_IDEController	23	2
■ Represents the capabilities of an Integrated Drive Electronics (IDE) controller device.		
Win32_IDEControllerDevice	7	0
■ Association class that relates an IDE controller and the logical device.		
Win32_InfraredDevice	23	2
■ Represents the capabilities and management of an infrared device.		

CLASS	PROPERTIES	METHODS
Win32_IRQResource	15	0
■ Represents an interrupt request line (IRQ) number on a Windows computer system.		
Win32_MemoryArray	39	2
■ Represents the properties of the computer system memory array and mapped addresses.		
Win32_MemoryArrayLocation	2	0
■ Relates a logical memory array and the physical memory array on which it exists.		
Win32_MemoryDevice	39	2
■ Represents the properties of a computer system's memory device along with its associated mapped addresses.		
Win32_MemoryDeviceArray	2	0
■ Relates a memory device and the memory array in which it resides.		
Win32_MemoryDeviceLocation	2	0
■ Association class that relates a memory device and the physical memory on which it exists.		
Win32_MotherboardDevice	22	2
■ Represents a device that contains the central components of the Windows computer system.		
Win32_OnBoardDevice	20	0
■ Represents common adapter devices built into the motherboard (system board).		
Win32_ParallelPort	26	2
■ Represents the properties of a parallel port on a Windows computer system.		
Win32_PCMCIAController	23	2
■ Manages the capabilities of a Personal Computer Memory Card Interface Adapter (PCMCIA) controller device.		
Win32_PhysicalMemory	30	0
■ Represents a physical memory device located on a computer as available to the operating system.		

CLASS	PROPERTIES	METHODS
Win32_PhysicalMemoryArray	27	1
■ Represents details about the computer system's physical memory.		
Win32_PhysicalMemoryLocation	3	0
■ Relates an array of physical memory and its physical memory.		
Win32_PNPAllocatedResource	2	0
■ Represents an association between logical devices and system resources.		
Win32_PNPDevice	2	0
■ Relates a device (known to Configuration Manager as a PNPEntity) and the function it performs.		
Win32_PNPEntity	22	2
■ Represents the properties of a Plug and Play device.		
Win32_PortConnector	20	0
■ Represents physical connection ports, such as DB-25 pin male, Centronics, or PS/2.		
Win32_PortResource	11	0
■ Represents an I/O port on a Windows computer system.		
Win32_Processor	44	2
■ Represents a device capable of interpreting a sequence of machine instructions on a Windows computer system.		
Win32_SCSIController	31	2
■ Represents a small computer system interface (SCSI) controller on a Windows system.		
Win32_SCSIControllerDevice	7	0
■ Relates a SCSI controller and the logical device (disk drive) connected to it.		
Win32_SerialPort	47	2
■ Represents a serial port on a Windows system.		
Win32_SerialPortConfiguration	29	0
■ Represents the settings for data transmission on a Windows serial port.		

CLASS	PROPERTIES	METHODS
Win32_SerialPortSetting	2	0
■ Relates a serial port and its configuration settings.		
Win32_SMBIOSMemory	38	2
■ Represents the capabilities and management of memory-related logical devices.		
Win32_SoundDevice	23	2
■ Represents the properties of a sound device on a Windows computer system.		
Win32_SystemBIOS	2	0
■ Relates a computer system (including data such as startup properties, time zones, boot configurations, or administrative passwords) and a system BIOS (services, languages, or system management properties).		
Win32_SystemDriverPNPEntity	2	0
■ Relates a Plug and Play device on the Windows computer system and the driver that supports the Plug and Play device.		
Win32_SystemEnclosure	37	1
■ Represents the properties associated with a physical system enclosure.		
Win32_SystemMemoryResource	10	0
■ Represents a system memory resource on a Windows system.		
Win32_SystemSlot	31	0
■ Represents physical connection points, including ports, motherboard slots, and peripherals, and proprietary connections points.		
Win32_USBController	23	2
■ Manages the capabilities of a USB controller.		
Win32_USBControllerDevice	7	0
■ Relates a USB controller and the *CIM_LogicalDevice* instances connected to it.		
Win32_USBHub	28	3
■ Represents the management characteristics of a USB hub.		

TABLE D-5 Network Device Classes

CLASS	PROPERTIES	METHODS
Win32_NetworkAdapter	36	2
■ Represents a network adapter on a Windows system.		
Win32_NetworkAdapterConfiguration	60	41
■ Represents the attributes and behaviors of a network adapter. The class is not guaranteed to be supported after the ratification of the Distributed Management Task Force (DMTF) common information model (CIM) network specification.		
Win32_NetworkAdapterSetting	2	0
■ Relates a network adapter and its configuration settings.		

TABLE D-6 Power Classes

CLASS	PROPERTIES	METHODS
Win32_AssociatedBattery	2	0
■ Relates a logical device and the battery it is using.		
Win32_Battery	33	2
■ Represents a battery connected to the computer system.		
Win32_CurrentProbe	35	2
■ Represents the properties of a current monitoring sensor (ammeter).		
Win32_PortableBattery	36	2
■ Represents the properties of a portable battery, such as one used for a notebook computer.		
Win32_PowerManagementEvent	4	0
■ Represents power management events resulting from power state changes.		
Win32_UninterruptiblePowerSupply	43	2
■ Represents the capabilities and management capacity of an uninterruptible power supply (UPS).		
Win32_VoltageProbe	35	2
■ Represents the properties of a voltage sensor (electronic voltmeter).		

TABLE D-7 Printing Classes

CLASS	PROPERTIES	METHODS
Win32_DriverForDevice	2	0
■ Relates a printer to a printer driver.		
Win32_Printer	86	9
■ Represents a device connected to a Windows computer system that is capable of reproducing a visual image on a medium.		
Win32_PrinterConfiguration	33	0
■ Defines the configuration for a printer device.		
Win32_PrinterController	7	0
■ Relates a printer and the local device to which the printer is connected.		
Win32_PrinterDriver	22	3
■ Represents the drivers for a Win32_Printer instance.		
Win32_PrinterDriverDll	2	0
■ Relates a local printer and its driver file (not the driver itself).		
Win32_PrinterSetting	2	0
■ Relates a printer and its configuration settings.		
Win32_PrintJob	24	2
■ Represents a print job generated by a Windows application.		
Win32_TCPIPPrinterPort	17	0
■ Represents a TCP/IP service access point.		

TABLE D-8 Telephony Classes

CLASS	PROPERTIES	METHODS
Win32_POTSModem	79	2
■ Represents the services and characteristics of a Plain Old Telephone Service (POTS) modem on a Windows system.		
Win32_POTSModemToSerialPort	7	0
■ Relates a modem and the serial port the modem uses.		

TABLE D-9 Video and Monitor Classes

CLASS	PROPERTIES	METHODS
Win32_DesktopMonitor ■ Represents the type of monitor or display device attached to the computer system.	28	2
Win32_DisplayConfiguration ■ Represents configuration information for the display device on a Windows system. This class is obsolete. In place of this class, use the properties in the *Win32_VideoController, Win32_DesktopMonitor*, and *CIM_VideoControllerResolution* classes.	15	0
Win32_DisplayControllerConfiguration ■ Represents the video adapter configuration information of a Windows system. This class is obsolete. In place of this class, use the properties in the *Win32_VideoController, Win32_DesktopMonitor*, and *CIM_VideoControllerResolution* classes.	14	0
Win32_VideoConfiguration ■ This class has been eliminated from Windows XP and later operating systems; attempts to use it generate a fatal error. In place of this class, use the properties contained in the *Win32_VideoController, Win32_DesktopMonitor*, and *CIM_VideoControllerResolution* classes.	30	0
Win32_VideoController ■ Represents the capabilities and management capacity of the video controller on a Windows computer system.	59	2
Win32_VideoSettings ■ Relates a video controller and video settings that can be applied to it.	2	0

TABLE D-10 COM Classes

CLASS	PROPERTIES	METHODS
Win32_ClassicCOMApplicationClasses ■ Association class. Relates a Distributed Component Object Model (DCOM) application and a Component Object Model (COM) component grouped under it.	2	0

CLASS	PROPERTIES	METHODS
Win32_ClassicCOMClass	6	0
■ Instance class. Represents the properties of a COM component.		
Win32_ClassicCOMClassSettings	2	0
■ Association class. Relates a COM class and the settings used to configure instances of the COM class.		
Win32_ClientApplicationSetting	2	0
■ Association class. Relates an executable and a DCOM application that contains the DCOM configuration options for the executable file.		
Win32_COMApplication	5	0
■ Instance class. Represents a COM application.		
Win32_COMApplicationClasses	2	0
■ Association class. Relates a COM component and the COM application where it resides.		
Win32_COMApplicationSettings	2	0
■ Association class. Relates a DCOM application and its configuration settings.		
Win32_COMClass	5	0
■ Instance class. Represents the properties of a COM component.		
Win32_ComClassAutoEmulator	2	0
■ Association class. Relates a COM class and another COM class that it automatically emulates.		
Win32_ComClassEmulator	2	0
■ Association class. Relates two versions of a COM class.		
Win32_ComponentCategory	6	0
■ Instance class. Represents a component category.		
Win32_COMSetting	3	0
■ Instance class. Represents the settings associated with a COM component or COM application.		
Win32_DCOMApplication	6	0
■ Instance class. Represents the properties of a DCOM application.		

CLASS	PROPERTIES	METHODS
Win32_DCOMApplicationAccessAllowedSetting	2	0
■ Association class. Relates the *Win32_DCOMApplication* instance and the user security identifiers (SIDs) that can access it.		
Win32_DCOMApplicationLaunchAllowedSetting	2	0
■ Association class. Relates the *Win32_DCOMApplication* instance and the user SIDs that can launch it.		
Win32_DCOMApplicationSetting	12	0
■ Instance class. Represents the settings of a DCOM application.		
Win32_ImplementedCategory	2	0
■ Association class. Relates a component category and the COM class using its interfaces.		

TABLE D-11 Desktop Classes

CLASS	PROPERTIES	METHODS
Win32_Desktop	21	0
■ Instance class. Represents the common characteristics of a user's desktop.		
Win32_Environment	8	0
■ Instance class. Represents an environment or system environment setting on a Windows computer system.		
Win32_TimeZone	24	0
■ Instance class. Represents the time zone information for a Windows system.		
Win32_UserDesktop	2	0
■ Association class. Relates a user account and desktop settings that are specific to it.		

TABLE D-12 Drivers Classes

CLASS	PROPERTIES	METHODS
Win32_DriverVXD	21	0
■ Instance class. Represents a virtual device driver on a Windows computer system.		

CLASS	PROPERTIES	METHODS
Win32_SystemDriver	22	10
■ Instance class. Represents the system driver for a base service.		

TABLE D-13 File System Classes

CLASS	PROPERTIES	METHODS
Win32_CIMLogicalDeviceCIMDataFile	4	0
■ Association class. Relates logical devices and data files, indicating the driver files used by the device.		
Win32_Directory	31	14
■ Represents a directory entry on a Windows computer system.		
Win32_DirectorySpecification	13	1
■ Instance class. Represents the directory layout for the product.		
Win32_DiskDriveToDiskPartition	2	0
■ Association class. Relates a disk drive and a partition existing on it.		
Win32_DiskPartition	34	2
■ Instance class. Represents the capabilities and management capacity of a partitioned area of a physical disk on a Windows system.		
Win32_DiskQuota	6	0
■ Association class. Tracks disk space usage for NTFS File System (NTFS) volumes.		
Win32_LogicalDisk	40	5
■ Represents a data source that resolves to an actual local storage device on a Windows system.		
Win32_LogicalDiskRootDirectory	2	0
■ Association class. Relates a logical disk and its directory structure.		
Win32_LogicalDiskToPartition	4	0
■ Association class. Relates a logical disk drive and the disk partition on which it resides.		

CLASS	PROPERTIES	METHODS
Win32_MappedLogicalDisk ■ Represents network storage devices that are mapped as logical disks on the computer system.	38	2
Win32_OperatingSystemAutochkSetting ■ Association class. Represents the association between a *CIM_ManagedSystemElement* instance and the settings defined for it.	2	0
Win32_QuotaSetting ■ Instance class. Contains setting information for disk quotas on a volume.	9	0
Win32_ShortcutFile ■ Represents files that are shortcuts to other files, directories, and commands.	34	14
Win32_SubDirectory ■ Association class. Relates a directory (folder) and one of its subdirectories (subfolders).	2	0
Win32_SystemPartitions ■ Association class. Relates a computer system and a disk partition on that system.	2	0
Win32_Volume ■ Instance class. Represents an area of storage on a hard disk.	2	0
Win32_VolumeQuota ■ Association class. Relates a volume to the per-volume quota settings.	2	0
Win32_VolumeQuotaSetting ■ Association class. Relates disk quota settings with a specific disk volume.	2	0
Win32_VolumeUserQuota ■ Association class. Relates per-user quotas to quota-enabled volumes.	2	0

TABLE D-14 Job Object Classes

CLASS	PROPERTIES	METHODS
Win32_CollectionStatistics ■ Association class. Relates a managed system element collection and the class representing statistical information about the collection.	2	0
Win32_LUID ■ Instance class. Represents a locally unique identifier (LUID).	2	0
Win32_LUIDandAttributes ■ Instance class. Represents a LUID and its attributes.	2	0
Win32_NamedJobObject ■ Instance class. Represents a kernel object that is used to group processes for the sake of controlling the life and resources of the processes within the job object.	4	0
Win32_NamedJobObjectActgInfo ■ Instance class. Represents the I/O accounting information for a job object.	19	0
Win32_NamedJobObjectLimit ■ Instance class. Represents an association between a job object and the job object limit settings.	2	0
Win32_NamedJobObjectLimitSetting ■ Instance class. Represents the limit settings for a job object.	14	0
Win32_NamedJobObjectProcess ■ Instance class. Relates a job object and the process contained in the job object.	2	0
Win32_NamedJobObjectSecLimit ■ Instance class. Relates a job object and the job object security limit settings.	2	0
Win32_NamedJobObjectSecLimitSetting ■ Instance class. Represents the security limit settings for a job object.	7	0
Win32_NamedJobObjectStatistics ■ Instance class. Represents an association between a job object and the job object I/O accounting information class.	2	0

CLASS	PROPERTIES	METHODS
Win32_SIDandAttributes	2	0
■ Instance class. Represents a SID and its attributes.		
Win32_TokenGroups	2	0
■ Event class. Represents information about the group SIDs in an access token.		
Win32_TokenPrivileges	2	0
■ Event class. Represents information about a set of privileges for an access token.		

TABLE D-15 Memory and Page File Classes

CLASS	PROPERTIES	METHODS
Win32_LogicalMemoryConfiguration	8	0
■ Instance class. This class is obsolete and has been replaced by the *Win32_OperatingSystem* class.		
Win32_PageFile	36	14
■ Instance class. Represents the file used for handling virtual memory file swapping on a Windows system.		
Win32_PageFileElementSetting	2	0
■ Association class. Relates the initial settings of a page file and the state of those settings during normal use.		
Win32_PageFileSetting	6	0
■ Instance class. Represents the settings of a page file.		
Win32_PageFileUsage	9	0
■ Instance class. Represents the file used for handling virtual memory file swapping on a Windows system.		
Win32_SystemLogicalMemoryConfiguration	2	0
■ Association class. This class is obsolete because the properties existing in the *Win32_LogicalMemoryConfiguration* class are now a part of the *Win32_OperatingSystem* class.		

TABLE D-16 Media and Audio Class

CLASS	PROPERTIES	METHODS
Win32_CodecFile	34	14
■ Instance class. Represents the audio or video codec installed on the computer system.		

TABLE D-17 Networking Classes

CLASS	PROPERTIES	METHODS
Win32_ActiveRoute	2	0
■ Association class. Relates the current IP4 route to the persisted IP route table.		
Win32_IP4PersistedRouteTable	9	0
■ Instance class. Represents persisted IP routes.		
Win32_IP4RouteTable	18	0
■ Instance class. Represents information that governs the routing of network data packets.		
Win32_IP4RouteTableEvent	2	0
■ Event class. Represents IP route change events.		
Win32_NetworkClient	6	0
■ Instance class. Represents a network client on a Windows system.		
Win32_NetworkConnection	17	0
■ Instance class. Represents an active network connection in a Windows environment.		
Win32_NetworkProtocol	23	0
■ Instance class. Represents a protocol and its network characteristics on a Windows computer system.		
Win32_NTDomain	27	0
■ Instance class. Represents a Windows NT domain.		
Win32_PingStatus	24	0
■ Instance class. Represents the values returned by the standard ping command.		
Win32_ProtocolBinding	3	0
■ Association class. Relates a system-level driver, network protocol, and network adapter.		

TABLE D-18 Operating System Event Classes

CLASS	PROPERTIES	METHODS
Win32_ComputerShutdownEvent	4	0
■ Represents computer shutdown events.		

CLASS	PROPERTIES	METHODS
Win32_ComputerSystemEvent	3	0
■ Represents events related to a computer system.		
Win32_DeviceChangeEvent	3	0
■ Represents device change events resulting from the addition, removal, or modification of devices on the computer system.		
Win32_ModuleLoadTrace	6	0
■ Indicates that a process has loaded a new module.		
Win32_ModuleTrace	2	0
■ Base event for module events.		
Win32_ProcessStartTrace	8	0
■ Indicates that a new process has started.		
Win32_ProcessStopTrace	8	0
■ Indicates that a process has terminated.		
Win32_ProcessTrace	8	0
■ Base event for process events.		
Win32_SystemConfigurationChangeEvent	3	0
■ Indicates that the device list on the system has been refreshed (a device has been added or removed, or the configuration has changed).		
Win32_SystemTrace	2	0
■ Base class for all system trace events, including module, process, and thread traces.		
Win32_ThreadStartTrace	11	0
■ Indicates that a new thread has started.		
Win32_ThreadStopTrace	4	0
■ Indicates that a thread has stopped.		
Win32_ThreadTrace	4	0
■ Base event class for thread events.		
Win32_VolumeChangeEvent	4	0
■ Represents a network-mapped drive event resulting from the addition of a network drive letter or mounted drive on the computer system.		

TABLE D-19 Operating System Settings Classes

CLASS	PROPERTIES	METHODS
Win32_BootConfiguration ■ Instance class. Represents the boot configuration of a Windows system.	9	0
Win32_ComputerSystem ■ Instance class. Represents a computer system operating in a Windows environment.	54	4
Win32_ComputerSystemProcessor ■ Association class. Relates a computer system and a processor running on that system.	2	0
Win32_ComputerSystemProduct ■ Instance class. Represents a product.	8	0
Win32_DependentService ■ Association class. Relates two interdependent base services.	3	0
Win32_LoadOrderGroup ■ Instance class. Represents a group of system services that define execution dependencies.	7	0
Win32_LoadOrderGroupServiceDependencies ■ Instance class. Represents an association between a base service and a load order group that the service depends on to start running.	2	0
Win32_LoadOrderGroupServiceMembers ■ Association class. Relates a load order group and a base service.	2	0
Win32_OperatingSystem ■ Instance class. Represents an operating system installed on a Windows computer system.	61	4
Win32_OperatingSystemQFE ■ Association class. Relates an operating system and product updates applied as represented in *Win32_QuickFixEngineering.*	2	0
Win32_OSRecoveryConfiguration ■ Instance class. Represents the types of information that will be gathered from memory when the operating system fails.	15	0

CLASS	PROPERTIES	METHODS
Win32_QuickFixEngineering	11	0
▪ Instance class. Represents system-wide Quick Fix Engineering (QFE) or updates that have been applied to the current operating system.		
Win32_StartupCommand	7	0
▪ Instance class. Represents a command that runs automatically when a user logs on to the computer system.		
Win32_SystemBootConfiguration	2	0
▪ Association class. Relates a computer system and its boot configuration.		
Win32_SystemDesktop	2	0
▪ Association class. Relates a computer system and its desktop configuration.		
Win32_SystemDevices	2	0
▪ Association class. Relates a computer system and a logical device installed on that system.		
Win32_SystemLoadOrderGroups	2	0
▪ Association class. Relates a computer system and a load order group.		
Win32_SystemNetworkConnections	2	0
▪ Association class. Relates a network connection and the computer system on which it resides.		
Win32_SystemOperatingSystem	3	0
▪ Association class. Relates a computer system and its operating system.		
Win32_SystemProcesses	2	0
▪ Association class. Relates a computer system and a process running on that system.		
Win32_SystemProgramGroups	2	0
▪ Association class. Relates a computer system and a logical program group.		
Win32_SystemResources	2	0
▪ Association class. Relates a system resource and the computer system on which it resides.		

CLASS	PROPERTIES	METHODS
Win32_SystemServices	2	0
■ Association class. Relates a computer system and a service program that exists on the system.		
Win32_SystemSetting	2	0
■ Association class. Relates a computer system and a general setting on that system.		
Win32_SystemSystemDriver	2	0
■ Association class. Relates a computer system and a system driver running on that computer system.		
Win32_SystemTimeZone	2	0
■ Association class. Relates a computer system and a time zone.		
Win32_SystemUsers	2	0
■ Association class. Relates a computer system and a user account on that system.		

TABLE D-20 Processes Classes

CLASS	PROPERTIES	METHODS
Win32_Process	45	6
■ Instance class. Represents a sequence of events on a Windows system.		
Win32_ProcessStartup	14	0
■ Instance class. Represents the startup configuration of a Windows process.		
Win32_Thread	22	0
■ Instance class. Represents a thread of execution.		

TABLE D-21 Registry Class

CLASS	PROPERTIES	METHODS
Win32_Registry	8	0
■ Instance class. Represents the system registry on a Windows computer system.		

TABLE D-22 Scheduler Job Classes

CLASS	PROPERTIES	METHODS
Win32_LocalTime	10	0
■ Instance class. Represents an instance in time represented as component seconds, minutes, day of the week, and so on.		
Win32_ScheduledJob	19	2
■ Instance class. Represents a job scheduled using the AT command and not the Windows NT schedule service.		

TABLE D-23 Security Classes

CLASS	PROPERTIES	METHODS
Win32_AccountSID	2	0
■ Association class. Relates a security account instance with a security descriptor instance.		
Win32_ACE	6	0
■ Instance class. Represents an access control entry (ACE).		
Win32_LogicalFileAccess	7	0
■ Association class. Relates the security settings of a file/directory and one member of its discretionary access control list (DACL).		
Win32_LogicalFileAuditing	7	0
■ Association class. Relates the security settings of a file/directory and one member of its system access control list (SACL).		
Win32_LogicalFileGroup	2	0
■ Association class. Relates the security settings of a file/directory and its group.		
Win32_LogicalFileOwner	2	0
■ Association class. Relates the security settings of a file/directory and its owner.		
Win32_LogicalFileSecuritySetting	6	2
■ Instance class. Represents security settings for a logical file.		

CLASS	PROPERTIES	METHODS
Win32_LogicalShareAccess	7	0
■ Association class. Relates the security settings of a share and one member of its DACL.		
Win32_LogicalShareAuditing	7	0
■ Association class. Relates the security settings of a share and one member of its SACL.		
Win32_LogicalShareSecuritySetting	5	2
■ Instance class. Represents security settings for a logical file.		
Win32_PrivilegesStatus	7	0
■ Instance class. Represents information about privileges required to complete an operation.		
Win32_SecurityDescriptor	5	0
■ Instance class. Represents a structural representation of a *SECURITY_DESCRIPTOR*.		
Win32_SecuritySetting	4	2
■ Instance class. Represents security settings for a managed element.		
Win32_SecuritySettingAccess	7	0
■ Instance class. Represents the rights granted and denied to a trustee for a given object.		
Win32_SecuritySettingAuditing	7	0
■ Instance class. Represents the auditing for a given trustee on a given object.		
Win32_SecuritySettingGroup	2	0
■ Association class. Relates the security of an object and its group.		
Win32_SecuritySettingOfLogicalFile	2	0
■ Instance class. Represents security settings of a file or directory object.		
Win32_SecuritySettingOfLogicalShare	2	0
■ Instance class. Represents security settings of a share object.		

CLASS	PROPERTIES	METHODS
Win32_SecuritySettingOfObject	2	0
■ Association class. Relates an object to its security settings.		
Win32_SecuritySettingOwner	2	0
■ Association class. Relates the security settings of an object and its owner.		
Win32_SID	5	0
■ Instance class. Represents an arbitrary SID.		
Win32_Trustee	5	0
■ Instance class. Represents a trustee.		

TABLE D-24 Service Classes

CLASS	PROPERTIES	METHODS
Win32_BaseService	22	10
■ Instance class. Represents executable objects that are installed in a registry database maintained by the Service Control Manager.		
Win32_Service	25	10
■ Instance class. Represents a service on a Windows computer system.		

TABLE D-25 Share Classes

CLASS	PROPERTIES	METHODS
Win32_DFSNode	25	10
■ Association class. Represents a root or junction node of a domain-based or stand-alone distributed file system (DFS).		
Win32_DFSNodeTarget	25	10
■ Association class. Represents the relationship of a DFS node to one of its targets.		
Win32_DFSTarget	25	10
■ Association class. Represents the target of a DFS node.		

CLASS	PROPERTIES	METHODS
Win32_ServerConnection ■ Instance class. Represents the connections made from a remote computer to a shared resource on the local computer.	12	0
Win32_ServerSession ■ Instance class. Represents the sessions that are established with the local computer by users on a remote computer.	13	0
Win32_ConnectionShare ■ Association class. Relates a shared resource on the computer and the connection made to the shared resource.	2	0
Win32_PrinterShare ■ Association class. Relates a local printer and the share that represents it as it is viewed over a network.	2	0
Win32_SessionConnection ■ Association class. Represents an association between a session established with the local server by a user on a remote machine and the connections that depend on the session.	2	0
Win32_SessionProcess ■ Association class. Represents an association between a logon session and the processes associated with that session.	2	0
Win32_ShareToDirectory ■ Association class. Relates a shared resource on the computer system and the directory to which it is mapped.	2	0
Win32_Share ■ Instance class. Represents a shared resource on a Windows system.	10	4

TABLE D-26 Start Menu Classes

CLASS	PROPERTIES	METHODS
Win32_LogicalProgramGroup ■ Instance class. Represents a program group in a Windows system.	7	0

CLASS	PROPERTIES	METHODS
Win32_LogicalProgramGroupDirectory	2	0
■ Association class. Relates logical program groups (groupings in the Start menu) and the file directories in which they are stored.		
Win32_LogicalProgramGroupItem	5	0
■ Instance class. Represents an element contained by a *Win32_ProgramGroup* instance that is not itself another *Win32_ProgramGroup* instance.		
Win32_LogicalProgramGroupItemDataFile	2	0
■ Association class. Relates the program group items of the Start menu and the files in which they are stored.		
Win32_ProgramGroup	6	0
■ Instance class. Deprecated. Represents a program group in a Windows computer system. Use the *Win32_LogicalProgramGroup* class.		
Win32_ProgramGroupContents	2	0
■ Association class. Relates a program group order and an individual program group or item contained in it.		
Win32_ProgramGroupOrItem	5	0
■ Instance class. Represents a logical grouping of programs on the user's Start\Programs menu.		

TABLE D-27 Storage Classes

CLASS	PROPERTIES	METHODS
Win32_ShadowBy	5	0
■ Association class. Represents the association between a shadow copy and the provider that creates the shadow copy.		
Win32_ShadowContext	5	0
■ Association class. Specifies how a shadow copy is to be created, queried, or deleted.		
Win32_ShadowCopy	5	0
■ Instance class. Represents a duplicate copy of the original volume at a previous time.		

CLASS	PROPERTIES	METHODS
Win32_ShadowDiffVolumeSupport	5	0
■ Association class. Represents an association between a shadow copy provider and a storage volume.		
Win32_ShadowFor	5	0
■ Association class. Represents an association between a shadow copy and the volume for which the shadow copy is created.		
Win32_ShadowOn	5	0
■ Association class. Represents an association between a shadow copy and where the differential data is written.		
Win32_ShadowProvider	5	0
■ Association class. Represents a component that creates and represents volume shadow copies.		
Win32_ShadowStorage	5	0
■ Association class. Represents an association between a shadow copy and where the differential data is written.		
Win32_ShadowVolumeSupport	5	0
■ Association class. Represents an association between a shadow copy provider with a supported volume.		
Win32_Volume	42	9
■ Instance class. Represents an area of storage on a hard disk.		
Win32_VolumeUserQuota	6	0
■ Association class. Represents a volume to the per volume quota settings.		

TABLE D-28 User Classes

CLASS	PROPERTIES	METHODS
Win32_Account	9	0
■ Instance class. Represents information about user accounts and group accounts known to the Windows system.		
Win32_Group	9	1
■ Instance class. Represents data about a group account.		

CLASS	PROPERTIES	METHODS
Win32_GroupInDomain	2	0
■ Association class. Identifies the group accounts associated with a Windows NT domain.		
Win32_GroupUser	2	0
■ Association class. Relates a group and an account that is a member of that group.		
Win32_LogonSession	9	0
■ Instance class. Describes the logon session or sessions associated with a user logged on to Windows NT or Windows 2000.		
Win32_LogonSessionMappedDisk	2	0
■ Association class. Represents the mapped logical disks associated with the session.		
Win32_NetworkLoginProfile	32	0
■ Instance class. Represents the network login information of a specific user on a Windows system.		
Win32_SystemAccount	9	0
■ Instance class. Represents a system account.		
Win32_UserAccount	16	1
■ Instance class. Represents information about a user account on a Windows system.		
Win32_UserInDomain	2	0
■ Association class. Relates a user account and a Windows NT domain.		

TABLE D-29 Event Log Classes

CLASS	PROPERTIES	METHODS
Win32_NTEventlogFile	39	16
■ Instance class. Represents data stored in a Windows NT/Windows 2000 log file.		
Win32_NTLogEvent	16	0
■ Instance class. Represents Windows NT/Windows 2000 events.		

CLASS	PROPERTIES	METHODS
Win32_NTLogEventComputer	2	0
■ Association class. Relates instances of *Win32_NTLogEvent* and *Win32_ComputerSystem*.		
Win32_NTLogEventLog	2	0
■ Association class. Relates instances of *Win32_NTLogEvent* and *Win32_NTEventlogFile* classes.		
Win32_NTLogEventUser	2	0
■ Association class. Relates instances of *Win32_NTLogEvent* and *Win32_UserAccount*.		

TABLE D-30 Windows Product Activation Classes

CLASS	PROPERTIES	METHODS
Win32_ComputerSystemWindowsProductActivationSetting	2	0
■ Association class. Relates instances of *Win32_ComputerSystem* and *Win32_WindowsProductActivation*.		
Win32_Proxy	6	1
■ Instance class. Contains properties and methods to query and configure an Internet connection related to Wi-Fi Protected Access (WPA).		
Win32_WindowsProductActivation	9	5
■ Instance class. Contains properties and methods related to WPA.		

TABLE D-31 Formatted Data Classes

CLASS	PROPERTIES	METHODS
Win32_PerfFormattedData	9	0
■ Represents abstract base class for the formatted data classes.		
Win32_PerfFormattedData_ASP_ActiveServerPages	9	0
■ Represents performance counters for the Active Server Pages device on the computer system.		
Win32_PerfFormattedData_ContentFilter_IndexingServiceFilter	12	0
■ Represents performance information about an Indexing Service filter.		

CLASS	PROPERTIES	METHODS
Win32_PerfFormattedData_ContentIndex_IndexingService ■ Represents performance data about the state of the Indexing Service.	20	0
Win32_PerfFormattedData_InetInfo_ InternetInformationServicesGlobal ■ Represents counters that monitor Internet Information Services (the Web service and the FTP service) as a whole.	20	0
Win32_PerfFormattedData_ISAPISearch_HttpIndexingService ■ Represents performance data from the HTTP Indexing Service.	17	0
Win32_PerfFormattedData_MSDTC_ DistributedTransactionCoordinator ■ Represents Microsoft Distributed Transaction Coordinator performance counters.	22	0
Win32_PerfFormattedData_NTFSDRV_SMTPNTFSStoreDriver ■ Represents global counters for the Microsoft Exchange NTFS Store driver.	22	0
Win32_PerfFormattedData_PerfDisk_LogicalDisk ■ Represents counters that monitor logical partitions of a hard or fixed disk drive.	32	0
Win32_PerfFormattedData_PerfDisk_PhysicalDisk ■ Represents counters that monitor hard or fixed disk drives on a computer.	30	0
Win32_PerfFormattedData_PerfNet_Browser ■ Represents counters that measure the rates of announcements, enumerations, and other browser transmissions.	29	0
Win32_PerfFormattedData_PerfNet_Redirector ■ Represents counters that monitor network connections originating at the local computer.	46	0
Win32_PerfFormattedData_PerfNet_Server ■ Represents counters that monitor communications using the Windows Internet Naming Service (WINS) Server service.	35	0

CLASS	PROPERTIES	METHODS
Win32_PerfFormattedData_PerfNet_ServerWorkQueues	26	0
■ Represents counters that monitor the length of the queues and objects in the queues.		
Win32_PerfFormattedData_PerfOS_Cache	26	0
■ Represents counters that monitor the file system cache, an area of physical memory that stores recently used data as long as possible to permit access to the data without having to read from the disk.		
Win32_PerfFormattedData_PerfOS_Memory	26	0
■ Represents counters that describe the behavior of physical and virtual memory on the computer.		
Win32_PerfFormattedData_PerfOS_Objects	26	0
■ Represents counts of the objects contained by the operating system such as events, mutexes, processes, sections, semaphores, and threads.		
Win32_PerfFormattedData_PerfOS_PagingFile	26	0
■ Represents counters that monitor the paging file(s) on the computer.		
Win32_PerfFormattedData_PerfOS_Processor	26	0
■ Represents counters that measure aspects of processor activity.		
Win32_PerfFormattedData_PerfOS_System	26	0
■ Represents counters that apply to more than one instance of component processors on the computer.		
Win32_PerfFormattedData_PerfProc_FullImage_Costly	17	0
■ Represents counters that monitor the virtual address usage of images executed by processes on the computer.		
Win32_PerfFormattedData_PerfProc_Image_Costly	17	0
■ Represents counters that monitor the virtual address usage of images executed by processes on the computer.		
Win32_PerfFormattedData_PerfProc_JobObject	22	0
■ Represents the accounting and processor usage data collected by each active named job object.		

CLASS	PROPERTIES	METHODS
Win32_PerfFormattedData_PerfProc_JobObjectDetails ■ Represents detailed performance information about the active processes that make up a job object.	36	0
Win32_PerfFormattedData_PerfProc_Process ■ Represents counters that monitor running application program and system processes.	36	0
Win32_PerfFormattedData_PerfProc_ ProcessAddressSpace_Costly ■ Represent counters that monitor memory allocation and use for a selected process.	46	0
Win32_PerfFormattedData_PerfProc_Thread ■ Represents counters that measure aspects of thread behavior.	21	0
Win32_PerfFormattedData_PerfProc_ThreadDetails_Costly ■ Represents counters that measure aspects of thread behavior that are difficult or time-consuming to collect.	10	0
Win32_PerfFormattedData_PSched_PSchedFlow ■ Represents flow statistics from the packet scheduler.	10	0
Win32_PerfFormattedData_PSched_PSchedPipe ■ Represents pipe statistics from the packet scheduler.	10	0
Win32_PerfFormattedData_RemoteAccess_RASPort ■ Represents counters that monitor individual Remote Access Service (RAS) ports of the RAS device on the computer.	10	0
Win32_PerfFormattedData_RemoteAccess_RASTotal ■ Represents counters that combine values for all ports of the RAS device on the computer.	10	0
Win32_PerfFormattedData_RSVP_ACSRSVPInterfaces ■ Represents the number of local network interfaces visible to and used by the Resource Reservation Protocol (RSVP) service.	10	0
Win32_PerfFormattedData_RSVP_ACSRSVPService ■ Represents RSVP or Audit Collection Services (ACS) service performance counters.	10	0

CLASS	PROPERTIES	METHODS
Win32_PerfFormattedData_SMTPSVC_SMTPServer ■ Represents counters specific to the Simple Mail Transfer Protocol (SMTP) Server.	10	0
Win32_PerfFormattedData_Spooler_PrintQueue ■ Represents performance statistics about a print queue.	22	0
Win32_PerfFormattedData_TapiSrv_Telephony ■ Represents the telephony system.	18	0
Win32_PerfFormattedData_Tcpip_ICMP ■ Represents counters that measure the rates at which messages are sent and received by using Internet Control Message Protocol (ICMP) protocols.	18	0
Win32_PerfFormattedData_Tcpip_IP ■ Represents counters that measure the rates at which IP datagrams are sent and received by using IP protocols.	18	0
Win32_PerfFormattedData_Tcpip_NBTConnection ■ Represents counters that measure the rates at which bytes are sent and received over the NetBIOS over TCP/IP (NBT) connection between the local computer and a remote computer.	18	0
Win32_PerfFormattedData_Tcpip_NetworkInterface ■ Represents counters that measure the rates at which bytes and packets are sent and received over a TCP/IP network connection.	18	0
Win32_PerfFormattedData_Tcpip_TCP ■ Represents counters that measure the rates at which TCP segments are sent and received by using the TCP protocol.	18	0
Win32_PerfFormattedData_Tcpip_UDP ■ Represents counters that measure the rates at which User Datagram Protocol (UDP) datagrams are sent and received by using the UDP protocol.	18	0
Win32_PerfFormattedData_TermService_TerminalServices ■ Represents Terminal Services summary information.	12	0

CLASS	PROPERTIES	METHODS
Win32_PerfFormattedData_TermService_ TerminalServicesSession	84	0
■ Represents Terminal Services per-session resource monitoring.		
Win32_PerfFormattedData_W3SVC_WebService	84	0
■ Represents counters specific to the World Wide Web Publishing Service.		

TABLE D-32 Raw Performance Monitor Classes

CLASS	PROPERTIES	METHODS
Win32_PerfRawData	9	0
■ Represents abstract base class for all concrete raw performance counter classes.		
Win32_PerfRawData_ASP_ActiveServerPages	9	0
■ Represents the Active Server Pages device on the computer system.		
Win32_PerfRawData_ContentFilter_IndexingServiceFilter	12	0
■ Represents performance information about an Indexing Service filter.		
Win32_PerfRawData_ContentIndex_IndexingService	20	0
■ Represents performance data about the state of the Indexing Service.		
Win32_PerfRawData_InetInfo_ InternetInformationServicesGlobal	20	0
■ Represents counters that monitor Internet Information Services (the Web service and the FTP service) as a whole.		
Win32_PerfRawData_ISAPISearch_HttpIndexingService	19	0
■ Represents performance data from the HTTP Indexing Service.		
Win32_PerfRawData_MSDTC_ DistributedTransactionCoordinator	22	0
■ Represents Microsoft Distributed Transaction Coordinator performance counters.		

CLASS	PROPERTIES	METHODS
Win32_PerfRawData_NTFSDRV_SMTPNTFSStoreDriver	22	0
■ Represents global counters for the Exchange NTFS Store driver.		
Win32_PerfRawData_PerfDisk_LogicalDisk	43	0
■ Represents counters that monitor logical partitions of a hard or fixed disk drive.		
Win32_PerfRawData_PerfDisk_PhysicalDisk	40	0
■ Represents counters that monitor hard or fixed disk drives on a computer.		
Win32_PerfRawData_PerfNet_Browser	29	0
■ Represents counters that measure the rates of announcements, enumerations, and other browser transmissions.		
Win32_PerfRawData_PerfNet_Redirector	46	0
■ Represents counters that monitor network connections originating at the local computer.		
Win32_PerfRawData_PerfNet_Server	35	0
■ Represents counters that monitor communications using the WINS Server service.		
Win32_PerfRawData_PerfNet_ServerWorkQueues	26	0
■ Represents counters that monitor the length of the queues and objects in the queues.		
Win32_PerfRawData_PerfOS_Cache	26	0
■ Represents counters that monitor the file system cache.		
Win32_PerfRawData_PerfOS_Memory	26	0
■ Represents counters that describe the behavior of physical and virtual memory on the computer.		
Win32_PerfRawData_PerfOS_Objects	26	0
■ Represents counts of the objects contained by the operating system such as events, mutexes, processes, sections, semaphores, and threads.		
Win32_PerfRawData_PerfOS_PagingFile	26	0
■ Represents counters that monitor the paging file(s) on the computer.		

CLASS	PROPERTIES	METHODS
Win32_PerfRawData_PerfOS_Processor	26	0
■ Represents counters that measure aspects of processor activity.		
Win32_PerfRawData_PerfOS_System	26	0
■ Represents counters that apply to more than one instance of a component processors on the computer.		
Win32_PerfRawData_PerfProc_FullImage_Costly	17	0
■ Represents counters that monitor the virtual address usage of images executed by processes on the computer.		
Win32_PerfRawData_PerfProc_Image_Costly	17	0
■ Represents counters that monitor the virtual address usage of images executed by processes on the computer.		
Win32_PerfRawData_PerfProc_JobObject	22	0
■ Represents the accounting and processor usage data collected by each active named job object.		
Win32_PerfRawData_PerfProc_JobObjectDetails	36	0
■ Represents detailed performance information about the active processes that make up a job object.		
Win32_PerfRawData_PerfProc_Process	36	0
■ Represents counters that monitor running application program and system processes.		
Win32_PerfRawData_PerfProc_ProcessAddressSpace_Costly	46	0
■ Represents counters that monitor memory allocation and use for a selected process.		
Win32_PerfRawData_PerfProc_Thread	21	0
■ Represents counters that measure aspects of thread behavior.		
Win32_PerfRawData_PerfProc_ThreadDetails_Costly	10	0
■ Represents counters that measure aspects of thread behavior that are difficult or time-consuming to collect.		
Win32_PerfRawData_PSched_PSchedFlow	10	0
■ Represents flow statistics from the packet scheduler.		

CLASS	PROPERTIES	METHODS
Win32_PerfRawData_PSched_PSchedPipe	10	0
■ Represents pipe statistics from the packet scheduler.		
Win32_PerfRawData_RemoteAccess_RASPort	10	0
■ Represents counters that monitor individual RAS ports of the RAS device on the computer.		
Win32_PerfRawData_RemoteAccess_RASTotal	10	0
■ Represents counters that combine values for all ports of the RAS device on the computer.		
Win32_PerfRawData_RSVP_ACSRSVPInterfaces	10	0
■ Represents the number of local network interfaces visible to and used by the RSVP service.		
Win32_PerfRawData_RSVP_ACSRSVPService	10	0
■ Represents RSVP or ACS service performance counters.		
Win32_PerfRawData_SMTPSVC_SMTPServer	10	0
■ Represents the counters specific to the SMTP server.		
Win32_PerfRawData_Spooler_PrintQueue	22	0
■ Represents performance statistics about a print queue.		
Win32_PerfRawData_TapiSrv_Telephony	18	0
■ Represents the telephony system.		
Win32_PerfRawData_Tcpip_ICMP	18	0
■ Represents counters that measure the rates at which messages are sent and received by using ICMP protocols.		
Win32_PerfRawData_Tcpip_IP	18	0
■ Represents counters that measure the rates at which IP datagrams are sent and received by using IP protocols.		
Win32_PerfRawData_Tcpip_NBTConnection	18	0
■ Represents counters that measure the rates at which bytes are sent and received over the NBT connection between the local computer and a remote computer.		
Win32_PerfRawData_Tcpip_NetworkInterface	18	0
■ Represents counters that measure the rates at which bytes and packets are sent and received over a TCP/IP network connection.		

CLASS	PROPERTIES	METHODS
Win32_PerfRawData_Tcpip_TCP	18	0
■ Represents counters that measure the rates at which TCP segments are sent and received by using the TCP protocol.		
Win32_PerfRawData_Tcpip_UDP	18	0
■ Represents counters that measure the rates at which UDP datagrams are sent and received by using the UDP protocol.		
Win32_PerfRawData_TermService_TerminalServices	12	0
■ Represents Terminal Services summary information.		
Win32_PerfRawData_TermService_TerminalServicesSession	84	0
■ Represents Terminal Services per-session resource monitoring.		
Win32_PerfRawData_W3SVC_WebService	84	0
■ Represents counters specific to the World Wide Web Publishing Service.		

Useful Microsoft .NET Framework Classes

DOCUMENTATION FOR THE .NET Framework can consume thousands upon thousands of printed pages. Luckily for environmentally minded individuals, these pages have not been printed (at least that I'm aware of). With a plethora of classes available, which ones should enterprise scripters use? The list in Table E-1 is a good place to start.

TABLE E-1 .NET Framework Classes and Their Use

.NET FRAMEWORK CLASS	CLASS USE
Collections.ArrayList	Implements the IList interface using an array whose size is dynamically increased as required.
Collections.Generic.Dictionary	Represents a collection of keys and values.
Collections.Queue	Represents a first-in, first-out collection of objects.
Collections.SortedList	Represents a collection of key-and-value pairs that are sorted by keys and accessible by key and index.
Collections.Stack	Represents a simple last-in, first-out (LIFO) nongeneric collection of objects.
Data.OleDb.OleDbCommand	Represents a SQL statement or stored procedure to execute against a data source.
Data.OleDb.OleDbConnection	Represents an open connection to a data source.
Data.OleDb.OleDbDataAdapter	Represents a set of data commands and a database connection that are used to fill the DataSet and update the data source.
Data.SqlClient.SqlCommand	Represents a Transact-SQL statement or stored procedure to execute against a SQL Server database.
Data.SqlClient.SqlConnection	Represents an open connection to a SQL Server database.

.NET FRAMEWORK CLASS	CLASS USE
Data.SqlClient.SqlDataAdapter	Represents a set of data commands and a database connection that are used to fill the DataSet and update a SQL Server database.
Data.SqlClient.SqlDataReader	Provides a way of reading a forward-only stream of rows from a SQL Server database.
DateTime	Represents an instant in time, typically expressed as a date and time of day.
Diagnostics.EventLog	Provides interaction with Windows event logs.
Diagnostics.Process	Provides access to local and remote processes and enables you to start and stop local system processes.
Diagnostics.ProcessStartInfo	Specifies a set of values that is used when you start a process.
Diagnostics.Stopwatch	Provides a set of methods and properties that you can use to accurately measure elapsed time.
DirectoryServices.DirectoryEntry	The *DirectoryEntry* class encapsulates a node or object in the Active Directory Domain Services hierarchy.
DirectoryServices.DirectorySearcher	Performs queries against Active Directory Domain Services.
Globalization.CultureInfo	Provides information about a specific culture (called a "locale" for unmanaged code development). The information includes the names for the culture, the writing system, the calendar used, and formatting for dates and sort strings.
Globalization.RegionInfo	Contains information about the country/region.
IO.StreamReader	Implements a TextReader that reads characters from a byte stream in a particular encoding.
IO.StringWriter	Implements a TextWriter for writing information to a string. The information is stored in an underlying StringBuilder.
IO.BinaryWriter	Writes primitive types in binary to a stream and supports writing strings in a specific encoding.
IO.Compression.DeflateStream	Provides methods and properties for compressing and decompressing streams using the Deflate algorithm.
IO.Compression.GZipStream	Provides methods and properties used to compress and decompress streams.
IO.DirectoryInfo	Exposes instance methods for creating, moving, and enumerating through directories and subdirectories.

.NET FRAMEWORK CLASS	CLASS USE
IO.FileStream	Exposes a stream around a file, supporting both synchronous and asynchronous read and write operations.
IO.FileSystemWatcher	Listens to the file system change notifications and raises events when a directory, or file in a directory, changes.
IO.MemoryStream	Creates a stream whose backing store is memory.
IO.StreamReader	Implements a TextReader that reads characters from a byte stream in a particular encoding.
IO.StreamWriter	Implements a TextWriter for writing characters to a stream in a particular encoding.
Net.IPAddress	Provides an IP address.
Net.IPEndpoint	Represents a network endpoint as an IP address and a port number.
Net.IPHostEntry	Provides a container class for Internet host address information.
Net.Mail.MailAddress	Represents the address of an electronic mail sender or recipient.
Net.Mail.MailMessage	Represents an e-mail message that can be sent using the *SmtpClient* class.
Net.Mail.SmtpClient	Allows applications to send e-mail by using the Simple Mail Transfer Protocol (SMTP).
Net.NetworkCredential	Provides credentials for password-based authentication schemes such as basic, digest, NT LAN Manager (NTLM), and Kerberos authentication.
Net.Sockets.Socket	Implements the Berkeley sockets interface.
Net.Sockets.TcpClient	Provides client connections for TCP network services.
Net.Sockets.UdpClient	Provides User Datagram Protocol (UDP) network services.
Net.WebClient	Provides common methods for sending data to and receiving data from a resource identified by a Uniform Resource Identifier (URI).
Random	Represents a pseudo-random number generator, a device that produces a sequence of numbers that meet certain statistical requirements for randomness.
Security.Principal.NTAccount	Represents a user or group account.

.NET FRAMEWORK CLASS	CLASS USE
Security.Principal.SecurityIdentifier	Represents a security identifier (SID) and provides marshaling and comparison operations for SIDs.
Security.Principal.WindowsPrincipal	Allows code to check the Windows group membership of a Windows user.
Security.SecureString	Represents text that should be kept confidential. The text is encrypted for privacy when being used and deleted from computer memory when no longer needed.
Text.ASCIIEncoding	Represents an ASCII character encoding of Unicode characters.
Text.RegularExpressions.Regex	Represents an immutable regular expression.
Text.StringBuilder	Represents a mutable string of characters.
Timers.Timer	Generates recurring events in an application.
Timespan	Represents a time interval.
URI	Provides an object representation of a URI and easy access to the parts of the URI.
Xml.XmlDocument	Represents an XML document.
Xml.XmlNodeReader	Represents a reader that provides fast, noncached, forward-only access to XML data in an XmlNode.
Xml.XmlTextWriter	Represents a writer that provides a fast, noncached, forward-only way of generating streams or files containing XML data that conforms to the W3C XML 1.0 and the Namespaces in XML recommendations.

WMI Error Messages

TABLE F-1 CONTAINS THE ranges of error messages that are returned by Windows Management Instrumentation (WMI).

TABLE F-1 WMI Error Range

VALUE RANGE	DESCRIPTION
0x800410xx - 0x800440	Errors that originate from within WMI itself. There are two common scenarios. The first scenario is when the specific WMI operation fails because of an error in the request. Typical WMI request errors include insufficient permissions to make the query. The second scenario for WMI errors are related to WMI infrastructure problems, such as incorrect common information model (CIM) or Distributed Component Object Model (DCOM) registration.
0x8007xxx	Errors originating in the core operating system. WMI might return this type of error because of an external failure, such as a DCOM security failure.
0x80040xxx	Errors originating in DCOM. For example, the DCOM configuration for operations to a remote computer might be incorrect.
0x80005xxx	Error originating from Active Directory Service Interfaces (ADSI) or Lightweight Directory Access Protocol (LDAP), such as an Active Directory access failure when using the WMI Active Directory providers.

Table F-2 contains some of the more common errors that might be received when working with WMI.

TABLE F-2 Common WMI Error Constants, Values, and Descriptions

CONSTANT	VALUE	DESCRIPTION
WBEM_E_FAILED	2147749889 (0x80041001)	Call failed.
WBEM_E_NOT_FOUND	2147749890 (0x80041002)	Object cannot be found.
WBEM_E_ACCESS_DENIED	2147749891 (0x80041003)	Current user does not have permission to perform the action.
WBEM_E_PROVIDER_FAILURE	2147749892 (0x80041004)	Provider has failed at some time other than during initialization.
WBEM_E_TYPE_MISMATCH	2147749893 (0x80041005)	Type mismatch occurred.
WBEM_E_OUT_OF_MEMORY	2147749894 (0x80041006)	Not enough memory for the operation.
WBEM_E_INVALID_PARAMETER	2147749896 (0x80041008)	One of the parameters to the call is not correct.
WBEM_E_NOT_AVAILABLE	2147749897 (0x80041009)	Resource, typically a remote server, is not currently available.

Index

Symbols and Numbers

A

E

O

P

S

About the Author

Ed Wilson is one of the Microsoft Scripting Guys and a well-known scripting expert. He writes the daily Hey Scripting Guy! article for the Scripting Guys blog on TechNet, as well as a weekly blog posting for Microsoft Press. He has also spoken at the TechEd technical conference and at Microsoft internal TechReady conferences. Ed is a Microsoft Certified Trainer who has delivered a popular Windows PowerShell workshop to Microsoft Premier Customers worldwide. He has written eight books, including five on Windows scripting, and all have been published by Microsoft Press. He has also contributed to nearly one dozen other books.

Ed holds more than twenty industry certifications, including Microsoft Certified Systems Engineer (MCSE) and Certified Information Systems Security Professional (CISSP). Prior to working for Microsoft, he was a senior consultant for a Microsoft Gold Certified Partner and specialized in Active Directory design and Microsoft Exchange Server implementation. In his spare time, Ed enjoys woodworking, underwater photography, and scuba diving.

Get Certified—Windows Server 2008

Ace your preparation for the skills measured by the Microsoft® certification exams—and on the job. With 2-in-1 *Self-Paced Training Kits*, you get an official exam-prep guide + practice tests. Work at your own pace through lessons and real-world case scenarios that cover the exam objectives. Then, assess your skills using practice tests with multiple testing modes—and get a customized learning plan based on your results.

EXAMS 70-640, 70-642, 70-646
MCITP Self-Paced Training Kit: Windows Server® 2008 Server Administrator Core Requirements
ISBN 9780735625082

EXAMS 70-640, 70-642, 70-643, 70-647
MCITP Self-Paced Training Kit: Windows Server 2008 Enterprise Administrator Core Requirements
ISBN 9780735625723

EXAM 70-640
MCTS Self-Paced Training Kit: Configuring Windows Server 2008 Active Directory®
Dan Holme, Nelson Ruest, and Danielle Ruest
ISBN 9780735625136

EXAM 70-647
MCITP Self-Paced Training Kit: Windows® Enterprise Administration
Orin Thomas, et al.
ISBN 9780735625099

EXAM 70-642
MCTS Self-Paced Training Kit: Configuring Windows Server 2008 Network Infrastructure
Tony Northrup, J.C. Mackin
ISBN 9780735625129

ALSO SEE

Windows Server 2008 Administrator's Pocket Consultant
William R. Stanek
ISBN 9780735624375

EXAM 70-643
MCTS Self-Paced Training Kit: Configuring Windows Server 2008 Applications Infrastructure
J.C. Mackin, Anil Desai
ISBN 9780735625112

Windows Server 2008 Administrator's Companion
Charlie Russel, Sharon Crawford
ISBN 9780735625051

Windows Server 2008 Resource Kit
Microsoft MVPs with Windows Server Team
ISBN 9780735623613

EXAM 70-646
MCITP Self-Paced Training Kit: Windows Server Administration
Ian McLean, Orin Thomas
ISBN 9780735625105

microsoft.com/mspress

Windows Server 2008— Resources for Administrators

Windows Server® 2008 Administrator's Companion

Charlie Russel and Sharon Crawford

ISBN 9780735625051

Your comprehensive, one-volume guide to deployment, administration, and support. Delve into core system capabilities and administration topics, including Active Directory®, security issues, disaster planning/recovery, interoperability, IIS 7.0, virtualization, clustering, and performance tuning.

Windows Server 2008 Resource Kit

Microsoft MVPs with Microsoft Windows Server Team

ISBN 9780735623613

Six volumes! Your definitive resource for deployment and operations—from the experts who know the technology best. Get in-depth technical information on Active Directory, Windows PowerShell™ scripting, advanced administration, networking and network access protection, security administration, IIS, and more—plus an essential toolkit of resources on CD.

Windows PowerShell Step by Step

Ed Wilson

ISBN 9780735623958

Teach yourself the fundamentals of the Windows PowerShell command-line interface and scripting language—one step at a time. Learn to use *cmdlets* and write scripts to manage users, groups, and computers; configure network components; administer Microsoft® Exchange Server 2007; and more. Includes 100+ sample scripts.

Windows Server 2008 Administrator's Pocket Consultant

William R. Stanek

ISBN 9780735624375

Portable and precise—with the focused information you need for administering server roles, Active Directory, user/group accounts, rights and permissions, file-system management, TCP/IP, DHCP, DNS, printers, network performance, backup, and restoration.

Internet Information Services (IIS) 7.0 Administrator's Pocket Consultant

William R. Stanek

ISBN 9780735623644

This pocket-sized guide delivers immediate answers for administering IIS 7.0. Topics include customizing installation; configuration and XML schema; application management; user access and security; Web sites, directories, and content; and performance, backup, and recovery.

ALSO SEE

Windows Server 2008 Hyper-V™ Resource Kit
ISBN 9780735625174

Windows® Administration Resource Kit: Productivity Solutions for IT Professionals
ISBN 9780735624313

Internet Information Services (IIS) 7.0 Resource Kit
ISBN 9780735624412

Windows Server 2008 Security Resource Kit
ISBN 9780735625044

Microsoft® Press

microsoft.com/mspress

Windows Server 2008 Resource Kit— Your Definitive Resource!

Windows Server® 2008 Resource Kit

Microsoft® MVPs with
Microsoft Windows Server Team

ISBN 9780735623613

Your definitive reference for deployment and operations—from the experts who know the technology best. Get in-depth technical information on Active Directory®, Windows PowerShell™ scripting, advanced administration, networking and network access protection, security administration, IIS, and other critical topics—plus an essential toolkit of resources on CD.

ALSO AVAILABLE AS SINGLE VOLUMES

Windows Server 2008 Security Resource Kit

Jesper M. Johansson et al. with Microsoft Security Team

ISBN 9780735625044

Windows Server 2008 Networking and Network Access Protection (NAP)

Joseph Davies, Tony Northrup, Microsoft Networking Team

ISBN 9780735624221

Windows Server 2008 Active Directory Resource Kit

Stan Reimer et al. with Microsoft Active Directory Team

ISBN 9780735625150

Windows® Administration Resource Kit: Productivity Solutions for IT Professionals

Dan Holme

ISBN 9780735624313

Windows Powershell Scripting Guide

Ed Wilson

ISBN 9780735622791

Internet Information Services (IIS) 7.0 Resource Kit

Mike Volodarsky et al. with Microsoft IIS Team

ISBN 9780735624412

What do you think of this book?

We want to hear from you!

To participate in a brief online survey, please visit:

microsoft.com/learning/booksurvey

Tell us how well this book meets your needs—what works effectively, and what we can do better. Your feedback will help us continually improve our books and learning resources for you.

Thank you in advance for your input!

Microsoft®
Press

Stay in touch!

To subscribe to the *Microsoft Press*® *Book Connection Newsletter*—for news on upcoming books, events, and special offers—please visit:

microsoft.com/learning/books/newsletter

Find the Right Resource for You

ADMINISTRATOR'S POCKET CONSULTANT	ADMINISTRATOR'S COMPANION	SELF-PACED TRAINING KIT	RESOURCE KIT

- Practical, portable guide for fast answers when you need them
- Focuses on core operations and support tasks
- Organized for quick, precise reference— to get the job done

- Comprehensive, one-volume guide to deployment and system administration
- Real-world insights, procedures, trouble shooting tactics, and workarounds
- Fully searchable eBook on CD

- Two products in one: official exam-prep guide + practice tests
- Features lessons, exercises, and case scenarios
- Comprehensive self-tests; exam-discount voucher; eBook on CD

- In-depth technical information and tools from those who know the technology best
- Definitive reference and best practices for deployment and operations
- Essential toolkit of resources, including eBook, on CD

Windows® 7 Administrator's Pocket Consultant
William R. Stanek
978-0-7356-2699-7

Microsoft® SQL Server® 2008 Administrator's Pocket Consultant, Second Edition
William R. Stanek
978-0-7356-2738-3

Microsoft Exchange Server 2010 Administrator's Pocket Consultant
William R. Stanek
978-0-7356-2712-3

Windows Small Business Server 2008 Administrator's Companion
Charlie Russel and Sharon Crawford
978-0-7356-2070-4

Windows Server® 2008 Administrator's Companion
Charlie Russel and Sharon Crawford
978-0-7356-2505-1

Microsoft Office SharePoint® Server 2007 Administrator's Companion
Bill English with the Microsoft SharePoint Community Experts
978-0-7356-2282-1

MCTS Self-Paced Training Kit (Exam 70-432): Microsoft SQL Server 2008—Implementation and Maintenance
Mike Hotek
978-0-7356-2605-8

MCITP Self-Paced Training Kit (Exams 70-640/642/643/647): Windows Server 2008 Enterprise Administrator Core Requirements
Holme, Ruest, Ruest, Northrup, Mackin, Desai, Thomas, Policelli, McLean, Mancuso, and Miller
978-0-7356-2572-3

MCTS Self-Paced Training Kit (Exam 70-652): Configuring Windows Server Virtualization
Ruest, Ruest, GrandMasters
978-0-7356-2679-9

Windows Server 2008 Hyper-V™ Resource Kit
Larson and Carbone with the Windows Virtualization Team at Microsoft
978-0-7356-2517-4

Windows Server 2008 Resource Kit
Microsoft MVPs with the Microsoft Windows Server Team
978-0-7356-2361-3

Windows 7 Resource Kit
Tulloch, Northrup, Honeycutt, Wilson, and the Windows 7 Team
978-0-7356-2700-0

Windows PowerShell™ 2.0
BEST PRACTICES

Expert recommendations, pragmatically applied.

Apply best practices for scripting Windows administrative tasks—and optimize your operational efficiency and results. This guide captures the field-tested solutions, real-world lessons, and candid advice of practitioners across the range of business and technical scenarios—and across the IT life cycle. Gain expert insights on what works, where to make tradeoffs, and how to implement the best scripting solutions for *your* organization.

Discover how to:

- Configure and customize the scripting environment
- Get scenario-based guidance for deployment
- Evaluate scripting needs; avoid common pitfalls
- Design functions and modules that optimize code reuse and flexibility
- Choose the right input and output methods
- Use scripts to simplify working with WMI and Active Directory®
- Learn best ways to handle errors, debug, and performance-test
- Manage script-execution policy, code-signing, and version control
- Write better help documentation
- Apply proven troubleshooting techniques

Companion media features:

- All the scripts referenced in the book
- Author Extras—additional problem-solving scripts you can customize
- Planning templates and tools
- Fully searchable eBook

*For **system requirements**, see the Introduction.*

microsoft.com/mspress

ISBN: 978-0-7356-2646-1

9 0 0 0 0

9 780735 626461

Part No. X16-38609

U.S.A. $59.99
[Recommended]

Operating Systems/Windows

About the Authors

Ed Wilson is a senior consultant at Microsoft® who has delivered popular scripting workshops to Microsoft customers and employees worldwide. Ed is well-known as one of the "Microsoft Scripting Guys" on Tech•Net, and he's written several books, including *Microsoft Windows PowerShell Step by Step* and *Windows PowerShell Scripting Guide*.

The **Windows PowerShell Teams at Microsoft** design, develop, and support the Windows PowerShell command-line and scripting environment.

MORE RESOURCES FOR IT PROFESSIONAL

Administrator's Pocket Consultant
- Practical, portable guide for fast answers when you need them
- Focus on core operations and support tasks
- Organized for quick, precise reference—to get the job done

Administrator's Companion
- Comprehensive, one-volume guide to deployment and system administration
- Real-world insights, procedures, troubleshooting tactics, and workarounds
- Fully searchable eBook on CD

Resource Kit
- In-depth technical information and tools from those who know the technology best
- Definitive reference and best practices for deployment and operations
- Essential toolkit of resources, including eBook, on CD

Self-Paced Training Kit
- Two products in one: official exam-prep guide + practice tests
- Features lessons, exercises, and case scenarios
- Comprehensive self-tests; trial software; eBook on CD

See inside cover

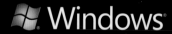

Windows®

Microsoft®